THE WISDOM
OF GENEROSITY

A READER IN AMERICAN PHILANTHROPY

WILLIAM J. JACKSON

EDITOR

BAYLOR UNIVERSITY PRESS

Cover Design by Nicole Weaver, Zeal Design
Cover Image: "Barn Raising" by Ann Mount. ©Bentley House Fine Art Publisher, Walnut Creek, California. Used with permission.

Library of Congress Cataloging-in-Publication Data

Jackson, William J. (William Joseph), 1943–
The wisdom of generosity : a reader in American philanthropy / William J. Jackson.
480 p. cm.
Includes bibliographical references and index.
ISBN 978-1-60258-059-6 (pbk.)
1. Generosity. 2. Humanitarianism. 3. Charities--United States. 4. Endowments--United States. I. Title.

BJ1533.G4J33 2008
177'.70973--dc22

2008010620

Printed in the United States of America on acid-free paper.

Dedicated to Marcia, my wife,
who for forty years has followed her own
wise and generous vision—
living a life of kindness and practicality.

CONTENTS

ANCIENT WRITINGS THAT INFLUENCED THE COLONISTS

A CONTEMPORARY ESSAY

EPILOGUE

PART II

Philanthropy and Liberty in the Enlightenment Era
1700 · 1800
· 55 ·

EPIGRAPH

STORIES

POEMS AND SONGS

SERMONS AND PHILANTHROPIC WRITINGS

PART III
Generous Spirit and the Development of Social Conscience
1800 · 1900
· 133 ·

EPIGRAPH

STORIES

PART IV
Giving in "The American Century" and Its Secularization
1900 · 2007
· 245 ·

THANKS, GOOD WILL, AND A GENEROUS HEART

TROUBLES, NEEDS, AND HOPEFUL REMEDIES

"On Father Eusebio Kino and the Southwest United States" is excerpted from Elna Bakker and Richard G. Lillard, *The Great Southwest: The Story of a Land and Its People* (Palo Alto, Calif.: American West, 1972) by permission of Monique Lillard.

"On the New England Mind" is reprinted by permission of the publisher from *The New England Mind: From Colony to Province* by Perry Miller, 399–401, Cambridge, Mass.: the Belknap Press of Harvard University Press, copyright © 1953 by the President and Fellows of Harvard College.

Excerpts from John Calvin, *Institutes of the Christian Religion* (Philadelphia: The Westminster Press, 1960) are used by permission of Westminster John Knox Press.

Helen Zunser, "A Smart Indian," is excerpted from "A New Mexico Village," *The Journal of American Folklore* 48.188 (1935). 176–178. Reprinted with permission from the American Folklore Society, Ohio State University.

"Not Ours to Give" is excerpted from *The Exploits of Ben Arnold* by Lewis F. Crawford, published by University of Oklahoma Press, 213–214.

Benjamin Kahn, "B'nai B'rith's Birth and Growth," from *Encyclopedia Judaica* 22 Volume Set 2nd edition by Fred Skolnik (Editor). 2006. Reprinted with permission of Gale, a division of Thomson Learning: www.thomsonrights.com. Fax 800-730-2215.

"George Peabody" is used with permission from Elizabeth Schaaf, Archivist and Curator from Archives of The Peabody Institute of The Johns Hopkins University.

"What Good Am I?" by Bob Dylan, on the album *Oh Mercy*. Copyright © 1989 Special Rider Music. "Chimes of Freedom" by Bob Dylan, on the album *Another Side of Bob Dylan*. Copyright © 1963; renewed 1992 by Special Rider Music. Used with permission from Special Rider Music.

Francis Abernethy, "The Golden Log: An East Texas Paradise Lost," from *The Golden Log, Publications of the Texas Folklore Society XXXI*. Eds. Mody C. Boatright, Wilson M. Hudson, and Allen Maxwell. Dallas: Southern Methodist University Press, 1962. 3–4.

Church Thomas, "Don't Forget the Best," from *The Golden Log, Publications of the Texas Folklore Society XXXI*. Eds. Mody C. Boatright, Wilson M. Hudson, and Allen Maxwell. Dallas: Southern Methodist University Press, 1962. 25–26.

"Oklahoma Oil Jokes" from *Bound for Glory* by Woody Guthrie, copyright © 1943 by E. P. Dutton, renewed © 1971 by Marjorie M. Guthrie. Used by permission of Dutton, a division of Penguin Group (USA) Inc.

Mody C. Boatright, "The Petroleum Geologist: A Folk Image," from *The Golden Log, Publications of the Texas Folklore Society XXXI*. Eds. Mody C. Boatright, Wilson M. Hudson, and Allen Maxwell. Dallas: Southern Methodist University Press, 1962. 66–68.

"Pieced-Up Rock," brief excerpt from pp. 27–28 from *Mules and Men* by Zora Neale Hurston, copyright © 1935 by Zora Neale Hurston; renewed © 1963 by John C. Hurston and Joel Hurston. Reprinted by permission of HarperCollins Publishers.

"Why Whites Have Everything: All a Matter of Money" from *Shuckin' and Jivin': Folklore from*

Permission for Thomas Hudson's painting of Robert Carter III given by Virginia Historical Society, Richmond, Va.

"Records of the Female Mutual Relief Society," with alterations to conform to modern conventions, from the Greensbury W. Offley Papers, American Antiquarian Society. Used by permission of Thomas Knoles, Marcus A. McCorison Librarian, American Antiquarian Society.

LIST OF ILLUSTRATIONS

Figure 1.1 "The Miser of the Nisqually," stoneware sculpture (24" X 10" X 5") by sculptor Jan Goodrich Rentenaar, Portland, Oregon. Used with permission.

Figure 1.2 Quaker Anthony Benezet instructing persecuted black children. Engraving. In public domain. Courtesy of Wikipedia Commons.

Figure 1.3 Early American farmer plowing. Engraving. In public domain. Library of Congress.

Figure 1.4 Bronze sculpture of Father Kino by Suzanne Silvercruys. Located in United States Capitol's Statuary Hall collection, Washington, D.C. Public domain. Photo by Rose Jackson.

Figure 1.5 Sculpture of the Stoic philosopher Seneca, owned by the Antikensammlung Berlin ("Berlin antiquities collection"), housed in the Altes Museum and Pergamon Museum in Berlin. Courtesy of Wikipedia Commons.

Figure 2.1 A Turkish Dervish in the 1860s. Amadeo Preziosi (1816–1882) was an Italian painter. Public domain. Courtesy of Wikipedia Commons.

Figure 2.2 Traditional depiction of Phyllis Wheatley. Public domain. Courtesy of Wikipedia Commons.

Figure 2.3 Liberty Goddess with flag, weathervane of molded and painted copper 21 inches high, made by Cushing and White, Waltham, Massachusetts, 1865. Adapted by the author from a Xerox of an auction advertisement.

Figure 2.4 Image based on a painting of Cotton Mather. Public domain. Courtesy of Wikipedia Commons.

Figure 2.5 Image based on a portrait of James Oglethorpe. Public domain. Courtesy of Wikipedia Commons.

Figure 2.6 Painting of John Wesley. Public domain. Courtesy of Wikipedia Commons.

Figure 2.7 Painting of Robert Carter III by Thomas Hudson, 1753. Oil on canvas. Virginia Historical Society space. Image rights owned by the Virginia Historical Society. www.vahistorical.org/ov/II-carter.htm. Used with permission.

Figure 2.8 Painting of George Washington. Public domain. Courtesy of Wikipedia Commons.

Figure 2.9 Painting of Benjamin Franklin. Public domain. Courtesy of Wikipedia Commons.

Figure 3.1 Portrait of Nathaniel Hawthorne from a publication in 1870. Public domain. Statue, Salem, Mass. Courtesy of Wikipedia Commons.

Figure 3.2 James Russell Lowell. Public domain. Courtesy of Wikipedia Commons.

Figure 3.3 Statute of Liberty. Official photo from Statue of Liberty State Park Web site. Public domain. Photo by Etienne Frossard, Brooklyn, New York.

Figure 3.4 Greensbury Washington Offley, a traditional portrait at the American Antiquarian Society, Worcester, Massachusetts. Used by permission.

Figure 3.5 Mission San Jose, with bell tower, San Antonio, Texas. Photo taken by author in July, 2006.

Figure 3.6 Thomas Jefferson portrait, public domain. Courtesy of Wikipedia Commons.

Figure 3.7 Ralph Waldo Emerson photo, public domain. Courtesy of Wikipedia Commons.

Figure 3.8 Henry David Thoreau photo, public domain. Courtesy of Wikipedia Commons.

Figure 3.9 "In the Bitter Cold," *Harper's Weekly*, 1858. (Also reproduced in *Make Way! 200 Years of American Women in Cartoons*, Monika Franzen, and Nancy Ethiel, Chicago: Chicago Review Press, 1988, p. 103.) Public domain.

Figure 3.10 "Sisters of Charity" Pe-ru-na advertisement from the latter part of the 19th century. Public domain. Adapted from a page of an old paper given to the author by the *Grapevine Sun* newspaper, Grapevine, Texas.

Figure 3.11 Cover of an undated booklet about Clara Barton. National Archives Red Cross Collection, box 004. Public domain.

Figure 3.12 Statue of George Peabody near the Royal Exchange in London. Courtesy of Wikipedia Commons.

Figure 3.13 Johnny Appleseed, illustration from "Johnny Appleseed—A Pioneer Hero" by W. D. Haley, *Harper's New Monthly Magazine*, no. CCVIII, November 1871, vol. XLIII, p. 830. Public domain.

Figure 3.14 Photo of Father Damien, Flemish Catholic priest, spiritual patron of lepers, outcasts, and HIV/AIDS patients, and patron folk saint of Hawaii. Public domain. Courtesy of Wikipedia Commons.

Figure 4.1 Cartoon images of Uncle Sam, from Alton Ketchum, *Uncle Sam: The Man and the Legend*, New York: Hill and Wang, 1959, pp. iii, 2, 3, 123. Used with permission.

Figure 4.2 Thomas Nast, engraving of "Uncle Sam's Thanksgiving." *The Art and Politics of Thomas Nast*, Morton Keller, New York: Oxford University Press, 1968, p. 64. Reprint of picture first published in 1869. Public domain.

Figure 4.3 Bob Dylan. Image courtesy of United States National Archives and Records Administration. Public domain. Courtesy of Wikipedia Commons.

Figure 4.4 President Ronald Reagan 1981. This image is a work of an employee of the Executive Office of the President of the United States, taken or made during the course of the person's official duties. As a work of the U.S. federal government, the image is in the public domain. Courtesy of Wikipedia Commons.

Figure 4.5 An Early Portrait of Booker T. Washington, from *Up from Slavery: An Autobiography*, Garden City: Doubleday & Company, 1901. Available at http://docsouth.unc.edu/washington/washing.html. Public domain.

Figure 4.6 Eldon Dedini cartoon from *The New Yorker*, October 26, 1992, p. 77. Used with permission.

Figure 4.7 Photo of Dr. Martin Luther King Jr., made available by the Library of Congress, from the New York World-Telegram and Sun Collection. Public Domain. Courtesy of Wikipedia Commons.

Figure 4.8 Helen Keller photograph. Public domain. Courtesy of Wikipedia Commons.

Figure 4.9 Painting by artist Robert Cenedella, "Santa Claus," 1989, oil on canvas 72" X 56". Used with permission. What do you think the crucified Santa and unopened gifts represent?

Figure 4.10 Kate Kretz, "Blessed Art Thou," 2006, 88" X 60," oil & acrylic on linen. "Angelina Jolie as a Madonna floating on clouds above the fluorescent-lit aisles of Wal-Mart." Used with permission from Kate Kretz.

PREFACE

When any original act of charity or of gratitude . . . is presented either to our sight or to our imagination, we are deeply impressed with its beauty and feel a strong desire in ourselves of doing charitable and grateful acts also.

THOMAS JEFFERSON*

Voices of America and Humanity's Wisdom

This story begins, for me, outside of America. I had to go far from home to learn about community service and to rediscover the generous heart of my native land.

When I was twenty-seven, I spent six months in a village outside Bangalore in South India. Much of that time I spent sketching, reading and writing, learning yoga, and sitting quietly. But nearly every day I did volunteer work at Divine Light School for the Blind, a small facility administered and staffed by Indian Christians from Kerala.

Every day I walked a mile along the bustling, sunny tar road to the simple compound of buildings. There I would help Venkatachali, the tall, thin, white-haired weaving master, prepare an old building to be used as a weaving classroom. And I read aloud George Eliot's novel *Silas Marner* (the story of a miser who loses his gold but finds an orphan child and happiness) to a blind teacher who rapidly transcribed it into Braille. Occasionally I would teach a class when a teacher was sick. One day I accompanied students on a field trip. We picnicked in Lal Bagh Botanical Gardens and visited the impressive State Legislature in Bangalore—not easy to describe, but I tried.

On my last day at the school, I distributed sweets and kazoos and was given a present of some tasty banana chips. At the end of that day, I felt an inner happiness well up that was more enjoyable than any other experience I'd ever known.

Returning home to America, I found myself attracted to service—visiting an old-age home in Vermont; cooking at Haley House, a Catholic Worker kitchen for the homeless in Boston; reading to a blind fellow graduate student at Harvard; volunteering at a soup kitchen in Indianapolis. And I met a variety of other volunteers, each with a different story.

Why do people help others? Are some reasons better than others? What faiths and philosophies come into play in acts of giving and serving? What American legacies from the past and contemporary emerging views regarding charitable and philanthropic acts help us understand more about these experiences?

This collection of many voices from America offers a means to reflect on the wide and deep spectrum of American generosity in thought and deed. Generosity, when considered as part of the spiritual wisdom of humanity, involves powerful ideas and metaphors. I have searched thousands of documents, newspapers, letters, diaries, books, poems, handbills, pamphlets, biographies, and other records of American history, searching for vivid examples of writings about generous giving and philanthropic acts in America. I have made use of university libraries and the Library of Congress in Washington, D.C.; the National Archives in College Park, Maryland; and the American Antiquarian Society in Worcester, Massachusetts.

I have crisscrossed the nation's valleys, river towns, fields, and mountains by highways and side roads to research this book. I was trying to rediscover America as I traveled through a variety of terrains, meeting Americans from ethnically diverse backgrounds in different regions of the country. I was not only seeking out texts but also wanting to meet the people, hear the music, and taste the food—take the pulse of the land. I wanted to find signs of the spirit of generosity in America, to help me mirror in this book what kind of place this country is. I found signs in many places—in nighttime fundraising fiestas on the San Antonio River, and in an old Poor House in rural Michigan. I saw it in the eyes of the homeless people waiting on the curb or leaning against the wall outside a Catholic shelter in Washington, D.C., five blocks from the Capitol, in the chilling autumn dusk. It was painted in murals on walls near the levee in Cape Girardeau, Missouri, and inscribed on placards in small parks, like Pliny Park in Brattleboro, Vermont, memorializing those who gave of themselves to their communities. I saw it in the colorful vitality of Graceland in Memphis, Tennessee, where Elvis' generosity is enshrined, and in a summer festival in the town square of Asheville, North Carolina. The spirit of generosity lives in charity dance marathons and walkathons; in raffles, fish fries, and bake sales; and in refugee aid and donations of canned goods to food banks. Look around America, and you see it in century-old buildings built by charitable and fraternal organizations. Each of us has a favorite example of this soulful architecture. Mine is the Lend-A-Hand Club on Main Street in Davenport, Iowa. As was said of Bachelor's Hall in Philadelphia, "It did from good and generous motives flow."

I thought of service activities in states such as Florida, California, Louisiana, Oregon, New York, and Pennsylvania that I'd visited over the years. I found signs of America's spirit in winter-coat giveaways and in soup kitchens; the signs are clear in charity auctions, Veteran's Day parades, blood drives, and food pantries; in the guidance of docents in museums and mentors in Big Brothers Big Sisters programs; and in the work of student volunteers of all sorts. Young people have shown a growing enthusiasm for service projects, including cleanup in the wake of Hurricane Katrina, and the City Year program in which youths dedicate a year of their lives to community service. The signs are in Goodwill stores, Red Cross relief operations, and Salvation Army bell ringers at Christmas time; in Meals on Wheels deliverers and hospice volunteers, secret Santas and anonymous benefactors; in support groups . . . Once you begin to focus on these signs, they multiply beyond counting, and you begin to realize how much fun, bonding, and community spirit is found in fund-raising events, which often involve song and dance and other forms of self-entertainment. Along the way I rediscovered the principle of helping one's neighbor—the good Samaritan parable—whenever I got lost and had to ask for help. I saw that kindness from strangers renews our faith in humanity and kindles our own generosity, moving us to "pay it forward." Friendliness, cooperation, the ability to give of oneself and "Love All, Serve All," as the House of Blues motto puts it—these are qualities for which Americans are rightly known and loved.

Humanity's wisdom traditions are often the deep background for any particular culture's inspiring spiritual ideas. Wisdom traditions buttress our struggles for justice, guide our striving for spiritual fulfillment, and give rise to powerful religious expressions. American generosity is inextricably part of humanity's wisdom traditions. America's spiritual wisdom has roots in Judaism and Christianity, in Rome and Greece, and also in other earlier civilizations, both Eastern and Western, as well as in Native American traditions. Humanity as a whole has a rich legacy of folk wisdom; consider any culture's unique proverbs, and you can see wisdom about helping others that has survived over the centuries.

We may want to appreciate America as an exceptional place, and we may recognize that the Judeo-Christian religions undergird unique ways of life, but why would we want to divorce the wisdom in American traditions from all other examples of human life? Obviously America is both an exception to, and a part of, human history. America was founded with unique goals and hopes conditioned by the times and experiences of her founders, but their inspiration was part of a spiritual wisdom with roots in classical Rome and Greece, Christian Palestine, and medieval England, with Muslim influences, not to mention Native American and African contributions. Immigrants from all parts of the world have added their own rich backgrounds to the mix that is American culture.

Enduring wisdom traditions are expressed in vivid images. Wisdom traditions are reflected in the stories that use images to keep alive ideas about giving and helping. Thus we can look at the images as a kind of record, a documentary memory that offers a way to discuss the imagination. In this book I pay special attention to metaphors in discourses, archetypal images in stories, symbols in verses, and sayings in order to explore American imagination in its formulations of the wisdom of generosity. The images reveal something of the visions behind the voices. They give us indications of some of the reasons why people serve and give to others, and they inspire people to share what they have in offerings of time, talent, and wealth.

Americans can benefit from learning more about our great country's past. What America has been reveals what America can be. Becoming better acquainted with the background, the historical context, gives us a framework useful in locating ideas, values, and knowledge in our discussions today. Histories of the origins, the formative era, and the growth and development of the nation give us a sense of the original thrust and also show how we remain a part of that trajectory today, seeking to fulfill its original dreams and promises. Thus, this reader offers resources, metaphorically speaking, for thinking about the genetics of American giving.

Some people despair of being able to take the pulse of America, saying America is just too large, with too many people to represent. But it is possible to listen to the voices of a nation and find coherence in its folk expressions and in the whole range of arts, from highbrow to popular and folk cultures. Not everyone can compose a national anthem, but sometimes a composer can find an anthem by reflecting the collective expression. Abraham Lincoln, Walt Whitman, Duke Ellington, Woody Guthrie, Bob Dylan, Carl Sandberg, Toni Morrison—all have mirrored America. Certainly it takes many voices to speak for America, so any attempt to represent candidly America's traditions of giving inevitably will be polyphonic.

I accept this challenge. For years I have jotted down notes to reflect the colorful voices I hear in America. I like the fact that any attempt to capture an aspect of "the multiauthored book of democracy," as someone once put it, will be a composite project. But how to organize a multitude of voices? What precedents are there to consider? I like medleys and collages, and B. A. Botkin's folklore collections and other culled items compiled and arranged by region have captivated me for many years. I like Studs Terkel's interviews, and Langston Hughes and Arna Bontemps' anthology of African American folk traditions, and collections of Native American tales, and various other gatherings of wisdom.[1] I like music that riffs out many variations on a single theme and poems like Wallace Stevens' "Thirteen Ways of Looking at a Blackbird," and the list poems of Walt Whitman. I greatly enjoy Ira Glass' radio program *This American Life*. And I like fractal images—geometric shapes in which the parts reflect the whole shape of a large complex image on smaller scales.[2] Such structures allow us to consider a topic with many aspects and nuances and their interrelationships. This book is thus a mosaic of pieces, organized in related clusters by time periods and themes.

The editor of an anthology is like a stage manager for the voices gathered, or a choreographer of sequences, allowing ideas to unfold and extend themselves. The editor is a shaper of pieces, finding wholeness by arranging parts—beginnings, middles, and endings—making an intricate jigsaw puzzle. The editor is a composer of a collage reflecting an immense and rich culture, and the composition process is complicated but rewarding. Even those readers who think they already know America well may discover much that is new here. In the words of Harry Truman, "The only thing new in the world is the history you don't know."[3] I hope some parts will resonate with your inner strings and move you to delve deeper.

I needed to cast a wide net indeed to catch something of the great sprawling reality of America's heart. This anthology is intended to paint swaths on a large canvas. It is deliberately inclusive of a wide spectrum of documentary glimpses of the oceanic dramas and personal moments of giving in America. It seeks to show American giving's representative forms and American generosity's vivid faces. It is a forum for U.S. philanthropy's eloquent and critical voices, its articulated reasons and results, its problems and its promises. By exploring in my introductions topics such as myths (deep background stories shaping sensibilities), key symbols of generosity and hospitality, American views on money and giving, and the historical context of the founders' ideas and the wisdom traditions they drew upon to form a workable compassionate democracy, I am considering our cultural psyche—its brightness and its shadows. Naturally, readers will agree with some views voiced here and disagree with others, and this natural difference of viewpoints will, I hope, help provoke engaging conversations.

When I arrived in New York City at the age of twenty in 1963 and walked the streets of the Lower East Side, it was natural to fall in love with the people. They were diverse and colorful, with different foods and styles of music. The Jews on Orchard Street, Puerto Ricans on Houston Street, Chinese on Mott, Italians in Little Italy, Eastern Europeans on Second Avenue—it was the American venture in full force, far less homogeneous than my home town, Rock Island, Illinois. It was America with vibrant intensity, like a Whitman poem, a Dos Passos epic novel, or a Hopper painting. It was a simple matter to fall in love with the people of America.

I was young, and times have gotten more complicated, but anyone who tries can still "hear America singing"[4] today. Every day we are within earshot of a great spectrum of personalities and giving and serving experiences: doctors and nurses, salesclerks and mechanics, truckers and secretaries, merchants and repairmen, preachers and politicians, roofers and restaurant workers, teachers and coaches. Listening to the richness and nuance, the depth and complexity of American voices in the twenty-first century can deepen our understanding and appreciation. I revel in the voices—past and contemporary—that I have found and amplified in this gathering, this unlikely chorus of discordant concord. Because any attempt to reflect America without a multitude of voices is unthinkable, unworkable, I have sought to gather many voices, utterances from many classes of Americans during many time periods, each with its own clarity and timbre, its own inspiration and reason.

F. Scott Fitzgerald wrote that America is "a willingness of the heart." But how is the American voluntary heart different from the willing heart of any other country? "Willingness"—to do what? To consume? Grow rich? Innovate and improvise? Extend equality? Give compassionate support to underdogs? Promote justice? Be a planetary police force? Further our own self-interest? Answer the plaintive cries of those in crisis? Each generation of Americans must specify its own "willingness of heart"—in a democracy, such commitment is necessary. It requires more than complaining, "bowling alone,"[5] and going through the motions of consumerism like sleepwalkers. It takes participation, learning about social issues, discussing alternative choices, voting. Styles of giving, modes of thinking about and symbolizing giving—these inevitably change over the centuries. New times bring new crises, stirring new willing responses of the heart. This collection gathers and celebrates the range of American voices of willingness of heart.

The voices of America are rich and sometimes unruly. They include "The Old Weird America" as cultural commentator Greil Marcus calls the folksongs and other American folk expressions from the first half of the twentieth century—the quirky creativity before the ages of electrification and technicolor and digital technologies emerged. The pieces I have collected here are all part of the American song—which is half pious hope and patriotism, half serious oration, and half jive and soulful rock and roll. (That is too many halves, but then, America has always been more than the sum of her parts.)

Generosity is a rich word that can describe a broad spectrum of actions. In this book, many of the stories and poems are about individual charitable acts. Essays and sermons offer a rationale for giving from theological or philosophical viewpoints. Other writings represent accounts of organized philanthropic ventures—group efforts, not-for-profit businesses done for the common good. Defining *philanthropy* as voluntary action for the public good, and exploring American ideas about philanthropic actions and giving, we rediscover the generous impulses in America's earlier phases and also distinguish a growing variety of examples up to and including the present time. Since "what's past is prologue,"[6] and originating events set up a trajectory of ideals and principles, awareness of the earlier phases of American philanthropy can help us understand better the world and circumstances in which we live and even suggest a leaping off point for new possibilities.

One underlying theme of this book, the research of which was supported in large part by the Lake Family Institute on Faith and Giving, is that giving often involves an act of faith. *Faith* is a word used in a variety of ways. There is much that is uncertain in life, but still we act, often taking "a leap of faith" to help others. Faith has been called the hope we have in things yet unseen. The word for faith in Judaism is *hesed*, holding to the covenant with God, with past traditions and generations yet to come. Faith in other worldviews also involves a remembrance of a vision, not just nebulous hope in invisible things. Faith is a following of inspiring teachings, appealing stories, memorable historic experiences. Faith can be a philosophical commitment to compassion and knowledge of our interconnectedness; faith in the power of love and the wisdom of altruism; faith in the kindness that can bring a better future.[7]

Much of my previous research in the last twenty years has been about the literature of South Indian *bhakti*—spiritual love and piety. This book on America is about charity and philanthropy. Literally, *philanthropy* means "love of humanity." Philanthropy encompasses the ideals and practices of helping your fellow man. Love, in both East and West, is often considered at once the great mystery of life and the reason for living.

Focus, Structure, and Contents

Expectations can distort experiences—both in receiving gifts and in reading books. So let me clarify something at the outset: this book is about the range of expressions on the topic of giving. I'm not trying to knit all the pieces together. It is together because all the parts are American. The topic of this anthology is the multiple voices exemplifying various sorts of giving, different kinds of acts of kindness, and also sometimes examples of the lack of generosity—the greed and selfishness that withholds the help that is needed. Generosity's shadow, selfish greed, which is the antithesis or failure of magnanimity, also reveals aspects of the character and importance of generosity. Examples of failures to be generous and their consequences can serve as lessons to help us avoid repeating mistakes. Therefore, the reader should expect some examples of miserliness along with all the examples of generosity. Having and giving, lacking and getting, appealing and showing how sharing is fulfilling—the whole range of experiences interests me.

Although each century differs in terms of historical situations and ways of expressing charity and philanthropy, each century's selections include stories; songs and verses; proverbs, sayings, and jokes; sermons, orations, and essays; biographical, historical narratives; and perspectives that help provide contexts and frameworks for understanding. The selections were made on the basis of their being representative examples of giving, vivid images and eloquent language, and enduring usefulness in the ongoing conversations about philanthropic issues. The sequential flow within each century goes approximately in this order:

1. An epigraph to set the century's tone
2. Stories, the most basic form of relating experiences, which lead us to reflections and conclusions naturally—we see acts of kindness and generosity played out in a narrative
3. Songs and verses, poetic ideas, and musical forms that entrance and intrigue, evoke and inspire
4. Proverbs, sayings, jokes, pithy wisdom, memorable bons mots, and summarized insights for contemplation
5. Sermons, orations, essays, abstract prosaic arguments, descriptions, discussions, and significant thinking about philanthropic issues

6. Biographical and historical narratives, personal accounts, and stories of organizations, all of which help provide contexts and examples of the philanthropic work of the time
7. An epilogue to tie up one century and lead toward the next

The passages and selections herein are all cultural artifacts from across four centuries, which document, reflect, and reveal aspects of America on topics related to giving
and helping. All are artifacts expressed in various dialects of the New World's American
English language. All are spun out of American consciousness, experiences in particular time periods. They are representative of their times. In a few cases, they were written outside America and then published and consumed in America. But in any case,
these passages were the kinds of writings and utterances that people in America heard,
read, discussed, remembered, and passed along. They were currents on the streams
of our culture, regardless of the varieties of genres they represent. I am democratic in
appreciating all the relevant genres of American voices. The introductions, in a variety
of ways, discuss the unique contributions, background, and thematic relevance of the
assembled pieces.

Exploring America's formative historical events and influential voices helps us understand aspects of the American psyche. Past inspirations serve the well-being of an ongoing community and are resources for the future; they are useful in discussions and in
developing further ideas enabling successive generations to meet their own challenges.
I have sought out and explored formative images shaping the American psyche as well
as later developments in U.S. history regarding benevolent activities. I use three lenses:
(1) history, to examine ideas and practices of the past; (2) enduring symbolic ideas of
spiritual wisdom, which form mankind's legacy from around the world; and (3) depth
psychology, to help explore images and imagination, symbolism and subjective experiences. To convey the sweep of four hundred years of American history is a tall order,
but representative pieces help reflect the changing contours of unfolding time periods.

1600–1700

The chronological beginning gives us an opportunity to reflect on our roots, with
Native American stories about the wisdom of nature and early expressions of
Christian charity. It was a time of indigenous people's ideas and Puritan beliefs and
also of the colonial-period settlers' necessities. This first selection of American voices
includes several Native American origin stories from different regions. It also includes
influential fables of Aesop known to the first settlers, translated passages from the
Roman philosopher Seneca's writings about gifts, as well as teachings from the Old and
New Testaments and writings of John Calvin.

Many of the writings convey a New World of hopes and concerns. Selected apho-
risms of Anne Bradstreet and portions of sermons and essays by such writers as John
Winthrop, Alexander Whitaker, William Penn, and Thomas Hooker reveal something of the adventurous Christian soul at this time. Images such as bread cast on the
waters, the good Samaritan's help to a wounded stranger, and Christ's blood freely
given offered inspiration. Also included are narratives such as accounts by Eusebio
Kino in the Southwest and explorer Captain John Smith. Brief pieces on "The New

England Mind," on Virginia, and on the California missions contextualize the writings in terms of regional differences.

Immigrants from different regions of England settled in different parts of early America, forming "powerful determinants of a voluntary society" still existing today.[8] Although less than twenty percent of today's U.S. population has British ancestry, the country's British genesis is nevertheless a key factor in determining some formative aspects of American culture. Besides the Native American background already in existence long before the Europeans arrived and the variety of British, French, and Dutch folkways, there were Puritan and Calvinist influences in the early New England states. There was also the African American presence. Some roots of African American traditions of giving and helping are traceable to West and Central Africa, regions known for longstanding reciprocal arrangements whereby those in need—for example, during a time of famine or loss of livelihood—become family-like dependents of people of means. Likewise there are ancient African organizations to help members of their own communities, and these mutual-aid practices found expression in the New World. Lacking African writings for the seventeenth century, I include writings of an antislavery Quaker, Anthony Benezet, which compile accounts of travelers describing the native generosity and friendliness of Africans in parts of the slave coast of West Africa where slave traders took them as captives.

1700–1800

During this era, we see ideals of philanthropy and liberty growing in the Enlightenment mind. This is the period of settling the land, the rise in stature of the revolutionary founders, and of early industrialism.

In this period, we hear more Native American stories, including a Winnebago trickster tale that warns against providing only for oneself. These stories were no doubt in circulation prior to this century, but they were widely told at this time. To include them here is a reminder of the important Native American presence in the eighteenth century. Furthermore, there are many short anonymous teaching stories on gratitude and generosity, including some from children's character-building literature in colonial America. Also there is a story of a group of women who sacrifice their comforts to contribute goods to the American Revolution. Songs and verses include "The Liberty Tree" by Thomas Paine, and a poem by Phillis Wheatley, a slave whose verses were admired by many, including George Washington. I present a selection of colorful verses on charity and philanthropy from newspapers of the period, and I have selected sermons and essays with passages on charity and on helping the poor by teaching them skills. "Universal Attributes of Women" by John Ledyard (1751–1789) takes a page from a world traveler's narrative praising women's kindness and hospitality worldwide as consistently exceeding men's compassion. New thinkers were emerging on the scene, and I include the insightful and visionary "Oration on Benevolence" by DeWitt Clinton (1769–1828), as well as John Wesley's directives concerning helping others. During this century, Benjamin Franklin is a prime example of new philanthropic contributions to public welfare. Also included are brief passages from letters of Washington and Jefferson on philanthropy as well as writing by James Oglethorpe, the philanthropist instrumental in founding Georgia as a hopeful place of refuge for English debtors. In all of these examples, there are some continuities with ideas and needs in our own time.⁹ Although agricultural practices have changed, reflections on the blessings of an abundant harvest, which close the section, have an ongoing resonance for this wealthy nation today.

1800–1900

This period is rich with voices of Americans' generous spirit and social conscience. It was the time of westward migration and the growth of cities; a time of burgeoning industrialism and romantic thinkers responding to the call of imagination; a time of Civil War and new waves of immigration and new social needs as the scale of communities expanded.

Voices of the nineteenth century tell tales and stories about generous givers from a variety of states. There are also poignant verses by Will Carleton, selections about gifts and doing good from Emily Dickinson and Walt Whitman, and hymns for the express purpose of benefitting widows and orphans. Lines from James Russell Lowell's popular "The Vision of Sir Launfal" show how America honored and perpetuated the knightly ideal of helping those in distress, stemming from Christian roots of caring. Longfellow's suggestive poem "Something Left Undone" and an anonymous poem, "The Beggar," about a Revolutionary War veteran present thoughts on conscience and our duty to those who gave much for our well-being. Another voice from this period is Ambrose Bierce's in his humorous poem "The Legatee." I include pieces by transcendentalist thinkers Thoreau, Emerson, and Whitman, philosopher-poets who were individualists about many topics, including charity. I have also selected passages from philanthropist Andrew Carnegie's "The Gospel of Wealth."

Brief biographies of notable givers such as Dorothea Dix, George Peabody, John Chapman, and Clara Barton are also included in this section. More than 150 years ago, Alexis de Tocqueville identified the associational and voluntary sector as the distinctive feature of American society. Amazingly, his writings still describe well some aspects of American life as we know it today. We see organized social service active in an account of a "Visit to an Insane Asylum" and "All-Night Missionary Gibbud's Story," and in Harriet Beecher Stowe's and Louisa May Alcott's writing about nurses. News stories of the 1800s include the story of David Minge, a Southern man who freed eighty slaves long before the Civil War and helped them start a new life. During this energetic century of change, many self-help and social-conscience organizations sprang up, and women's voices began to be heard more.

1900 to the Present

This section offers voices of giving during "The American Century" and in our own postmodern times. This is the time of the secularization of philanthropy, of new media and celebrities. There are voices reflecting on duties of the wealthy, and new pragmatic ways to help the poor, such as social entrepreneurship with new businesses geared to change the world for the better. There is a plentiful and varied treasury of examples of giving from which to select.

The voices of the twentieth century gathered here include Texas folktales like "The Golden Log," which is a little like the old Northwest Indian myth of a collapsing bridge that marked the loss of a more innocent time. Both can be read as cautionary tales about what leads to the disastrous end of an era of cooperation and appreciation of the common good. You will see folktales from Louisiana, New Mexico, and Tennessee, and African American folktales on tithing. I include such examples of generosity as "The Legend of the Lone Ranger" by Fran Striker, which became a 1950s TV show; Oklahoma Oil Stories; an anecdote from Huey P. Long; and a black folk sermon collected by Zora Neal Hurston. I have offered songs and verses about gifts and giving and helping others—Robert Frost's "The Gift Outright" and Gwendolyn Brooks' poem "The Lovers of the Poor," which describes philanthropists from the viewpoint of the poor, some of Peter Maurin's verses, lyrics by Bob Dylan, and Stuart Scharf's "Give a Damn."

Included are sermons and essays by spiritual leaders and social activists, such as W. E. B. Dubois, Jane Addams, and Martin Luther King, Jr., as well as an important but neglected passage by William James on the importance of saintly individuals. There is James Hillman on service, Wendell Berry on the agricultural basis of the abundance that makes generosity possible, and Gary Snyder on how a man with nothing nevertheless found what he had to contribute to society. Also the voices of philosopher of science Lewis Thomas on altruism, and cosmologist Brian Swimme on the exemplary generosity of the sun. John D. Rockefeller on "The Difficult Art of Giving" represents a classic on giving. This century is so rich with voices, a few must suffice to suggest the range: Booker T. Washington on the art and science of getting donations; Thomas Moore's reflections on service, and "Gestures of Grace" about doing good in the neighborhood by Margaret Davis. From twentieth-century news stories, I include an article on organ donation. I also offer brief accounts of several charitable foundations, stories of service organizations,[10] and economist Jeffrey Sachs' ideas on eliminating world poverty. More and more celebrities, sports heroes, and politicians are drawing attention to worthy causes.

By compiling this anthology, I hope to contribute to the process in which charitable giving and the study of philanthropy becomes more self-aware. By knowing more of the past, being conscious of connections, and identifying forgotten or unrecognized aspects of philanthropy, the neglected legacies of generosity become part of the conversations today. Reflections on the controversies, paradoxes, and conundrums of giving make us aware of philanthropy's nuances in the real world. Giving is not just dependent on spontaneous feelings of empathy for motivation.[11] We learn principles of caring for others by example, by stories told in a tradition, by family members, by proverbs, and by cultural works depicting values, ideals, and duties. Participation in service contributes to understanding philanthropy, too. Reading about it alone, the student would lack some dimensions. Hence "service learning." If actual experiences of service and giving are concurrently pursued, readers will enhance their understanding of this book's contents.

At the institutional level, there are norms, rules, laws, and official expectations—directives that say "Thou shalt." At the individual-psyche level, stories and other symbolic expressions provide both anchors that situate us and archetypes that inspire us. At the microbiology level, mirror neurons enable sympathy, and such molecular processes as the activation of serotonin receptors give us satisfaction in the helpful parts we play in society. Society and individual, learning and feeling, conscious living up to expectations and deep subconscious processes of which we are not always aware—these work together to make a whole.

When possible, I list Internet sites where full texts are available, since today more readers have computers than have access to old printed materials from the eighteenth century, for example. I have occasionally added quotation marks and other punctuation to centuries-old texts for the sake of clarity. Where necessary, I have contemporized spellings as well. In some cases I have also added my own titles to passages extracted from longer texts to indicate the theme and content.

The range of the English language is amazingly rich, as this collection reminds us. Behind each example there are literatures and precedents, and sometimes regional and ethnic dialects. A deceptively simple folk tale may harbor deep truths. The highly rhetorical oration often resonates with images and references from the Bible, Shakespeare, and other literary classics. This collection revels in the diversity and richness of our shared language.

Debts of Gratitude

I typically begin research projects with a hope and trust that interesting things will come to light as I search through out-of-the-way materials. I'm grateful that I have not been disappointed—it has been rewarding to find new perspectives on America. Many unexpected "gifts" of significant writings and interesting ideas have come to me along the way, as well as thought-provoking surprises.[12] I have learned from the insights and suggestions of friends and colleagues, as well as from conducting research at archives and historical sites in a number of states. Some of this book I found in my own memories, in my bones' marrow; some was in the American air; and some was kept safe in the coolness of antiquary collections. I have foraged and browsed, hunted and gathered, incorporated and digested and arranged historical and philosophical points from many sources. The selections can be browsed according to interest, need, and impulse, rather than necessarily read in a completely linear fashion.

The medieval Sufi poet Saadi, a master of metaphor and parable, wrote that once a friend gave him a piece of aromatic clay as a gift. He questioned the clay: "Are you musk or ambergris or what? I'm entranced by your perfume." The fragrant clay answered: "I was once a mere lowly piece of clay, but then I was befriended by a rose—the sweet smell of my companion permeated me and has become associated with my very being—otherwise I would be nothing but a lump of clay." This story about keeping good company is also about the presence of spirit in matter. Without my inspiring teachers, I would not have many of the good things I hope you will find in this work. I've picked up good ideas from the great people I've been fortunate to know. I wish to thank, for example, the Lake Institute Advisory Board, Bill Enright, Carol Johnston, Elizabeth Lynn, Rabbis Dennis and Sandy Sasso, Don Johnson, and Scott Alexander, David Smith, and Fred Kniss.

Philosopher Jacob Needleman's book *The Soul of America* was an inspiration to me in the early stages of this project. I am indebted to his work, which I recommend to those seeking understanding of America's spiritual roots.

As the first Lake Scholar, I wish to express my gratitude to the Lake Institute for the support given to me during this three-year appointment. The Lake Institute on Faith and Giving offers a public forum for exploring connections between individual philanthropy and faith, particularly within the major religious traditions. Its mission is to foster greater understanding of the ways in which faith inspires and informs giving. The goal is to encourage donors, whatever their religious orientation or spiritual practice, to become more thoughtful in their personal philanthropy. Established in 2002 within the Center on Philanthropy at Indiana University, the Institute honors the memory and legacy of Thomas and Marjorie Lake, who through their volunteer activity and charitable support played an influential role in enhancing the quality of life for citizens and communities within and beyond Indianapolis and Indiana. The Lake Institute carries out its mission through an expanding program of educational offerings, research, and public forums, including the annual Thomas H. Lake Lecture, the Distinguished Visitors program, seminars and educational programs, and the appointment of a Lake Scholar in residence at the Center on Philanthropy.

My friend Jillian Vandermarks encouraged me to explore the theme of giving in my own life. Thinking and writing about my own American experiences has given me grounding and, I hope, kept me from being overly abstract and one-sidedly academic. Bill Enright, Director of the Lake Family Institute, helped me do the work involved in the research, writing, and publishing of this book. Members of the Department of Religious Studies at Indiana University-Purdue University at Indianapolis (IUPUI)—Tom Davis, Ted Mullen, Johnny Flynn, Edward Curtis, Rachel Wheeler, David Craig, Matthew Condon, Peter Thuessen, and Kelly Hayes—offered helpful feedback. Philip Goff, director of the Center for the Study of American Religion and Culture, encouraged me and gave useful advice as this project unfolded, and Jan Shipps, IUPUI professor emeritus, helped me find useful Mormon materials, as did Jill Derr. Thanks to Rabbi Geoffrey Dennis, and to Dr. Gary Zola and Kevin Proffitt, at the American Jewish Archives in Cincinnati. Philanthropic Studies graduate student Thomas Southard read parts of this work at an early stage and helpfully shared his responses. Al Lyons, my research assistant on this project, helped me locate passages and helped me think about them as well; he worked on all the behind-the-scenes work that goes into a book. Debbie Dale was very helpful, especially in typing up passages from old newspapers and other rare publications, which were often difficult to decipher. My friend from graduate school days, North Carolinian Carl Ernst, and Vermont neighbor James Newell, my Illinois cousin Daniel Fetes, and my Iowan brother, the artist Thomas C. Jackson—all gave helpful suggestions and encouraging feedback. And many thanks also to Casey Blaine, Diane Smith, and Mary Ann Jeffreys at Baylor University Press for all their help.

My intention has been to compose this book not just by imposing an organization on the material but by finding principles of organization that grow from the materials themselves. The prose and poetry in this book are meant to reveal both similarities and contrasts in attitudes and values about giving. I hope you find pleasant surprises and forgotten truths, as well as lost and neglected moments of heroism and wisdom and that you recognize your America and other Americas, too. My job has been to find ways to let inspired voices speak out and find their listeners, allowing us to rediscover the varied ways Americans have been generous, generation after generation. I can only say to India (where a great teacher showed me the beauty of service) and to my own country: "When I was deep in poverty you taught me how to give."[13]

OUR ROOTS IN THE WISDOM OF NATURE AND CHRISTIAN CHARITY

1600 · 1700

EPIGRAPH

BELLE DEACON (1905–1995)

[This contemporary Alaskan poet's verses celebrate the importance of old stories—enduring wisdom that helps us survive. First Nations people tell stories about the forces of nature when speaking of abundance and gratitude and giving. Enduring traditional stories have a subtle guiding quality. In particular, stories of giving set up patterns of empathic response and customs of neighborliness.]

The People's Stories

They said this about the way my stories go.
In the time of long ago:
"If you don't fall asleep, you can obtain the old wisdom"
that was being told to us when I was a child.
"Even if you are sleepy, you should try to stay awake.
And you shouldn't fidget.
You should just think about everything.
Then you'll get the old wisdom that was told
    to us in the past."
After we'd thought about it a little,
"Tell it to us," they would say to us.
When we start to tell it, it is like a bright light ahead of us,
just as though it were written as we speak.

Belle Deacon, "Deg Hit'an Gixudhoy (The People's Stories)," *Engithidong Xugixudhoy (Their Stories of Long Ago)*. Fairbanks: Alaska Native Language Center and Iditarod Area School District, 1987.

STORIES

NORTHWEST NATIVE AMERICAN (1)

[Flood stories involve archetypal images of origin and cyclical renewal, as seen in this Pacific Northwest Indian tale of the Great Flood. The Nisqually tribe traditionally lived around Puget Sound and from ancient times revered Mount Tacoma as a sacred place. Tacoma, meaning "White Mountain" (now called Mount Rainer), is in Washington State and rises to 14,411 feet above sea level. Nisqually stories speak of Tacoma's heights as the refuge for the survivor of the great flood that covered the earth when the Whulge (waters of Puget Sound) rose so high after the long rain. In the second story, the inordinate love of wealth—here seen in the form of hiaqua, a wampumlike medium of exchange—is a source of trouble for humans. Many cultures have stories of greed distorting people's relationships. After finding the wealth he always dreamed of, the old Nisqually miser must go through a storm and nearly die before he can be freed from his overly acquisitive nature. Only then is he ready to play an important part in his tribe, giving to others and finding fulfillment. Note that rock shapes seen in the crater correspond to the spirits. In the Nisqually world-view, there is one Great Spirit and many emanations of this Spirit—spirits of places, such as Mount Tacoma, and spirits of creatures, such as salmon and elk.]

After the Storm

At that time, long ago, the waters had drowned all the other people, and then the waves rose up and tried to capture the last man climbing higher up Mount Tacoma's slopes. The waves kept rising, and the man was up to his chest in cold water, with his hope fading. He grew fearful that the next wave would knock him back into the dark, turbulent waters. But then the tamanous (spirit) of the peak gazed with sympathy upon the man and turned his feet to stone to anchor him against the storm. When the storm stopped and the waters subsided, the man stood there still, his feet now a part of the peak of Tacoma, and he felt sad that he could not return to the valley where the air was mild and flowers would soon be in bloom. The Great Spirit of all things came and caused the man to feel drowsy. As the man rested in peaceful sleep, the Great Spirit took a rib from the man's chest and formed it into a woman. The Great Spirit then detached the man from the rock where his feet had been attached. When the man awoke, he was happy to see the woman, and he took her to a forest by the seashore, where they began life anew; the rebirth of the human race began there.

A Miser Becomes Generous

Long ago, there lived on the shore of the Whulge an old man famous for his prowess in hunting and fishing, but even more so for his unusual attraction to hiaqua. Hiaqua was like the wampum of the East Coast tribes—it was made of small shells cut off at both ends and strung together. As currency of exchange, hiaqua gave its owner the ability to trade for all the goods men want and need. Possession of hiaqua brought esteem, status, even a reputation for wisdom. The old man prized hiaqua more than anything else, and he traded the meat and fish he obtained in his skillful hunting and fishing for hiaqua with an insatiable desire to accumulate more and more. He never gave any to his wife, always burying it in a secret place. He was known as a miser constantly seeking to enlarge his hoard.

One day the old man was hunting on the slopes of Tacoma and as usual was thinking about hiaqua: *Where can I get more of those wonderful beads?* He was too preoccupied with his plans to sell the game he got to starving widows to pay homage to the spirit of Tacoma. The spirits of snowy heights up there by the sky were offended by his irreverent presence. The old man presumed to demand of the spirits, "Can't you tell me how to find hiaqua?" The elk was the old man's spirit guide, and later that day he saw elk tracks going up the slopes. He began to think that the elk was telling him how to find a great treasure in the crater up at the top of Tacoma.

The old man went home and told his wife what he was thinking.

The next day, taking an elk horn to use as a digging tool, the old man set out, climbed high to the peak, and reached the snow-covered hollow of the crater's rim. There he saw a salmon-shaped rock, a kamas (edible bulb) root-shaped rock, and a rock shaped like the head of an elk.

The old man took the shapes up there as a sign from the spirit of Tacoma and began to dig in the snow near the base of the elk head. He soon found the beautiful and valuable hiaqua treasure he had been dreaming of, what he had been seeking for so long. He gleefully grabbed string after string of the precious pure white shell beads and wrapped them around his arms and waist and neck. He was so engrossed with his newfound wealth that he did not see that thirteen gigantic otters had emerged from the dark lake and were sitting in a circle to watch. At every thirteenth stroke of the elk horn digging into the earth, the otters slapped their tails on the ground, but the old man paid them no mind.

Figure 1.1 "The Miser of the Nisqually"

Weighed down with more hiaqua than he had ever imagined, the old man decided to start on his way back home. He did not offer even one bead, let alone one string, of hiaqua to the spirits there; he did not offer a string to the stone salmon, kamas root, or elk head. The otters slid back into the lake and began to vigorously slap the waters with their thick tails. A dark mist began to rise, and the spirit of Tacoma angrily began to wage a storm as the old man tried to go home. The spirits chased and harassed the old man as he tried to hurry away. The winds seemed like hands grabbing the hiaqua as a kind of offering. The storm let up briefly, but then it returned in full force, harsher than before. He kept going and relieved himself of more and more of his burden as he went, as if he had no choice if he wanted to survive.

It became very dark, and eventually he reached some woods just as the last handful of beads was being torn from his fist; he opened his hand and flung the hiaqua into the insistent winds. Exhausted and depressed, he dropped to rest on some moss, and he slept deeply for a long, long time. . . .

When the old man awoke, he recognized the spot as being the same place he had started from the morning before. He stretched, and his joints felt stiff as he moved around. Hungry, he ate some kamas bulbs and had a smoke. He felt different somehow. His hair was all matted now, and strangely, it came all the way down to his knees. "The spirit of Tacoma was playing tricks on me," he said to himself. His mind was quiet now, calm and contented. Hiaqua was not on his mind. The storm had cleansed him of all his obsessive greed. He was free from the burdens and habits he used to have. The whole world seemed bright and beautiful; everything was fresh and new.

The old man continued on his way home but the woods looked different now. At dusk he arrived at a prairie where his lodge had been. A very old woman with strings of hiaqua was cooking salmon and singing near the door. The old man recognized her voice. She looked a lot like his wife, but much older. She told him: "You left here many years ago. I lost track of just how many. It must be at least thirty years now! I remained faithful and waited for you all this time. I took my mind off my fears and sorrows by trading kamas bulbs and herbs. Look, I've become prosperous!"

The old man did not care about material wealth any more. He was happy to be at home now, contented with his mind more at peace than ever before. He remembered the hiaqua he had buried long ago and dug it up, because it could be useful in helping people who were in need. The old man was now glad to give freely whatever he had to offer, whether that meant sharing material goods or insights from his store of wisdom. A simple life with love for others, veneration for the spirit, and respect and thanks for the forces of nature was all he needed now to feel satisfied.

People came from near and far to ask how best to spear salmon, hunt elk, and pay homage to the Great Spirit. The old man was now the great medicine man of the Nisqually, and the people looked to him for guidance and help. Within a year of his return, a child was born to his wife. The old man lived a long time, and on his death bed he whispered this story of his life to his son.

Written by William J. Jackson, based on several tellings, including Charles M. Skinner, *Myths and Legends of Our Own Land*, vol. 2. Philadelphia: J.B. Lippincott, 1896, 242–45. Also Theodore Winthrop's version in *Sights and Scenes in Oregon, Washington and Alaska for Tourists*. Omaha, Neb.: Passenger Department, Union Pacific Railway Co., 1888, 24–28.

NORTHWEST NATIVE AMERICAN (2)

[Cultures both East and West tell stories of a golden age before a fall when life was harmonious and people lived in a childlike state of happiness. Life was naturally in order without a structure of laws and penalties. Desire, loss of amity, and eruptions of conflict bring the age of cooperation crashing to an end. In this story, a generous old woman brings a temporary reprise, but then greedy enmity returns. The forces of conflict rebound with a vengeance, causing terrible problems, while the signs of generosity are rewarded and encouraged but fail to prevail. Human nature is stubborn, the story seems to say, and the forces of good must bide their time and hope for a new day.]

Collapse of a Bridge

In the earliest times, according to the Northwest tribes, the great Creator being Tyhee Sahale, a single governing spirit living in the sky, capricious, now helpful, now angry, along with his two sons arrived at what is now known as the Dalles in Oregon. They came by way of the great river now known as the Columbia. Seeing the beautiful land thereabouts, the sons both desired it and fought with each other. Their father solved the quarrel by taking his bow and aiming one arrow to the north and then aiming another to the west, telling his sons to go find them. The son who traveled north became the ancestor of the Klickitats. The one who traveled West became the ancestor of the Mult-nomahs. Tyhee Sahale lifted up the earth between these two regions, forming what are now called the Cascade Mountains, so that the sons would not clash.

The Columbia River symbolized the flow of peace shared by the tribes, and Sahale made a stone bridge, called the Bridge of the Tomanawos, to arch across the chasm so that those on both sides could be friends and trade goods and exchange news. As the people multiplied, they lost the ability to live in peace and caused more and more trouble. Tylee Sahale became disgusted with both tribes, the sun stopped shining, and cold winds blew snow over the land. Without fire, the tribes began to freeze. Only one old woman named Loowit had fire.

Loowit's neighbors all went to her, seeking flame to light their fires, and she gener-ously accommodated them. Then Sahale, seeing this kindness, told Loowit she was the guardian of the sacred flame and to guard it well on the stone bridge. He also told her to ask for a reward for peacefully sharing her fire. Loowit said her wish was for "youth and beauty," and instantly she became young and beautiful.

Everything went well for a while, but then Loowit's charms attracted two great chiefs—Pahtoe, leader of the north side of the Columbia River, and Wyeast, leader of the Multnomah people on the southwest side. Because they both wanted her, Pahtoe and Wyeast fought over Loowit, stirring up enmity between their tribes. Their conflicts disturbed the earth, causing it to rumble and crack and hurl red-hot molten rock, as if to mock the people's rage. Sick and tired of the chieftains' and their peoples' destructive acts and shedding of blood, the Creator caused the bridge of the gods to collapse, to keep the tribes apart.

The two brothers and the girl, crushed in the destruction of the stone bridge, whose debris formed the Cascades in the river, were transformed. Chief Wyeast became snow-crested Mount Hood, and Chief Pahtoe turned into snow-peaked Mount Adams. Beau-tiful young Loowit became the peak of Mount St. Helen. The mountains peer out coldly at each other forever in a lasting memorial of the rifts caused by human faults. The bridge that once allowed easy crossing of the Columbia is now only a memory. For a long time, people could see the stones from the fallen bridge in the rapids of the Columbia; now a dam has caused the water to deepen there.

Some say that even after much time had passed, Pahtoe and Wiyeast as mountain peaks still angrily quarreled over Loowit! Now their tantrums caused sheets of flame to burst out of their peaks, and they hurled great rocks at each other. But Pahtoe and Wiyeast were not able to throw the rocks far enough. The rocks dropped down into the Great River, the Columbia, damming it up. Ever since then, the river has become nar-row and very swift running at that point now known as the Dalles.

Written by William J. Jackson, based on a story heard by his wife, Marcia Jackson, in Portland, Oregon, and on information in Katherine Berry Judson, ed., *Myths and Legends of the Pacific Northwest*. Lincoln: University of Nebraska Press, 1997, 47–49. Alternate version at www.mtsthelens.net/MtStHelensNet/bridgeofgods.html, "Tragic Triangle: The Love Story of Loowit: Legend of the Bridge of the Gods . . ."

NORTHWEST NATIVE AMERICAN (3)

[Coyote is a trickster figure in the stories of Western Native Americans. Like Raven, Coyote is an archetypal image of the quirky reality of existence, always surprising. As Raven liberated imprisoned light so the universe could be seen, Coyote liberates the salmon so there can be a generous distribution for the well-being of the whole. But tricksters remind us we should never feel too secure in a dynamic universe. Like Nature herself, the Coyote giveth and the Coyote taketh away. Nature can be generous, but we must play our part with respect and moderation, not taking nature's great giveaway for granted and being wasteful. Coyote in this story seeks fair distribution of resources. Salmon was a staple food for Native Americans in the Northwest, so this is no trivial tale, but one of survival. Coyote is generally wild and unpredictable, like the weather, but here he is on the side of the poor and against those who take unfair advantage simply because they can. The "Skookums" referred to in this story are spirits or monsters.]

Coyote Frees the Salmon from Klamath River

Then Coyote went to Klamath River [in what is now southern Oregon and northern California]. He found the people very poor. They had no food. The river was full of salmon, but the people could not get any. Three Skookums had built a dam to prevent the salmon from coming up the river. So the Skookums had all the fish, but the people had none. Coyote was very angry. Coyote said, "Before many suns, fish shall come up the river. The people shall have all the salmon they need."

Then Coyote went to the mouth of the river. The Skookums saw him. They thought he was only a skulking coyote. Coyote whined for some of their fish. The Skookums would not give him any. Coyote came close to their camp. The Skookums drove him away. But Coyote saw where the Skookums kept the key of the dam. That was what he had wanted when he whined for fish.

Next morning, one Skookum started down to open the trap and let in a fish for herself. Coyote ran out of the tepee, jumped between Skookum's feet and tripped her up. Skookum fell, and the key fell out of her hand. Coyote picked up the key and went to the dam. Coyote opened the dam and let the fish through. The salmon went upstream into the country of the Cahrocs. Then the people had food to eat.

Afterward Coyote broke down the dam. Ever since then, salmon go every year up that river.

Katherine Berry Judson, ed., *Myths and Legends of the Pacific Northwest*. Lincoln: University of Nebraska Press, 1997, 123–24.

ALASKAN

[Holding together with others and sharing food generously are themes dramatized in the following story. Note the patterns that relate to philanthropy. For example, the man's wife does not share, which leads to troubles. The man, on the other hand, values the humble find of the fin, which sustains him, and he shows his gratitude by being generous. Repaying what was given, he returns the good deed many times over. Such stories teach values of cooperating with others and giving what we are able to those in need; they also sug-

gest what we should expect as the result of our selfish actions. *These values seem to have been pervasive among Native Americans. Far to the south in the Bahaman Islands where Columbus encountered indigenous people, a similar ethos prevailed. Columbus wrote that the Indians were free with their belongings, giving whatever the Europeans wanted, "with as much love as if their hearts went with" each of the gifts they gave.]*

Man Saved by Salmon Fin

A man and his wife lived in a village on a river somewhere. When the man hunted he brought all kinds of animals home. One time when he hunted he got some sheep. It was in the fall and he got two rams. He brought the fat meat home and let his wife put it away in the cache. He told her, "When people are out of food give them a little piece from one of those sheep." The people had food all winter, but they got short in the springtime. When they were out the man asked his wife, "Where are those sheep we put away in case people ran out of food?" She answered, "They are gone already." She had eaten them herself without the man knowing. When they were out of food the husband got sick and lost weight because his wife had not saved the meat as he had told her.

When the people were going in springtime to their summer camps the wife left her husband in the house. He stayed there for a few days and then said, "I'm going for a walk away from here while I can still move." After he went for a while he came to a place where some people had stayed overnight. He looked for some food, but he found none from where the people had been. He went to where a dog had been tied, looked around, and finally found the bone from a fin of a dried salmon. He ate it, bone and all. After his stomach got better he went again.

A little farther over he saw a camp with people and they let him stay with them. The people had a lot of food. He ate, gained weight, and got his health back. He started hunting again and bringing food home for the people. One time he got a wolf. Before he went back to camp he took the wolf to the place where he had eaten the salmon bone and left it there, saying, "I have returned what I found." He told the people about it when he went back to camp. He told them to go look at that place where the wolf was every time they had a chance. After he told them that he found out that they were the people who had stayed overnight at that place before they moved up. The people went down and found the wolf at the dog's pole, so they took it home. A few days later when they went down to see the pole again they found a wolverine there. Every time the man went out hunting he took something by that dog's pole. Whenever he hunted he always gave meat to the people; he wanted to feed everybody.

Collected by Paul Monroe in the form of an Eskimo oral tradition from Carl Stalker, in Edwin S. Hall Jr., *The Eskimo Storyteller: Folktales from Noatak, Alaska*. Knoxville: University of Tennessee Press, 1975, 358–59.

HAWAIIAN

[All living beings have a constant need for water and food—that is life's primal predicament. Many cultures have a story of a primordial sacrifice, a symbol of life feeding on life and the gift of nourishment that makes survival possible. Feelings of gratitude and indebtedness can lead to sharing and generosity, as in this first story, said to have been transmit-

ted over the generations for as long as Hawaiians have inhabited their islands. Stories of the rewards of feeding a stranger, a theme in the second tale, are told in Hindu, Buddhist, Muslim, and other cultures. The New Testament advises, "Be not forgetful to entertain strangers: for thereby some have entertained angels unawares" (Heb 13:2). Even today, self-sacrifice is highly valued by native Hawaiians, as we see in the true story of Hawaiian folk hero Eddie Would Go. Eddie was a young man who gave his life trying to help rescue the crew of a fleet of double-hulled voyaging canoes during a storm in 1978. Myths have this quality—they are retold and relived generation after generation with new names and new dress, but basically the same theme.]

The Breadfruit Tree

The god Ku, who was of polygamous nature, once came to Hawaii and married a Hawaiian woman, with whom he lived many years and raised a large family. He did not tell the woman that he was a god; he worked on the land like anybody else.

A time came when food was scarce and no one could get enough to eat. Ku's wife and children were starving. Ku was sorry for them. He told his wife that he could get food for them by going himself on a long journey, but that he could never return to them. At first his wife would not hear of it, but she finally consented to his going when she heard the children crying for hunger. Ku said, "Let us go into the yard." There he said goodbye to the woman and told her that he was going to stand on his head and would disappear into the earth. Then she must wait until his toes appeared out of the ground. Out of them would grow food for the family. He stood on his head and began to sink into the ground, first his head and shoulders, finally his whole body disappeared.

His wife watched the spot every day and watered it with her tears.

One day a sprout appeared and from it a tree grew so rapidly that in a few days the family had the food that Ku had promised. It was the breadfruit. The wife and children ate all they wanted. Only they could pick the fruit; if anyone else tried, the tree would run back into the ground. After a time sprouts grew about the parent tree and these were given to friends and neighbors to plant in their own gardens. Thus Ku's gift blessed his people.

(This old oral tradition was written down by folktale collector Laura Green.)

The Breadfruit Offering

Two girls who were roasting breadfruit in the upland plain boasted of their gods. "Laka is my god, a beneficient god!" said one.

"Kapo is my god, an amiable god!" said her companion.

While they were thus praising their gods an old woman appeared. She said to the first girl, "Give me some of your breadfruit."

"No," answered the girl, "my breadfruit belongs to Laka."

"Is Laka a powerful god?"

"Yes, a powerful god indeed!"

"Give me some water from your gourd."

"No, indeed! This water belongs to Laka."

The old woman turned to the second girl and asked her for breadfruit. Knowing that she had not vowed the breadfruit to her favorite god, she gave it gladly. When the old woman had eaten she asked for water from her gourd and received it. When she rose to go, before leaving she said to the girl who had treated her kindly, "Go home and tell your parents to store food in their house and to hang up flags for ten days at the corners of the house."

When the girl told her family what the old woman had said they knew that it was no old woman but Pele herself. [Pele is the goddess of the power in the volcano which rises up and flows across the land to the sea.] They were glad that the girl had been kind to her. They obeyed all her commands, and at the expiration of ten days fire from the volcano appeared above Ma-ku'a-we'o-we'o. The lava flowed over Ka-u district and destroyed many homes but spared the house and family of the kind-hearted girl.

Parents and grandparents teach their offspring not to be stingy, not to answer strangers rudely. Some day they may offend Pele and evil befall them.

Mary Wiggin Pukui, comp. and trans., *Hawaiian Folk Tales*, 3rd ser. Poughkeepsie, N.Y.: Vassar College, 1933, 127, 167.

CHEROKEE

[This story, about disagreement and anger, is resolved by gifts. The Great Spirit gives different kinds of berries, and finally strawberries, to the wife, and the wife in turn gives strawberries to her remorseful husband, restoring domestic tranquility. Gifts often serve to dissolve discord and reconcile quarrelers. Various ritual gifts were given as a sign of reconciliation between warring parties—wampum was one form of wealth given at such times. In a sense, all the fruits of the earth are gifts to humanity; received in a spirit of sharing, they can serve as a bond.]

How Red Strawberries Brought Peace in the Woods

There is a river in Arkansas called Strawberry River because its bank is full of wild strawberries. It is a strange stream because near its mouth it flows forward and backward, which no other river in Arkansas does. The Cherokee Indians who used to hunt around the Strawberry River tell a good story of how the strawberries came to the land.

The Great Spirit looked around and saw the endless sky and the green land, and he said man and woman were needed on that land. So he created a warrior and gave him a squaw for a wife.

The two lived together in peace for a long time. He hunted and fished and the woman planted then reaped and cooked food.

Then one day they had a quarrel about a little thing, and so the trouble began. Every day they quarreled a little more. Soon they quarreled about everything.

This kept on for a long time until one day the woman was so angry, she left the man when he was out hunting. She set out for the Sun land that was far off in the east.

When the man came home, he did not find his wife in the wigwam. He looked all around; she was not there. Only her footsteps showed where she had gone. He followed them, but even though he ran fast he could not reach her, she was so far ahead.

She was far, far ahead, running all the time, not looking back.

The man ran all the time too. He ran so fast, he became tired and hungry. The Great

Spirit saw him and was sorry for him.

"Why do you run like that?" he asked the man.

"I am running to catch up to my wife who ran away from our wigwam."

"Why did she run away?"

The man was silent.

Then the Great Spirit said, "She ran away because you two quarreled all the time."

"That is true," the man said. "I will not quarrel again. I am not angry any more."

"If you will not quarrel and not be angry, I will bring her back to you."

The Great Spirit ran in front of the woman and put before her a fine patch of elderberries blooming blue and ripe. She looked at them and kept on running.

Again the Great Spirit ran before her and set in her path some bushes full of blackberries.

The woman came to them, looked at them, and ran on.

The Great Spirit raced ahead of her, all the time putting in her way bushes of all kinds of berries, but she just looked at them and kept on running very fast.

Then the Great Spirit put before her, low on the ground, a bed of beautiful red strawberries. She had never seen the glossy red fruit and had never smelled the strawberry perfume. She bent down to pick some and put them in her mouth. They tasted sweet and good, and she kept on bending down to pick them and eat them. This gave the man a chance to come nearer. One time, as she bent down, she looked backward and saw him running to her.

Then the years they had lived together without quarreling came back to her. She saw the many days they had lived in peace. She forgot all about quarrels and wanted to go back to him. She sat down near a river where the water flowed forward and backward and waited. He came nearer all the time and she wanted more and more to go home with him. She picked up many strawberries and held them in her hands, waiting for him. He came up and she held the red berries up to him. He took them and ate them. They were sweet and smelled nice. He thanked her.

"These berries are very good and I am glad that you gave them to me. I will not quarrel again with you," he said.

"No, we must not quarrel again and be angry," the woman said.

They ate more strawberries together and then they went home.

The strawberries spread all over, and Indians and white folks have been eating them ever since. That is why near the river in Arkansas where the water flows forward and backward so many wild glossy-red strawberries grow and people call it the Strawberry River.

M. A. Jagendorf, *Folk Stories of the South*. New York: Vanguard, 1972, 33–35.

POEM

BENJAMIN TOMPSON (1642–1714)

[These passages are from the prologue to an epic poem, first published in 1676. The poem voices dismay at the decline in piety, the loss of spiritual commitment, and the turn toward luxury, ease, and pleasure. The loss of religious fervor mourned here laments the treatment

of others less fortunate and the brutalization that warfare brings. Tompson mourns a loss of familial friendliness, generous sharing, and a simpler life of more innocent and less greedy concerns. It's uncertain whether the idealistic picture of the good old days he paints ever existed. But nostalgia for the pristine beginning and regret for ideals betrayed are recurrent feelings that cannot be denied and often impel people to use their resources to recover the vitality of well-being in their communities. Peter Buckley in 1651 wrote of America as "a city on a hill" where wise and holy people would live according to God's covenant. William Stoughton wrote in 1668 of the colonists as chosen people: "God hath sifted a whole nation, that he might send choice grain into this wilderness." But Tompson describes a decline and wishes to remind New World settlers of the early high ideals.]

New England's Crisis

. . . the dainty Indian maize
Was eat with clamshells out of wooden trays,
Under thatched huts, without the cry of rent,
And the best sauce to every dish, content.

These golden times (too fortunate to hold)
Were quickly sinned away for love of gold.
'Twas then among the bushes not the street,
If one in place did an inferior meet,
"Good morrow, brother! Is there aught you want?
Take freely of me, what I have you ha'n't."

These times were good, merchants cared not a rush
For other fare than jonakin and mush.
Although men fared and lodged very hard,
Yet innocence was better than a guard. . . .
. . . the noise of war
Was from our towns and hearts removed far.
No bugbear comets in the crystal air
To drive our Christian planters to despair.
Freeness in judgement, union in affection,
Dear love, sound truth, they were our grand protection.

Benjamin Tompson, *New England's Crisis*. Boston: The Club of Odd Volumes, 1894. Also at http://etext.lib.virginia.edu/subjects/eaw/poems/tomptext.htm.

COLONIAL AND PURITAN STORIES

ANTHONY BENEZET (1713–1784)

[Anthony Benezet, a descendent of French Protestants who endured persecution, championed the causes of persecuted oppressed people, including slaves from Africa, Acadi-

ans, and Native Americans. He became a Quaker at fourteen, and matured as a teacher, author, and philanthropist during the years he spent in America. He has been called the most prolific antislavery writer and most influential advocate of African American rights of his times. The passages below are from his book on Guinea and the slave trade. Slaves were brought to the New World beginning in the early 1600s. The earliest slaves' songs and stories about giving were not written down, but it is known that some slaves were Muslim, with the custom of zakat, giving alms. In early America, the Muslim slaves brought from Africa practiced customs still found today. Muslim women in Georgia saved small amounts of rice and sugar each day, if they were able to, and made rice-ball cakes as charity gifts (sakara) for children. More information on this is found in Sylviane A. Diouf's Servants of Allah: African Muslims Enslaved in the Americas. Although documents spelling out the exact words of African slaves in the 1600s are rare, some descriptions by Europeans exist. The following passages describe the customs and ethos of Africans taken as slaves. The Europeans who took them claimed they were helping civilize barbarians by enslaving them, yet the captives' African customs of friendship, generosity, and decency are described as nobler than the ways of those who used their fellow human beings as merchandise. Benezet's writing is both an indictment of European slave traders and a reminder of African customs.]

Africans Captured in Slave Trade Described as Civil and Charitable

From Chapter 2:

[William Smith:] "The country about D'Elmina and Cape Coast, is much the same for beauty and goodness, but more populous; and the nearer we come towards the Slave Coast, the more delightful and rich all the countries are, producing all sorts of trees, fruits, roots, and herbs, that grow within the Torrid Zone."

J. Barbot also remarks, with respect to the countries of Ante and Adom, "That the soil is very good and fruitful in corn and other produce, which it affords in such plenty, that besides what serves for their own use, they always export great quantities for sale; they have a competent number of cattle, both tame and wild, and the rivers abundantly stored with fish, so that nothing is wanting for the support of life, and to make it easy."

In the Collection it is said, "That the inland people on that part of the coast, employ themselves in tillage and trade, and supply the market with corn, fruit, and palm wine; the country producing such vast plenty of Indian corn, that abundance is daily exported, as well by Europeans as Blacks resorting thither from other parts."

Figure 1.2 Quaker Anthony Benezet instructing persecuted black children.

"These inland people are said to live in great union and friendship, being generally well tempered, civil, and tractable; not apt to shed human blood, except when much provoked, and ready to assist one another."

*   *   *

Next adjoining to the Slave Coast, is the kingdom of Benin, which, though it extends but about 170 miles on the sea, yet spreads so far inland, as to be esteemed the most potent kingdom in Guinea. By accounts, the soil and produce appear to be in a great measure like those before described; and the natives are represented as a reasonable good-natured people. Artus says, "They are a sincere, inoffensive people, and do no injustice either to one another, or to strangers." William Smith confirms this account, and says, "That the inhabitants are generally very good-natured, and exceeding courteous and civil. When the Europeans make them presents, which in their coming thither to trade they always do, they endeavour to return them doubly."

*   *   *

[In Benin] The King and great Lords subsist several poor at their place of residence on charity, employing those who are fit for any work, and the rest they keep for God's sake; so that here are no beggars.

*   *   *

. . . [I]n Kongo and Angola, the soil is in general fruitful, producing great plenty of grain, Indian corn, and such quantities of rice, that it hardly bears any price, with fruits, roots, and palm oil in plenty.

The natives are generally a quiet people, who discover a good understanding, and behave in a friendly manner to strangers, being of a mild conversation, affable, and easily overcome with reason.

*   *   *

From Chapter 5:

From the foregoing accounts, as well as other authentic publications of this kind, it appears that it was the unwarrantable lust of gain, which first stimulated the Portugueze, and afterwards other Europeans, to engage in this horrid traffic. By the most authentic relations of those early times, the natives were an inoffensive people, who, when civilly used, traded amicably with the Europeans. It is recorded of those of Benin, the largest kingdom in Guinea, that they were a gentle, loving people; and Reynold says, "They found more sincere proofs of love and good will from the natives, than they could find from the Spaniards and Portugueze . . ."

*   *   *

It was long after the Portugueze had made a practice of violently forcing the natives of Africa into slavery, that we read of the different Negroe nations making war upon each other, and selling their captives. And probably this was not the case, till those bordering on the coast, who had been used to supply the vessels with necessaries, had become corrupted by their intercourse with the Europeans, and were excited by drunkenness and avarice to join them in carrying on those wicked schemes, by which those unnatural wars were perpetrated; the inhabitants kept in continual alarms; the country laid waste; and, as William Moor expresses it, "infinite numbers sold into slavery." But that the Europeans are the principal cause of these devastations, is particularly evidenced by one, whose connexion with the trade would rather induce him to represent it in the fairest colours, to wit, William Smith, the person sent in the year 1726 by the African company to survey their settlements, who, from the information he received of one of the factors, had resided ten years in that country, says, "That the discerning natives account it their greatest unhappiness, that they were ever visited by the Europeans."—"That we christians introduced the traffick of slaves; and that before our coming they lived in peace." If instead of making slaves of the Negroes, the nations who assume the name and character of christians, would use their endeavours to make the nations of Africa acquainted with the nature of the christian religion, to give them a better sense of the true use of the blessings of life, the more beneficial arts and customs would, by degrees, be introduced amongst them; this care probably would produce the same effect upon them, which it has had on the inhabitants of Europe, formerly as savage and barbarous as the natives of Africa.

*   *   *

From Chapter 9:

[In Astley's Collection … the author] speaking of the Mandingos settled at Galem, which is situated 900 miles up the Senegal, after saying that they carry on a commerce to all the neighbouring kingdoms, and amass riches, adds, "That excepting 'the vices peculiar to the Blacks,' they are a good sort of people, honest, hospitable, just to their word, laborious, industrious, and very ready to learn arts and sciences." Here it is difficult to imagine what vices can be peculiarly attendant on a people so well disposed as the author describes these to be. . . . [Peter Kolben writes that the Hottentots] ". . . are eminently distinguished by many virtues, as their mutual benevolence, friendship, and hospitality; they breathe kindness and good will to one another, and seek all opportunities of obliging. Is a Hottentot's assistance required by one of his countrymen? He runs to give it. Is his advice asked? He gives it with sincerity. Is his countryman in want? He relieves him to the utmost of his power." Their hospitality extends even to European strangers: in travelling thro' the Cape countries, you meet with a cheerful and open reception, in whatsoever village you come to. In short, he says, "The integrity of the Hottentots, their strictness and celerity in the execution of justice, and their charity, are equalled by few nations. In alliances, their word is sacred; there being hardly any thing they look upon as a fouler crime than breach of engagements. Theft and adultery they punish with death." They firmly believe there is a God, the author of all things, whom they call the God of gods. . . .

*   *   *

Father Tachard, a French Jesuit, famous for his travels in the East Indies, in his account of these people, says, "The Hottentots have more honesty, love, and liberality for one another, than are almost anywhere seen amongst christians."

Anthony Benezet, *Some Historical Account of Guinea, Its Situation, Produce, and the General Disposition of Its Inhabitants, An Inquiry into the Rise and Progress of the Slave Trade, Its Nature and Lamentable Effects*. Philadelphia: 1771; reprinted in London: 1772. For full text and notes to quotations: www.gutenberg.org/files/11489/11489-8.txt.

CAPTAIN JOHN SMITH (1580–1631)

[Historian Moses Coit Tyler asserted that one of the first characteristics England noted in American literature was "what proved to be the incurable American habit of talking back to her." (Moses Coit Tyler, A History of American Literature [New York: Putnam, 1879], 29.) He pointed to the tone of an early seventeenth-century letter written by Captain John Smith to British authorities as an example. Smith, whose A True Relation of Virginia was the first book written in America, wrote in a way that, in Tyler's view, suited the personality of a famed adventurer. In the following passage, Smith writes of being sickened by seeing the gold fever of greed. The age of exploration and colonization was partly fueled with philanthropic ideals—to save pagan souls, to give families ruined financially a new beginning, to civilize barbaric wildernesses. It was also partly fueled by dreams of finding gold. In his narratives, John Smith often referred to himself in the third person, as we see below.]

A Drunken Ship with Gilded Dirt

. . . The worst mischief was our gilded refiners, with their golden promises, made all men their slaves in hope of recompense. There was no talk, no hope, nor work, but dig gold, wash gold, refine gold, load gold. Such a brute of gold, as one mad fellow desired to be buried in the sands, least they should by their art make gold of his bones. Little need there was and less reason, the ship should stay, their wages run on, our victual consume 14 weeks, that the Mariners might say, they built such a golden Church, that we can say, the rain washed near to nothing in 14 days. Were it that Captain Smith would not applaud all those golden inventions, because they admitted him not to the sight of their trials, nor golden consultations I know not: but I heard him question with Captain Martin and tell him, except he would shew him a more substantial trial, he was not enamored with their dirty skill. Breathing out these and many other passions, never any thing did more torment him, than to see all necessary business neglected, to fraught such a drunken ship with so much gilded dirt . . .

John Smith, *Narratives of Early Virginia 1606–1625*, ed. Lyon Gardiner Tyler. New York: Barnes & Noble, 1966, 136–37.

ALEXANDER WHITAKER (1585–1616)

[Whitaker, a theologian from Cambridge, arrived in Virginia in 1611. Among his converts in the colony was Pocahontas. The sermons Whitaker sent back to England include statements that recognize both the humanity and the sinfulness of the Indians. In this writing, he explains the reasons for giving, and pleads for generosity to the Indians. He explores the question of why God made the rewards of good acts to come after much time has passed.

Bread has many associations in Judeo-Christian traditions. It is the "staff of life" and also represents spiritual sustenance. Jesus said "I am the living bread . . . the bread . . . is my flesh." Our word "companions" comes from the words "sharers of bread." Bread is the staple food of the West, and later it came to mean "money" in American slang. Whitaker does not mention the bread of communion, a central Christian metaphor, but for many readers it will resonate in the background because it is such a familiar religious image. The sermon's style is serious and somber, with formal language, yet it is a long fantasy on the strange image of tossing bread onto the waters and then expecting it to multiply. Whitaker expends much talk in explaining the symbolic enigma. When common sense says "take care of yourself; keep your goods for yourself," it is paradoxical advice to cast it on wider waters. Resolving that conundrum, Whitaker explores the larger picture and promises a great return in the long run to those with the necessary faith. Casting one's bread, one finds the grail. The words in italics were reminders to Whitaker to emphasize those parts of his speech in intensity, to get the meaning across.]

Good News from Virginia

Cast thy bread upon the water: for after many days thou shalt find it. —Eccl 11:1

Be bold my Hearers to contemn riches, and frame your selves to walk worthy of God; for none other be worthy of God, but those that lightly esteem of riches.

Nakedness is the riches of nature; virtue is the only thing that makes us rich and honorable in the eyes of wise men. Poverty is a thing which most men fear, and covetous men cannot endure to behold: yet poverty with a contented mind is great riches: he truly is the only poor man, not that hath little, but which continually desireth more. Riches (as they are esteemed) have no limits, but still cry, *plus vitra*, still more. . . .

Wherefore . . . Solomon . . . said . . . *Behold all is vanity, and vexation of the spirit. In the fifth Chapter, He that loveth silver, shall not be satisfied with silver; and he that loveth riches, shall be without the fruit of it. And what good cometh to the owners thereof, but the beholding thereof with their eyes.* And he addeth, *The satiety of the rich will not suffer him to sleep.* Again, *There is an evil sickness that I have seen under the sun, Riches reserved to the owners thereof, for their evil.* Now in the beginning of this chapter, he hath let down a remedy to both these evils, whereby our riches may be made constant unto us: we may take pleasure and profit by them, and our posterity through many descents may enjoy them after us. *Cast thy bread* (sayeth he) *upon the waters*: why? *For after many days thou shalt find it.*

The sentence is Rhetorical, full of figures, and needs some explaining. Bread in Scripture is usually taken for all kind of meat and drink, as may appear, Gen.18.5. And in divers other places: but here (I take it) it is more generally put for all kind of Alms, of what nature soever: not only for meat and drink, money, apparel, or the like, but also for any kind of thing, whereby we may relieve the necessity of our neighbor. *Waters* also are here metaphorically put for all those men, who stand in need of the alms of our liberality, whether they be such as cannot, but gladly would requite us, or else such as being able, forget to be thankful.

So that the plain meaning of the words is this. Give liberally thine alms to all sorts of men, that may stand in need of thy help: hide not thine eyes at the miserable state of the afflicted; neither stop thine ear at the cry of the poor, though they be not able to recompense thy well-doing: reproach not thine enemy, when he is punished, but rather overcome his evil deeds with thy goodness; neither suffer any to return empty handed from thee, whom God shall offer to thy liberality. For though thou canst not presently expect a plentiful reward of thy well-doing, though the persons, to whom thou hast cast thine alms, be not able to requite thee, or forgetful of good turns, yet be assured of it, that God beholdeth thy charity, and will at his appointed time requite thee, even in this world, if it be good for thee, thou shalt taste of his bounty, but in the world to come he hath reserved for thee a most glorious crown of blessed immortality. This is the soul and substance of this short sentence.

The words naturally divide themselves into two principal parts. A Commandment to be Liberal and Charitable: and a promise of reward, which hereafter we shall find. The Commandment also containeth in it five points, touching the doctrine of Liberality.

1. The duty to be performed, *Cast thy bread*: be liberal to all.
2. The manner of bestowing our alms, by casting it away.
3. What is to be given, *Bread*; all things needful, yea, and of the best kind.
4. Who may be liberal: even those that have it: *Thy bread*, it must be thine own.
5. To whom we must be liberal; to all, yea, to the *Waters*.

First, we will briefly speak of these five points of this Commandment as they lie in order; and then directly come unto the promise more particularly. The enjoined duty is *Liberality,* which sometimes is termed *Alms:* sometimes more largely is used for all kind of good works, and very often is signified by the names of *Charity* and *Brotherly love:* all which being in sense and signification one, shall in the naming of them, be used all as one. *Liberality* is the true practice of Christian *Humanity* and *Brotherly courtesy,* one towards another. A virtue commanded by God, and commended by the examples of the best; which makes us accepted of God, and desired of men. *Faith* gives comfort to my soul, and ministers peace to my conscience: Hope teacheth me not to be hasty, but to wait patiently the appointed time of God; but the practice of *Love* maintains and moreover is beneficial unto others, yea, profitable to all. *Now abideth Faith, Hope and Love, even these three;* but the greatest of these is Love. Wherefore hath God made men great, and filled their coffers with his treasures, but that they should as faithful stewards of God's store, liberally provide for the necessity of his Saints. The richest man in the world, hath no right by nature to the things he doth possess; for naked he came into the world, and he must return naked out of the same again. Why then hath God made thee rich, and commended that to thy liberality which was not thine own; but that thou shouldst be bountiful to those whom he hath made poor?

What goodness or excellency did God see in thee, more than in the poorest reasonable creature, before thou yet wast, that he should make thee rich, and him poor? Doth it not befall to thee, as to the fool? Ye verily, *the condition of men* in this case, and *the condition of beasts is all one: As one dieth, so dieth the other; all go to one place, and all was of the dust;* and all shall return to the dust. But that which Nature hath not distinguished, the wisdom and bounty of God hath by a property of calling altered, and lending his treasures to the rich men of the world, hath showed to them an example of his Liberality, to this end, that they might be open-handed to others, distributing as faithful stewards of his gifts, according to the necessity of the Saints. Wherefore our Savior Christ proclaimeth, *Who is a faithful servant and wife, whom his master hath made ruler over his household to give them meat in season. Blessed is that servant, whom his master when he cometh shall find so doing.* Saint Paul exhorteth us to do good to all, but specially to the household of faith: and writeth to *Timothy,* to *charge them that be rich in this world, that they do good, and be rich in good works, ready to distribute and communicate.* He showeth *Titus* also, that the end of our *Redemption is, that we might be Zealous of good works:* and therefore willeth him to affirm, *That they which have believed in God, might be careful to show forth good works, etc. . . .*

Cast thy bread, etc. What? hath God given us goods to cast them away? Yea verily, for Solomon sayeth, There is a time to seek, and a time to lose; a time to keep, and a time to cast away. Which time of losing and casting away the Scripture, here noteth. But by this word of casting away, is meant no violent rejecting, or negligent losing of some things that we hate or do not greatly esteem: but a liberal giving away of such things as we do possess: which may appear by these reasons . . .

. . . The Doctrine handled is touching *Liberality,* allegorically compared to the seed of bread (for so bread may be here understood) which husbandmen cast not away, but sow as well in moist, as in drier grounds: and to *Tremelius* doth interpret them. Now as husbandmen do not cast away their seed, which they fling into the ground, for hatred or neglect, but under hope of God's blessing: even so *liberal men* exercising the *works* of charity, do not cast away their alms, as one that casteth a bone to a dog, or flingeth dead flowers from him, etc. But freely bestow the alms of God without pride, vainglory, or disdain, yea, without hope of any restitution, or any other recompense, besides the acceptance of God, and the reward which God shall give unto him in this life, but especially in the great day of his harvest. And with this doth agree that saying of Solomon, *There is that scattereth and is more increased.* So that the spirit of God teacheth us by this word of casting, how we may scatter our good deeds and bestow our alms, as that they may be accepted of God and profitable unto us. As, many ask and receive not, because they ask amiss: so the most that cast away find not, because they be illiberal in their liberality, or because they give amiss. . . .

Our great Master Christ, the mouth of God to man, handling the doctrine of liberality in his Sermon on the mount, hath taught us many rules touching the right manner of giving alms, which we may refer to these five points.

First, that we give in faith, for without faith it is unpossible to please God; therefore without faith our alms cannot please God: the sum of which faith is this: first, that God will accept of us and our alms for his son Jesus Christ's sake, for no work of any man can please God, before the man be approved of him, and then all our good deeds shall be accepted of him. . . .

The second rule in giving is, that we give in Love, which whosoever lacketh cannot give aright, and sayeth Saint Paul, Though I feed the poor with all my goods and have not love; it profiteth me nothing. The sum of which love is, that out of mere pity, compassion and fellow-feeling of our neighbor's wants, we call our bread to him; not for constraint of law, and custom of parishioners, neither for any sinister respect of praise or vainglory. Wherefore the same Paul sayeth, He that distributeth, let him do it with simplicity: and our Savior Christ commandeth, that when thou doest thine alms, let not thy left hand know what thy right hand doth.

Thirdly, we must give our alms bountifully and with a cheerful mind: but as everyone wisheth in his heart, so let him give, not grudging or of necessity, for God loveth a cheerful giver: He that soweth sparingly shall reap also sparingly; and he that soweth liberally shall reap also liberally. . . .

The fourth rule of right giving, ariseth from hence, which is, that we give our alms with discretion. First, that we communicate such things as the need of our neighbor requireth; the thirsty man must have drink, the hungry and naked, meat and apparel, the imprisoned for debt, money and the like. Secondly, we must not defer the time of our relief, lest that we give too late, when the case of our neighbor is past help: *Bis dat qui cito dat:* ["He gives twice who gives quickly."] The Physician comes too late when the patient is dead. But a word spoken in season is like apples of gold and pictures of silver: whilst thou may, then do good, thou knowest not then what may befall afterward. Thirdly, we must choose such a place as may be void of vainglory and hypocrisy. Our left hand may not know what our right hand doth: Honors may be openly given for the encouragement of others; but alms-deeds must be given in secret: then thy Father that seeth in secret shall reward thee openly. The last rule of giving is, that we give in Justice. . . . That we give not other men's goods . . . The true feasting is to break thine own bread to the hungry, to bring the poor that wander into thine house.

The next point to be handled is, wherein we are to be liberal, what we are to give: Solomon hath shut up under the name of Bread, whereby (as I said before) is meant all things wherein we may receive the necessities of our neighbors: for if a man shall cast his drink, apparel, gold, and the like upon the waters, he shall after many days find them: but *Solomon* included all these alms under the name of *bread*, because he would enforce this doctrine under one Allegory of sowing, and therefore doth suite his phrase with words of most significance. Again, bread is the staff of good nourishment, and the most usual kind of alms which we give. This article then of this Commandment is, that if our neighbors do stand in need of our help in anything wherein we may help them; we are not to withhold our hand from them, but to cast our alms liberally unto them. . . .

The wants of our neighbors' outward state are most and everywhere common. First, we must freely give to the poor, as clothes to the naked, liberal gleanings to the stranger, fatherless and widow; Justice in Judgement to the oppressed, etc.

Secondly, we must freely lend whereby we may be oftentimes as beneficial to our neighbor as by giving. Concerning which our Savior Christ sayeth, From him that would borrow of thee, turn not away thy face. And the commandment of God is, Thou shalt open thy hands to thy poor brother, and lend him sufficient for his need which he hath.

Thirdly, we must freely forgive and remit the due debt which our neighbor doth owe unto us, if it so fall out that God bring him into decay and extreme poverty. . . .

The fourth point in order to be considered is, who may properly give alms which may easily be determined, if we consider the divers kinds of good works which we have now lately rehearsed . . . *Everyone may be a giver of alms.* For he that hath not riches of wealth and cannot give much, let him give a little according to the measure of his ability. Wherefore our Savior Christ commendeth the liberality of the poor widow, which cast into the treasury but two mites, which was all that she had.

Those also that have not money and goods to help their neighbor, let them lend the help of their bodily labor, of their callings, or the virtues of their soul and body unto them, and this was Peter's Alms. . . .

This is the doctrine, and I beseech God to stir up your minds to the practice of liberality in all things towards all men. And remember the poor estate of the ignorant inhabitants of Virginia. Cast forth your alms (my brethren of England) and extend your liberality on these charitable works, which God hath called you to perform. Let not the servants of superstition, that think to merit by their good works (as they term them) go beyond us in well doing; neither let them be able to open their mouths against us, and to condemn the religion of our Protestation, for want of charitable deeds. . . . Those that cannot help in monies by reason of their poverty, may venture their persons hither, and here not only serve God, but help also these poor Indians, and build a sure foundation for themselves, but if you can do neither of these, then send your earnest prayers to God for the prosperity of this work. . . .

And this is the rule of *St. Paul,* do good to all, but specially to the household of Faith. Though the children of God be chiefly to be respected: yet are we not to withhold our alms from anyone, if they need our help. The rule of Christ is answerable: Give him that asketh, and from him that would borrow of thee turn not away. Do good to them that hate you, and pray for them which hurt you, and persecute you. And so Paul expoundeth this rule of Christ: *If thine enemy hunger, feed him, if he thirst give him drink.* If then we must feed and clothe our enemies and persecutors, how much more our friends and helpers; it remaineth then that we must do good to all. . . .

. . . Wherefore my brethren, put on the bowels of compassion, and let the lamentable estate of these miserable people enter in your consideration: One God created us, they have reasonable souls and intellectual faculties as well as we; we all have Adam for a common parent. . . . But if any of us should misdoubt that this barbarous people is uncapable of such heavenly mysteries, let such men know that they are far mistaken in the nature of these men, for besides the promise of God, which is without respect of persons made as well to unwise men after the flesh, as to the wise, etc. let us not think that these men are so simple as some have supposed them: for they are of body lusty, strong, and very nimble: they are a very understanding generation, quick of apprehension, sudden in their dispatches, subtle in their dealings, exquisite in their inventions, and industrious in their labor. I suppose the world hath no better mark-men with their bows and arrows than they be. . . . They have a rude kind of Commonwealth, and rough government, wherein they both honor and obey their Kings, Parents, and Governors, both greater and less, they observe the limits of their own possessions, and encroach not upon their neighbors' dwellings. Murder is a capital crime scarce heard of among them: adultery is most severely punished, and so are their other offenses. These unnurtured grounds of reason in them, may serve to encourage us: to instruct them in the knowledge of the true God, the rewarder of all righteousness, not doubting but that he was powerful to save us by his word, when we were nothing, will be merciful also to these sons of Adam in his appointed time, in whom there be remaining so many footsteps of God's image. Wherefore you wealthy men of this world, whose bellies God hath filled with his hidden Treasure: trust not in uncertain riches, neither cast your eyes upon them; for riches taketh her to her wings as an Eagle, and flieth to Heaven. *But be rich in good works ready to distribute or communicate. . . .*

For after many days thou shalt find it. Hitherto have we spoken of the commandment and the several branches of the same: Now follows the reason of this Commandment which the Holy Ghost useth here to stir up unto liberality, which is taken from the reward which we shall have of our well-doing, for after many days thou shalt find it, the sum of which reason is, that though God do not presently reward our well-doing, but do deter the requital of it for many days, yet thy good works shall not perish, but God at the appointed time, shall abundantly recompense thy liberality. Out of this reason we may gather two notable conclusions touching the reward of liberality. First we may conclude from hence, that God doth not always give a present reward to the good works; he doth for the most part defer his rewards many days, sometimes many years, yea sometimes even till death itself, when he will never cease to reward us according to our works, with unspeakable joys of blessed immortality. And the wisdom of God doth thus defer his rewards for most singular reasons. For if God should presently reward good works, who then would not be a prodigal giver, who then would be a faithful giver? For when a man is certain of present gain he will not spare to give abundantly, because he seeth an exceeding profit ready to be put into his hands for so doing: and this would stir up the most covetous wretch in the world to be liberal, gaping out of mere covetousness, after an over-plus of reward. Wherefore God hath made the time and condition of his rewards doubtful, that we might not be covetous of the benefit: but that he might exercise our faith, and teach us with patience of hope to expect the appointed time of his reward. The principal point of perfect charity is, that we give in faith, whose true nature is to depend upon God for the good success of our alms, *for Faith is the ground of things that are hoped for, & the evidence of things that are not seen.* . . .

. . . It is the property of true charity to neglect the present reward. For Love the mother of liberality is not covetous, but is bountiful, it believeth all things, it hopeth all things . . .

Alexander Whitaker, *Good News from Virginia* (London: 1613). Facsimile edition. New York: Scholars' Facsimiles and Reprints, 1976.

LEADERS OF VIRGINIA (1620)

[Some forms of seventeeth-century American philanthropy were very pragmatic, as the next example illustrates. In 1620 the leaders of Virginia offered help to parentless destitute children in England—seven years of apprenticeship in the new colony, an arrangement they hoped would bring mutual benefits. The orphans would learn skills and have their needs provided for, and at the end of the apprenticeship, they would work an additional seven years; they would then receive liberty and half of the cattle and fruits of the earth that they had helped to increase and produce, as well as twenty-five acres of land in Virginia. The new colony would gain in the increase of its productive population, and the needy children would have gainful employment and learn how to make a worthwhile life for themselves. Below is part of the offer that leaders of the new colony penned and sent to the Virginia Company of London.]

A Benevolent Plan for Orphan Apprentices

It is intended and fully resolved that this next spring the number of one hundred children more . . . shall be sent and transported by the said Virginia Company out of the City of London unto Virginia, aforesaid, and that toward the charge of transporting and appareling the same children, the like collection of £ 500, of men godly and charitably disposed toward the said plantation, which do reside within the said city and the suburbs thereof, the same shall be paid to the Virginia Company for the purpose aforesaid. Now, therefore, for the good of the same children, and in consideration of the premises, it is fully concluded and ordered and decreed at a great and general Quarter Court this day held by the Treasurer, Council, and company of Virginia, that the said hundred children last mentioned shall be sent at the Virginia Company's charge, and during their voyage shall have their provision sweet and good and well appareled, and all other things necessary for the voyage; and that every of the same children shall be there placed apprentices with honest and good masters—that is to say, the boys for the term of seven years or more, so as their apprenticeships may expire at their several ages of one-and-twenty years or upward, and the maids or girls for the term of seven years, or until they shall attain their several ages of one-and-twenty years, or be married, to be by the same masters during that time educated and brought up in some good crafts, trades, or husbandry, whereby they may be enabled to better their living and maintain themselves when they shall attain their several ages or be out of their apprenticeships; and during their apprenticeships shall have all things provided for them as shall be fit and requisite, as meat, drink, apparel, and other necessaries.

And, further, that at the expiration of their several apprenticeships, every of the said children shall have freely given unto them and provided for them, at the said Company's charge, provision of corn for victuals for one whole year, and shall also have a house ready built to dwell in, and be placed as a tenant in some convenient place upon so much land as they can manage; and shall have one cow and as much corn as he or she will plant, and 40s. to apparel them, or apparel to that value; and shall also have convenient weapons, munition and armor for defense, and necessary implements and utensils for household, and sufficient working tools and instruments for their trades, labor, and husbandry in such sort as other tenants are provided for.

Moreover, that every of the said children last mentioned, which shall have thus served their apprenticeships and be placed and provided for as aforesaid, shall be tied to be tenants or farmers in manner and form aforesaid for the space of seven years after their apprenticeships ended, and during that time of their labor and pains therein they shall have half of all the increase, profit, and benefit that shall arise, grow, and increase by the management thereof, as well the fruits of the earth, the increased of the cattle as otherwise, and the other moiety thereof, to go and remain to the owners of the land, in lieu and satisfaction of a rent to be paid for the same land so by them to be occupied; and that at the expiration of the same last seven years every of the said children to be at liberty either to continue tenants or farmers of the Company upon the same lands, if they will, at the same rates and in the manner aforesaid, or else provide for themselves elsewhere.

And, lastly, that either of the same children, at the end of the last seven years, shall have moreover five-and-twenty acres of land, to be given and allotted to them in some convenient place or places within the English plantations in Virginia aforesaid, to hold in fee simple by socage tenure to every of them and their heirs forever freely, for the rent of *6d.* for every five-and-twenty acres by way of quit rent in lieu of all services in regard of the tenure. All which premises we, the said Treasurer, Council, and Company, do order and decree, and faithfully promise shall be justly and truly performed toward the said children according to the true intent and meaning thereof.

R. A. Brock, ed., *Abstract of the Proceedings of the Virginia Company of London, 1619–1624.* Richmond: Virginia Historical Society, 1888, 1:39–42.

JOHN WINTHROP (1588–1649)

[Aboard the flagship Arabella in 1630, Puritan leader John Winthrop wrote a sermon setting forth this well-reasoned argument for loving and helping others with a persuasive appeal to Christian archetypes of sympathy. Delivering the hortatory message on the high seas as the ship sailed across the Atlantic toward the New World, he distilled New Testament teachings to give the colonists a vision of their purpose in a strange land. He contemplated their deepest reasons for leaving England and articulated Puritan goals in founding a community in the New World. The model he proposed offered a reminder of Christian values and took account of the fears and hopes involved in the momentous mission they had undertaken. The principles he hoped would serve as the organizing force of the community express a vision of the new Puritan commonwealth being planted in America. The word charity as Winthrop used it meant loving-kindness, not donating money to help the poor. Loving others involves treating them as we would wish to be treated. Winthrop was a successful Cambridge-educated lawyer from a wealthy family in the cloth trade. Disgusted by the corruption of the church and the court, Winthrop became the first governor of the Massachusetts Bay Colony and is known as "the Founding Father of New England." It is said that he personified well the characteristic Puritan dynamic of eagerness to attain success in the world entwined with fervor for attaining salvation in the hereafter. He was a believer in profit and prosperity as a sign that God was blessing one's endeavors. Below we see his views on charity. The image of a community knitted together by Christ and forming a glorious body joined by love was powerful and persuasive to fervent religious believers of this community, and it was capable of nurturing strong bonds among them. Italicized words in the text show quotations from the Bible and parts of the sermon Winthrop intended to emphasize when he preached it.]

A Model of Christian Charity (Excerpts)

Object. The wise man's Eyes are in his head, saith Solomon, *and foreseeth the plague;* therefore he must forecast and lay up against evil times when he or his may stand in need of all he can gather.

Ans. This very Argument Solomon useth to persuade to liberality, Eccl: *Cast thy bread upon the waters ,* and *for thou knowest not what evil may come upon the land.* Luke 26: *Make you friends of the riches of iniquity;* you will ask how this shall be? very well. For first he that gives to the poor, lends to the lord and he will repay him even in this life an hundredfold to him or his.—*The righteous is ever merciful and lendeth and his seed enjoyeth the blessing;* and besides we know what advantage it will be to us in the day of account when many such witnesses shall stand forth for us to witness the improvement of our talent. . . .

*   *   *

. . . [T]he Lord looks that when he is pleased to call for his right in any thing we have, our own interest we have, must stand aside till his turn be served. For the other, we need look no further then to that of John 1: *He who hath this world's goods and seeth his brother to need and shuts up his compassion from him, how dwelleth the love of God in him,* which comes punctually to this conclusion; if thy brother be in want and thou canst help him, thou needst not make doubt, what thou shouldst do; if thou lovest God thou must help him.

    Quest. What rule must we observe in lending?
    Ans. Thou must observe whether thy brother hath present or probable or possible means of repaying thee, if there be none of those, thou must give him according to his necessity, rather then lend him as he requires; if he hath present means of repaying thee, thou art to look at him not as an act of mercy, but by way of Commerce, wherein thou art to walk by the rule of justice; but if his means of repaying thee be only probable or possible, then is he an object of thy mercy, thou must lend him, though there be danger of losing it, Deut 15:7: *If any of thy brethren be poor, thou shalt lend him sufficient.* That men might not shift off this duty by the apparent hazard, he tells them that though the year of Jubilee were at hand (when he must remit it, if he were not able to repay it before) yet he must lend him and that cheerfully. *It may not grieve thee to give him* (saith he) and because some might object, why so I should soon impoverish myself and my family, he adds with all thy work; for our Saviour, Matt 5:42: *From him that would borrow of thee turn not away.*

    Quest. What rule must we observe in forgiving?
    Ans. Whether thou didst lend by way of commerce or in mercy, if he hath nothing to pay thee, must forgive, (except in cause where thou hast a surety or a lawful pledge) Deut 15:2: Every seventh year the Creditor was to quit that which he lent to his brother if he were poor as appears ver. 8. *Save when there shall be no poor with thee.* In all these and like cases, Christ was a general rule, Matt 7:22: *Whatsoever ye would that men should do to you, do ye the same to them also.*

    Quest. What rule must we observe and walk by in cause of community of peril?
    Ans. The same as before, but with more enlargement towards others and less respect

Figure 1.3 Early American farmer plowing

towards ourselves and our own right. Hence it was that in the primitive Church they sold all, had all things in common, neither did any man say that which he possessed was his own. . . . *He who shutteth his ears from hearing the cry of the poor, he shall cry and shall not be heard;* Matt 25: *Go ye cursed into everlasting fire &c. I was hungry and ye fed me not,* 2 Cor 9:16: He that soweth sparingly shall reap sparingly. Having already set forth the practice of mercy according to the rule of God's law, it will be useful to lay open the grounds of it also, being the other part of the Commandment and that is the affection from which this exercise of mercy must arise, the Apostle tells us that this *love is the fulfilling of the law,* not that it is enough to love our brother and so no further; but in regard of the excellency of his parts giving any motion to the other as the soul to the body and the power it hath to set all the faculties on work in the outward exercise of this duty; as when we bid one make the clock strike, he doth not lay hand on the hammer, which is the immediate instrument of the sound, but sets on work the first mover or main wheel; knowing that will certainly produce the sound which he intends. So the way to draw men to the works of mercy, is not by force of Argument from the goodness or necessity of the work; for though this cause may enforce, a rational mind to some present act of mercy, as is frequent in experience, yet it cannot work such a habit in a soul, as shall make it prompt upon all occasions to produce the same effect, but by framing these affections of love in the heart which will as naturally bring forth the other, as any cause doth produce the effect.

The definition which the Scripture gives us of love is this. *Love is the bond of perfection,* first it is a bond or ligament. Secondly it makes the work perfect. There is no body but consists of parts and that which knits these parts together, gives the body its perfection, because it makes each part so contiguous to others as thereby they do mutually participate with each other, both in strength and infirmity, in pleasure and pain. To instance in the most perfect of all bodies; Christ and his Church make one body;

the several parts of this body considered a part before they were united, were as disproportionate and as much disordering as so many contrary qualities or elements, but when Christ comes, and by his spirit and love knits all these parts to himself and each to other, it is become the most perfect and best proportioned body in the world, Eph 4:16: *Christ, by whom all the body being knit together by every joint for the furniture thereof, according to the effectual power which is in the measure of every perfection of parts, a glorious body without spot or wrinkle;* the ligaments hereof being Christ, or his love, for Christ is love, 1 John 4:8. So this definition is right. *Love is the bond of perfection.*

John Winthrop, "A Modell of Christian Charity." Boston: Collections of the Massachusetts Historical Society, 1838, 3rd ser., 7:31–48. Accessible at http://history.hanover.edu/texts/winthmod.html. (Word spellings have been modernized).

On ROGER WILLIAMS (1603–1683)

[Moses Coit Tyler studied at Yale and wrote a two-volume history of American literature that became a classic. This piece from that history is about early settler Roger Williams. Williams grew up near Newgate, in London, where many Puritans were put to death, and this may have turned his sympathy toward religious liberty. He studied at Cambridge University and became a chaplain to a wealthy family. He was married and soon went with his wife to the Massachusetts Bay Colony. When his preaching put him at odds with the strict Puritans, he was almost deported. Befriended by Indians, he settled at the headwaters of Narragansett Bay, founding a settlement at Providence. Williams was a generous man who argued that forced conversion of the Indians was a kind of rape. Both the Indians and the newcomers had reasons to be generous—their stories and wisdom traditions taught them this. An anonymous writer in early Maryland wrote, "Experience hath taught us, that by kind and fair usage, the Natives are not only become peaceable, but also friendly, and have upon all occasions performed as many friendly Offices to the English in Maryland, and New-England, as any neighbor or friend uses to do in the most civil parts of Christendom: therefore any wise man will hold it in a far more just and reasonable way to treat the People of the Country well." (From A Relation of Maryland, printed in London, 1635.) There were early settlers who were conscientious in respecting and appreciating the humanity and helpfulness of the Native Americans. There were also hostile Indians and belligerent settlers, and they antagonized one another. The ravens in the quoted verse are references to the providential support given to the prophet Elijah in the desert, a story from the Old Testament. In Williams' verse, they are symbolic of the Native Americans who helped him survive.]

History of American Literature by Moses Coit Tyler

With respect to the sympathy of Roger Williams with the Indians, it concerns us, at present, to note that it did not exhaust itself in the invention of a legal opinion on their behalf: throughout his whole life, early and late, he put himself to much downright toil and self-denial for their benefit, both in body and in soul. He and John Eliot had come to New England in the same year, 1631, but at least a dozen years before John Eliot had entered upon his apostolic labors among the Indians,

Roger Williams had lodged "with them in their filthy, smoky holes . . . to gain their tongue," and had preached to them in it. "My soul's desire," he said, "was to do the natives good." Later, he knew from his own experience, that it was possible for the English to live at peace with the Indians; when, however, that peace was broken, though he wished the English to acquit themselves manfully and successfully, he evermore stood between them and their vanquished foes, with words of compassion. In 1637, amid the exasperation caused by the Pequot war, the voice of Roger Williams was heard imploring the victors to spare. "I much rejoice," he writes to the governor of Massachusetts, "that . . . some of the chiefs at Connecticut, . . . are almost adverse from killing women and children. Mercy outshines all the works and attributes of Him who is the Father of Mercies." In another letter he expresses the hope that all Christians who receive as slaves the surviving Pequots, may so treat them "as to make mercy eminent." In still another letter he invokes mercy upon the miserable Pequots, "since the Most High delights in mercy, and great revenge hath been already taken." This, to the end of his life, was his one cry in the midst of all storms of popular wrath and revenge.

And the benignity of Roger Williams was large enough to go out toward other people than the Indians. His letters, public and private, are a proof that the sight of any creature in trouble, was enough to stir his heart and his hand for quick relief. His best clients appear to have been those who had no other advocate, and who could pay no fees: poor people; sick ones; wanderers; "the dead, the widows, and the fatherless"; and, especially, all who had been turned adrift for the crime of having an independent thought. Nay, his generosity threw its arms not only around those who were then actually unfortunate, but even around those who might ever become so; and for them, too, he tried to make tender provision. In 1662, the people of Providence resolved to divide among themselves the lands that still remained common. When Roger Williams heard of this, he wrote a warm-hearted and moving appeal to them, as his "loving friends and neighbors," beseeching them that as he first gave to them all the lands, so they would permit some to remain unappropriated, as a possession in reserve for such homeless persons as, driven from any country for conscience' sake, might thereafter flee to them for refuge: "I earnestly pray the town to lay to heart, as ever they look for a blessing from God on the town, on your families, your corn and cattle, and your children after you, . . . that after you have got over the black brook of some soul-bondage yourselves, you tear not down the bridge after you, by leaving no small pittance for distressed souls that may come after you."

[In William's book] *A Key into the Language of America: or, An help to the language of the natives in that part of America called New England,* "If nature's sons, both wild and tame, / Humane and courteous be, / How ill becomes it sons of God / To want humanity!" [Williams wrote]: "It is a strange truth that a man shall generally find more free entertainment and refreshing amongst these barbarians, than amongst thousands that call themselves Christians"; and he hints gratefully at the hospitality he had found among American savages even when he had experienced some lack of it among his own countrymen: "God's providence is rich to his, / Let none distrustful be; / In wilderness, in great distress, / These ravens have fed me."

Moses Coit Tyler, *History of American Literature*, vol. 1, chap. 3 and 4. New York: G. P. Putnam's Sons, 1879. [Tyler quotes the verses from "A Key to the Language of America," reprinted in Narr. Club Pub. I. 1–222, and there edited by J. Hammond Trumbull, 39, 46.]

PETER STUYVESANT (ca. 1600–1672) AND OTHERS

[Peter Stuyvesant, the son of a Dutch minister, became Director-General of New Netherland colony (now New York) in 1647. Stuyvesant perceived non-Reformed religious groups as a threat to the colony and sought to suppress them, but Dutch law and colonial tradition guaranteed religious freedom. Directors of the Dutch West India Company in Amsterdam revoked Stuyvesant's rulings and ordered him to accept Jews from Dutch Brazil seeking refuge in New Netherland. This acceptance was ordered on the basis of "reason and equity," as well as common sense—to thrive, the sparsely populated colony needed more inhabitants. It was also ordered on the basis of the Jews' good reputation and their financial investments in the Dutch West India Company. Furthermore, it was contingent on the agreement of the Jews to provide for themselves and to seek no help or support from the Dutch Church colonists already established there. Thus, the Jewish philanthropic tradition in the New World became self-organized early in order to shoulder responsibility independently for the welfare of the Jewish community. In the text below, the term "Portuguese nation" refers to Sephardic Jews, as does "this nation." Pernambuco, which had been the stronghold of Dutch Brazil, was captured by Portuguese invaders in 1654, despite intense efforts of the Jews there to help the Dutch keep it. The indigence of the fleeing Jews was the result of their having been robbed by pirates while journeying to New Netherland.]

Correspondence Regarding the First Jews in New Amsterdam, and Their Need to Provide for Themselves

1. Peter Stuyvesant, Manhattan, to the Amsterdam Chamber of Directors, September 22, 1654

The Jews who have arrived would nearly all like to remain here, but learning that they, (with their customary usury and deceitful trading with the Christians) were very repugnant to the inferior magistrates, as also to the people having the most affection for you; the Deaconry also fearing that owing to their present indigence they might become a charge in the coming winter, we have, for the benefit of this weak and newly developing place and the land in general, deemed it useful to require them in a friendly way to depart; praying also most seriously in this connection, for ourselves as also for the general community of your worships, that the deceitful race—such hateful enemies and blasphemers of the name of Christ—be not allowed further to infect and trouble this new colony, to the detraction of your worships and the dissatisfaction of your worships' most affectionate subjects.

2. From an Advocate of the Jews to Honorable Lords, Directors of the Chartered West India Company, Chamber of the City of Amsterdam, January 1655

The merchants of the Portuguese nation residing in the City respectfully remonstrate to your Honors that it has come to the knowledge that your Honors raise obstacles to the giving of permits or passports to the Portuguese Jews to travel and go to reside in New Netherland, which if persisted in will result to the great disadvantage of the Jewish nation. It can also be of no advantage to the general Company but rather damaging.

There are many of the nation who have lost their possessions at Pernambuco and have arrived from there in great poverty, and part of them have been dispersed here and there. So that your petitioners had to expend large sums of money for their necessaries of life, and through lack of opportunity all cannot remain here to live . . .

It is well known to your Honors that the Jewish nation in Brazil have at all times been faithful and have striven to guard and maintain that place, risking for that purpose their possessions and their blood. . . .

Your Honors should also please consider that many of the Jewish nation are principal shareholders in the Company. They having always striven their best for the Company, and many of their nation have lost immense and great capital in its shares and obligations. As foreign nations consent that the Jewish nation may go to live and trade in their territories, how can your Honors forbid the same and refuse transportation to this Portuguese nation who reside here . . . and this to a land that needs people for its increase? . . .

Therefore the petitioners request, for the reasons given above . . . that your Honors be pleased not to exclude but to grant the Jewish nation passage to and residence in that country; otherwise this would result in a great prejudice to their reputation. Also that . . . the Jewish nation be permitted, together with other inhabitants, to travel, live, and traffic there, and with them enjoy liberty on condition of contributing like others . . .

3. Rev. Johannes Megapolensis, New Amsterdam to the Classis the Governing Board of the Dutch Reformed Church, Amsterdam, Holland, March 18, 1655

Last summer some Jews came here from Holland, in order to trade. Afterwards some Jews, poor and healthy, also came there on the same ship with Domine Theodorus Polheijmis. It would have been proper that these had been supported by their own nation, but they have been at our charge, so that we have had to spend several hundred guilders for their support. They came several times to my house, weeping and bewailing their misery, and when I directed them to the Jewish merchant they said that he would not lend them a single stiver. Now again in the spring some have come from Holland, and report that a great many of that lot would yet follow and then build here their synagogue. This causes among the congregation here a great deal of complaint and murmuring. These people have no other god than the unrighteous Mammon, and no other aim than to get possession of Christian property, and to win all other merchants by drawing all trade towards themselves. Therefore, we request your Reverences to obtain from the Lords Directors that these godless rascals, who are of no benefit to the country, but look at everything for their own profit, may be sent away from here. For, as we have here Papists, Mennonites and Lutherans among the Dutch; also many Puritans or Independents, and many Atheists and various other servants of Baal among the English under this Government, who conceal themselves under the name of Christians; it would create a still greater confusion, if the obstinate and immovable Jews came to settle here.

4. The West India Company to Peter Stuyvesant, April 26, 1655
Honorable, Prudent, Pious, Dear, Faithful . . .

We would have liked to effectuate and fulfill your wishes and request that the new territories should no more be allowed to be infected by people of the Jewish nation, for we foresee therefrom the same difficulties which you fear. But after having further weighed and considered the matter, we observe that this would be somewhat unreasonable and unfair, especially because of the considerable loss sustained by this nation, with others, in the taking of Brazil, as also because of the large amount of capital which they still have invested in the shares of this company. Therefore after many deliberations we have finally decided and resolved to apostille upon a certain petition presented by said Portuguese Jews that these people may travel and trade to and in New Netherland and live and remain there, provided the poor among them shall not become a burden to the company or to the community, but be supported by their own nation. You will now govern yourself accordingly.

—The Directors of the West India Company Department of Amsterdam

5. Peter Stuyvesant, New Amsterdam, to the Board of the West India Company, Amsterdam, October 30, 1655.

To give liberty to the Jews will be very detrimental there, because the Christians there will not be able at the same time to do business. Giving them liberty, we cannot refuse the Lutherans and Papists.

Jacob Rader Marcus, ed., *The Jew in the American World: A Source Book.* Detroit, Mich.: Wayne State University Press, 1996, 1:29–33.

EZECHIEL CARRE (c. 1660–after 1697)

[Ezechiel Carre was a Huguenot clergyman who had previously served as minister of a congregation in Roche-Chalais, France, his native land. (The term "Huguenot" in the sixteenth and seventeenth centuries was used to refer to members of the Protestant Reformed Church of France, who were historically known as French Calvinists.) In 1686 he emigrated with twenty-five other French refugee families to the short-lived settlement of Frenchtown in East Greenwich, Rhode Island. The group of Huguenots, led by their able minister Carre and a physician, Pierre Ayrault, purchased land west of Narragansett Sound. In 1690, Carre's book about "The Doctrine the Jesuits teach the Savages of the New World," with a preface by Cotton Mather, was published in Boston. It was the first French book printed in North America. In his sermon below, Carre delves into the symbolism of the parable of the good Samaritan. In a later part of the sermon not included here, he discusses how symbolically Jesus is like the good Samaritan coming to the rescue of sinners, saving them, healing them, generously restoring their well-being. Note the phrase "Turks and Pagans" near the end; seventeenth and eighteenth century literature commonly used "Turk" to represent non-Christian believers in God. Note also the idea near the end that is similar to Chaucer's line: at death each man "must forego all that he has, save only that which he has invested in good works." This is a familiar idea, repeated over the centuries— "At death, you only take with you what you gave away." The italicized words are Carre's own reminders of points to emphasize when delivering the sermon.]

The Charitable Samaritan (1689)

There was . . . a man wounded by Robbers in the High-way of Jerusalem, there was a Priest and a Levite so uncompassionate as not to succour him, which through their neglect a Samaritan did. But these surprising occurrences represented excellent Mysteries in a spiritual sense. I have then two things to examine in this Text. . . . I will show the Literal Sense. . . . On the other hand I will discover the Mystical sense here hidden. God give us grace, that being animated by the example of this Samaritan, which we have this day set before our eyes, we may always manifest our Charity towards our Neighbours, and even towards our most cruel Enemies, that so we may one day inherit eternal Life. Amen. . . .

. . . Covetousness is the fountain of all sorts of evils, 'tis the Mother of Theft, Robbery, Murder, Violence, Inhumanity, etc., for these Wretches after they had wounded this man with many wounds, leave him half dead. . . . By chance there came down a Priest that way, and saw this man thus murdered just expiring, and he passed by on the other side; so likewise a Levite coming to the place, and seeing him, passed by on the other side of him. . . .

These two were Brethren to the wounded man, of the same blood, of the same Nation, of the same Religion; and if these Wretches would do no good for Strangers, yet at least they ought to have done it for their dying Brother.

These two men who read the Law, and expounded it every day, ought not they to have kept in mind that excellent passage of Scripture, *Thou shalt not hide thy self from thine own flesh?* Nevertheless those uncompassionate men turned away and passed on the other side.

Ah my Brethren! It appears from hence, that there is a great difference between the Preaching Charity, and the practicing of it. God had entrusted his Oracles with this Priest and Levite; it was they who ought to have instructed others but if it be they do not what they Preach all their Discourses, *are but a sounding brass, and a tinkling cymbal.* . . .

. . . They went more upon the observation of the ceremonies, than upon the exercise of Charity, which is an unjust preference . . . oftentimes we dispense with a Duty which is contrary to our worldly interest, under pretext of another although much inferior to it; without considering that the lesser should give way to the greater. By this rule of . . . true Piety, this Priest and this Levite were under an obligation to have left their Titles and their offerings, to have relieved this poor Wretch.

Behold a Samaritan far better instructed in the Law of Charity, who passing by the same way, is touched with Compassion, and drawing near to his poor dying Wretch, *bound up his Wounds.* . . . See the difference between these two sorts of people, this Priest and Levite were persons chosen by God for the practice of this Charity, but they did it not. Oh God! *What ingratitude* is here? And the Samaritan on the other hand without any obligation (thank that of Piety) does it; here observe that oftentimes, those whom God calls to be *Exemplary* to others do their duty the least of any. . . .

He might have reasoned with himself, If I should come near this dying man they may accuse me for killing of him, at the least they will have evil thoughts of me, because of the hatred which is between our Nations; *but Charity is not suspicious*; he never stands to reason, because his heart is touched besides he might (to hinder his giving any thing to this poor wounded man) have said, I have need of it myself, I may give that which I may one day find the want of; But *Charity seeks not her own interest*. She adores Providence, she causes to hope that God will make good with real advantage all those Goods which we generously expend for the relief of the poor, as he did of old to the Widow of Zarephath. (1 Kings 17)

After all, this Samaritan in his drawing near this wounded man to relieve him, did so not out of ostentation, for he appears alone on the way, but merely from the consideration of this man's misery; many give their *Alms to be seen of men*, and if they come near the poor to bestow any thing, it is through vain glory; and it is properly their *ambition that gives their Alms, and not their Charity;* but here it was the *heart* that gave, *He was touched with Compassion for the poor man.*

It doth well appear that his piety was sincere, since it produced such great effects, *he bound up his wounds, pouring in oil and wine and set him on his own beast, and brought him to an inn and took care of him, & this wine and Oil* the poor Samaritan carried with him for his own nourishment; but how dear so ever his Ailments be to him, he willingly sacrifices them to the recovering of this wounded man.

He did not as those do, who come to the poor with useless promises, and store of wishes, but *give them nothing.* Oh great abuse! This man doth not so; but coming unto him *he bound up his wounds.* Behold what Charity is here! Men have commonly a loathing of such things, but Charity [inspires them] to go beyond all these repugnancies of nature. He does more, he *poured in oil and wine.* These are remedies made use of for wounds; God having given to these two excellent Creatures not only the virtues to preserve the health of a man, but also to restore it when amiss.

But he stops not there, *he set him on his own beast, and brought him to an inn,* he willingly incommodes himself to ease the wounded man, he saw that his feet could not carry him, and therefore helped him upon his horse, and for fear lest some accident should happen to him by the way, he conducted him himself, and led him to such a place as government had established for the conveniency of Travellers; no sooner is he arrived there, but *he took care of him.*

He thought himself not discharged of his duty towards this man, if through his neglect, his wounds should have been exasperated, he therefore looks to him afresh.

But being obliged to *depart on the morrow, he took out two-pence, and gave them to the Host, and said unto him, take care of him, and whatever thou spendest more, when I come again, I will repay thee.*

This Samaritan you see spared nothing, no, not that which men love most, his money he paid the Host; he recommends the wounded person to his care, and promises at his return to make him a full payment for all the time that he should be with him. How excellent a period hath Charity? How general? How distinguished? Every thing in it contributed to the benefit of this poor wretch; with his heart he was moved to compassion, with his hands he bound up his wounds, with his feet he drew near to relieve him, with his money he paid for him, and left wherewithal afterward for his entertainment. . . .

. . . Jesus Christ must come in a short time to render to each according to his works . . . to him that hath shall be given, whosoever then shall have an overplus of his talents, shall receive so much the more. 'Tis in the same fence he here promises to restore to his servants the overplus.

*   *   *

I make no doubt but you will consent with me in this, and in your heart blame this want of Charity in the Priest and Levite, who passed by without succouring this poor man; but you consider not that every day you do the same; all those times that you know the necessity of your Brethren and do not concern yourselves about the remedy thereof, do not say that you know not any that are poor and indigent, or that have need of your help, Ah! Have you not them every day before your eyes? Many whom the robbers of Persecution have reduced almost to the condition of this poor wounded man in my Text (that is to say) who are *half dead* with miseries, for they cannot properly be said to live that are in such a condition; they may be said to be half dead. How many times have you passed by them with an heart as indifferent as this Priest and this Levite showed to this wounded man, not withstanding, they are your Brethren, of the same blood, of the same Nation, of the same Religion. Ah my Brethren, you ought to lay their poverty to heart, since it is caused for the best of all causes in the World, to wit, that of Jesus Christ: how much should that move us since thereby Christ presents occasion to us to exercise our Charity in such manner as may be most agreeable to God how much should it animate us. . . .

But Christians, limit not your Charity only to your Brethren, else what do you more than the Turks and Pagans. Do good to all even to your very Enemies, imitate this Samaritan towards this Jew. These two Nations (as you know) hated one another mortally, and were of different Religions; nevertheless this Samaritan passes all that by, and shows to this poor afflicted man, all the good Offices he was capable to perform. Let the very seeing the miserable, suffice you for the finding objects worthy of your pity.

And for to overcome the utmost efforts of the hard-heartedness of mankind, remember what Jesus Christ hath done for you, he strips himself of his glory, he made himself poor and miserable, yea mortal, for the Love he bore to you; will you then refuse to give him some small portion of your Temporal Goods? For in as much as you give it unto one of these little ones, you give it unto him. *The poor are the Treasurers of Jesus Christ; he charges to his own account that which you bestow on them, and he will largely pay you the Interest another Day. If you advance some part of your goods to the poor, he will Restore you an hundred fold in the world to come.*

He will do much more, he hath promised to give you Heaven for a cup of cold water. Of all the Goods you possess, you shall carry nothing with you, you shall have nothing Remaining to you but what you have (as it were) Deposited into the hands of our Lord, then make to your selves Friends of this incorruptible Riches, so that when you fail, they may receive you into Everlasting Habitations. AMEN.

Ezechiel Carre, *The Charitable Samaritan: A sermon on the tenth chapter of Luke, verses 30–35, Pronounced in the French Church at Boston,* tran. N. Walter. Boston: Samuel Green, 1689. Copy held by the New York Public Library.

ANNE BRADSTREET (1612–1672)

[Anne Bradstreet received an unusually extensive education in England, thanks to her father's position as a steward of the Earl of Lincoln. Married at sixteen, she arrived in Massachusetts at eighteen, where she found a hard life and a culture that shocked her genteel sensibilities. She assuaged her homesickness by writing poetry. Bradstreet's writing does not reflect the New World's public life much; rather than being distinctively American, her poetry reflects a British mind-set. In her meditations, she draws examples from everyday life: bed, ship, storm, shadow, husks, wells. She was a colonial Puritan woman, a mother of eight children, a social critic, and, as we see below, a wise poet with sobering philosophical ideas, humility, and spirituality. Here are selections from her meditations on doing good and ideas exploring conscience and beneficial tendencies in human nature. In her epitaph for her mother's grave, she rhymed that her mother had been "A friendly neighbor, pitiful to poor, whom she fed and clothed with her store." Bradstreet admired the practice of good deeds and the exercise of useful talents, as seen in her following words of wisdom.]

Meditations Divine and Moral

II. Many can speak well, but few can do well. We are better scholars in the Theory than the practique part, but he is a true Christian that is a proficient in both.

III. Youth is a time of getting, middle age of improving, and old age of spending; a negligent youth is usually attended by an ignorant middle age, and both by an empty old age. He that hath nothing to feed on but vanity and lies must needs lie down in the Bed of sorrow.

IV. A ship that bears much sail, and little or no ballast, is easily overset; and that man, whose head hath great abilities, and his heart little or no grace, is in danger of foundering.

XVII. Few men are so humble as not to be proud of their abilities; and nothing will abase them more than this,—What hast thou, but what thou hast received? Come give an account of thy stewardship.

XLVII. A shadow in the parching sun, and a shelter in a blustering storm, are of all seasons the most welcome; so a faithful friend in time of adversity, is of all other most comfortable.

XLVIII. There is nothing admits of more admiration, than God's various dispensation of his gifts among the sons of men, betwixt whom he hath put so vast a disproportion that they scarcely seem made of the same lump, or sprung out of the loins of one Adam. . . . And no other reason can be given of all this, but it so pleased him, whose will is the perfect rule of righteousness.

XLIX. The treasures of this world may well be compared to husks, for they have no kernel in them, and they that feed upon them, may soon stuff their throats, but cannot fill their bellies; they may be choked by them, but cannot be satisfied with them.

LV. We read of ten lepers that were Cleansed, but of one that returned thanks: we are more ready to receive mercies than we are to acknowledge them: men can use great importunity when they are in distresses, and show great ingratitude after their successes; but he that ordereth his conversation aright, will glorify him that heard him in the day of his trouble.

LXVIII. The gifts that God bestows on the sons of men, are not only abused, but most Commonly employed for a Clean Contrary end, than that which they were given for, as health, wealth, and honor, which might be so many steps to draw men to God in consideration of his bounty towards them, but have driven them the further from him, that they are ready to say, we are lords, we will come no more at thee. If outward blessings be not as wings to help us mount upwards, they will Certainly prove Clogs and weights that will pull us lower downward.

LXXXIV. Well doth the Apostle call riches deceitful riches, and they may truly be compared to deceitful friends who speak fair, and promise much, but perform nothing, and so leave those in the lurch that most relied on them: so is it with the wealth, honors, and pleasures of this world, which miserably delude men and make them put great confidence in them, but when death threatens, and distress lays hold upon them, they prove like the reeds of Egypt that pierce instead of supporting, like empty wells in the time of drought, that those that go to find water in them, return with their empty pitchers ashamed.

LXXVII. God hath by his providence so ordered, that no one Country hath all Commodities within it self, but what it wants, another shall supply, that so there may be a mutual Commerce through the world. As it is with Countries so it is with men, there was never yet any one man that had all excellences, let his parts, natural and acquired, spiritual and moral, be never so large, yet he stands in need of something which another man hath, (perhaps meaner than himself,) [*sic*] which shows us perfection is not below, as also, that God will have us beholden one to another.

Anne Bradstreet, *The Works of Anne Bradstreet in Prose and Verse*, ed. John Harvard Ellis. New York: Peter Smith, 1932, 48, 51, 59, 60, 63, 69, 70–71, 73.

EUSEBIO FRANCISCO KINO (1645–1711)

[In the South and Far West, Spanish missionaries and government officials worked as a team in the seventeenth and eighteenth centuries to spread Christian doctrine and the rule of Spain. The Spanish government supported missions with money and military protection, and missionaries established missions on the frontier to convert, pacify, and bring Native Americans to European civilization. The missions built churches and put into place whole systems of agriculture and craftsmanship, including cattle raising, tanning and weaving, fruit growing, and caring for sheep, goats, and horses. They taught music, reading, and writing and sought to turn tribes of Indians into Christian citizens. Father Kino, a Jesuit missionary in Mexico and what is now New Mexico and Arizona, wrote a book about a fellow priest who had served in that region before him—Francisco Saeta. Kino believed Saeta was an exemplary missionary; he seems to have been more selfless and charitable than the controversial but better known Junipero Serra, who came a generation later and was remembered by some Indians as having mistreated native people, aiding colonial rule with a system of forced labor and the eradication of Indian culture. Kino describes in the passage below Saeta's missionary venture, which he found inspiring, and shows how self-sacrifice for others is affirmed as the true gift of Christianity.]

"Bloodless Martyrdom" for the Padre

Little by little [the Indians] are convinced by the works which they see with their own eyes as these are more effective than the words which they hear. As we said before, everything that is good or bad travels rapidly throughout the whole Indian territory. They ask one another: "how are you getting along with the Father?" If the answer is that "all goes well—that our Father teaches prayer and doctrine and that he preaches about the Word of God and the path to heaven; that he celebrates Mass for us; baptizes us; confesses us; marries us; visits our sick; administers the holy oils; buries our dead; provides us with food and clothing; likes, takes care of us, defends and protects us; that our Father has not come to seek chocolate and silver, but only our souls, and that he is willing to live and die with us in order to take us to heaven with him," once reports like these are made very many new conversions follow in a short time, all of which verifies what St. Gregory said—if every Christian were what he should be by example and through a disciplined life, the whole world would soon be Christian. . . . The missionary who deals with poor, uneducated, and timid savages does not lose the value accruing to a profound ministry. For God himself has assured us "That he who does something for the least of mine, does for me" (Matt 25:40). Whatever we do for his little ones, we do to God Himself; thus we serve and please God through the poor. . . . Let the blessed crown of a prolonged bloodless martyrdom be the distinguishing motive and special goal of these new missions wherever a sudden and bloody martyrdom . . . is wanting.

Kino's Biography of Francisco Javier Saeta, S. J., tran. Carles W. Polzer. St. Louis: St. Louis University, 1971, 207, 215, 217.

On FATHER EUSEBIO KINO AND THE SOUTHWEST UNITED STATES

[This piece, from Bakker and Lillary's book about the Southwest region of the United States, discusses the character and contributions of Father Eusebio Kino. Eusebio Francisco Kino was born in Segno in 1644, in what is now Italy—at the time it was a valley in Tirol, Austria. Kino's widely varied interests included astronomy, mathematics, and cartography, all of which helped him to prove that Baja California is a peninsula. His missionary journeys in the Southwest covered over fifty thousand square miles. He established over twenty missions and country chapels in Northwest Mexico and Southwest United States. Kino is remembered for helping the Pima Indians in matters of agriculture and defense and for opposing the use of Indians as slave labor in northern Mexico's silver mines. Father Kino died at Mission Magdalena in Sonora on March 15, 1711. His name today adorns many towns, streets, monuments, and landmarks in the Southwest in memory of his years of service there. His legendary generosity, giving away his belongings to those in need whom he met on his way, is still celebrated today in the Southwest region. A century before John Chapman planted his apple orchards in the East and Midwest, Father Kino left his bright legacy of sharing in the Southwest. The dark side of the European contact could be symbolized by Coronado Onate, as we see below.]

The Great Southwest (excerpt) by Elna Bakker and Richard G. Lillary

Between 1687 and 1711, came the activities of Father Eusebio Kino, S. J. This Austrian from the Tyrol, a Renaissance man, had been offered a professorship in mathematics at a Bavarian university before he went to Mexico as a Missionary. He worked in Baja California until he transferred his energies to the desert mainland, with a headquarters at Missia Nuestra Señora de los Dolores on the Rio San Miguel. During his twenty-four years there he made fifty journeys, some a thousand miles long, exploring from the Rio Sonora to the Gila and from San Pedro to the Colorado. Sometimes he rode forty or more miles in a day, traveling with few soldiers and sometimes only with Papagos, Pimas, Sobaipuris, or the tall Yumas and Series. He converted and baptized thousands of Indians in scores of tribes, founded missions, and built churches. To feed the missions, he became in effect a benign cattle king, founding a score of ranches from Santa Barbara, deep in Chihuahua to San Xavier del Bacnea Tucson. He inspired Father Juan Maria Salvatierra S. J., founder of the permanent missions in Baja California, and he was the careful historian, in *Celestial Favors*, of his own imperial labors in the arid borderlands.

Kino had even fewer Spanish colonists than the Franciscans had in the Chihuahua Trail, so even more than they he was carrying out the Spanish policy of colonizing the frontier by incorporating the natives into the system. He was working for both church and state as he brought European civilization, including fruits and vegetables, to the civilizations already there. He urged the king to the "reduction" of Apacheria by means of missionary effort. He hoped to see trade ties develop eastward and westward, with the Indians and Spanish in Nuevo Mejico and the Indians in Alto California. In 1710 he was urging Philip V to push the conversion of California and to create Nueva Navarra in the region of Pimeria Alta; his map of this area is famous. A fellow Jesuit wrote that this busy many-sided man, who would sit up all night reading, "neither smoked nor took snuff not wine . . . nor had any other bed than the sweat blankets of his horse for a mattress, and two dollar blankets. He never had more than two coarse shirts, because he gave everything as alms to the Indians."

✳   ✳   ✳

In the central elements of civilization, the Europeans, like their Mexican and Anglo descendents, had nothing basic to give the New World natives, who already had systems of farming and hunting, government, religion, education, ethics, family rela-

tionships, crafts and arts. While there were great variations and contrasts in everything from physique to language, the evidence from the earliest records is that at first the Indian, from Apaches to Zunis, kept their word. Until they sensed or experienced aggression, they were hospitable. They gave or sold food to exploring parties, provided guides, pointed out water holes, and sometimes provided expert and advanced medicinal assistance. Many tribes, notably those that irrigated, were inclined to peace rather than to use of arms. . . . What the Spanish brought in were new systems of organization, physical novelties, and social disasters. . . . Time after time the Spanish leaders broke their word, teaching treachery to the natives and inaugurating four hundred years of sieges, battles, solitary killings and mass slaughters. . . . Shortly after Onate arrived in New Mexico, he assaulted a town of the Keres people, 1,500 persons in 200 houses in their almost impregnable Troy, a mesa 357 feet high—Acoma. Apparently a small band of Spanish men had precipitated a bloody fight with some Acoma warriors, who killed Juan de Zaldivar, the Spanish leader, and a dozen companions. A revenge party led by Juan's brother Vincente contrived to reach the top of the mesa, where they killed 600 to 800 Acomans and captured 70 to 80 warriors and 500 or more women and children.

Figure 1.4 Bronze sculpture of Father Kino

They murdered some natives and threw their bodies over the cliff, hanged two Indians without cause and burned the town. At the trial of the captives in Santo Domingo, Onate ordered that all males more than twenty-five year old have a foot cut off and be given twenty years of "personal service"—slavery. All females age twelve or older were to be sold for twenty years of personal service. Two Hopis captured at Acoma lost their right hands and were sent home as a warning to others. Several scores of young girls captured at Acoma were delivered to the viceroy in Cuidad Mejico, who distributed them among convents. After dispensing this justice and teaching the infidels a moral lesson, Onate turned to founding missionary districts and assigning a friar to each.

Spaniards like Onate came from a Europe of caste and slavery, of almost incessant wars and cruelty. The first to arrive freshly remembered wars against the Moors and the conquest of Granada, Mexico, and Peru. As time went on their followers remembered the series of wars between their Holy Roman Emperor Charles V and King Francis I of France, wars against peasants and Turks, the Thirty Years War and other wars of the Reformation, wars over the Austrian and the Spanish successions, conquest and genocide in the Netherlands, the Napoleonic wars—wars—and the prolonged tortures of the Inquisition. It was the bloodthirsty occidental tradition of brutal, big scale international intrigue and devastation sanctioned by rhetorical holiness, that the small nomadic nations and city-states of the desert mesa sand villages were commanded to submit to.

Elna Bakker and Richard G. Lillary, *The Great Southwest: The Story of a Land and Its People*. Palo Alto, Calif.: American West Publishing, 1972, 142–43, 147–49.

WILLIAM PENN (1644–1718)

[William Penn, a Quaker, was the son of a British admiral to whom Charles II owed money. Charles repaid the debt in 1681 with the charter for a new colony, which Penn named Pennsylvania at the king's insistence. Penn welcomed people of all religious faiths who needed a place to settle with true religious freedom. The Quaker faith, also known as the Religious Society of Friends, is a religious movement that began in eighteenth-century England, led by George Fox and other like-minded men who believed in more spiritual independence than did the authoritarian Puritans. Quakers believed in "that of God [which is] in everyone," and they prayed to be moved by the spirit within. They became known as peacemakers, champions of underdogs, and charitable reformers. Penn lived in America for four years and left a lasting legacy. In his writings, Penn encouraged others to do good instead of living out their lives in mere trivial pursuits. He believed that "True Godliness" excites people to mend the world, repairing social wrongs. Some of his ideas influenced the writing of the American Constitution. Penn believed in making an effort: "No pain, no palm; no thorns, no throne; no gall, no glory; no cross, no crown." In Penn's book, Fruits of Solitude, he wrote many brief meditations and reflections to encourage thinking about virtues.]

No Cross, No Crown

The best recreation is to do good: and all Christian customs tend to temperance, and some good and beneficial end; which more or less may be in every action (1 Pet 1:15; Heb 10:25; 1 Pet 4:9-11; Matt 25:36, 37). For instance, if men and women would be diligent to follow their respective callings; frequent the assemblies of religious people; visit sober neighbours to be edified, and wicked ones to reform them; be careful in the tuition of their children, exemplary to their servants; relieve the necessitous, see the sick, visit the imprisoned; administer to their infirmities and indispositions, endeavour peace amongst neighbours: also, study moderately such commendable and profitable arts, as navigation, arithmetic, geometry, husbandry, gardening, handicraft, medicine, &c.; and that women spin, sew, knit, weave, garden, preserve, and the like housewife and honest employments, the practice of the greatest and noblest matrons, and youth, among the very heathen: helping others, who for want are unable to keep servants, to ease them in their necessary affairs; often and private retirements from all worldly objects, to enjoy the Lord: secret and steady meditations on the divine life and heavenly inheritance; which to leave undone and prosecute other things, under the notion of recreations, is impiety; it is most vain in any to object, that they cannot do these always, and therefore why may not they use these common diversions? for I ask, what would such be at? what would they do? and what would they have? They that have trades have not time enough to do half of what hath been recommended. And as for those who have nothing to do, and indeed do nothing, which is worse, but sin, which is worst of all, here is variety of pleasant, of profitable, yea, of very honourable employments and diversions for them. Such can with great delight sit at a play, a ball, a masque, at cards, dice, &c., drinking, revelling, feasting, and the like, an entire day; yea, turn night into day, and invert the very order of the creation, to humour their lusts (Amos 6:3-8); and were it not for eating and sleeping, it would be past a doubt, whether they would ever find time to cease from those vain and sinful pastimes, till the hasty calls of death should summon their appearance in another world: yet do they think it intolerable and hardly possible, for any to sit so long at a profitable or religious exercise.

*   *   *

[L]et it be sufficient for us to say, that when people have first learned to fear, worship, and obey their Creator, to pay their numerous vicious debts, to alleviate and abate their oppressed tenants; but above all outward regards, when the pale faces are more commiserated, when the famished poor, the distressed widow, and helpless orphan, God's works and your fellow-creatures, are provided for; then, I say, if then, it will be time enough for you to plead the indifferency of your pleasures . . . to visit the sick, see the imprisoned, relieve the needy, &c. are such excellent properties in Christ's account, that thereupon He will pronounce such blessed, saying, "Come, ye blessed of my Father, inherit the kingdom prepared for you," &c. (Matt 25:34-41). So that the great are not, with the leviathan in the deep, to prey upon the small, much less to make a sport of the lives and labour of the lesser ones, to gratify their inordinate senses.

William Penn, *No Cross, No Crown* (n.p., 1682), chap. 15 and 18. http://www.gospeltruth.net/Penn/nocrossnocrownch18.htm.

Fruits of Solitude
Part I : Bounds of Charity

47. Lend not beyond thy Ability, nor refuse to lend out of thy Ability; especially when it will help others more than it can hurt thee.

48. If thy Debtor be honest and capable, thou hast thy Mony again, if not with Encrease, with Praise: If he prove insolvent, don't ruin him to get that, which it will not ruin thee to lose: For thou art but a Steward, and another is thy Owner, Master and Judge.

49. The more merciful Acts thou dost, the more Mercy thou wilt receive; and if with a charitable Imployment of thy Temporal Riches, thou gainest eternal Treasure, thy Purchase is infinite: Thou wilt have found the Art of Multiplying [the term used by alchemists for increasing precious metals] indeed.

Frugality or Bounty

50. Frugality is good if Liberality be join'd with it. The first is leaving off superfluous Expences; the last bestowing them to the Benefit of others that need. The first without the last begins Covetousness; the last without the first begins Prodigality: Both together make an excellent Temper. Happy the Place where ever that is found.

Part II : Of Charity

281. Charity has various Senses, but is Excellent in all of them.

282. It imports; first, the Commiseration of the Poor, and Unhappy of Mankind, and extends an Helping-Hand to mend their Condition.

283. They that feel nothing of this, are at best not above half of Kin to Human Race; since they must have no Bowels, which makes such an Essential Part thereof, who have no more Nature.

284. A Man, and yet not have the Feeling of the Wants or Needs of his own Flesh and Blood! A Monster rather! And may he never be suffer'd to propagate such an unnatural Stock in the World.

285. Such an Uncharitableness spoils the best Gains, and two to one but it entails a Curse upon the Possessors.

286. Nor can we expect to be heard of God in our Prayers, that turn the deaf Ear to the Petitions of the Distressed amongst our fellow Creatures.

287. God sends the Poor to try us, as well as he tries them by being such: And he that refuses them a little out of the great deal that God has given him, Lays up Poverty in Store for his own Posterity.

288. I will not say these Works are Meritorious, but dare say they are Acceptable, and go not without their Reward: Tho' to Humble us in our Fulness and Liberality too, we only Give but what is given us to Give as well as use; for if we are not our own, less is that so which God has intrusted us with.

289. Next, CHARITY makes the best Construction of Things and Persons, and is so far from being an evil Spy, a Back-biter, or a Detractor, that it excuses Weakness, extenuates Miscarriages, makes the best of every Thing; forgives every Body, serves All, and hopes to the End.

290. It moderates Extreams, is always for Expediences, labors to accommodate Differences, and had rather suffer than Revenge: And so far from Exacting the utmost Farthing, that it had rather lose than seek her Own Violently.

291. As it acts Freely, so, Zealously too; but 't is always to do Good, for it hurts no Body.

292. An Universal Remedy against Discord, and an Holy Cement for Mankind.

293. And lastly, 'T is Love to God and the Brethren, which raises the Soul above all worldly Considerations; and, as it gives a Taste of Heaven upon Earth, so 't is Heaven in the Fulness of it hereafter to the truly Charitable here.

294. This is the Noblest Sense Charity has, after which all should press, as that more Excellent Way.

295. Nay, most Excellent; for as Faith, Hope and Charity were the more Excellent Way that Great Apostle discovered to the Christians, (too apt to stick in Outward Gifts and Church Performances) so of that better Way he preferred Charity as the best Part, because it would out-last the rest, and abide for ever.

296. Wherefore a Man can never be a true and good Christian without Charity, even in the lowest Sense of it: And yet he may have that Part thereof, and still be none of the Apostle's true Christian, since he tells us, That tho' we should give all our Goods to the Poor, and want Charity (in her other and higher Senses) it would profit us nothing.

297. Nay, tho' we had All Tongues, All Knowledge, and even Gifts of Prophesy, and were Preachers to others; ay, and had Zeal enough to give our Bodies to be burned, yet if we wanted Charity, it would not avail us for Salvation.

298. It seems it was his (and indeed ought to be our) Unum Necessarium, or the One Thing Needful, which our Saviour attributed to Mary in Preference to her Sister Martha, that seems not to have wanted the lesser Parts of Charity.

299. Would God this Divine Virtue were more implanted and diffused among Mankind, the Pretenders to Christianity especially, and we should certainly mind Piety more than Controversy, and Exercise Love and Compassion instead of Censuring and Persecuting one another in any Manner whatsoever.

William Penn, *Fruits of Solitude*. Cambridge, Mass.: Harvard University Press, 1909, Part I "Bounds of Charity," http://www.bartleby.com/1/3/109.html. Part I, "Frugality or Bounty," http://www.bartleby.com/1/3/110.html. Part II "Charity," http://www.bartleby.com/1/3/226.html.

ANCIENT WRITINGS THAT INFLUENCED THE COLONISTS

AESOP (620–560 BC)

[Knowledge of Aesop's fables was widespread among the British immigrants from the colonial period of America onward; they had been popular in both Latin and English since the Middle Ages. Aesop, according to Greek history and legends, was an Ethiopian philosopher and slave from Phrygia who lived in Samos in the sixth century B.C. According to one later legend, he was born ugly and mute, but his generosity to an attendant of Isis prompted the goddess to give him the ability to compose fables. His brief morality tales and animal stories with life lessons were part of classical learning and quite influential. Even a child could understand, remember, and tell these stories that taught social lessons about sharing, cooperating, and helping others.]

Four Fables on Greed and Good Deeds

The Miser and His Gold

Once upon a time there was a Miser who used to hide his gold at the foot of a tree in his garden; but every week he used to go and dig it up and gloat over his gains.

A robber, who had noticed this, went and dug up the gold and decamped with it. When the Miser next came to gloat over his treasures, he found nothing but the empty hole. He tore his hair, and raised such an outcry that all the neighbours came around him, and he told them how he used to come and visit his gold. "Did you ever take any of it out?" asked one of them.

"Nay," said he, "I only came to look at it."

"Then come again and look at the hole," said a neighbour; "it will do you just as much good."

[Moral:] Wealth unused might as well not exist.

The Old Woman and the Wine-Jar

An old woman found an empty jar which had lately been full of prime old wine and which still retained the fragrant smell of its former contents. She greedily placed it several times to her nose, and drawing it backwards and forwards said, "O most delicious! How nice must the Wine itself have been, when it leaves behind in the very vessel which contained it so sweet a perfume!"

[Moral:] The memory of a good deed lives.

The Serpent and the Eagle

An Eagle swooped down upon a Serpent and seized it in his talons with the intention of carrying it off and devouring it. But the Serpent was too quick for him and had its coils round him in a moment; and then there ensued a life-and-death struggle between the two. A countryman, who was a witness of the encounter, came to the assistance of the eagle, and succeeded in freeing him from the Serpent and enabling him to escape. In revenge, the Serpent spat some of his poison into the man's drinking-horn. Heated with his exertions, the man was about to slake his thirst with a draught from the horn, when the Eagle knocked it out of his hand, and spilled its contents upon the ground.

[Moral:] "One good turn deserves another."

The Lion and the Mouse

A lion was awakened from sleep by a Mouse running over his face. Rising up angrily, he caught him and was about to kill him, when the Mouse piteously entreated, saying: "If you would only spare my life, I would be sure to repay your kindness." The Lion laughed and let him go. It happened shortly after this that the Lion was caught by some hunters, who bound him by strong ropes to the ground. The Mouse, recognizing his roar, came and gnawed the rope with his teeth and set him free, exclaiming:

"You ridiculed the idea of my ever being able to help you, expecting to receive from me any repayment of your favor; now you know that it is possible for even a Mouse to confer benefits on a Lion."

[Moral:] No act of kindness, no matter how small, is ever wasted.

Aesop, *Three Hundred Aesop's Fables*, tran. George Fyler Townsend. London: Routledge and Sons, 1867. Available online at http://www.pacificnet.net/~johnr/aesop/.

SENECA, ROMAN PHILOSOPHER (4 B.C.–A.D. 65)

[Bear in mind when reading the next passages that New England's earliest settlers owned few books: the Bible; the revered works of Calvin, especially the Institutes; and possibly popular Puritan works like Arthur Dent's Plain Man's Pathway to Heaven and Lewis Bayly's Practice of Piety. They also owned Latin classics by Cicero, Virgil, and Ovid. Seventeenth-century Puritans also knew the writings of the Roman Stoic philosopher and playwright Seneca. Born in Spain, educated in Rome, Seneca was a tutor to Nero, then a minister to him, and finally was suspected of plotting against him. William Hubbard, a Puritan minister in Ipswich Massachusetts from 1642 to 1704, considered Seneca to have been "the best of Heathen Philosophers." References to moralist philosophers such as Seneca are rife in the writings of colonial New England. He influenced America's Founding Fathers in the eighteenth century, as well as philosophers such as Emerson and Thoreau. Carlos Fuentes noted that "the ancient stoic philosophy from Roman Iberia is deep indeed in the soul of Hispanics" who migrated to America's Southwest. Seneca's wisdom was not isolated; human beings around the world, including ancient Greeks and Asians, developed a wisdom of spirituality and humanheartedness. One of the principles of this wisdom, which envisions the reasons for giving, is that there is a unity in the universe, an interrelatedness of the parts of the whole—like the ecological web of life seen in modern science. Therefore, generosity is part of organic reality. The health and well-being of the whole (family, community, nation) is one's larger Self. Various terms such as "God" and "love," "justice" and "harmony," "oneness" and "spirit" refer to this aspect of existence. In Christianity, this is also symbolized by "the mystical body of Christ," the vine, and the tree of life. The human being's larger Self includes other living beings, therefore the teaching is to "Love one another," and "Do unto others as you would have them do unto you," and "Love your neighbor as yourself." Seneca's teachings share similarities with Christian ones. In this wisdom view, the goodness in a person is part of an eternal principle, a sacred transcendent divine reality, or the expression of a spirit shared with others. In Seneca's philosophy, happiness is founded on wisdom and goodness. Seneca's teachings encourage people to give as they would receive—something like the golden rule.]

Of Benefits

A benefit is a good office, done with intention and judgment; that is to say, with a due regard to all the circumstances of what, how, why, when, where, to whom, how much, and the like. Or, otherwise, it is a voluntary and benevolent action, that delights the giver in the comfort it brings to the receiver. The very meditation of it breeds good blood and generous thoughts, and instructs us in all the parts of honor, humanity, friendship, piety, gratitude, prudence and justice.

In short, the art and skill of conferring benefits is, of all human duties, the most absolutely necessary to the well-being both of reasonable nature and of every individual; as the very cement of all communities, and the blessing of particular ones.

He that does good to another man does good also to himself; not only in the consequence, but in the very act of doing it; for the conscience of well-doing is an ample reward.

Of Intentions and Effects

The good-will of the benefactor is the fountain of all benefits; Nay, it is the benefit itself, or at least the stamp that makes it valuable and current. The obligation rests in the mind, not in the matter; and all those advantages which we see, handle, or hold in actual possession by the courtesy of another are but several modes or ways of explaining and putting the good-will in execution.

There needs no great subtlety to prove that both benefits and injuries receive their value from the intention, when even brutes themselves are able to decide this question. Tread upon a dog by chance, or put him to pain upon the dressing of a wound; the one he passes by as an accident, and the other, in his fashion, he acknowledges as a kindness. But offer to strike at him, though you do him no hurt at all, he flies yet in the face of you, even for the mischief that you barely meant it.

My friend is taken by pirates; I redeem him; and after that he falls into other pirates' hands. His obligation to me is the same still as if he had preserved his freedom. And so, if I save a man from any misfortune, and he falls into another; if I give him a sum of money which is afterward taken away by thieves; it comes to the same case. Fortune may deprive us of a benefit, but the benefit itself remains inviolable.

If the benefit resided in the matter, that which is good for one man would be so for another. Whereas many times the very same thing given to several persons works contrary effects, even to the difference of life or death; and that which is one body's cure proves another body's poison. Besides that, the timing of it alters the value; and a crust of bread upon a pinch, is a greater present than the imperial crown.

And the same reason holds good even in religion itself. It is not the incense, or the offering, that is acceptable to God, but the purity and devotion of the worshipper. Neither is the bare will, without action, sufficient, that is, where we have the means of acting; for in that case it signifies as little to wish well without well-doing, as to do good without willing it. There must be effect as well as intention, to make me owe a benefit.

In fine, the conscience alone is the judge, both of benefits and injuries.

And so it is with the good we receive, wither without, or beside, or contrary to intention. It is the mind, and not the event, that distinguishes from an injury.

Of Judgment in the Bestowal of Benefits

We are to give by choice, and not by hazard. My inclination bids me to oblige one man; I am bound in duty and justice to serve another. Here it is a charity, there it is pity; and elsewhere, perhaps, encouragement.

There are some that want, to whom I would not give; because, if I did, they would still want. To one man I would barely offer a benefit, but I would press it upon another.

To say the truth, we do not employ money to more profit than that which we bestow; and it is not to our friends, our acquaintances or countrymen, nor to this or that condition of man, that we are to restrain our bounties, but wheresoever there is a man, there is a place and an occasion for a benefit. We give to some that are good already; to others, in hope to make them so; but we must do all with discretion. For we are as well answerable for what we give as for what we receive. Nay, the misplacing of a benefit is worse than the not receiving of it; for the one is another man's fault, but the other is mine.

The error of the giver does oft-time excuse the ingratitude of the receiver; for a favor ill-placed is rather a profusion than a benefit.

I will choose a man of integrity, sincere, considerate, grateful, temperate, well-natured, neither covetous nor sordid; and when I have obliged such a man, though not worth a groat [small coin] in the world, I have gained my end.

If we give only to receive, we lose the fairest objects for our charity: the absent, the sick, the captive, and the needy. When we oblige those that can never pay us again in kind, as a stranger upon his last farewell, or a necessitous person upon his death-bed, we make Providence our debtor, and rejoice in the conscience even of a fruitless benefit. So long as we are affected with passions, and distracted with hopes and fears, and with our pleasures, we are incompetent judges where to place our bounties. But when death presents itself, and that we come to our last will and testament, we leave our fortunes to the most worthy. He that gives nothing but in hopes of receiving, must die intestate [without a legal will].

* * *

The rule is, we are to give as we would receive, cheerfully, quickly, and without hesitation; for there is no grace in a benefit that sticks to the fingers.

It was well said of him that called a good office, that was done harshly, and with an ill will, a stony piece of bread. It is necessary for him that is hungry to receive it, but it almost chokes a man in going down. There must be no pride, arrogance of looks, or tumor of words in the bestowing of benefits.

Whatsoever we bestow, let it be done with a frank and cheerful countenance. A man must not give with his hand, and deny with his looks. He that gives quickly, gives willingly.

Many benefits are great in show, but little or nothing in effect when they come hard, slow, or at unawares. That which is given with pride and ostentation, is rather an ambition than a bounty.

Figure 1.5 Stoic philosopher, Seneca

He must be a wise, a friendly, and a well-bred man that perfectly acquits himself in the art and duty of obliging; for all his actions must be squared according to the measures of civility, good-nature, and discretion.

Of Requital

Diogenes walked naked and unconcerned through the middle of Alexander's treasures and was, as well in other men's opinions as in his own, even above Alexander himself, who at that time had the whole world at his feet. For there was more that the one scorned to take than the other had it in his power to give; and it is a greater generosity for the beggar to refuse money than for a prince to bestow it.

Nor is it to be said that "I cannot requite such a benefactor because I am poor, and have it not." I can give good counsel, a conversation wherein he may take both delight and profit, freedom of discourse without flattery, kind attention, where he deliberates, and faith inviolable where he trusts. I may bring him to a love and knowledge of truth, deliver him from the errors of his credulity, and teach him to distinguish betwixt friends and parasites.

Of How the Receiver Should Act

There are certain rules in common betwixt the giver and the receiver. We must do both cheerfully, that the giver may receive the fruit of his benefit in the very act of bestowing it. The more glorious part, in appearance, is that of the giver; but the receiver has undoubtedly the harder game to play in many regards.

There are some from whom I would not accept a benefit; that is to say, from those upon whom I would not bestow one. For why should I not scorn to receive a benefit where I am ashamed to own it?

It is a pain to an honest and a generous mind to lie under a duty of affection against inclination. I do not speak here of wise men, that love to do what they ought to do, that have their passions at command, that prescribe laws for themselves and keep them when they have done; but of men in a state of imperfection, that may have done a good will perhaps to be honest, and yet be overborne by the contumacy of their affections.

We must therefore have a care to whom we become obliged; and I would be much stricter yet in the choice of a creditor for benefits than for money. In the one case, it is but paying what I had, and the debt is discharged. In the other, I do not only owe more, but when I have paid that, I am still in arrear, and this law is the very foundation of friendship.

Of Ingratitude

The principle causes of ingratitude are pride and self-conceit, avarice, envy, etc. It is a familiar exclamation, "It is true he did this or that for me, but it came so late, and it was so little, I had even as good been without it. If he had not given it to me, he must have given it to somebody else; it was nothing out of his own pocket." Nay, we are so ungrateful that he that gives us all we have, if he leaves anything to himself, we reckon that he does us injury.

Not to return one good office for another is inhuman; but to return evil for good is diabolical. There are too many even of this sort who, the more they owe, the more they hate. There is nothing more dangerous than to oblige those people; for when they are conscious of not paying the debt, they wish the creditor out of the way.

But what is all this to those who are so made, as to dispute even the goodness of Heaven, which gives us all, and expects nothing again, but continues giving to the most unthankful and complaining.

Without the exercise and the commerce of mutual offices we can be neither happy nor safe, for it is only society that secures us. Take us one by one, a prey even to brutes as well as to one another. Nature has brought us into the world naked and unarmed. We have not the teeth or the paws of lions or bears to make ourselves terrible. But with the two blessings of reason and union we secure and defend ourselves against violence and fortune. This it is that comforts us in sickness, in age, in misery, in pains, and in the worst of calamities. Take away this combination, and mankind is dissociated and falls to pieces.

The Wisdom of the Stoics: Selections from Seneca . . . [tran. Roger L'Strange in the seventeenth century], ed. Frances and Henry Hazlitt. Lanham, Md.: University Press of America, 1984, 51–59.

PASSAGES ON GIVING FROM THE BIBLE

[The first generations of New World settlers were powerfully instructed by the Bible, which they considered to be revelation. Such parables as the widow's mite and the good Samaritan were known to all. Christian teachings of help and generosity were familiar from sermons, conversations, and reading. The teachings that one hand should not know what the other does and that one should not hide one's light under a bushel, yet one should pray in one's closet—using religion not for display but for the welfare of one's soul—were ideals shaping the colonial ethos. The following passages are indicative of Judeo-Christian teachings on helping those in need. Many charity sermons were preached in this and the next centuries to remind people of these teachings and to encourage them to donate to good causes.]

Old Testament

The poor shall never cease out of the land: therefore I command thee, saying, Thou shalt open thine hand wide unto thy brother, to thy poor, and to thy needy, in thy land.

—DEUT 15:11

Thou shalt not see thy brother's ass or his ox fall down by the way, and hide thyself from them: thou shalt surely help him to lift them up again. —DEUT 22:4

Who am I, and what is my people, that we should be able to offer so willingly after this sort? for all things come of thee, and of thine own have we given thee.

—1 CHR 29:14

Did not I weep for him that was in trouble? was not my soul grieved for the poor?

—JOB 30:25

The wicked borroweth, and payeth not again: but the righteous sheweth mercy, and giveth. —PS 37:21

He that oppresseth the poor reproacheth his Maker: but he that honoureth him hath mercy on the poor. —PROV 14:31

New Testament

If any man will sue thee at the law, and take away thy coat, let him have thy cloke also. And whosoever shall compel thee to go a mile, go with him twain. —MATT 5:40-41

Give to him that asketh thee, and from him that would borrow of thee turn not thou away. —MATT 5:42

Love your enemies, bless them that curse you, do good to them that hate you.

—MATT 5:44

When thou doest thine alms, do not sound a trumpet before thee. —MATT 6:2

Then Jesus beholding him loved him, and said unto him, One thing thou lackest: go thy way, sell whatsoever thou hast, and give to the poor, and thou shalt have treasure in heaven: and come, take up the cross, and follow me.

And he was sad at that saying, and went away grieved: for he had great possessions. —Mark 10:21-22

And Jesus looked round about, and saith unto his disciples, How hardly shall they that have riches enter into the kingdom of God!

And the disciples were astonished at his words. But Jesus answereth again, and saith unto them, Children, how hard is it for them that trust in riches to enter into the kingdom of God!

It is easier for a camel to go through the eye of a needle, than for a rich man to enter into the kingdom of God. —Mark 10:23-25

[Jesus] answereth and saith unto them, He that hath two coats, let him impart to him that hath none; and he that hath meat, let him do likewise. —Luke 3:11

Be kindly affectioned one to another with brotherly love; in honour preferring one another;

Not slothful in business; fervent in spirit; serving the Lord;

Rejoicing in hope; patient in tribulation; continuing instant in prayer;

Distributing to the necessity of saints; given to hospitality. —Rom 12:10-13

Though I bestow all my goods to feed the poor, and though I give my body to be burned, and have not charity, it profiteth me nothing. —1 Cor 13:3

Brethren, we do you to wit of the grace of God bestowed on the churches of Macedonia;

How that in a great trial of affliction the abundance of their joy and their deep poverty abounded unto the riches of their liberality. —2 Cor 8:1-2

Being confident of this very thing, that he which hath begun a good work in you will perform it until the day of Jesus Christ. —Phil 1:6

Let us consider one another to provoke unto love and to good works: —Heb 10:24

Pure religion and undefiled before God and the Father is this, To visit the fatherless and widows in their affliction, and to keep himself unspotted from the world. —Jas 1:27

What doth it profit, my brethren, though a man say he hath faith, and have not works? can faith save him?

If a brother or sister be naked, and destitute of daily food,

And one of you say unto them, Depart in peace, be ye warmed and filled; notwithstanding ye give them not those things which are needful to the body; what doth it profit?

Even so faith, if it hath not works, is dead, being alone. —Jas 2:14-17

The Holy Bible, King James Version.

JOHN CALVIN (1509–1564)

[Calvin's writings, especially the Institutes, were among the very few printed publications owned by the first generations of New England Christians. John Calvin, the son of a lawyer in France, studied at the University of Paris and became a staunch leader of Puritan Protestantism. This passage from the Institutes of the Christian Religion (1536) shows the strict standards from the early church that Calvin upheld in his Reformation vision for the Christian church. Riches were to be spent on the poor, not on institutional luxuries. In this text, the poor are said to have a right to the wealth that is in the church's keeping.]

Institutes of the Christian Religion

You will frequently find both in the decrees of synods and in ancient writers that all that the church possesses, either in lands or in money, is the patrimony of the poor. And so this song is often sung there to bishops and deacons, that they should remember that they are not handling their own goods but those appointed for the need of the poor; and if in bad faith they suppress or waste them, they shall be guilty of blood. Accordingly, they are admonished to distribute these goods to whom they are owed, with the greatest awe and reverence, as if in God's presence, without partiality. Hence arise those grave protestations in Chrysostom, Ambrose, Augustine, and other bishops like them, by which they affirm their uprightness among the people.

But it is fair and sanctioned also by the law of the Lord, that those who work for the church be supported at public expense (1 Cor 9:14; Gal 6:6); and some presbyters in that age also consecrating their inheritances to God made themselves voluntarily poor. Consequently, the distribution was then such that the ministers did not lack food, and the poor were not neglected. Yet provision was meanwhile made that the very ministers, who ought to give others an example of frugality, should not have so much as to abuse it to the point of luxury and indulgence, but only enough to meet their needs. For those clergy who can be supported by their parents' possessions, says Jerome, if they receive anything belonging to the poor, commit sacrilege, and by such an abuse they eat and drink judgment upon themselves (1 Cor 11:29).

*   *   *

At first they [church leaders] spent very little on the embellishment of sacred things; afterward, although the church became gradually richer, they still kept moderation in this respect. Whatever money was given to it still remained intact for the poor, should any great need arise. Thus Cyril, when famine seized the province of Jerusalem and the distress could not otherwise be relieved, sold vessels and vestments, and spent the money on poor relief. Similarly Acacius, bishop of Amida, when a great multitude of Persians was well-nigh dying from famine, calling together his clergy, delivered this famous speech: "Our God needs neither plates nor cups, for he neither eats nor drinks." Then he melted the vessels to obtain both food and the price of ransom for the pitiable folk. Jerome also, when he inveighs against excessive splendor of churches, honorably mentions Exuperius, bishop of Toulouse in his day, who carried the Lord's body in a wicker basket and his blood in a glass vessel, but suffered no poor man to hunger. What I just now said of Acacius, Ambrose states about himself, for when the Arians reproached him for having broken the sacred vessels to ransom prisoners, he used this wonderful excuse: "He who sent out the apostles without gold also gathered churches without gold. The church has gold not to keep but to pay out, and to relieve distress. What need to keep what helps not? Or are we ignorant of how much gold and silver the Assyrians carted off from the Temple of the Lord (2 Kgs 18:15-16)? Would it not be better for the priest to melt it to sustain the poor, if other aid is lacking, than for a sacrilegious enemy to bear it away? Will not the Lord say, 'Why have you allowed so many needy to die of hunger? Surely you had gold with which to minister sustenance. Why were so many prisoners carried off and not ransomed? Why were so many killed by the enemy? It were better for you to preserve vessels of living men than of metals.' To these you cannot give reply, for what would you say? 'I was afraid lest the temple of God lack ornament.' He would reply: 'The sacraments do not require gold, nor do those things please with gold that are not bought with gold. The ornament of the sacraments is the ransom of prisoners.'" To sum up, What the same man said in another place we see to be very true: "Whatever, then, the church had was for the support of the needy." Likewise: "The bishop had nothing that did not belong to the poor."

John Calvin, *Institutes of the Christian Religion*. Philadelphia: Westminster, 1960, vol. 2, bk. 4, sec. 6, p. 1074, and sec. 8, pp. 1075–76.

A CONTEMPORARY ESSAY

On THE NEW ENGLAND MIND

[The following passage offers a sense of the New England roots of American culture. Twentieth-century historian Perry Miller developed a deep understanding of the New England ethos. Born in Chicago in 1905, he "discovered America," or rather, realized how much he wanted to study and write about early America, when he was a sailor far from home, in Africa. He studied history and taught at Harvard, becoming a pre-eminent authority on colonial New England, writing many books that bring the era to life for readers. He was (posthumously) awarded the Pulitzer Prize in 1966. During the seventeenth century, Puritan attitudes toward poverty involved Christian charity but also a sense that the Hand of Providence was evident in people's plights. Miller traces the change from the high hopes of John Winthrop for a better life for disadvantaged people to the compromise of Cotton Mather, accepting that the disadvantaged would always exist and have troubles, even in a New World, suggesting that high ideals were adjusted in the face of real experiences in America.]

The New England Mind: Puritan Attitudes toward Poverty
by Perry Miller

The founders had been anything but democrats: yet leaders of the Great Migration universally assumed that were God to bless the covenant of the people, those whom Winthrop unhesitatingly called "the meaner sort" would thrive more in New England than in old. Indeed, that the meaner would advance, while those able to invest estates in the civic enterprise stood to lose, was an axiomatic assumption of the men who took upon themselves the burden of command—a conception of *noblesse oblige* to which shrewd traders like John Hull and Samuel Sewall were still bound. But we have recorded with what a shock the second generation realized that somehow, despite the rich opportunities of land and sea, despite the ethic of pious labor, New England had a pauper class on its hands. Clerical theorists of the covenant then responded by denouncing those who ground the faces of the poor, excoriated capitalists, and sublimated consternation into redemption by suffering. For a generation or more, this eloquence carried the community; precisely because the jeremiad, by insistently arraigning social evils, never gave over the hope of rectification—never gave over expounding in concrete detail just what enormities would be chastised and what trials rewarded—it never saw poverty as the inescapable burden of the poor. It always said that, come the reformation, indigence would be abolished. Possibly in the last half of the century this formula continued to be effective because penury still stopped short of destitution. But early in the eighteenth century, the preachers themselves had to admit that oppression of the poor had become a habit, and by the wearisome repetition of their complaint confess that such injustices, being merely deplorable, would never be redressed. A certain cynicism crept into the forensic delivery, as preachers strove to find the lot of the poor not really so bad as their own lamentations had earlier pictured it. In New England, Cotton Mather learned to say, the poor—although greatly increased and much afflicted—are more comfortably provided for than elsewhere; they ought, instead of complaining, to say, "God hath not so dealt with the rest of the poor in our Nation, or scarce in any Nation." In 1719 Benjamin Colman stepped out of his pulpit to tell the town authorities that they should establish a regular market: the fathers, he admitted, had not seen this necessity, but "they were not quite enough Men of this world for us"; though they took great care for our minds and souls, they "were a little too Negligent of those mortal Bodies." A market would, he felt, improve virtue and good morals, but there was, he conceded, a danger that once goods were spread out in such display, the poor would be tempted to buy the best. To this objection he could answer only by revealing what had gradually become the tacit premise of clerical admonitions to that class:

> They that are poorer in worldly state should and must give way to the Rich. Who but they ordinarily should buy the dearest and best of the kind? Providence means it for them. It is the Government of Heaven; let us submit to it. God has given into their hand more abundantly . . . Now & then we that are poorer may taste of the best too and be thankful. But we should be willing to live low, where God has set us.

Seldom did a cleric let himself speak so openly (the frankness of this statement needs to be balanced against the courtly sanity Colman exhibited in the smallpox argument). Neverless, the disguise wore progressively thinner; there wanted little wit indeed to perceive that commiseration from the pulpit, in the sign of an ordered and unalterable philosophy of society, meant only that the poor were poor.

"God is said to be the maker of the Rich and Poor" thus became the social content of official Puritanism. The poor should not repine, said Increase Mather, because though they be mean in the eye of the world ("it may be they go in Leather Cloathes"), they may by their piety prove blessings to society "and keep off destroying Judgments." Complacency was implied, on the one hand, by exhortations to the rich to give more abundantly to charity (in these years that word took on the restricted meaning unknown to John Winthrop) and by funereal praises of those who had devoted their estates to the poor (accompanied with shocked exclamations that there were some "unto whom God gave riches, but they have not Willed so much as one Penny to the Poor, or to any Pious use") and, on the other, by a number of works addressed, shamelessly, to the poor as an incurable class. By 1716 Cotton Mather deigned to tell them that "To Receive Alms, with such a lowly Mind, as becomes them who need them is as great a Grace, as to Bestow them." They should thank God that He has commanded "us" to help: "Your Benefactor is but the Instrument of Heaven in what is done for you"; should you, after this bounty, become vicious, "or if you should Steal, as the Poor sometimes do," you will suffer spiritual pangs. Mather was not yet a Gradgrind, but he was closer to him than to the first legislators of the colonies; there was not yet an Oliver Twist to ask for more, but Mather tried to forestall him: beware of this, he warned the poor, if you cannot bear poverty on earth, "with a Submission of Souls to the Thing Appointed for you, 'tis very certain, your Preparation for Heaven, has but very Dark Symptoms upon it." As for the hope—or at least the expectation—that had stirred the meaner sort among the immigrants, that egalitarian prospect was postponed: "The Grave, the Grand Leveller, will quickly bring the rich and the Poor to be upon Equal Terms; One shall not be upon Higher Ground than another, when Both are Laid under Ground." The language of these passages—of which there are thousands—shows the equanimity with which, along with mechanical admonitions against oppression, the inherited philosophy of class distinction had subsided into a single dimension. "If Great Things are carv'd out unto one person, and Small Things unto another, it is the Hand of Divine Providence that has the carving of them." Strangely enough, a few who went "in Leather Cloathes" were reluctant to submit to such carving.

Perry Miller, *The New England Mind*. Cambridge, Mass.: Harvard University Press, 1983, 399–401.

EPILOGUE

[This passage offers a reminder about human mortality and a state-ment of resolve that has inspired Americans for generations, urging them to contribute to others' well-being without procrastination. The passage is often repeated in speeches, collections of spiritual writing, and on posters and other artifacts. It is usually attributed to William Penn, although its source was most likely another Quaker, Stephen Grellet, 1773–1855.]

I Expect to Pass Through

I expect to pass through life but once. If therefore, there be any kindness I can show, or any good thing I can do to any fellow being, let me do it now, and not defer or neglect it, as I shall not pass this way again.

PART II

PHILANTHROPY AND LIBERTY IN THE ENLIGHTENMENT ERA

1700 · 1800

EPIGRAPH

ANONYMOUS

Philanthropy

True Charity can never fail,
But will o'er Time and Death prevail:
Were Prophecies and Tongues to cease,
The Man of Love shall live in peace,

Of ev'ry Virtue, ev'ry Grace,
True Charity is first in place;
And love to God and Man will be
The ground of ALL FELICITY!

Herald of the United States, Warren, R. I., 1793-07-20, 27:316.

STORIES

WINNEBAGO TRIBE

[We have seen examples of Native American traditions in the 1600s. The encounters of Native Americans with European settlers continued well beyond that time. The following three stories are reminders that Native Americans offered examples of another way of life, with customs of liberty and generosity making a strong impact on colonists. In the seventeenth and eighteenth centuries, when Europeans arrived in the New World, the Ho-chunk tribe (also known as the Winnebago) was a Siouan-speaking people living in what is now Wisconsin. "Ho-Chunk" comes from a word meaning "large fish," referring to the sturgeon, which thrived in Lake Winnebago and sustained the Indians there. The tribe today has a reservation in western Iowa and Northeastern Nebraska, but many Winnebagos also live in Wisconsin and Minnesota. Winnebago stories of trickster figures have been collected and studied by a number of twentieth-century scholars. The one presented below demonstrates the values of sharing and cooperating, along with the foolishness of out-smarting oneself in a selfish quest for personal advantage. Instead of bluntly saying "share your food" and "help your neighbor," this story shows, through the humor and drama of trickster fooling trickster, the disastrous results of not sharing, not cooperating—conveying a warning in a memorable way. "Wak'djunk'aga" means "the tricky one."]

Wak'djunk'aga's Appetite Incites Greed and Causes Him Grief

One time Trickster, Wak'djunk'aga, was hungry and went out looking for food. He built a fire and sat down and fantasized about many kinds of food, and then heard two birds in a nearby tree discussing how Coyote, who lived nearby, had a special trap for getting prey, and so he had lots of food stored up for himself, even while nearby villagers were starving because they couldn't find any game.

Trickster figured he could steal Coyote's magical trap and then always have plenty to eat. Near a bush, he made a hole deep in the ground and covered it over with tree branches, weeds, and bark. Then he went to find Coyote, acting as if he needed his help to capture some fat squirrels. Coyote agreed, and they set off together, and when they got near the bush, Trickster said, "You sneak up on them now—they're behind that bush over there." Coyote, though he had plenty of food already, was greedy for more, and he quietly crawled over to the bush and fell down into the Trickster's freshly dug hole. Trickster covered the hole with dirt and danced around, making warrior whoops and hollers.

The two birds saw this trick and went to the starving villagers and told them how Coyote had been hoarding all the game, using a magical trap to do it. Some of the villagers went to find the trap and the food. Trickster saw them and asked them what they were doing there.

The villagers said, "We're just now having a great feast—everyone here is invited. We're here to find guests."

Trickster said, "Let's go!" figuring he'd find Coyote's hoard of food later and eat it all himself.

The villagers described to the Trickster all the kinds of food being prepared, and

Trickster's mouth watered to hear about them.

The villagers said, "We have prepared a special wigwam just for you, our guest, to stay in."

Trickster happily ran inside the wigwam and immediately stumbled over a stone and tumbled down into a deep hole—the earth swallowed him whole, and he had no way out.

The villagers said, "Lies and deception used to get more food than you need will cause misfortune in the end, hurting the one with the greed."

Wording by William J. Jackson, based on a tale in David Lee Smith, *Folklore of the Winnebago Tribe*. Norman: University of Oklahoma Press, 1997, 38–39.

ONEIDA TRIBE

[Generosity sometimes involves difficult choices. This story is one of self-sacrifice, undertaken so that one child's people could live. The transformation of the girl into flowers is reminiscent of other, more mythological stories, such as that of Sedna, a goddess figure in Eskimo stories. Sedna, trying to escape an unhappy marriage, is divided into pieces, and her body parts become the creatures of the sea.

We feel indebted and bound to a reverent remembrance of the heroes and heroines who protected our ancestors' lives—their gift is evident in each breath we take. Consider two examples of other Americans who gave their lives so others would survive. David O. Dodd (d. 1864) was a 17-year-old rebel spy in Arkansas during the Civil War who refused to divulge the names of his leader or his informants. He accepted hanging as his punishment so his compadres could live. John Luther "Casey" Jones (d. 1900), the famous locomotive engineer hero, died while doing his duty, with one hand on the whistle rope and the other on the airbrake lever. Casey stayed at his post on the train, knowing it would crash, in order to give those on board time to jump off. Anyone who gives the last full measure of his or her devotion—dying for the lives of others—performs a most magnanimous act. Such a life becomes a legend, and the person's words—like Nathan Hale's "I only regret that I have but one life to lose for my country"—proverbial. The hero's deeds are preserved in folktales, songs, paintings, and other arts, including a stained-glass window, in the case of David O. Dodd. Our sacrifices for future generations will also be revered as sacred gifts, just as our failure to take precautions to preserve lives will arouse resentment. In each generation, much depends on ordinary people finding within themselves deeper resources for caring about others.]

Memory of the Sacrifice of Aliquipiso

The Oneida people were in hiding, besieged by their old enemies, the Mingos. They had abandoned their villages after being mercilessly attacked and were concealed in secret caves and on inaccessible cliffs, where they were starving. They could not go far to gather food, or the Mingos would kill them.

An Oneida girl named Aliquipiso came forward with a solution. "Let me go to the Mingoes and lead them to that place down there below this cliff. There you can crush them all."

It is said that the leaders listened closely and considered her plan and that the sachems put purple and white wampum around her neck, saying, "Aliquipiso, the great spirit has blessed you. You show great bravery and vision. We will always keep you in our hearts."

Aliquipiso said good-bye to the elders and her family and went to find the Mingos. They captured her and told her she must reveal the hiding places of the Oneidas. If she agreed, she would be accepted by them and live as an adopted member of their tribe. When she refused, they tortured her.

After much torture, she agreed to lead them to her people.

"If you try to trick us, you will die," they threatened her.

The Mingo warriors followed Aliquipiso, and approaching the cliff, she said to the Mingos, "Come here, and I will show you the secret way up."

Then she called to her own people's warriors: "Our foes are here—destroy them!" Huge stones and boulders fell, and no one at the foot of the cliff escaped. Many Mingo warriors died that day, and never again did the Mingoes attack the Oneidas. They retreated to their own hunting grounds.

The story of Aliquipiso's courage and self-sacrifice has been told by Oneidas generation after generation.

The Oneidas say that the Great Mystery transformed Aliquipiso's hair to the plant known as woodbine, an herb that all agree is "good medicine." The Oneidas say that from Aliquiposo's body, sacrificed by her for her people's survival, came the honeysuckle flower, known in their language as "brave woman's blood." It is a perennial reminder of her courageous generosity.

Wording by William J. Jackson, based on a story told by the Oneidas, and in Paula Gunn Allen, ed., *Spider Woman's Granddaughters: Traditional Tales and Contemporary Writing by Native American Women*. New York: Fawcett Columbine, 1989, 63–64, and "The Warrior Maiden" at http://www.manataka.org/page66.html (an alternate version).

AMERICAN STORY

[This eighteenth century tale is about hospitality. It is a story sympathetic to the Native Americans, written for the education of young people in the colonies. Although the style may seem stilted today, the storyteller speaks in a straightforward manner and makes an important point about the danger of dismissing others as less than us, unworthy of our help. The same point, which was made by the parable of the Good Samaritan, is made again and again in the experiences and stories of each generation. Native American hospitality was widely recorded in the seventeenth and eighteenth centuries. Protestant clergyman Daniel Gookin, in Historical Collections of the Indians in New England, published in 1674, wrote of New England Indians, "They are much given to hospitality in their way. If any strangers come to their houses, they will give him the best lodging and diet they have; and the strangers must be first served, by themselves. The wife makes ready, and by her husband's direction, delivers to the strangers, according to their quality, or his affection." The first generations of settlers often misunderstood the Indians' systems of gifts and hospitality, their methods of land use, and their religious beliefs. The tale shows how stereotypes are unjust, causing us to reevaluate assumptions about the categories "civil" and "savage." In the last line, the Indian says the opposite of what he means—he really is telling the miser to expand his sympathy.]

Revenge Sweetened by Generosity

If there was no inward complacency to be experienced in the performance of a generous action; if it was not a moral obligation due to our fellow creatures; if it was not consistent with the principles of a pure religion, still there are other incitements which may render it wise and politic to alleviate the cries of distress, however mean or apparently contemptible the object. We do not, however, recommend our youthful readers to form their notions of liberality on the selfish consideration of interest; nor to render them universally profuse. There are some cases where it is almost criminal to lavish benefits; for pecuniary aids harden the vicious, and contribute to make an indolent character a still more unworthy member of society; for others, seeing laziness fatten on the spoils of the bountiful, catch the contagion, and renounce the profits and the sweets of honest industry. We may as well be niggardly as give without discrimination; except under circumstances where a drop of water, or a crust of bread, would suffice to nourish an exhausted suppliant.

Some short time since, an Indian in North America, having hunted a whole day without success, found himself towards evening, seriously overcome by hunger and thirst. In this unpleasant dilemma, he approached the cottage of a white man, who resided on the borders of the woods: there he made known his wants to the master of the house; and concluded by humbly desiring a morsel or two of bread. "I have none!" answered the white man, in a surly tone.

"Give me, then, a cup of small beer?" said the famishing Indian.

"Indeed I will not," replied he.

"I am so faint," replied the *Savage*, "that a glass of water, even, will be acceptable!"

"Be gone, you Indian dog!" answered the white man: "I will not give you any thing."

About six months after this occurrence, the white man went out to hunt, with several of his neighbors; from all of whom he was separated by accident. It happened too, in a thick forest, to the turnings of which he was a perfect stranger: for a long time, therefore, did he rove about, and elevate his voice in vain; the hopes of being enabled to extricate himself, did not seem to coincide with probability. When, however, the bewildered hunter was sinking in despair, he fortunately perceived an Indian hut, the owner of which he requested to guide him home.

"It is too late, Sir," said the Indian. "You cannot reach your house tonight. Be contented, therefore, to tarry in my habitation till tomorrow. Everything that I have, shall be at your service."

This strayed huntsman cheerfully accepted the Indian's offer. He partook of such refreshments as the hut afforded; and afterwards stretched his weary body on a bed of skins, which the host's family had carefully collected for that purpose.

Next morning, the Indian conducted his guest out of the wood, and showed him the direct road which led to his own village. When they were about taking leave of each other, the Indian stepped before his companion; and, looking full in his face, desired him to consider, whether, or not, they were total strangers? "Have you never seen me before, Sir?" said the Indian.

At that instant, the white man recognized, in his benefactor, the very man to whom he had so recently denied a glass of cold water! The very who, fatigued and hungry, he had driven with indignation from his door. He was disconcerted; and shame so fully possessed his soul, that he could find no means of apologizing for his inhumanity: of course, he continued a mortifying silence; while the Indian, big with the pride of conscious superiority, thus concluded his triumph.

"When now," said he, "you again see any of my Tribe oppressed by hunger of thirst, and they ask you for a bit of bread; or for a drop of water, say to them, 'Go about your business, you Indian dog!'"

Pleasing Incitements to Wisdom and Virtue, Conveyed through the Medium of Anecdote, Tale and Adventure: Calculated to Entertain, Fortify, and Improve the Juvenile Mind. Translated chiefly from the German. Philadelphia: Reprinted by James Humphreys from the London Edition, 1800.

ANONYMOUS

[Muslim influences were at work in the American imagination in the eighteenth century. We often think of historic encounters with Islam in terms of the Crusades, but there have been positive contacts as well. This story bears likenesses to stories in the Thousand and One Nights, the only Arabic work thus far to enjoy widespread popularity in the West. American newspaper readers of the eighteenth century read these Muslim culture stories for entertainment, drawing spiritual and moral lessons from them. In this story, the fault of greediness is not immediately punished, but in the end repeated mistakes do not pass with impunity. The dervish (a term for Muslim holy men from Persia or Turkey, living austerely and begging for alms) is the very soul of generosity and patience. The youth in this story should have felt gratitude for the dervish's forgiveness, but he did not and so suffered the consequences. The ultimate result of greed and thievery is great loss. In this literature, wisdom and morals are taught with an entertaining flourish, like medicine concealed in a tasty food.]

Ingratitude and Avarice Punished

A Dervish venerable by his age, fell ill in the house of a widow, who lived in extreme poverty in the suburbs of Balsora (Basra in Iraq). He was so touched with the care and zeal with which she had assisted him, that at his departure he said to her, "I have remarked that you have where-with to subsist upon alone, but that you have not enough to share it with your only son, the young Abdalla. If you will trust him to my care, I will do all that is possible to acknowledge in his person the obligations I have to you." The good woman received his proposal with joy, and the Dervish departed with the young man.

Abdalla a hundred times testified his gratitude to him, but the old man always said to him, "My son, it is by actions that gratitude is proved: I shall see at a proper time and place whether you are so grateful as you profess to be."

One day as they continued their travels, they found themselves in a solitary place, and the Dervish said to Abdalla, "We are now at the end of our journey." The Dervish striking a light, made a small fire, into which he cast a perfume. [The Dervish] then prayed for some moments, after which the earth opened, and the Dervish said to him, "Thou may now enter, my dear Abdalla; remember it is in thy power to do me a great service, and that this perhaps is the only opportunity thou canst ever have of testifying to me thou art not ungrateful. Do not de dazzled by what thou will find there, think only of seizing upon an iron candlestick with twelve branches, which thou will find close to a door, that is absolutely necessary to me. Come up immediately, and bring it to me."

Abdalla promised everything, and descended boldly into the vault; but forgetting what had been so expressly commanded of him, whilst he was filling his vest and bosom with the gold and jewels which this vault inclosed in prodigious heaps, the opening by which he entered closed of itself; he had, however, presence of mind enough to seize on the iron candlestick: He searched many ways to get out, at length, after much pain and inquietude, he was fortunate enough to find a narrow passage, which led him out of his obscure cave, though it was not until he had followed it a considerable way that he perceived a small opening, covered with briars and thorns, through which he came out.

Figure 2.1 Dervish in a bazaar

He looked on all sides to see if he could perceive the Dervish, but not seeing him, nor remembering any of the places through which they had passed, he went on as fortune directed him, and was extremely astonished to find himself before the door of his mother's house. She immediately enquired after the holy Dervish. Abdalla told her frankly the danger he had run to satisfy his unreasonable desires; he afterwards showed her the riches; while they contemplated on these treasures with avidity, and, dazzled with their luster, formed a thousand projects in consequence of them, they all vanished away before their eyes. It was then that Abdalla sincerely reproached himself with his ingratitude and disobedience; as he did thus, he placed the candlestick in the midst of the room.

When night was come, without reflecting, he placed a light in it, immediately they saw a Dervish appear, who turned round for an hour and disappeared, after having thrown them an aspre, or small Turkish coin. Abdalla, who meditating all the day upon what he had seen the night before, was willing to know what would happen the next night if he put a candle in each of the branches: He did so, and twelve Dervishes appeared; they turned round also for an hour, and each of them threw an aspre. He constantly every night repeated the same ceremony, which had always the same success. This trifling sum was enough to make him and his mother subsist tolerably; but thinking it but a small advantage they drew from the candlestick, he resolved to carry it back to the Dervish, in hopes that he might obtain of him the treasure he had seen, or at least what had vanished from his sight, by restoring him a thing for which he had testified so ardent a desire. He was so fortunate as to remember his name, and that of the city where he dwelt. He took leave of his mother, and departed immediately with the candlestick, which furnished him with necessaries on the road. When he arrived at *Magrabi,* his first care was to enquire in what house the Dervish dwelt. He got intelligence, and repaired thither immediately, and found fifty porters who kept the gates of his palace, each having a staff, with a head of gold in their hands; the palace was filled with slaves and domestics; in fine, the court of a prince could not expose to view greater magnificence. Abdalla then enquired for the Dervish; he was soon conducted to an agreeable pavilion where the Dervish was seated. "Thou art but an ungrateful wretch," said he [the Dervish] to him. "If thou had known the true use of this candlestick never would thou have brought it me. I will make thee sensible of its true virtue." Immediately he placed a light in each of its branches, and when the twelve Dervishes had turned for some time, he gave each of them a blow with a cane, and in a moment they were converted into twelve large heaps of diamonds and other precious stones. "This," said he, "is the proper use to be made of this miraculous candlestick; but to prove to thee that curiosity was the only occasion of my search for it; here are the keys of my magazine, tell if the insatiable miser would not be satisfied with them."

Abdalla obeyed him, and examined twelve magazines, which were so full of all manner of riches, that he could not distinguish what merited his admiration most; regret of having restored the candlestick and not finding the use of it, pierced the heart of Abdalla; the Dervish seemed not to perceive it, but on the contrary loaded him with caresses. When the eve of the day which he had fixed for his departure was come, the Dervish said to him, "Abdalla, I owe thee a mark of my gratitude for taking so long a journey with a view of bringing me the thing I desired; thou may depart, thou shall find tomorrow, at the gates of my palace, one of my horses to carry thee; I make thee a present of it, as well as of a slave, who shall conduct to thy house two camels loaded with gold and jewels." Abdalla said to him all that a heart sensible to avarice could express, when its passion was satisfied, and went to lay down until the morning arrived, which was the time fixed for his departure. During the night he was still agitated, without being able to think on any thing else but the candlestick, and what it produced: He determined at length to seize on the candlestick, which was not difficult, the Dervish having trusted him with the keys of the magazine; he knew where the candlestick was placed; he took it and hid it at the bottom of one of the sacks, which he filled with pieces of gold, and other riches he was allowed to take, and loaded it as well as the rest upon his camels, and after returning the Dervish his keys, departed with his horse, his slave and two camels.

When he had gone some days journey he sold his slave, resolving not to have a witness of his former poverty, nor of the source of his present riches; he bought another, and arrived without any other obstacle at his mother's. His first care was to place the loads of the camels and the candlestick in the most private room in the house, and in his impatience to feed his eyes with his great opulence, he placed lights immediately in the candlestick; the twelve Dervishes appearing, he gave each of them a blow with all his might; but he had not remarked, that the Dervish when he struck them had the cane in his *left* hand: Abdalla, by a natural motion, made use of his right, and the Dervishes, instead of becoming heaps of riches, immediately drew from beneath their robes, each a formidable club, with which they struck him so hard, and so often, that they left him almost dead, and disappeared, carrying with them all his treasure, the camels, the horse, the slave, and the candlestick.

Solomon Soberside, *Entertaining Histories for Young Masters and Misses*. Worcester, Mass.: Centinel, 1796, 34–45.

RICHARD JOHNSON (d. 1793)

[Richard Johnson, a printer, began writing around 1770 and supported his family by authoring dozens of books. He often preached about the virtue of prudence, and in The Adventures of a Silver Penny advised, "Be good-natured and affable, and ever ready to

assist the unfortunate as far as your condition will prudently admit." He wrote The Blossoms of Morality, from which the following piece comes, late in 1788. In it, he adapted a Muslim story to teach children about having a good character. Although Johnson lived in England, his books were popular in America, and so this story, published in New York, is included here. It reminds us that generosity and gratitude are highly valued in many parts of the world and must be appreciated by those who seek to encourage social harmony and a thriving economy.]

Generosity Rewarded

Of all the graces that contribute to adorn the human mind, there are perhaps none more estimable than generosity and gratitude. To define the exact boundary between generosity and profusion, is not perhaps easy, since every one will explain it by the ideas they have of their own motives for action; yet how far soever avarice may have deprived some men of every spark of generosity, yet those very men fail to expect it from others, and are sure to complain bitterly of those who do not display it in all their actions.

Nothing can equal the pleasure arising from the glow of a generous heart, which is prompted to a noble action, solely from the love of virtue, and who wishes not to make of it a worldly parade.

Fame is often purchased by generous donations, which would never have been given, had not popular idolatry been the main object in view; while others, like the generous man in the following tale, consulted only the approbation of his own honest feelings.

One of the caliphs of Egypt, being in the field of battle, was unexpectedly surrounded by a great number of rebels, who were preparing to give the fatal blow, which would at once have finished his life, and put an end to his mortal career. Fortunately for him, an Arab happened to be near the spot, with other soldiers of his party, who seeing the situation of the caliph rushed upon the rebels, and attacked them with such fury, that they were all soon put to flight.

The name of this Arab was Nadir, who had for some months lived a wandering life in the most retired and unfrequented places, in order to escape the vengeance of the caliph against whom he had joined the people in a late insurrection.

This generous conduct of Nadir was so much admired by all the Arabians, that the sires still relate it to their children among their evening tales. This adventure had the happy effect of perfectly reconciling Nadir to the caliph, who, charmed with the generosity of a man who had saved his life, at the very instant he might have destroyed it, promised to place in him an implicit confidence. "But," said the caliph, "let me hear how you have passed your time during your state of banishment."

"I have been a wandering fugitive," replied Nadir, "ever since your family were elevated to the throne of this empire, conscious that the sword of vengeance was at all times hanging over my head, it became natural for me to seek security in retirement. I found refuge for some time in the house of a friend at Basra; but fearing that my stay in that city might be dangerous, I one night quitted it under the favor of a disguise, and pursued my journey towards the desert.

"I had escaped the vigilance of the guards, and thought myself out of all danger, when a man of a suspicious countenance seized my camel's bridle, and expressed his suspicions, that I was the man the caliph was in search of, and for the apprehension of whom a very considerable reward had been promised.

"I answered that I was not the man he was in quest of."

"Is not your name Nadir?" said he. This disconcerted me, and I could no longer deny myself to be the object of his pursuit.

I put my hand into my bosom, and pulling out a jewel of some value, "Receive," said I, "this trifling token of my gratitude, for the important service I hope you will now do me, in keeping silence, and favoring my escape. Should fortune again smile on me, I will share my prosperity with you."

He took my diamond, and examined it very attentively. "Before I put this diamond into my turban, as your gift," said he, "I would wish you to answer me one question honestly. I have heard you have been a liberal man, and always ready to assist the poor and necessitous; but did you ever give away one half of your wealth at one time?" I answered in the negative, and he renewed his questions, till he came down to one tenth, when I replied, that I believed I had, at one time, given away more than one tenth of my whole fortune.

"If that be the case (said the man, as soon as I had made him that reply), that you may know there is at least one person in the realm, more bountiful than yourself, I, who am nothing better than a private soldier, and receive only two dollars per month, return you your jewel, which must certainly be worth three thousand times that money." Having thus said he threw me back my diamond, and pursued his journey.

Astonished at so benevolent and generous an action, I rode after him, and begged him to return. "Generous friend," said I to him, "I would rather be discovered, and forfeit my head, than be thus vanquished in point of generosity. Magnanimous stranger, either I must follow you all day, or you must accept of this tribute of my gratitude."

He then turning about, said to me, "Were I to take from you your diamond, I should consider myself as a robber on the highway, since you receive no value for it. Let me advise you to lose no time, but make the best of your way to your proposed retreat." He continued inflexible, and we parted.

The caliph knew not which to admire most, the generosity of Nadir or the soldier. A proclamation was published, ordering the generous soldier to appear at the caliph's court, that he might receive the reward of his virtues; but all was to no effect, as no one came forward to claim the glorious reward. However, about a twelvemonth afterwards, when Nadir attended the caliph at a general review, a private soldier received a blow from his officer, for holding down his head as the caliph passed. This drew the attention of Nadir, who, after looking steadfastly in the face of the offending soldier, leaped from his horse, and caught him in his arms.

To conclude, this proved to be the man who had so generously treated Nadir, and had endeavored to shun the reward of his virtues. The caliph paid him singular honors on the spot, and at last raised him to the highest rank in his army.

Richard Johnson, *The Blossoms of Morality*. New York: Longworth, 1800.

ANONYMOUS

[This is an unusual story of a stranger's kind care and the idea that "no good deed goes unpunished." Note that the gentlewoman giving a helping hand was inspired by Hindu spirituality—"the sublime enthusiasm of Eastern morality"—showing us that not all Anglo-Saxons of the eighteenth century were solely informed by Christian teachings. It

seems to imply that a gossipy, insensitive world often bruises and brutalizes our humane feelings and that we are in danger of growing callous in defending ourselves from unkind, suspicious, and malicious chatterboxes. "Pancreatic" usually means the secretion of the pancreas, which has enzymes that aid digestion; in this story, "pancreatic" seems to be a pun on the kind woman's sympathy for "all creation."]

Philanthropy

I happened to be very ill at that time, and sitting by the fire-side one morning in my lodgings, when I received a very polite care, in a female hand, unknown, acquainting me, that having been struck with that rich vein of philanthropy, she was pleased to say, which flowed like milk and honey through all my writings, Mr.____ would be much obliged, and flattered, if I would afford her an opportunity of a personal acquaintance with the author, by doing her the favour of drinking tea with her that evening.

I was too weak to venture abroad. I wrote her word so . . . assured her that I longed equally for the pleasure of an acquaintance with any person, whose heart and mind seemed to sympathize with those affections she was so kind to compliment me, and intreated the honour of a *sans ceremonie* visit from her, upon this occasion, that very evening.

She condescended to accept my invitation, and came accordingly. She visited me every day while I continued confined—which kindness I returned, most punctually, as soon as I was able to go abroad.

She was a woman of sense and virtue—not lively, but possessed of that charming sort of even cheerfulness, which naturally flows from goodness—*Nems conscia recti.* She was reserved, and, like a ghost, would rarely speak till spoken to. She had, like a lute, all the passive powers of music in her, but wanted the master's hand to bring them forth.

She had quitted England very young—before her tender affections had been rendered callous, by the collisions of the world. She had been carried into India, where she continued, till those sentiments had ripened into principle, and were inspired with all the sublime enthusiasm of eastern morality.

She seemed to be unhappy. This added a tenderness to my esteem for her—I guessed, but inquired not her private history, and she communicated nothing. She would repine, but not resent. She had no gall to boil over—her overflowings were of the pancreatic juices only.

From that time we held a constant and refined intercourse, while she remained in the kindness, and a friendly correspondence in this world—I prophecy!—She happened to be another man's wife too.

But the charity that had attracted, with the virtue that united us, were not able to screen us from the censure of base minds: neither her own fair character, nor the memento of my ghostly appearance, were sufficient bars to slander . . .

Unsigned, *Rivington's New-York Gazetteer*, June 24, 1773, 10:1.

BENJAMIN WEST (1738–1820)

[Isaac Bickerstaff was a pseudonym that bibliographer Charles Evans attributed to Benjamin West, a leading American portrait painter of his day. Isaac Bickerstaff was a pen name

first used by Jonathon Swift in 1708; Richard Steele later used it in The Tatler, a London pub-lication. In America, Benjamin West used the name when he was editor of Bickerstaff's Boston Almanac. The following dialogue, from West's 1773 almanac, presents ironic arguments on the reasoning of miserliness and prodigality. Each cannot see the other's view and speaks with humorous vehemence, criticizing and exercising self-justification. This eighteenth cen-tury dialogue of polar opposite views on approaches to giving represents irreconcilably differ-ent personalities or sides of human nature that reappear in every generation.]

A Dialogue between a Miser and Prodigal

Miser. What, young Spendthrift! You are as profuse as ever, I see.

Prodigal. Prithee, old Mannon! Look to thyself: Thou hast faults anew to mend.

Miser. Why art thou not a fool, to squander so much gold away upon thy desires, when thou hast so little in thy pockets?

Prodigal. And art thou not a madman, to wear such shabby cloaths, when thou hast so much money in thy bags.

Miser. Thou will live to want what thou threwest away upon back and belly; they will be thy ruin.

Prodigal. Thy back and belly call thee madman, for thou dost starve them: Thou art now in want of the money thy bags contain: Thou darest not touch it: Thy gold hast already ruined thee.

Miser. Thou fool! the money in my coffers is my great comfort. Be wise; and learn to live like me.

Prodigal. Thou madman! Learn to live like thee! I can but do that when all my gold is gone.

Miser. Thou spendthrift! To how many persons art thou indebted, and how many duns hast thou every day!

Prodigal. Thou Miser! dost thou not live indebted to thyself, and does not thy belly dun thee every hour?

Miser. Thou wilt soon be in jail.

Prodigal. Thou art in one already; for thy very soul is imprisoned in the chest where thy bags are.

Miser. Thou wilt die a beggar.

Prodigal. Thou dost live one.

Miser. Thy children will curse thee when thou art dead.

Prodigal. Thine curse thee whilst thou art alive, and will rejoice when thou art gone to the devil.

Benjamin West, *Bickerstaff's Boston Almanack*. Boston: John Fleming, printer, 1773.

ANONYMOUS

[Children's literature in eighteenth-century America was primarily instructional, a kind of educational entertainment. The hero of the first story is a child determined to care for the poor, even if it means incurring the displeasure of her father. Though giving is not done for self-advancement, the tale shows generosity naturally rewarded—the girl rises in life. Good-ness brings more goodness. The second story is about a child's kindness toward an animal,

teaching that caring attention nurtures life. The moral seems to be that living things sup-ported with loving care will grow and thrive, while those neglected and slighted will wither and decline. The word "churl" in the story is an old term for a miserly person.]

A Gift for Children
Story of the Young Cottager

On a warm summer's day, as Rose, a poor girl sat singing at her wheel in the shade of the wood, she heard a deep groan among the trees. She stopped her wheel, and for a moment listened, but all being still, she went on with her work. In a few minutes, she again heard a groan as of a person in distress. She started up and went towards the place, to discover the occasion of the sound; but having looked about some time without success, she returned to her work. Again the groans saluted her ears, and she resolved to find the cause. Pursuing a narrow winding path, she at length beheld an old man, in the agonies of distress, stretched on the ground, and his head supported by the roots of a tree. The tender hearted Rose hastened to him, and stooped down, attempted to raise his head into her lap; when the poor man faintly spoke the word water, Rose guessed by this that he wanted drink, and ran to her father's cottage, where she took her bowl of new milk and bro't to the poor suffering old man. He drank freely, and was soon refreshed so as to thank Rose for her kind concern.

Rose asked him how he came to be in that situation. He replied that on his way from New York to Hartford, he was seized with a violent fever, and lay sick for several days, in which time all his money was spent. That after his money was gone, his land-lord would no longer lodge and take care of him and being obliged to travel before he had gained his strength, he was soon fatigued, and almost fainted; being just able to crawl in to the shade of the woods.

When the compassionate girl heard this story, she ran home and bro't some brown bread, which was all her father's cottage afforded. This she softened with milk, and sit-ting down by his side, fed him with it. He soon revived so as to be able to walk to a shed which some workmen had raised in the neighbourhood. Here he lay down upon the straw, while Rose went to inform her father; who had just come home. Rose entreated her father to assist the poor old man, and give him a bed, till he should be well enough to go on his journey. "Give him a bed," said her father; "this would be a fine thing indeed. What will the town say, when my own family becomes a charge upon them? I am sure we are poor enough already and want help more than we are able to give it."

"But," said Rose, "our minister tells us to do all the good we can, and pity those that are in distress."

"Yes, yes," said the father, "he should preach that to rich folks. Poor folks have nothing to give. It is well if we can maintain ourselves, and not come upon the town [as beggars]."

"But father," said Rose, "it will cost us but little to let the miserable old man lodge a few nights in the house; and besides the minister says God will return us fourfold, what we give to the poor."

"O fie, child," answered the old churl, "let me hear no more of your *helping the poor*. We are poor enough ourselves."

"I am sure, sir, if you could only see how *very poor* this man is, you would be glad to afford him a little relief."

"Peace, girl," said her father, "and eat your porridge."

Rose, seeing she could not prevail on her hard-hearted father to lend the man any assistance, resolved to do what she could herself. She therefore ate but little of her porridge, and when her father was gone out, she carried the rest to the poor man in the shed. Rose found him in a calm sleep, and not being willing to wake him, she sat down by his side, till he awoke, and then kindly presented him a little refreshment. This would not satisfy her feeling heart; but seeing him exposed to the damp air of the evening, she went and bro't him some clothes to cover him in the night.

In this manner, the good girl provided for the poor sick man, by giving him a part of her own portion of food every day, till he had quite recovered, and was able to pursue his journey. When he departed, he burst into a flood of tears, and blessed her a thousand times for her kindness. He said, he could express his gratitude only by words, and tears of joy, but he was sure heaven would reward her virtue.

This generous conduct of Rose was soon reported in the neighbouring villages, and every one was pleased and delighted with Rose. In a few years her amiable conduct made her the admiration of all who knew her; and a wealthy young farmer being charmed with her virtues, offered her his heart, his hand, and his fortune. Thus was Rose raised from poverty, by her virtuous and good conduct, and now lives in wealth and plenty—the joy of her husband, and the pattern of all good wives.

The Lamb

Little Phebe, a poor shepherd's daughter, was sitting one morning by the side of a great road, holding upon her lap a porringer of milk, in to which she as dipping some brown bread for her breakfast.

During this little repast, a carrier came the same way, who was driving twenty live lambs to market, in a cart. These poor little animals, heaped one upon another with their legs tied, and their heads drooping, filled the air with the most sorrowful bleatings, which went to the very heart of Phebe, though the carrier heard them without pity. When he came up to her, he flung a poor little lamb before her, that he was carrying by the heels upon his shoulder. "There, child," cried he, "there's a good-for-nothing beast for you, that has just died, to cheat me of a crown. Take it, if you will, and make yourself a feast with it."

Phebe immediately left off eating her breakfast and, putting the porringer and the bread on the ground took the lamb in her arms, and looked at it with the utmost compassion.

"Poor little creature!" cried she; "yet why should I be sorry for you? To-day, or to-morrow, they would only have taken a great knife, and cut your poor throat; and now, instead of that, you have nothing more to go through." While she was talking to it in this manner, the lamb, growing warm again in her arms, began to open its eyes and move, she made a faint bleating cry, as if pining for its dam.

It would be difficult to describe the joy of Phebe at the sound of its voice. She wrapped it up in her apron, then covered it over again with her fustian coat, and bent her neck almost down upon her knees to keep it warmer, breathing, at the same time, with all her might, into its nostrils. By little and little, she felt the poor animal revive, and her own heart beat with joy every time it showed any signs of life. Encouraged by this success, she rolled up some crumbs in her hands, put them in to her porringer, and taking them out with her fingers, contrived, though, not without much difficulty, to force them between its teeth, though they were shut very close. The lamb, who was only dying from want, felt itself a little strengthened by this nourishment. She now began to stretch out her legs, and shake her head and her tale, and perk up her ears; and soon after, she was so much better as to stand upon her feet; and then, seeing the porringer with Phebe's breakfast, she went and drank out of it herself, to the great delight of the little girl. In short, a quarter of an hour had hardly passed, before she was so well recovered, as to cut a thousand capers round her new little mistress. Phebe, in a transport of joy, took her in her arms, running with her into the cottage, showed her to her mother. "Little Baalam," as she now called her, became from this time the object of all her cares, she always shared with her the bread and milk she was allowed from her own meals; and she would not have parted with this one little lamb, for the largest flock of sheep in the village. Baalam was so grateful for her kindness, that she was never a step distant from her, the most plaintive bleating spoke her sorrow at the parting.

The pity and good nature of Phebe, however, had still a greater recompence. Baalam was soon the mother of several other little lambs, who, in their turn grew the mother of more: so that, in a few years, Phebe had a very pretty flock of sheep, entirely her own; which fed the family with their milk and supplied them with clothes from their wool.

Anonymous, *A Gift for Children*. Norwich, Conn.: John Sterry, 1796, 3–6, 8–10.

CLAUDE SAVARY (1750–1788)
AND M. CHENIER (18C)

[The following accounts, the first taken from a book and republished in a newspaper, and the second published originally in a newspaper, praise Arabs for their hospitality and generosity. Both were probably published to widen the horizons of stay-at-home farmers and merchants. Claude Savary was a French explorer and Orientalist. Some scholars today would say his Orientalist view expressed here says more about Euro-American imagination of the time than about Arabs. They see it as romantic praise of the "noble savage untouched by corrupting influences of civilization." But it may also be an honest attempt by a traveler to learn and teach about people in other parts of the world, using the only history and vocabulary with which the author was familiar. The second account, by M. Chenier (who may have been the French consul in Morocco around this time), shows surprise at the possibility of cooperation instead of enmity. Orientalists, in seeing Arabs as noble exotic others, also attempted to report a situation with universal human implications. We are all potentially helpers of strangers in need of directions and other necessities, and, as travelers, we too are strangers potentially in need of help. We depend on others just as others depend on us.]

Character of a Tribe of the Arabs,
from [Claude] Savary's Letters on Egypt, 1792

A part of the Arabs, who may be called cultivators, live under the government of their Scheiks [*sic*], who possess several principalities in the Thebais. This word, which signifies old man, is the most illustrious token of their power. They are still, as heretofore, the judges, the pontiffs, and the sovereigns of their people. They govern more like fathers of families than kings. These venerable patriarchs usually take their repasts at the doors of their houses, or their tents, and invite all who present themselves. On rising from table they cry with a loud voice, In the name of God, let him that is hungry come near and eat; nor is the invitation a barren compliment. Every man, whoever he be, has a right to seat himself, and to partake of the food he finds there.

The Arabs give the same reception to strangers and travellers who come near their tents that Abraham did to the angels (Gen 18). Servants wash their feet; the women knead unleavened bread, which they bake upon the ashes, and they are served with roasted sheep, milk and honey, and the best of everything they are possessed of. [The slight impositions levied by the Scheiks through their territories, do not oppress their subjects. They enjoy their affection. The Arab comes and exposes his affairs at their tribunal. They are not complicated, and the light of natural reason, aided by the simple and clear laws of the Coran, suffice to terminate them on the spot. Their judgments are almost always dictated by equity. Under this paternal government, man possesses all his liberty, and is no further attached to his Prince than by the ties of respect and gratitude. He may speak freely to him, therefore, and censure or commend him according to the circumstances . . .]

These Arabs are the best people in the world. They are ignorant of the vices of polished nations. Incapable of concealment, they are strangers to tricks and falsehood. Lofty and generous they openly repulse an insult with an armed hand, and never revenge themselves by treachery. Hospitality amongst them is sacred. Their houses and their tents are open to all travellers of every religion. They treat their guests with as much respect and affection as their own relations.

Herald of the United States, Worcester, R.I., 1792-02-11, 5:20.

Generosity and Hospitality of Lions (1792)

M. Chenier, in this present state of Morocco, relates the following story of a Lion. I have been assured, says the author, that an Arab, who went to hunt the lion, having proceeded far into the forest, happened to meet with two lion's whelps, that came to caress him; the hunter stopped with the little animals and waiting for the coming of sire or dam, took out his breakfast and gave them a part. The lioness arrived unperceived by the huntsman, so that he had not time, or perhaps wanted the courage, to take his gun. After having for some time, looked at the man that was feasting the young, the lioness went away, and soon after returning, bearing with her a sheep, which she laid at the huntsman's feet.

The Arab, thus become one of the family, took this occasion of making a good meal, skinned the sheep, made a fire, and roasted a part, giving the entrails to the young; the Lion in his turn came also, and, as of respecting the rights of hospitality, shewed no tokens whatever of ferocity. Their guest the next day, having finished his provisions, returned, and came to a resolution never more to kill any of those animals. He stroked and caressed the whelps at taking leave of them, and the dam and the sire accompanied him until he was safely out of the forest.

Vermont Journal and Universal Advertiser 1792-01-24, vol. 9, 443:3. (Also in *Dunlap's American Daily Advertiser* 1792-01-07, 4040:2. And the *Morning Ray* 1792-01-03, vol. 1, 11:3.)

NORTH CAROLINA STORY

[In this retelling of an old Southern story based on actual events, North Carolina women during the American Revolution nobly renounce British tea and clothing. Their acts inspire generosity in local merchants to also make sacrifices and to offer goods to support the revolutionary effort. The story reminds us that every little bit helps, that a journey of a thousand miles begins with one step, and that it is fitting to sacrifice luxuries for causes we care about. The decision of the North Carolinians is based on an idea later summed up well by Mahatma Gandhi, "Live simply, that others may simply live."]

The Revolution of the Ladies of Edenton

This is a velvety tale that actually happened down South in North Carolina. Folks there and folks in every Southern state love to tell it, for it is a happening of which every man, woman, and child in North Carolina, as well as every other state, is proud. To this day, wherever the story is told, it brings a warm and grand smile to the face and to the heart: the Edenton Tea Party, the first famous revolution by women in our land.

Surely you have heard of the Boston Tea Party, where merchantmen and citizens decided to throw the English tea into the bay rather than buy it and pay the tax. The same was done by the Edenton ladies—just as patriotic and just as determined to forego tea drinking until the unjust taxes by the English were lifted.

There were Penelope Barker and Elizabeth King, there were Sarah Valentine, Miss Johnston, and a host of others with equally rounded names who cried that America must be free of British tyranny.

The whole town of Edenton in North Carolina was boiling with political fervor and fury. Old and young were set free themselves and run their own government. And when the women were not asked to the political meetings that were going on, they decided to have their own political meetings. So they met in their homes when they came together to knit and embroider, to talk, and to drink tea.

At all these get-togethers there was tea—English tea! No social visit or friendly gathering was ever complete without tea. Now, with talk of British tyranny, talk of throwing off the British yoke—what of British tea?

One day, in that eventful year of 1774, Mistress Penelope Barker and Mistress King and a few other fine ladies were sitting over sweet cakes and cups of tea. They talked, not of laces and recipes and fashion, but of British tyranny and American determination to be freed from it.

"We too must join our men fighting for freedom," spoke Mistress Barker. She was fearless and free in her talk.

"That we certainly must. I don't know just what we can do, but there must be some work for us women," said Mistress King.

Such was the talk throughout Edenton. The seed was planted deep, and soon the fruits began to grow.

The next afternoon when the ladies were together, they decided to form a militant patriotic organization to help the men ready to fight at the battlefront. Thus began the famous feminine revolution of the ladies of Edenton against "British Tea."

The women were gathered at the home of Mistress Elizabeth King. There was a large number of them, over fifty. Talk was loud and strong. Eyes shone and faces flushed.

Mistress Penelope Barker was elected president.

The talk was different from the talk men had at their patriotic meetings and soon they formed their own plan of battle against the British.

"The Ladies of Edenton," for reasons of patriotism and the desire to help the fight of the thirteen colonies in their battle for independence, decided unanimously they would not conform to the pernicious custom of drinking the tea come from England. And the aforesaid "Ladies of Edenton" would not promote or encourage "ye wear of any manufacture from England until such time that all acts which tend to enslave this, our native country, shall be repealed."

These were the very words the ladies of Edenton used on October 25, 1774, and all the women of the town, high and low, lived up to the resolution fully.

Instead of tea they now brewed dried leaves of raspberry vines and to them this tasted sweeter than the tea from England, for it was sweetened and flavored with patriotism and love of country.

The fervor of action burned high after this patriotic deed. When the ladies declared their tea-independence of England, the men of Edenton dispatched to beleaguered Boston a shipload of corn, flour, and pork. One of Edenton's merchant princes gave one of his ships for George Washington to use, and Dr. Williamson, at his own cost, bought cargoes of medical and other supplies for the Revolutionary army. Many others followed suit.

Such were the results of the revolution of the Edenton ladies. Do you wonder that the story is in the land of folktales where such stories are told over and over again!

M. A. Jagendorf, *Folk Stories of the South*. New York: Vanguard, 1972, 182–84.

THOMAS PERCIVAL (1740–1804)

[These stories from popular children's literature teach how a life driven not by greed but by generosity and doing what is right leads to fulfillment and satisfaction. Percival was born in Warrington, England, and studied medicine at Edinburgh University. Best known in England and America for his work in medical ethics and social reform, Percival also published a highly acclaimed anthology for children, A Father's Instructions, on both sides of the Atlantic. Aside from examples in religious literature, there are few writings today in children's stories or popular culture where such values are so prominent.]

A Father's Instructions
Liberality

You have seen the husbandman *scattering* his seed upon the furrowed ground! It springs up, is gathered into his barns, and crowns his labours with joy and plenty.—Thus the man who distributes his fortune with generosity and prudence, is amply repaid by the gratitude of those whom he obliges, by the approbation of his own mind, and the favour of God.

Honesty and Generosity

A poor man, who was door-keeper to a house in Milan, found a purse which contained two hundred crowns. The man who had lost it, informed by a public advertisement, came to the house, and giving sufficient proof that the purse belonged to him, the door-keeper restored it. Full of joy and gratitude, the owner offered his benefactor twenty crowns, which he absolutely refused. Ten were then proposed, and afterwards five; but the door-keeper still continuing inexorable, the man threw his purse upon the ground, and in an angry tone cried, "I have lost nothing, nothing at all, if you thus refuse to accept of a gratuity." The door-keeper then consented to receive five crowns, which he immediately distributed among the poor.

Thomas Percival, *A father's instructions; consisting of moral tales, fables, and reflections; designed to promote the love of virtue, a taste for knowledge, and an early acquaintance with the works of nature.* Philadelphia: Thomas Dobson, 1788, 21, 29.

POEMS AND SONGS

EIGHTEENTH-CENTURY VERSES AND SKETCHES ON CHARITY AND PHILANTHROPY

[Eighteenth-century newspapers included many verses and reflections about giving. Usually unsigned, though sometimes written by local poets who used their initials or pen names, these writings encouraged good deeds and uplifting aid as the flowering of the human spirit. The writings below praise kindness toward others and consider generosity a sign of greatness of soul. Sometimes these were set to music and presented in benefit performances, as with An Ode below, which calls on the heavens to witness the acts of kindness and envisions how charity can improve unfortunate conditions and offer hope of a better life. This literature helped convey the reasons for giving.]

On Charity

That breast which melts at other's woe,
　Alone can real pleasure know,
Alone is blest and calm;
This sure is charity refin'd,
Which pitying heals the wounded mind,
　And pours on grief rich balm.
This will each other loss supply,
And please When other beauties fly,
　Which now our hearts alarm;
When fades the bloom of Nancy's face,
With all her elegance and grace
and every other charm.

Middlesex Gazette, Middletown, Conn., 1787-02-26, vol. 2, 69:4.

Elegy by Henry James Pye

The various blessings bounteous heaven bestows,
With gratitude and charity repay:
Relieve thy suffering friend, or share his woes,

But from his failings turn thine eyes away.

Cumberland Gazette, Falmouth, Maine, 1791-01-24, 4.

READER! He was indeed A MAN!
Although passing his life on the rough domain
of Neptune,
He possessed the keenest Sensibility;
His Heart,
Open as the full blown Rose,
Was the
Temple of true Benevolence, and unupbraiding Charity.

Federal Gazette & Baltimore Daily Advertiser, Baltimore, Md., 1798-08-29, vol. 9, 1496:2.

An Ode by Mr. Rea

From seats of bliss, in realms above,
Where goodness feeds on peace and love,
 And virtue finds reward;
Ye smiling throng, whose pious toil
With grace enrich'd your natal soil,
 This charity regard

Benevolence the heart expands;
Munificence, with liberal hands,
 "The debt of love fulfils:"
Religion triumphs as she finds
Her virtues living on her mind,
 A balm for human ills.

The sinking widows meet relief,
The hapless orphans lose their grief,
 Their tears no more are seen:
Safe in their country's tender arms,
Secur'd from poverty's alarms,
 They join the cheerful scene.

In rapture here their eyes behold
The publick heart with love unfold,
 By precepts most divine:
The image of their parents there,
Supports their hope, forbids despair,
 And in high lustre shines.

Rea, "An Ode," sung at the Lecture of the Congregational Charitable Society, in Boston, on the 12th of February, 1795.

A Fragment (Vision of the figure of Charity Embodied)

I could never look upon the figure of Charity without emotion. It is an object which melts the heart to tenderness, and quickens the feelings to that exquisite sensibility, that is neither pleasure or pain.

There she sits—one infant clings to her breast—another laughs at her knee—a third wantons by her side.

Complacency smiles upon her smooth cheek.

Tranquility beams upon her right eye—

She appears animated, but not from the self-gratification of passions. The comforts and ease she communicates to others, satisfies her wishes.

From mental happiness, not from sensual pleasures, she experiences delight. Her raptures are those of the soul!

Just so did the wife of a late Sea-Captain appear the day after the storm, wherein her husband, and two daughters perished.

Alas! How changed!

Grief and despair have distracted her senses—

The storm whistles in her brain—

She hears the raging of the sea, and no warmth can thaw the cold that chills her heart—

The hurricane that destroyed the object of her love hath ceased—

The clouds that overwhelmed them with snow are dissipated—

The frost that numbed their limbs hath thawed—

The waves that swallowed them up have subsided—

The sun, which retired from the scene of horror, hath returned to comfort the world, and shines forth again.

All is calm—

But what power shall calm the trouble of this widow's breast?

From whence shall a ray of comfort beam upon her afflictions?

The merciful interposition of Heaven alone can lessen the bitterness of her grief.

Vermont Journal, Windsor, Vt., 1787-04-16, vol. 4, 194:3.

Generosity

If considered in a large and extensive sense, or as a first principle, of all the qualities that raise and ennoble a character, Generosity is the most striking and lovely. It pervades the whole soul, and gives a lustre to every action, wherever it actuates a mind by nature formed with sensibility; it elevates the man of liberal education and polished manners to a degree little below the angelic race.

'Tis the offspring of heaven—the elder brother of Charity—Sympathy is its sister, and Love its darling companion.

Compassion and Benevolence are in its train, and Sincerity its constant attendant. Happy, happy would it be for the world, was it oftener to be met with!

How many evils and calamities would it remove or alleviate—how many animosities and contentions would it stifle in the birth!

True generosity discards all the long catalogue of vices that disgrace human nature, and spread a dark shade over the intellectual and moral world; envy and malice fly before it.

A stranger to cruelty, hypocrisy, and dissimulation, it dwells only in the bosom of those where no vice can be found.

It relieves the oppressed, it protects the weak; yet it triumphs not. 'Tis ever bold in a good cause, and shrinks not from danger when fortitude is required. It comforts and animates the depressed, gives the tear of pity to the dejected, and commiserates the unfortunate, whom passion or imprudence have led into the paths of vice and misery; it makes every allowance for the failings of mankind, and treats not even the abandoned with severity.

It delights in the prosperity of all around, and partakes of their joy; oftentimes it is confounded with liberality—but liberality is only a beautiful feature in its countenance; it rises still higher, and implies everything amiable in the soul; it counteracts the common principle of self-love, and induces the possessor of it to sacrifice his own inclination to another's benefit.—*The gay libertine* will frequently boast of this virtue, and value himself upon the goodness of his heart; but he deserves not the character, for he cannot in any situation, indulge in his favorite pleasures, without acting an ungenerous part.—The covetous and spendthrift have no claim to it. The revengeful and haughty know not its pleasures. *Generosity!* 'Tis a godlike principle, 'tis magnanimity guided by discretion, tempered by meekness; 'tis true dignity allied to humility; 'tis universal philanthropy—the inmate of good souls, the distinguishing badge of *great soul.*

Middlesex Gazette, Middletown, Conn., 1787-01-22, vol. 11, 64:2.

PHILLIS WHEATLEY (1753–1784)

[Phillis Wheatley, born in Africa, was sold into slavery at age seven. Taken to America, she worked as the slave of a Boston merchant. She spoke English well and wrote poetry by age sixteen, publishing Poems on Various Subjects in 1773 to wide acclaim. The following excerpt is from a poem about love as the cause of all works of mercy. The poem personifies Love to dramatize how the greatness of human affection is a divine power. Because this divine power includes all kinds of love, it encompasses human kindness and charity. Wheatley asks: What image shows the Eternal most? And answers: wonder-inspiring infinite Love, with wise providence and praiseworthy mercy, for which humanity often fails to be sufficiently thankful. Writing during the Enlightenment period, she argues that reason is undeniably great, but it is not all.]

Thoughts on the Works of Providence

"Let there be light," he said: from his profound
Old *Chaos* heard, and trembled at the sound:
Swift as the word, inspir'd by pow'r divine,

Behold the light around its Maker shine,
The first fair product of th' omnific God,
And now through all his works diffus'd abroad.

As reason's pow'rs by day our God disclose,
So we may trace him in the night's repose:

Say what is sleep? and dreams how passing strange!
When action ceases, and ideas range
Licentious and unbounded o'er the plains,
Where *Fancy's* queen in giddy triumph reigns.
Hear in soft strains the dreaming lover sigh

To a kind fair, or rave in jealousy;
On pleasure now, and now on vengeance bent,
The lab'ring passions struggle for a vent.
What pow'r, O man! thy *reason* then restores,
So long suspended in nocturnal hours?
What secret hand returns the mental train,
And gives improv'd thine active pow'rs again?
From thee, O man, what gratitude should rise!
And, when from balmy sleep thou op'st thine eyes,
Let thy first thoughts be praises to the skies.

Figure 2.2 Traditional depiction of
Phyllis Wheatley

How merciful our God who thus imparts
O'erflowing tides of joy to human hearts,
When wants and woes might be our righteous lot,
Our God forgetting, by our God forgot!

Among the mental pow'rs a question rose,
"What most the image of th' Eternal shows?"
When thus to *Reason* (so let *Fancy* rove)
Her great companion spoke immortal *Love*.

"Say, mighty pow'r, how long shall strife prevail,
And with its murmurs load the whisp'ring gale?

Refer the cause to *Recollection's* shrine,
Who loud proclaims my origin divine,
The cause whence heav'n and earth began to be,
And is not man immortaliz'd by me?
Reason let this most causeless strife subside."
Thus *Love* pronounc'd, and *Reason* thus reply'd.

"Thy birth, coelestial queen! 'tis mine to own,
In thee resplendent is the Godhead shown;
Thy words persuade, my soul enraptur'd feels
Resistless beauty which thy smile reveals."

Ardent she spoke, and, kindling at her charms,
She clasp'd the blooming goddess in her arms.

Infinite *Love* where'er we turn our eyes
Appears: this ev'ry creature's wants supplies;

This most is heard in *Nature's* constant voice,
This makes the morn, and this the eve rejoice;
This bids the fost'ring rains and dews descend
To nourish all, to serve one gen'ral end,
The good of man: yet man ungrateful pays
But little homage, and but little praise.

To him, whose works array'd with mercy shine,
What songs should rise, how constant, how divine!

Phillis Wheatley, *Poems on Various Subjects, Religious and Moral.* Philadelphia: J. Crukshank, 1786, verses 76–130.

THOMAS PAINE (1737–1809)

[Thomas Paine was one of a cadre of revolutionary thinkers who foresaw the possibility of more freedom and equality for the common man. Influenced by Jean Jacques Rousseau and living in a time of exasperation with tyranny and oppression of the poor, Paine envisioned new possibilities of liberty. The Goddess of Liberty image was on the rise in men's minds in the 1700s. Paintings, poems, and rhetorical prose personified the exciting ideal of freedom in emblems of Liberty. There were Liberty Poles set up in villages, and Liberty Trees designated as meeting places in the colonies. Paine inspired with his writings about liberty, persuading colonists with pamphlets such as "Common Sense" that they could identify themselves as Americans, not British dependents of the king. Thomas Paine helped Liberty become the soul image of America, unifying the people and giving them courage to take the next step. Liberty and Philanthropy were seen almost as sisters in the eighteenth century—both are muses for those who seek justice; both are ideals; both are about striving for a better life. Love of humanity and insistence upon self-determination (rather than enduring oppression) go hand in hand. When artistically depicted, both had a hopeful inspiring glow.]

Liberty Tree

IN a chariot of light, from the regions of day,
The Goddess of Liberty came,
Ten thousand celestials directed her way,
And hither conducted the dame.
A fair budding branch from the gardens above,
Where millions with millions agree,
She brought in her hand as a pledge of her love
And the plant she named Liberty Tree.

The celestial exotic stuck deep in the ground,
Like a native it flourished and bore;
The fame of its fruit drew the nations around,
To seek out this peaceable shore.

Unmindful of names or distinctions they came,
For freemen like brothers agree;
      With one spirit endued, they one friendship pursued,
      And their temple was Liberty Tree.

Beneath this fair tree, like the patriarchs of old,
Their bread in contentment they ate,
Unvexed with the troubles of silver or gold,
The cares of the grand and the great.
With timber and tar they Old England supplied,
And supported her power on the sea:
Her battles they fought, without getting a groat,
For the honor of Liberty Tree.

But hear, O ye swains ('tis a tale most profane),
How all the tyrannical powers,
Kings, Commons, and Lords, are uniting amain
To cut down this guardian of ours.
From the East to the West blow the trumpet to arms,
Thro' the land let the sound of it flee:
Let the far and the near all unite with a cheer,
In defense of our Liberty Tree.

Figure 2.3 Liberty Goddess with flag

First published in the *Pennsylvania Magazine* (1775), http://www.19.5degs.com/ebook/liberty-tree/872.

ANONYMOUS (1790)

[This poem dramatizes the thanks of the widows of Marblehead, Massachusetts, for the charity that helped sustain them in their time of need. Presumably the women were the widows of fishermen whose lives were often threatened at sea by inclement weather. The joy experienced after doing something for others is mysterious; there is no single word in English to denote it. The glow of satisfaction, the warm feeling of a good conscience approving, a sense of fellowship that is fulfilled in deed—these are blissful feelings that dawn as subtle rewards for those who rescue others from penury and alleviate others' misery. The last four lines of the following poem are especially eloquent in suggesting this truth; they still speak to us over two centuries later.]

On the Prize of fifteen hundred dollars being drawn by the poor widows of Marblehead, written there

Whence this increase of wealth? What bounteous hand
Grants more than sanguine Hope could e'en demand?
Nor *Chance*, nor *Fortune* shall the merit claim,
Those fancied forms to *Folly* owe their name:
Such airy phantoms ill deserve our lays;

A nobler object calls forth all our praise.
That Pow'r Supreme, who knows no great or small,
But looks unchang'd with equal eye on all—
Who lifts the poor from their unnoted state,
And humbles at his will th' aspiring great—
Whose hand divine hath held us in its span,
And fed, and cloth'd us since our lives began—
Hath, sure, this last rich gift in kindness sent,
To be improv'd, and not it riot spent;
A further proof of Heav'n's indulgent care,
In which our poorer neighbours ought to share.
Accept, Great God, what thankful hearts can give,
For life and health, and all the means to live!
Much thou hast added to our former store;
O keep us still as humble as before!
What thou hast lent, direct us how to use,
And teach us when to give, and when refuse.
To others freely let our bounty flow,
But not beyond Discretion's limits go.
Then let us live as useful as we can—
Grateful to God—beneficent to man—
Possess obscure the bliss of doing good,
Never so well explain'd as understood.

Massachusetts Sentinel, April 24, 1790, http://earlyamerica.com/earlyamerica/past/index.html.

SERMONS AND PHILANTHROPIC WRITINGS

COTTON MATHER (1663–1728)

[Cotton Mather, a Puritan minister, was a member of a prominent early New England family. This piece was first published in Boston in 1710. It influenced, among others, Benjamin Franklin, a man who grew beyond Puritanism to a belief in the religious value of charitable deeds rather than in the outward show and talk of one's religion. In this work, Mather urges care for the poor and deprived, encouraging compassionate commiseration, showing good neighborliness by sharing food, giving work, and enabling education. Mather teaches lessons about giving selflessly without desire for reward. Note that he teaches doing good not only as a Bible teaching, but also as a Quranic injunction. He imagines good deeds' effects extending beyond our limited awareness, using the image of concentric circles expanding on the surface of a pond: "A stone falling into a pool—one circle and service will produce another till they extend—who can tell how far?" In Mather's view, charity begins at home, with each man starting his own work of good acts by correcting the faults of his own soul. A person can then be charitable to others—carefully giving alms, helping the poor find work, assisting neighbors in times of need, performing good deeds as a form of praise. In this view, religious life is basically constructive, improving the well-being of

others in this life, as well as in the hereafter. St. Gregory of Nazianzen, referred to below, was a fourth-century Doctor of the Church.]

Bonifacius, an Essay upon the Good

. . . None but a Good Man, is really a Living Man; And the more Good any Man does, the more he really Lives. All the rest is Death; or belongs to it. Yea, you must Excuse me, if I say, The Mahometan also shall condemn the Man, who comes not into the Principles of this Book. For I think, it occurs no less than Three Times in the Alcoran [Qur'an]: God Loves those that are inclined to do Good . . .

Methinks, this excellent zeal should be carried into our Neighborhood. Neighbors! you stand related unto one another. And you should be full of devices that all the neighbors may have cause to be glad of your being in the neighborhood. We read: "The righteous is more excellent than his neighbor." But we shall scarce own him so, except he be more excellent *as* a neighbor. He must excel in the duties of good neighborhood. Let that man be better than his neighbor who labors to be a better neighbor, to do most good unto his neighbor.

And here first: the poor people that lie wounded must have wine and oil poured into their wounds. It was a charming stroke in the character which a modern prince had given to him: "To be in distress is to deserve his favor." O good neighbor, put on that princely, that more than royal quality! See who in the neighborhood may deserve thy favor. We are told: "This is pure religion and undefiled" (a jewel that neither is counterfeit nor has any flaws in it), "to visit the fatherless and widows in their affliction." The orphans and widows, and so all the children of affliction in the neighborhood, must be visited and relieved with all agreeable kindness.

Neighbors—be concerned that the orphans and widows in your neighborhood may be well provided for. They meet with grievous difficulties, with unknown temptations. While their next relatives were yet living, they were, perhaps, but meanly provided for. What must they now be in their more solitary condition? Their condition should be considered, and the result of the consideration should be: "I delivered the orphan that had no helper, and I caused the heart of the widow to sing for joy."

By consequence, all the afflicted in the neighborhood are to be thought upon. Sirs, would it be too much for you at least once in a week to think: "What neighbor is reduced into pinching and painful poverty? Or in any degree impoverished with heavy losses?" Think: "What neighbor is heartbroken with sad bereavements, bereaved of desirable relatives?" And think: "What neighbor has a soul buffeted and hurried with violent assaults of the wicked one?" But then think: "What shall be done for such neighbors?"

First: you will pity them. The evangelical precept is: "Have compassion one of another—be pitiful." It was of old, and ever will be, the just expectation: "To him that is afflicted, pity should be shown." And let our pity to them flame out in our prayer for them. It were a very lovely practice for you, in the daily prayer of your closet every evening, to think: "What miserable object have I seen today that I may do well now to mention for the mercies of the Lord?"

But this is not all. 'Tis possible, 'tis probable, you may do well to visit them: and when you visit them, comfort them. Carry them some good word which may raise a gladness in an heart stooping with heaviness.

And lastly: give them all the assistances that may answer their occasions. Assist them with advice to them, assist them with address to others for them. And if it be needful, bestow your alms upon them: "Deal thy bread to the hungry; bring to thy house the poor that are cast out; when thou seest the naked, cover him." At least Nazianzen's charity, I pray: *Si nihil habes, da lacrymulam*—"if you have nothing else to bestow upon the miserable, bestow a tear or two upon their miseries." This little is better than nothing . . .

In moving for the devices of good neighborhood, a principal motion which I have to make is that you consult the spiritual interests of your neighborhood as well as the temporal. Be concerned lest the deceitfulness of sin undo any of the neighbors. If there be any idle persons among them, I beseech you, cure them of their idleness. Don't nourish 'em and harden 'em in that, but find employment for them. Find 'em work; set 'em to work; keep 'em to work. Then, as much of your other bounty to them as you please.

If any children in the neighborhood are under no education don't allow 'em to continue so. Let care be taken that they may be better educated, and be taught to read, and be taught their catechism and the truths and way of their only savior.

One more: if any in the neighborhood are taking to bad courses—lovingly and faithfully admonish them. If any in the neighborhood are enemies to their own welfare or families—prudently dispense your admonitions unto them. If there are any prayerless families, never leave off entreating and exhorting them till you have persuaded them to set up the worship of God. If there be any service of God or of His people to which anyone may need to be excited, give him a tender excitation. Whatever snare you see anyone in, be so kind as to tell him of his danger to be ensnared, and save him from

Figure 2.4 Painting of Cotton Mather

it. By putting of good books into the hands of your neighbors, and gaining of them a promise to read the books—who can tell what good you may do unto them! It is possible you may in this way, with ingenuity and with efficacy, administer those reproofs which you may owe unto such neighbors as are to be reproved for their miscarriages. The books will balk nothing that is to be said on the subjects that you would have the neighbors advised upon.

Finally: if there be any base houses, which threaten debauch and poison and confound the neighborhood, let your charity to your neighbors make you do all you can for the suppression of them.

That my proposal to do good in the neighborhood and as a neighbor may be more fully formed and followed, I will conclude it with minding you that a world of self denial is to be exercised in the execution of it. You must be armed against selfishness, all selfish and squinting intentions in your generous resolutions. You shall see how my demands will grow upon you.

First: you must not think of making the good you do a pouring of water into a pump to draw out something for yourselves. This might be the meaning of our savior's direction: "Lend, hoping for nothing again." To lend a thing, properly is to hope that we shall receive it again. . . . If any man by burnings or shipwrecks or other disasters had lost his estate, his friends did use to lend him considerable sums of money, to be repaid not at a certain day but when he should find himself able to repay it without inconvenience. Now, they were so cunning that they would rarely lend upon such disasters unto any but such as they had hope would recover out of their present impoverishment, and not only repay them their money but also requite their kindness, if ever there should be need of it. The thing required by our savior is: "Do good unto such as you are never like to be the better for."

But then, there is yet an higher thing to be demanded. That is: "Do good unto those neighbors who have done hurt unto you." So says our savior: "Love your enemies; bless them that curse you; do good to them that hate you, and pray for them which despitefully use you and persecute you." Yea, if an injury have been done you, improve it as a provocation to do a benefit unto him who did the injury. This is noble! It will bring marvelous consolations! Another method might make you even with your forward neighbors: this will set you above them all. It were nobly done if, in the close of the day when you are alone before the Lord, you make a particular prayer for the pardon and prosperity of any person from whom you may have suffered any abuse in the day. And it would be nobly done if, at last calling over the catalogue of such as have been abusive to you, you may be able to say (the only intention that can justify your doing anything like to keeping a catalogue of them!): "There is not one of these but I have done him, or watched to do him, a kindness." Among the Jews themselves there were the Hasideans, one of whose institutions it was to make this daily prayer unto God: *Remitte et condona omnibus qui vexant nos* ("Forgive all who trouble and harass us"). Christians—go beyond them! Yea, Justin Martyr tell us, in primitive times they did so: "Praying for their enemies."

But I won't stop here. There is yet an higher thing to be demanded. That is: do good unto those neighbors who will speak ill of you after you have done it. So says our savior: "Ye shall be the children of the highest: he is kind unto the unthankful and unto the evil." You will every day find, I can tell you, monsters of ingratitude. Yea; if you distinguish any person with doing for him something more than you have done for others, it will be well if that very person do not at some time or other hurt you wonderfully. Oh! the wisdom of divine providence in ordering this thing! Sirs, it is that you may do good on a divine principle: good merely for the sake of good! "Lord, increase our faith!"

And God forbid that a Christian faith should not come up to a Jewish! There is a memorable passage in the Jewish records. There was a gentleman of whose bounty many people every day received reliefs and succors. One day he asked: "Well, what do our people say today?" They told him: "Why, the people partook of your kindnesses and services, and then they blessed you very fervently." "Did they so?" said he, "Then I shall have no great reward for this day." Another day he asked: "Well, and what say our people now?" They told him: "Alas, good sir, the people enjoyed your kindnesses today, and when all was done, they did nothing but rail at you." "Indeed!" said he, "Now for this day I am sure that God will give me a good and great reward."

Though vile constructions and harsh invectives be never so much the present reward of doing the best offices for the neighborhood, yet, my dear Boniface, be victorious over all discouragements. "Thy work shall be well rewarded," saith the Lord.

If your opportunities to do good reach no further, yet I will offer you a consolation, which one has elegantly thus expressed: "He that praises God only on a ten-stringed instrument, with his authority extending but unto his family and his example but unto his neighborhood, may have as thankful an heart here, and as high a place in the celestial choir hereafter, as the greatest monarch that praiseth God upon a ten-thousand-stringed instrument, upon the loud sounding organ having as many millions of pipes as there be people under him." . . . A stone falling into a pool—one circle and service will produce another till they extend—who can tell how far?

Cotton Mather, *Bonifacius*. Boston, 1710. Entire essay available online at ksghome.harvard. edu/~phall/08.%20Mather.pdf. [For an essay on Ben Franklin and Cotton Mather as two aspects of American thought see John H. Lienhard, "Benjamin Franklin and Cotton Mather" at http://www. uh.edu/engines/epi1611.htm.]

JUPITER HAMMON (1711–1806)

[Jupiter Hammon, a poet and a slave, was the first black writer to be published in America. His masters, the Lloyd family of Long Island, were Christians who encouraged Hammon to use his talents and become educated. He studied on his master's estate with Nehemiah Bull, a Harvard graduate and, later, a noted clergyman in New England. Hammon was a religious thinker of great faith, and his works are a kind of Christian preaching in poetry and prose. Though Hammon did not seek freedom for himself, he decried the injustice of slavery and called for it to be phased out of American life. He advocated that slaves concentrate on living Christian lives and winning an eternal reward that would not depend on skin color or social status: "If we should ever get to Heaven, we shall find nobody to reproach us for being black or being slaves." His religion gave him consolation and reason to hope for a better future. Hammon's writings suggest he had a generous spirit toward both God and humanity.]

An Address to the Negroes of the State of New York

Now I acknowledge that liberty is a great thing, and worth seeking for, if we can get it honestly, and by our good conduct, prevail on our masters to set us free: Though for my own part I do not wish to be free, yet I should be glad, if others, especially the young negroes were to be free, for many of us, who are grown up slaves, and have always had masters to take care of us, should hardly know how to take care of ourselves; and it may be more for our own comfort to remain as we are. That liberty is a great thing we may know from our own feelings, and we may likewise judge so from the conduct of the white-people, in the late war. How much money has been spent, and how many lives has been lost, to defend their liberty. I must say that I have hoped that God would open their eyes, when they were so much engaged for liberty, to think of the state of the poor blacks, and to pity us. He has done it in some measure, and has raised us up many friends, for which we have reason to be thankful, and to hope in his mercy. What may be done further, he only knows, for *known unto God are all his ways from the beginning* . . . Now my brethren it seems to me, that there are no people that ought to attend to the hope of happiness in another world so much as we do. Most of us are cut off from comfort and happiness here in this world, and can expect nothing from it. Now seeing this is the case, why should we not take care to be happy after death. Why should we spend our whole lives in sinning against God: And be miserable in this world, and in the world to come. If we do thus, we shall certainly be the greatest fools. We shall be slaves here, and slaves forever. We cannot plead so great temptations to neglect religion as others. Riches and honours which drown the greater part of mankind, who have the gospel, in perdition, can be little or no temptations to us.

We live so little time in this world that it is no matter how wretched and miserable we are, if it prepares us for heaven. What is forty, fifty, or sixty years, when compared to eternity. When thousands and millions of years have rolled away, this eternity will be no nigher coming to an end. Oh how glorious is an eternal life of happiness! And how dreadful, an eternity of misery. Those of us who have had religious masters, and have been taught to read the Bible, and have been brought by their example and teaching to a sense of divine things, how happy shall we be to meet them in heaven, where we shall join them in praising God forever. But if any of us have had such masters, and yet have lived and died wicked, how will it add to our misery to think of our folly. If any of us, who have wicked and profane masters should become religious, how will our estates be changed in another world.

Jupiter Hammon, "An Address to the Negroes of the State of New-York" (n.p., 1787), 13, 18–20, http://etext.lib.virginia.edu/readex/20400.html.

JAMES OGLETHORPE (1696–1785)

[Georgia was the last of the original thirteen English colonies established on the North American mainland. British imperial officials needed a buffer colony between the colony of South Carolina and Spanish Florida to the south. This was one motive for Georgia's establishment. The British Crown invested heavily in founding the colony, viewing it as a strategic move, but the founders of Georgia, led by James Oglethorpe, conceived of it more as a refuge for English debtors and criminals. They hoped to establish the colony with utopian philosophy and no slavery, no vast plots of land controlled by a single owner, and without rum. It was planned as a place where new beginnings could flourish without the social ills of poverty and excessive privilege. In the first decades of the eighteenth century, half of England lived in abject poverty, giving rise to pirates and other kinds of rebels and desperadoes. Oglethorpe had faith in the New World's potential to provide a new life for those seeking the opportunity. In Oglethorpe's writing, note his references to the conscious precedent of Roman colonies and the precedent of the colony William Penn founded.]

Founding Vision for Georgia as a Humanitarian Refuge (1733)
Some Account of the Designs of the Trustees for Establishing
the Colony of Georgia in America.

In *America* there are fertile lands sufficient to subsist all the useless Poor in *England,* and distressed Protestants in Europe; yet Thousands starve for want of mere sustenance. The distance makes it difficult to get thither. The same want that renders men useless here, prevents their paying their passage; and if others pay it for 'em, they become servants, or rather slaves for years to those who have defrayed the expense. Therefore, money for passage is necessary, but is not the only want; for if people were set down in America, and the land before them, they must cut down trees, build houses, fortify towns, dig and sow the land before they can get in a harvest; and till then, they must be provided with food, and kept together, that they may be assistant to each other for their natural support and protection.

The Romans esteemed the sending forth of Colonies, among their noblest works; they observed that Rome, as she increased in power and empire, drew together such a conflux of people from all parts that she found herself over-burdened with their number, and the government brought under an incapacity to provide for them, or keep them in order. Necessity, the mother of invention, suggested to them an expedient, which at once gave ease to the capital, and increased the wealth and number of industrious citizens, by lessening the useless and unruly multitude; and by planting them in colonies on the frontiers of their empire, gave a new Strength to the whole; and *This* they looked upon to be so considerable a service to the commonwealth, that they created peculiar officers for the establishment of such colonies, and the expense was defrayed out of the public treasury.

FROM THE CHARTER.—His Majesty having taken into his consideration, the miserable circumstances of many of his own poor subjects, ready to perish for want: as likewise the distresses of many poor foreigners, who would take refuge here from persecution; and having a Princely regard to the great danger the southern frontiers of South Carolina are exposed to, by reason of the small number of white inhabitants there, hath, out of his Fatherly compassion towards his subjects, been graciously pleased to grant a charter for incorporating a number of gentlemen by the name of *The Trustees for establishing the Colony of Georgia in America.* They are empowered to collect benefactions; and lay them out in clothing, arming, sending over, and supporting colonies of the poor, whether subjects on foreigners, in Georgia. And his Majesty farther grants all his lands between *Savannah and Alatamaha,* which he erects into a Province by the name of GEORGIA, unto the Trustees, in trust for the poor, and for the better support of the Colony. At the desire of the Gentlemen, there are clauses in the Charter, restraining them and their successors from receiving any salary, fee, perquisite, or profit, whatsoever, by or from this undertaking; and also from receiving any grant of lands within the said district, to themselves, or in trust for them. There are farther clauses granting to the Trustees proper powers for establishing and governing the Colony, and liberty of conscience to all who shall settle there.

The Trustees intend to relieve such unfortunate persons as cannot subsist here, and establish them in an orderly manner, so as to form a well regulated town. As far as their fund goes, they will defray the charge of their passage to Georgia; give them necessaries, cattle, land, and subsistence, till such time as they can build their houses and clear some of their land. They rely for success, first on the goodness of Providence, next on the compassionate disposition of the people of England; and, they doubt not, that much will be spared from luxury, and superfluous expenses, by generous tempers, when such an opportunity is offered them by the giving of £20 to provide for a man or woman, or £10 to a child for ever.

*   *   *

For the continuing of the relief which is now given, there will be lands reserved in the Colony; and the benefit arising from them is to go to the carrying on of the trust. So that, at the same time, the money by being laid out preserves the lives of the poor, and makes a comfortable provision for those whose expenses are by it defrayed; their labor in improving their own lands, will make the adjoining reserved lands valuable; and the rents of those reserved lands will be a perpetual fund for the relieving more poor people. So that instead of laying out the money upon lands, with the income thereof to support the poor, this is laying out money upon the poor; and by relieving those who are now unfortunate, raises a fund for the perpetual relief of those who shall be so hereafter.

There is an occasion now offered for every one, to help forward this design; the smallest benefaction will be received, and applied with the utmost care:—every little will do something; and a great number of small benefactions will amount to a sum capable of doing a great deal of good.

If any person, moved with the calamities of the unfortunate, shall be inclined to contribute towards their relief, they are desired to pay their benefactions into the Bank of England, on account of the Trustees for establishing the Colony of Georgia in America; or else, to any of the Trustees, who are, &c.

Peter Force, *Tracts* , vol. 1, no. 2. Washington, D.C., 1836, 4–7. http://personal.pitnet.net/ primarysources/oglethorpe.html.

JAMES OGLETHORPE'S LIFE (1696–1785)

[The life of James Oglethorpe shows how a philanthropic thrust was integral to the founding of some communities in early America. His story reveals an aspect of America's origins that often has been forgotten. To better understand how America originated in hopes for a better life, it is useful to recall that England had many social problems in the eighteenth century, and a rigid class hierarchy made it difficult for the unfortunate to determine their own destinies. Oglethorpe's dreams of a society where those shackled by debt could find freedom and prosperity were more possible to fulfill in the New World, where a strong sense of beginning anew was alive at that time.]

"... for Others": The Founding of Georgia

James Edward Oglethorpe lived a colorful and adventurous life in times of great historic change. He was born in 1696 into a wealthy English family with status and power. His father and brothers were members of Parliament. At ten he served as a footguard for the queen, for whom his mother was a lady-in-waiting. At fifteen he went to train at Lampres Military Academy near Paris. In 1714 his mother sent him to Oxford University, where he excelled at archery and languages. In 1716 Oglethorpe took part in the war between Turkey and Austria, becoming a lieutenant colonel at twenty-one.

When two of his brothers died and he returned from war, he inherited the family estate called Westbrook and became a responsible landowner. He contributed to local projects such as funding the upkeep of communal fire engines, buying new water buckets. He enjoyed the gardens on the estate, and the vineyard there thrived, becoming the largest in all of England. Honor duels and sword fights were part of maintaining a nobleman's lifestyle in those days and gave a precarious quality to life. Oglethorpe was once imprisoned for six months because he killed a man in a brawl. He became a member of Parliament at twenty-six and was appointed to many committees. Politically concerned with problems of poverty, he gave generously to improve lives. He defended colonists' rights and was opposed to slavery. In 1728 he became the driving power in the Parliamentary Prison Discipline Committee.

He was also concerned about issues such as housing for the poor, putting forth legislation allowing the poor to rent cottages slated for destruction. One of his friends, writer Robert Castell, was thrown into a debtors' prison, where he contracted smallpox and died. Distraught at this turn of events, Oglethorpe formed a committee to look into harsh prison practices such as the chaining of prisoners in rooms with poor ventilation. (In 1869 Parliament finally ended the practice of sending indebted people to prisons where they were unable to earn money to pay their debts.)

Responding to the plight of unemployed poor people on the streets of London, various seventeenth- and eighteenth-century thinkers thought the answer was America. John Smith's 1606 Virginia colony was intended to give people a fresh start. John Hammond, who realistically noted in his writings such as *Leah and Rachel* that Virginia and Maryland had their share of rogues, troublemakers, and criminal settlers, also said they were models of industry and opportunity, offering a far better life. British men of privilege wrote and shouted, "England Forever!" but disadvantaged risk-takers of the seventeeth and eighteenth centuries considered their situation and said, "America instead is better!" George Alsop, for example, wrote enthusiastically of the colonies as offering a better life, hope for the poor and distressed. Oglethorpe agreed and thought he could help start a colony in the New World for the poor and disadvantaged.

Figure 2.5 Portrait of James Oglethorpe

In 1730 Oglethorpe with others formed the Georgia Society with a charter to found a colony in the New World. There was a region south of South Carolina and north of Spanish Florida that had good soil and a mild climate, excellent for growing rice and tobacco. It would also serve as a buffer between the other colonies and the Spanish. The colonists would be debtors seeking a second chance instead of living on London's bleak streets or languishing in the debtors' prison. It took time for the idea to gain support, but in 1732 George II gave land to Oglethorpe's Georgia Society, and they, as the twenty-one trustees of the Georgia colony, began to organize in earnest. They agreed to take no salary or seek other personal gain from the venture. The seal they agreed upon displayed the motto "Not for Themselves but for Others." Oglethorpe and the other trustees gave money and goods, tools for farming, seeds and plants, clothes, and other necessities of a new life.

In November 1732 the ship *Ann* set sail from England with Oglethorpe and the first Georgia colonists. The grant included all the land between the Altamaha and Savannah rivers and from the headwaters of these rivers to the "south seas." The ship arrived at what is now Charleston, South Carolina, on January 13, 1733. While the new colonists recouped their energy, Oglethorpe explored the terrain of Georgia and met with the son of a former governor of South Carolina, Musgrove, who helped Oglethorpe negotiate a land agreement with the Creek Indians with whom he traded.

Leaders of the South Carolina government helped the new colony, the thirteenth in the New World, get started by donating livestock, rice, and money, and they were not the only good neighbors—the native Americans there, the Yamacraw tribe, helped the Georgia colonists survive during the first difficult years. Peaches and cotton grew especially well there and in time became major export crops. Although Oglethorpe prohibited slavery and rum in the colony, the colonists thought slaves would make the colony more prosperous and life easier.

Oglethorpe, as city planner for Savannah, designed the city with a number of squares or small parks surrounded by buildings. Gradually, the colony grew. In 1733 a ship with forty-two Jewish travelers arrived in Savannah, seeking to join the new colony. Among these new arrivals was a physician, who treated the colonists suffering from various illnesses. Soon Irish, German Lutherans from Austria, Swedes, Dutch, and Scottish immigrants joined the colony.

Oglethorpe established the first Masonic lodge in the colony of Georgia, which is now said to be "the oldest continuously operating English constituted lodge of Freemasons in the Western Hemisphere." The charitable work of Freemasons is well known, and Oglethorpe's philanthropic work included advocating for the welfare of children, the rights of sailors, the poor of England, the plight of prisoners, and the relief of debtors.

During a trip to England in 1734 and 1735, Oglethorpe obtained official regulations prohibiting rum and slavery in Georgia, even though this went against the stated wishes of some of the colonists. Oglethorpe, accompanied by religious leaders John Wesley and Charles Wesley, returned to Georgia.

In 1739 England declared war against Spain, drawing Oglethorpe into the conflict. He led one unsuccessful advance against St. Augustine, Florida, in 1740 but then went on to successfully defeat the Spanish in the battle of Bloody Marsh near Fort Frederica on St. Simons Island in 1742, establishing Georgia's regional survival. After a second failed attack upon the Spanish at St. Augustine in 1743, and due to complaints by the colonists about his rules and rigid leadership style, Oglethorpe was recalled to England. Ultimately, all the charges against him were dropped, but he never returned to Georgia. In 1750 he stopped resisting the demands of the Georgia colonists to allow slavery in their society.

Wording by William J. Jackson, based on information in several books including Cookie Lommel, *James Oglethorpe, Humanitarian and Soldier*. Philadelphia: Chelsea House, 2001, 7–40; Phinizy Spalding, *Oglethorpe in America* (Athens: University of Georgia Press, 1984); and Phinizy Spalding and Harvey H. Jackson, eds., *Oglethorpe in Perspective*. Tuscaloosa: University of Alabama Press, 2006.

JOHN WESLEY (1703–1791)

[Wesley was an Anglican clergyman, theologian, and early leader in the Methodist movement. Saved from a fire in his father's rectory at the age of five, Wesley was left with a deep conviction that Providence had marked him for great things. He lived in England until 1735, and then went to Savannah, Georgia, hoping to help colonists live spiritual lives and to convert the Indians. Discouraged by his lack of success, he returned to England in 1738, where a mystical experience during a Moravian meeting in Aldersgate transformed his spiritual outlook. Influenced by a number of spiritual lessons and trends, Wesley preached and practiced outreach, believing that his purpose in life was to spark a revival in the Anglican Church. His ministry sought out and welcomed the disreputable poor, those considered beyond the pale of respectable society and ordinary churches. The redemption of the straying, abandoned ones proved the power of the gospel. Organizing disciples into small groups, Wesley appointed leaders to teach them the Methodist faith and the way to live righteous lives. The groups joined together into larger congregations, so members belonged to a community something like an extended family. One modern scholar, Christopher P. Momany, has suggested that Wesley's General Rules offers a useful paradigm for

postmodern ethics. Wesley was a thrifty and giving person, and charity was a key point in his life and teachings. In his understanding, supporting services for the needy, such as orphanages and hospitals, was a practical way of avoiding the temptations that often come with excessive wealth. He saw the trappings of wealth as too often in conflict with the ethos of Methodism, which he said was a path of the heart. Following Wesley's leadership, Methodists became increasingly active in social-justice issues such as prison reform and abolitionism. His ideal of making the best effort one is capable of to help others remains an inspiring high standard for those resolving to engage in charitable activities. Wesley's Rule urges believers to "Do all the good you can,/By all the means you can,/In all the ways you can,/In all the places you can,/At all the times you can,/To all the people you can,/As long as ever you can."]

Nature, Design, and General Rules of the United Societies

1. In the latter end of the year 1739, eight or ten persons came to me in London, who appeared to be deeply convinced of sin, and earnestly groaning for redemption. They desired (as did two or three more the next day) that I would spend some time with them in prayer, and advise them how to flee from the wrath to come; which they saw continually hanging over their heads. That we might have more time for this great work, I appointed a day when they might all come together, which from thenceforward they did every week, namely, on Thursday, in the evening.

To these, and as many more as desired to join with them, (for their number increased daily), I gave those advices, from time to time, which I judged most needful for them; and we always concluded our meeting with prayer suited to their several necessities. 2. This was the rise of the United Society, first in London, and then in other places. Such a society is no other than "a company of men having the form and seeking the power of godliness, united in order to pray together, to receive the word of exhortation, and to watch over one another in love, that they may help each other to work out their salvation." 3. That it may the more easily be discerned, whether they are indeed working out their own salvation, each society is divided into smaller companies, called classes, according to their respective places of abode.

There are about twelve persons in every class; one of whom is styled the Leader. It is his business, (1) To see each person in his class once a week at least, in order to inquire how their souls prosper; to advise, reprove, comfort, or exhort, as occasion may require; to receive what they are willing to give toward the relief of the poor. (2) To meet the Minister and the Stewards of the society once a week; in order to inform the Minister of any that are sick, or of any that walk disorderly, and will not be reproved; to pay to the Stewards what they have received of their several classes in the week preceding; and to show their account of what each person has contributed. 4. There is one only condition previously required in those who desire admission into these societies,—a desire "to flee from the wrath to come, to be saved from their sins:" But, wherever this is really fixed in the soul, it will be shown by its fruits. It is therefore expected of all who continue therein, that they should continue to evidence their desire of salvation, First, by doing no harm, by avoiding evil in every kind; especially that which is most generally practiced: Such is, the taking the name of God in vain; the profaning the day of the Lord, either by doing ordinary work thereon, or by buying or selling; drunkenness, buying or selling spirituous liquors, or drinking them, unless in cases of extreme necessity; fighting, quarreling, brawling; brother going to law with brother; returning evil for evil, or railing for railing; the using many words in buying or selling; the buying or selling unaccustomed goods; the giving or taking things on usury, that is, unlawful interest; uncharitable or unprofitable conversation, particularly speaking evil of Magistrates or of Ministers; doing to others as we would not they should do unto us; doing what we know is not for the glory of God, as the "putting on of gold or costly apparel;" the taking such diversions as cannot be used in the name of the Lord Jesus; the singing those songs, or reading those books, which do not tend to the knowledge or love of God; softness, and needless self-indulgence; laying up treasures upon earth; borrowing without a probability of paying; or taking up goods without a probability of paying for them. 5. It is expected of all who continue in these societies, that they should continue to evidence their desire of salvation, Secondly, by doing good, by being, in every kind, merciful after their power; as they have opportunity, doing good of every possible sort, and as far as is possible, to all men;—to their bodies, of the ability which God giveth, by giving food to the hungry, by clothing the naked, by visiting or helping them that are sick, or in prison;—to their souls, by instructing, reproving, or exhorting all they have any intercourse with; trampling under foot that enthusiastic doctrine of devils, that "we are not to do good unless our heart be free to it:" By doing good especially to them that are of the household

Figure 2.6 Portrait of John Wesley

of faith, or groaning so to be; employing them preferably to others, buying one of another; helping each other in business; and so much the more, because the world will love its own, and them only: By all possible diligence and frugality, that the gospel be not blamed: By running with patience the race that is set before them, "denying themselves, and taking up their cross daily;" submitting to bear the reproach of Christ, to be as the filth and off-scouring of the world; and looking that men should "say all manner of evil of them falsely for the Lord's sake." 6. It is expected of all who desire to continue in these societies, that they should continue to evidence their desire of salvation. Thirdly, by attending upon all the ordinances of God. Such are, the public worship of God; the ministry of the word, either read or expounded; the supper of the Lord; family and private prayer; searching the Scriptures; and fasting, or abstinence. 7. These are the General Rules of our societies; all which we are taught of God to observe, even in his written word, the only rule, and the sufficient rule, both of our faith and practice. And all these, we know, his Spirit writes on every truly awakened heart. If there be any among us who observe them not, who habitually break any of them, let it be made known unto them who watch over that soul as they that must give an account. We will admonish him of the error of his ways; we will bear with him for a season: But then if he repent not, he hath no more place among us. We have delivered our own souls.

John Wesley, Charles Wesley. May 1, 1743. http://www.godrules.net/library/wesley/274wesley_h7.htm. "General Rules" for the "United Societies," which were the nucleus of the Methodist Discipline, and continue to be the basis of the faith. 1743.

JONATHAN EDWARDS (1703–1758)

[Jonathan Edwards was a Congregational preacher and evangelical theologian. He studied at Yale and was ordained a minister in 1727. He led a series of revivals in the 1730s that culminated in the First Great Awakening, in which preachers used the levers of guilt and a sense of urgency toward salvation, as well as a need for moral living, to lift people to intense religious feelings. His sermon "Sinners in the Hands of an Angry God" inspired "fear of the Lord," which in the Bible is said to be the beginning of wisdom. In his notes for the following two sermons, we see his use of powerful Christian symbols. In the first, he explores how water flowing freely is an apt symbol for God's generosity, and how Christ's blood was as freely given as abundant water. The promise is that if the soul accepts freely given grace, one will find the grail of redemption. In the second, he explains how Christians can be charitable toward Christ by serving and helping others in his stead, and how those who are giving will be rewarded. Typically, his sermons were sketched out as texts of ideas and images on which to improvise as he spoke to congregations.]

Waters of Life: The Promise of a Gift More Plentiful Than a River[†]
Sermon on Psalms 1:3, *"He shall be like a tree planted by the Rivers of Water"*

As the waters of a river run easily and freely so the love of Christ. [He] freely came into the world, laid down his life and endured those dreadful sufferings. His blood was freely shed. Blood flowed as freely from his wounds as water runs down in a river. The chief and most excellent things that Christ bestows are the influences of his Spirit on their hearts to enlighten and sanctify and comfort. These all come freely from Christ like the waters of a River. Christ willingly gives his people that look to him and trust in him light and life in their souls. There is an abundance of water. Christ is like a river in the great plenty and abundance of his love and grace . . .

The tree that spreads out its roots by a river has water enough—no need of rain or any other water. So the true saint finds enough in Christ. Great plenty of water enough to supply a great multitude of persons with drink to satisfy all their thirst, to supply the roots of a multitude of trees. So [it is] for all the saints. [The] waters of a river don't fail, [it] flows constantly, day and night. Waters that run upon the [ground from the] showers of rain or melting of snows soon dry up. But [not so the water of a river.] Little brooks dry up in a very dry time. But the waters of a great river continue, running continually and from one age to another and are never dry. So Christ never [leaves] His saints that love Him and trust in Him [*sic*] . . .

He never leaves off to take care. The grace of Christ in the heart shall always continue. Christ never will take away his spirit from them. That inward life and comfort that Christ gives the hearts of his saints shall continue to all eternity. When the death comes, that comfort and Happiness shall continue. When the end of the world comes yet their comforts shall be like a river that shall not be dried up. The soul [of the saint] is joined to Christ and they are made one. As the water enters into the roots, so Christ and they are made one. As the water enters into the roots, so Christ enters the heart and soul of a godly man and dwells there. The spirit of Christ comes into the very heart of a saint as water to the roots of a tree . . .

Water gives life and keeps it alive, makes it grow, makes it grow beautiful, fruitful.

[†] Title is the author's own.

A tree planted [by a river] is green in time of great drought when other trees wither. So the soul of a true Saint in time of affliction. At death. At the end of the world. [The greenness never fails.]

Transcribed by Rachel Wheeler, Sermon on Psalm 1:3, August 1751, Jonathan Edwards Collection, General Collection. New Haven: Yale University, Beinecke Rare Book and Manuscript Library.

Much in Deeds of Charity [The Christian Promise]

When Christ was upon earth he was poor. He was an object of charity. And during the time of his public ministry he was supported by the [charity] of some of his followers, and particularly certain women, as we read, Luke 8:2-3, "And certain women, which had been healed of evil spirits and infirmities, Mary called Magdalene, out of whom went seven devils, And Joanna the wife of Chuza Herod's steward, and Susanna, and many others, which ministered unto him of their substance." And these women were rewarded by being peculiarly favored with gracious manifestations, which Christ made of himself to them. He discovered himself first to them after his resurrection, before any of the twelve disciples. They first saw a vision of glorious angels who spoke comfortably to them, and then Christ appeared to them and spake peace to them, saying, "All hail [. . . .] Be not afraid." And they were admitted to come and hold him by the feet and worship him (Matt 28:9[–10]).

So Mary and Martha and Lazarus were a family that were charitable to Christ, used joyfully to entertain him at their house and make the best provision for him that they could. And they were a family remarkably distinguished by Christ's presence and the manifestations of his love.

And though we can't now be charitable to Christ in person as they were, because he is not here, nor does he now stand in need, yet we may be charitable to Christ now as well as they then. For though Christ is not here, he has left others in his room to be his receivers, and they are the poor, and has told us that he shall look upon what is done to them as done to him; so that Christ is poor yet in his members, and we may relieve him and be in a way to receive the same benefit by it that those did that were charitable to him when he was on earth.

*　　*　　*

When such deeds are done from right principles, God will give spiritual discoveries as a free reward. Though the goodness and excellency of the reward be infinitely greater than the worth of what is given in charity, yet for Christ's sake it shall be accepted and shall receive such an exceeding great reward. For there is no man that gives a cup of [water in Christ's name who loses his reward] (Mark 9:41). For God rewards good persons—pressed down, {and shaken together, and running over} [Luke 6:38]. Yea, he rewards an hundredfold; yea, and much more than so. When we give to others earthly good things, God will reward us with heavenly good things. This Christ promises, Luke14:[13-]14, "when thou makest a feast, invite the poor, the maimed, the lame, the blind: and thou shalt be blessed; for they cannot recompense thee: but thou shalt be recompensed at the resurrection of the just." And God often gives persons foretastes of those future rewards while here. Treasure is this way laid up in heaven and, therefore, heavenly blessings shall flow down from heaven upon them while they are here.

Wilson H. Kimnach, Kenneth P. Minkema, and Douglas A. Sweeney, eds., *The Sermons of Jonathon Edwards: A Reader*. New Haven: Yale University Press, 1999, 201–3.

ANONYMOUS

[In the mid-eighteenth century, colonial American industry was not very advanced; the industrious use of natural resources was just beginning to unfold. At this time, charity was often seen as helping the poor find good work so they could sustain themselves. The idea "give a man a fish and he'll have a meal, but teach a man to fish and he'll feed himself every day" is suggested in saying that it is a praiseworthy form of charity to give a poor man employment. Self-sufficiency is the enduring answer, and the author here suggests a way to accomplish that goal. "Our affluence is not our virtue, nor is their poverty their crime" is one of many abiding lines found in this essay. Perhaps this piece, which proposes encouraging the poor to produce their own food and to produce linen from flax, was influenced by experiments that had been tried in England. For example, philanthropist Thomas Firm (1632–1697) established a workhouse in London for the poor, refugees, and released prisoners, where seventeen hundred workers produced linen. He wrote a pamphlet about his experiment in 1681. This essay bears the marks of hopeful American pragmatism, an enthusiasm for hard work and thrift, producing useful goods and thereby doing well.]

Industry and Frugality Proposed as the Surest Means to Make a Rich and Flourishing People

That particular Branch of Benevolence which we call *Patriotism*, or the *Love of our Country*, may be looked upon as one of the noblest Virtues that ever inhabited the human breast. Where it has had opportunity to exert itself in any considerable degree, it has seldom failed to make those famous who have been possessed of it. Public reverence and honors have been their Reward whilst living, and statues and monumental inscriptions have preserved their memory when dead.

All nations have, at some time or other, cultivated and encouraged this principle, because, at some time or other, all nations have reaped the greatest advantages from it. The ancients, both *Greeks* and *Romans*, carried it to the highest pitch. Among them, he was a happy man who could devote himself to sure and speedy destruction for the good of his country.

Dulce et decorum est pro patria mori [It is sweet and fitting to die for one's homeland.] was a Lesson they were early taught, and which they never suffer'd to slide out of their Mind. While this Spirit prevail'd, those states, in which it did prevail, arose to be the most eminent in the World. The *public Good* was then the aim of every Man: This was the Point in which all their views center'd, and to which all their Actions were directed. But when they once came to lose sight of *this Point*, and to look on themselves as so many Individuals, distinct from the Public, they soon set up and pursued particular interests of their own, and the Public was always neglected and often sacrificed to these private Pursuits, when it came in Competition with them. Thus was their Union dissolved and their Strength dissipated. The Bundle became untied and those Arrows which, when united, could hardly be bent, now separate and single, were easily broken.

There never was a Time, perhaps, that call'd more loudly for the Exercise of this public spirit, of which we have been speaking, than the present . . . God has given us a pleasant land and a fruitful one. He has not indeed seen fit to exempt it from the general curse, which the fall of our first parents drew on the world; nor has he exempted us from our share in that curse. If we eat our bread, we must eat it in the sweat of our face;

and the thorns and thistles that our fields bring forth to us, are not so much a proof of the ground's bitterness as of our sloth. We must reap our corn before we can fill our barns, and we must plough and sow before we can hope to reap. But if we will sit with folded arms, expecting the earth spontaneously to heap its fruits in our lap, we shall be, as it is fit we should be, certainly disappointed. We inhabit, as I have already said, a fertile region. Our land is good and, with proper culture, capable of producing every thing we want.

*   *   *

Nature, we see, has done enough for us; it is our business to improve her gifts. Let us increase our industry and abate our extravagance, and cry of poverty will soon cease. I say, let us establish industry and frugality, and prosperity will soon follow them. By these have the weakest states been raised to wealth and power, while the opposite vices of sloth and luxury have sunk the most opulent ones into poverty and ruin. It would be wasting time to descend to particular instances, because it is an observation no man can fail of making who has gone through but a few pages of history, either ancient or modern. And Nature is constant and uniform; the same Cause, with the same Circumstances, will always produce the same Effect. What has preserved and aggrandiz'd others, will preserve and aggrandize us, and what has impoverish'd and ruin'd them, will impoverish and ruin us. Let us therefore shun Luxury and sloth as the Rock on which they have split. Let us follow industry and frugality; these will lead us, as they have led them, to wealth and power.

The number of those who are *really* poor, and who must be maintained by the public alms, is indeed a great burden on the province. But this burden lies heavier on some of our towns than on others, and heaviest of all on our metropolis, the town of Boston. It is a Load they can neither bear nor shake off from their Shoulders. It seems to be increasing on them while their Strength is declining; and tho' they may for a Time stagger under it, they must sink at last, unless some Way be found either to alleviate their Burden or to recruit their Strength. Now whatever lessens the number of their poor will effect one, and whatever renders their poor useful will effect both. This will be taking from the weight of one scale, and at the same time adding to that of the other. When we cast a look into the houses of our poor, what scenes of distress do we often behold! Numbers of wretches hungry and naked, shivering with cold and, perhaps, languishing with disease. But still they wear the human shape, and are part of our own species, and humanity will not suffer them to perish. The change of a few circumstances, quite accidental as to us, might have lodged us in their cold cottages and given them possession of our comfortable dwellings. Our affluence is not our virtue, nor is their poverty their crime. Such reflections as these must warm our breasts with compassion and excite us to do all we can to alleviate miseries which might have been our own.

Very little need be said in order to kindle this compassionate temper towards the poor. There are few countries, perhaps none in the world, where it prevails in a greater degree than among ourselves; and God forbid I should say any thing to check it. No; may this laudable spirit still prevail, and continue to be, as it has been, an honor to us. But yet I may be allowed to say, that it requires Prudence to direct it to *right* Objects, and to regulate it, both as to the Manner and *Degree* in which we are to exercise it. And here it may be affected in general, that *that* is a less beneficial Charity which maintains the Poor, than *that* which enables the Poor to maintain themselves. The latter is certainly less precarious, more diffuse and more lasting. The *former* is confined to *one*

Object, the *latter* is extended to *many*, because it makes *that Object* useful to many. He therefore is more truly charitable who gives the poor employment, than he who gives them money. He is a better friend to the community, he is a better friend to the poor themselves. Indeed where age or sickness or any other infirmity, either of body or mind, has rendered the poor unable to work, here we can have no expectation from them. To these we must open our hand freely, but we must open it with discretion. We may be bountiful to them without being profuse. We may afford them the necessaries, we may afford them the comforts, without furnishing them with the luxuries of life. But when those apply to us for alms, who are hearty and strong, and labor under no malady but that of laziness, we may, we *ought* to deny them. These are the very persons, the apostle tells us, should not eat, because they will not work; and to feed and clothe such, while they continue idle, is rather to transgress than fulfill the law of charity. We may indeed be told by such persons, that they cannot get employment, and that they would be glad to work, if they could. This, I believe is not often really the case. But if it has been so heretofore, it is like to be so no longer. A scheme is now projected, by which a door will be opened to let all our poor into employment; and women and children, who are our most common and idle beggars, may now find work proper for their sex and age.

I have often beheld, with concern, the Swarms of Children, of both Sexes, that are continually strolling and playing about the Streets of our Metropolis, clothed in Rags, and brought up in Idleness and Ignorance; and who must probably come, in a very short Time, from picking of Sticks to picking of Pockets. This is certainly a Disgrace to that great Town; and I have long wonder'd that no Remedy has been applied to so pernicious an Evil, and which, at the same Time, will so easily admit of a Cure. To this End nothing more is required, than lodging a Power in some proper Persons, to take up such Children and (whether their unnatural Parents will or no) to place them out to such Trades of Employments as may in Time enable them to acquire an honest Subsistence. The Objection, that this would infringe the natural Rights of Mankind, is weak and frivolous. There are few Laws that do not, in some Way or other and in some Degree, affect these rights, and every Man, that becomes a Member of any community, gives up some Part of them. Without doing so, it is impossible for us to enjoy the Benefits of Society, or to reap any Advantage from the wisest and best Regulations. The Americans were as free a People as any under the Sea. They knew the Worth of Liberty, and were jealous of it in the highest Degree. Yet they, free as they were, had a Law that inflicted severe Penalties on Idleness. This Law was made by that wise man Solon, and it impower'd certain Magistrates to call any Man before them, and to examine into his ordinary Expenses and the Means by which he was enabled to support them. Far from looking on this as a Diminution of their Liberty, they submitted to it, as a wise Institution, and doubtless experienced the good effect of it.

* * *

Let us improve our lands to the utmost. Let these supply us with corn for the bread we eat, and with flax for the linen we wear, and at the same time, let us retrench some of our unnecessary expenses, and we must, even under all our other disadvantages, soon become a rich and flourishing people. I therefore repeat it again, and I wish I could repeat it till it was universally believed, let us banish Luxury and Sloth; let a Spirit of Industry and Frugality prevail, especially among the Poor; and let every Scheme that has a Tendency to introduce and confirm this Spirit among them, be assisted and encouraged by the Rich; then, and not till then, shall the State of our Affairs change for the better, and a new and lovely Scene shall open to our view. Our trees shall bend beneath their load, and our fields and pastures shall be clothed with corn and grass. Our barns shall be filled with the fruits of the earth, and our flocks and herds shall be multiplied exceedingly. In our towns, trade and commerce, especially the most profitable branches of them, shall revive and flourish, and the busy hand of industry shall be everywhere in motion. Our tradesmen shall no longer complain for want of work, nor for want of their money when their work is done. The cheerful laborer shall sing over his daily task, because he will be sure of his wages, because he will be sure they were earned. A general satisfaction shall run through all ranks of men; good offices shall become reciprocal and common; the rich shall be better served and poor better paid.

And what heart would not leap at such a prospect! What hand would not contribute to the purchase of it! A prospect, not like others to be obscured by mists and clouds, and which at best, by being often viewed, become indifferent, perhaps tiresome, to the eye. This, on the contrary, will be ever improving; it will brighten with time, and be continually presenting us with fresh beauties, and fresh delights. Happy is the eye that shall behold it, but happier the hand that shall be instrumental in procuring it.

Unsigned, *Industry and Frugality Proposed as the Surest Means to Make a Rich and Flourishing People.* Boston: Thomas Fleet, 1753.

DEWITT CLINTON (1769–1828)

[Dewitt Clinton served in the New York state legislature from 1797 to 1802, when he was elected to the U.S. Senate. He soon resigned to serve as mayor of New York, a post he held until 1815. A statesman and an eloquent writer, Clinton wrote letters to The Federalist under the pen name "A Countryman" on issues such as the contradiction of slavery and constitutional equality. Tall, dignified, and well-spoken, Clinton is remembered for his efforts to link the Atlantic Ocean to the Great Lakes and was called "the father of the Erie Canal." In the following speech from 1794, he pokes holes in cynicism and locates the principle of benevolence in an image of the divine living within each person; he also discusses humility and suggests how great philanthropists and institutions might contribute to human welfare. In the final paragraphs he shows that he is a visionary thinker, suggesting a great international meeting about the welfare of the world, envisioning an early idea for a sort of United Nations. He also envisions an international university, and considers the transformations made possible by individuals' benevolent activities, picturing something like the Peace Corps as a future volunteer endeavor for service-minded Americans. "The immortal Howard" mentioned below refers to John Howard, a British philanthropist and prison reformer.]

An Oration on Benevolence

The progressive improvement of human affairs opens a prospect so grand and so interesting, promises such permanence and such practicability, as naturally to induce an enquiry into the most efficient mode of maturing it to perfection. As the universal extension of the principle of benevolence presents itself as the only method of accomplishing this great event; and as our fraternity rests its principal merits upon, and has been uniformly and highly and honorably distinguished for, the exercise of this sublime virtue, you will excuse me if I presume to offer a few thoughts upon it; and when describing the nature and effects of benevolence, I feel confident of experiencing the benefit of yours, if I should fail in those flights of fancy—that elevation of style and that profundity of remark, which become a man speaking on a subject that unites in its praise—all the modes of imagination, all the faculties of the understanding, and all the virtues of the heart.

*   *   *

In contemplating the subject proposed, we at the first glance behold mankind divided, not only in speculation but in action, into two great parties. The one side espousing the cause of disinterested benevolence and the other declaring that interest and selfishness govern the universe. A well regulated self-love might unquestionably answer all the purposes of creation, and it is certainly not fair promiscuously to class the advocates of this opinion with those who espouse the system of misanthropy, especially as the general complexion of our conduct receives its color and its glow from self-love: There is something however extremely pleasing to a noble mind, independent of its benign influence to view man as capable of disinterested benevolence: It elevates him in the scale of being and breaks down the partition that separates him from the order of spirits; It places him on a lofty eminence, from which he can look down without any other sigh than the sigh of pity, upon the perishable goods of mortality.

He who supposes that all our actions are bottomed upon interest or vanity will naturally conduct himself according to his opinion. If charity proceeds from ostentation, patriotism from ambition and friendship from interest in others—why should they not emanate from the same sources in himself. He will thus pass through the world a stranger to all the endearing charities of life—dead to the noblest feelings of the soul and deaf to the enchanting voice of virtuous pleasure. The delights of love will be viewed by him as an article of commerce or an union of convenience—the ties of friendship will be rendered subservient to views of profit and vanity—the good of country will be sacrificed to the calls of ambition—philanthropy will give way to the most detestable selfishness—the world will receive its hue from his jaundiced eye of suspicion—and like an unfortunate traveler cast upon a desert of society—useless to mankind, useless to himself. If this doctrine has such a pernicious practical influence upon individuals, the evil increases with tenfold fury when extended to nations.

*   *   *

The deduction is plain: There must exist in the soul a regard for the welfare of mankind independent of interested views. To conceive a selfish scheme, we must consider—we must investigate—we must combine ideas—but the moral sense like a flash of lightning bursts in upon us: We either instantly glow with anger or lose ourselves in admiration: It is an emanation from the divinity—the Promethean fire brought down from Heaven—the working of the image of God within us . . .

It is in the season of infancy that we must look for genuine nature; then the character first opens, and shows itself; then the power of interest is feeble and the artifices of ambition obvious. The inhabitant of the woods, who has never mingled in the corruptions of society, exhibits amidst the awful ferocities of his disposition some of the genuine characters of man, but in contemplating him we must carefully distinguish between the vices, which grow out of the different stages of society, and the inherent propensities of the heart. Misfortune also serves to reduce us to the level of nature, and to render us acquainted with ourselves; it has been well remarked by an acute observer that the most unfeeling man he ever met with, was one whose whole life was a series of fortunate events. To the recluse and the solitary we may also with propriety look for the lessons of nature; here the collision of intercourse has not worn off the feelings and destroyed the emotions of the heart. In these various conditions and stations, we see the principle of benevolence strongly operative; we find the mind thus unadulterated by a commerce with the world, replete with the kindest wishes and most friendly sentiments. The first emotions of the infant heart beat in unison with friendship and benevolence. The hospitable savage, to relieve his forlorn guest, will part with his last morsel and hazard the horrors of famine. The child of affliction will often forget his own misfortunes in sympathizing with the distresses of others; and the recluse, on his first appearance in the bustle of the world, fraught with the most benevolent sentiments, will alas, too soon experience that his opinions are too pure for the corruptions of society.

If the principle of benevolence is so pure and so hallowed, how excellent must be its practice! The power of dispensing good approaches the attributes of the deity, and the pleasures resulting from the relief of the distressed are so ecstatic and delightful as to form the most striking foretaste of the joys of Heaven.—The sun itself, with all its cheering rays and vivifying influence, is not so glorious a sight as the spectacle of a good man distributing his bounty—and to him we must look up as the truly great, for in the calm eye of reason he stands pre-eminently towering above the victorious general or the throned monarch. The state of office, the pomp of power, the splendor of wealth or a long train of illustrious ancestors may not attend him, but what are these compared to the pleasures of sensibility or the smiles of Heaven?

*   *   *

Benevolence seems to invest a man with magic charms; wherever he goes kind wishes attend him: it forms a good criterion of the whole frame and temper of his soul with which all the other virtues rise and will almost necessarily be connected. "Tell me," says a feeling writer, of a compassionate man, "you represent to me a man of a thousand other good qualities, on whom I can depend, whom I may safely trust with my wife, my children, my fortune and reputation!"

The draughts of life, according to the allegory of the Poets, proceed from the vessels of good and evil that stand on each side of Jupiter and whenever they are found pure and unmixed, they flow from the vessel on the left hand. Admirable description of the miseries of life! Unalloyed felicity we never experience, but affliction in all the forms of terror in all the channels of bitterness, attacks us: It approaches us in the shape of disease and poverty, presents itself in the dress of oppression and calumny, assails us in the loss of friends and reputation, and menaces us in all the incalculable forms with which imagination can array the victims of her influence. The prison, the house of madness, the retreat of poverty, the horrid gibbet, and the blood streaming scaffold, bear dreadful testimony to her mighty power. To restrain her baneful influence and to draw the draughts of life from the vessel of good on the right hand of Jupiter, are the objects of the benevolent man. In this grand expedition of humanity, the immortal Howard established beyond doubt the being and beauty of benevolence; he rose sublimely from the couch of affluence and ease—encountered the insolence of fools and the ridicule of misanthropists—the dungeon's groans and the tyrant's frowns—braved the horrors of disease, the storms of heaven and the tempests of the ocean; and wherever he went, chains fell from the hands of slavery and the tears of the prison were changed into smiles—the blessings of all good men followed his footsteps and even despots, dis-armed by the sublimity of his virtues, deigned to listen from their thrones to the tale of sorrow and to stretch forth the lenient hand of relief.

In the application of the benevolent principle to the conduct of nations, so many pleasing ideas rush upon the mind as to hazard the conception of visionary and chimerical speculations. To pave the way for the introduction of this sublime virtue in the administration of the affairs of a nation, the will of the community not the will of an individual ought to be the controlling power: The sentiments of the people are always right, whereas those of an individual, especially in an elevated station, are too much under the government of sinister impressions. Next to a good disposition to conduct right political affairs may be ranked competent ability; The diffusion of knowledge is therefore also requisite to produce this great improvement; which when effected, the conduct of a nation to itself and to other nations will afford a fight upon which celestial spirits will look with admiration.

In the first place, it will be the ardent object of the community to increase the quantity of happiness, and secondly to diminish the influence of misery among its members. With this view, schools of virtue and seminaries of learning will be founded—agriculture, commerce, and manufactures encouraged—the polite arts and the useful sciences patronized—and the rights of nature and the rights of religion respected: With this design, it will also be the object of the Nation to assuage physical evils by the establishment of hospitals, alms-houses and public granaries, and to alleviate by proper correctives the moral ills which prevail. The shackles of slavery will then fall to the ground and the horrid instruments of capital punishment be only seen on the descriptive canvas.—The proud crest of oppression will be leveled to the dust—the chicanery of law banished from the feats of distributive justice—and the long catalogue of crimes which disgraces our statute books considered as the forgery of misanthropists or as the invention of diabolical spirits.

After viewing this sublime prospect of a nation happy in itself, let us behold the sublimer spectacle of all the nations of the world happy in each other.

No longer will the melancholy yew and the doleful cypress overshade the martial field—no longer will the voice of discord like Ate hot from hell cry havoc and let loose the dogs of war—no longer will the din of arms and the clash of conflicting hosts "grate thunder" on the ear—but benevolence daughter of Heaven will compose the tempests of nations and extend the olive branch of peace over the Universe.

The first anticipation that presents itself, is a Congress of Ambassadors from all the nations of the world, to consult upon the means of augmenting the mass of human happiness; and let not this idea receive the contemptuous sneer of high-pretending wisdom before it is brought to the touchstone of imagination, for it is only an extension of the confederacies of bordering states, and amplification of the design of Henry the Great of France to unite the views of the European Nations.

By this mighty congress of nations, a free commerce will be universally established; trade will be left open to the channels which nature points out; Duties and premiums and prohibitions will be no more; Commerce will seek the regions of industry and skill, and the wants of mankind will be supplied upon the basis of their virtues.

A university, for the illumination of the world, will also be founded; to which as the store-house of knowledge the learned of all nations will resort as formerly they did to ancient Egypt. Here the European, the Asiatic, the African, and the American Literati will assemble and communicate to each other, the discoveries, the curiosities and the knowledge of their respective continents; here the prejudices of country will vanish before the talisman of merit; here the ground of emulation will be widened; and it will be no longer contended whether a Frenchman or a Englishman but whether a Native of the Eastern or Western Hemisphere shall bear away the palm of genius and the trophies of knowledge.

Great improvements must also take place, which far surpass the momentum of power that a single nation can produce, but will with facility proceed from their united strength. The hand of art will change the face of the Universe; Mountains, deserts, and oceans will feel its mighty force. It will not then be debated whether hills shall be prostrated, but whether the Alps and the Andes shall be leveled? Nor whether sterile fields shall be fertilized, but whether the deserts of Africa shall feel the power of cultivation? Nor whether rivers shall be joined, but whether the Caspian shall see the Mediterranean, and the waves of the Pacific lave the Atlantic Shores?

DeWitt Clinton, "An Oration on Benevolence, delivered before the Society of Blackfriars, in the City of New York, at their anniversary festival," November 10, 1794 (printed by Friar McLean, 1795).

"ASTERIO" (n.d)

[The writer who used the pen name "Asterio" seems to have written this piece to provoke readers' consciences. The author reminds us that misfortune is part of the human condition and recalls Christian teachings calling for care of those in need. Asking if those unmoved by the distress of others have forgotten that their own families might someday be in need, Asterio says that sometimes giving alms is done as a mere display of one's status, but that it can also be done in such a way that it is the sign of "a Christian heart." Asterio ends with rousing praise of Charity, enthusiastic about Charity's effects and expressing the wish that others might realize true Charity's greatness.]

An Essay on Charity

As we are creatures of one Almighty Creator, and partakers of the same common nature, it behoves us to sympathize with the afflicted, to relieve the distresses of the needy, and to cultivate and cherish a principle of philanthropy. Who that has any bowels of compassion can refrain from extending his charity to the poor and needy?

As misfortunes are incident to human life, those who are in circumstances to procure sustenance for themselves, may soon be deprived of the means, and reduced to extreme poverty and distress. None are certain that prosperity will smile on them through life; for prosperity and adversity by turns succeed each other, as rain does fair weather and fair weather rain. The man who is in competent circumstances one year, may the next be destitute of the necessaries and conveniences of life. In this situation he may be also visited with physical evils, and be disabled by sickness and infirmity to procure food and raiment for himself and family. To persons thus situated, does not humanity itself teach us to stretch a helping hand? Scripture confirms the suggestions of humanity, and points it out as our indispensable duty "to feed the hungry and to clothe the naked."

For a moment let us figure to our imagination a widow with her fatherless children around her, asking for a morsel of bread to allay their keen appetites: she has none to give! Fain would she relieve their wants, but fortune has proved unfavourable to her; she has lost the support of her family, the object of her affections and the consolation of her declining years: she is left to the charity of the community. And are there not some of those who banish from their breasts every principle of benevolence? Who are so selfish as to be destitute of the bowels of compassion towards those who are deserving and stand in need of charity? Would such persons but reflect, that this might be the situation of their own families, would they not then be excited to extend charity to those who labour under calamities? Would they not also think it hard, if this was to be their own situation, and others should refuse to bestow on them a little of their superfluity?

But methinks such a scene as this would stimulate the most uncharitable breast to distribute. Can it be possible, that human beings could be so unmoved at distress, as not to impart according to their ability? If there be any such, let them carry in their remembrance, that it is the language of divine revelation, that those who shut their bosoms against the necessities of their fellow creatures, are devoid of vital piety: "Who so hath this world's good, and seeth his brother stand in need, and shutteth up his bowels of compassion from him, how dwelleth the love of God in him?"

Charity is indeed an amiable virtue; it discovers a spirit of sympathy and love towards our fellow creatures: it gives an additional luster to other qualities of the mind, and is generally an evidence of a Christian heart; generally, I say, but not always; for persons may bestow alms from ostentatious views, hoping thereby to purchase fame among men.

Charity may also proceed from a mere softness or tenderness of the natural temper, in which sense the exercise of it cannot be called a virtue.

But what is this charity, when compared to charity bestowed by a religious heart, teeming with sympathy and love towards all objects of commiseration?

A charitable temper, as well as practice, is productive of happy effects—It enlarges the soul, and improves it in goodness: by this means the humane and social affections are cultivated—It softens the roughness of human nature, meliorates the heart, and learns us to think, act and feel as becomes rational begins.—OH CHARITY! DIVINE CHARITY! may thy influence warm and possess every breast! Mayest thou prevail through every clime, and stimulate the unfeeling mortal to sympathize with the distressed!

Asterio, "An Essay on Charity," *New York Magazine, or Literary Repository*, December 1793, 6, 12, p. 711.

ANONYMOUS

[This 1793 essay raises questions about sympathy. What do humans owe their fellow humans? Using examples from world history and legends to illustrate his points, the author urges readers to expand their magnanimity. He uses the image of ripples made by a stone dropped in water, as Cotton Mather did, but in this piece the image is used to convey the idea that there are concentric circles we owe our kindness to—at the center there is the family; extending out there are relatives, friends, countrymen; and further away we relate compassionately to strangers, and ultimately all humanity. The author shows an expansive large-hearted American outlook.]

Essay on Philanthropy

Homo sum; nihil humani a me alienum puto.
A man I am; to me all Men are Friends. —TERENCE

Goodness is one of the most noble attributes of the Supreme Being. Let us strive to copy it in ourselves, in as great a degree as feeble mortals can, and we shall find the source of true happiness. I see, indeed, nothing but the testimony of a pure conscience that can be compared to the secret satisfaction the friend of the world enjoys; I mean, the humane man, the man that takes pleasure in making others happy.

* * *

I run over all ages to find, in the historic monuments they have left us, men of this character; but how few do I find! You will see, however, an illustrious specimen of it in the following example.

The Emperor Cambi of China, being out a hunting, and having gone astray from his attendants, met with a poor old man, who wept bitterly, and appeared afflicted from some extraordinary disaster. He rode up to him, moved at the condition he saw him in; and, without making himself known, asked what was the matter with him. "Alas! Sir," replied the old man; "though I should tell you the cause of my distress, it is not in your power to remedy it."

"Perhaps, my good man," said the Emperor, "I may be of greater help to you than you think; make me your confidant, you do not know what may happen to your advantage."

"Well, good Sir, if you would soon know," answered the old man, "I must tell you that all my sufferings are owing to a Governor of one of the Emperor's pleasure houses. Finding a little estate of mine, near that royal house, to suit his conveniency, he seized upon it, and reduced me to the state of beggary you see me in. Not contented with this inhuman treatment, he forced my son to become his slave, and so robbed me of the only support of my old age. This, Sir, is the reason of my tears."

The Emperor was so affected by this speech, that, fully resolved to take vengeance of a crime committed under the sanction of his authority, he asked immediately the old man if they were far from the house he spoke of; and, the old man answering they were not above half a league, he said he had a mind to go there with him himself, to exhort the governor to restore to him his estate and his son, and that he did not despair of persuading him to it. "Persuade him!"

Replied the old man: "Ah, sir, remember, if you please, I told you that mean belongs to the Emperor. It is neither safe for you nor me to propose any thing like what you say to him; he will only treat me the sores for it, and you will receive some insult from him, which I beg you would not expose yourself to."

"Be under no concern on my account," replied the Emperor, "I am determined to go upon this business, and I hope we shall soon see a better issue to our negotiation than you imagine."

The old man, who perceived visible marks in this unknown person of that something which illustrious birth impresses on the aspect of those of rank, believed he should not more oppose his good intentions, and only objected, that, being broke down with old age and a foot, he was not able to keep up with the walk of the horse the Emperor was mounted on.

"I am young," answered the Emperor; "do you get a horseback and I will go a foot." The old man not accepting the offer, the Emperor hit upon the expedient of taking him behind him; but the old man again excusing himself, that, his poverty having deprived him of the means of changing linen and clothes, he might communicate to him vermin he could not keep himself clear of: "Come; friend," said the Emperor, "be in no trouble about that; get behind me; a change of clothes will presently rid me of all communication of the kind."

At length the old man mounted, and both soon arrived at the house they rode to. The Emperor asked for the governor, who, appearing, was greatly surprised when the Prince, in accosting him, discovered to him, to make himself known, the embroidered dragon he wore on his breast, which his hunting garb had kept concealed. It happened to render more famous, as it were, this memorable action of justice and humanity, that most of the Grandees, who followed the Emperor to the chase, there met about him, as if assigned a place of rendezvous. Before this grand assembly he severely reproached the old man's persecutor with his signal injustice, and, after obliging him to restore to him his estate and son he ordered his head to be instantly cut off. He did more: He put the old man in his place, admonishing him to take care lest fortune changing his manner, another might hereafter avail himself of his injustice as he now had of the injustice of another.

The Emperor's whole conduct was truly noble, justice influenced by humanity; and this act of humanity in him principally regarded the concern men feel forth human species in general, for this single reason, that they are men like themselves, without being united either by the ties of blood, of love or friendship; though we must not exclude in the Emperor the sacred tie between the Sovereign and subject, by which they are bound to consult a reciprocal welfare.

It is just we should have a superior tenderness for a father, a wife, a child, or a friend; but there is a sort of affection which we owe to all mankind, as being members of the same family, of which God is the Creator and Father. Let us illustrate this by the circular undulations which the fall of a stone causes on the surface of a clear and tranquil water. The agitation in the center, by communicating itself afar off, forms a great number of tremulous circles, the faintness of whole imprecation is in proportion to the largeness of their circumference, till the last seems to have escaped from our sight. Here is an image of the different degrees of our affections. We love principally that which touches us the more nearly, and less and less, in proportion to the distance. We consider mankind, with relation to us, as divided into different classes; everyone of which, increasing gradually, consists of greater numbers than the former: we place ourselves in the smallest, which is surrounded by others more extended; and from thence we distribute to the different orders of men which they contain, different degrees of affection, more or less strong, in proportion to their distance from us, in such manner as that the last has hardly any share of it. These different classes may be ranked in the following order: A wife, children, friends, relations, men of the same religion; the next are those of the same trade or profession as ourselves; the other classes comprehend our neighbours, fellow citizens and countrymen: The last of which includes all the rest, is the universal class of mankind.

The Massachusetts Magazine; or, Monthly Museum of Knowledge and Rational Entertainment. Boston: Isaiah and Ebenezer T. Andrews, January 1793; 5, 1, pp. 33–35.

THOMAS PAINE (1737–1809)

[Brilliant theorist of liberty and democracy, Thomas Paine had spiritual tastes that were nonconformist and critical of blindly following traditions, whether regarding a hereditary monarchy or a violent God. Paine's friends included visionary poet and artist William Blake and political philosopher Samuel Adams. Paine wrote the well-known treatise The Age of Reason between 1793 and 1795, although his work was interrupted in 1794 while in prison for opposing the execution of Louis XVI. Paine was admired both in his own time and in later generations. Abraham Lincoln said he never tired of reading Paine, and Thomas Alva Edison said he considered Paine to be the greatest political thinker. The following passage reveals his personality and his religious leanings and aversions. He questions the logic and images of the Christian story and speaks with reverence of Quaker philanthropy. As a deist, he believed in a transcendent Deity but did not see the Bible as the exclusive source of all truth. In his view, creation, the world of nature, was the great revelation. As seen in the following excerpt, Paine saw Jesus as characterized by philanthropy, love of humanity. He explains how for a deist such as himself religion means contemplating the Deity's power, wisdom, and goodness in his works and spending one's life imitating the Deity.]

The Age of Reason

It is somewhat curious that the three persons whose names are the most universally recorded were of very obscure parentage. Moses was a foundling; Jesus Christ was born in a stable; and Mahomet was a mule driver. The first and the last of these men were founders of different systems of religion; but Jesus Christ founded no new system. He called men to the practice of moral virtues, and the belief of one God. The great trait in his character is philanthropy. . . .

From the time I was capable of conceiving an idea, and acting upon it by reflection, I either doubted the truth of the christian system, or thought it to be a strange affair; I scarcely knew which it was: but I well remember, when about seven or eight years of age, hearing a sermon read by a relation of mine, who was a great devotee of the church, upon the subject of what is called Redemption by the death of the Son of God. After the sermon was ended, I went into the garden, and as I was going down the garden steps (for I perfectly recollect the spot) I revolted at the recollection of what I had heard, and thought to myself that it was making God Almighty act like a passionate man, that killed his son, when he could not revenge himself any other way; and as I was sure a man would be hanged that did such a thing, I could not see for what purpose they preached such sermons. This was not one of those kind of thoughts that had any thing in it of childish levity; it was to me a serious reflection, arising from the idea I had that God was too good to do such an action, and also too almighty to be under any necessity of doing it. I believe in the same manner to this moment; and I moreover believe, that any system of religion that has anything in it that shocks the mind of a child, cannot be a true system.

It seems as if parents of the christian profession were ashamed to tell their children any thing about the principles of their religion. They sometimes instruct them in morals, and talk to them of the goodness of what they call Providence; for the Christian mythology has five deities: there is God the Father, God the Son, God the Holy Ghost, the God Providence, and the Goddess Nature. But the christian story of God the Father putting his son to death, or employing people to do it, (for that is the plain language of the story), cannot be told by a parent to a child; and to tell him that it was done to make mankind happier and better, is making the story still worse; as if mankind could be improved by the example of murder; and to tell him that all this is a mystery, is only making an excuse for the incredibility of it.

How different is this to the pure and simple profession of Deism! The true deist has but one Deity; and his religion consists in contemplating the power, wisdom, and benignity of the Deity in his works, and in endeavouring to imitate him in every thing moral, scientifical, and mechanical.

The religion that approaches the nearest of all others to true Deism, in the moral and benign part thereof, is that professed by the Quakers: but they have contracted themselves too much by leaving the works of God out of their system. Though I reverence their philanthropy, I can not help smiling at the conceit, that if the taste of a Quaker could have been consulted at the creation, what a silent and drab-colored creation it would have been! Not a flower would have blossomed its gaieties, nor a bird been permitted to sing.

Thomas Paine, *The Age of Reason*, chaps. 8 and 13. http://libertyonline.hypermall.com/Paine/AOR-Frame.html.

JOHN WOOLMAN (1720–1772)

[A member of an old New Jersey family, John Woolman was a Quaker preacher who traveled around the colonies, preaching in remote areas of the frontier. Woolman stated that his desire to protect living things came from an incident in his youth, when he killed a family of robins. Like others of his faith, he believed slavery was a sin, and he worked to convince all Quakers to condemn it. Later, when Woolman's own business grew so large and demanding that it hampered his ability to answer his calling to speak of faith to others, he simplified, switching from retail trade to tailoring and tending his orchard. His life and writing show a deep sympathy for people in humble circumstances and a belief that moderation and simplicity encourage the sharing of resources with others. Woolman embraced such causes as protesting the French and Indian War, the prevention of cruelty to animals, and the refusal to pay taxes that would go to support war. Preaching to Quakers often and writing spiritual reflections in his journals, he expressed his conscientious concerns in the troubling age in which he lived. The chapters below are from Woolman's book calling on the wealthy to be compassionate in their relations to the poor.]

A Plea for the Poor

Chapter Two [On Unfairness and Injustices]

Wealth Desired for its own sake obstructs the increase of virtue, and large possessions in the hands of selfish men have a bad tendency, for by their means too small a number of people are employed in things useful; and therefore they, or some of them, are necessitated to labour too hard, while others would want business to earn their bread were not employments invented which, having no real use, serve only to please the vain mind.

*   *   *

Men who have large possessions and live in the spirit of charity, who carefully inspect the circumstance of those who occupy their estates, and regardless of the customs of the times regulate their demands agreeable to universal love—these, by being righteous on a principle, do good to the poor without placing it as an act of bounty. Their example in avoiding superfluities tends to incite others to moderation. Their goodness in not exacting what the laws or customs would support them in tends to open the channel to moderate labour in useful affairs and to discourage those branches of business which have not their foundation in true wisdom.

To be busied in that which is but vanity and serves only to please the unstable mind tends to an alliance with them who promote that vanity, and is a snare in which many poor tradesmen are entangled. To be employed in things connected with virtue is most agreeable to the character and inclination of an honest man.

While industrious, frugal people are borne down with poverty and oppressed with too much labour in useful things, the way to apply money without promoting pride and vanity remains open to such who truly sympathize with them in their various difficulties.

Chapter Three [On Universal Love]

Our gracious Creator cares and provides for all his creatures. His tender mercies are over all his works; and so far as his love influences our minds, so far we become— interested in his workmanship and feel a desire to take hold of every opportunity to lessen the distresses of the afflicted and increase the happiness of the creation. Here we have a prospect of one common interest from which our own is inseparable that to turn all the treasures we possess into the channel of universal love becomes the business of our lives. Men of large estates whose hearts are thus enlarged are like fathers to the poor, and in looking over their brethren in distressed circumstances and considering their own more easy condition, find a field for humble meditation and feel the strength of those obligations they are under to be kind and tender-hearted toward them.

Poor men eased of their burdens and released from too close an application to business are at liberty to hire others to their assistance, to provide well for their animals, and find time to perform those visits amongst their acquaintance which belongs to a well-guided social life.

When these reflect on the opportunity those had to oppress them, and consider the goodness of their conduct, they behold it lovely and consistent with brotherhood; and as the man whose mind is conformed to universal love hath his trust settled in God and finds a firm foundation to stand on in any changes or revolutions that happen amongst men, so also the goodness of his conduct tends to spread a kind, benevolent disposition in the world.

Chapter Four [The Golden Rule]

Our blessed Redeemer, in directing us how to conduct one towards another, appeals to our own feeling: "Whatsoever ye would that other men should do to you, do ye even so to them" (Matt 7:12). . . .

If a wealthy man, on serious reflection, finds a witness in his own conscience that there are some expenses which he indulgeth himself in that are in conformity to custom, which might be omitted consistent with the true design of living, and which was he to change places with those who occupy his estate he would desire to be discontinued by them—whoever are thus awakened to their feeling will necessarily find the injunction binding on them: "Do thou even so to them."

Divine love imposeth no rigorous or unreasonable commands, but graciously points out the spirit of brotherhood and way to happiness, in the attaining to which it is necessary that we go forth out of all that is selfish.

Chapter Eight [Using Riches Wisely]

To labour for an establishment in divine love where the mind is disentangled from the power of darkness is the great business of man's life. Collecting of riches, covering the body with fine-wrought, costly apparel, and having magnificent furniture operates against universal love and tends to feed self, that to desire these things belongs not to the children of the Light.

He who sent ravens to feed Elijah in the wilderness, and increased the poor widow's small remains of meal and oil, is now as attentive to the necessities of his people as ever, that when he numbers us with his people and saith, "Ye are my sons and daughters" (2 Cor 6:18)—no greater happiness can be desired by them who know how gracious a Father he is. The greater part of the necessaries of life are so far perishable that each generation hath occasion to labour for them; and when we look toward a succeeding age with a mind influenced by universal love, we endeavour not to exempt some from those cares which necessarily relate to this life, and give them power to oppress others, but desire they may all be the Lord's children and live in that humility and order becoming his family. Our hearts being thus opened and enlarged, we feel content in a use of things as foreign to luxury and grandeur as that which our Redeemer laid down as a pattern.

By desiring wealth for the power and distinction it gives and gathering it on this motive, a person may properly be called a rich man, whose mind is moved by a draft distinguishable from the drawings of the Father and cannot be united to the heavenly society, where God is the strength of their life, before he is delivered from this contrary drawing. "It is easier," saith our Saviour, "for a camel to go through a needle's eye than for a rich man to enter the kingdom of God" (Mark 10:25). Here our Lord uses an instructing similitude, for as a camel considered under that character cannot pass through a needle's eye, so a man who trusteth in riches and holds them for the sake of the power and distinction attending them cannot in that spirit enter the kingdom. Now every part of a camel may be so reduced as to pass through a hole as small as a needle's eye, yet such is the bulk of the creature, and the hardness of its bones and teeth, that it could not be completed without much labour. So man must cease from that spirit which craves riches, and be reduced into another disposition, before he inherits the kingdom, as effectually as a camel must cease from the form of a camel in passing through the eye of a needle.

When our Saviour said to the rich youth, "Go sell that thou hast and give to the poor" (Mark 10:21), though undoubtedly it was his duty to have done so, yet to confine this of selling all as a duty on every true Christian would be to limit the Holy One. Obedient children who are entrusted with much outward substance wait for wisdom to dispose of it agreeable to his will, in whom "the fatherless findeth mercy" (Hos 14:3). It may not be the duty of everyone to commit at once their substance to other hands, but rather from time to time to look round amongst the numerous branches of the great family, as his stewards who said, "Leave thy fatherless children; I will preserve them alive; and let thy widows trust in me" (Jer 49: 11). But as disciples of Christ, however entrusted with much goods, they may not conform to sumptuous or luxurious living. For if possessing great treasures had been a sufficient reason to make a fine show in the world, then Christ our Lord, who had an unfailing storehouse, and in a way surpassing the common operations in nature supplied thousands of people with food, would not have lived in so much plainness.

John Woolman, *A Plea for the Poor or A Word of Remembrance and Caution to the Rich*, 1793. http://www.umilta.net/woolmanplea.html.

CADWALLADER COLDEN (1688–1776)

[Born in Ireland of Scottish parents, Colden studied in Edinburgh and London before sailing for Philadelphia in 1710. He moved to New York in 1718 and became the surveyor general of the province of New York shortly thereafter. He spent much of his time on the frontier interacting with Iroquois Confederation Indians, especially the Mohawks. These experiences led to the writing in 1722 of History of the Five Indian Nations of Canada. Colden was a multifaceted thinker whose written works include philosophy, natural history, ethics and medicine, as well as physics and theories of the nature of the universe. Later in life, he studied botany, making significant contributions to the field, and also became lieutenant governor of New York in 1760. In the first sentence of the piece below, note that the word "affect" meant "seek" in the usage of the time. Note also that Colden finds parallels between the Native American customs of hospitality and gift giving and the practices of ancient Greeks described by the epic poet Homer.]

Hospitality among the Mohawks[†]

Their great men, both sachems and captains, are generally poorer than the common people; for they affect to give away and distribute the presents or plunder they get in their treaties or in war, so as to leave nothing to themselves . . . .

The Five Nations have such absolute notions of liberty, that they allow of no kind of superiority of one over another, and banish all servitude from their territories. They never make any prisoner a slave; but it is customary among them to make a compliment of naturalization into the Five Nations . . . . The hospitality of these Indians is no less remarkable than their other virtues; as soon as any stranger comes, they are sure to offer him victuals. If there be several in company, and come from afar one of their best houses is cleaned and given up for their entertainment. Their complaisance, on these occasions, goes even farther than Christian civility allows of, as they have no other rule for it, than the furnishing their guest with everything they think will be agreeable to him . . . .

I can . . . give two strong instances of the hospitality of the Mohawks, which fell under my own observations; and which show that they have the very same notion of hospitality, which we find in the ancient poets. When I was last in the Mohawks' country, the sachems told me, that they had an Englishman among their people, a servant who had run from his master in New York. I immediately told them that they must

[†] Title is the author's own.

deliver him up. No, they answered, we never serve any man so, who puts himself under our protection. On this I insisted on the injury they did thereby to his master; and they allowed it might be an injury, and replied, though we never will deliver him up, we are willing to pay the value of the servant to the master. Another man made his escape from the jail of Albany, where he was in prison on an execution for debt; the Mohawks received him, and, as they protected him against the sheriff and his officers, they not only paid the debt for him, but gave him land, over and above sufficient for a good farm, whereon he lived when I was last there. To this it may be added, all their extraordinary visits are accompanied with giving and receiving presents of some value; as we learn likewise from Homer was the practice of old times.

Cadwallader Colden, *The History of the Five Indian Nations of Canada*, vol. 1. New York: Allerton, 1922, ix–xlii.

WILLARD THORP (1899–1990)

[Thorp was a distinguished literary historian and educator from New York, educated at Hamilton College, Harvard, and Princeton. He taught English at Princeton for over two decades and published books, reviews, and articles in literary and philology journals. He edited a colorful anthology on the South, from which the following selection is taken. Hospitality is a kind of generosity recognized around the world, and Southern hospitality is legendary. Welcoming and entertaining visitors lavishly consumed profits and left hosts teetering on bankruptcy, yet the custom continued. Unfortunately, in the eighteenth and first two-thirds of the nineteenth centuries, this largesse was based on the economy of slavery.]

Southern Hospitality and Planters' Generosity

The young aristocrat was also brought up to have a strong sense of obligation to his kin. The number of Southern words and expressions relating to the ties of family—kinfolks, blood kin, kissing kin, kissing cousins, connections, "Virginia cousins"—testifies to the strength of the code in this respect. In the early days planter families intermarried, as feudal houses always do, in order to bring two great fortunes together. Political power was also increased by these interfamily connections. The planter squire obligated to help his less fortunate kin was sometimes impoverished or made a bankrupt by assuming the debts of a brother or nephew . . . .

It is useless to argue whether Southerners are more hospitable than the people of other parts of the country, but it is true that in plantation days they could afford to entertain guests lavishly. The stores of food raised on the place were not for export but were intended for the groaning table of the mansion. Visiting kin, neighbors from the other side of the country, the preacher, the stranger within the gates, were welcome. Some planters, it is recorded, had the roads patrolled by slaves on the lookout for acceptable travelers who might wish to dine and spend the night. There were house slaves in abundance to do the fetching and carrying, the laundering and barbering, and even to provide entertainment. The open-handed hospitality of some planters drove them into debt. F. B. Simkins notes, in *A History of the South*, that "George Washington, although an efficient and successful businessman and farmer, discovered that most of the profits of his Mount Vernon estate not consumed by his slaves were eaten up by the stream of relatives, friends, and distinguished travelers who passed his way."

Willard Thorp, *A Southern Reader*. New York: Alfred A. Knopf, 1955, 244.

ROBERT CARTER III (1728–1804)

[In 1782, as the tide of opinion increasingly turned against slavery in America, the Commonwealth of Virginia officially authorized private manumissions. In years that followed, thousands of slaves were freed. Robert Carter III was a slave owner who found this new legal situation agreeable to his sentiments. The eccentric grandson of land-rich "King" Carter, Robert Carter III inherited sixty-five thousand acres and many slaves when he turned twenty-one. He had no formal education, but Baptist and Swedenborgian teachings may have contributed to his realization that slavery was wrong, along with his feelings about owning his half brother, "Baptist Billy." During a smallpox epidemic, Carter survived a high fever that lasted four days; he emerged from the experience feeling that he had seen God. He delved into the world's religions and decided the simple Christian faith of his slaves was the most inspiring and genuine. Carter freed the 452 slaves he owned in stages, according to age. Carter's manumission at that time was a generous act born out of noble sentiments, but the persistence of slavery as an institution made the world the freed slaves entered inhospitable and their new lives hard. Carter moved to Baltimore after freeing his slaves and before dying requested an unmarked grave, presumably because he sought no prominence after death. The following legal document outlines the gradual release of specific slaves on different dates to cause "the least possible disadvantage" to Carter's fellow citizens.]

Deed of Gift

Whereas I Robert Carter of Nomony-Hall in the County of Westmorland and Common Wealth of Virginia am possessed as my absolute property, off, in and to many Negroes and mulatto Slaves whose number, Names, Situations and ages will fully appear by a Schedule hereunto annexed: And whereas I have for some time past been convinced that to retain them in Slavery is contrary to the true Principles of Religion and Justice, and that therefore it was my duty to manumit them if it could be accomplished without infringing the Laws of my County, and without being of disadvantage to my Neighbours and the community at large: And whereas the general assembly on the Common Wealth of Virginia did in the year 1782 enact a Law entitled "An Act to authorize the Manu mission of Slaves" now be it remembered that I the said Robert Carter do under the said Act for my-self my Heirs Executors and Administrators emancipate from Slavery all such of my Slaves enumerated in the aforesaid Schedule (as are under the age of 45 years) but in the Manner and as herein after particularly mentioned and set forth, that is to say: that forasmuch as I have with great care and attention endeavoured to discouver that mode of Manumission from Slavery which can be effected consonant to law and with the least possible disadvantage to my fellow citizens I have determined to discharge my-self from this act of justice and duty by declaring that my slaves shall not receive an immediate but a gradual emancipation in the following manner—viz; fifteen of my slaves under the age of 45 beginning at the oldest and descending according to their age, are hereby—

Emancipated and set free on the 2nd day of January 1792: And Fifteen more of my slaves shall be liberated and set free on the 1st day of January 1793 and so annually in every year upon the 1st day of January (unless when that happens on a Sunday and then on the next succeeding Day) until the year 1801 inclusive by which means, 150 of my slaves within the age restricted by the act aforesaid will be manumitted; regard still being had in all the subsequent Manumissions that the oldest of my slaves be the first emancipated: and whereas it will be found from the schedule aforesaid that a large number of my male and female slaves are at present under the ages of 21 and 18 years I do hereby declare that such and every of the Male Negroes shall be emancipated and set free when he or they shall attain the age of 21 years, and such and every of the females when she or they shall have attained to the age of 18 years respectively accord-ing to the said schedule and the aforesaid act of Assembly: In Wit-ness whereof I have hereunto set my hand and affixed my seal this 1st Day of August 1791—Robt. Carter. (seal)

Figure 2.7 Painting of Robert Carter III

And whereas sundry female slaves mentioned in the annexed schedule have been delivered of children since the 1st Day of Janu-ary, 1791—which children are considered as slaves in the Com-monwealth aforesaid—and to provide for the children that may be so born I do now declare that all the males and females that may be born of the aforesaid women in the course of the present year 1791—shall be free—that is to say the males in the year 1812 females in the year 1809 or as many of them as may be then living—as witness my hand and seal the day and year above written—

Robert Carter, "Deed of Gift." Durham, N.C.: Duke University Rare Book, Manuscript and Special Collections Library, Robert Carter Papers, reel 32, bound vol. 11, 1791. "Deed of Emancipation." 1 August 1791. Robert Carter Papers, vol. 11. Durham, N.C.: Duke University. [DK-11A1, 1:2–3]

GEORGE WASHINGTON (1732–1799)

[As commander in chief in the Revolutionary War, George Washington showed leadership and courage in the struggle for independence. But, like the Roman leader Cincinnatus, who led in battle then returned to his farm, Washington did not assume power after serving, but

rather withdrew, handing over his sword to the Continental Congress. At the Constitutional Convention, his presence prevented the parties from splintering into factional chaos. He did not push himself forward, but rather let the people choose him, as he believed befitted a democracy. Washington demonstrated a sense of self that was encompassing, allowing him to identify with the nation as a whole, much as Abraham Lincoln did in the next century. Trained in self-discipline by his wilderness experiences, and being a man of impressive physical strength, ambitious to earn his society's respect by striving for excellence, Washington became "the Father of America." The following passages from his papers reflect his philanthropic concerns and values. His ideas include the necessity of the nation to have godly charity, humility, and peacefulness if it seeks to be happy; the importance of being philanthropic, industrious, economical, and having useful arts, rather than employing provocations to violence when seeking to promote mankind's happiness; the power of love and peace; and from his last will and testament, the giving of some of his resources to establish a university accessible to young Americans. Like a good number of other revolutionary war leaders and founding fathers, including Ben Franklin, John Hancock, Paul Revere, Ethan Allen, and Edmund Burke, Washington was a member of the Freemasons, a fraternal benevolent association dedicated to the promotion of the principles of "Brotherly Love, Relief, and Truth."]

Passages on Philanthropy

I now make it my earnest prayer, that God would have you and the State over which you preside, in his holy protection, that he would incline the hearts of the Citizens to cultivate a spirit of subordination and obedience to Government—to entertain a brotherly affection and love for one another, for their fellow Citizens of the United States at large, and particularly for their Brethren who have served in the Field, and finally, that he would most graciously be pleased to dispose us all, to do Justice, to love Mercy, and to demean ourselves with that Charity, Humility, and Pacific temper of mind which were the Characteristicks of the Divine Author of our blessed Religion, and without an humble imitation of whose example in these things, we can never hope to be a Happy Nation.

—George Washington to John Hancock (circular), 11 June 1783. "The Papers of George Washington." http://gwpapers.virginia.edu/documents/constitution/1784/hancock.html.

* * *

While I reiterate the professions of my dependence upon Heaven as the source of all public and private blessings; I will observe that the general prevalence of piety, philanthropy, honesty, industry, and economy seems, in the ordinary course of human affairs, particularly necessary for advancing and conforming the happiness of our country. While all men within our territories are protected in worshipping the Deity according to the dictates of their consciences; it is rationally to be expected from them in return, that they will be emulous of evincing the sanctity of their professions by the innocence of their lives and the beneficence of their actions; for no man, who is profligate in his morals, or a bad member of the civil community, can possibly be a true Christian, or a credit to his own religious society.

—Letter to the General Assembly of Presbyterian Churches, May 1789 to Caleb Gibbs, vol. 30. "The Writings of George Washington from the Original Manuscript Sources 1745–1799, John C. Fitzpatrick, Editor." http://www.alexanderhamiltoninstitute.org/lp/Washington/electronic%20books/Volume%2030.htm.

* * *

And if, instead of the provocations to war, bloodshed and desolation (oftentimes unjustly given), the strife of nations, and of individuals, was to excel each other in acts of philanthropy, industry and economy; in encouraging *useful* arts and manufactures, promoting thereby the comfort and happiness of our fellow men, and in exchanging on liberal terms the products of one Country and clime, for those of another, how much happier would mankind be.

—May 26,1794 to the Earl of Buchan, vol. 33. "The Writings of George Washington from the Original Manuscript Sources 1745–1799, John C. Fitzpatrick, Editor." http://www.alexanderhamiltoninstitute. org/lp/Washington/electronic%20books/Volume%2033.htm.

On War and Love

[from a letter written late in life to a French friend who had recently been in battle]

Figure 2.8 Painting of George Washington

While you have been making love, under the banner of Hymen, the great Personages in the North have been making war, under the inspiration, or rather under the infatuation of Mars. Now, for my part, I humbly conceive, you have had much the best and wisest of the bargain. For certainly it is more consonant to all the principles of reason and religion (natural and revealed) to replenish the earth with inhabitants, rather than to depopulate it by killing those already in existence, besides it is time for the age of Knight-Errantry and mad-heroism to be at an end. Your young military men, who want to reap the harvest of laurels, don't care (I suppose) how many seeds of war are sown; but for the sake of humanity it is devoutly to be wished, that the manly employment of agriculture and the humanizing benefits of commerce, would supersede the waste of war and the rage of conquest; that the swords might be turned into plough-shares, the spears into pruning hooks, and, as the Scripture expresses it, "the nations learn war no more."

Washington, letter to Marquis de Chastellux April 25–May 1, 1788. #147. http://oll.libertyfund.org/ Texts/LFBooks/Washington0268/Collection/HTMLs/0026_Pt09_Chap09.html#hd_lf026.head.147.

Washington's Last Will and Testament

That as it has always been a source of serious regret with me, to see the youth of these United States sent to foreign Countries for the purpose of Education, often before their minds were formed, or they had imbibed any adequate ideas of the happiness of their own; contracting, too frequently, not only habits of dissipation and extravagance, but principles unfriendly to Republican Government & to the true and genuine liberties of mankind; which, thereafter are rarely overcome. For these reasons, it has been my ardent wish, to see a plan devised on a liberal scale which would have a tendency to spread systematic ideas through all parts of this rising Empire, thereby to do away with local attachments and State prejudices, as far as the nature of things would, or indeed ought to admit, from our National Councils. Looking anxiously forward to the accomplishment of so desirable an object as this is (in my estimation) my mind has not been able to contemplate any plan more likely to effect the measure than the establishment of a UNIVERSITY in a central part of the United States, to which the youth of fortune and talents from all parts thereof might be sent for the completion of their Education, in all the branches of polite literature in arts and Sciences, in acquiring knowledge in the principles of politics & good government; and (as a matter of infinite Importance in my judgment) by associating with each other, and forming friendships in Juvenile years, be enabled to free themselves in a proper degree from those local prejudices and habitual Jealousies which have just been mentioned; and which, when carried to excess, are never failing sources of disquietude to the Public mind, & pregnant of mischievous consequences to this Country: Under these impressions, so fully dilated.

Item: I give and bequeath in perpetuity the fifty shares which I hold in the Potomac Company (under the aforesaid Acts of the Legislature of Virginia) towards the endowment of a UNIVERSITY to be established within the limits of the District of Columbia, under the auspices of the General Government, if that Government should incline to extend a fostering hand towards it; and until such Seminary is established, and the funds arising on these shares shall be required for its support, my further Will & desire is that the profit accruing there from shall, whenever the dividends are made, be laid out in purchasing Stock in the Bank of Columbia or some other Bank, at the discretion of my Executors; or by the Treasurer of the United States for the time being under the direction of Congress; provided that honorable body should Patronize the measure, and the Dividend proceeding from the purchase of such stock is to be vested in more stock, and so on, until a sum adequate to the accomplishment of the object is obtained, of which I have not the smallest doubt, before many years passes away; even if no aid or encouragement is given by Legislative authority, or from any other source.

Item: The hundred shares which I held in the James River Company, I have given, and now confirm in perpetuity to, and for the use and benefit of Liberty-Hall Academy, in the County of Rockbridge, in the Commonwealth of Virginia . . .

Last Will and Testament by George Washington http://teachingamericanhistory.org/library/index. asp?document=36

BENJAMIN FRANKLIN (1706–1790)

[Franklin is sometimes called the quintessential American. His life and his writing, as in his almanacs and autobiography below, are affirmations of public service. Living in a time and place of great opportunities, Franklin believed in upward mobility and pragmatism. He believed that one can help oneself by helping others, that if each person pursues his own interests, society as a whole profits. Franklin was an inventor and innovator who inspired others to solve problems and make discoveries. His vision of the ideal society was a community that would work so well that the need for charity would be outmoded. From humble origins, he nicknamed himself "Poor Richard" when he wrote almanacs to inform and educate ordinary people. The almanacs included proverbs with themes of social give-and-take, and affirmations of the rewarding life of virtue and service. He promoted values of industry, frugality, moderation, and sobriety because they yielded good results. By industrious labor and thrifty habits, he thought people could attain freedom from want and security in a world of uncertainty. Franklin thought of God as "the Great Benefactor,"

and he believed that people could most appropriately express thanks to God "by the only means in their power, promoting the happiness of His other children." Franklin in one of his writings lists virtues but does not include generous giving among them. Franklin explained his philosophy: "I am for doing good to the poor, but I . . . think the best way of doing good to the poor is, not making them easy in poverty, but leading . . . them out of it." His autobiography was a means of discussing ideas that might improve others' lives. In it he describes founding the Junto club for the mutual improvement of its members, a library, a fire company, programs for upkeep of the streets, a hospital, and an academy, among other things. Self-help, mutual aid, cooperative action, civic duty, civil society—Franklin was there first. He was influenced by Quakers and played the part when foreigners thought of him as a Quaker sage. His ideas to ensure fairness, as well as his attention to details and tireless ingenuity, are still inspiring.]

Poor Richard's Almanac

"The poor have little, beggars none, the rich too much, enough
not one." (1733)

"Who pleasure gives/Shall joy receive." (1734)

"Tell a miser he's rich and a woman she's old, you'll get no money of
one, nor kindness of t'other." (1737)

"The noblest question in the world is What Good may I do in it?"
(1737)

"Defer not thy well doing: be not like St. George, who is always on
horseback, and never rides on." (1738)

"Love, and be lov'd." (1739)

"Great Beauty, great Strength and great Riches, are really and truly of
no great use; a right Heart exceeds all." (1739)

"Serving God is Doing Good to Man, but Praying is thought an
easier Service, and therefore more generally chosen." (1753)

"Gifts much expected, are paid, not given." (1753)

---

http://usinfo.state.gov/usa/infousa/facts/loa/bfcont.htm.

Franklin's Autobiography

Chapter 7

About this time, our club meeting, not at a tavern, but in a little room of Mr. Grace's, set apart for that purpose, a proposition was made by me, that, since our books were often referr'd to in our disquisitions upon the queries, it might be convenient to us to have them altogether where we met, that upon occasion they might be consulted; and by thus clubbing our books to a common library, we should, while we lik'd to keep them together, have each of us the advantage of using the books of all the other members, which would be nearly as beneficial as if each owned the whole. It was lik'd and agreed to, and we fill'd one end of the room with such books as we could best spare. The number was not so great as we expected; and tho' they had been of great use, yet some inconveniences occurring for want of due care of them, the collection, after about a year, was separated, and each took his books home again.

And now I set on foot my first project of a public nature, that for a subscription library. I drew up the proposals, got them put into form by our great scrivener, Brockden, and, by the help of my friends in the Junto, procured fifty subscribers of forty shillings each to begin with, and ten shillings a year for fifty years, the term our company was to continue. We afterwards obtain'd a charter, the company being increased to one hundred: this was the mother of all the North American subscription libraries, now so numerous. It is become a great thing itself, and continually increasing. These libraries have improved the general conversation of the Americans, made the common tradesmen and farmers as intelligent as most gentlemen from other countries, and perhaps have contributed in some degree to the stand so generally made throughout the colonies in defense of their privileges.

Chapter 8

It will be remark'd that, tho' my scheme was not wholly without religion, there was in it no mark of any of the distinguishing tenets of any particular sect. I had purposely avoided them; for, being fully persuaded of the utility and excellency of my method, and that it might be serviceable to people in all religions, and intending some time or other to publish it, I would not have any thing in it that should prejudice any one, of any sect, against it. I purposed writing a little comment on each virtue, in which I would have shown the advantages of possessing it, and the mischiefs attending its opposite vice; and I should have called my book THE ART OF VIRTUE, because it would have shown the means and manner of obtaining virtue, which would have distinguished it from the mere exhortation to be good, that does not instruct and indicate the means, but is like the apostle's man of verbal charity, who only without showing to the naked and hungry how or where they might get clothes or victuals, exhorted them to be fed and clothed.—James 2: 15, 16. ["If a brother or sister be naked, and destitute of daily food, And one of you say unto them, Depart in peace, be ye warmed and filled; notwithstanding ye give them not those things which are needful to the body; what doth it profit?"]

Chapter 9

About this time I wrote a paper (first to be read in Junto, but it was afterward publish'd) on the different accidents and carelessnesses by which houses were set on fire, with cautions against them, and means proposed of avoiding them. This was much spoken of as a useful piece, and gave rise to a project, which soon followed it, of forming a company for the more ready extinguishing of fires, and mutual assistance in removing and securing the goods when in danger. Associates in this scheme were presently found, amounting to thirty. Our articles of agreement oblig'd every member to keep always in good order, and fit for use, a certain number of leather buckets, with strong bags and baskets (for packing and transporting of goods), which were to be brought to every fire; and we agreed to meet once a month and spend a social evening together, in discoursing and communicating such ideas as occurred to us upon the subject of fires, as might be useful in our conduct on such occasions.

The utility of this institution soon appeared, and many more desiring to be admitted than we thought convenient for one company, they were advised to form another, which was accordingly done; and this went on, one new company being formed after another, till they became so numerous as to include most of the inhabitants who were men of property; and now, at the time of my writing this, tho' upward of fifty years since its establishment, that which I first formed, called the Union Fire Company, still subsists and flourishes, tho' the first members are all deceas'd but myself and one, who is older by a year than I am. The small fines that have been paid by members for absence at the monthly meetings have been apply'd to the purchase of fire-engines, ladders, fire-hooks, and other useful implements for each company, so that I question whether there is a city in the world better provided with the means of putting a stop to beginning conflagrations; and, in fact, since these institutions, the city has never lost by fire more than one or two houses at a time, and the flames have often been extinguished before the house in which they began has been half consumed.

Chapter 11

Peace being concluded, and the association business therefore at an end, I turn'd my thoughts again to the affair of establishing an academy. The first step I took was to associate in the design a number of active friends, of whom the Junto furnished a good part; the next was to write and publish a pamphlet, entitled Proposals Relating to the Education of Youth in Pennsylvania. This I distributed among the principal inhabitants gratis; and as soon as I could suppose their minds a little prepared by the perusal of it, I set on foot a subscription for opening and supporting an academy; it was to be paid in quotas yearly for five years; by so dividing it, I judg'd the subscription might be larger, and I believe it was so, amounting to no less, if I remember right, than five thousand pounds.

Figure 2.9 Painting of Benjamin Franklin

In the introduction to these proposals, I stated their publication, not as an act of mine, but of some publick-spirited gentlemen, avoiding as much as I could, according to my usual rule, the presenting myself to the publick as the author of any scheme for their benefit.

The subscribers, to carry the project into immediate execution, chose out of their number twenty-four trustees, and appointed Mr. Francis, then attorney-general, and myself to draw up constitutions for the government of the academy; which being done and signed, a house was hired, masters engag'd, and the schools opened, I think, in the same year, 1749.

The scholars increasing fast, the house was soon found too small, and we were looking out for a piece of ground, properly situated, with intention to build, when Providence threw into our way a large house ready built, which, with a few alterations, might well serve our purpose. This was the building before mentioned, erected by the hearers of Mr. Whitefield, and was obtained for us in the following manner.

It is to be noted that the contributions to this building being made by people of different sects, care was taken in the nomination of trustees, in whom the building and ground was to be vested, that a predominancy should not be given to any sect, lest in time that predominancy might be a means of appropriating the whole to the use of such sect, contrary to the original intention. It was therefore that one of each sect was appointed, viz., one Church-of-England man, one Presbyterian, one Baptist, one Moravian, etc., those, in case of vacancy by death, were to fill it by election from among the contributors. The Moravian happen'd not to please his colleagues, and on his death they resolved to have no other of that sect. The difficulty then was, how to avoid having two of some other sect, by means of the new choice.

Several persons were named, and for that reason not agreed to. At length one mention'd me, with the observation that I was merely an honest man, and of no sect at all, which prevail'd with them to chuse me. The enthusiasm which existed when the house was built had long since abated, and its trustees had not been able to procure fresh contributions for paying the ground-rent, and discharging some other debts the building had occasion'd, which embarrass'd them greatly. Being now a member of both sets of trustees, that for the building and that for the Academy, I had a good opportunity of negotiating with both, and brought them finally to an agreement, by which the trustees for the building were to cede it to those of the academy, the latter undertaking to discharge the debt, to keep for ever open in the building a large hall for occasional preachers, according to the original intention, and maintain a free-school for the instruction of poor children. Writings were accordingly drawn, and on paying the debts the trustees of the academy were put in possession of the premises; and by dividing the great and lofty hall into stories, and different rooms above and below for the several schools, and purchasing some additional ground, the whole was soon made fit for our purpose, and the scholars remov'd into the building.

In 1751, Dr. Thomas Bond, a particular friend of mine, conceived the idea of establishing a hospital in Philadelphia (a very beneficent design, which has been ascrib'd to me, but was originally his), for the reception and cure of poor sick persons, whether inhabitants of the province or strangers. He was zealous and active in endeavouring to procure subscriptions for it, but the proposal being a novelty in America, and at first not well understood, he met with but small success.

At length he came to me with the compliment that he found there was no such thing as carrying a public-spirited project through without my being concern'd in it. "For," says he, "I am often ask'd by those to whom I propose subscribing, Have you consulted Franklin upon this business? And what does he think of it? And when I tell them that I have not (supposing it rather out of your line), they do not subscribe, but say they will consider of it." I enquired into the nature and probable utility of his scheme, and receiving from him a very satisfactory explanation, I not only subscrib'd to it myself, but engag'd heartily in the design of procuring subscriptions from others. Previously, however, to the solicitation, I endeavoured to prepare the minds of the people by writing on the subject in the newspapers, which was my usual custom in such cases, but which he had omitted.

The subscriptions afterwards were more free and generous; but, beginning to flag, I saw they would be insufficient without some assistance from the Assembly, and therefore propos'd to petition for it, which was done. The country members did not at first relish the project; they objected that it could only be serviceable to the city, and therefore the citizens alone should be at the expense of it; and they doubted whether the citizens themselves generally approv'd of it. My allegation on the contrary, that it met with such approbation as to leave no doubt of our being able to raise two thousand pounds by voluntary donations, they considered as a most extravagant supposition, and utterly impossible.

On this I form'd my plan; and asking leave to bring in a bill for incorporating the contributors according to the prayer of their petition, and granting them a blank sum of money, which leave was obtained chiefly on the consideration that the House could throw the bill out if they did not like it, I drew it so as to make the important clause a conditional one, viz., "And be it enacted, by the authority aforesaid, that when the said contributors shall have met and chosen their managers and treasurer, and shall have raised by their contributions a capital stock of value (the yearly interest of which is to be applied to the accommodating of the sick poor in the said hospital, free of charge for diet, attendance, advice, and medicines), and shall make the same appear to the satisfaction of the speaker of the Assembly for the time being, that then it shall and may be lawful for the said speaker, and he is hereby required, to sign an order on the provincial treasurer for the payment of two thousand pounds, in two yearly payments, to the treasurer of the said hospital, to be applied to the founding, building, and finishing of the same."

This condition carried the bill through; for the members, who had oppos'd the grant, and now conceiv'd they might have the credit of being charitable without the expense, agreed to its passage; and then, in soliciting subscriptions among the people, we urg'd the conditional promise of the law as an additional motive to give, since every man's donation would be doubled; thus the clause work'd both ways. The subscriptions accordingly soon exceeded the requisite sum, and we claim'd and receiv'd the public gift, which enabled us to carry the design into execution. A convenient and handsome building was soon erected; the institution has by constant experience been found useful, and flourishes to this day; and I do not remember any of my political manoeuvres, the success of which gave me at the time more pleasure, or wherein, after thinking of it, I more easily excus'd myself for having made some use of cunning.

Some may think these trifling matters not worth minding or relating; but when they consider that tho' dust blown into the eyes of a single person, or into a single shop on a windy day, is but of small importance, yet the great number of the instances in a populous city, and its frequent repetitions give it weight and consequence, perhaps they will not censure very severely those who bestow some attention to affairs of this seemingly low nature. Human felicity is produc'd not so much by great pieces of good fortune that seldom happen, as by little advantages that occur every day.

Thus, if you teach a poor young man to shave himself, and keep his razor in order, you may contribute more to the happiness of his life than in giving him a thousand guineas. The money may be soon spent, the regret only remaining of having foolishly consumed it; but in the other case, he escapes the frequent vexation of waiting for barbers, and of their sometimes dirty fingers, offensive breaths, and dull razors; he shaves when most convenient to him, and enjoys daily the pleasure of its being done with a good instrument. With these sentiments I have hazarded the few preceding pages, hoping they may afford hints which some time or other may be useful to a city I love, having lived many years in it very happily, and perhaps to some of our towns in America.

* * *

I am for doing good to the poor, but I differ in opinion about the means. I think the best way of doing good to the poor is, not making them easy in poverty, but leading or driving them out of it.

"The Autobiography of Benjamin Franklin," http://www.earlyamerica.com/lives/franklin. "On the Price of Corn and Management of the Poor November 27–29, 1766," http://www.historicaldocuments. com/OnthePriceofCorn.htm.

JOHN LEDYARD (1751–1789)

[This piece praises women's inspiring kindness. John Ledyard was an American adventurer whose world travels included the last voyage undertaken by Captain Cook. He is said to have failed at most of the plans and ideas he hoped to implement, but his writings earned the respect of Thomas Jefferson. The passage from Ledyard's journal below reminds us of an age-old gold standard for compassion: good women's hearts.]

Universal Attributes of Women

I have observed among all nations, that the Women ornament themselves more than men; that the Woman, wherever found, is the same kind, civil, obliging, humane, tender being; that she is ever inclined to be gay and cheerful, timorous and modest. They do not hesitate, like Man, to do a generous action of any kind; not haughty nor arrogant, nor supercilious, but full of courtesy, and fond of society; industrious, economical, ingenious; more liable in general to err than man, but in general, also, more virtuous, and performing more good actions than he. I never addressed myself, in the language of decency and friendship to a Woman, whether civilized or savage, without receiving a decent and friendly answer. With Man it has often been otherwise.

In wandering over the barren plains of inhospitable Denmark, through honest Sweden, frozen Lapland, rude and churlish Finland, Russia and the wide-spread regions of the wandering Tartar, of hungry, dry, cold, wet or sick, Woman was ever friendly to me, and uniformly so; and to add this virtue, so worthy of the appellation of Benevolence, these actions have been performed in so free and kind in a manner that, if I was dry, I drank the sweet draught and, if hungry, ate the coarse morsel with a double relish. Those who have been used to contemplate the female character only in Societies highly civilized and polished may think differently from me but having viewed in almost every parcel of the Globe, in the uttermost obscurity in unadorned Simplicity where nature only dictates, and where her page is clear and legible they would agree with me that with less variety of character than man the number is not great that is above or below this description.—Ledyard's Siberian Journal

John Ledyard, *Brazos Courier*, Texas, Tuesday, July 14, 1840, p. 2. Also found in *The Last Voyage of Captain Cook: The Collected Writings of John Ledyard*, ed., James Zug. Washington: National Geographic, 2005, 186–87.

MASON LOCKE WEEMS (1759–1825)

[Mason Locke Weems, a member of the Freemasons benevolent fraternal organization, was an imaginative writer with a wealth of fanciful images. It was Weems who dramatized and embellished the life of George Washington with legendary motifs we know today, such as the tale of cutting down a cherry tree and saying, "I cannot tell a lie." Weems approached history like a playwright, heightening the impact of the ideas he wished to discuss by illustrating them with his vivid imagination. This essay offers hope and enthusiasm for the American venture and an affirmation that "Jews or Gentiles, Christians or Mahometans" are all protected by the Constitution. In his view, the inspiring ideals of equality, liberty, and philanthropy belong together. Weems argued against the excesses of

fanatical "party spirit" and urged cooperation for the well-being of America. Where there is hateful polarity, he asserted, there can be little generosity and concern for the welfare of the nation as a whole; the new nation thrives with a broadminded cooperative outlook. The following pamphlet by Weems may have been based on an oration. Peter Francisco, mentioned below, was well known at the time. He lived from 1760 to 1831 and was a celebrated Revolutionary War soldier, called a "one man army." This tall dark and swash-buckling figure is remembered for helping win battles and killing eleven men in one battle with his oversized sword.]

The Philanthropist; or, a Good Twelve Cents Worth of Political Love Powder, for the Fair Daughters and Patriotic Sons of America

All Men Are Equal

"SOHO! What the plague have we got here now? All men equal! All men equal!!! Here's a pretty love powder for us truly—An arrant dose of Jacobinism I'll warrant it, sufficient to poison the nation."

This is just what I apprehended; for some gentlemen, the moment they hear mention of EQUALITY, fancy they see a host of hungry fans-culottes in full march for desolation, equaling all property, leveling all distinctions, knocking down kings, clapping up beggars, and waving the tri-coloured flag of anarchy, confusion and wretchedness, over the ruins of happiness and order.

From such equality, good Lord, deliver us! But the equality now in question is as different from that, as is a spirit of heaven from a goblin damn'd. 'Tis an equality of mutual dependence, of civil obligation, of social affection, of dutiful obedience to the laws, and of harmonious co-exertion to make ourselves and our country happy.

When I say that all men are equal, I allude not to the endowments of mind or body. For, whether we consider the size, strength and activity of the latter—there is certainly a surprising inequality among men.

As to SIZE—Some are dwarfs, mere pigmies, hardly a match for cranes—while others, the giant sons of earth, lift their mighty forms, terrible to look on.

As to STRENGTH—Some are so very feeble, that the weight of a grasshopper is burthensome—while others, like Sampson [sic], among the Hebrews, or Peter Francisco, who among ourselves, possess a degree of bodily force that is truly astonishing.

As to ACTIVITY—Some men swift footed as the roe-buck can bound across the fields with the motion of the winds, scarcely injuring the tender grass in their rapid course; while others snail slow in progress, can scarcely drag their torpid limbs along. . . .

Equally great is the difference between different persons, in the powers and qualities of their minds.

As to UNDERSTANDING—Some are so very dull that it is a hard matter to teach them a sum in the rule of three; while others quickly drink dry the shallow fountains of human knowledge, and then boldly strike out into the main ocean of the Almighty's works. Witness our great RITTENHOUSE, of whom it was well said by the vice-President of the United States, that, "though he never made a world, yet he came nearer to it than any man ever did."

And witness too our sage FRANKLIN, who, though bro't up a poor Printer's boy, soon learnt the art to chain the thunderbolts of heaven, and to bid fierce lightnings play harmlessly about our buildings. "E coelo fulmina eripuit, sceptraque tyrannis."

As to ELOQUENCE—Some, like our famous PATRICK HENRY, can lead the passions of men about, with as much ease as a countryman calls his pigs after him; while another hardly has utterance sufficient to declare his passion to a pretty milk-maid.

As to HUMANITY—One is so tender hearted, that like the amiable Dr. GOLDSMITH, he can say to a little captive fly, "go poor thing, there is surely room enough in this great world for you and me"; while another can pickle the raw hide of a poor slave, for breaking a tea-cup.

As to BENEVOLENCE—This, like the man of ROSS, will sell his elegant pictures and plate, to assist his distressed tenant; while that, will distress his tenant, selling even the bed from under his sick wife and children, to raise money for gawdy pictures and plate.

Thus there appears a most surprising inequality between men, both in mind and body; an inequality almost as great as that between angels and men, or between men and children. This inequality is so very striking, that some, when told, that all men are equal, burst out into a hearty laugh, treating it as a silly French conceit.—Such gentlemen will perhaps keep up the laugh when they hear that this inequality among men, as individuals, is the very cause of their equality as a social body.—That great philosopher, Paul of Tarsus, has explained this seeming paradox in a most beautiful and masterly manner. He compares the various members in the body of society to the members in the human body.—"We have all many members in one body; some of these occupy a high place, as the head; some a low, as the feet; some appear to enjoy great honor; the eye which sees beautiful objects, the ear which hears sweet sounds: while others, the poor feet, are obliged to plod on the ground liable to be bruised by stones or defiled by mud." But notwithstanding this apparently great inequality among the members, they have not just cause of pride or discontent. The foot has no reason to envy the eye, nor the eye to insult the foot. They are all equally dependent on one another, equally necessary to the perfection of the body, and to each other's welfare. For, what could the eyes do without the feet? Or how could the feet go without the eyes? With the like admirable wisdom, God has placed together the members which compose the great body of society.—Some are rich, some poor, some wise, some ignorant, some strong, some feeble. These though seemingly very unequal, are yet perfectly equal, in their mutual dependence, in their absolute need of one another. The wise are like eyes, to see, for the ignorant; the poor, like the feet, to plod; some, like the head, to contrive; others, like the arms, to execute. Some were made to direct; others to obey; these to labour with their head, and those with their hands. None of these can do without the rest. As in the body, the dead cannot say to the foot, "I have no need of you"; so in society, the richest man, nay, the greatest king cannot say to the poorest tradesman, "I have no need of you"; for the laced coat that glitters on his back, the sword which graces his side, the chariot in which he rolls, the palace wherein he lives, the books that amuse his mind, the music that enchants his ear; all these, and the ten thousand other conveniences and elegancies of his life are the joint production of as many different artificers. Were it not for these ingenious poor men, what would become of the greatest monarch on earth? Why, he would soon find himself a most necessitous and wretched being. To be more sensibly convinced of this, let us suppose the proudest Nebuchadnezzar that ever scoffed contempt on his poor subjects, to be placed in a situation where he could derive no assistance from them, and mark the figure his haughty kingship makes. "With a flint tomahawk he hacks down a dozen or two of saplings; these he sets up on end, ties at the top, and covers with bark and mud, leaving a hole just big enough for himself and his dog to creep in and out at. This is his wigwam, his castle, his palace. In the midst of this he kindles up a fire, around which he yawns and dozes away his gloomy winters. With no clothes but skins torn from the quivering limbs of Wolves and Bears, no food but acorn: and the carcasses of such animals as he has mastered by his club and bow; no music but hissing serpents, screaming wild cats, or the storm howling thro the forest."

Thus destitute is the condition, thus imperfect the happiness of the man who has none to help him. His abilities, though the greatest ever bestowed on man, are infinitely insufficient to procure those innumerable felicities of which his kind Creator has rendered him capable. His body embraces a number of senses, such as feeling, hearing, tasting, etc. which are so many pleasant inlets to a vast variety of gratifications; add to this, his mind, with its capacities, for all the far sublimer pleasures of knowledge, virtue, beauty, painting, poetry, harmony, etc. so numerous, that nature herself with all her exhaustless treasures can hardly supply them.

But how utterly impossible it is for an individual to acquire all these things for himself, must instantly occur to any one who considers what a world of industry, time and ingenuity it takes to invent and carry to perfection a single art of science: then how passing absurd to think that any one man though armed with the strength of Sampson [sic] and wisdom of Solomon, can manage the thousand arts and sciences which exalt the citizen above the savage, which sweeten and embellish life, and which from the most helpless of the animal creation render man the lord of the world! No: this is the work, not of ONE, but of MYRIADS; a work to be effected by men not as solitary, scattered individuals, but as the members of a compact all powerful society.

Let us now view them in their associated state. Convinced of their extreme feebleness while alone, they come together for mutual safety and benefit. The various talents which God has distributed among them individually, are now brought into the common flock and exerted for the general good. Some contribute great bodily strength, others increase that strength by the aid of art and ingenious inventions: the old counsel the young, the wise teach the ignorant, the bold encourage the timid; and as fifty thousand men, taken individually, have but little strength or terror, but consolidated into an army, furnished with proper weapons aided by discipline, and led on by brave commanders, they become unspeakably formidable. So, when the talents and strength of thousands (though insignificant in the individual) are collected into one great social body, aided by arts and acting in harmonious concert, they acquire a force that is truly astonishing, and can with ease accomplish things beyond the reach of imagination. . . .

*   *   *

This great doctrine, "the natural equality of men," founded in our equal wants and equal inability to supply them, suggests the great duty of exerting ourselves for the common benefit. He who neglects this deserves not to be called a good man, for he withholds from the community the blessings which he might confer, & by meanly withdrawing his shoulders from the common burden, he cruelly throws too great a part of it upon others. Such a man, instead of rising as is foolishly imagined, by such a life of idleness and dissipation, degrades himself into the condition of an ungrateful beggar, who lives upon the labours of others without making any return.

And besides, what can sink a man more even in his own eyes, than that he has done nothing to serve his neighbors, to benefit his poor relations, to educate and establish his own children, or to advance the interest and glory of his country; in fine, that he has buried his talents, defeated the kind intentions of heaven in bestowing them, and that if he were cut off by death, his place would not be missed, nay, the world would be happily delivered from an useless burden.

On the other hand, what nobler satisfaction can any person enjoy than in the reflection, that, no day passes over his head but sees him diligently employed in promoting his own and the happiness of mankind: that he not only supplies others with many of the good things of this life, but endeavors by his good example to raise their joyful views to a far brighter world. An exalting consideration this, and one equally open to the poor and to the rich; for as in the natural body, the smallest joint, the smallest nerve and fibre, contributes to the strength, elegance and usefulness of the whole; so in the social body, the general peace and happiness depend on the good behavior of the lower classes, especially as they are by far the most numerous. Hence it is not to be doubted, that the meanest laborer, the poorest slave, who cheerfully exerts himself in the duties of his place, has a right to share with the most exalted of the sons of men, that glorious title—the friend of mankind and the servant of God.

This great doctrine, "natural equality of men," sweeps away all ground of pride from the rich, and of dejection from the poor.

*　　*　　*

Since then no individual has either time or talents to procure the materials of a happy life, without an affectionate union with his fellow men in society—it is very plain that God intended man for society, and it is as plainly his intention that good laws and government should be introduced among them. As in the human body those numberless sinews which give it all its motions, are not left at liberty to distort and convulse it at pleasure, but are wisely confined by ligamentous bandages which will not allow their irregular and dangerous cramps: just so the members of the political body require to be confined within the bounds of their duty and usefulness. The weakness of human nature renders this necessary; for when men leaving their caves and dens first came together, they were neither Solomons nor Saints, but a rude selfish race, too ready to lay light hands on whatever pleased them, and to knock down all who displeased them; and that this day there are but too many of the same Mohawk principles, ready to rob, to slander, and even to murder their neighbors in duels. Yes, the Iron restraint of the laws is necessary; and laws require rulers to execute them—for it would never do for a whole country to quit their ploughs and convene to make laws to punish criminals. Certain persons must be elected by the people and invested with their authority to make good laws and to see them rigorously executed, "to the terror of evil doers and to the praise of them that do well." . . .

O how goodly a thing it is to see a whole nation living thus together in unity! A single instrument of music artfully touched, affords much delight, but how much more delightful to hear an hundred different instruments all mingling their sweet notes in one grand concert! So, to see one man living prudently and happily, affords a heartfelt satisfaction; but to see thousands and millions living harmoniously together, under the same excellent laws, all cheerfully engaged at their several works, and moving on smoothly in their proper ranks: the rulers wisely leading, the people dutifully following, and all lovingly accompanying one another. . . .

Another consideration which must rivet the souls of all reasonable men to our constitution, is that charming delicacy, that profound and equal respect, with which she treats the religious opinions of her children. Even in that government, which is looked on as the most equitable in the Eastern world (I mean Great Britain), the people are at daggers drawn about religion. . . .

But, thanks to God, we have none of these pontifical villainies to wean our affections from our country, or from one another. We are perfectly at liberty to worship our Maker, every man according to the dictates of his own conscience; and provided we act up to the high character of good citizens, our excellent constitution stands equally a wall of fire around all whether we be Jews or Gentiles, Christians or Mahometans. . . .

O blessed land of well secured liberty, of equal laws, of moderate taxes, and of universal toleration! Where no king can trample, no statesman oppress, nor priest can persecute us; but where all, like an equal band of brothers, cheerfully cultivating our several talents, may enjoy more happiness than can be found in any other nation on earth! What dutiful son can think of all these thy truly republican favors without clasping thee to his heart as thy dearest best of mothers, who gave us our birth, nursed our helpless infancy, supports our manhood, and lavishes on us a profusion of every earthly good. Or what prodigal son who considers the husks fed on by the poor in other lands, but their plenteousness of bread at thy table O Columbia, but must instantly exclaim, "I will arise, and will go to the arms of my country." Volney assures us, that in the Holy land the people are so wretchedly poor, that to avoid starving they use so much cockle and wild seeds in their bread as often sickens them, and that he actually saw at the gates of the once flourishing Damascus a couple of meager, half-naked wretches contending with hungry dogs over the carcass of a dead camel. O that we did but know in this our day the many felicities we enjoy under this our government, and did but love the government as we ought!

But how shall we manifest our love? By splitting into parties and mortally hating one another? No, god forbid; for a furious party spirit is the greatest judgment, the heaviest curse that can befall our country. It extinguishes love in the best hearts, and in the worst it blows up the coals of hatred to ten fold fury. It makes even good men shy of one another and breaks off the sweetest friendship. This vile spirit deforms every thing; by giving a hardness to the features and a fierceness to the eyes it turns the loveliest woman into a Fright, and the comeliest man into a Demon. It pollutes the most sacred places, introducing unnatural strife even there where sweetest harmony should ever found; in our streets and at our tables. It fills our newspapers which were meant to be the vehicles of innocent amusement and calm instruction, with the bitterest abuse, provoking to bloody battles and murderous duels. It confounds all the great distinctions of worth and villainy in characters; the vilest creature, the basest Arnold, if on our side, is cried up as an angel; while an angel if he oppose us, though never so decently and for ever so good reasons, is branded as a miscreant!

Mason Locke Weems, *The Philanthropist; or a Good Twelve Cents Worth of Political Love Powder, for the Fair Daughters and Patriotic Sons of America.* Dumfries, Va., s.n., 1799.

ANONYMOUS

[This philosophical reflection, offering inspiration to cultivate appreciation for life's blessings, was a kind of writing eighteenth-century newspapers provided for farmers and other laborers to enrich their minds. It celebrates the rural life central to the American experience in the 1700s. The symbol of harvest is old and deep. It involves ideas of Providence,

goodness, faithfulness, giving, and receiving. Appreciating rural experiences, natural abundance, and thanksgiving for the good life lived close to nature, this philosophy counts and praises the rewards of country life. Thomas Jefferson and others held an agricultural ideal for America, with perennial values. It was a way of life unenthralled with the random wheel of fortune where fashion changes every year—where would that take the nation? Values of seasons, cultivation and harvest, prospering with the fruits of one's labor—these offered secure changes. But America would change—with inventions, industrial development, fashions reshaped for competitive markets, experiments and technologies, new imports and media, new investment styles—and these would before long make the farm seem rather old-fashioned. Gratitude and the distribution of goods to those in need usually go hand in hand. Agricultural symbolism is less understandable in the world today, but it is part of a "conversation with the land" that has long been important in American life. In our time, authors such as Wendell Berry and Wes Jackson keep this rural ideal alive, as does an inscription on one government building in Washington, D.C., that affirms that the family farm has long been a hopeful way to live a fulfilled life. The old days of that lifestyle are mostly over now, but its symbolic value lives on.]

Reflections on Harvest

To the Farmer

The great Governor of the Universe manifests himself in all his works; but in none more conspicuously, than in the regular returns of harvest. They who regard not the hand, which guides the seasons, directs the influence of the heavens, and spreads the earth with timely supplies for its numerous inhabitants, are represented, in the sacred oracles, as fixed in infidelity, or fallen into more than brutal stupidity.

The fruits of the earth, which are necessary to the support of animal life, evidently depend on causes, beyond the reach and control of human power.—Useless is the labor of man without the friendly disposition of the seasons. These are in no degree, under our direction. The whole management of the natural world is in superior hands. There is nothing within the narrow sphere of human agency, that, in the least, contributes to cause or restrain the showers of heaven; to increase or moderate the heat of the sun; to continue or change the course of the winds. The productions of nature are to us as full and direct a proof of the existence and government of a Deity, as was the creation of the world to those superior beings, who stood by, and beheld it rising under his almighty hand.

Harvest gives us a display of divine wisdom. That rational creatures may know how to order their conduct, God governs the world by general established laws. If the seasons were thrown into confusion, or the regular succession of them frequently interrupted, we could never judge how to plan and pursue our labors; when to sow our seed, or to expect a harvest; of what provision to make in one season for our subsistence, until the return of the next. But as the system of the divine government is uniform and steady, or subject only to small and occasional variations, we can form with judgment, and prosecute with success, our designs. We see the seasons ordered with wisdom superior to ours. Experience often convinces us, how erroneously we have judged; and yet all our experience has not made us wise enough to judge perfectly for the future. A plentiful harvest may follow seasons, which to us appear unfavorable; and the fruits of the field are frequently cut short after the most promising prospects. There are many things in the natural world so entirely out of our sight, that to determine the precise manner in which the seasons should be ordered, is far beyond our sagacity. The weather which seems unfavorable, may be necessary for the removal or prevention of evils unsuspected by us, which if permitted to operate, would be fatal to the fruits of the earth: Or that, which is unfriendly to particular soils, may be adapted to general fertility; or that, which produces a scanty harvest in one season, may contribute to the fruitfulness of succeeding years.

An occasional scarcity may answer important moral purposes. It reminds us that there is a power above; teaches us our dependence; awakens a spirit of industry; urges frugality; gives opportunity for the exercise of benevolence; and prepares us to receive, with more sensible gratitude, the future bounties of heaven.

Harvest reminds us of the goodness of that Being on whom we depend. The benevolence of his nature we learn from those effects of it which we see and enjoy. When we see a man of affluence dispersing his charities among the indigent, we rejoice that there is so much power in the hands of one, who has so kind a heart. How much greater evidence have we of the goodness of Almighty God, who opens his hand and satisfies the desires of every living creature.

The *faithfulness* of God is conspicuous in the regular returns of harvest. He has made us dependent on his care; and while we trust his care, in the exercise of that prudence and industry, which his providence prescribes, seasonable supplies are not denied.

The promise delivered to mankind 4000 years ago, that "while the earth remaineth summer and winter, seed time and harvest shall not fail," we see continually made good. There have been partial famines: But these have oftener been artificial than providential—oftener the effect of war, ravage, plunder, monopoly and oppression, than of an interruption in the course of nature. Such a general failure of seed time or harvest by the inclemency of the seasons, as could be called an infraction on the earth of the promise, has never been known. Every harvest is a fresh instance of the faithfulness of God, and a fresh encouragement to confidence in his care.

Cumberland Gazette, Portland, Maine, 1791-08-08 p. 1.

EPILOGUE

BLACK HAWK (1767–1838)

[This Sauk and Fox tribal leader lived in what is now Rock Island, Illinois, on the Mississippi River. Abraham Lincoln as a young man was an officer in the Black Hawk War, which was fought to push Black Hawk and his tribe out of the Mississippi Valley area. In this traditional origin story, which Black Hawk told in his autobiography, we see two hunters' generosity reciprocated by gifts that their whole tribe could share. Many Native American stories reveal the value they placed on the food that sustained them; they revered with gratitude the sacred source of that food. Thanksgiving is a theme in many Native American ceremonies and is a value central to a traditional way of life.]

Story of the Gift of Corn and Beans

When our corn is getting ripe, our young people watch with anxiety for the signal to pull roasting ears, as none dare touch them until the proper time. When the corn is fit for use another great ceremony takes place, with feasting and returning thanks to the Great Spirit for giving us Corn.

I will now relate the manner in which corn first came. According to tradition handed down to our people, a beautiful woman was seen to descend from the clouds, and alight upon the earth, by two of our ancestors who had killed a deer, and were sitting by a fire roasting a part of it to eat. They were astonished at seeing her, and concluded that she was hungry and had smelt the meat. They immediately went to her, taking with them a piece of the roasted venison. They presented it to her, she ate it, telling them to return to the spot where she was sitting at the end of one year, and they would find a reward for their kindness and generosity. She then ascended to the clouds and disappeared. The men returned to their village, and explained to the tribe what they had seen, done and heard, but were laughed at by their people. When the period had arrived for them to visit this consecrated ground, where they were to find a reward for their attention to the beautiful woman of the clouds, they went with a large party, and found where her right hand had rested on the ground corn growing, where the left hand had rested beans, and immediately where she had been seated, tobacco.

The two first have ever since been cultivated by our people as our principal provisions, and the last is used for smoking. The white people have since found out the latter, and seem to relish it as much as we do, as they use it in different ways: Smoking, snuffing and chewing.

We thank the Great Spirit for all the good he has conferred upon us. For myself, I never take a drink of water from a spring without being mindful of his goodness.

Autobiography of Ma-ka-tai-me-she-ki-kiak, or Black Hawk, available at Project Gutenberg, http://www.gutenberg.org/catalog/world/readfile?fk_files= 9061&pageno=1, p. 33.

PART III

Generous Spirit and the Development of Social Conscience

1800 · 1900

EPIGRAPH

MCGUFFEY'S ECLECTIC SECOND READER

[William Holmes McGuffey (1800–1873) graduated from Washington College in Pennsylvania. He taught in Ohio frontier schools before teaching ancient languages at Miami University in Oxford, Ohio; later he served as president of several colleges in Ohio and taught courses in moral philosophy from 1845 until his death. His collections of didactic stories and verses reflect his philosophy of education and became standard elementary-school textbooks in most states of the union. The McGuffey Readers enjoyed great popularity—over 125,000,000 copies were sold. The verses below distinguish true charms, encouraging students to be cheerful, helpful, and compassionate.]

True Beauty

> Beautiful faces are they that wear
> The light of a pleasant spirit there;
> Beautiful hands are they that do
> Deeds that are noble, good and true;
> Beautiful feet are they that go
> Swiftly to lighten another's woe.

William Holmes McGuffey, *McGuffey's Eclectic Second Reader.* Cincinnati, Ohio: Truman and Smith, 1836, lesson 6.

STORIES

HONESTUS

[The traditions of Judaism, written in the Torah and the Talmud, and in later writings by religious leaders and philosophers like Moses Maimonides, encourage helping others in a variety of ways. The Torah teaches that he who mocks the poor blasphemes God. Maimonides distinguished eight levels of Tzedakah or charity, from the least to the best: (1) Giving grudgingly; (2) Giving cheerfully, but less than one should; (3) Giving only after being asked; (4) Giving without being asked; (5) Giving where the recipient knows who the donor is; (6) Giving where the recipient does not know who the donor is; (7) Giving where neither the donor nor the recipient know each other; (8) Giving in a way that allows the recipient to provide for himself. The following is a story of reciprocity and generosity. The old man gives, not for reward—but he prospers nevertheless. Although Honestus is a pen name and the anecdote is not written as a news story, the author claimed personal knowledge of the events, recording this as a story about generosity with a happy ending that Americans should know about. Newspapers of the day had looser standards, and sometimes the lines between reporting and moralizing were blurred.]

The Benevolent Jew

At the close of the last century and the beginning of this [1799–1800], a brisk trade was carried on by the Americans between the United States and the Mediterranean sea. The ships and vessels being neutral, usually touched at the English port of Gibraltar. The Swan Tavern was the principal hotel of the place, and there the shipmasters and supercargoes of the American vessels in port usually congregated.

Every day an old Jew, with a beard frosted by time, tall, meagre, and bent with age, and clad in a coarse and beggarly gabardine, with a small basket filled with the best Havanah cigars hanging from his arm, might be seen standing on the pavement near the door of the Swan, motionless as a statue. He solicited no custom, and spoke not, save only to answer when asked the price of his cigars.

Amongst the shipmasters in the trade was Capt. B., of Newport, Rhode Island—a man of family, yet a whole-souled, liberal, dashing young sailor. Capt. B. smoked the best Havanahs, and drew largely upon old Isaac's basket, and usually flung a piece of money of much more worth than the cigars he took, without asking the price or waiting for the change.

A short time before the peace of Amiens when all the French ports were blockaded, Capt. B. was captured when attempting to enter the port of Marseilles, and sent into Gibraltar for trial. It was soon known in Marseilles, and sent into Gibraltar for trial. It was soon known in Gibraltar, that owing to Capt. B's expressing his indignation in no measured terms on seeing his private stores and wines sent on board the capturing ship immediately after capture, before the trial and condemnation (piracy by the law), he had been treated with great cruelty, robb'd of all his private property, even to his instruments, books and part of his clothing. The Americans in port furnished him with what money they could spare to employ counsel to defend his cause and pay his expenses: but during the time which elapsed pending the trial, it was all expended, and at its termination he was without a dollar to pay his bills, and not an American in port.

The day after the condemnation of his ship, when Capt. B. was pacing his chamber in the third loft of the Swam, in no enviable state of mind or feeling, a ruined man, without means to pay his bill or his expenses back to his destitute wife and children— there was a rap at the door.

"Come in."

The door opened, and disclosed old Isaac the Jew, with his basket of best Havanahs on his arm; he looked cautiously to the right and left along the corridors, stept hastily into the room, and closed the door.

"You need not bring your cigars to me, Isaac; I have no money to give you for cigars now."

"I know it, Capt. B., and I have not come to sell you cigars. I know the English have robb'd you of everything, and it is my duty to bear a portion of your loss. When you were prosperous you dealt liberally with the poor old Jew."—Then drawing from under his vest a leather purse, said: "Here is money to pay your expenses back to your country; take it and return to your wife and children. Should God permit you to become prosperous again while I live, I know you will return it; if not, I shall not need it."

Capt. B. was dumb-founded with amazement and indescribable emotions.

"This is too much, Isaac! I cannot take it!" Then after a struggle with his pride and his distress, he poured the purse of gold upon the table and counted its contents—sixty odd doubloons (one thousand dollars!). It was some time before Isaac could prevail upon him to accept any of his proffered relief. At last, reflection upon his destitute situation, and the distressing condition of his beloved wife and children, carried the day, and he took barely sufficient to pay his bills at Gibraltar and his expenses to his home, forcing back the remainder upon the benevolent old Jew.

Happily he did not permit false pride to conceal the circumstance; and so long as I continued in the trade, old Isaac the Jew, was always at his post near the door of the Swan with his basket of best Havanahs, and never lacked customers when there were any Americans in port—for they knew the story of the Benevolent Jew.

Honestus, "Original anecdote of an occurrence which fell within the observation of the writer," *Brazos Courier* (Brazoria, Tex.), December 1, 1840.

HONESTUS

[Stories such as this, derived from the Arabian classic One Thousand and One Nights, were published in frontier newspapers. Retold here by an American writer, the original is found in the 277th–279th nights. The author seems to have studied Persian; Azrael's repeated words, "firmaun nicht," are likely the author's memory of "farman nist," meaning in Persian, "it is not commanded." This material was often used in a moralizing fashion. The creative literary response of European writers to One Thousand and One Nights, such as in William Beckford's short novel, Vathek, was to mine it both for romantic atmosphere and for teaching lessons in morality. The approach taken by literary popularizers was not simply to depict an exotic East seen in entirely opposite terms from Europe; rather, underlying human concerns, such as the foolishness of vanity and self-importance, were often highlighted and portrayed. But whether to satisfy an interest in the exotic or a hunger for ultimate meanings, such sto-

ries captured the imagination. The story below explores the wisdom of humility and knowing one's limits—"you can't take it with you," we say today; you will have to let go of all you
piled up. So use resources wisely and humbly to improve the lives of those in need today; time
will destroy all vain attempts to create a material paradise.]

The Persian Fable of the Garden of Irim

When Shudad, Monarch of Persia and Lord over all the earth, heard one of his
Emirs read to him a description of Paradise, he said: "For me there is no need of
such a paradise, I can build a better Paradise for myself."

Then he ordered fifty of his Emirs and great officers of the things of this world, to
go forth into all parts of the earth and seek out the most beautiful spot upon it for the
site of his paradise.

And he caused Firmauns [decrees] to be written to the Kings of Strombolo (Con-
stantinople), of Rome, China, and to all of the Kings and potentates of the whole world,
commanding them that they should bring to him all that could be found of the things
beautiful, precious or rare in all their dominions, as materials for the construction of
his Paradise.

After many years, the Emirs of Shudad, with reverence and prostrations, reported
to him that they had selected an elevated plain in Khorassan as the most eligible of all
earthly places for the site of his Paradise.

Then Shudad commanded that all of the most cunning artificers of the whole earth
should be gathered together to construct the object of his desires, who caused to be constructed a magnificent Palace, with bricks of yellow gold, and bricks of white silver, laid
alternate, to delight the eye: and they erected on either side massive pillars of silver, with
capitols, frieze, and cornice, composed of diamonds and other precious stones set in gold,
as a faint indication of the splendor of the court of the mighty Monarch of all the earth.

And they planted a garden with trees alternate. The one composed of precious
stones, with leaves of emerald green, and imitation fruit of ruddy rubies, and other
gems of fruit-like colour: the other of fruit-bearing trees, of choicest kinds: the one to
delight the eye, the other to regale the palate.

And they builded around about the garden, an high wall, twenty cubits in height, of
the glazen and painted bricks of China, of many colours; and on the inner side thereof,
they faced it with plates of mirror, to give the splendour of the garden unbounded
extent in the eyes of the beholder.

Then after two hundred years of incessant exertion of all the skill of all the human
race, the Kings of all the kingdoms, the Emirs, and Lords, and great officers of state,
with great reverence, and thousands of prostrations, approached the august presence of
Shudad, to inform him that his Paradise was ready for his reception.

Then Shudad set forth in great state to take possession of his Paradise.

First went five hundred thousand of the most valiant warriors of all mankind,
mounted upon the most beautiful, vigorous, and fleet horses of the desert breed, with
housings glittering with gold and silver; their diamond-pointed spears too dazzling to
look upon.

Then came two hundred thousand elephants with howdahs of crimson cloth and
gold, filled with a multitude of mailed warrior guards, clad in scarlet cloth embroidered
with silver; whose gleaming scimitars of Damascus steel obscured the rays of the sun.

Next came two hundred thousand camels, bearing huge panniers filled with bread, and cakes, and meats, and fruits, which were cast to the right, and to the left, on either hand, amongst the famishing multitudes; countless as the stars in the firmament of heavens, or the sand on the sea shore, who had been gathered together to construct this Paradise for Shudad.

Then came two hundred thousand of the most beautiful boys of all the kingdoms of all the earth; sweeping the dust from the way over which the great monarch Shudad, Lord of all the earth, was to pass.

Then came two hundred thousand beautiful faun-eyed Virgins, surpassing in loveliness all that mortal men had before seen; fairer than the stories of Paradise; strewing roses and fragrant flowers in the path of Shudad.

Then came Shudad, surrounded by an hundred thousand Kings, Potentates, Lords, Emirs, and great officers of state, in all the splendour the whole world could supply.

Thus Shudad, the great Monarch of Persia, and Lord over all things earthly, approached the great gate of the Paradise he had ordered to be constructed . . . [H]e heard a rude voice call to him—"Halt, Shudad!!"

Shudad turned his head with an angry visage, and saw near him a terrific figure, with an awful countenance, of whom he demanded—"Who art thou! That darest to speak in such a rude tones to the Monarch of all the World?"

"Azrael! (the angel of death) and am come to seize thine impure spirit!!"

Shudad trembled!! Then in a supplicating tone said, "Grant me, I pray, so much time that I may enter the Paradise which has been so many years preparing for me and regale my senses with its beauties."

"Firmaun Nicht!" Then with one foot in the stirrup, the other on the ground, the impure spirit of the infidel-minded Shudad, was sped to the regions of eternal anguish, and fire fell from Heaven and consumed all that was upon that plain!!! . . .

. . . When of late years, I flatter myself with the hope, that by my exertions in this life, and my efforts in Texas, I may secure a little Paradise of peace and comfort for my family, of my own creation, out of this wilderness, and offer up a prayer to God to be permitted to effect it, the thought flashes through my mind; before that prayer be granted, you will hear the astounding words of Azreal—*"Firmaun nicht!"*

When I see men endeavouring to enrich themselves by the ruin of their neighbors, by efforts to appropriate to themselves the hard earned property of others because of some alledged defect in legal formalities, and hear them exult in anticipations of the wealth, and enjoyment, they expect to derive from it, it occurs to my mind, that before they enter into possession of the joys they pray for—they will hear the appalling words of Azreal—*"Firmaun nicht!"*

When I hear citizens offering aspirations to God, that they may live long enough, to see the loan effected, the currency raised to par, and peace and prosperity reign throughout Texas, me thinks, before you realize those prayers without maintaining the sound principles of immutable right, and electing honest men to manage your affairs, you will hear in the voice of Azrael—*"Firmaun nicht!!!"*

Well! What moral is to be gathered from all this.—Why! That the sum of human effort, is the Grave.

Honestus, "The Persian Fable of the Garden of Irim", *Brazos Courier* (Brazoria, Tex.), November 17, 1840. The original story in Richard F. Burton's translation from *The Book of the Thousand Nights and a Night* is available online at http://www.wollamshram.ca/1001/Vol_4/vol4.htm.

SOUTHWEST FOLK TALE

[In eighteenth- and nineteenth-century Southwestern culture, a guest was considered a blessing, even if the host was living in poverty. The guest was good luck and should be welcomed, fed, and entertained. In this folk tale, a stranger is given refuge from a night snowstorm, offered a bed, and given a crust of bread in the morning. Surprise gifts left by the stranger are rewards for generous souls who seek no reward. Offerings of hospitality, however humble, are signs of a healthy outlook endowed with the promise of a good future. Various cultures around the world, including India and Arabia, have prided themselves on their customs of welcoming strangers who visited their homes; a miserly reaction to the needs of a wanderer in one's domain bodes ill; even small efforts to help are meaningful signs of a gracious life.]

Stranger's Gift

The wind blew hard as the snow fell against the chinked house near San Antonio Mountain, on the border between New Mexico and Colorado. The señora put two more stones into the boiling pot of water that heated over the fire in the fireplace. Stone soup for dinner—again. All she knew how to fix from nothing was stone soup. The señora was tired of stone soup. She was tired of her husband coming home late from his hard work in the town. She was tired of carrying around her crying children. She was tired.

There came a sound of horses outside. She stood up, and with her body weary, she went to the door. Her husband was coming down the road. He was whistling and smiling to the driver of a wagon. Her husband called out to the stranger, "Have a good evening!"

The two men shook hands and spoke. He waved to his weary wife, and she closed the door.

She went to the fire, picked up another hearthstone, and put it in the boiling pot. She knew they would have company for dinner. She set another place at the table.

Her oldest child started to whimper, and the baby started to cry. She moved her weary bones to the other side of the room and picked up the baby. The older one she settled in her lap as she sat in the broken rocking chair.

The thin door opened and in walked her husband and the stranger. The stranger was old, withered, but had a youthful face. She put the baby down and pushed her oldest in front of her to greet the stranger. The stranger nodded to the oldest child, bowed his head in respect to the senora, and sat down in the only straight-backed chair in their one-room home. The woman said nothing, but took another cracked wooden bowl from the dusty mud shelf and placed it near the fire to warm.

The husband hummed a fine song. He was happy, for a guest was good luck.

The stranger sat and waited for the stone soup. He ate it carefully. Each spoonful was tasted as a delicacy, and each swallow was done slowly.

"Señora, this is truly the finest stone soup I have ever had. Thank you for inviting me in."

The señora smiled. Her husband finished quickly and asked if he could bring the horses out of the winter snow. There was a dry place under the leaning front portal that was not much, but would keep the snow off the horses' backs.

The stranger and the husband went outside. The señora stood up and cleared the table. The stone soup had done her some good, too. She was less tired, less weary, and some of her husband's song stuck in her mind. The two men returned, covered with snow. They were laughing and slapping each other on the back to get off the loose snow.

The señora took down some old clothes from the high mud shelf and shook them out. She laid them down near to the fire and asked the stranger to take their bed. They would sleep on the floor. The stranger refused and insisted on sleeping on the floor. The husband laughed and took his señora to their bed just inches away from where the stranger lay sleeping.

The señora woke early and fixed the stranger some warm, stale bread wrapped in a clean rag. The stranger thanked the señora. "Thank you for your generosity."

He went out to hitch his wagon to the horses. The husband woke and hurried out the door to help the stranger.

The señora sang as she woke the children. She danced with the baby, she laughed at her oldest child's funny stories, and she let the weariness fall from her body.

The husband hurried back inside. He closed the door. His eyes were filled with wonder. "He is gone. There are no tracks. He is gone without a trace. There is wood under the portal where the horses were, and there is more, there is much more."

The señora pulled a torn quilt around her shoulders and followed her husband outside. There, under the portal, were wooden boxes of food, wooden boxes of clothes, and a beautiful music box!

Teresa Pijoan, *La Cuentista: Traditional Tales in Spanish and English.* Santa Fe, N. Mex.: Red Crane Books, 1994, 30–32.

HELEN ZUNSER (1906–1976)

[Helen Zunser, whose married name was Helen Zunser Wortis, was a folklorist who collected Mexican-American folktales. This story, which explores relations between the rich and the poor, makes reference to the wealthy man's hope of buying gold cheaply from the Indian. During the nineteenth century, gold was discovered in and around New Mexico, and Indians often sold gold for less than the going rate. In this trickster story, the poor man has the last laugh, outwitting the stingy wealthy man long enough to eat a free meal. The listener to such stories usually roots for the underdog, delighting to hear how he gains an advantage. The rich might forget the New Testament teaching that when they have a feast, they should invite the poor and disadvantaged, but such stories serve as reminders to encourage that generosity.]

The Smart Indian [A New Mexican Trickster Tale]

Once there were a rich man, he too rich, and when he had a daughter he make a promise to God that when his daughter get married he invite only rich men to the fiesta, and no poor mens. So when she got married, all the rich mens came but no poor mens. He put some men outside, and they chase away all the poor mens in torn coats. So all the poor mens sit outside, and can't go in to the fiesta. Now there was a Indian, and he come up and he was very hungry. And he see all the poor mens sitting there and he says, "Where can I get something to eat?" and some of the poor mens say, "Go to the fiesta, there's a lot eat." But some others say no, only rich mens go to that fiesta. So the Indian he stand and think awhile, and then say, "I go to the fiesta anyhow." So he went up and the mens say, "Where you going ?" and he say, "I'm going to the fiesta." And they say, "You can't, only rich mens can come." So the Indian say, "I must speak to the rich man," and they say, "You can't speak to him," but he says, "I must speak to him." So they go in to the rich man and say, "There's an Indian here who say he want to come to the fiesta." So the rich man says, "Tell him to go way." So they go back and tell the Indian. "Go back, come tomorrow." So the Indian say, "I must speak to he rich man if only a few words." So the rich man come and the Indian say, "Do you want to buy some gold?" Now the rich man always thinking of money, and he says, "Come in, come in," and he puts him down at a table, and gives him plenty to eat, because he think he get the gold cheap. When he finished he puts him at another table, and gives him plenty to drink, and then the Indian say, "I'm full." So then the rich man goes down to his store, and he says, "Have you gold to sell? Where is the gold?" But the Indian say, "Oh no, I just wanted to know. Now if I find gold I know you will buy it. I bring it here." So the rich man is too mad and he beat the Indian and throw him out, but the Indian don't care; his belly full.

Helen Zunser, "A New Mexico Village," *The Journal of American Folklore* 48, no. 188 (1935): 176–78. Also in B. A. Botkin, ed., *A Treasury of Western Folklore*. New York: Crown, 1964, 694.

LEWIS F. CRAWFORD (1870–1936)

[Lewis Crawford was a historian and folklorist. The following tale, from one of his books, is about taking and giving, ownership and limits. The Indian has something the white man wants and knows something the white man does not. Spotted Tail will not exhibit largesse with what belongs to his descendent, and he will not personally profit from pretending to own what is another's. (Like the Onondaga Nation tradition, which demands considering consequences seven generations into the future when making decisions, Spotted Tail is seriously conscientious.) His stance raises the question: What man with a conscience would freely dispense great natural treasures belonging to others? This story from the nineteenth century was told in the Dakotas and reminds us of our obligation to future generations.]

Not Ours to Give

The Indians were much more penetrating and intelligent than we often give them credit for being. Take, for instance, Spotted Tail's little joke. The commission had proposed to lease the Black Hills for mining purposes for a hundred years, paying only a nominal rental. One day the commissioners had been driven out to the treaty tent in a government ambulance drawn by six mules. Most of the Indians were gone, but just as the ambulance was starting back, Spotted Tail rode up to it on his horse. The driver stopped and Senator Allison put out his head and asked what was wanted. Spotted Tail answered, "I want those mules."

"But you can't have them," protested the senator. "They don't belong to us and we can't sell them."

"I don't want to buy them," returned Spotted Tail. "I want to borrow them."

"For how long?"

"A hundred years."

"Why, you're crazy. There wouldn't be anything left of them in a hundred years.

And besides they belong to the Great Father, to the whole nation. We couldn't let you have them."

"That is what I expected you to say," said Spotted Tail. "The Black Hills don't belong to the chiefs, either. They belong to all of us. We can't loan them or give them away."

Lewis F. Crawford, *Rekindling Camp Fires: The Exploits of Ben Arnold Connor, Wa-Si-Cu Tam-A-He-Ca*. Bismark, N. Dak.: Capital Book, 1926, 213–14.

ANONYMOUS (1800)

[These selections from a children's book teach lessons, such as the understanding and transformation that is possible when a magnanimous giving spirit encounters those in desperate need, the workings of just desserts, and the repayment of good deeds. These stories, although told in an old-fashioned style, teach morals that hold up even two centuries later. They may strike us as simplistic and heavy handed, but they are recognizable as teaching parables about topics that remain relevant. Helping neighbors in their time of need may enable their children to grow up unscarred by trauma; causing violent harm to the disadvantaged will come back to haunt the privileged; we should never assume that we are the most generous and considerate ones and others are not up to our standard of excellence. In all these cases, it is good to be generous and humble in interacting with neighbors and fellow passengers on our journeys; we never know when we might need some help ourselves.]

Pleasing Incitements to Wisdom and Virtue

The Hungry Family

A farmer, returning from the corn mill, was attacked by a person whom he discovered to be one of his neighbours. The ruffian, elevating a cudgel, demanded of him the bag of flour which he was carrying home; but, the Farmer, no ways intimidated, sprang from his horse; and seizing the robber by the throat, exclaimed—"You see, villain! That it is in my power to punish your temerity!"

Robber—"Do so; or, deliver your flour. I want it: we are starving; I, my children, and my wife!"

Farmer—"Ah! Are you perishing of hunger? That is another matter. But still I would not have you be a thief.—Take the bag.—I make you a voluntary present of it. I will even help to place it on your shoulder. Be gone. And do not forget to keep your own counsel."

The horse, being eased of his burden, set off, on a full gallop, to the farm-yard. The farmer's wife, seeing the animal without her husband, ran, in the greatest confusion, to communicate her apprehensions to her domestics. Before, however, any measures could be taken, she had the satisfaction of feeling her good man enter the house, in a state of the utmost tranquility. She instantly asked him, how it happened that the horse came home alone.

Farmer—"Hold your tongue!"

Wife—"And where is the flour?"

Farmer—"Be still, I say!—wait till I can speak to you in private."

As soon as they were alone, the Farmer related the whole adventure to his wife; and ended with saying—"Assuredly this man and his family must labour under the greatest distress, or he would never have dared to attack me; knowing as he does, that, in point of strength, I am able to overpower, with ease, two or three like himself!"

The amiable woman, without staying to make any observations on what she had heard, took up a large loaf, and covered it with her apron. When about to quit the house, she whispered her husband thus—"As their hunger is so pressing, it will be hard for them to stay while the flour is baked."

She immediately proceeded to the house of her neighbour; and there, the first object which struck her was the little children devouring the dough around their mother; who, half-famished, was making it into bread. She presented the poor woman with the loaf; and, adding a few shillings to that seasonable relief, left the dismal habitation before the astonished mother could pour forth the overflowings of a heart that throbbed with gratitude. By these acts of well-timed magnanimity, the despairing husbandman acquired new vigour and new spirits: he became doubly diligent in the discharge of his daily occupations; this continues to secure him a moderate competency; he trembles on recurring to his narrow escape; and blesses, daily, his philanthropic benefactor.

From this Narrative, my little Readers will see the solid benefits which generosity—under particular circumstances—may confer; and, as they grow up towards a state of manhood, it will teach them the necessity of endeavouring to distinguish Misfortunes from Crimes.

The Wickedness of Youth Punished in Age

It is our hope that all mischievous children seeing their folly will amend. To facilitate this, we deem it our duty to show them the consequences which have followed vice in particular instances; and to infer from thence, that such consequences, however dreadful, are always within the bounds of possibility. The history which I am about to relate is well known among the inhabitants of a certain village in the West of England; and I have here presented it, in a connected form, as a terror to the bad, and as comprising incidents calculated to astonish and fortify the good.

Dick Wildman was the son of a country miller, who bestowed little or no education on his child. Possessing vulgar ideas himself, he thought, it unnecessary to put Dick in the way of acquiring any superior notions; for if the lad, when in his early years, excelled in mischievous contrivances, he was certain of obtaining his father's approbation, whoever might be the unfortunate object of his wit. Richard, however, possessed good natural abilities; but they were perverted, for want of proper cultivation, added to the influence of pernicious examples.—Ah! How happy are those children who receive in time the salutary correction and reproof of prudent parents or guardians! How miserable those little innocents, who are reared under the direction of fathers and of mothers who can only boast of their ignorance, their cunning, and even their dishonesty!—How often do the children suffer for the follies, or the crimes, of those who gave them birth! While the real criminals elude, sometimes, the hand of misfortune, and the laws' inflictions! These are considerations that ought to interest, in a most particular manner, all the youthful readers of Richard Wildman's history: it will show them the fatal consequences of imitating the vicious pursuits of others, by whomsoever they may be excited, or allured from the sober sentiments of virtue and goodness.

To contrive and execute roguish tricks, formed the entire study of Dick Wildman; but, then, he was certain of countenance; dreaded no authority; was ignorant of the consequences; and was not subjected to any rational employment, with relation either to business or to learning. He frequently drove sharp nails through the shoes of his father's journeyman, whose custom it was to work in a pair of slippers; and when this wicked urchin saw the blood trickle down, or heard the rustic's cries, from the sudden anguish which he felt, then was his happiness complete; the child triumphed; and the parent laughed.

This, however, was a pleasure which could not always prove successful: the man became more wary; and little Richard deemed him an ill-natured fellow. Thus disappointed at home, he searched abroad for amusements; and, at length, in the company of two or three more, as idle as himself, he exercised his brutality on the lame, the helpless, and the blind.—Once in particular, having noticed the hut of a poor old woman, who partly subsisted on parish pay, they discharged a volley of stone through the window; one of which, striking the back part of the poor creature's skull, fractured it, and occasioned her death, before the accident was discovered. Seeing the unhappy object of their vengeance fall, they precipitately left the spot; and extorted a promise from each other to keep the matter secret. A Coroner's Inquest was afterwards held on the body: but their being no witnesses of the fatal transaction, besides the party concerned, as no signs of a burglarious attempt appeared, and as no one could possibly attribute that catastrophe to the wickedness of children, the Verdict was given—"Willful Murder, committed by a person or persons unknown!"

Dick's companions felt the turpitude of their conduct; and, from that time, never threw a stone, nor again molested the peaceful passenger. But his sensations were of a more hardened kind; for, shortly afterwards, a distressed man, approaching the mill door, and imploring charity, Dick answered him, with deceitful indications of benevolence: "Lay down your bag, poor man!" said he, "and follow me. I will relieve your necessities!" The unsuspecting beggar did as he was directed: but, having entered an outhouse, Richard turned the key upon him, and ran immediately to the bag, the contents of which—composed of dry pieces of bread, cheese, &c.—he presented to his father's pigs, and then filled up the deficiency with rubbish.

Having thus far succeeded in a scheme which he considered as inimitable, the wicked rogue set his prisoner at liberty. The poor man, quickly discovering the injurious exchange which had been made, cried and lamented most bitterly. His loss, indeed, amounted to nothing considerable; but, then, it was his all. The demolition of a poor man's last crust, is, comparatively, as piercing to the mind of sensibility, as an overwhelming storm, which destroys the remaining property of an adventurous merchant. The latter, indeed, is hardly ever subjected to actual want, however dreadful his misfortunes: but when indigence cannot replace the loss of bread, the most agonizing dissolution necessarily ensues; and the author of such a willful injury may be said to have struck a dagger into the human heart.

Unconscious of this truth, young Wildman laughed heartily at the beggar's distress—at that distress which his own villainy had occasioned. He robbed the poor wretch of his earthly all, under the semblance, too, of charity, which he never intended to bestow. The amiable part of my little readers may now suppose that this ruffian in miniature had perpetrated as much cruelty as malice could possibly devise. But, alas! The despairing beggar, in an attempt to make known his sufferings to the miller, was

assailed by the yard-dog, urged on and encouraged by the abominable Richard.—
Dreadful, indeed, were the sufferer's cries at that moment; his hat fell off; his stick
dropped from his hand; every feature of his countenance expressed dismay and terror.
This, however, added Richard's exultation; and it with pain and reluctance we say, that
a new transport escaped his eyes, on beholding the animal tear off the calf of Poverty's
enfeebled leg!

To dwell longer on Dick Wildman's juvenile achievements, would be to swell the
indignation of all those who may have read thus far. The recital, I trust, would not
entertain; and enough has been disclosed for the purposes of caution.

Let us now view him as a man. His father died; and he succeeded him as a miller.—
Tyrannical and cruel towards others, he despised or was rather careless of danger himself;
and sometimes encountered difficulties which a person of more gentleness and prudence
would have avoided. Venturing one hard winter, on a loose piece of ice, close by his mill,
it gave way, and he fell under the water, against some iron spikes, which pretty deeply
penetrated that fleshy part of his body: his skull was fractured by means of a sharp stone;
and both his legs broken, having been jammed between timbers that were placed for confining the water. In this deplorable condition Wildman was dragged out by his servant,
scarcely exhibiting any signs of life. Proper medical means were, however, employed: and
he recovered his senses, to be conscious, as it were, of the magnitude of those inflictions, which had been reserved as just punishment for his youthful offenses. Both his
legs were afterwards amputated; he could only walk with the aid of crutches—those aids
of which he had so often robbed the crippled and the blind—and, finding that a long
illness had exhausted his finances, he flew to the brandy-bottle for relief: this expedient, indeed, exhilarated his spirits for a time; but, causing an inflammation in his eyes,
he was deprived of the benefit of sight.—Thus, poor, leg-less, blind, diseased, famishing,
and weak, Dick Wildman begged from door to door: afraid of every step he took, and
suspecting those answers which he solicited, for fear that some miscreant, of a similar
disposition to his own, should conduct him headlong into that pit which he had formerly
prepared, when the helpless and the infirm happened to attract his notice. Too late, this
monster perceived the atrocity of his conduct: but, convinced of it at length, he frequently
exclaim'd that Providence had justly rendered him that shocking spectacle, as a punishment for his crimes, and as a dreadful example to others!

The Compassionate Jew

Nothing is perhaps more ridiculous, if not more culpable, than to mock our fellow-
creatures, because their religious opinions, or their manners, differ from our own.
To obtain respect ourselves, we must pay deference to others, of whatever nation, or
persuasion: for numerous facts have demonstrated, that virtue, and every good quality
which adds dignity to the human form, are to be found in the most distant regions of
this terraqueous globe.

A party of gay young men, last summer, returning to London in one of the Gra-
vesend boats, regaled themselves with bread and ham, during the course of their passage.
Next to these frolicsome youths sat a Jew and a poor soldier; the latter of whom, having
a good appetite, and no provision to satisfy the cravings of nature, often cast a wistful
eye at the delicious slices which were circulating within the reach of his olfactory organs.
He sighed too; but sighed, alas! in vain. The Jew, however, did not escape the gentlemen's

attention; and, being tinctured with the vulgar prejudice of which we have before spoken, one among them cried, sneeringly, "Smouch, will you have some ham?"

"If you please, gentlemen," answered the Jew.

"How! You do not dare, surely, to swallow pork?"

"A piece of ham, nevertheless," answered the Jew, "will prove highly acceptable."

Astonished at his ready acquiescence, they cut him a slice; and he received it on a biscuit, which he drew from his pocket, in order to avoid touching the meat, agreeably to his law. This increased the party's surprise. "What!" said one of them, "would you keep the ham at so respectful a distance form your fingers? How, then, will you dare to eat it?"

The Jew, without answering this question, gave the young gentlemen his thanks for their kindness; and then turned to the soldier, saying, "See there, my friend! That is for you.—Now it is in your power to say, that a Jew has feasted you on ham!" After this, directing his eyes to the youthful wits, he thus addressed them: "Gentlemen, have you not learnt compassion from Jesus and his Apostles? Thank God! I have been better instructed by Moses and the Prophets."

Pleasing Incitements to Wisdom and Virtue, conveyed through the medium of anecdote, tale, and adventure: calculated to entertain, fortify, and improve the juvenile mind. Philadephia: James Humphreys, 1800, 33–36, 68–77, 104–11.

ANONYMOUS (ca. 1818)

[Often the differences that hold us apart are skin deep, based on artificial conventions rather than on deep-seated essentials. We have natural affinities and bonds of kinship that crises may reveal. The war crisis referred to in this story was the War of 1812. It offers four women the experience of "communitas," or deep togetherness, a sort of initiation outside usual routines to a potential state of transformation. In helping one another, the four different kinds of Protestants forge bonds of enduring friendship rich in soulful sharing. The reader considering the kinship of the four "charitable sectarians" imagines that the reconciliation of their differences and their joining together in acts of kindness would please the deity whom the different women worship. Discovery of their common humanity comes as a relief, providing them with a realization of underlying unity. This story portrays broadminded sympathy as a harmonizing power. Those kept apart by differences of doctrine and denomination are sometimes brought together by the bond of sharing in service to others. The story was published in The Christian Disciple, a Unitarian newspaper.]

The Charitable Sectarians

During the late unhappy war (all wars indeed are unhappy), many families and individuals fled from the seacoast into the country, to escape the dangers which were threatened by the hovering enemy. In one of the villages but a few miles from the metropolis, four females found themselves brought together, and boarding beneath a single roof. It happened that they were all of different persuasions in religion. One was a Baptist, another an Episcopalian, a third a Unitarian, and the fourth a Congregational Calvinist. They were all, moreover, in the habit of devoting an hour after breakfast every morning to secluded religious exercises and meditations. The Episcopalian lady found simple food for her devotion in the liturgy and lessons of her church. The Baptist spent the whole hour in devout and fervent prayers, intermingled with the profoundest self-examination. The Calvinist, beside her usual act of worship, spent the remainder of the time on Scott's Bible; while the Unitarian, after repeating with the greatest earnestness and deliberation the Lord's prayer, and reading two or three chapters in the gospels, sat down to a volume of Buckminster's Sermons.

It was not until after they had lived together almost a week, that they became informed of each other's way of thinking. On the first Sabbath morning after their residence in the country, their conversation naturally turned on religious topics.

Upon the mutual disclosure of their sentiments which followed, it was very evident that the cordial familiarity and esteem they had begun to feel and express for each other, was suddenly changed into an oppressive embarrassment and reserve. They walked silently to meeting, and sustained for some days after, a suspension of their friendly conversations.

And what could there have been, that is connected with religion, which should thus counteract some of the most delightful and amiable tendencies of human nature? The most favorable answer that can be given is, the immense importance of the subject itself, which makes us abhor the slightest deviation from what we conceive to be the right on matters of eternal interest. On the other hand, the most unfavorable solution of the problem consists in the prejudices of our education, and the very narrow range to which our knowledge is confined. Perhaps the exact truth lies in both of these explanations united. The four ladies who are the subjects of our narrative, were, as we before intimated, all susceptible of pious impressions. They all considered religion the most interesting, the most momentous business of their lives. Hence, so easily do our minds associate ideas which present themselves together—so readily do we imagine that the connection is natural and unavoidable, when it is only arbitrary and accidental, they had each fallen into the almost unavoidable mistake of attaching a title of salvation to the secular forms in which they had been nursed and brought up.—The Baptist had connected all her thoughts of heaven, of holiness, and of favor in the sight of God, with the ceremony of Baptism by immersion and exclusive communion.

The Episcopalian, who had scarcely ever heard of such a practice, but who had seen the table of the Lord open to all who chose to approach it, could hardly imagine that sentiments of piety might find any way of utterance except in the established formularies of her church.

The Calvinist, who had a humble and sincere assurance of her individual election, found it impossible to believe that the Deity chooses to operate upon the heart of man in any other than one definite, unvarying mode.

And the Unitarian, while she consoled herself with more enlarged, and, as she conceived, scriptural conceptions of the Deity, was inclined to suppose that God would not regard with a favorable eye, those whose opinions of him were so opposite to her views of divine truth and divine benevolence.

Actuated by these views and feelings it is not surprising that they should experience that sudden chill which diffused itself through their intercourse for a few days after the discovery of their religious sentiments. But there is something in human nature, which God himself has given us, which rises above the petty distinctions created by our ignorance, our follies and our passions. It was not long before the Baptist found, that all those virtues and graces upon which she valued herself, as being derived from the immediate and irresistible communications of the spirit of God, were exercised and displayed in equal force by the Unitarian. It was not long before the Calvinist saw, that though the Episcopalian made no pretenses to personal election, yet she gave such evidences of her sincerity, her warm piety, her heavenly-mindedness, and in short her almost perfect and godly preparation for another world, that no speculative belief could possibly make her better. It was not long before the Episcopalian perceived how little necessary connection subsists between a form of words and the vital religion of the heart. Nor was it long ere the Deity could not be angry with misconceptions concerning his nature since the most exact ideas we can form of him here below must be infinitely short of truth and reality,

The Baptist fell sick. And what became of distinctions then? Which of the others was the most tender, the most sedulous, the most Christian then? Which made the most unwearied efforts to soothe her anxieties, to compose her mind, and to administer every comfort her situation required? And when the crisis of her disease came on, whose prayers for her restoration were most frequent and fervent, whose religious conversation was most prudent, rational, and decisive, and edifying? Ask the Baptist, who has since happily recovered. She will tell you that friend, sister, religious teacher and guide were all so united, and yet so distributed amongst the three, that she forgot her distance from home, and would not have called her minister from the charge of his flock, if it had been in her power.

The Calvinist heard of the safe return of a brother, who had been fighting the battles of his country. So ready and sincere were the congratulations of her three companions, that she experienced no alarm at feeling some of the straitest and gloomiest of her doctrines giving way within her mind. She began to wish for the possibility of their salvation; every thing conspired to raise the wish into a belief; and when at length she perceived that some higher, broader, and more liberal principle than an assent to words of man's device is the basis of the Christian character, she felt something like an oppression taken off from her heart, and knew indeed what it was to be called from darkness into marvellous light.

The Episcopalian had set a plan of charity on foot. She met from her sectarian friends all the encouragement that could stimulate her zeal. They advised with her; they assisted her both with pecuniary means, and with personal exertions. How little reflection in her did it require to perceive that every virtue and every grace did not emanate from the liturgy! Reflection? There was none required. Conviction came. She was convinced, she felt that there could be Christians, and yet—(the concession cost her heart not one sigh), not Episcopalians.

The Unitarian received tidings of the death of her father in a distant land. In the tears of her companions she saw no flaming persecution; in their sympathy she heard no uncharitable denunciations; in the consolations they offered, she had no occasion to reproach them with fundamental mistakes and narrow views. She could not help believing, that how much soever their heads retained of error, their hearts still savored of the simplicity that is in Christ.

Besides the foregoing circumstances, there was another, which had a powerful tendency to reconcile the jarring inclination and ungracious feelings which the difference of their persuasions had at first excited. It was the manifest existence of faults and foibles in them all. One of them (for we shall be too courteous to specify names here), was occasionally peevish and fretful; another was a little given to slander; a third was too provokingly caustic in her raillery; and the fourth was somewhat inclined to injurious suspicions. Now it would not have been a great exertion of good sense in each of them to become persuaded, that neither exclusive communion at the Lord's table, nor the use of the best forms of prayer, nor the belief that God is but one person, could give either of them a prerogative to indulge in any one of the above mentioned vices.—And while they mutually forgave and mutually chid each other, they acknowledged the insufficiency and arrogance of those claims which ascribed moral perfection to one form of worship rather than another; and the more they corrected their faults, the more they were loosened from their bigotry.

Who does not remember the sweet tidings of returning peace? How did all hearts rejoice, and how few felt their joy diminished by a counteracting pang! But there were a few, and among them were the four heroines, into whose religious privacy and intercourse we have now had the presumption to intrude. They will, however, forgive our interference, if any of our readers should learn a lesson from the simple narrative and simpler reflections which have been now woven for their instruction. We shall wind up our tale by only remarking, that the bitterness which these four friends experienced at parting for their respective homes, was alleviated by the sense of the mutual benefits they had received. They have kept up an occasional correspondence to this day; and while neither of them has incurred the charge of apostatizing from her particular persuasion, they still cherish, and endeavor to disseminate, as far as lies in their power, this sentiment, that, as the Deity has allowed angels of different orders and degrees to chant his praises in heaven, so he is not displeased at the sincere attempts (all of them indeed imperfect) which are made by different sects on earth, to celebrate his name.

"The Charitable Sectarians," *The Christian Disciple* 4, no.2 (1818): 40–43.

FATHER MATHEW (1790–1856)

[It is not always clear how best to help others or, even, if our interference may cause harm. Sarah Orne Jewett wrote, "There is always a hope that 'our unconscious benefactions may outweigh our unconscious cruelties,' but . . . we seldom really know how much we have to do with other people's lives." In this account by the charismatic Irish priest Father Mathew, there seems to be an unquestionable clarity about helping another. A poor woman devotes her energies to caring for an abandoned orphan; the clergyman envies her rewards for this. Father Mathew was a temperance leader who conducted a speaking tour in America from 1849 to 1851, receiving warm welcomes in New York and Washington.]

Rewards of a Poor Woman's Kindness

A poor woman found in the streets a male infant, which she brought to me, and asked imploringly what she was to do with it. Influenced, unhappily by cold caution, I advised her to give it to the church wardens. It was then evening. On the ensuing morning, early, I found this poor woman at my doors. She was a poor water-carrier. She cried bitterly, and said, "I have not slept one wink all night, for parting with that child which God had put in my way, and, if you will give me leave, I will take him back again." I was filled with confusion at the pious tenderness of this poor creature, and I went with her to the parish nurse for the infant, which she brought to her home with joy, exclaiming, in the very words of the prophet, "poor child, though my mother has forgotten thee, I will not forget thee." Eight years have elapsed since she brought to her humble home that exposed infant, and she is now blind from the constant exposure to wet and cold; and ten times a day may be seen that poor water-carrier passing with her weary load, led by this little foundling boy. O merciful Jesus, I would gladly sacrifice the wealth and power of this wide world, to secure to myself the glorious welcome that awaits this poor blind water-carrier on the great accounting day! Oh, what compared to charity like this, the ermined robe, the ivory sceptre, the golden throne, the jewelled diadem!

Charles E. Little, comp., *Historical Lights: Six Thousand Quotations from Standard Histories and Biographies*. New York: Funk & Wagnalls, 1886, qt. #781, p. 93.

CHARLES F. LUMMIS (1859–1928)

[Generosity is forced from an unnamed rich man in this local legend collected by Charles Lummis when he traveled across America in the latter part of the nineteenth century. The rich man falsely raised expectations, and needy men, requiring not empty promises but honesty, work, and bread, made him pay up, threatening him with "dancing in the air." Since philanthropy, by most definitions, is voluntary, this is the least philanthropic kind of giving. While vigilantism is never to be condoned, the story is a realistic and sad reminder that if we don't willingly do the good that we are able to do with our wealth, we may find ourselves in precarious circumstances, our contribution extorted from us.]

The Millionaire and the Miners

In 1877 a wealthy Detroiter went home from his mines in Leadville, Colorado, and told some very large stories. His exaggerated and bragging accounts led several hundred poor men to return with him to Leadville, where he glibly promised them employment. They got there only to find the camp already crowded with unemployed men dependent on the charity of the miners. Most of them were without means, and soon starvation stared them in the face. When the miners learned the situation, they made the braggart millionaire a frontier call. An impolite rope was stretched over a cedar branch, and one end discommoded his neck. "Now," said the visitors, "you fooled these men out here to starve, by your blowing. They've got no work and no way to get home. Give them fifty dollars apiece to take them back to Detroit, or you'll dance on nothing in less'n two minutes."

The millionaire was mulish and they swung him up once, twice, three times. At the third elevation he gasped surrender, and signed a check for the required amount. A trustyman galloped off toward distant Denver, and in a few days was back with the money to send the befooled Detroiters home.

Charles F. Lummis, *A Tramp Across the Continent*. New York: Scribner's Sons, 1892, 54–55.

NATHANIEL HAWTHORNE (1804–1864)

[Hawthorne was born in Salem, Massachusetts, the son of a sea captain. Growing up, Nathaniel must have imbibed the culture of New England Congregationalism. He made his living working at the Boston Custom House and then at the Salem Custom House. His novel The Scarlet Letter (1850) gained him respectability as a writer, and he went on

to write other novels and stories. His allegories are sometimes enigmatic, stimulating the reader to puzzle over questions they suggest. In the story below, children and adults treat a plaything differently, with consequences. The story raises age-old questions: Is an act philanthropic if one gives with the intention of changing the recipient, wishing him to become more like oneself? Are such motives an inevitable part of giving, since we all have a sense of selfhood? Is the ideal of selfless giving always better? Views differ. Some evangelical charity projects involve changing recipients' faith, seeking conversions to Christianity. Members of other traditions, such as Judaism, typically see this as self-centered and therefore not as altruistic as giving with no strings attached. Hawthorne's playful fable suggests that having a "common sense" simplistic view of our effects on others is not always wise, and looking at others with self-centered presuppositions does not always result in their best interests being served. If we treat others solely through the lens of our own values, wishes, and conventions, our interventions may lead to disaster. What at first sight seems like a good intention, on closer examination may involve delusions. Stories like this allow us to reflect extensively on such philanthropic issues.]

The Snow-Image: A Childish Miracle

One afternoon of a cold winter's day, when the sun shone forth with chilly brightness, after a long storm, two children asked leave of their mother to run out and play in the new-fallen snow. The elder child was a little girl, whom, because she was of a tender and modest disposition, and was thought to be very beautiful, her parents, and other people who were familiar with her, used to call Violet. But her brother was known by the style and title of Peony, on account of the ruddiness of his broad and round little phiz [meaning face], which made everybody think of sunshine and great scarlet flowers. The father of these two children, a certain Mr. Lindsey, it is important to say, was an excellent but exceedingly matter-of-fact sort of man, a dealer in hardware, and was sturdily accustomed to take what is called the common-sense view of all matters that came under his consideration. With a heart about as tender as other people's, he had a head as hard and impenetrable, and therefore, perhaps, as empty, as one of the iron pots which it was a part of his business to sell. The mother's character, on the other hand, had a strain of poetry in it, a trait of unworldly beauty,—a delicate and dewy flower, as it were, that had survived out of her imaginative youth, and still kept itself alive amid the dusty realities of matrimony and motherhood.

So, Violet and Peony, as I began with saying, besought their mother to let them run out and play in the new snow; for, though it had looked so dreary and dismal, drifting downward out of the gray sky, it had a very cheerful aspect, now that the sun was shining on it. The children dwelt in a city, and had no wider play-place than a little garden before the house, divided by a white fence from the street, and with a pear-tree and two or three plum-trees overshadowing it, and some rose-bushes just in front of the parlor-windows. The trees and shrubs, however, were now leafless, and their twigs were enveloped in the light snow, which thus made a kind of wintry foliage, with here and there a pendent icicle for the fruit.

"Yes, Violet,—yes, my little Peony," said their kind mother, "you may go out and play in the new snow."

Accordingly, the good lady bundled up her darlings in woolen jackets and wadded sacks, and put comforters round their necks, and a pair of striped gaiters on each little pair of legs, and worsted mittens on their hands, and gave them a kiss apiece, by way of a spell to keep away Jack Frost. Forth sallied the two children, with a hop-skip-and-jump, that carried them at once into the very heart of a huge snow-drift, whence Violet emerged like a snow-bunting, while little Peony floundered out with his round face in full bloom. Then what a merry time had they! To look at them, frolicking in the wintry garden, you would have thought that the dark and pitiless storm had been sent for no other purpose but to provide a new plaything for Violet and Peony; and that they themselves had been created, as the snow-birds were, to take delight only in the tempest, and in the white mantle which it spread over the earth.

At last, when they had frosted one another all over with handfuls of snow, Violet, after laughing heartily at little Peony's figure, was struck with a new idea.

"You look exactly like a snow-image, Peony," said she, "if your cheeks were not so red. And that puts me in mind! Let us make an image out of snow,—an image of a little girl,—and it shall be our sister, and shall run about and play with us all winter long. Won't it be nice?"

"Oh yes!" cried Peony, as plainly as he could speak, for he was but a little boy. "That will be nice! And mamma shall see it!"

"Yes," answered Violet; "Mamma shall see the new little girl. But she must not make her come into the warm parlor; for, you know, our little snow-sister will not love the warmth."

And forthwith the children began this great business of making a snow-image that should run about; while their mother, who was sitting at the window and overheard some of their talk, could not help smiling at the gravity with which they set about it. They really seemed to imagine that there would be no difficulty whatever in creating a live little girl out of the snow. And, to say the truth, if miracles are ever to be wrought, it will be by putting our hands to the work in precisely such a simple and undoubting frame of mind as that in which Violet and Peony now undertook to perform one, without so much as knowing that it was a miracle. So thought the mother; and thought, likewise, that the new snow, just fallen from heaven, would be excellent material to make new beings of, if it were not so very cold. She gazed at the children a moment longer, delighting to watch their little figures,—the girl, tall for her age, graceful and agile, and so delicately colored that she looked like a cheerful thought more than a physical reality; while Peony expanded in breadth rather than height, and rolled along on his short and sturdy legs as substantial as an elephant, though not quite so big. Then the mother resumed her work. What it was I forget; but she was either trimming a silken bonnet for Violet, or darning a pair of stockings for little Peony's short legs. Again, however, and again, and yet other agains, she could not help turning her head to the window to see how the children got on with their snow-image.

Indeed, it was an exceedingly pleasant sight, those bright little souls at their task! Moreover, it was really wonderful to observe how knowingly and skilfully they managed the matter. Violet assumed the chief direction, and told Peony what to do, while, with her own delicate fingers, she shaped out all the nicer parts of the snow-figure. It seemed, in fact, not so much to be made by the children, as to grow up under their hands, while they were playing and prattling about it. Their mother was quite surprised at this; and the longer she looked, the more and more surprised she grew.

"What remarkable children mine are!" thought she, smiling with a mother's pride; and, smiling at herself, too, for being so proud of them. "What other children could have made anything so like a little girl's figure out of snow at the first trial? Well; but now I must finish Peony's new frock, for his grandfather is coming to-morrow, and I want the little fellow to look handsome."

So she took up the frock, and was soon as busily at work again with her needle as the two children with their snow-image. But still, as the needle travelled hither and thither through the seams of the dress, the mother made her toil light and happy by listening to the airy voices of Violet and Peony. They kept talking to one another all the time, their tongues being quite as active as their feet and hands. Except at intervals, she could not distinctly hear what was said, but had merely a sweet impression that they were in a most loving mood, and were enjoying themselves highly, and that the business of making the snow-image went prosperously on. Now and then, however, when Violet and Peony happened to raise their voices, the words were as audible as if they had been spoken in the very parlor where the mother sat. Oh how delightfully those words echoed in her heart, even though they meant nothing so very wise or wonderful, after all!

But you must know a mother listens with her heart much more than with her ears; and thus she is often delighted with the trills of celestial music, when other people can hear nothing of the kind.

"Peony, Peony!" cried Violet to her brother, who had gone to another part of the garden, "bring me some of that fresh snow, Peony, from the very farthest corner, where we have not been trampling. I want it to shape our little snow-sister's bosom with. You know that part must be quite pure, just as it came out of the sky!"

"Here it is, Violet!" answered Peony, in his bluff tone,—but a very sweet tone, too,—as he came floundering through the half-trodden drifts. "Here is the snow for her little bosom. O Violet, how beau-ti-ful she begins to look!"

"Yes," said Violet, thoughtfully and quietly; "our snow-sister does look very lovely. I did not quite know, Peony, that we could make such a sweet little girl as this."

The mother, as she listened, thought how fit and delightful an incident it would be, if fairies, or still better, if angel-children were to come from paradise, and play invisibly with her own darlings, and help them to make their snow-image, giving it the features of celestial babyhood! Violet and Peony would not be aware of their immortal playmates,—only they would see that the image grew very beautiful while they worked at it, and would think that they themselves had done it all.

"My little girl and boy deserve such playmates, if mortal children ever did!" said the mother to herself; and then she smiled again at her own motherly pride.

Nevertheless, the idea seized upon her imagination; and, ever and anon, she took a glimpse out of the window, half dreaming that she might see the golden-haired children of paradise sporting with her own golden-haired Violet and bright-cheeked Peony.

Now, for a few moments, there was a busy and earnest, but indistinct hum of the two children's voices, as Violet and Peony wrought together with one happy consent. Violet still seemed to be the guiding spirit, while Peony acted rather as a laborer, and brought her the snow from far and near. And yet the little urchin evidently had a proper understanding of the matter, too!

"Peony, Peony!" cried Violet; for her brother was again at the other side of the garden. "Bring me those light wreaths of snow that have rested on the lower branches of the pear-tree. You can clamber on the snowdrift, Peony, and reach them easily. I must have them to make some ringlets for our snow-sister's head!"

"Here they are, Violet!" answered the little boy. "Take care you do not break them.

Well done! Well done! How pretty!"

"Does she not look sweetly?" said Violet, with a very satisfied tone; "and now we must have some little shining bits of ice, to make the brightness of her eyes. She is not finished yet. Mamma will see how very beautiful she is; but papa will say, 'Tush! nonsense!—come in out of the cold!'"

"Let us call mamma to look out," said Peony; and then he shouted lustily, "Mamma! mamma!! mamma!!! Look out, and see what a nice 'ittle girl we are making!"

The mother put down her work for an instant, and looked out of the window. But it so happened that the sun—for this was one of the shortest days of the whole year—had sunken so nearly to the edge of the world that his setting shine came obliquely into the lady's eyes. So she was dazzled, you must understand, and could not very distinctly observe what was in the garden. Still, however, through all that bright, blinding dazzle of the sun and the new snow, she beheld a small white figure in the garden, that seemed to have a wonderful deal of human likeness about it. And she saw Violet and Peony,—indeed, she looked more at them than at the image,—she saw the two children still at work; Peony bringing fresh snow, and Violet applying it to the figure as scientifically as a sculptor adds clay to his model. Indistinctly as she discerned the snow-child, the mother thought to herself that never before was there a snow-figure so cunningly made, nor ever such a dear little girl and boy to make it.

"They do everything better than other children," said she, very complacently. "No wonder they make better snow-images!"

She sat down again to her work, and made as much haste with it as possible; because twilight would soon come, and Peony's frock was not yet finished, and grandfather was expected, by railroad, pretty early in the morning. Faster and faster, therefore, went her flying fingers. The children, likewise, kept busily at work in the garden, and still the mother listened, whenever she could catch a word. She was amused to observe how their little imaginations had got mixed up with what they were doing, and carried away by it. They seemed positively to think that the snow-child would run about and play with them.

"What a nice playmate she will be for us, all winter long!" said Violet. "I hope papa will not be afraid of her giving us a cold! Sha'n't you love her dearly, Peony?"

"Oh yes!" cried Peony. "And I will hug her, and she shall sit down close by me and drink some of my warm milk!"

"Oh no, Peony!" answered Violet, with grave wisdom. "That will not do at all. Warm milk will not be wholesome for our little snow-sister. Little snow people, like her, eat nothing but icicles. No, no, Peony; we must not give her anything warm to drink!"

There was a minute or two of silence; for Peony, whose short legs were never weary, had gone on a pilgrimage again to the other side of the garden. All of a sudden, Violet cried out, loudly and joyfully,—"Look here, Peony! Come quickly! A light has been shining on her cheek out of that rose-colored cloud! And the color does not go away! Is not that beautiful!"

"Yes; it is beau-ti-ful," answered Peony, pronouncing the three syllables with deliberate accuracy. "O Violet, only look at her hair! It is all like gold!"

"Oh certainly," said Violet, with tranquility, as if it were very much a matter of course. "That color, you know, comes from the golden clouds, that we see up there in the sky. She is almost finished now. But her lips must be made very red,—redder than her cheeks. Perhaps, Peony, it will make them red if we both kiss them!"

Accordingly, the mother heard two smart little smacks, as if both her children were kissing the snow-image on its frozen mouth. But, as this did not seem to make the lips quite red enough, Violet next proposed that the snow-child should be invited to kiss Peony's scarlet cheek.

"Come, 'ittle snow-sister, kiss me!" cried Peony.

"There! she has kissed you," added Violet, "and now her lips are very red. And she blushed a little, too!"

"Oh, what a cold kiss!" cried Peony.

Just then, there came a breeze of the pure west-wind, sweeping through the garden and rattling the parlor-windows. It sounded so wintry cold, that the mother was about to tap on the window-pane with her thimbled finger, to summon the two children in, when they both cried out to her with one voice. The tone was not a tone of surprise, although they were evidently a good deal excited; it appeared rather as if they were very much rejoiced at some event that had now happened, but which they had been look-ing for, and had reckoned upon all along.

"Mamma! mamma! We have finished our little snow-sister, and she is running about the garden with us!"

"What imaginative little beings my children are!" thought the mother, putting the last few stitches into Peony's frock. "And it is strange, too that they make me almost as much a child as they themselves are! I can hardly help believing, now, that the snow-image has really come to life!"

"Dear mamma!" cried Violet, "pray look out and see what a sweet playmate we have!"

The mother, being thus entreated, could no longer delay to look forth from the window.

Figure 3.1 Portrait of Nathaniel Hawthorne

The sun was now gone out of the sky, leaving, how-ever, a rich inheritance of his brightness among those purple and golden clouds which make the sunsets of winter so magnificent. But there was not the slightest gleam or dazzle, either on the window or on the snow; so that the good lady could look all over the garden, and see everything and everybody in it. And what do you think she saw there? Violet and Peony, of course, her own two darling children. Ah, but whom or what did she see besides? Why, if you will believe me, there was a small figure of a girl, dressed all in white, with rose-tinged cheeks and ringlets of golden hue, playing about the garden with the two children! A stranger though she was, the child seemed to be on as familiar terms with Violet and Peony, and they with her, as if all the three had been playmates during the whole of their little lives. The mother thought to herself that it must certainly be the daughter of one of the neighbors, and that, seeing Violet and Peony in the garden, the child had run across the street to play with them. So this kind lady went to the door, intending to invite the little runaway into her comfortable parlor; for, now that the sunshine was withdrawn, the atmosphere, out of doors, was already growing very cold.

But, after opening the house-door, she stood an instant on the threshold, hesi-tating whether she ought to ask the child to come in, or whether she should even speak to her. Indeed, she almost doubted whether it were a real child after all, or only a light wreath of the new-fallen snow, blown hither and thither about the garden by the intensely cold west-wind. There was certainly something very singular in the aspect of the little stranger. Among all the children of the neighborhood, the lady could remember no such face, with its pure white, and delicate rose-color, and the golden ringlets tossing about the forehead and cheeks. And as for her dress, which was entirely of white, and fluttering in the breeze, it was such as no reasonable woman would put upon a little girl, when sending her out to play, in the depth of winter. It made this kind and careful mother shiver only to look at those small feet, with nothing in the world on them, except a very thin pair of white slippers. Nevertheless, airily as she was clad, the child seemed to feel not the slightest inconvenience from the cold, but danced so lightly over the snow that the tips of her toes left hardly a print in its surface; while Violet could but just keep pace with her, and Peony's short legs compelled him to lag behind.

Once, in the course of their play, the strange child placed herself between Violet and Peony, and taking a hand of each, skipped merrily forward, and they along with her. Almost immediately, however, Peony pulled away his little fist, and began to rub it as if the fingers were tingling with cold; while Violet also released herself, though with less abruptness, gravely remarking that it was better not to take hold of hands. The white-robed damsel said not a word, but danced about, just as merrily as before. If Violet and Peony did not choose to play with her, she could make just as good a playmate of the brisk and cold west-wind, which kept blowing her all about the garden, and took such liberties with her, that they seemed to have been friends for a long time. All this while, the mother stood on the threshold, wondering how a little girl could look so much like a flying snow-drift, or how a snow-drift could look so very like a little girl.

She called Violet, and whispered to her.

"Violet my darling, what is this child's name?" asked she. "Does she live near us?"

"Why, dearest mamma," answered Violet, laughing to think that her mother did not comprehend so very plain an affair, "this is our little snow-sister whom we have just been making!"

"Yes, dear mamma," cried Peony, running to his mother, and looking up simply into her face. "This is our snow-image! Is it not a nice 'ittle child?"

At this instant a flock of snow-birds came flitting through the air. As was very natural, they avoided Violet and Peony. But—and this looked strange—they flew at once to the white-robed child, fluttered eagerly about her head, alighted on her shoulders, and seemed to claim her as an old acquaintance. She, on her part, was evidently as glad to see these little birds, old Winter's grandchildren, as they were to see her, and welcomed them by holding out both her hands. Hereupon, they each and all tried to alight on her two palms and ten small fingers and thumbs, crowding one another off, with an immense fluttering of their tiny wings. One dear little bird nestled tenderly in her bosom; another put its bill to her lips. They were as joyous, all the while, and seemed as much in their element, as you may have seen them when sporting with a snow-storm.

Violet and Peony stood laughing at this pretty sight; for they enjoyed the merry time which their new playmate was having with these small-winged visitants, almost as much as if they themselves took part in it.

"Violet," said her mother, greatly perplexed, "tell me the truth, without any jest. Who is this little girl?"

"My darling mamma," answered Violet, looking seriously into her mother's face, and apparently surprised that she should need any further explanation, "I have told you truly who she is. It is our little snow-image, which Peony and I have been making. Peony will tell you so, as well as I."

"Yes, mamma," asseverated Peony, with much gravity in his crimson little phiz; "this is 'ittle snow-child. Is not she a nice one? But, mamma, her hand is, oh, so very cold!"

While mamma still hesitated what to think and what to do, the street-gate was thrown open, and the father of Violet and Peony appeared, wrapped in a pilot-cloth sack, with a fur cap drawn down over his ears, and the thickest of gloves upon his hands. Mr. Lindsey was a middle-aged man, with a weary and yet a happy look in his wind-flushed and frost-pinched face, as if he had been busy all the day long, and was glad to get back to his quiet home. His eyes brightened at the sight of his wife and children, although he could not help uttering a word or two of surprise, at finding the whole family in the open air, on so bleak a day, and after sunset too. He soon perceived the little white stranger sporting to and fro in the garden, like a dancing snow-wreath, and the flock of snow-birds fluttering about her head.

"Pray, what little girl may that be?" inquired this very sensible man. "Surely her mother must be crazy to let her go out in such bitter weather as it has been to-day, with only that flimsy white gown and those thin slippers!"

"My dear husband," said his wife, "I know no more about the little thing than you do. Some neighbor's child, I suppose. Our Violet and Peony," she added, laughing at herself for repeating so absurd a story, "insist that she is nothing but a snow-image, which they have been busy about in the garden, almost all the afternoon."

As she said this, the mother glanced her eyes toward the spot where the children's snow-image had been made. What was her surprise, on perceiving that there was not the slightest trace of so much labor!—no image at all!—no piled up heap of snow!—nothing whatever, save the prints of little footsteps around a vacant space!

"This is very strange!" said she.

"What is strange, dear mother?" asked Violet. "Dear father, do not you see how it is? This is our snow-image, which Peony and I have made, because we wanted another playmate. Did not we, Peony?"

"Yes, papa," said crimson Peony. "This be our 'ittle snow-sister. Is she not beau-ti-ful? But she gave me such a cold kiss!"

"Poh, nonsense, children!" cried their good, honest father, who, as we have already intimated, had an exceedingly common-sensible way of looking at matters. "Do not tell me of making live figures out of snow. Come, wife; this little stranger must not stay out in the bleak air a moment longer. We will bring her into the parlor; and you shall give her a supper of warm bread and milk, and make her as comfortable as you can. Meanwhile, I will inquire among the neighbors; or, if necessary, send the city-crier about the streets, to give notice of a lost child."

So saying, this honest and very kind-hearted man was going toward the little white damsel, with the best intentions in the world. But Violet and Peony, each seizing their father by the hand, earnestly besought him not to make her come in.

"Dear father," cried Violet, putting herself before him, "it is true what I have been telling you! This is our little snow-girl, and she cannot live any longer than while she breathes the cold west-wind. Do not make her come into the hot room!"

"Yes, father," shouted Peony, stamping his little foot, so mightily was he in earnest, "this be nothing but our 'ittle snow-child! She will not love the hot fire!"

"Nonsense, children, nonsense, nonsense!" cried the father, half vexed, half laughing at what he considered their foolish obstinacy. "Run into the house, this moment! It is too late to play any longer, now. I must take care of this little girl immediately, or she will catch her death-a-cold!"

"Husband! dear husband!" said his wife, in a low voice,—for she had been looking narrowly at the snow-child, and was more perplexed than ever,—"there is something very singular in all this. You will think me foolish,—but—but—may it not be that some invisible angel has been attracted by the simplicity and good faith with which our children set about their undertaking? May he not have spent an hour of his immortality in playing with those dear little souls? And so the result is what we call a miracle. No, no! Do not laugh at me; I see what a foolish thought it is!"

"My dear wife," replied the husband, laughing heartily, "you are as much a child as Violet and Peony."

And in one sense so she was, for all through life she had kept her heart full of childlike simplicity and faith, which was as pure and clear as crystal; and, looking at all matters through this transparent medium, she sometimes saw truths so profound that other people laughed at them as nonsense and absurdity.

But now kind Mr. Lindsey had entered the garden, breaking away from his two children, who still sent their shrill voices after him, beseeching him to let the snow-child stay and enjoy herself in the cold west-wind. As he approached, the snow-birds took to flight. The little white damsel, also, fled backward, shaking her head, as if to say, "Pray, do not touch me!" and roguishly, as it appeared, leading him through the deepest of the snow. Once, the good man stumbled, and floundered down upon his face, so that, gathering himself up again, with the snow sticking to his rough pilot-cloth sack, he looked as white and wintry as a snow-image of the largest size. Some of the neighbors, meanwhile, seeing him from their windows, wondered what could possess poor Mr. Lindsey to be running about his garden in pursuit of a snow-drift, which the west-wind was driving hither and thither! At length, after a vast deal of trouble, he chased the little stranger into a corner, where she could not possibly escape him. His wife had been looking on, and, it being nearly twilight, was wonder-struck to observe how the snow-child gleamed and sparkled, and how she seemed to shed a glow all round about her; and when driven into the corner, she positively glistened like a star! It was a frosty kind of brightness, too, like that of an icicle in the moonlight. The wife thought it strange that good Mr. Lindsey should see nothing remarkable in the snow-child's appearance.

"Come, you odd little thing!" cried the honest man, seizing her by the hand, "I have caught you at last, and will make you comfortable in spite of yourself. We will put a nice warm pair of worsted stockings on your frozen little feet, and you shall have a good thick shawl to wrap yourself in. Your poor white nose, I am afraid, is actually frost-bitten. But we will make it all right. Come along in."

And so, with a most benevolent smile on his sagacious visage, all purple as it was with the cold, this very well-meaning gentleman took the snow-child by the hand and led her towards the house. She followed him, droopingly and reluctant; for all the glow and sparkle was gone out of her figure; and whereas just before she had resembled a bright, frosty, star-gemmed evening, with a crimson gleam on the cold horizon, she now looked as dull and languid as a thaw. As kind Mr. Lindsey led her up the steps of the door, Violet and Peony looked into his face,—their eyes full of tears, which froze before they could run down their cheeks,—and again entreated him not to bring their snow-image into the house.

"Not bring her in!" exclaimed the kind-hearted man. "Why, you are crazy, my little Violet!—quite crazy, my small Peony! She is so cold, already, that her hand has almost frozen mine, in spite of my thick gloves. Would you have her freeze to death?"

His wife, as he came up the steps, had been taking another long, earnest, almost awe-stricken gaze at the little white stranger. She hardly knew whether it was a dream or no; but she could not help fancying that she saw the delicate print of Violet's fingers on the child's neck. It looked just as if, while Violet was shaping out the image, she had given it a gentle pat with her hand, and had neglected to smooth the impression quite away.

"After all, husband," said the mother, recurring to her idea that the angels would be as much delighted to play with Violet and Peony as she herself was,—"after all, she does look strangely like a snow-image! I do believe she is made of snow!"

A puff of the west-wind blew against the snow-child, and again she sparkled like a star.

"Snow!" repeated good Mr. Lindsey, drawing the reluctant guest over his hospitable threshold. "No wonder she looks like snow. She is half frozen, poor little thing! But a good fire will put everything to rights!"

Without further talk, and always with the same best intentions, this highly benevolent and common-sensible individual led the little white damsel—drooping, drooping, drooping, more and more out of the frosty air, and into his comfortable parlor. A Heidenberg stove, filled to the brim with intensely burning anthracite, was sending a bright gleam through the isinglass of its iron door, and causing the vase of water on its top to fume and bubble with excitement. A warm, sultry smell was diffused throughout the room. A thermometer on the wall farthest from the stove stood at eighty degrees. The parlor was hung with red curtains, and covered with a red carpet, and looked just as warm as it felt. The difference betwixt the atmosphere here and the cold, wintry twilight out of doors, was like stepping at once from Nova Zembla to the hottest part of India, or from the North Pole into an oven. Oh, this was a fine place for the little white stranger!

The common-sensible man placed the snow-child on the hearth-rug, right in front of the hissing and fuming stove.

"Now she will be comfortable!" cried Mr. Lindsey, rubbing his hands and looking about him, with the pleasantest smile you ever saw. "Make yourself at home, my child."

Sad, sad and drooping, looked the little white maiden, as she stood on the hearth-rug, with the hot blast of the stove striking through her like a pestilence. Once, she threw a glance wistfully toward the windows, and caught a glimpse, through its red curtains, of the snow-covered roofs, and the stars glimmering frostily, and all the delicious intensity of the cold night. The bleak wind rattled the window-panes, as if it were summoning her to come forth. But there stood the snow-child, drooping, before the hot stove!

But the common-sensible man saw nothing amiss.

"Come wife," said he, "let her have a pair of thick stockings and a woollen shawl or blanket directly; and tell Dora to give her some warm supper as soon as the milk boils. You, Violet and Peony, amuse your little friend. She is out of spirits, you see, at finding herself in a strange place. For my part, I will go around among the neighbors, and find out where she belongs."

The mother, meanwhile, had gone in search of the shawl and stockings; for her own view of the matter, however subtle and delicate, had given way, as it always did, to the stubborn materialism of her husband. Without heeding the remonstrances of his two children, who still kept murmuring that their little snow-sister did not love the warmth, good Mr. Lindsey took his departure, shutting the parlor-door carefully behind him. Turning up the collar of his sack over his ears, he emerged from the house, and had barely reached the street-gate, when he was recalled by the screams of Violet and Peony, and the rapping of a thimbled finger against the parlor window.

"Husband! husband!" cried his wife, showing her horror-stricken face through the window-panes. "There is no need of going for the child's parents!"

"We told you so, father!" screamed Violet and Peony, as he re-entered the parlor. "You would bring her in; and now our poor—dear-beau-ti-ful little snow-sister is thawed!"

And their own sweet little faces were already dissolved in tears; so that their father, seeing what strange things occasionally happen in this every-day world, felt not a little anxious lest his children might be going to thaw too! In the utmost perplexity, he demanded an explanation of his wife. She could only reply, that, being summoned to the parlor by the cries of Violet and Peony, she found no trace of the little white maiden, unless it were the remains of a heap of snow, which, while she was gazing at it, melted quite away upon the hearth-rug.

"And there you see all that is left of it!" added she, pointing to a pool of water in front of the stove.

"Yes, father," said Violet looking reproachfully at him, through her tears, "there is all that is left of our dear little snow-sister!"

"Naughty father!" cried Peony, stamping his foot, and—I shudder to say—shaking his little fist at the common-sensible man. "We told you how it would be! What for did you bring her in?"

And the Heidenberg stove, through the isinglass of its door, seemed to glare at good Mr. Lindsey, like a red-eyed demon, triumphing in the mischief which it had done!

This, you will observe, was one of those rare cases, which yet will occasionally happen, where common-sense finds itself at fault. The remarkable story of the snow-image, though to that sagacious class of people to whom good Mr. Lindsey belongs it may seem but a childish affair, is, nevertheless, capable of being moralized in various methods, greatly for their edification. One of its lessons, for instance, might be, that it behooves men, and especially men of benevolence, to consider well what they are about, and, before acting on their philanthropic purposes, to be quite sure that they comprehend the nature and all the relations of the business in hand. What has been established as an element of good to one being may prove absolute mischief to another; even as the warmth of the parlor was proper enough for children of flesh and blood, like Violet and Peony,—though by no means very wholesome, even for them,—but involved nothing short of annihilation to the unfortunate snow-image.

But, after all, there is no teaching anything to wise men of good Mr. Lindsey's stamp. They know everything,—oh, to be sure!—everything that has been, and everything that is, and everything that, by any future possibility, can be. And, should some phenomenon of nature or providence transcend their system, they will not recognize it, even if it come to pass under their very noses.

"Wife," said Mr. Lindsey, after a fit of silence, "see what a quantity of snow the children have brought in on their feet! It has made quite a puddle here before the stove. Pray tell Dora to bring some towels and mop it up!"

Nathaniel Hawthorne, *The Snow Image and Other Stories*, http://www.gutenberg.org/etext/513.

POEMS AND SONGS

ANONYMOUS

[In this poem, a veteran of the War for Independence wanders in his old age without the necessities that would make life enjoyable and give him dignity. The ingratitude of a nation that benefited from his sacrifice makes a haunting image of neglect and betrayal. Treating him like someone disgraced, a beggar to be shunned, is an incongruity that calls to the conscience of society, insisting on more generosity and remembrance. Prior to the War of 1812, Revolutionary War veterans were given little support; local militias were honored locally, but the Continental Army was not highly esteemed nationally. Regard for aging veterans grew along with nationalist feelings that spread among the American people after the War of 1812, and many agreed that pensions would be fair recompense. The Revolutionary War Pension Act of 1818 showed this change of attitude. Despite a scandal in 1820 regarding the program, twenty thousand Revolutionary War veterans began to receive pensions. However, not all did, including the subject of the poem below. The description of the scarred man is touching—he has been wounded by the lion of war, and as a frail survivor begging for food, he is rendered as not much better off than those wounded mortally.]

The Beggar [A Revolutionary War Veteran]

A few weeks since, a mendicant appeared in our village, pale and emaciated, and convulsed with spasmodic affections, brought on to all appearance, by an irritation of wounds received in the battles of our independence. The many and deep scars with which his skull and breast, and arms, were disfigured, evinced that the tragedy of our revolution had been to him no bloodless drama. He asked not for the means to pamper appetite. His face bespoke him an honest and temperate man. He begged only for humanity's sake, a pittance to support nature, till he could reach his few surviving friends, further North. It was an affecting sight to see an old man—a veteran of that sacred war, (in which he had lost three sons)—begging alms to aid him on the spot, where, in the wretched hovel which he could call his last prayer for his own, ungrateful country, cover his face with his tattered mantle, and die.

> And thou hast seen, thou say'st, old man,
> The Lion in his ire;
> When from his strain'd and bloodshot eye,
> Flash'd out vindictive fire.

> And thou hast heard, old man, thou say'st
> The terror of his roar,
> That echo'd mid our mountain rocks,
> and rang along the shore.

> And thou hast stood unblenchingly [unblinkingly]
> His gristly [ghastly] front before—

When carnage wav'd her dripping wing,
And drenched the earth with gore.

God help thee, father! For the world
Is pitiless and cold—
It sheltereth not the shelterless—
Revereth not the old.

Aye, it can gaze upon the front
That battle's stamp hath seal'd
And leave unfill'd the withered hand,
Too weak its blade to wield.

Why left they not thy welt'ring corpse
On Bunker's smoking steep—
When through thy brow the death-shot plough'd
That furrow broad and deep?

Or why on Yorktown's crimson plain
Didst thou not yield thy breath?
Far better, had that bloody sleep
Been the long sleep of death.

Then hadst thou bled as Warren bled,
And like Montgomery died—
Thy name been chronicled among
The heroes of our pride.

God give thee, father, words to beg—
Choking with shame—thy food;
Those scars proclaim thy country's weal—
Those rags, her gratitude.

"The Begger," *Vermont American.* Reprinted in *Texas Gazette* 1, no. 33 (July 31, 1830): 4.

ANONYMOUS (WRITING FOR EPISCOPAL CHARITY CHILDREN)

[Charitable institutions dependent on voluntary contributions will often present musical programs, plays, sermons, and other events as ways to communicate their needs and thank donors. The styles change over the centuries; what donors two centuries ago found touching might today seem overly sentimental. But the goal was the same—to raise funds and express thanks. By putting ideas and feelings about the experiences of orphans into rhythms and rhymes sung in a melody suitable for a hymn, the two composers below crystallize human experiences, eliciting sympathy and expressing triumphal joy. The celebration of compassion in ritual-like public performances is a way to expand the circle of sympathy and generosity.]

A Hymn to Be Sung at St. George's Chapel 1804

Chill'd by the blasts of adverse fate;
 Oppressed by sorrow's gloom;
The soothing voice of parent love
 All hush'd within the Tomb.

Without us, want his vigils kept;
 Within us, silent woe;
Our infant minds in fearful thought
 Made every shade a foe.

God's pitying eye our troubles saw,
 And instantly relief
Broke through the wint'ry clouds of woe,
 And scatter'd every grief.

Beneath his heavenly wings we find
 A calm and sure retreat;
O, then, let ev'ry Orphan breast
 With grateful transport beat!

Let raptur'd Angels bend to hear
 The mercies we have found;
From human woe wipe off the tear,
 And spread the joyful sound.

We thank thee Halleluiah
We bless thee Hallelujah
We praise thee, O Lord Hallelujah
Forevermore Amen.

"Hymn to be sung by the Episcopal Charity Children at St. George's Chapel," New York, Dec. 2, 1804; sermon and collection for the benefit of that benevolent institution.

ANONYMOUS

Hymn to be Sung by the Scholars of the Methodist Charity School, New York City

Blest are the hands that pity show,
 The hearts that love retain.
That calm the widow'd mother's woe,
 And soothe the Orphan's pain.

To walk in wisdom's ways delight,

And open Mercy's door;
That guide the steps of youth aright,
And save the humble poor.

May Heav'nly love, and Gospel truth,
With their Celestial rays,
Inspire the hearts of age and youth
With gratitude and praise.

Stanzas 4–6, November, 1810. Bieber Handbill Collection, Center for American History, University of Texas at Austin.

WILL CARLETON (1845–1912)

[William McKendree Carleton grew up on a Michigan farm. He wrote books of poems celebrating rural American life, such as Farm Ballads (1873) and Farm Legends (1875), and won recognition as a poet who spoke for the people of the countryside. Carleton wrote "Over the Hill to the Poor-house" just after the Civil War. At that time, poorhouses offered organized support, food, and shelter for the destitute. Typically, small towns contributed to county or regional poorhouses. The poorhouse in the poem is a cobblestone structure that still stands on the outskirts of Hillsdale, Michigan. Some say Carleton wrote this poem after talking with the elderly lady who had once owned it. This county poor farm was in existence for fifteen years when a fire in 1869 gutted the stone house, leaving only the walls. The original building was restored and used to shelter the poor until 1955. The poem's story, that of a mother spending time at her respective children's home until finally she was sent to the poor house, is poignant. Reading the poem and hearing the ballad recited in public is said to have caused a significant number of Americans to keep their elderly parents at home, diminishing the population in poorhouses for a time. Like the poems of the veteran-beggar and the orphans above, it sings with the voice of pathos. This kind of literature was meant to be a warning: provide for yourself and for others in need; those unable to will be left at the mercy of strangers.]

Over the Hill to the Poor-house

Over the hill to the poor-house I'm trudgin' my weary way—
I, a woman of seventy, and only a trifle gray—
I, who am smart an' chipper, for all the years I've told,
As many another woman that's only half as old.

O'er the hill to the poor-house—I can't quite make it clear!
Over the hill to the poor-house—it seems so horrid queer!
Many a step I've taken a-toilin' to and fro,
But this is a sort of journey I never thought to go.

What is the use of heapin' on me a pauper's shame?
Am I lazy or crazy? Am I blind or lame?

True, I am not so supple, nor yet so awful stout:
But charity ain't no favor, if one can live without.

I am willin' and anxious an' ready any day
To work for a decent livin', an' pay my honest way;
For I can earn my victuals, an' more too, I'll be bound,
If any body only is willin' to have me round.

Once I was young an' han'some—I was, upon my soul—
Once my cheeks was roses, my eyes as black as coal;
An [sic] I can't remember, in them days, of hearin' people say,
For any kind of a reason, that I was in their way.

'Tain't no use of boastin', or talkin' over free,
But many a house an' home was open then to me
Many a han'some offer I had from likely men,
And nobody ever hinted that I was a burden then.

And when to John I was married, sure he was good and smart,
But he and all the neighbors would own I done my part;
For life was all before me, an' I was young an' strong,
And I worked the best that I could in tryin' to get along.

And so we worked together; and life was hard, but gay,
With now and then a baby for to cheer us on our way;
Till we had half a dozen, an' all growed clean an' neat,
An' went to school like others, an' had enough to eat.

So we worked for the child'rn, and raised 'em every one;
Worked for 'em summer and winter, just as we ought to've done;
Only perhaps we humored 'em, which some good folks condemn.
But every couple's child'rn's a heap the best to them.

Strange how much we think of our blessed little ones!—
I'd have died for my daughters, I'd have died for my sons;
And God he made that rule of love, but when we're old and gray,
I've noticed it sometimes somehow fails to work the other way.

Strange, another thing: when our boys an' girls was grown,
And when, exceptin' Charley, they'd left us there alone;
When John he nearer an' nearer come, an' dearer seemed to be,
The Lord of Hosts he come one day an' took him away from me.

Still I was bound to struggle, an' never to cringe or fall—
Still I worked for Charley, for Charley was now my all;
And Charley was pretty good to me, with scarce a word or frown,
Till at last he went a-courtin', and brought a wife from town.

She was somewhat dressy, an' hadn't a pleasant smile—
She was quite conceity, and carried a heap o' style;
But if ever I tried to be friends, I did with her, I know;
But she was hard and proud, an' I couldn't make it go.

She had an edication, an' that was good for her;
But when she twitted me on mine, 'twas carryn' things too fur;
An' I told her once, 'fore company (an' it almost made her sick),
That I never swallowed a grammar, or 'et a 'rithmetic.

So 'twas only a few days before the thing was done—
They was a family of themselves, and I another one;
And a very little cottage one family will do,
But I never have seen a house that was big enough for two.

An' I never could speak to suit her, never could please her eye,
An' it made me independent, an' then I didn't try;
But I was terribly staggered, an' felt it like a blow,
When Charley turned ag'in me, an' told me I could go.

I went to live with Susan, but Susan's house was small,
And she was always a-hintin' how snug it was for us all;
And what with her husband's sisters, and what with child'rn three,
'Twas easy to discover that there wasn't room for me.

An' then I went to Thomas, the oldest son I've got,
For Thomas' buildings'd cover the half of an acre lot;
But all the child'rn was on me—I couldn't stand their sauce—
And Thomas said I needn't think I was comin' there to boss.

And then I wrote to Rebecca, my girl who lives out West,
And to Isaac, not far from her—some twenty miles at best;
And one of 'em said 'twas too warm there for anyone so old,
And t'other had an opinion the climate was too cold.

So they have shirked and slighted me, an' shifted me about—
So they have well-nigh soured me, an' wore my old heart out;
But still I've born up pretty well, an' wasn't much put down,
Till Charley went to the poor-master, an' put me on the town.

Over the hill to the poor-house—me child'rn dear, good-by [sic]!
Many a night I've watched you when only God was nigh;
And God'll judge between us; but I will al'ays pray
That you shall never suffer the half I do to-day.

county.info/ history0053.asp.

ANONYMOUS

[This handbill, distributed to potential patrons by a child soliciting donations for her blind father and her family, is a plea for sympathy and aid. The poem's personal terms and artful rhymes tug at the heartstrings. The story, printed on a single sheet, saved the child from repeating the story many times over each day; as well, it was offered as a souvenir or token of appreciation for contributions of small change, making the encounter more of a two-way exchange. Today we sometimes encounter on city streets individuals with hearing loss or other disabilities, giving passersby a card illustrating hand signals used by the deaf and soliciting aid. Some argue there is give and take in all philanthropy—the giver might gain public respect, self-esteem, and sometimes a token.]

Helping Father

Kind friend, my father's blind,
And has been, oh so long!
And I know you will not mind,
To buy my little song.

My song is not so very long
That you will tire before you read it.
And I hope it won't be wrong to buy,
Although you do not need it.

I try to sell it all day long,
From one place to another,
But I don't mind it much you know,
Because I'm helping father.

I have a little brother too,
The sweetest little darling,
With rosy cheeks and bright brown eyes
And hair that's always curling.

I'd like to stay at home with him,
My darling little brother,
But then I can't do that you know,
For I want to help my father.

So now kind friend, please buy my song,
And thus you'll help another,
And I know you'll never regret
Helping poor blind father.

PRICE—Anything you choose to give.

Card (with "Beggar's Poem" written in pencil above title), undated, likely early nineteenth century or later. Barker Collection, Center for American History, University of Texas at Austin.

A. W. HARMON (19th century)

[A. W. Harmon was a poet living in Maine whose work was published in broadsides. Author of topical pieces such as the lyrics to "The Granite Mill Fire at Fall River, Massachusetts" (sung to the tune of the popular ballad "Young Edmond"), Harmon penned the following poem and likely knew well the person it describes. Distributed by the disabled man to potential donors, these verses record the former blacksmith's plea for sympathy and contributions, making an appeal to the New Testament injunction to give to those in need. The poem's ending promises rewards both in this life and in the hereafter (on the other "shore") to those who befriend the needy. The promise of blessings combines with the sympathy evoked by the description of the blind man's brighter past and glum present.]

Pity the Sorrowful

"Concerning his sickness, caused by lifting, which injured his spine, affecting his head and eye-sight badly, confining him to his bed and a dark room for three years."

> Good people all, I pray draw near
> Attend a while and you shall hear
> What pain and anguish seized my head,
> And threw me down on a sick bed—
>
> Affecting thus my eye-sight bad,
> And causing me to feel quite sad,
> Shut up in a dark room, and I
> Could not behold the earth or sky.
>
> While others could their friends behold
> And travel round from pole to pole,
> Enjoy themselves from day to day,
> In a dark room I had to lay.
>
> I cannot see as others see,
> One thing appears like two to me;
> Had I ten thousand, with delight
> I'd give it all for health and sight.
>
> Engaged at Blacksmith's work was I,
> With eager hopes and spirits high,
> Hopes master of my trade to be,
> But ah how soon my hopes did flee.
>
> And I grew sick and had to leave,
> Could work no more which did me grieve.
> My spine was injured, and my sight

Grew dimmer thro' from morn to night.

Dreary and lonesome every day,
Distress and anguish on me lay,
One glimmering hope was left me still,
In life some place I yet should fill.

Was to my bed three years confined
With inflammation on my spine,
Ah who my feelings can relate,
Or thus imagine my sad fate.

Six months in a dark room I lay,
My strength was wasting fast away,
Knew nothing what was going on,
My intellectual powers were gone.

Distress and anguish filled my breast,
I could obtain but little rest.
Affected badly was my sight,
Yet hope from me too not her flight.

Better to give than to withhold,
We in the Bible so are told—
God loves the giver, the free man
Who helps the needy when he can.

Come you that do these verses read,
Come be a friend in time of need.
And God will bless you evermore,
And fill your basket and your shore.

~~~~~~

Handbill, 1800–1819. Barker collection, Center for American History, University of Texas at Austin.

HENRY WADSWORTH LONGFELLOW (1807–1882)

[Born in Portland, Maine, educated at Bowdoin College, and appointed to a professorship at Harvard University, Longfellow was one of the most popular and prolific poets of the nineteenth century. This poet, linguist, and educator contributed significantly to the cultural flowering of New England during the time leading up to the end of the Civil War. The influential Unitarian thinker William Ellery Channing wrote of Longfellow, "he did not belong to any one sect but rather to the community of those free minds who loved the truth." Longfellow wrote that "We often excuse our own want of philanthropy by giving the name of fanaticism to the more ardent zeal of others," and he advised, "Give what you have. To someone it may be better than you dare to think." He wrote the following poem on the topic of our unfinished business. The good we humans

could do but do not, is imagined here as something waiting. Lost opportunities dog the conscience and eventually overshadow us. The poem urges us to exert ourselves in our endeavors and reminds us that the fundamental task of helping to mend the world is never done.]

Something Left Undone

Labor with what zeal we will,
Something still remains undone,
Something uncompleted still
Waits the rising of the sun.

By the bedside, on the stair,
At the threshhold, near the gates,
With its menace or its prayer,
Like a medicant it waits;

Waits, and will not go away;
Waits, and will not be gainsaid;
By the cares of yesterday
Each to-day is heavier made;

Till at length the burden seems
Greater than our strength can bear,
Heavy as the weight of dreams
Pressing on us everywhere.

And we stand from day to day,
Like the dwarfs of times gone by,
Who, as Northern legends say,
On their shoulders held the sky.

~~~~~~

Henry Wadsworth Longfellow, "Something Left Undone," http://www.hwlongfellow.org/poems_poem.php?pid=57.

TECUMSEH (1768–1813)

[Tecumseh's contemporaries considered him unique in wisdom and noble spirit. "He who attracted most my attention was a Shawnee chief, Tecumseh—a more sagacious or a more gallant warrior does not I believe exist. He was the admiration of everyone who conversed with him," wrote a contemporary, British major general Sir Isaac Brock. Later generations of Native Americans find in him an inspiring image of dignity, expressing ideals of self-help and fierce determination. Tecumseh's magnanimity, the generosity of his great spirit, was a gift to generations of Native Americans and others who revere his heartening memory to this day. To give respect to all, to abuse no one and no thing are philanthropic acts. (Similarly, Muslims believe that not harming others is a form of philanthropy.)]

Tecumseh's Death Song

So live your life that the fear of death can never enter your heart. Trouble no one about their religion; respect others in their view, and demand that they respect yours. Love your life, perfect your life, beautify all things in your life. Seek to make your life long and its purpose in the service of your people. Prepare a noble death song for the day when you go over the great divide. Always give a word or a sign of salute when meeting or passing a friend, even a stranger, when in a lonely place. Show respect to all people and grovel to none. When you arise in the morning give thanks for the food and for the joy of living. If you see no reason for giving thanks, the fault lies only in yourself. Abuse no one and no thing, for abuse turns the wise ones to fools and robs the spirit of its vision. When it comes your time to die, be not like those whose hearts are filled with the fear of death, so that when their time comes they weep and pray for a little more time to live their lives over again in a different way. Sing your death song and die like a hero going home.

"Chief Tecumseh," http://www.indigenouspeople.net/tecumseh.htm.

WALT WHITMAN (1819–1892)

[Whitman was born on Long Island and moved to Brooklyn at age four. He read widely and was intrigued by Emerson's essays. His notebooks show he experimented with a new kind of poetry to convey an unrestrained sense of selfhood. Bringing a distinctive voice to American poetry, a voice that eventually became accepted as expressing a quintessentially American outlook, Whitman reflected the largeness and diversity of the country and its people. He had an expansive imagination, a generosity of spirit illustrated by nursing and giving gifts to the wounded of the Civil War, and a wisdom reflecting his experiences of bustling, burgeoning nineteenth-century America but leavened by other cultures as well. He had a rare ability to speak honestly, with an unfettered original American voice mirroring the world. Whitman expresses his esteem for the gift of poetic vision, which opens others' eyes to the wonders of existence. His statement that charity and personal force are the only investments worth anything was backed up by his own life of serving. His soulful, candidly sung life was an example of giving, sharing, and appreciating life in America. Whitman was not only a New World poet but also a kind of American prophet. Philosopher Jacob Needleman observed, "Our idea of equality, Whitman tells us, is a trace, an echo of the ancient doctrine of inner transcendence that was brought to the world by the teachings of wisdom, Jesus no less than Buddha or the sages and saints of India and China."]

Love and Give

This is what you shall do: Love the earth and sun and the animals, despise riches, give alms to every one that asks, stand up for the stupid and crazy, devote your income and labor to others, hate tyrants, argue not concerning God, have patience and indulgence toward the people, take off your hat to nothing known or unknown or to any man or number of men, go freely with powerful uneducated persons and with the young and with the mothers of families, read these leaves in the open air every season of every year of your life, re-examine all you have been told at school or church or in any book, dismiss whatever insults your own soul; and your very flesh shall be a great poem and have the richest fluency not only in its words but in the silent lines of its lips and face and between the lashes of your eyes and in every motion and joint of your body.

Walt Whitman, preface to *Leaves of Grass*. New York: Library of America, 1993, 11.

To Rich Givers

WHAT you give me, I cheerfully accept,
    A little sustenance, a hut and garden, a little money—these, as I rendezvous with my poems;
    A traveler's lodging and breakfast as I journey through The States—Why should I be ashamed to own such gifts? Why to advertise for them?
    For I myself am not one who bestows nothing upon man and woman;
    For I bestow upon any man or woman the entrance to all the gifts of the universe.

Walt Whitman, *Leaves of Grass*. Philadelphia: David McKay, 1900, 181.

MABEL DOWN (NORTHAM) BRINE (1816–1913)

[Brine was an author of children's literature. Her poem "Somebody's Mother," written in 1878, suggests that we should think of others as being like ourselves, of the same human family. The mother is each child's first love and friend, helper, playmate, and soul mate. Expanding the feelings of gratitude and love for our parents, we can care for the welfare of others in the world; by reflecting on our own experiences of wishing our loved ones to have necessities and comforts, we expand our empathy to the welfare of others. Brine's simple poem, which seeks to open an embracive vision that awakens kindness and helpfulness, was memorized by grade-school students for classroom recitation. It is an example of a kind of inspirational literature aimed at refining sensibilities, which has played a significant role in cultivating the compassion that often inspires philanthropic activities in America and in the rest of the world. The poem ends on a note of mutual fulfillment, in reciprocal good will.]

Somebody's Mother

The woman was old and ragged and gray
And bent with the chill of the Winter's day.

The street was wet with a recent snow
And the woman's feet were aged and slow.

She stood at the crossing and waited long,
Alone, uncared for, amid the throng

Of human beings who passed her by
Nor heeded the glance of her anxious eyes.

Down the street, with laughter and shout,
Glad in the freedom of "school let out,"

Came the boys like a flock of sheep,
Hailing the snow piled white and deep.

Past the woman so old and gray
Hastened the children on their way.

Nor offered a helping hand to her—
So meek, so timid, afraid to stir

Lest the carriage wheels or the horses' feet
Should crowd her down in the slippery street.

At last came one of the merry troop,
The gayest laddie of all the group:

He paused beside her and whispered low,
"I'll help you cross, if you wish to go."

Her aged hand on his strong young arm
She placed, and so, without hurt or harm,

He guided the trembling feet along,
Proud that his own were firm and strong.

Then back again to his friends he went,
His young heart happy and well content.

"She's somebody's mother, boys, you know,
For all she's aged and poor and slow.

"And I hope some fellow will lend a hand
To help my mother, you understand,

"If ever she's poor and old and gray,
When her own dear boy is far away."

And "somebody's mother" bowed low her head
In her home that night, and the prayer she said

Was "God be kind to the noble boy,
Who is somebody's son, and pride and joy!"

Mabel Down (Northam) Brine, "Somebody's Mother," www.theotherpages.org/poems/brine01.html.

JAMES RUSSELL LOWELL (1819–1891)

[Born in Cambridge, Massachusetts, Lowell, the son of a Unitarian minister, enjoyed a childhood close to nature. After graduating from Harvard in 1838, he began writing poetry while studying law and became known as one of the five "Fireside Poets." Maria White Lowell, his wife, was also a poet, and both were outspoken abolitionists. The poem below was one of the writings that kept alive in nineteenth-century America the romance and sublime ideals of the Knights of the Round Table. It was one of his most popular poems, reprinted many times. Lowell in these passages brings out the legend's Christian roots. The verses refer to the teaching of Jesus: "Who feeds the least of these feeds me." To meditate

and act upon the meaning of that teaching is a pursuit of deepening spiritual wisdom; the religious idea is that in serving fellow human beings, one serves the spirit that informs and unites all. The quest for the grail was a prime old-world archetype, and themes of nobility, self-sacrifice, and rescuing those in distress continue to be associated with this story.]

The Vision of Sir Launfal

VII

As Sir Launfal mused with a downcast face,
A light shone round about the place;
The leper no longer crouched at his side,
But stood before him glorified,
Shining and tall and fair and straight
As the pillar that stood by the Beautiful Gate,—
Himself the Gate whereby men can
Enter the temple of God in Man.

Figure 3.2 Portrait of James Russell Lowell

VIII

His words were shed softer than leaves from the pine,
And they fell on Sir Launfal as snows on the brine,
That mingle their softness and quiet in one
With the shaggy unrest they float down upon;
And the voice that was softer than silence said,
"Lo, it is I, be not afraid!
In many climes, without avail,
Thou hast spent thy life for the Holy Grail;
Behold, it is here,—this cup which thou
Didst fill at the streamlet for me but now;
This crust is my body broken for thee;
This water his blood that died on the tree;
The Holy Supper is kept, indeed,
In whatso we share with another's need,—
Not what we give, but what we share,—
For the gift without the giver is bare;
Who gives himself with his alms feeds three,—
Himself, his hungering neighbor, and me."

James Russell Lowell, "The Vision of Sir Launfal," *The Poetical Works of James Russell Lowell.* Boston: Houghton Mifflin, 1978, 108–11, vs. 301–27. Also available online at http://www.gutenberg.org/files/17948/17948-8.txt.

AMBROSE BIERCE (1842–1914)

[Bierce was an editorial writer and satirist, a rhymester and short-story writer. He worked as a journalist in San Francisco and Washington, D.C., and disappeared in Mexico in December 1913, never to be heard from again. His sarcasm and ever-ready criticism earned him

the nickname "Bitter Bierce." The piece below is a humorous poem about a bequest. It lampoons a trickster figure, a man who was generous to himself as the most deserving because of an odd stipulation in a rich philanthropist's will. America seems to have more than her share of con men, and it is easy to imagine the modern trickster figure in his three-piece suit as an incarnation of Coyote or another traditional trickster. Bierce satirizes gifts left in wills, the attempt to create impressions of virtue, even lawyers and judges, leaving us with an amusing if cynical example of someone who believes it is better to receive than to give.]

The Legatee

In fair San Francisco a good man did dwell,
And he wrote out a will, for he didn't feel well.
Said he: "It is proper, when making a gift,
To stimulate virtue by comforting thrift."

So he left all his property, legal and straight,
To "the cursedest rascal in all of the State."
But the name he refused to insert, for, said he:
"Let each man consider himself legatee."

In due course of time that philanthropist died,
And all San Francisco, and Oakland beside—
Save only the lawyers—came each with his claim,
The lawyers preferring to manage the same.

The cases were tried in Department Thirteen,
Judge Murphy presided, sedate and serene,
But couldn't quite specify, legal and straight,
The cursedest rascal in all of the State.

And so he remarked to them, little and big—
To claimants: "You skip!" and to lawyers: "You dig!"
They tumbled, tumultuous, out of his court
And left him victorious, holding the fort.

'Twas then that he said: "It is plain to my mind
This property's ownerless—how can I find
The cursedest rascal in all of the State?"
So he took it himself, which was legal and straight.

Ambrose Bierce, "The Legatee," http://www.theotherpages.org/poems/bierce01.html.

THOMAS BAILEY ALDRICH (1836–1907)

[Aldrich was a prolific writer, born in Portsmouth, New Hampshire, to parents from old New England families. He worked as an editor at several major New York and Boston

magazines, including the Atlantic Monthly. His stories and poems won a wide audience, and his novels and memoirs also enjoyed popularity. His Story of a Bad Boy, said to be the first realistic narrative treatment of an American boy in literature, helped inspire Mark Twain to write Tom Sawyer. His pithy poem below holds a truth about being the best kind of host. Hospitality involves the generosity of extending a warm welcome, which makes the guest feel at home, not as an other, but as a family member.]

Hospitality

When friends are at your hearthside met,
Sweet courtesy has done its most
If you made each guest forget
That he himself is not the host.

Thomas Bailey Aldrich, "Hospitality," *Poems*. New York: AMS Press, 1970 (reprinted from 1907 edition, Houghton Mifflin), 200.

EMMA LAZARUS (1849–1887)

[Emma Lazarus, a Jewish-American poet who was a passionate defender of Russian immigrant rights and protester against anti-Semitism, penned what is probably the most famous written depiction of Liberty. Her poem about the spirit of America as represented in the Statue of Liberty dramatically conveys a vision of welcome and refuge. This colossus is not like the famous Greek colossus statue of Rhodes depicting the wide strides of a huge conqueror but is a "mighty woman with a torch, whose flame is the imprisoned lightning," a power of the skies held fast and ready for use. And in this poem, Liberty's name is "Mother of Exiles," and the glowing torch offers a worldwide awakening to understanding a new world of life's possibilities. The Liberty goddess envisioned in this poem is said to be uninterested in the old world but rather asks for tired, poor, huddled masses yearning to breathe more freely, the "wretched refuse" of crowded distant shores, homeless seekers of home. Sixteen years after Lazarus' death, a plaque inscribed with her poem celebrating America's generous love of humanity was affixed to the pedestal of the statue, where it remains today.]

The New Colossus

Not like the brazen giant of Greek fame,
With conquering limbs astride from land to land;
Here at our sea-washed, sunset gates shall stand
A mighty woman with a torch, whose flame
Is the imprisoned lightning, and her name
Mother of Exiles. From her beacon-hand
Glows world-wide welcome; her mild eyes command
The air-bridged harbor that twin cities frame.
"Keep ancient lands, your storied pomp!" cries she
With silent lips. "Give me your tired, your poor,
Your huddled masses yearning to breathe free,

Figure 3.3 Statue of Liberty

The wretched refuse of your teeming shore.
Send these, the homeless, tempest-tost to me,
I lift my lamp beside the golden door!"

Emma Lazarus, "The New Colossus," at the Statue of Liberty National Monument, http://www.libertystatepark.com/emma.htm.

WORDS OF WISDOM

AMERICAN PROVERBS

[Proverbs distill insights and observations that are sometimes valid for centuries. How do they begin and spread? Memorable ideas that are well said oft become self-perpetuating memes. A vivid image or catchy rhyme, even a half rhyme, helps an observation endure. Proverbs are worthy of contemplation because they are condensed wisdom. They are found in everyday speech, spoken by grandparents and mentors, critics and cultural commentators. Some proverbs crossed borders, entering the English language from other cultures; all the below were commonly heard in 1800s America.]

A beggar is never out of his road.

A beggar's empty wallet is heavier than a full one.

A beggar's purse is bottomless.

A day without bread is a long day indeed.

A forced kindness deserves no thanks.

A friend in need is a friend indeed.

A little help is better than a lot of pity.

Beggars can never be bankrupt.

Beggars can't be choosers.

Charity begins at home.

Charity is a virtue of the heart and not of the hand.

Charity is its own reward.

Charity's not a bone you throw your dog

> but a bone you share with your dog.

Each day provides its own gifts.

Heaven helps those who help themselves.

If you can't help, at least don't hinder.

It's an easy matter for a stingy man to get rich, but what's the use?

It's better to tell your money where to go than to ask where it went.

Let him who gives nothing be silent, and him who receives speak.

Never bite the hand that feeds you.

No good deed goes unpunished.

The Lord loves a cheerful giver.

The reason some people are stingy is also the reason they are rich.

'Tis better to give than to receive.

True generosity is the ability to give without thought of reward.

You only take with you what you gave away.

Collected by the author/editor from various sources including dictionaries, journals, essays, newspapers, and the Internet.

NEWSPAPER BRIEFS ON CHARITY from the 1800s

[These brief reflections about charity indicate that editors of nineteenth-century American newspapers knew their audiences were keenly interested in the topic. Some points are practical, some philosophical, some poetic, and some about specific religious doctrines, but all reveal something about how people thought about giving and caring in the nineteenth century. Most of these examples show that Americans in the 1800s saw charity as a universal value, rather than viewing it from a narrow sectarian angle. As Mark Twain is supposed to have said: "If we should deal out justice only, in this world, who would escape? No, it is better to be generous, and in the end more profitable, for it gains gratitude for us, and love."]

Charity

As an important object of this highly respectable association is not generally known, we beg leave to call the attention of our readers, to the piece, in this day's paper, over the signature of "Benevolus."—Charity is twice blest—it blesses him that gives, and him that receives.

Boston Gazette 12, no. 25 (May 27, 1802): 3.

Pars beneficii est, quod petitur, si cito neges. Syrus
"It is something like kindness immediately to refuse, what it is intended to deny."—It is charity not to excite a hope, when it must end in disappointment.

Boston Gazette 35, no. 44 (November 25, 1811): 4.

It was a common saying of Julius Caesar, "that no music was so charming in his ears as the requests of his friends, and the supplication of those in want of his assistance."

It would be well for many who profess to be Christians, did they imitate more closely this pagan.

Boston Gazette 47, no. 26 (March 17, 1817): 4.

There is an assertion, affirmed by a writer of great celebrity, to the infinite honor of the lower orders of society, viz. That *all* which the RICH give to the poor in private beneficence is but a *mite* and a *trifle* when compared with what the POOR GIVE TO ONE ANOTHER.

Boston Commercial Gazette 50, no. 25 (September 10, 1818): 2.

An Inscription over a calm and clear Spring in Blenheim Gardens:

> Charity
> Here quench your thirst, and mark in me
> An emblem of true Charity;
> Who while my bounty I bestow,
> Am neither seen, or heard, to flow:
> Yet ever full, supplied from heaven,
> For every cup of water given. TW 1818

Boston Gazette 49, no. 16 (February 9, 1818): 4.

Moral Charity

To give what you scarcely know how to apply, can hardly be called an exercise of that charity, "which seeketh not her own." It is by the sacrifice of our pleasures, or by the imitation of our desires and accustomed comforts that we fulfill the two injunctions of letting our moderation be known to all men," and of "doing to others as we would they should do unto us."

Boston Commercial Gazette 52, no. 11 (July 22, 1819): 4.

Private Charity

A man was accused of being niggardly, and never bestowing anything in charity. His friend undertook to defend his character, by saying, that his alms deeds were done in private, not pharisaically; and concluded, as follows: what he gives, he gives: and that is nothing to anybody.

Boston Commercial Gazette 52, no. 16 (August 9, 1819): 1.

Selected Verses

> Give me the cheek which, red or pale,
> Proclaims Compassion near,
> Which melts with sorrow's bitter tale,
> And sheds the heavenly tear.
>
> Not the light, foolish face, which shines
> In pleasure's brightest hour,

But in adversity would pine,
Under affliction's power. . . .

But may the partner of my choice
All melting kindness be,
A sprightly form, a soothing voice,
Employ'd in Charity.

Arkansas Gazette 1, no. 24 (March 29, 1820): 4.

The Just

Ten thousand charities exist; but the just is that which consists in a sober care for the virtues as well as the wants of men. That gives just enough to encourage industry. That supplies a whole life, by being ready at the time of need; and that encourages and respects economy, when the happiness of life requires it.—This charity blows no trumpet, rings no bells, and forms no association but for its instant occasions. The warm blood of life flows. All rise to their full duty, and the poor are caught before they fall.

Boston Commercial Gazette 53, no. 6 (January 3, 1820): 4.

On Pauperism and Poor Houses

The real causes of pauperism are the want of employment, incapacity of body or mind to labor, native indolence, and the excessive indulgence of the stronger appetites and inclinations. None of these are aided or strengthened, in the remotest degree, by any considerations that may be suggested by Christian institutions. The two first we all know, are not; they exist through necessity and cannot be altered by any such devices. The other causes do not operate to any great extent.

Cincinnati Inquirer, 1821.

Turkish Charity

The fourth commandment of the Koran is that every believer shall give the fortieth part of his income to his poor relations, if he has any, if not, to his poor neighbors. So well is this commandment observed that beggars are very rare in Turkey. They extend their charity to the animal creation. They have often been known to buy birds in the market and set them at liberty under the beautiful superstition that the souls of those birds will one day bear witness to their kindness before the throne of God. This is almost equal to the affecting superstition of the Afghans who burn incense and spread flowers over the sepulchre, believing that the spirits of the departed sit each at the head of his own grave enjoying the fragrance of the incense and perfume. . . . The fourth chapter of the Koran contains the following injunctions: "Shew kindness to thy parents, to thy relations, to orphans, to the poor, to thy neighbor who is a relative to thee, and to thy neighbor who is a stranger to thee; to thy familiar companion, to the traveller, and to the captive whom thy right hand has taken; for God loveth not the proud, the vain-glorious, the covetous, or those who bestow their wealth in order to be seen of men." In compliance with the spirit of these injunctions, the Turks voluntarily repair the roads, make cisterns for the comfort of the traveller, and the most devout amongst them erect sheds by the wayside, beneath whose shade the way-faring man may rest. And yet these men are savage *barbarians*, and the whole world cheers the amiable Russians in their march of rapacity, extortion and plunder!

Vermont Gazette 19, no. 36 (August 19, 1828): 1.

On Charity

Charity does not consist in creeds of strict or liberal import; but in the temper of heart with which they are adopted, and propagated. Dr. Beecher.

Baltimore Patriot 33, no. 149 (June 22, 1829): 2.

Charity, the vital principle of religion, is often the most absent member of the church.

Baltimore Patriot 36, no. 1 (July 1, 1830): 2.

A Religious Life

The beauty of a religious life is one of its greatest recommendations. What does it profess? Peace to all mankind—It teaches us those arts which will render us beloved and respected, which will contribute to our present comfort as well as our future happiness. Its great ornament is charity—it inculcates nothing but love and simplicity of affection; it breathes nothing but the purest spirit of delight—in short it is a system perfectly calculated to benefit the heart, improve the mind, and enlighten the understanding. This is religion, pure and undefiled—pure from bigotry, and undefiled by hypocrisy.

Vermont Gazette 49, no. 2510 (September 13, 1831): 1.

Charity the Best Fruit of Faith

Contempt and want are easy to be borne; but who can bear respect and abundance.

A wide extended charity is the best fruit that faith can produce on earth.

Farmer's Cabinet 34, no. 45 (July 8, 1836): 1.

The Compass

Charity and faith make up one perfect pair of compasses, that can take the true latitude of a Christian heart; faith is the one foot, pitched in the centre immoveable; while charity walks about in a perfect circle of beneficence; these two never did, never can go asunder. Warrant me your love. I dare warrant your faith. Bishop Hall.

Farmer's Cabinet 50, no. 1 (August 13, 1851): 1.

Charity

Whether we name thee charity, or love,
Chief grace below, and all-in-all above . . .

Who seeks to praise thee, and to make thee known
To other hearts, must have thee in his own. 1863

Farmer's Cabinet 61, no. 50 (July 9, 1863): 1.

Give and it shall be given unto you; your charity should seek the poor before the poor seek your charity.

Farmer's Cabinet 58, no. 2 (August 10, 1859): 1.

The charities unpublished on earth are the brightest pages written down by the Recording Angel above.

Farmer's Cabinet 66, no. 35 (March 19, 1868): 1.

The Gospel an Impulsive and Universal Benevolence

The Gospel is a constraining power, and the sympathies which it awakens are co-extensive with the wants and woes of a suffering race. To do good to all men, is the distinguishing and the necessary feature of the religion which emanates from the bosom of Infinite Love; and I hazard nothing in saying, that the instance remains to be found, where the soul that has truly submitted to the power of the cross, has not been impelled to seek, in some particular form, the well-being of others. No community ever received the Gospel savingly, that has not gone forth in its sympathies and its efforts to administer to the great world beyond itself. . . .

Farmer's Cabinet 67, no. 14 (October 22, 1868): 1.

Further Thoughts on Charity

Charity does not study fashion in her methods; but let her come in whatever awkward guise she may, she is always beautiful.

Farmer's Cabinet 72, no. 25 (December 31, 1873): 1.

Truth is the ground of science, the scale to charity, the type of eternity, and the fountain of grace.

Farmer's Cabinet 75, no. 41 (March 17, 1877): 1.

A good man will be doing good wheresoever he is. His trade is a compound of charity and justice.

Farmer's Cabinet, no. 13 (October 2, 1877): 1. [Farmer's Cabinet was published in New Hampshire 1802–1879.]

Charity ever finds in the act reward, and needs no trumpet in the receiver.

Farmer's Gazette 77, no. 7 (August 20, 1878): 1.

ACCOUNTS OF AMERICAN GENEROSITY
AND COOPERATION

ALEXIS DE TOCQUEVILLE (1805–1859)

[Born to an aristocratic Norman family, Tocqueville studied law in Paris, and in 1831–1832, as a young researcher visiting America's prison system, he wrote of the patterns he saw emerging here in the early nineteenth century. Many American attitudes and behaviors that he characterized are as true today as they were almost two centuries ago. He famously noted the spirit of American volunteerism: "If an accident happens on the highway, everybody hastens to help the sufferer . . . If some great and sudden calamity befalls a family, the purses of a thousand strangers are at once willingly opened and small but numerous donations pour in to relieve their distress" (Democracy in America, pt. 2, bk. 3, chap. 4). Rather than being swayed by rhetorical idealism about virtue and self-sacrifice, Tocqueville's Americans see private advantage coinciding with general interest—each one who helps at a barn raising finds the whole town advancing in prosperity. They do good to others not because they are holy angelic people, but because it's the smart thing to do; each gains from the good he or she does. Tocqueville's observation of Americans reaching out, acting as integral parts of a society, is familiar to us today. We live in more complicated times, sometimes disconnected from this sense of belonging and the need for pitching in. We may not notice the person with a flat tire as we race by, talking on a cell phone and running late. But every generation has people who rise to the task, keeping the American ideal alive.]

How the Americans Combat Individualism by the Principle
of Self-interest Rightly Understood

When the world was managed by a few rich and powerful individuals, these persons loved to entertain a lofty idea of the duties of man. They were fond of professing that it is praiseworthy to forget oneself and that good should be done without hope of reward, as it is by the Deity himself. Such were the standard opinions of that time in morals.

I doubt whether men were more virtuous in aristocratic ages than in others, but they were incessantly talking of the beauties of virtue, and its utility was only studied in secret. But since the imagination takes less lofty flights, and every man's thoughts are centered in himself, moralists are alarmed by this idea of self-sacrifice and they no longer venture to present it to the human mind.

They therefore content themselves with inquiring whether the personal advantage of each member of the community does not consist in working for the good of all; and when they have hit upon some point on which private interest and public interest meet and amalgamate, they are eager to bring it into notice. Observations of this kind are gradually multiplied; what was only a single remark becomes a general principle, and it is held as a truth that man serves himself in serving his fellow creatures and that his private interest is to do good.

I have already shown, in several parts of this work, by what means the inhabitants of the United States almost always manage to combine their own advantage with that of their fellow citizens; my present purpose is to point out the general rule that enables them to do so. In the United States hardly anybody talks of the beauty of virtue, but they maintain that virtue is useful and prove it every day. The American moralists do not profess that men ought to sacrifice themselves for their fellow creatures because it is noble to make such sacrifices, but they boldly aver that such sacrifices are as necessary to him who imposes them upon himself as to him for whose sake they are made.

They have found out that, in their country and their age, man is brought home to himself by an irresistible force; and, losing all hope of stopping that force, they turn all their thoughts to the direction of it. They therefore do not deny that every man may follow his own interest, but they endeavor to prove that it is the interest of every man to be virtuous. I shall not here enter into the reasons they allege, which would divert me from my subject; suffice it to say that they have convinced their fellow countrymen.

Montaigne said long ago: "Were I not to follow the straight road for its straightness, I should follow it for having found by experience that in the end it is commonly the happiest and most useful track." The doctrine of interest rightly understood is not then new, but among the Americans of our time it finds universal acceptance; it has become popular there; you may trace it at the bottom of all their actions, you will remark it in all they say. It is as often asserted by the poor man as by the rich. In Europe the principle of interest is much grosser than it is in America, but it is also less common and especially it is less avowed; among us, men still constantly feign great abnegation which they no longer feel.

The Americans, on the other hand, are fond of explaining almost all the actions of their lives by the principle of self-interest rightly understood; they show with complacency how an enlightened regard for themselves constantly prompts them to assist one another and inclines them willingly to sacrifice a portion of their time and property to the welfare of the state. In this respect I think they frequently fail to do themselves justice, for in the United States as well as elsewhere people are sometimes seen to give way to those disinterested and spontaneous impulses that are natural to man; but the Americans seldom admit that they yield to emotions of this kind; they are more anxious to do honor to their philosophy than to themselves. . . .

The principle of self-interest rightly understood is not a lofty one, but it is clear and sure. It does not aim at mighty objects, but it attains without excessive exertion all those at which it aims. As it lies within the reach of all capacities, everyone can without difficulty learn and retain it. By its admirable conformity to human weaknesses it easily obtains great dominion; nor is that dominion precarious, since the principle checks one personal interest by another, and uses, to direct the passions, the very same instrument that excites them.

The principle of self-interest rightly understood produces no great acts of self-sacrifice, but it suggests daily small acts of self-denial. By itself it cannot suffice to make a man virtuous; but it disciplines a number of persons in habits of regularity, temperance, moderation, foresight, self-command; and if it does not lead men straight to virtue by the will, it gradually draws them in that direction by their habits. If the principle of interest rightly understood were to sway the whole moral world, extraordinary virtues would doubtless be more rare; but I think that gross depravity would then also be less common. The principle of interest rightly understood perhaps prevents men from rising far above the level of mankind, but a great number of other men, who were falling far below it, are caught and restrained by it. Observe some few individuals, they are lowered by it; survey mankind, they are raised.

I am not afraid to say that the principle of self-interest rightly understood appears to me the best suited of all philosophical theories to the wants of the men of our time, and that I regard it as their chief remaining security against themselves. Towards it, therefore, the minds of the moralists of our age should turn; even should they judge it to be incomplete, it must nevertheless be adopted as necessary.

I do not think, on the whole, that there is more selfishness among us than in America; the only difference is that there it is enlightened, here it is not. Each American knows when to sacrifice some of his private interests to save the rest; we want to save everything, and often we lose it all. Everybody I see about me seems bent on teaching his contemporaries, by precept and example, that what is useful is never wrong. Will nobody undertake to make them understand how what is right may be useful?

No power on earth can prevent the increasing equality of conditions from inclining the human mind to seek out what is useful or from leading every member of the community to be wrapped up in himself. It must therefore be expected that personal interest will become more than ever the principal if not the sole spring of men's actions; but it remains to be seen how each man will understand his personal interest. If the members of a community, as they become more equal, become more ignorant and coarse, it is difficult to foresee to what pitch of stupid excesses their selfishness may lead them; and no one can foretell into what disgrace and wretchedness they would plunge themselves lest they should have to sacrifice something of their own well-being to the prosperity of their fellow creatures.

I do not think that the system of self-interest as it is professed in America is in all its parts self-evident, but it contains a great number of truths so evident that men, if they are only educated, cannot fail to see them. Educate, then, at any rate, for the age of implicit self-sacrifice and instinctive virtues is already flitting far away from us, and the time is fast approaching when freedom, public peace, and social order itself will not be able to exist without education.

Alexis de Tocqueville, *Democracy in America*, tr., Henry Reeve. New York: D. Appleton, 1899, bk. 2, chap. 8. Also available at http://xroads.virginia.edu/~HYPER/DETOC/ch2_08.htm.

GREENSBURY WASHINGTON OFFLEY (1808–1896)

[*African American clergyman and author Greensbury Washington Offley was born in Centerville, Maryland. He never went to school but learned to read through informal instruction and self-education, and many respected people of his time spoke highly of his ideas and moral worth. In 1847 he began working as an agent for the African Methodist Episcopal Zion Church in Worcester, Massachusetts, raising funds for the establishment of a church. At the end of the Civil War he was involved in fundraising for missionary work to be carried out among newly freed slaves in the South. He wrote a brief autobiography and a book titled God's Immutable Declaration of His Own Moral and Assumed Natural Image and Likeness in Man. The following is a charter for a self-help society he helped form, found in one of his notebooks. The society exemplifies the sort of voluntary American self-interest organization about which Tocqueville wrote. People in America found ways to join together in order to provide for themselves; even with few resources, they strove to take care of themselves.]*

Records of the Female Mutual Relief Society

Preamble

For as much as union is strength and strength is need(ed) to carry out any important enterprise, those who would accomplish it must be united in feeling and sentiment. Common sympathy is the great Principle established by our Lord. When he was on Earth he went about Doing good. It is with a view to carry out this principle in deeds of mutual sympathy for the mutual relief of mutual suffering that we the undersigned do form ourselves into a society and adopt the following Constitution.

Figure 3.4 Portrait of Greensbury Washington Offley

Constitution.

Art. 1st. This society shall be called the female Relief Society....

Art. 2. The object of this society shall be to administer to the relief of its members when sick and needy and in case of Death to aid in securing them a respectable Burial.

Art. 5. Any female of respectable character Belonging to the church and congregation . . . may Become a member of this society By signing the Constitution and paying fifty cents in advance and twelve and a half cents monthly. . . .

Art. 6. Any Person who has Been a member of this Society one year and has paid their Monthly dues regularly and shall be taken sick and unable to Work or attend their Daily Business shall Be entitled to Receive One Dollar Per Week for four weeks, if sick after that they shall receive what the society feel able to give them.

Art. 7. All the Meetings of this society shall Be opened by Reading a Portion of scripture or the new Testament and Prayer. . . .

Reverend Greensbury Washington Offley, Notebook, Offley papers. Worcester, Mass.: American Antiquarian Society, 1866.

LORIN W. BROWN (d. 1978)

[Brown is one of the foremost folklorists of Hispano Folklife in New Mexico. Here, Brown describes how a wealthy leader brings a church bell into existence. The bell is a symbolic center of a congregation's religious life, a ringing signal calling worshipers to periodic prayer. The occasion of its arrival traditionally requires a fitting ritual, a feast of thanksgiving. The bell, revered as a sign of the sacred life of the community, is precious, described as a newly delivered baby. The rich man gives the bulk of the gold, but the villagers give rings and other jewelry, and this adds to the bell's clear tone. This piece voices the festive mood, the wonder, the momentousness of the event. The generosity of the wealthy can bring fulfillment to a community, if practiced with genuine care and awareness of people's needs, rather than as a means to exert power over those who are indebted.]

The Christening of a Bell

The bell that hangs in the adobe bell tower atop the old church was cast in the patio of one of the villagers and hung in the tower after a christening ceremony. For this ceremony, Don Pedro Cordova and his wife, Dona Ramona, served as *padrino* and *madrina* of the bell, giving it a name just as if it were some baby for whom they were sponsors. As the wealthiest couple of the little settlement, no one disputed them this honor, especially since Don Pedro had contributed the greater part of the gold and silver that had gone into the melting pot. . . . True, others of the village had donated

Figure 3.5 Mission San Jose

rings and ornaments of gold and silver to the melting pot to give the bell a sweeter, clearer tone, but Don Pedro had given thirty gold *escudos* and some silver coin, a large sum even in those days. However, in those days of barter, money was of little use.

In those days, what gold and coin came into Don Pedro's hands was of small use to him, so that when it occurred to him to donate a bell to the church, he found use for some of his hoard.

The caster of bells built his oven in Don Pedro's patio, and under the latter's watchful eyes stoked his oven so as to melt the different metals. A cast of clay had been prepared into which the molten metal was poured. A period of suspense ensued while the metal cooled. Perhaps the bell would be cracked or some bubble would render it useless and necessitate recasting.

Everyone rejoiced when the first casting was a success and immediately began to prepare for the christening of the bell and the ceremony and feasting which would be part of that event.

On the morning of the christening ceremony, the little village seethed with excitement. Visitors from nearby villages and outlying farms arrived in ever-increasing numbers—afoot, on horseback, and in creaking *carretas*—all eager to join in the festivities and anticipating the social interchange that a gathering of this kind was certain to produce. Bake ovens were emptied of loaves of enticing fragrant bread, together with steaming pots of *panocha*, cakes, and baked meats. Don Pedro, as *padrino*, had ordered that a huge repast be prepared so everyone could eat and drink his fill. Whole beefs, sheep, and kids were roasted to satisfy the hunger of the assembling crowd.

The appearance of the sexton on the church roof and the sound he made as he banged on a copper pan, the improvised bell soon to be discarded, signified that mass would soon be said, and giving them time to get ready before the last signal was sounded. Everybody who possibly could, crowded into the little church after the new bell had been carried in on a small platform, the whole gaily decorated with ribbons and wreaths of flowers. After mass, Don Pedro and his wife, resplendent in their finery, followed the bell as it was carried before the officiating priest.

The christening of the bell differed in no way from the christening of a baby. . . .

Lorin W. Brown, *Hispano Folklife of New Mexico: The Lorin W. Brown Federal Writers' Project Manuscripts* (Albuquerque: University of New Mexico Press, 1978), 101–3.

TIMOTHY FLINT (1780–1840)

[Born in North Reading, Massachusetts, Flint studied at Harvard University, graduating in 1800. An ordained Christian minister, he performed missionary work in the Mississippi Valley from 1815 until 1825. His first book about life on the frontier, Recollections of the Last Ten Years, was published in 1826. Flint also wrote romantic novels of the frontier, including the excerpt below from Francis Berrian, or The Mexican Patriot, about life in what is now Texas. The narrator argues with people he encounters in Mexico, enthusiastically praising American philanthropic and civic life. Flint points to the public buildings and canals being constructed, and the visible increase in comforts, knowledge, and wealth in the new nation. He insists that Americans are not as avaricious as their reputations seem to indicate and points out how in wartime, American sailors sacrificed their lives for their country. The narrator of the novel asks outsiders to come see for themselves the way Americans are seriously engaged in fine arts and religious life. To go away from home can cause us to appreciate home and to share our newfound enthusiasm with others who share our homeland.]

Proud of America's Civil Society[†]

For a man to know the force of his patriotism, it is necessary that he should be in a foreign country, and hear his own vilified. . . . "I am not going," I observed [in answer to someone prejudiced about America], "to answer and refute in detail all the charges which you have brought against us. It is true, in reply to the sweeping charge of avarice, that we are a money-getting people; and, unfortunately, your country has taken, as samples of ours, only the people whose sole business abroad is to make money. These men, perhaps, carry the desire of acquisition to avarice and a passion. But it is by no means, as you suppose, an universal trait. No country, according to its wealth, much less according to its age, has so many noble public and private charities. There is no country in which so much indulgence is shown to beggars, in which the poor have so much consideration, and whose regulations furnish them with so much comfort. Acts of private generosity are not so apt to be blazoned there, for the very reason that they are common, and that they who perform them feel that they are only acting in common with a multitude of others, and shrink from public applause. If you would know whether we have the spirit of public munificence among us, you must see, as I have seen, our public buildings, and our works of public utility and comfort in our cities. To know if we have public enterprise, you must see those canals that wed the lakes with the ocean, and the commencement of those projects that are to unite the long courses of the western streams with the Atlantic waters. To judge if we are a happy people, you must traverse, as I have done, the Union from one extreme

---

[†] Title is the author's own.

to the other, and see everywhere the increasing comfort, knowledge, and opulence of ten millions of people, among whom property, equal rights, comfortable existence, contentment, cheerfulness, and hope are, as I believe, more generally and plentifully diffused, than among any other people of the same numbers on our globe. You suppose that there are among us no pursuits, but those dictated by avarice. . . . The annals of no age or country, I dare affirm, can furnish a more general and striking contempt of money, and of everything but glory, a more entire disregard of every mean and sordid motive, and even of life itself, than the history of our marine in our late war with Great Britain. In the history of what other country will you find authenticated reports of wounded sailors voluntarily dropping into the sea after battle, and alleging as a reason for doing so, that they were wounded past the hope of cure, and could do nothing more for their country? There is, I believe, no country where a miser is regarded with more contempt, and a rich man, merely as such, with less respect. Nothing blasts the reputation sooner, than to be reputed the slave of avarice. We are reputed, beyond the seas, and by many of the bigoted and prejudiced of the parent country, to be destitute of all taste for the fine arts and for literature, and even the dawning of patronage and literary munificence. . . . That we produce our full share of the materials of excellence in the fine arts, let the fact attest, that more than an equal proportion of the distinguished British painters of the last age, and the promising geniuses of the present, were, and are natives of the United States. . . . In that region where I was bred, it has been generally conceded, that a greater proportion of the people attend public worship, as a habit, than in any other country. Religion has a more general influence upon morals and sentiments. Of consequence, fewer crimes are committed, and there are fewer public executions, than elsewhere. In short, the whole country, with some very limited regions excepted, presents such a spectacle of order, quiet, and peaceable industry, and regular advancement in comfort and improvement of every kind, as, I firmly believe, is not to be seen in an equal degree in any other country. You should see, before you condemn us. . . ."

Timothy Flint, *Francis Berrian, or, The Mexican Patriot*. Boston: Cummings, Hilliard, 1826, 104–06, 108.

ANONYMOUS

[Although slavery was legal during the first centuries of America's existence, some individuals experienced a change of heart and acted upon their consciences' realizations. As related in the previous section of this book, Virginia planter Robert Carter, a signer of the Declaration of Independence, freed five hundred slaves in 1791. The following news article tells of another man, David Minge, who freed eighty slaves and gave them provisions to help them start new lives.]

Extraordinary Munificence [About David Minge 1825]

A paragraph has lately gone the round of the papers, announcing that a gentleman of Virginia had emancipated upward of eighty slaves, and chartered a vessel to send them, at his own expense, to Hayti; but without giving the name of the author of so distinguished an act of munificence. We think it due to justice to supply this deficiency, and to add the following facts which have been communicated to us by gentlemen familiar with them, as well as by Captain Russell, one of the owners of the brig *Hannah and Elizabeth*, of Baltimore, the vessel chartered.

The gentleman who has thus distinguished himself, is Mr. David Minge of Charles City County, near Sandy point, on James river. Capt. Russell informs that there were put on board the Hannah and Elizabeth, eighty seven colored people of different ages, from three months to forty years, being all the slaves which Mr. Minge owned except two old men, whom he had likewise manumitted, but who being past service he retains and supports them. The value of these negroes, at the prices now going, might be estimated at about twenty six thousand dollars! And Mr. Minge expended previous to their embarkation, about 1200 dollars in purchasing ploughs, hoes, iron and other articles of husbandry for them, besides providing them with several suits of clothes to each, provisions, groceries, cooking utensils, and every thing which he supposed they might require for their comfort during the passage, and for their use after their arrival out— he also paid $1600 for the charter of the vessel.

But Mr. Minge's munificence does not end here. On the bank of the river, as they were about to go on board, he had a peck of dollars brought down, and calling them all around him, under a tree, distributed the hoard among them in such sums and under such regulations that each individual did, or would, receive seven dollars. By this provision, Mr. M. calculated that his emigrants would be enabled to commence the cultivation of the soil immediately after their arrival. Without being dependent on President Boyer for any favor whatever, unless the permission to improve the government lands might be considered.

Mr. Minge is about 24 or 25 years of age, unmarried, and unencumbered in every respect; possesses an ample fortune, and has received the benefits of a collegiate education at Harvard University. He assigned no other motive for having freed his slaves, and for his subsequent acts of generosity towards them, than that he conceived it would be doing a service to send them out of it; that they had all been good servants, but that he was rich enough without them.

We have heard of splendid sacrifices at the shrine of philanthropy; aged men on quitting the stage of moral existence have bequeathed large endowments to public charities, and princely legacies to religious and moral institutions. But where shall we find an instance of the kind attributable to a man of Mr. Minge's age? The case we believe is without parallel.

"Extraordinary Munificence," *Eastern Argus* 1, no. 89, Portland, Maine (August 5, 1825): 2.

On MORMONS

[The American Joseph Smith (1805–1844) was the prophet of Mormonism, or "the Church of Jesus Christ of Latter-Day Saints." Mormons practice tithing, donating one tenth of their income to the church each year. A large part of this money goes to church buildings and maintenance, and for education and missionary work. Mormons are a close-knit community, cooperating in barn raisings and pitching in to help others in times of need. A dramatic historic example of this collective effort in a crisis is related below by Howard Christy, professor emeritus at Brigham Young University in Provo, Utah, a historian of the Mormon church in America. One firsthand account of rescuing migrating Mormons stranded in snowstorms on their way to Salt Lake City recalled: "We harnessed up and

started and met them about ten miles East of the Pacific Springs. They were in a very sad condition, a great many badly frozen. We used all the care and attention we could to make them as comfortable as possible. My only blanket I gave to a sick girl to keep her warm. We made good headway towards the Valley and arrived on the 30th of November, thankful that the Lord had brought us safely through the cold and snow to our families"
(Thomas Steed, The Life of Thomas Steed from His Own Diary, 1826–1910, published in Farmington, Utah, 1935). Although many people died, if not for the volunteers who set out into the extreme winter mountains to help their imperiled brothers and sisters, many more would have been lost. The event, poignant with suffering and sorrows, was also the stage on which the "proudest single event" of the pioneering Mormons occurred.]

Rescue from Freezing: 1856 Mormon Handcart Company Disaster[†]
by Howard A. Christy

The large backlog of needy LDS [Latter-day Saints] converts awaiting passage from Europe and reduced tithing receipts at home persuaded Brigham Young in 1855 to instruct that the "poor saints" sailing from Liverpool to New York and taking the train to Iowa City should thence "walk and draw their luggage" overland to Utah. In 1856 five such Mormon pioneer handcart companies were organized to make the 1,300-mile trip on foot from the western railroad terminus at Iowa City to Salt Lake City.

Success seemed assured when the first two companies, totaling 486 immigrants pulling 96 handcarts, arrived safely in Salt Lake City on September 26, 1856. They accomplished the trek in under sixteen weeks. The third company, and presumably the last of the season, made up of 320 persons pulling 64 handcarts, arrived on October 2. But at that point the two remaining companies, totaling 980 people and 233 handcarts, were still on the way, having started dangerously late. One of these companies, under James G. Willie, left Iowa City on July 15, crossed Iowa to Florence (Omaha), Nebraska, then, after a week in Florence, headed out onto the plains. The last company, under Edward Martin, departed Florence on August 25. Three independent wagon companies, carrying 390 more immigrants, also started late.

A week after the departure of the Martin Company, Franklin D. Richards, an apostle who had organized the handcart effort as president of the European Mission, also departed Florence with sixteen other returning missionaries. This party, on horseback and in fast carriages, passed the Martin Company on September 7, the Willie Company on September 12, and arrived in Salt Lake City on October 4.

Richards's report that many more immigrants were coming was a shock: the late-starting immigrants would not be adequately clothed for the cold weather they would surely experience; they, like those in all previous lightly supplied handcart companies, would be perilously short of food; and, as they were unexpected, the last resupply wagons, which were routinely dispatched into the mountains to meet immigrant companies, had already returned.

Anticipating the worst, President Young mobilized men and women gathered for general conference and immediately ordered a massive rescue effort. A party of twenty-seven men, led by George D. Grant, left on October 7 with the first sixteen of what ultimately amounted to 200 wagons and teams. Several of the rescue party, including Grant, had been among the missionaries who had ridden in from the East five days before.

[†] Title is the author's own.

Two weeks later, one of the earliest blizzards on record struck just as both the handcart companies and the independent wagon companies were entering the Rocky Mountains in central Wyoming. After several days of being lashed by the fierce blizzard, people in the exposed handcart companies began to die.

Grant's rescue party found the Willie Company on October 21—in a blinding snowstorm one day after they had run out of food. But the worst still lay ahead, when, after a day of rest and replenishment, the company had to struggle over the long and steep eastern approach to South Pass in the teeth of a northerly gale. Beyond the pass, the company, now amply fed and free to climb aboard empty supply wagons as they became available, moved quickly, arriving in Salt Lake City on November 9. Of the 404 still with the company, 68 died and many others suffered from severe frostbite and near starvation.

Those of the Martin Company, three-fourths of them women, children, and the elderly, suffered even more. When the storm hit on October 19, they made camp and spent nine days on reduced rations waiting out the storm. Grant's party, after leaving men and supplies with the Willie Company, plunged farther east through the snow with eight wagons in search of the Martin Company. A scouting party sent out ahead of the wagons found them 150 miles east of South Pass.

The company, already in a desperate condition, was ordered to break camp immediately. The supply wagons met them on the trail, but the provisions were not nearly enough and, after struggling 55 miles farther, the company once again went into camp near Devil's Gate to await the arrival of supplies.

In the meantime, the rescue effort began to disintegrate. Rescue teams held up several days by the raging storm turned back, fearing to go on and rationalizing that the immigrant trains and Grant's advance party had either decided to winter over or had perished in the storm.

The Martin Company remained in camp for five days. When no supplies came, the company, now deplorably weakened, was again forced out on the trail. It had suffered fifty-six dead before being found, and it was now losing people at an appalling rate.

Relief came barely in time. A messenger ordered back west by Grant reached and turned around some of the teams that had abandoned the rescue. At least thirty wagons reached the Martin Company just as it was about to attempt the same climb to South Pass that had so sorely tested the Willie Company. Starved, frozen, spent, their spirits crushed, and many unable to walk, the people had reached the breaking point.

But now warmed and fed, with those unable to walk riding in the wagons, the company moved rapidly on. The Martin Company, in a train of 104 wagons, finally arrived in Salt Lake City on November 30. Out of 576, at least 145 had died and, like the Willie Company, many were severely afflicted by frostbite and starvation.

Elements of the three independent wagon companies and the rescue effort straggled into Salt Lake City until mid-December—except for twenty men, under Daniel W. Jones, who remained for the winter at Devil's Gate to guard freight unloaded there by the independent wagon companies, in part to make room for exhausted members of the Martin Company. The Jones party suffered misery and starvation at Devil's Gate. At one point they were reduced to eating rawhide until friendly Indians gave them some buffalo meat.

The decision to send out the Willie and Martin companies so late in the season was extremely reckless. In mid-November President Brigham Young angrily reproved those who had authorized the late start or who had not ordered the several parties back to

Florence when they still had the opportunity, charging "ignorance," "mismanagement," and "misconduct." Though terrible, the suffering could have been far worse. Had the rescue effort not been launched immediately—well before the storm struck—the handcart companies would probably have been totally destroyed.

Six more handcart companies crossed the plains after 1856. To demonstrate that the idea was still viable, seventy missionaries made the trip in the opposite direction in the spring of 1857. Five companies, totaling 1,076 immigrants with 223 handcarts, crossed west with little difficulty: two in 1857, one in 1859, and two in 1860. In all, 2,962 immigrants walked to Utah with handcarts. About 250 died along the way—all but about 30 of those in the Willie and Martin companies.

For Latter-day Saints, the handcart story, particularly the account of the Willie and Martin companies, has darkened the collective memory of the westering saga. But that episode is also remembered for the unparalleled gallantry exhibited by so many, immigrants and rescuers alike. Of particular note is the superb performance of the women; their courage and mettle contributed enormously to the eventual survival of both companies. It was at once the most ill-advised and tragic, the most heroic, and arguably the proudest single event in the Mormon pioneer experience.

Howard A. Christy, "Handcart Companies," *Encyclopedia of Mormonism*, vol. 2, ed. Daniel H. Ludlow. New York: Macmillan Publishing Company, 1992, 571–73.

GIVING, PHILANTHROPY, AND SERVICE TO OTHERS

THOMAS JEFFERSON (1743–1826)

[Founding father, third president, philosophical Renaissance man, inventor, writer of the Declaration of Independence, designer of Monticello, and founder of the University of Virginia, Jefferson was a richly multifaceted person. Raised Anglican, he was an ardent Deist with Unitarian leanings in adult life, revering Jesus as a great moral teacher but not as the divine Son of God. He edited a version of the New Testament, eliminating the miracles and highlighting the moral teachings. Jefferson placed great philosophical importance on inner resources: conscience, free will, the ability to reason and to strive inwardly to discern the moral path, and bringing political organization into coordination with spiritual vision. He had an American sense of humanity's divine nature, and he recognized that in each person were weaknesses and flaws as well as a power of consciousness with potentially great depth and awareness. He articulated the American opportunity of organizing a spiritual democracy, giving high place to the sense of communal self that members of a democratic society are capable of developing. American philosopher Jacob Needleman has said that the enigma of our nation's destiny is found in the concerns with which Jefferson wrestled: Can people come together and work within a form of spiritual democracy, striving toward the goal of a progressive interior opening of the conscience? Can Americans as time goes on search for spiritual democracy within political democracy? Can we harmonize inner and outer needs and obligations when they are in conflict? Jefferson made serious contributions to thinking about these philosophical/spiritual issues. The following, from an appeal to Congress and from his letters, discusses concerns such as the importance of offer-

ing hospitality to refugees, the duty of those with means to be charitable, and the need for giving to institutions within reach of one's own ability to see how the money is spent.]

Passages on Philanthropy

"And shall we refuse the unhappy fugitives from distress that hospitality which the savages of the wilderness extended to our fathers arriving in this land? Shall oppressed humanity find no asylum on this globe?"

1801 appeal to Congress to ease naturalization laws.

* * *

Private charities, as well as contributions to public purposes in proportion to every one's circumstances, are certainly among the duties we owe to society.

From a letter to Charles Christian. Washington ed. vi, 44. Monticello, 1812

* * *

We are all doubtless bound to contribute a certain portion of our income to the support of charitable and other useful public institutions. But it is a part of our duty also to apply our contributions in the most effectual way we can to secure their object. The question, then, is whether this will not be better done by each of us appropriating our whole contributions to the institutions within our reach, under our own eye; and over which we can exercise some useful control? Or, would it be better that each should divide the sum he can spare among all the institutions of his State, or of the United States? Reason, and the interest of these institutions themselves, certainly decide in favor of the former practice. This question has been forced on me, heretofore, by the multitude of applications which have come to me from every quarter of the Union on behalf of academies, churches, missions, hospitals, charitable establishments, &c. Had I parcelled among them all the contributions which I could spare, it would have been for each too feeble a sum to be worthy of being either given or received. If each portion of the State, on the contrary, will apply its aids and its attentions exclusively to those nearest around them, all will be better taken care of. Their support, their conduct, and the best administration of their funds, will be under the inspection and control of those most convenient to take cognizance of them, and most interested in their prosperity.

Figure 3.6 Painting of Thomas Jefferson

Letter to Samuel Kerchival. Washington ed. v, 489. Monticello, 1810.

* * *

It is a duty certainly to give our sparings to those who want; but to see also that they are faithfully distributed, and duly apportioned to the respective wants of those receivers. And why give through agents whom we know not, to persons whom we know not, and in countries from which we get no account, when we can do it at short hand, to objects under our eye, through agents we know, and to supply wants we see?

Letter to Mr. Megear. Washington ed. vii, 286. Monticello, 1823.

*   *   *

The general relation in which I, some time since, stood to the citizens of all our States, drew on me such multitudes of applications as exceeded all resource. Nor have they abated since my retirement to the limited duties of a private citizen, and the more limited resources of a private fortune. They have obliged me to lay down as a law of conduct for myself, to restrain my contributions for public institutions to the circle of my own State, and for private charities to that which is under my own observation; and these calls I find more than sufficient for everything I can spare.

Letter to Charles Christian. Washington ed. vi, 44. Monticello, 1812.

*   *   *

Thomas Jefferson, Letters 1195–99 in *The Jeffersonian Cyclopedia*. Thomas Jefferson Collection, University of Virginia Library, http://etext.lib.virginia.edu/toc/ modeng/public/JefCycl.html.

JOHN B. GOUGH (1817–1886)

[Born in England, Gough immigrated to America when he was twelve. As a young man, he lost his means of livelihood and went into debt. Personal losses drove him to drink, and by twenty-five he was endangering his life with self-destructive alcoholic behavior. Once he overcame his addiction, Gough became famous for his lectures and writings about the dangers of intoxicants. The temperance movement he championed was part of the Second Great Awakening, which brought more religious fervor to everyday life in America. By around 1860, millions of Americans had responded to preachers calling for the exertion of more will power and a greater sense of personal responsibility in facing temptations. In the passage below, Gough writes about those who sacrifice their own comforts to advance a noble cause and how their effect is out of proportion to their small numbers. The human race owes a debt of gratitude to reformers who have helped societies with acts of self-giving.]

What Is a Minority?

What is a minority? The chosen heroes of this earth have been in a minority. There is not a social, political, or religious privilege that you enjoy today that was not bought for you by the blood and tears and patient suffering of the minority. It is the minority that has stood in the van of every mortal conflict, and achieved all that is noble in the history of the world.

John B. Gough, *The Portable Dragon: The Western Man's Guide to the I Ching*, ed. R. G. H. Siu. Cambridge, Mass.: MIT Press, 1971, 225.

RALPH WALDO EMERSON (1803–1882)

[America's first great philosopher, Emerson, is known as a transcendentalist. His father was a Unitarian minister, and Emerson himself served as a minister at Second Church of Boston. Philosophically and theologically, he expressed views that reflected the new American experiences rather than a repetition of British culture and a rehash of European

works. His thoughtful intuitive essays, mosaics of insights, are of enduring interest, still today provoking thoughtful responses and sparking new ideas in readers. Transcendentalist philosophy was idealistic in some ways, seeing the individual's spirit as part of the oversoul, but it was ambivalent on the topic of philanthropy, because self-reliance was so important, and reform was considered more possible within the individual than in the world at large. When Emerson contemplates a custom such as gift giving, as below, he reports from an honest account of experiences and from wide learning, offering unique perspectives. He analyzes traditional items given as gifts, probing their meaning and value; he distinguishes true gifts from trivial ones and notes discrepancies between gifts and intentions, the gap between the act and the ideas attempting to be expressed. He celebrates the inherent power of love.]

Gifts

Gifts of one who loved me—
T'was high time they came;
When he ceased to love me,
Time they stopped for shame.

It is said that the world is in a state of bankruptcy; that the world owes the world more than the world can pay, and ought to go into chancery [court of equity] and be sold. I do not think this general insolvency, which involves in some sort all the population, to be the reason of the difficulty experienced at Christmas and New Year and other times, in bestowing gifts; since it is always so pleasant to be generous, though very vexatious to pay debts. But the impediment lies in the choosing. If at any time it comes into my head that a present is due from me to somebody, I am puzzled what to give, until the opportunity is gone. Flowers and fruits are always fit presents; flowers, because they are a proud assertion that a ray of beauty outvalues all the utilities of the world. These gay natures contrast with the somewhat stern countenance of ordinary nature: they are like music heard out of a work-house. Nature does not cocker us; we are children, not pets; she is not fond; everything is dealt to us without fear or favor, after severe universal laws. Yet these delicate Bowers look like the frolic and interference of love and beauty. Men use to tell us that we love flattery even though we are not deceived by it, because it shows that we are of importance enough to be courted. Something like that pleasure, the flowers give us: what am I to whom these sweet hints are addressed? Fruits are acceptable gifts, because they are the flower of commodities, and admit of fantastic values being attached to

Figure 3.7 Photo of Ralph Waldo Emerson

them. If a man should send to me to come a hundred miles to visit him and should set before me a basket of fine summer-fruit, I should think there was some proportion between the labor and the reward.

For common gifts, necessity makes pertinences and beauty every day, and one is glad when an imperative leaves him no option; since if the man at the door have no shoes, you have not to consider whether you could procure him a paint-box. And as it is always pleasing to see a man eat bread, or drink water, in the house or out of doors, so it is always a great satisfaction to supply these first wants. Necessity does everything well. In our condition of universal dependence it seems heroic to let the petitioner be the judge of his necessity, and to give all that is asked, though at great inconvenience. If it be a fantastic desire, it is better to leave to others the office of punishing him. I can think of many parts I should prefer playing to that of the Furies. Next to things of necessity, the rule for a gift, which one of my friends prescribed, is that we might convey to some person that which properly belonged to his character, and was easily associated with him in thought. But our tokens of compliment and love are for the most part barbarous. Rings and other jewels are not gifts, but apologies for gifts. The only gift is a portion of thyself. Thou must bleed for me. Therefore the poet brings his poem; the shepherd, his lamb; the farmer, corn; the miner, a gem; the sailor, coral and shells; the painter, his picture; the girl, a handkerchief of her own sewing. This is right and pleasing, for it restores society in so far to the primary basis, when a man's biography is conveyed in his gift, and every man's wealth is an index of his merit. But it is a cold life-less business when you go to the shops to buy me something which does not represent your life and talent, but a goldsmith's. This is fit for kings, and rich men who represent kings, and a false state of property, to make presents of gold and silver stuffs, as a kind of symbolical sin-offering, or payment of blackmail.

. . . We do not quite forgive a giver. The hand that feeds us is in some danger of being bitten. . . . He is a good man who can receive a gift well. We are either glad or sorry at a gift, and both emotions are unbecoming. Some violence I think is done, some degradation borne, when I rejoice or grieve at a gift. I am sorry when my independence is invaded, or when a gift comes from such as do not know my spirit, and the act is not supported; and if the gift pleases me overmuch, then I should be ashamed that the donor should read my heart, and see that I love his commodity, and not him. The gift, to be true, must be the flowing of the giver unto me, correspondent to my flowing unto him. When the waters are at level, then my goods pass to him, and his to me. All his are mine, all mine his. I say to him, How can you give me this pot of oil or this flagon of wine when all your oil and wine is mine, which belief of mine this gift seems to deny? Hence the fitness of beautiful, not useful things, for gifts. This giving is flat usurpation, and therefore when the beneficiary is ungrateful, as all beneficiaries hate all Timons [*Timon of Athens*, by Shakespeare, is a play about an embittered man who hates man-kind], not at all considering the value of the gift but looking back to the greater store it was taken from—I rather sympathize with the beneficiary than with the anger of my lord Timon. For the expectation of gratitude is mean, and is continually punished by the total insensibility of the obliged person. It is a great happiness to get off without injury and heart-burning from one who has had the ill-luck to be served by you. It is a very onerous business, this of being served, and the debtor naturally wishes to give you a slap. A golden text for these gentlemen is that which I so admire in the Buddhist, who never thanks, and who says, "Do not flatter your benefactors."

The reason of these discords I conceive to be that there is no commensurability between a man and any gift. You cannot give anything to a magnanimous person. After you have served him he at once puts you in debt by his magnanimity. The service a man renders his friend is trivial and selfish compared with the service he knows his friend stood in readiness to yield him, alike before he had begun to serve his friend, and now also. Compared with that good-will I bear my friend, the benefit it is in my power to render him seems small. Besides, our action on each other, good as well as evil, is so incidental and at random that we can seldom hear the acknowledgments of any person who would thank us for a benefit, without some shame and humiliation. We can rarely strike a direct stroke, but must be content with an oblique one; we seldom have the satisfaction of yielding a direct benefit which is directly received. But rectitude scatters favors on every side without knowing it, and receives with wonder the thanks of all people.

I fear to breathe any treason against the majesty of love, which is the genius and god of gifts, and to whom we must not affect to prescribe. Let him give kingdoms of flower-leaves indifferently. There are persons from whom we always expect fairy-tokens; let us not cease to expect them. This is prerogative, and not to be limited by our municipal rules. For the rest, I like to see that we cannot be bought and sold. The best of hospitality and of generosity is also not in the will, but in fate. I find that I am not much to you; you do not need me; you do not feel me; then am I thrust out of doors, though you proffer me house and lands. No services are of any value, but only likeness. When I have attempted to join myself to others by services, it proved an intellectual trick—no more. They eat your service like apples, and leave you out. But love them, and they feel you and delight in you all the time.

Ralph Waldo Emerson, *The Selected Writings*. New York: Modern Library, 1968, 402–05.

HENRY DAVID THOREAU (1817–1862)

[One of America's premier philosophers, greatest naturalists, and most probing social commentators, Thoreau was educated at Harvard, as well as self-educated, learning from world literature, including Hindu, Buddhist, and Muslim sources. Thoreau's voice of candor has an evergreen freshness; he saw things for himself and opposed hypocrisy and falseness, keeping his distance from conventional pieties that did not ring true for him. On the topic of giving, he believed charity might have a demeaning effect on the receiver. He kept a sense of higher destiny, liberated from conventional worldly values' limits. His poverty and humble simplicity were essential to his sense of freedom, and yet his work and life left us gifts that keep on giving. Note Thoreau's reference to Persian literature (the Gulistan by the Sufi poet Sa'di) at the end of the essay; it reminds us of the international influences in his thinking. His criticisms of false philanthropy are cautions to be considered anew today. His embrace of causes such as care for wilderness areas, antislavery, and Native American rights make him a sort of American patron saint of ecology and human rights. He died at forty-five, leaving behind many insightful writings and the example of a conscientious life. Largely unread in his own lifetime, Thoreau has become a perennial favorite, continually spurring new readers to examine their consciences and work fearlessly for what they hold dear.]

Philanthropy

I confess that I have hitherto indulged very little in philanthropic enterprises. I have made some sacrifices to a sense of duty, and among others have sacrificed this pleasure also. There are those who have used all their arts to persuade me to undertake the support of some poor family in the town; and if I had nothing to do—for the devil finds employment for the idle—I might try my hand at some such pastime as that. However, when I have thought to indulge myself in this respect, and lay their Heaven under an obligation by maintaining certain poor persons in all respects as comfortably as I maintain myself, and have even ventured so far as to make them the offer, they have one and all unhesitatingly preferred to remain poor. While my townsmen and women are devoted in so many ways to the good of their fellows, I trust that one at least may be spared to other and less humane pursuits. You must have a genius for charity as well as for any thing else. As for Doing-good, that is one of the professions which are full. Moreover, I have tried it fairly, and, strange as it may seem, am satisfied that it does not agree with my constitution. Probably I should not consciously and deliberately forsake my particular calling to do the good which society demands of me, to save the universe from annihilation; and I believe that a like but infinitely greater steadfastness elsewhere is all that now preserves it. But I would not stand between any man and his genius; and to him who does this work, which I decline, with his whole heart and soul and life, I would say, Persevere, even if the world call it doing evil, as it is mostly likely they will.

I am far from supposing that my case is a peculiar one; no doubt many of my readers would make a similar defense. At doing something—I will not engage that my neighbors shall pronounce it good—I do not hesitate to say that I should be a capital fellow to hire; but what that is, it is for my employer to find out. What *good* I do, in the common sense of that word, must be aside from my main path, and for the most part wholly unintended. Men say, practically, Begin where you are and such as you are, without aiming mainly to become of more worth, and with kindness afore-thought to go about doing good. If I were to preach at all in this strain, I should say rather, Set [*sic*] about being good. As if the sun should stop when he had kindled his fires up to the splendor of a moon or a star of the sixth magnitude, and go about like a Robin Goodfellow, peeping in at every cottage window, inspiring lunatics, and taint-ing meats, and making darkness visible, instead of steadily increasing his genial heat and beneficence till he is of such brightness that no mortal can look him in the face, and then, and in the meanwhile too, going about the world in his own orbit, doing it good, or rather, as a truer philosophy has discovered, the world going about him getting good. When Phaeton, wishing to prove his heavenly birth by his beneficence, had the sun's chariot but one day, and drove out of the beaten track, he burned several blocks of houses in the lower streets of heaven, and scorched the surface of the earth, and dried up every spring, and made the great desert of Sahara, till at length Jupiter hurled him headlong to the earth with a thunderbolt, and the sun, through grief at his death, did not shine for a year.

There is no odor so bad as that which arises from goodness tainted. It is human, it is divine, carrion. If I knew for a certainty that a man was coming to my house with the conscious design of doing me good, I should run for my life, as from that dry and parching wind of the African deserts called the simoom, which fills the mouth and nose and ears and eyes with dust till you are suffocated, for fear that I should get some of his good done to me—some of its virus mingled with my blood. No—in this case I would rather suffer evil the natural way. A man is not a good *man* to me because he will feed me if I should be starving, or warm me if I should be freezing, or pull me out of a ditch if I should ever fall into one. I can find you a Newfoundland dog that will do as much. Philanthropy is not love for one's fellow-man in the broadest sense. [Philan-thropist John] Howard was no doubt an exceedingly kind and worthy man in his way, and has his reward; but, comparatively speaking, what are a hundred Howards to *us*, if their philanthropy does not help *us* in our best estate, when we are most worthy to be helped? I never heard of a philanthropic meeting in which it was sincerely proposed to do any good to me, or the like of me . . .

Be sure that you give the poor the aid they most need, though it be your example which leaves them far behind. If you give money, spend yourself with it, and do not merely abandon it to them. We make curious mistakes sometimes. Often the poor man is not so cold and hungry as he is dirty and ragged and gross. It is partly his taste, and not merely his misfortune. If you give him money, he will perhaps buy more rags with it. I was wont to pity the clumsy Irish laborers who cut ice on the pond, in such mean and ragged clothes, while I shivered in my more tidy and somewhat more fashionable garments, till, one bitter cold day, one who had slipped into the water came to my house to warm him, and I saw him strip off three pairs of pants and two pairs of stockings ere he got down to the skin, though they were dirty and ragged enough, it is true, and that he could afford to refuse the *extra* garments which I offered him, he had so many *intra* ones. This ducking was the very thing he needed. Then I began to pity myself and I saw that it would be a greater charity to bestow on me a flannel shirt than a whole slop-shop on him. There are a thousand hacking at the branches of evil to one who is striking at the root, and it may be that he who bestows the largest amount of time and money on the needy is doing the most by his mode of life to produce that misery which he strives in vain to relieve. It is the pious slave-breeder devoting the proceeds of every tenth slave to buy a Sunday's liberty for the rest. Some show their kindness to the poor by employing them in

Figure 3.8 Photo of Henry David Thoreau

their kitchens. Would they not be kinder if they employed themselves there? You boast of spending a tenth part of your income in charity; may be you should spend the nine tenths so, and done with it. Society recovers only a tenth part of the property then. Is this owing to the generosity of him in whose possession it is found, or to the remissness of the officers of justice?

Philanthropy is almost the only virtue which is sufficiently appreciated by mankind. Nay, it is greatly overrated; and it is our selfishness which overrates it. A robust poor man, one sunny day here in Concord, praised a fellow-townsman to me, because, as he said, he was kind to the poor; meaning himself. The kind uncles and aunts of the race are more esteemed than its true spiritual fathers and mothers. I once heard a reverend lecturer on England, a man of learning and intelligence, after enumerating her scientific, literary, and political worthies, Shakespeare, Bacon, Crowell, Milton, Newton, and others, speak next of her Christian heroes, whom, as if his profession required it of him, he elevated to a place far above all the rest, as the greatest of the great. They were Penn, Howard, and Mrs. [Elizabeth] Fry [famous philanthropists and social reformers of the time]. Every one must feel the falsehood and cant of this. The last were not England's best men and women; only, perhaps, her best philanthropists.

I would not subtract any thing from the praise that is due to philanthropy, but merely demand justice for all who by their lives and works are a blessing to mankind. I do not value chiefly a man's uprightness and benevolence, which are, as it were, his stem and leaves. Those plants of whose greenness withered we make herb tea for the sick, serve but a humble use, and are most employed by quacks. I want the flower and fruit of a man; that some fragrance be wafted over from him to me, and some ripeness flavor our intercourse. His goodness must not be a partial and transitory act, but a constant superfluity, which costs him nothing and of which he is unconscious. This is a charity that hides a multitude of sins. The philanthropist too often surrounds mankind with the remembrance of his own cast-off griefs as an atmosphere, and calls it sympathy. We should impart our courage, and not our despair, our health and ease, and not our disease, and take care that this does not spread by contagion. From what southern plains comes the voice of wailing? Under what latitudes reside the heathen to whom we would send light? Who is that intemperate and brutal man whom we would redeem? If any thing ail a man, so that he does not perform his functions, if he have a pain in his bowels even—for that is the seat of sympathy—he forthwith sets about reforming—the world. Being a microcosm himself he discovers—and it is a true discovery, and he is the man to make it—that the world has been eating green apples; to his eyes, in fact, the globe itself is a great green apple, which there is danger awful to think of that the children of men will nibble before it is ripe; and straightway his drastic philanthropy seeks out the Esquimaux and the Patagonian, and embraces the populous Indian and Chinese villages; and thus, by a few years of philanthropic activity, the powers in the mean while using him for their own ends, no doubt, he cures himself of his dyspepsia, the globe acquires a faint blush on one or both of its cheeks, as if it were beginning to be ripe, and life loses its crudity and is once more sweet and wholesome to live. I never dreamed of any enormity greater than I have committed. I never knew, and never shall know, a worse man than myself.

I believe that what so saddens the reformer is not his sympathy with his fellows in distress, but, though he be the holiest son of God, is his private ail. Let this be righted, let the spring come to him, the morning rise over his couch, and he will forsake his generous companions without apology. My excuse for not lecturing against the use of tobacco is, that I never chewed it; that is a penalty which reformed tobacco-chewers have to pay; though there are things enough I have chewed, which I could lecture against. If you should ever be betrayed into any of these philanthropies, do not let your left hand know what your right hand does, for it is not worth knowing. Rescue the drowning and tie your shoe-strings. Take your time, and set about some free labor.

Our manners have been corrupted by communication with the saints. Our hymn-books resound with a melodious cursing of God and enduring him forever. One would say that even the prophets and redeemers had rather consoled the fears than confirmed the hope of man. There is nowhere recorded a simple and irrepressible satisfaction with the gift of life, any memorable praise of God. All health and success does me good, however far off and withdrawn it may appear; all disease and failure helps to make me sad and does me evil, however much sympathy it may have with me or I with it. If then, we would indeed restore mankind by truly Indian, botanic, magnetic, or natural means, let us first be as simple and well as Nature ourselves, dispel the clouds which hang over our own brows, and take up a little life into our pores. Do not stay to be an overseer of the poor; but endeavor to become one of the worthies of the world.

I read in the Gulistan, or Flower Garden [*sic*], of Sheik Sadi [*sic*] of Shiraz, that "[T]hey asked a wise man, saying: Of the many celebrated trees which the Most High God has created lofty and umbrageous, they call none azad [*sic*], or free, excepting the cypress, which bears no fruit; what mystery is there in this? He replied, Each has its appropriate produce, and appointed season, during the continuance of which it is fresh and blooming, and during their absence dry and withered; to neither of which states is the cypress exposed, being always flourishing; and of this nature are the azads, or religious independents.—Fix not thy heart on that which is transitory; for the Dijlah, or Tigris, will continue to flow through Baghdad after the race of caliphs is extinct: if thy hand has plenty, be liberal as the date tree; but if it affords nothing to give away, be an azad, or free man, like the cypress."

Henry David Thoreau, *A Week on the Concord and Merrimack Rivers; Walden, or Life in the Woods; The Maine Woods; Cape Cod*, ed. Robert F. Sayre. New York: Library of America, 1985, 379–85. Accessable at http://thoreau.eserver.org/walden1e.html.

CHIEF SEATTLE (1786–1866)

[Born on Blake Island, Washington, Seattle was a leader of the Squamish and Duwamish tribes of Puget Sound. He is remembered as a man who showed courage in times of trouble and as an eloquent orator with a voice that carried far—both literally and figuratively. The following speech was paraphrased from notes written by Henry Smith, a respected physician, poet, and journalist present at this speech. Though controversial, it is an expression of American experiences. Seattle's ideas expand our sense of caring for the land. It is doubtful that one can care for fellow humans if one does not care for the earth, which sustains all life. An expansive view of philanthropy includes caring for the natural world upon which all depend.]

Treaty Oration 1854

To us the ashes of our ancestors are sacred and their resting place is hallowed ground. You wander far from the graves of your ancestors and seemingly without regret. Your religion was written upon tables of stone by the iron finger of your God so that you could not forget. The Red Man could never comprehend nor remember it. Our religion is the traditions of our ancestors—the dreams of our old men, given them in solemn hours of night by the Great Spirit; and the visions of our sachems; and it is written in the hearts of our people.

Your dead cease to love you and the land of their nativity as soon as they pass the portals of the tomb and wander way beyond the stars. They are soon forgotten and never return. Our dead never forget the beautiful world that gave them being. . . .

We will ponder your proposition [to purchase the remaining Salish lands], and when we decide we will let you know. But should we accept it, I here and now make this condition that we will not be denied the privilege without molestation of visiting at any time the tombs of our ancestors, friends and children. Every part of this soil is sacred in the estimation of my people. Every hillside, every valley, every plain and grove, has been hallowed by some sad or happy event in days long vanished. The very dust upon which you now stand responds more lovingly to their footsteps than yours, because it is rich with the blood of our ancestors and our bare feet are conscious of the sympathetic touch. . . . Even the little children who lived here and rejoiced here for a brief season will love these somber solitudes and at eventide they greet shadowy returning spirits.

And when the last Red Man shall have perished, and the memory of my tribe shall have become a myth among the White man, these shores will swarm with the invisible dead of my tribe, and when your children's children think themselves alone in the field, the store, the shop, upon the highway, or in the silence of the pathless woods, they will not be alone. . . . At night when the streets of your cities and villages are silent and you think them deserted, they will throng with the returning hosts that once filled and still love this beautiful land. The White Man will never be alone. Let him be just and deal kindly with my people, for the dead are not powerless. Dead, did I say? There is no death, only a change of worlds.

Henry A. Smith, *Sunday Star* (Seattle), October 29, 1887.

NANCY HOARD-LINCOLN SALISBURY
(Mrs. Stephen Salisbury)

[In the following journal entry, a wife expresses gratitude to her husband for giving her the wherewithal to help support those in need, including her own mother. This expression of humble thanks reminds us of the days when women had little financial independence and had to rely on their husbands' beneficence. The Salisbury family was well known over several generations for their philanthropic contributions to the town of Worcester, Massachusetts.]

Charity Begins at Home

I have been made very happy today by my dearest husband's thoughtful consideration of my mother, and the probability of her wanting more means than she could conveniently command to complete the repairs she is making upon her house. He has therefore put into my hands the sum of one hundred dollars which I intend to forward to her by today's mail. I fancy I can see her grateful emotion as she opens the letter and is made aware of this kind and thoughtful attention. I thank my Heavenly Father most fervently for all his bountiful gifts and especially do I feel grateful when I'm enabled to contribute to the happiness of my friends, and to the comfort and necessities of the poor, who almost daily ask my assistance and Charity.

Mrs. Stephen Salisbury (Nancy Hoard-Lincoln), *Journal 1952*, vol. 13, box 63, Salisbury Family papers, June 26, 1852. Worcester, Mass.: American Antiquarian Society.

HISTORICAL BACKGROUND
FOR THE NINETEENTH CENTURY

DANIEL J. BOORSTIN (1914–2004)

[This passage by historian Daniel J. Boorstin provides historical background for the growth of charitable institutions and social concerns in nineteenth-century America. In the first three decades of the 1800s, evangelical activism in the Second Great Awakening shifted focus away from the Calvinist stress on sin as a damnable fault; rather, sin began to be seen as

human activity, and there was more faith in human ability to do good rather than evil. Personal salvation was preached in fiery sermons in camp meetings, which were held by different denominations in several regions. At first these evangelical revivals were little concerned with society as a whole. Much in the religious and moral ethos of the nineteenth century seemed individualist, with change only possible through appeals to the hearts of individuals. But the benevolence groups that grew in later decades, promoting the temperance movement, prison reform, antislavery, peace, and changes in education, were conscience-stirred offshoots of the Second Great Awakening. There was a progression of thinking among American evangelicals: Samuel Hopkins (1721–1803), who studied theology with Jonathon Edwards, characterized holiness as "disinterested benevolence." In his view, the fruits of genuine conversion were deeds done in the spirit of "disinterested benevolence" for the good of the entire community. Nathanial W. Taylor (1786–1858) modified the Calvinist teachings to bring them more into harmony with the sentiments of the Second Awakening. Charles Finney (1792–1875) was a great evangelist who took Taylor's work and preached about working for God's kingdom in this life, and soon Walter Rauschenbusch (1861–1918) would be articulating the social gospel—Christian responsibility for a practical realization of religious ideals in this world. Thus did the concept of charity develop, from individual gifts to individuals to institutions practically self-organizing to help others on a larger scale, as shown in Boorstin's following overview of nineteenth-century charity.]

The Quick-Grown, Fluid Community: The Booster Spirit

In nineteenth century England a number of cities like London, Birmingham, and Manchester grew with unprecedented rapidity. But this speed was slow compared to the contemporary growth of many American cities, which became metropolises almost before geographers had located them on their maps. The population of Illinois, for example, more than quadrupled between 1810 and 1820, more than trebled between 1820 and 1830, and again between 1830 and 1840. The city of Chicago (then Fort Dearborn), which around 1830 counted a hundred people, by 1890 had passed the million mark. Though it had taken a million years for mankind to produce its first city of a million inhabitants, Americans—or perhaps we should say Chicagoans—accomplished this gargantuan feat within a single lifetime. Similar phenomena occurred not only in Chicago but in dozens of other places—in Omaha, Cincinnati, Denver, Kansas City, St. Louis, and Dallas, to mention only a few.

Such fantastic growth itself fostered a naive pride in community, for men literally grew up with their towns. From this simple fact came a much maligned but peculiarly American product: the Booster Spirit. The spirit which had grown in the nineteenth century was pretty conscious of itself by about 1900 when the word "booster" was invented. In cities of explosive growth, group needs were urgent and rapidly changing. Sewage disposal, water supply, sidewalks, parks, harbor facilities, and a thousand other common needs at first depended on the desires, the willingness, and the good will of individuals. Could people who had very little governmental machinery do these things for themselves and their neighbors? Could they rapidly change the scale and the ends of their thinking about their town? Were they willing? By saying "Yes," they proved that they were a community.

Hardly less remarkable than this sudden intensity of community feeling in upstart cities was the fluidity of the population and the readiness with which people came and went. During a single day in the summer of 1857, thirty-four hundred immigrants arrived in Chicago on the Michigan Central Railroad alone. People came not only from the eastern and southern United States but from Ireland, Germany, and Scandinavia, and, very soon, too, from Poland, Italy, China, and other remote places. People who came so readily sometimes also left soon and in large numbers. Such cities flourished partly because they were distribution points-spigots from which people poured into the spongelike hinterland.

Thus was nourished the Booster Spirit, distinctively American not only in intensity and volubleness but in the readiness with which it could be detached from one community and attached to another. Booster loyalties grew rapidly; yet while they lasted, they seemed to have an oaklike solidity. Here today and there tomorrow. Chicago today; tomorrow Omaha, Denver, or Tulsa. "But while I'm here, I'm with you 150 percent." "We'll outgrow and outshine all the rest!" Never was a loyalty more fervent, more enthusiastic, more noisy—or more transferable. This was the voluntary, competitive spirit. . . .

The keynote of all this was community. American history had helped empty the word of its connotations of selflessness. Notice how irrelevant were the antitheses of "Individualism" versus "Socialism," "The Man" versus "The State." Governments here were not the transformed instruments of hereditary power. American businessmen were eager and ingenious at finding ways for federal, state, or local government to serve their enterprises—whether they were New England shippers, western lumbermen, transcontinental railroad builders, manufacturers, or simple farmers or merchants. Of course, this was not because they were socialists but rather because, starting from the fact of community, they could not help seeing all agencies of government as additional forms through which specific community purposes could be served.

Daniel J. Boorstin, *The Decline of Radicalism.* New York: Random House, 1963, 49–52.

SERVING THE NEEDS OF THE VULNERABLE IN THE NINETEENTH CENTURY

HELEN CAMPBELL (1839–1918) AND THOMAS W. KNOX (1835–1896)

[Campbell and Knox were social reformers and commentators who gathered an anthology of sketches and vignettes depicting people in need and in trouble, as well as those who tried to help them. As America grew, so, too, grew the scale of social problems. Attempts to come to terms with this fact may today sound odd to us. For example, William Paley bespoke a common attitude toward nineteenth-century charities when he wrote, "I use the term Charity . . . to signify the promoting the happiness of our inferiors." "Charity in this sense I take to be the principal province of virtue and religion: for, whilst worldly prudence will direct our behavior towards our superiors, and politeness towards our equals, there is little beside the consideration of duty, or an habitual humanity which comes into the place of consideration, to produce a proper conduct towards those who are beneath us, and dependent on us" ("Charity," The Principles of Moral and Political Philosophy. London: R. Faulder, 1785, 1st ed.; bk. 3, pt. 2, chap. 1, 191–92). But with various attempts, the institutionalization of

philanthropy evolved. Helping and serving our fellow human beings takes many forms. The following pieces are examples of conditions and caregivers in nineteeth-century America.]

Three Accounts from *Darkness and Daylight*

Visit to an Insane Asylum

(Forty-five years after Dorothea Dix made her report to Congress, social reformer Helen Campbell visited the insane asylum on one of the New York islands.)

Twenty acres of land belong to the asylum, and are cultivated to the highest pitch by the patients. Flowers are everywhere, and the greenhouse is another source of pleasure to the workers in it. The water-supply flows through submarine pipes from the Croton reservoir and is abundant. In the new cook-house, soup is boiled in set kettles through which steam pipes pass, and is carried to the dining-room in huge pails. The dietary is a generous one. Soup predominates, but it is of the most nourishing order, and there is no limit as to quantity. Knives and forks are allowed to very few, and tin plates have proved the best form of dish, as they cannot be broken. . . .

Till very lately there was small provision for amusement, but the attendant physicians realized long ago how vital a factor this was in cure, and begged for larger quarters. A large and airy hall has at last been built, and here at least once a week all who are not too excited by numbers gather together, dance, sing, or are given some light entertainment. The delight in this is a thing that passes on from one week to the next.

As in every asylum, there is one who believes herself the Queen of Heaven, and daily receives dispatches from God; and one who owns it and everything in it, doctors included. Across the room sits a patient who receives guests affably and announces herself as the widow of President Garfield. A rag doll on the little table by her bed is one of her forty-five children, all of whom are grown up and doing well,—most of them, she says, in fine positions.

Near her is a little woman with twinkling blue eyes and a particularly merry laugh, who dances with delight, but pauses at intervals to whisper of the horrors she could tell if she were disposed.

"Murders by the score,—yes, by the score," she says, looking suspiciously about her; "but the victims are thrown into the river at once, so that no one has to mention it. Take care; I shall be heard,"—and she laughs again and nods to her partner, a silent man, who chuckles to himself at intervals and moves his lips noiselessly.

Under the trees sits a one-armed French soldier who believes he is one of Napoleon's marshals and that the Emperor is to come again. An Irish philosopher, a graduate of Dublin University, and here from drink and opium, owns the island, but lends it by the day to the institutions.

"To-morrow, may be, I'll have 'em all pulled down," he says reflectively. "I'm thinking foine gyardens would look better and more cheerful like, but there's no hurry. Whin the time comes there's enough to carry out me orders and no bother to meself. There's no hurry at all, and I wouldn't be discommoding the Doctors, not I."

Down the long walk comes a group of women out with an attendant, all of them in the asylum uniform of calico, less unpleasant than the bed-ticking dresses of the workhouse prisoners, a detachment of whom are working here. One little woman, walking with bent head, raises it suddenly and emits a piercing toot. She thinks herself a steam engine and whistles periodically, to the rage of the others, who recognize her delusion but are wholly unconscious of their own.

So it goes, and for each is the story of a blighted life and often the ruin of other lives closely bound to theirs. It is a pauper asylum, and fifty years ago all know what fate would have been theirs.

All-Night Missionary Gibbud's Story— Reformer in the Alleys and Saloons

[In the 1880s and 1890s in America there was a growing literature about itinerants, including many fictional accounts about vagabonds and homeless beggars. In 1842 Nathaniel Hawthorne wrote in a notebook that so much want and wretchedness was abroad in the world that we should believe people when they say they need our assistance. Even if they're lying, a kind act does us more good than miserliness would. He thought vagrants "should be permitted to roam through our land of plenty, scattering the seeds of tenderness and charity—as birds of passage bear the seeds of precious plants from land to land, without ever dreaming of the office which they perform." For several decades this idea was what charity meant to many, but with the growth of socially conscious religious outreach missions, charity became more institutionalized. Also, during the period 1885–1915, modern philanthropy emerged on the national scene, as wealthy tycoons began to give significant funding to charitable causes.]

(Under this heading, the social reformer Helen Campbell quotes the following first-person account in her book *Darkness and Daylight*.)

I had been holding meetings in a small room in the midst of the slums of Baxter Street [in New York City], going out into the alleys, saloons, and dives of the neighborhood, and literally compelling the people to come in. I made frequent visits after dark to "Hell Gate," "Chain and Locker," and "Bottle Alley," resorts for sailors and low characters, and invited them to the meeting. The proprietors, though in a bad business, generally treated me with courtesy though I sometimes succeeded in taking nearly all their customers away.

One summer night I started out to gather in my audience. The streets were full. . . . A "mud-gutter" band in front of one of the dance-halls was making discordant music, while children of all ages, from the babe just out of the mother's arms to the young girl in her teens, jostled each other in a rude attempt at dancing. Bare-headed colored women, in soiled calico dresses, with sleeves rolled up, stopped, before entering the brothels, to join with rough-looking sailors in a "break-down." From a cellar-way leading to filthy underground apartments came the noise of a piano, drummed by unskilled hands, while the painted women at the door tried to induce victims to enter.

I had just come out of the place named "Hell Gate" when I saw a partially intoxicated woman supporting herself against a lamp post, and near by stood a burly negro. The woman was tall and thin, and it was plain even then that consumption was doing its fatal work. She had no hat, no shoes; a dirty calico dress was all the clothing she had on, and that was not in condition to cover her nakedness. Her hair was matted and tangled, her face bruised and swollen; both eyes were blackened by the fist of her huge negro companion, who held her as his slave and had beaten her because she had not brought him as much money as he wanted. I invited her to the meeting and passed on. Near the close of the service she came in; with tearful eyes she listened to the story of Jesus, and was one of the first to request prayers. After the meeting she expressed a desire for a better life, but she had no place to go, save to the dens of infamy from which she came. I decided at once to take her to the Florence Night Mission, and, accompanied by a friend who had assisted me in the meeting, we started.

We were going toward the horse-cars, and congratulating ourselves that we had gotten away unobserved, when we were confronted by the very negro from whom we sought to escape. With an oath he demanded,

"Whar you folks takin' dat gal to?"

It was a fearful moment, near midnight, a dark street, and not a soul in sight. I expected every moment that he would strike me. I was no match for him. Signaling my friend to go on with the girl, and taking the negro by the coat, I said excitedly.

"I am taking her to a Christian home—to a better life. If ever you prayed for any one, pray for her; I know you are a bad man, but you ought to be glad to help any girl away from this place. So pray for her as you have never prayed before."

All this time my friend and the woman were going down the street as fast as possible. I had talked so fast that the negro did not have a

Figure 3.9 "In the Bitter Cold"

chance to say a word, and before he could recover from his astonishment I ran on. He did not attempt to follow.

Four cares were hailed before one would let us on. The drivers would slacken up, but, seeing the woman's condition, would whip up their horses and drive on. Finally, when the next driver slackened, we lifted our frail burden to the platform before he could prevent us.

Arriving at the Mission, we helped her up the steps and rang the bell; she turned to me and said, "You will be proud of me some day." I smiled then, as I thought the chances of being proud of her were slim, but how many times since, when vast audiences have been moved to tears by the pathos of her story, or spellbound by her eloquence, have I indeed been proud of her.

She was admitted to the house, giving the assumed name of Nellie Conroy. For nine years she had lived in Baxter Street slums, becoming a victim to all the vices that attend a dissipated life until at last she became an utter wreck. Everything was done for her at the Mission, and in time permanent employment was found.

Some time after, word reached the Mission that Nellie had left her place and gone back to her old haunts in Baxter Street. A card with the address of "The Florence" was left at one of her resorts, and the whole matter was forgotten, until late one night the doorbell of the Mission rooms softly rang, and the poor wretched object admitted proved to be Nellie. At the meeting the next night she was the first to come forward. When asked to pray, she lifted her pale face to heaven and quoted, with tearful pathos, that beautiful hymn:

> The mistakes of my life have been many,
> The sins of my heart have been more:
> And I scarce can see for weeping,
> But I'll knock at the open door.

Then followed a touching prayer, a humble confession of sin, an earnest pleading for pardon, a quiet acceptance of Christ by faith, a tearful thanksgiving for knowledge of sins forgiven.

Her life from that time until her death—nearly two years later—was that of a faithful Christian. She gave satisfaction to her employers; she was blessed of God in her testimony at the Mission, and soon she was sought after by churches, temperance societies, and missions to tell what great things the Lord had done for her.

* * *

At her funeral many Christian workers and friends gathered to do honor to her remains. Many converts from the slums who had been won to Christ by her testimony were among the mourners, and not a few came to look on that pale face who still lived in sin and shame, but who sincerely loved one who had so often entreated them to turn and live.

Volunteer Fireman

[There are many colorful stories of experiences shared by volunteers and members of self-help cooperatives. This one describes the experience of someone working in the theatre who also was a volunteer fireman. When it was time to go onstage, the fire alarm began ringing, and so, wearing a variety of bright period costumes, the actors and extras hurried to help save a burning building.]

Thomas Knox, a nineteenth-century New York journalist, interviews a former member of the city's old volunteer fire department.

The volunteer firemen were recruited from all kinds of trades and occupations. It was an invariable rule with them to answer every fire alarm at whatever hour it was sounded, no matter what they were doing at the time.

"One time," said an old fire-laddie, "Barnum, the showman, was giving a play called 'Moll Pitcher, or the Battle of Monmouth,' at this old museum at the corner of Broadway and Ann Street. There were Red-coats and Continentals in uniform, and no end of Indians with feathers and war paint and tomahawks in the battle scene, and a lot of us that ran with an engine a little way down Ann Street had hired out for 'supes' [supernumeraries or extras] to make up the 'armies' that went on the stage.

Well, one day, just as we were all dressed in our stage costumes and it was almost time for us to march on the stage for the great battle, the fire-bell rang out a signal for a fire in our district. We didn't stop for anything, but went yelling down the stairs and out into the street just as we were—the most motley crowd of firemen that ever turned out at a fire. We met the engine coming up Ann Street, grabbed the rope, and went on to the fire with the rest of the boys. How the small boys did scamper out of the way, and how folks did stare at us, especially at the Indians in war paint and feathers, and the Red-coats in their gay uniforms; but we kept at our work and put out the fire and then went back to the Museum, though by that time the play was over. Barnum was awful mad at first, as his battle scene was all broken up, but next morning the story was in the papers and he got such a good advertisement out of the affair for nothing, that he was all serene again by the time of the afternoon performance."

Helen Campbell and Thomas Knox. *Darkness and Daylight,* (first published, Hartford: A.D. Worthington, 1892; Detroit: Singing Tree Press, 1969), 237–39, 376–79, 527–28. Also in *Witnessing America*, 260, 401–5, 459–60.

CATHARINE BEECHER (1800–1878)
AND HARRIET BEECHER STOWE (1811–1896)

[The Beecher sisters, dedicated social reformers, accomplished much in their lifetimes. Harriet, a mother of seven children, found time to write thirty books. In childhood she nearly memorized One Thousand and One Arabian Nights, repeating them to her siblings nightly at bedtime. When Lincoln met her, he called her "the little woman who wrote the book that started this great war," referring to her novel Uncle Tom's Cabin as a catalyst for the Civil War. Raised as a Congregationalist but eventually becoming an Episcopalian, Harriet wrote out of a Christian sense of injustice and also as a lover of America. She aided runaway slaves and established schools and boarding houses for freed slaves. Catharine realized her mission at age twenty-four: "to find happiness in living to do good." She helped organize the Ladies Society for Promoting Education in the West, which founded several women's colleges. In the following passages put together by the sisters, ideal imaginings and philosophical aspirations about nursing are contrasted with the actual experiences of nurses by juxtaposing selections by two different authors: Ann Preston and Louisa May Alcott. Ann Preston, a Quaker, studied medicine, became dean of Philadelphia Female Medical College, trained the first African American and Native American women physicians and founded the Women's Hospital in Philadelphia. Louisa May Alcott, the great American novelist, is famous for Little Women and other works of fiction.]

Nurses
Ann Preston *(The ideal)*

The good nurse is an artist. O the pillowy, soothing softness of her touch, the neatness of her simple, unrustling dress, the music of her assured yet gentle voice and tread, the sense of security and rest inspired by her kind and hopeful face, the promptness and attention to every want, the repose that like an atmosphere encircles her, the evidence of heavenly goodness, and love that she diffuses!

Louisa May Alcott *(The real)*

November 1862—Thirty years old. Decided to go to Washington as a nurse if I could find a place. Help needed, and I love nursing, and must let out my pent-up energy in some new way. Winter is always a hard and a dull time, and if I am away there is one less to feed and warm and worry over.

I want new experiences, and am sure to get 'em if I go. So I've sent in my name, and bide my time writing tales, to leave all snug behind me, and mending up my old clothes,—for nurses don't need nice things, thank Heaven!

Figure 3.10 "Sisters of Charity" Pe-ru-na advertisement

December—On the 11th I received a note from Miss Hannah M. Stevenson telling me to start for Georgetown next day to fill a place in Union Hotel Hospital. Mrs. Ropes of Boston was matron, and Miss Kendall of Plymouth was a nurse there, and though a hard place, help was needed. I was ready, and when my commander said "March!" I marched. Packed my trunk, and reported in Boston that same evening.

We had all been full of courage till the last moment came, then we all broke down. I realized that I had taken my life in my hand, and might never see them all again. I said, "Shall I stay, Mother?" as I hugged her close. "No, go! And the Lord be with you!" answered the Spartan woman, and till I turned the corner she bravely smiled and waved her wet handkerchief on the door-step. Shall I ever see that dear old face again?

So I set forth in the December twilight, with May and Julian Hawthorne as escort, feeling as if I was the son of the house going to war.

All went well, and I got to Georgetown one evening very tired. Was kindly welcomed, slept in my narrow bed with two other room-mates, and on the morrow began my new life by seeing a poor man die at dawn, and sitting all day between a boy with pneumonia and a man shot through the lungs. A strange day, but I did my best, and when I put mother's little black shawl round the boy while he sat up panting for breath, he smiled and said, "You are real motherly, ma'am." I felt as if I was getting on. The man only lay and stared with his big black eyes, and made me very nervous. But all were well behaved, and I sat looking at the twenty strong faces as they looked back at me,—hoping that I looked "motherly" to them; for my thirty years made me feel old, and the suffering round me made me long to comfort every one.

January 1863—I never began the year in a stranger place than this; five hundred miles from home, alone among strangers, doing painful duties all day long, & leading a life of constant excitement in this great house surrounded by 3 or 4 hundred men in all stages of suffering, disease & death. Though often home sick, heart sick & worn out, I like it—find real pleasure in comforting tending & cheering these poor souls who seem to love me, to feel my sympathy though unspoken, & acknowledge my hearty good will in spite of the ignorance, awkwardness, & bashfulness which I cannot help showing in so new & trying a situation. The men are docile, respectful, & affectionate, with but few exceptions, truly lovable & manly many of them. John Suhre a Virginia blacksmith is the prince of patients, & though what we call a common man, in education & condition, to me is all that I could expect or ask from the first gentleman in the land. Under his plain speech & unpolished manner I seem to see a noble character, a heart as warm & tender as a woman's, a nature fresh & frank as any child's. He is about thirty, I think, tall & handsome, mortally wounded & dying royally, without reproach, repining, or remorse. Mrs. Ropes & myself love him & feel indignant that such a man should be so early lost, for though he might never distinguish himself before the world, his influence & example cannot be without effect, for real goodness is never wasted.

Monday 4th—I shall record the events of a day as a sample of the days I spend:—

Up at six, dress by gaslight, run through my ward & fling up the windows though the men grumble & shiver, but the air is bad enough to breed a pestilence & as no notice is taken of our frequent appeals for better ventilation, I must do what I can. Poke up the fire, add blankets, joke, coax, & command, but continue to open doors & windows as if life depended on it, mine does, & doubtless many another, for a more perfect pestilence-box than this house I never saw—cold, damp, dirty, full of vile odors from wounds, kitchens, wash rooms, & a jumble of good, bad, & indifferent nurses, surgeons & attendants to complicate the Chaos still more.

After this unwelcome progress through my stifling ward I go to breakfast with what appetite I may, find the inevitable fried beef, salt butter, husky bread & washy coffee, listen to the clack of eight women & a dozen men, the first silly, stupid or possessed of but one idea, the last absorbed in their breakfast & themselves to a degree that is both ludicrous and provoking.

Till noon I trot, trot, giving out rations, cutting up food for helpless "boys," washing faces, teaching my attendants how beds are made or floors swept, dressing wounds, taking Dr. Fitz Patrick's orders (privately wishing all the time that he would be more gentle with my big babies), dusting tables, sewing bandages, keeping my tray tidy, rushing up & down after pillows, bed linen, sponges, books & directions, till it seems as if I would joyfully pay down all I possess for fifteen minutes rest.

At twelve the big bell rings & up comes dinner for the boys who are always ready for it & never entirely satisfied. Soup, meat, potatoes & bread is the bill of fare. Charley Thayer the attendant travels up & down the room serving out the rations, saving little for himself yet always thoughtful of his mates & patient as a woman with their helplessness. When dinner is over some sleep, many read & others want letters written. This I like to do for they put in such odd things & express their ideas so comically I have great fun interiorly while as grave as possible exteriorly. A few of the men word their paragraphs well & make excellent letters. John's was the best of all I wrote. The answering of letters from friends after some one has died is the saddest & hardest duty a nurse has to do.

Supper at five sets every one to running that can run & when that flurry is over all settle down for the evening amusements which consist of newspapers, gossip, Drs last round, & for such as need them the final doses for the night. At nine the bell rings, gas is turned down & day nurses go to bed. Night nurses go on duty, & sleep & death have the house to themselves. *(From the diary of Louisa May Alcott.)*

Catharine E. Beecher and Harriet Beecher Stowe, *The American Woman's Home*. Hartford: Harriet Beecher Stowe Center, 2002, 254.

On CLARA BARTON

[Clarissa Harlowe Barton was born in Oxford, Massachusetts, to parents who were abolitionists and Universalists. Clara grew up on the family farm and learned nursing skills by tending her brother after he was badly injured. In 1861 Barton formed an agency to supply necessities to soldiers wounded in the Civil War. President Lincoln put her in charge of activities to search for missing Union soldiers in 1865. Along with others in Washington, D.C., Barton founded the American Red Cross in 1881. In 1882 she campaigned for official acceptance of the Red Cross by the government and for the American ratification of the Geneva Convention, which protected soldiers injured in war. Barton led the Red Cross for twenty-three years, during which time it helped the U.S. armed forces in the Spanish-American war. She also won acceptance of the inclusion of peacetime relief work in the mission of the International Red Cross. Matthew J. Greevy, in a 1938 poem written in the voice of Clara Barton, wrote, "My humble spirit marches at all times; / I am, I am, / The Red Cross of the United States of America."]

The American Red Cross, Its Forerunners and Its Founder

Although the Civil War may be said to have been the indirect cause of the American branch of the International Red Cross, which was founded in Geneva in 1864, it was Clara Barton who was directly responsible for its confirmation in the United States Senate in March, 1882.

Prior to this date, there were numerous organizations which can honestly be called the forerunners of the Red Cross in this country. The Soldiers' Aid Society of Cleveland, Ohio, founded on April 20th, 1861, has the distinction of being the first group of women organized solely for the relief of the soldiers. Allied clubs and organizations soon sprang up all over the North and the South. Some, however, were composed of men only.

Two of the most important and far-reaching of all these groups were the U.S. Christian Commission and the U.S. Sanitary Commission. The former was an outgrowth of the Army Committee of the New York Men's Christian Association and was founded by the Board of Directors of the last named institution on May 27, 1861. The following June two male delegates were sent to Washington where they were given permission to enter the army hospitals and administer any aid possible. Others soon joined this Army Committee and "hospital stores, and comforts of all sorts" were distributed. The Army Committee's "Jamaica wagon" with its library and provisions became as well known on the dust-laden streets of Washington and the surrounding camps as were the wagons of the Christian Commission which was soon to supplant this Army Committee. The true purpose of the organization was "to promote spiritual and temporal welfare. It embraced all the states . . . and both body and soul." Laymen as well as ministers volunteered their services without remuneration and were sent to battlefields, hospitals, and camps. Not only did they minister to the souls of the dying, but under fire they gathered the wounded from the field and assisted the surgeons "at the amputating table." Branches were organized all over the country as the War went into its second year, and the organization contributed an important part to the mental and physical morale of the sick and wounded.

The Woman's Central Association of Relief, an auxiliary branch of the U.S. Sanitary Commission was, perhaps, more comparable to the present-day Red Cross than any of the numerous other organizations. The Commission itself was approved by President Lincoln on June 13, 1861. Simon Cameron, the Secretary of War, gave permission to the Chairman, the Reverend Henry W. Bellows, D.D., for "The Commission, in connection with a Surgeon of the U.S.A. . . . to direct its inquiries to the principles and practices connected with the inspection and recruits and enlisted men; the sanitary condition of the volunteers; to the means of preserving and restoring the health, and of securing the general comfort and efficiency of troops; to the proper provision of cooks, nurses, and hospitals; and to other subjects of like nature."

Figure 3.11 Cover of an undated booklet about Clara Barton

The Woman's Central Association of Relief selected a hundred women out of several hundred candidates who were specially trained under distinguished physicians and surgeons in the New York hospitals. The Commission then asked the War Department to receive these nurses on salary as they were needed, but made it perfectly clear that they would not proceed to Washington "until directly called for by the Medical Bureau, and that the Government would not be financially responsible in any way until they were actually in service."

Branches were formed throughout the North with central offices in key cities. "Food, clothing, bedding, bandages, sponges, pads, wine and spirits, Hospital furniture, etc." were sent to these main branches where they were packed and sent to distribution points. Thus, this organization can be said to have performed many of the duties of the modern Red Cross.

Functioning at the same time as Clara Barton, but working for the United States Government were Dorothea Lynde Dix and Dr. Mary Edwards Walker. Miss Dix, who was fifty-nine years of age, had spent most of her life in administering to and founding hospitals for the mentally deficient. Early in the summer of 1861 she was appointed "Superintendent of Women Nurses" and was authorized "to select and assign woman nurses to general or permanent military hospitals." In July, 1862, this appointment was renewed by Surgeon-General Hammond, and she was empowered to appoint one female nurse to every two male nurses, but her responsibilities in other directions were curtailed and she was held directly responsible to her chief. . . .

Practically every woman in the Confederacy was a potential Red Cross nurse or worker during the War. Clubs were formed in church cellars where bandages, hospital supplies and even uniforms were turned out in great quantities. Wealthy women from every state donated their money and time to the founding and running of hospitals. Outstanding among these was Capt. Sally Tompkins of Virginia, the only woman to receive a commission in the Army of the Confederacy. Capt. Tompkins took over the beautiful Robertson residence in Richmond and equipped it as the Robertson Hospital, with the donor herself in charge. There were, in fact, very few Southern ladies who did not spend part of each day in the hospitals where they performed any menial task they were assigned.

But it is Clarissa Harlowe Barton who has always been considered the mother of the American Red Cross. Her experience began when she was a young girl for she was devoted to a bed-ridden brother whom she watched over and nursed for many years. Perhaps it was her tender love for him and her sympathy for him in his helplessness that so ably fitted her for the superb job which awaited her in the future.

Fortunately, Miss Barton was on hand in Washington when the ragged, footsore, and hungry men of the Sixth Massachusetts Regiment marched up Pennsylvania Avenue [during the Civil War] after they had had to fight their way through crowds of Southern sympathizers in Baltimore. She immediately advertised for provisions and set up the prototype of the present-day canteens. She worked independently until July, 1862, when Surgeon-General Hammond gave her permission to "go upon the sick transports in any direction, for the purpose of distributing comforts for the sick and wounded, and nursing them." During all the War years she managed to get supplies to the battlefields where she distributed them personally and cared for the wounded. . . .

Perhaps it was the American Association for the Relief of Misery on the Battlefields, which was founded in 1866 by the Reverend Dr. Henry W. Bellows and a group of men who had served with him on the Sanitary Commission, that spurred Miss Barton on to the belated organization of the Red Cross. It was the aim of this group to win the Government's support and eventually influence our acceptance of the Geneva Treaty, but the War Department stubbornly refused to override Secretary Seward's decision against its adoption. Undaunted, Miss Barton went on working alone. . . . Finally on May 20, 1881, under the presidency of James A. Garfield, a National Society of the Red Cross was organized, but because of the President's assassination, the Geneva Convention was not adopted until March of the following year. At last, Miss Barton had succeeded in establishing the magnificent organization now known as the American Red Cross. It was fitting that she should have been elected its first president.

Clara Barton was author of the American amendment to the Constitution of the Red Cross, which provides that the society shall distribute relief not only in war but in times of other calamities such as famines, floods and earthquakes.

"The American Red Cross Is Born," in *News from Home*, ed. Kenneth H. Dunshee, 5:2. New York: Home Insurance Company, 1944. Red Cross papers, National Archives, box 1, folder 004.

On DOROTHEA "DRAGON" DIX

[The life of New England teacher and social reformer Dorothea Dix illustrates the hope for healing famously expressed by Lincoln: "With malice toward none; with charity for all . . . to bind up the nation's wounds; to care for him who shall have borne the battle, and for his widow, and his orphan—to do all which may achieve and cherish a just and lasting peace, among ourselves, and with all nations." Dix came from a dysfunctional family for whom she cared for years. Dix's father was a traveling Methodist preacher in Maine, but Methodism was not the path that appealed to her. When staying with her grandmother in Boston, Dix was attracted to the sermons of Unitarian minister William Ellery Chan-

ning, who preached God's love rather than God's wrath. Channing also thought that public charities weakened poor people's motivation and encouraged begging; he championed ventures that helped the poor become self-sufficient. Dix was inspired by his ideas. At thirty-nine, encountering the dismal conditions of women suffering in a jail and learning of the treatment of vulnerable people in other institutions, Dix began work to improve the lives of the disadvantaged, helping found thirty-two mental hospitals, over a dozen schools for the feeble minded, and a nurses' training school. She became known as "the most effective advocate of humanitarian reform in American mental institutions" of her time. (V. Viney and S. Zorich, "Contributions to the History of Psychology XXIX—Dorothea Dix," Psychological Reports 50 (1982): 211–18.)]

The Soft-Spoken Crusader by Suzanne LeVert

A noted social reformer, Dix became the Union's Superintendent of Female Nurses during the Civil War. The soft spoken yet autocratic crusader had spent more than 20 years working for improved treatment of mentally ill patients and for better prison conditions. A week after the attack on Fort Sumter, Dix, at age 59, volunteered her services to the Union and received the appointment in June 1861 placing her in charge of all women nurses working in army hospitals. Serving in that position without pay through the entire war, Dix quickly molded her vaguely defined duties.

She convinced skeptical military officials, unaccustomed to female nurses, that women could perform the work acceptably, and then recruited women. Battling the prevailing stereotypes—and accepting many of the common prejudices herself—Dix sought to ensure that her ranks not be inundated with flighty and marriage-minded young women by only accepting applicants who were plain looking and older than 30. In addition, Dix authorized a dress code of modest black or brown skirts and forbade hoops or jewelry.

Even with these strict and arbitrary requirements, relaxed somewhat as the war persisted, a total of over 3,000 women served as Union army nurses. Called "Dragon Dix" by some, the superintendent was stern and brusque, clashing frequently with the military bureaucracy and occasionally ignoring administrative details. Yet, army nursing care was markedly improved under her leadership.

Dix looked after the welfare of both the nurses, who labored in an often brutal environment, and the soldiers to whom they ministered, obtaining medical supplies from private sources when they were not forthcoming from the government. At the war's conclusion, Dix returned to her work on behalf of the mentally ill.

Accessible at http://www.civilwarhome.com/dixbio.htm. Source Catherine Clinton, *Scholastic Encyclopedia of the Civil War*. New York: Scholastic, 1999, 31.

EMILY BLACKWELL (1826–1910)

[Susan B. Anthony and Elizabeth Cady Stanton founded the National Women's Suffrage Association in 1869. The struggle for women's rights in the latter nineteenth century included not only the right to vote, but the right to study medicine and work in fields that had been exclusively dominated by men. Emily Blackwell and her sister Elizabeth were pioneers in the medical profession in America. Elizabeth was the first American woman

to earn a medical degree. Emily also wanted to study medicine and tried for six years to be accepted in a medical-school program before getting into Rush Medical College in Chicago, where she studied for one year. Pressure from the Illinois medical community caused Rush to terminate Blackwell's studies. Blackwell then completed her medical training and received her degree from Western Reserve University School of Medicine (now Case Western Reserve University) in 1854. Emily and Elizabeth, along with another doctor, Marie Zakrzewska, founded the New York Infirmary for Indigent Women and Children in Greenwich Village. This was the first hospital in America operated solely for women and by women. Analyzing women's conditions and needs, Emily Blackwell's hopeful and intelligent voice in this passage from a pamphlet illumines a way forward, explaining with righteous insistence why women at this time needed to join forces.]

Women Unite!

There is a lack of combination—of *esprit de corps*—among women, which contrasts strongly with what we find among men. No man stands alone. He has his trade-union, his club, his political affiliations and business connections with his fellows, be it on a higher or lower level, in a narrower or wider sphere. Women have nothing of all this. . . .

Combination and united action are, if possible, more essential to women than to men. The strength of women is purely that of moral force. So long as brute strength is the controlling force in society women have no place or chance in it. They are simply sacrificed to the physical needs of the race. But civilization means the predominance of moral over physical force, and the more complete this ascendancy, the better opportunity is there for the development of women to their full perfection. But to reach this end they must develop and exert their own moral force. This must be done not only by individual but by collective action. The highest must realize that she is outraged by the degradation of the lowest and that her own status is rendered insecure by the industrial misery and isolation of the workers below her. Every woman must learn that her position depends upon the general idea which society entertains of the nature, the powers, the qualities of womanhood, and that every class and rank of women contributes its quota toward forming this general estimate which decides the standing of each individual. Every woman should feel that it is incumbent on her to do her part toward raising this estimate, not only by her personal work and conduct but by the strength which comes through union, and should lend her aid to organized efforts for self-help and self-protection.

The Temperance Unions are almost the only example of any widely combined effort of women to exert an organized influence in any special direction. There should be even more universal organizations for other ends. If every girl knew as a matter of course that in each city, however large, or village, however small, there was an organization to which she could apply and find advice, information, and moral support when needed, she would not feel that she had to struggle alone against the influence too strong for her. If working women could be brought together in unions, in clubs, in organizations in which they found fellowship and the support that comes of companionship and intercourse they would not be so weak, so single handed in the struggle for existence. . . .

Emily Blackwell, M.D., (Excerpt from) "Need of Combination among Women for Self-Protection," *Philanthropist* (189?): 2, 7–8. Woodbridge, Conn.: Research Publications, c1985; 19th century legal treatises; no. 7133.

CHARITABLE ORGANIZATIONS

B'NAI B'RITH

[Benjamin Kahn was a rabbi and the international director of the B'nai B'rith Hillel Founda-
tions in Washington, D.C., as well as the director of the Jewish Studies Program at Ameri-
can University. Kahn's account below concerns the founding of the B'nai B'rith (Hebrew for
"Children of the Covenant") Jewish charitable organization and its activities in the nineteeth
century. Seemingly patterned on the fraternal organization model of the Freemasons, which
had long been in existence in America, B'nai B'rith connected the various charitable customs
of religious and ethnic Judaism in the New World diaspora to form a more organized type
of philanthropy. In 1901 B'nai B'rith joined forces with the Baron de Hirsch Fund to help
resettle immigrant Jews to inland communities, so that they would not all settle in big cities
on the East Coast. In later years B'nai B'rith started its Department of Adult Jewish Educa-
tion and undertook publications programs. B'nai B'rith has also offered social services for
veterans and has organized programs for the disabled for decades. The motto of B'nai B'rith
is "Charity, Fraternal Love and Harmony." The Jewish tradition of "Tikkun Olam," meaning
"Repair the world," has been an important aspiration from ancient times.]

B'nai B'rith's Birth and Growth by Benjamin Kahn

B'nai B'rith was founded on Oct. 13, 1843, by 12 men who met in a café on the Lower East Side of New York to establish a new fraternal order for U.S. Jews who then numbered 15,000 souls. The first president was Isaac Dittenhoefer, but Henry Jones, his successor, is credited as the chief founder. The founders chose B'nai B'rith ("Sons of the Covenant") as the name of their new organization and the Menorah as its insignia. They formulated its aims in the following preamble to the B'nai B'rith constitution; "B'nai B'rith has taken upon itself the mission of uniting persons of the Jewish faith [originally 'Israelites'] in the work of promoting their highest interests and those of humanity; of developing and elevating the mental and moral character of the people of our faith; of inculcating the purest principles of philanthropy, honor, and patriotism; of supporting science and art; alleviating the wants of the poor and needy; visiting and attending the sick; coming to the rescue of victims of persecution; providing for, pro-tecting, and assisting the widow and orphan on the broadest principles of humanity."

These purposes were implemented during the 19th and the early 20th century via a program dominated by mutual aid, social service, and philanthropy. In 1865 the order made a substantial grant to aid cholera epidemic sufferers in Erez Israel, and six years later to provide food, clothing, and medical supplies for victims of the Chicago fire. The organization established orphanages, homes for the aged, and hospitals. After 1881, when the mass immigration from Eastern Europe poured in to the country, B'nai B'rith sponsored Americanization classes, trade schools, and relief programs. Hitherto B'nai B'rith had consisted primarily of German Jews, but the changing character of the U.S. Jewish population, and of the 20th century, gave a new complexion to the constituency of the order, its program, and its structure. In 1897, when B'nai B'rith's membership numbered slightly more than 18,000, B'nai B'rith Women came into being with the founding of a ladies' auxiliary chapter in San Francisco. By 1968 B'nai B'rith women had over 1,000 chapters in 22 countries, with a membership of 135,000, with 90% of the chapters in North America.

Encyclopedia Judaica. Jerusalem: Keter Publishing House, 1972, 4:1144–45.

THE KNIGHTS OF COLUMBUS

[Humble beginnings mark the origins of a number of charitable institutions that have since grown large and become established across America. As described below, a handful of friends in a church basement saw a need and agreed to work together, beginning a movement that made a difference in the world around them. The imagery of knighthood is strong in a number of American organizations: the Knights of Pythias, the Knights of Columbus, the imagery of Knights Templar in the Freemasons, and the Knights of the Holy Eucharist, to name a few. Knights, as we saw in the introduction to Russell's "Sir Launfal," are associated with a noble spiritual quest, with service to others and willingness to live a life of self-sacrifice. The following account sketches the beginnings and charitable mission of the well-known Catholic charitable organization, the Knights of Columbus, dedicated to the principles enshrined in their motto: "Unity, Charity, and Fraternity."]

Knights of Columbus

History. Growth of the Knights of Columbus: On Oct. 2, 1881, a small group of men met in the basement of St. Mary's Church on Hillhouse Avenue in New Haven, Connecticut. Called together by their 29-year-old parish priest, Father Michael J. McGivney, these men formed a fraternal society that would one day become the world's largest Catholic family fraternal service organization. They sought strength in solidarity, and security through unity of purpose and devotion to a holy cause: they vowed to be defenders of their country, their families and their faith. These men were bound together by the ideal of Christopher Columbus, the discoverer of the Americas, the one whose hand brought Christianity to the New World. Their efforts came to fruition with the incorporation of the Knights of Columbus on March 29, 1882. . . .

The Order has been called "the strong right arm of the Church," and has been praised by popes, presidents and other world leaders, for support of the Church, programs of evangelization and Catholic education, civic involvement and aid to those in need.

http://www.kofc.org/about/history/index.cfm.

United in Charity. At the annual Supreme Council meeting in Texas in 2004, Supreme Knight Carl A. Anderson introduced United in Charity, a general, unrestricted endowment to support and ensure the overall long-term charitable and philanthropic goals of the Order.

Every year, the Order receives special requests from the Catholic Church and organizations closely aligned with our mission of support for the Church.

Now, such requests must be met from the general funds of the Order or in combination with specific appeals, as for example the Gulf States Disaster Relief fund—and the demand at times far exceeds the supply. The funds from United in Charity would help support these vital endeavors in the future.

http://www.kofc.org/un/about/charities/index.html.

THE LEND-A-HAND CLUB OF DAVENPORT, IOWA

[Local philanthropic enterprises were on the rise across America in the late 1800s. One source of the intensified philanthropic activity was Edward Everett Hale (1822–1909), whose father was the grandnephew of Nathan Hale, Revolutionary War martyr spy. Hale was a prodigy, entering Harvard at age thirteen, and graduating second in his class at age seventeen. A much-admired Unitarian minister, Hale was known for his social conscience, charisma, and pragmatic liberal theology, encouraging people to care for one another. He was a prolific writer, an effective preacher of hundreds of sermons, and the versatile author and editor of over sixty books. Before the Civil War, he was involved in the antislavery movement. Hale's sermons and magazine writings inspired many people; historians say he raised the tone of America's cultural and ethical life during the fifty years he eloquently spoke out to encourage humanitarian causes. Engaged in work on popular education, including organizing chautauquas and voicing his concern for the well-being of working-class homes, Hale brought a new standard to thinking about American values and spreading ideas about helping those in need. He also wrote for newspapers, editing for the Boston Daily Advertiser and the Christian Examiner, and he founded in 1886 his Lend-a-Hand Journal, the first national social-work journal in America. Hale wrote, "I am only one, but I am one. I cannot do everything, but I can do something. And because I cannot do everything, I will not refuse to do the something that I can do. What I can do, I should do. And what I should do, by the grace of God, I will do." In one story he wrote, "Look up and not down, forward and not back, look out and not in, lend-a-hand." Hale's ideas about reaching out to others were broadcast all across America and inspired the formation of several kinds of service organizations. The following is one example.]

The Founding of a Club to Improve the Lives of Local Working Girls

On December 25, 1887, ten women got together at a brown-bag lunch in Davenport, Iowa, to discuss how they could help improve the lives of local working girls—young women, some as young as fourteen (there were no child-labor laws then), arriving in Davenport without families or connections, just starting out as members of the work force. The meeting was organized by physician Jennie McCowen, who graduated with honors in 1876 from the State University of Iowa and began work on the medical staff at Iowa State Hospital for the Insane at Mount Pleasant and later moved to Davenport. Some of the women who met that day—a doctor, a teacher, a laundress, a dressmaker, a canning-factory girl, and two matrons of institutions—were professionals, and others were members of a King's Daughters Circle. (The Order of the Daughters of the King was founded in 1885 by Margaret J. Franklin at the Church of the Holy Sepulchre in New York City, an Episcopal church, and was dedicated to prayer and service.) The group discussed ways to help young women who, from the moment they arrived as strangers in town, had to deal with lodging, food, education, cultural adjustment, and a place to eat lunch and enjoy recreation. This lunch meeting led to the forming of a club called The Working Women's Lend-A-Hand Club.

At first the Club was housed in a small room in a building at Second and Brady. Girls who needed a place to spend time when they were not working brought their lunch parcels there during their noon break, or they could purchase lunch in the lunchroom for a few cents. Before long, plans began to develop for a larger facility—a boarding home where working girls could live. Such a home was opened at 708 Brady Street in 1901. That first year, one hundred girls applied to live there but could not be accommodated in the thirteen lodging rooms, so Club members began to think about a new and bigger building. Davenporters supported fund-raising events, including international pageants at the Opera House and a moonlight excursion on the Mississippi in 1911. The Davenport *Democrat and Leader* newspaper asked a conscience-probing question: "What if your girl were starting out in a strange city with small means and no friends? Would such an organization as the Lend-a-Hand be worthwhile?" Davenporters answered with their wallets, contributing more than was hoped for to the Club for enlarged facilities.

In June 1922 the new Club was built—a large rectangular brick building at 105 South Main Street by the Mississippi River—with eighty dormitory-style rooms and a sun parlor facing the river on each floor. It was not only a home for working women, but also the elderly and handicapped. It had a cafeteria and private dining rooms and boasted a modern swimming pool—over 16,000 people swam there in the first year alone. The Club offered members classes in German, English, domestic science, current events, arts and crafts, and needlework and crochet; it also served as a home for Girl Scout activities and musical programs for the community. The Club offered services to handicapped girls and ran an employment bureau as well.

Programs expanded, helping stranded women, women who had been victims of abuse, and women needing counseling and language instruction to start new lives. In the 1930s, the lounge, cafeteria, and swimming and meeting facilities were opened to all women. In 1987 the Club celebrated its hundredth-year anniversary by once again expanding.

William J. Jackson, based on articles from the Special Collections department of Davenport Public Library, and *Davenport Times Democrat*, December 2, 1965, 23-4.

THE FRATERNAL ORDER OF EAGLES

[During the latter 1800s, many fraternal organizations sprang up and spread across America. The Grange, for example, founded in 1867 to foster improvement of farmers' economic and social position, became popular in rural America. Like the Masons and other organizations already popular in the eighteenth century, these groups offered socializing networks where friends could meet and people could avail themselves of opportunities to help their communities and better the lives of those in need. The following is a colorful account of one such American fraternal organization, the Fraternal Order of Eagles. The eagle is an important emblem of America, a patriotic symbol in decorations and oratory. Under the banner of eagles, people across America have been

involved in supporting a variety of noble causes, some of which are mentioned below. The Eagles motto is "People Helping People."]

The Order of Good Things

It was over 100 years ago on February 6th, 1898 the Fraternal Order of Eagles was founded by six theater owners sitting on a pile of lumber in Moran's shipyard in Seattle, Washington. Competitors in the theater industry, they met to discuss a musicians strike. After deciding what to do on that issue, they decided to bury the hatchet and form an organization dubbed "The Order of Good Things."

The first meetings were held on the stages of various local theaters and after the business was settled a keg of beer was rolled out and all enjoyed a few hours of social activities. A few weeks later as their numbers grew they chose the Bald Eagle as their official emblem and changed the name to "The Fraternal Order of Eagles." The membership formed a Grand Aerie in April 1898, secured a charter, drew up a constitution and by-laws and elected its first president, John Cort.

Most of the first Eagle members were connected with the theatre, actors, stagehands, playwrights, etc., and as they went on tour they carried the story of the new order with them across the United States and Canada. This is the reason the Eagles grew so quickly and all the way across the country. Many cities in the east have low Aerie numbers such as New York #40, Philadelphia #42 and Buffalo #46.

The idea spread like wildfire. The order was unique in its concept of brotherhood and its early success has been attributed to its establishment of a sick and funeral benefit (no Eagle was ever buried in a "Potter's Field"), along with provisions for an Aerie physician and other "fringe benefits," unknown in other fraternal organizations up to that time.

As the Eagles grew, so did its responsibilities to its members. Its first Constitution and By-Laws were merely copied from those previously used by a defunct fraternal organization and it took later members like Frank Hering—the "Father of Mother's Day," and long time editor of the national Eagle Publication—to revise the By-Laws and make them unique from any other organization.

Hering, a member of South Bend Aerie No. 435, who had been Notre Dame's first Athletic Director and a great football quarterback and baseball player, wrote the order's funeral service. When he died in 1943 his stirring words were recited over his own body by Grand Worthy President Lester Loble. It was men like Hering who kept the Eagles from going under during the difficult days at the turn of the century and built the solid foundation it rests on today.

Over the years, the Eagles have fought and won many bitter battles for a Workman's Compensation Act, Mothers and Old Age pensions, Social Security laws and "Jobs After 40" and are still fighting to liberalize present social benefits along with combating vicious diseases plaguing mankind through their sponsorship of the Art Ehrmann Cancer Fund, Max Bear Heart Fund, Jimmy Durante Children's Fund, "Doc" Dunlap Kidney Fund and the Diabetes Fund.

Many great social and political leaders have belonged to the Eagles. President Theodore Roosevelt was one of the many who joined and praised the order for its humanitarian accomplishments, as did a later Roosevelt—Franklin Delano. President Harry S. Truman often reiterated that the Eagles were his type of organization—one founded by, and for the common man.

As you learn about our history, you will see we are just like you. Proud, Caring, People Helping People, that understand that the needs of the many will always outweigh the needs of the few.

Fraternal Order of Eagles Web site at http://www.foe.com/history/history.html.

PHILANTHROPIC AND SAINTLY GIVERS

On GEORGE PEABODY

[George Peabody began working at age eleven as a stock boy in a store in his New England hometown. At nineteen he became a partner in a dry-goods business that became very successful. From 1850 onward, as the values of scientific understanding and capitalism grew increasingly important, philanthropy became less exclusively a domain of religion and moral reform. Institutes to further education and research were established by the endowments of wealthy industrialists and financiers. With his wealth, Peabody engaged in philanthropic activities to improve society, encourage self-help for the poor, and promote education and public access to information. Some have called him the father of modern philanthropy. He was honored in England, where a statue of him still stands in London, and in America, where he received the Congressional Medal of Honor in 1867. His hometown, South Danvers, is now known as Peabody, Massachusetts.]

George Peabody—Nineteenth-century Philanthropist
by Elizabeth Schaaf

George Peabody, founder of the Peabody Institute, was born in Danvers, Massachusetts, in 1795, into a family of modest means. With only four years of formal education and no family connections, he achieved enormous international success as an investment banker in London. He is considered by many to be the founder of modern philanthropy.

While serving as a volunteer in the War of 1812, Peabody met Elisha Riggs of Baltimore. In 1814, Riggs supplied financial backing to found the wholesale dry goods firm of Peabody, Riggs, and Company. In 1816, Peabody moved to Baltimore and took offices in Old Congress Hall on Baltimore and Sharp Streets. Baltimore would be his home for the next 20 years. The thriving Baltimore business soon established branches in Philadelphia and New York. Seeking still wider business opportunities, George Peabody traveled to England in 1827 to purchase wares and to negotiate the sale of American cotton in Lancashire. In 1837, the year Queen Victoria ascended the throne, he took up residence in London.

In 1838, Peabody played an important role in the rescue of the financial fortunes of the state of Maryland and other states by his support of their bonds, at a time when the market was flooded with such instruments. Peabody was able to sell Maryland bonds to Baring Brothers by assuring the company of the state's good faith and credit and then bought a quantity of the securities himself. He also campaigned for the states to honor their commitments and, when they did, he made a fortune on the bonds he had bought when much of the public thought them worthless.

In 1851, Britain, which had been moving towards free trade, staged *The Great Exhibition of the World of Industry of All Nations* in London in the daring new exhibition hall, dubbed the "Crystal Palace" by the British press. The purpose of the exhibition was to show off British products to new foreign markets. President Fillmore provided transportation for American goods to the Exhibition, but Congress, still suspicious of the British, refused funds for U.S. participation in this "speculative venture." The American exhibits languished in their crates while the British press heaped scorn on the former colony. Peabody recognized the importance of his country's taking part and put up £3,000 (about $15,000) of his own funds to install the American exhibits. His investment paid off handsomely, as immense crowds flocked to see Colt's revolver, Cyrus McCormick's reaping machine, fine daguerreotypes, and other wonders.

Figure 3.12 Statue of George Peabody

During this period, British society was reeling under the impact of industrialization and uncontrolled urban growth, with the homeless and destitute increasing at an appalling rate. The problems plaguing England spurred the adoption of the Poor Laws and gave rise to a host of charitable causes. Charles Dickens' writings reminded the more affluent of the plight of the poor. The Ragged Schools received Lord Shaftesbury's parliamentary backing and Angela Burdett-Coutts' financial support. George Peabody knew these people and shared their concerns.

Peabody's philanthropic activities began after the Great Exhibition. All of them were aimed towards improving society, and particularly at providing the less fortunate with the means to improve themselves. Unlike many philanthropists of the period, his activities were not intended to promote religious beliefs; in fact, he clearly stated that his institutions were not to be used to nurture sectarian theology or political dissension. An 1831 letter to his nephew, David Peabody, probably provides the best insight into the reasons for his philanthropy:

> *Deprived, as I was, of the opportunity of obtaining anything more than the most common education, I am well qualified to estimate its value by the disadvantages I labour under in the society in which my business and situation in life frequently throws me, and willingly would I now give twenty times the expense attending a good education could I possess it, but it is now too late for me to learn and I can only do to those that come under my care, as I could have wished circumstances had permitted others to have done by me. . . .*

. . . Peabody founded and supported numerous institutions in New England and elsewhere. At the close of the Civil War, he established the Peabody Education Fund to "encourage the intellectual, moral, and industrial education of the destitute children of the Southern States." However, his grandest beneficence was to Baltimore where he achieved his earliest success.

Elizabeth Schaaf, Archivist of the Peabody Institute, http://www.peabodyhistorical.org/gpeabody. htm. (emphasis original)

Although he was a shrewd merchant, and for the most part made a point of ignoring all direct requests for charity, Peabody had qualities which made him highly attractive to both men and women and especially to young people. His deeply lined face and snow-white hair seemed an index to his character—acute, strong, yet benevolent. He was kindly, generous both to his numerous relatives (he never married) and to the objects of his great benefactions, and, though simple in his personal tastes, moved urbanely in London society. Moreover, in his business dealings there was no trace of the dishonorable practices to which the great American financiers of the next generation sometimes stooped.

"George Peabody 1795–1869," http://rjohara.net/peabody/gpeabody.

W. T. STEAD

[William Thomas Stead was a controversial journalist and a well-known pacifist and spiritualist. He was said to be the most famous passenger on the Titanic when it sank. Railroad tycoon Jay Gould, about whom he penned the passage below, was also a controversial public figure. When he died at fifty-eight, journalists noted that he left 70 million dollars to his children and none to the country where he made his fortune. The turning points in Gould's amassing of a fortune have often been characterized as crooked and devious. Note the animal images in Stead's character sketch below exploring Gould's contributions to society—"a vulture, a viper, a wolf"—and also the image of royalty in the statement "the millionaire is the king." This portrayal reflects ambivalence; in America, status, nobility, and wealth are associated with largesse, yet, too, there is sometimes resentment. Stead implies that Gould could have given more and also that he could have been more conscious of his public image as a giver. Gould's religion was indeterminate; he was not a churchgoer and was said to be quiet and private in regard to his religious beliefs. His wife and children were Episcopalians. As a philanthropist, Gould seems to have been less conscientious and less effective and influential than Peabody, Carnegie, and Rockefeller, who paid more attention to the choices and effects of their giving.]

Was Jay Gould a Good Philanthropist?

The whole carnivora has been ransacked to find analogies for Jay Gould. He has been a vulture, a viper, a wolf, a fox, a bear, and no one knows what other animals of prey. There is little doubt that Jay Gould did not shed crocodile tears over his victims any more than Napoleon did over the Prussians and Austrians whom he crushed at Jena and Austerlitz. But, just as it is possible for great warriors to be very humane, so it is possible for eminent financial operators to preserve their "bird in their breast," and, as a matter of fact, many of the kings of Wall street and of the Bourse [the European stick exchange] have in the midst of their acquisition preserved a love of their fellow men as well as for their fellow men's cash.

. . . As an individual, as a husband, as a father, and as a florist, he may have been ideal. But it is as a millionaire he must be judged, and as a millionaire he must be condemned or acquitted. That is to say, the judgment will go for or against Jay Gould, not upon the method in which he utilized the faculties and opportunities which are common to the whole human family, but as to the use he made of the exceptional faculties and opportunities that lay within his reach. In the plutocratic democracy, such as the United States, the millionaire is the king. His friends have again and again asserted that no man in the whole country was more powerful than Jay Gould. What use did he make of his millions? They say that he employed them to develop the resources of the great Southwest, to extend the telegraph system, and to generally promote the material welfare of the country. Well and good; that may be true, but of course there is another side to all this, and there are many who maintain that, even from a material progress point of view, the United States would have got on better if Jay Gould had never come out of the cellar in which his father locked him the first time he played truant. Those who take this view have a curious confirmation in the fact that within a week of Jay Gould's death the value of the stocks in which his fortune was locked up increased greatly. It was estimated at no less than $400,000.

But is that all? His friends reply that he used his wealth not merely for the promotion of the material development of the United States, but for the prevention of panics, and in many cases for the saving of his friends from imminent ruin.

It may be so; the millionaire, with all his moneybags round about him, is driven by the instinct of self-preservation to endeavor to prevent catastrophes which would certainly impair the value of his securities.

Then, as to the saving of his friends, that is quite possible. All those who were in the inner circle declare that he was kindly dispositioned and inclined to help where he could.

His Charities

Then they say further that, despite the evidence afforded by his will, in which $70,000,000 were left to his heirs, without a single cent being devoted to public charities or works of beneficence, that he had been extremely generous during his lifetime. But in strict accordance with the evangelical precept, he had not let his left hand know what his right hand did. It may be so, but it is to be regretted that he did not carry out other evangelical precepts, for nothing could be greater than the secrecy with which he covered all such beneficence. The secrecy is, indeed, so great that most people believe that no such beneficence existed. On one occasion it is said that he gave $10,000 to a Presbyterian building fund, and that stands out as almost the only gift of any importance that he is said to have made. Dr. Green declares that his noble impulse and generous benefactions are known only to those who were intimately acquainted with him. The directors of the Missouri also lay stress upon these personal qualities of which the world knows nothing:

> Of the personal qualities of Mr. Gould we may record the just estimate of those who, by long and intimate association with him, have been made, as we believe, fit judges. Mr. Gould was a man of tried personal and moral courage, a kind, considerate and generous friend, modest and gentle in demeanor, moderate in speech, judicial and just in his judgments. To those whose business and

personal relationship to him had been longest and closest he was most endeared.

According to Mr. Morosini:

> Mr. Gould gave away many fortunes in his lifetime. He always concealed his generous deeds, because rich men are besieged by beggars all the time. In one instance I was made the agent in a gift of $65,000 to one man out West whom Mr. Gould wished to befriend. No one ever heard of it. Several years ago it was telegraphed from Richmond that some unknown Northern man had responded to the appeal of those in charge at Mount Vernon and had purchased additional acres of land to be added to the old Washington estate. It turned out that Mr. Gould had bought the property and turned it over to the Mount Vernon people.

Thurlow Reed's Testimony

The most remarkable statement, however, is that of the well-known philanthropist, the late Mr. Thurlow Weed, who in 1879 spoke as follows on this subject: "I am Mr. Gould's philanthropic adviser. Whenever a really deserving charity is brought to my attention, I explain it to Mr. Gould. He always takes my word as to when and how much to contribute. I have never known him to disregard my advice in such matters. His only condition is that there shall be no public blazonry of his benefactions. He is a constant and liberal giver, but doesn't let his right hand know what his left hand is doing. Oh, there will be a full page to his credit when the record is opened above."

If so, it is to be sincerely hoped that it will be to his credit hereafter, for it certainly has not been put to his credit at present. As an illustration of this, take the following extract from the sermon preached by the Rev. G. Inglehart, in Park Avenue Methodist Episcopal Church on the Sunday after his death:

> Gould, with his seventy millions, was one of the colossal failures of our time. He was a purely selfish man. His greed consumed his charity. He was like death and hell—gathering in all, giving back . . .

What Millionaires Might Do

What could not these men do if they were to band themselves together in a sacred league to make war upon all those things which they themselves would unanimously agree were evils afflicting mankind? They will reply, no doubt, that they have not so much as a moment, to think of the disposition of such vast questions. The task that absorbs their time and consumes their energies is that of seeing that their investments are safe, and that their constantly accruing millions are profitably invested. Mr. Russell Sage, in September, 1890, said: "Mr. Gould cannot begin to use even a small portion for his own personal use even a small part of the interest which his dividend money alone would yield. He must reinvest it, and he does reinvest it. It is safe to say that he takes this money as the dividend period comes around and buys other securities." In other words, they have got so much to do in the getting and hoarding that they have neither inclination nor time, or they have no time even if they have the inclination to concern themselves about its disposition. Such a position is a dangerous one for them to take up. Great wealth, unless greatly used, will not be left long in the administration of individual men. If it be true that the getting and hoarding absorbs the whole of the gray matter in the millionaire's brain, then we shall not have long to wait before we shall see the crystallizing of the inarticulate unrest of the suffering multitude in the conviction that there should be a division of labor, and that while the millionaire should be allowed to get his millions, the elected representatives of the democracy should decide the way in which it should be spent and distributed. The millionaire would thus be relieved of the burden of looking after his millions, and could devote the whole of his time and energy to the more congenial task of amassing them.

W. T. Stead, "Jay Gould," *The American Review of Reviews*, February, 1893, http://www.attackingthedevil.co.uk/reviews/gould.php.

ANDREW CARNEGIE (1835–1919)

[Born in Scotland, Carnegie migrated to America in 1848 and became a major business-man in the steel industry and later a great philanthropist. All members of his immediate family were lapsed Calvinists who found spiritual inspiration in sources such as the teachings of Swedenborg and Channing. Carnegie was not dominated by Calvinist stern-ness, but in business he was sober and industrious—and very successful. He gave away most of his fortune while he was alive. He liked to provide for those who worked hard to become self-sufficient, believing that giving to unworthy causes did more harm than good. He donated funds to found free public libraries and supported schools and universities in America and abroad. He funded scientific-research centers, paid for museums, and financed efforts for world peace. He had strong ideas about the values of accumulating wealth and how to help society, as seen below. He asserted that "the kept Dollar is a stink-ing fish," after he had attained his great wealth and was busy distributing it to the best effect. His book on this topic, The Gospel of Wealth, is a well-known classic.]

The Gospel of Wealth and Best Fields for Philanthropy
Part I: The Problem of the Administration of Wealth

The problem of our age is the proper administration of wealth, that the ties of brotherhood may still bind together the rich and poor in harmonious relationship. The conditions of human life have not only been changed, but revolutionized, within the past few hundred years. In former days there was little difference between the dwelling, dress, food, and environment of the chief and those of his retainers. The Indians are today where civilized man then was. When visiting the Sioux, I was led to the wigwam of the chief. It was like the others in external appearance, and even within the difference was trifling between it and those of the poorest of his braves. The contrast between the palace of the millionaire and the cottage of the laborer with us today measures the change which has come with civilization. This change, however, is not to be deplored, but welcomed as highly beneficial. It is well, nay, essential, for the progress of the race that the houses of some should be homes for all that is highest and best in literature and the arts, and for all the refinements of civilization, rather than that none should be so. Much better this great irregularity than universal squalor. Without wealth there can be no Maecenas. The "good old times" were not good old times. Neither master nor servant was as well situated then as today. A relapse to old conditions would be disastrous to both—not the least so to him who serves—and would sweep away civilization with it. But whether the change be for good or ill, it is upon us, beyond our power to alter, and, therefore, to be accepted and made the best of. It is a waste of time to criticize the inevitable.

* * *

The price which society pays for the law of competition, like the price it pays for cheap comforts and luxuries, is also great; but the advantages of this law are also greater still than its cost—for it is to this law that we owe our wonderful material development, which brings improved conditions in its train. But, whether the law be benign or not, we must say of it, as we say of the change in the conditions of men to which we have referred: It is here; we cannot evade it; no substitutes for it have been found; and while the law may be sometimes hard for the individual, it is best for the race, because it insures the survival of the fittest in every department. We accept and welcome, therefore, as conditions to which we must accommodate ourselves, great inequality of environment; the concentration of business, industrial and commercial, in the hands of a few; and the law of competition between these, as being not only beneficial, but essential to the future progress of the race. Having accepted these, it follows that there must be great scope for the exercise of special ability in the merchant and in the manufacturer who has to conduct affairs upon a great scale. That this talent for organization and management is rare among men is proved by the fact that it invariably secures enormous rewards for its possessor, no matter where or under what laws or conditions. The experienced in affairs always rate the man whose services can be obtained as a partner as not only the first consideration, but such as render the question of his capital scarcely worth considering: for able men soon create capital; in the hands of those without the special talent required, capital soon takes wings. Such men become interested in firms or corporations using millions; and, estimating only simple interest to be made upon the capital invested, it is inevitable that their income must exceed their expenditure and that they must, therefore, accumulate wealth. Nor is there any middle ground which such men can occupy, because the great manufacturing or commercial concern which does not earn at least interest upon its capital soon becomes bankrupt. It must either go forward or fall behind; to stand still is impossible. It is a condition essential to its successful operation that it should be thus far profitable, and even that, in addition to interest on capital, it should make profit. It is a law, as certain as any of the others named, that men possessed of this peculiar talent for affairs, under the free play of economic forces must, of necessity, soon be in receipt of more revenue than can be judiciously expended upon themselves; and this law is as beneficial for the race as the others.

Objections to the foundations upon which society is based are not in order, because the condition of the race is better with these than it has been with any other which has been tried. Of the effect of any new substitutes proposed we can-not [sic] be sure. The Socialist or Anarchist who seeks to overturn present conditions is to be regarded as attacking the foundation upon which civilization itself rests, for civilization took its start from the day when the capable, industrious workman said to his incompetent and lazy fellow, "If thou dost not sow, thou shalt not reap," and thus ended primitive Communism by separating the drones from the bees. One who studies this subject will soon be brought face to face with the conclusion that upon the sacredness of property civilization itself depends—the right of the laborer to his hundred dollars in the savings-bank, and equally the legal right of the millionaire to his millions. Every man must be allowed "to sit under his own vine and fig-tree, with none to make afraid," if human society is to advance, or even to remain so far advanced as it is. To those who propose to substitute Communism for this intense Individualism, the answer therefore is: The race has tried that. All progress from the barbarous day to the present time has resulted from its displacement. Not evil, but good, has come to the race from the accumulation of wealth by those who have had the ability and energy to produce it. But even if we admit for a moment that it might be better for the race to discard its present foundation, Individualism,—that it is a nobler ideal that man should labor, not for himself alone, but in and for a brotherhood of his fellows, and share with them all in common, realizing Swedenborg's idea of heaven, where, as he says, the angels derive their happiness, not from laboring for self, but for each other,—even admit all this, and a sufficient answer is, This is not evolution, but revolution. It necessitates the changing of human nature itself—a work of eons, even if it were good to change it, which we cannot know.

It is not practicable in our day or in our age. Even if desirable theoretically, it belongs to another and long-succeeding sociological stratum. Our duty is with what is practicable now—with the next step possible in our day and generation.

*　　*　　*

There are but three modes in which surplus wealth can be disposed of. It can be left to the families of the decedents; or it can be bequeathed for public purposes; or, finally, it can be administered by its possessors during their lives. Under the first and second modes most of the wealth of the world that has reached the few has hitherto been applied. Let us in turn consider each of these modes. The first is the most injudicious. In monarchical countries, the estates and the greatest portion of the wealth are left to the first son, that the vanity of the parent may be gratified by the thought that his name and title are to descend unimpaired to succeeding generations. The condition of this class in Europe to-day teaches the failure of such hopes or ambitions. The successors have become impoverished through their follies, or from the fall in the value of land. Even in Great Britain the strict law of entail has been found inadequate to maintain an hereditary class. Its soil is rapidly passing into the hands of the stranger. Under republican institutions the division of property among the children is much fairer; but the question which forces itself upon thoughtful men in all lands is, Why should men leave great fortunes to their children? If this is done from affection, is it not misguided affection? Observation teaches that, generally speaking, it is not well for the children that they should be so burdened. Neither is it well for the State. Beyond providing for the wife and daughters moderate sources of income, and very moderate allowances indeed, if any, for the sons, men may well hesitate; for it is no longer questionable that great sums bequeathed often work more for the injury than for the good of the recipients. Wise men will soon conclude that, for the best interests of the members of their families, and of the State; such bequests are an improper use of their means.

It is not suggested that men who have failed to educate their sons to earn a livelihood shall cast them adrift in poverty. If any man has seen fit to rear his sons with a view to their living idle lives, or, what is highly commendable, has instilled in them the sentiment that they are in a position to labor for public ends without reference to pecuniary considerations, then, of course, the duty of the parent is to see that such are provided for in moderation. There are instances of millionaires' sons unspoiled by wealth, who, being rich, still perform great services to the community. Such are the very salt of the earth, as valuable as, unfortunately, they are rare. It is not the exception, however, but the rule, that men must regard; and, looking at the usual result of enormous sums conferred upon legatees, the thoughtful man must shortly say, "I would as soon leave to my son a curse as the almighty dollar," and admit to himself that it is not the welfare of the children, but family pride, which inspires these legacies.

As to the second mode, that of leaving wealth at death for public uses, it may be said that this is only a means for the disposal of wealth, provided a man is content to wait until he is dead before he becomes of much good in the world.

*　　*　　*

Poor and restricted are our opportunities in this life, narrow our horizon, our best work most imperfect; but rich men should be thankful for one inestimable boon. They have it in their power during their lives to busy themselves in organizing benefactions from which the masses of their fellows will derive lasting advantage, and thus dignify their own lives. The highest life is probably to be reached, not by such imitation of the life of Christ as Count Tolstoi gives us, but while animated by Christ's spirit, by recognizing the changed conditions of this age, and adopting modes of expressing this spirit suitable to the changed conditions under which we live, still laboring for the good of our fellows, which was the essence of his life and teaching, but laboring in a different manner.

This, then, is held to be the duty of the man of wealth: To set an example of modest, unostentatious living, shunning display or extravagance; to provide moderately for the legitimate wants of those dependent upon him; and, after doing so, to consider all surplus revenues which come to him simply as trust funds, which he is called upon to administer, and strictly bound as a matter of duty to administer in the manner which, in his judgment, is best calculated to produce the most beneficial results for the community—the man of wealth thus becoming the mere trustee and agent for his poorer brethren, bringing to their service his superior wisdom, experience, and ability to administer, doing for them better than they would or could do for themselves. . . .

The best uses to which surplus wealth can be put have already been indicated. Those who would administer wisely must, indeed, be wise; for one of the serious obstacles to the improvement of our race is indiscriminate charity. It were better for mankind that the millions of the rich were thrown into the sea than so spent as to encourage the slothful, the drunken, the unworthy. Of every thousand dollars spent in so-called charity today, it is probable that nine hundred and fifty dollars is unwisely spent—so spent, indeed, as to produce the very evils which it hopes to mitigate or cure. A well-known writer of philosophic books admitted the other day that he had given a quarter of a dollar to a man who approached him as he was coming to visit the house of his friend. He knew nothing of the habits of this beggar, knew not the use that would be made of this money, although he had every reason to suspect that it would be spent improperly. This man professed to be a disciple of Herbert Spencer; yet the quarter-dollar given that night will probably work more injury than all the money will do good which its thoughtless donor will ever be able to give in true charity. He only gratified his own feelings, saved himself from annoyance—and this was probably one of the most selfish and very worst actions of his life, for in all respects he is most worthy.

In bestowing charity, the main consideration should be to help those who will help themselves; to provide part of the means by which those who desire to improve may do so; to give those who desire to rise the aids by which they may rise; to assist, but rarely or never to do all. Neither the individual nor the race is improved by almsgiving. Those worthy of assistance, except in rare cases, seldom require assistance. The really valuable men of the race never do, except in case of accident or sudden change. Everyone has, of course, cases of individuals brought to his own knowledge where temporary assistance can do genuine good, and these he will not overlook. But the amount which can be wisely given by the individual for individuals is necessarily limited by his lack of knowledge of the circumstances connected with each. He is the only true reformer who is as careful and as anxious not to aid the unworthy as he is to aid the worthy, and, perhaps, even more so, for in almsgiving more injury is probably done by rewarding vice than by relieving virtue. . . .

Thus is the problem of rich and poor to be solved. The laws of accumulation will be left free, the laws of distribution free. Individualism will continue, but the millionaire will be but a trustee for the poor, intrusted for a season with a great part of the increased wealth of the community, but administering it for the community far better than it could or would have done for itself. The best minds will thus have reached a stage in the development of the race in which it is clearly seen that there is no mode of disposing of surplus wealth creditable to thoughtful and earnest men into whose hands it flows, save by using it year by year for the general good. This day already dawns. Men may die without incurring the pity of their fellows, still sharers in great business enterprises from which their capital cannot be or has not been withdrawn, and which is left chiefly at death for public uses; yet the day is not far distant when the man who dies leaving behind him millions of available wealth, which was free for him to administer during life, will pass away "unwept, unhonored, and unsung," no matter to what uses he leaves the dross which he cannot take with him. Of such as these the public verdict will then be: "The man who dies thus rich dies disgraced."

Such, in my opinion, is the true gospel concerning wealth, obedience to which is destined some day to solve the problem of the rich and the poor, and to bring "Peace on earth, among men good will."

Andrew Carnegie, *The Gospel of Wealth and Other Timely Essays*. Cambridge, Mass.: Harvard University Press, 1962, 14–21, 25–29. Accessible at http://www.webpal.org/a_reconstruction/lets/carnegie/content.htm.

...This is where the children of honest poverty have the most precious of all advantages over those of wealth. The mother, nurse, cook, governess, teacher, saint, all in one; the father, exemplar, guide, counselor, and friend! Thus were my brother and I brought up. What has the child of millionaire or nobleman that counts compared to such a heritage?

Andrew Carnegie, *Autobiography of Andrew Carnegie*. Boston: Northeastern University Press, 1986, 30. Accessible at http://www.wordowner.com/carnegie/chapter2.htm.

On JOHN CHAPMAN (1775–1847)

[By planting apple orchards on the frontier, John Chapman (later nicknamed Johnny Appleseed) prepared the way for an America of family farms. This dedication to nurturing rural life was challenged by Johnny Smokestackseed, Johnny Railroadseed, Johnny Oilwellseed, and Johnny Steelmillseed, who soon left their own marks on the landscape.

The "little home on the prairie," which John Chapman hoped to make more happy and comfortable, was a part of American life in the early 1800s, but before long, the slums in fast-growing cities were also a part of America. Johnny Appleseed's life of service made him a folk hero and, for some, a generous folk saint. In 1946 Walt Disney made a short cartoon about Johnny Appleseed, and there have since been a variety of plays, poems, songs, and events celebrating his life. In Fort Wayne, Indiana, where he was buried, there is an annual Johnny Appleseed festival. He is one of the early American heroes who offered gentleness, generosity in giving material goods, and an example of friendliness and spiritual inspiration to ongoing generations. William D'Arcy Haley (1828–1890), a Unitarian minister and writer, collected information about John Chapman's life from people who had met him and composed the following memorial to him.]

Johnny Appleseed—A Pioneer Hero
by W. D. Haley

The "far West" is rapidly becoming only a traditional designation: railroads have destroyed the romance of frontier life, or have surrounded it with so many appliances of civilization that the pioneer character is rapidly becoming mythical. The men and women who obtain their groceries and dry-goods from New York by rail in a few hours have nothing in common with those who, fifty years ago, "packed" salt a hundred miles to make their mush palatable, and could only exchange corn and wheat for molasses and calico by making long and perilous voyages in flat-boats down the Ohio and Mississippi rivers to New Orleans. Two generations of frontier lives have accumulated stores of narrative which, like the small but beautiful tributaries of great rivers, are forgotten in the broad sweep of the larger current of history. The march of Titans sometimes tramples out the memory of smaller but more useful lives, and sensational glare often eclipses more modest but purer lights. This has been the case in the popular demand for the dime novel dilutions of Fenimore Cooper's romances of border life, which have preserved the records of Indian rapine and atrocity as the only memorials of pioneer history. But the early days of Western settlement witnessed sublimer heroisms than those of human torture, and nobler victories than those of the tomahawk and scalping-knife. Among the heroes of endurance that was voluntary, and of action that was creative and not sanguinary, there was one man whose name, seldom mentioned now save by some of the few surviving pioneers, deserves to be perpetrated.

The first reliable trace of our modest hero finds him in the Territory of Ohio, in 1801, with a horse-load of apple seeds, which he planted in various places on and about the borders of Licking Creek, the first orchard thus originated by him being on the farm of Isaac Stadden, in what is now known as Licking County, in the State of Ohio. During the five succeeding years, although he was undoubtedly following the same strange occupation, we have no authentic account of his movements until we reach a pleasant spring day in 1806, when a pioneer settler in Jefferson County, Ohio, noticed a peculiar craft, with a remarkable occupant and a curious cargo, slowly dropping down with the current of the Ohio River. It was "Johnny Appleseed," by which name Jonathan Chapman was afterward known in every log-cabin from the Ohio river to the Northern lakes, and westward to the prairies of what is now the State of Indiana. With two canoes lashed together he was transporting a load of apple seeds to the Western frontier, for the purpose of creating orchards on the farthest verge of white settlements. With his canoes he passed down the Ohio to Marietta, where he entered the Muskingum, ascending the stream of that river until he reached the mouth of the Walhonding, or White Woman Creek, and still onward, up the Mohican, into the Black Fork, to the head of navigation, in the region now on the line of the Pittsburg and Fort Wayne Railroad, in Ohio. A long and toilsome voyage it was, as a glance at the map will show, and must have occupied a great deal of time, as the lonely traveler stopped at every inviting spot to plant the seeds and make his infant nurseries. These are the first well-authenticated facts in the history of Jonathan Chapman, whose birth, there is good reason for believing, occurred in Boston, Massachusetts, in 1775. According to this, which was his own state-ment in one of his less reticent moods, he was, at the time of his appearance on Licking Creek, twenty-six years of age, and whether impelled in his eccentricities by some abso-lute misery of the heart which could only find relief in incessant motion, or governed by a benevolent monomania, his whole after-life was devoted to the work of planting apple seeds in remote places. The seeds he gathered from the cider-presses of Western Pennsylva-nia; but his canoe voyage in 1806 appears to have been the only occasion upon which he adopted that method of transporting them, as all his subsequent journeys were made on foot. Having planted his stock of seeds, he would return to Pennsylvania for a fresh sup-ply, and, as sacks made of any less substan-tial fabric would not endure the hard usage of the long trip through forests dense with underbrush and briers, he provided himself

Figure 3.13 Johnny Appleseed

with leathern bags. Securely packed, the seeds were conveyed, sometimes on the back of a horse, and not infrequently on his own shoulders, either over a part of the old Indian trail that led from Fort Duquesne to Detroit, by way of Fort Sandusky, or over what is styled in the appendix to "Hutchin's History of Bognet's Expedition in 1864" the "second route through the wilderness of Ohio," which would require him to traverse a distance of one hundred and sixty-six miles in a west-northwest direction from Fort Duquesne in order to reach the Black Fork of the Mohican.

* * *

In personal appearance Chapman was a small, wiry man, full of restless activity; he had long dark hair, a scanty beard that was never shaved, and keen black eyes that sparkled with a peculiar brightness. His dress was of the oddest description. Generally, even in the coldest weather, he went barefooted, but sometimes, for his long journeys, he would make himself a rude pair of sandals; at other times he would wear any cast-off foot-covering he chanced to find—a boot on one foot and an old brogan or a moccasin on the other. It appears to have been a matter of conscience with him never to purchase shoes, although he was rarely without money enough to do so. On one occasion, in an unusually cold November, while he was traveling barefooted through mud and snow, a settler who happened to possess a pair of shoes that were too small for his own use forced their acceptance upon Johnny, declaring that it was sinful for a human being to travel with naked feet in such weather. A few days afterward the donor was in the village that has since become the thriving city of Mansfield, and met his beneficiary contentedly plodding along with his feet bare and half frozen. With some degree of anger he inquired for the cause of such foolish conduct, and received for reply that Johnny had overtaken a poor, barefooted family moving Westward, and as they appeared to be in much greater need of clothing than he was, he had given them the shoes. His dress was generally composed of cast-off clothing, that he had taken in payment of apple-trees; and as the pioneers were far less extravagant than their descendants in such matters, the homespun and buckskin garments that they discarded would not be very elegant or serviceable. In his later years, however, he seems to have thought that even this kind of second-hand raiment was too luxurious, as his principal garment was made of a coffee sack, in which he cut holes for his head and arms to pass through and pronounced it "a very serviceable cloak, and as good clothing as any man need wear." In the matter of head-gear his taste was equally unique; his first experiment was with a tin vessel that served to cook his mush, but this was open to the objection that it did not protect his eyes from the beams of the sun; so he constructed a hat of pasteboard with an immense peak in the front, and having thus secured an article that combined usefulness with economy, it became his permanent fashion.

Thus strangely clad, he was perpetually wandering through forests and morasses, and suddenly appearing in white settlements and Indian villages; but there must have been some rare force of gentle goodness dwelling in his looks and breathing in his words, for it is the testimony of all who know him that, not withstanding his ridiculous attire, he was always treated with the greatest respect by the rudest frontiers-man, and, what is a better test, the boys of the settlements forbore to jeer at him. With grown-up people and boys he was usually reticent, but manifested great affection for little girls, always having pieces of ribbon and gay calico to give to his little favorites. Many a grandmother in Ohio and Indiana remember the presents she received when a child from poor homeless Johnny Appleseed. When he consented to eat with any family he would never sit down to the table until he was assured that there was an ample supply for the children; and his sympathy for their youthful troubles and his kindness toward them made him friends among all the juveniles of the borders.

The Indians also treated Johnny with the greatest kindness. By these wild and sanguinary savages he was regarded as a "great medicine man," on account of his strange appearance, eccentric actions, and especially the fortitude with which he could endure pain, in proof of which he would often thrust pins and needles into his flesh. His nervous sensibilities really seem to have been less acute than those of ordinary people, for his method of treating the cuts and sores that were the consequences of his barefooted wanderings through briers and thorns was to sear the wound with a red-hot iron, and then cure the burn. During the war of 1812, when the frontier settlers were tortured and slaughtered by the savage allies of Great Britain, Johnny Appleseed continued his wanderings, and was never harmed by the roving bands of hostile Indians. On many occasions the impunity with which he ranged the country enabled him to give the settlers warning of approaching dangers in time to allow them to take refuge in their brick-houses before the savages could attack them. Our informant refers to one of these instances, when the news of Hull's surrender came like a thunder-bolt upon the frontier. Large bands of Indians and British were destroying every thing before them and murdering defenseless women and children, and even the block-houses were not always a sufficient protection. At this time Johnny traveled day and night, warning the people of the approaching danger. He visited every cabin and delivered this message: "The Spirit of the Lord is upon me, and he hath anointed me to blow the trumpet in the wilderness, and sound an alarm in the forest; for, behold, the tribes of the heathen are round about your doors, and a devouring flame followeth after them." The aged man who narrated this incident said that he could feel even now the thrill that was caused by this prophetic announcement of the wild-looking herald of danger, who aroused the family on a bright moonlight midnight with his piercing voice. Refusing all offers of food and denying himself a moment's rest, he traversed the border day and night until he had warned every settler of the approaching peril.

His diet was as meager as his clothing. He believed it to be a sin to kill any creature for food, and thought that all that was necessary for human sustenance was produced by the soil. He was also a strenuous opponent of the waste of food, and on one occasion, on approaching a log-cabin, he observed some fragments of bread floating upon the surface of a bucket of slops that was intended for the pigs. He immediately fished them out, and when the housewife expressed her astonishment, he told her that it was an abuse of the gifts of a merciful God to allow the smallest quantity of any thing that was designed to supply the wants of mankind to be diverted from its purpose.

* * *

He would describe the growing and ripening fruit as such a rare and beautiful gift of the Almighty with words that became pictures, until his hearers could almost see its manifold forms of beauty present before them. To his eloquence on this subject, as well as to his actual labors in planting nurseries, the country over which he traveled for so many years is largely indebted for its numerous orchards. But he denounced as absolute wickedness all devices of pruning and grafting, and would speak of the act of cutting a tree as if it were a cruelty inflicted upon a sentient being.

Not only is he entitled to the fame of being the earliest colporteur on the frontiers, but in the work of protecting animals from abuse and suffering he preceded, while in his smaller sphere, he equaled the zeal of the good Mr. Bergh. [Henry Bergh founded the American Society for Animal Protection.] Whenever Johnny saw an animal abused or heard of it, he would purchase it and give it to some more humane settler, on condition that it should be kindly treated and properly cared for. It frequently happened that the long journey into the wilderness would cause the new settlers to be encumbered with lame and broken-down horses, that were turned loose to die. In the autumn Johnny would make a diligent search for all such animals, and, gathering them up, he would bargain for their food and shelter until the next spring, when he would lead them away to some good pasture for the summer. If they recovered so as to be capable of working, he would never sell them, but would lend or give them away, stipulating for their good usage. His conception of the absolute sin of inflicting pain or death upon any creature was not limited to the higher forms of animal life, but every thing that had being was to him, in the fact of its life, endowed with so much of the Divine Essence that to wound or destroy it was to inflict an injury upon some atom of Divinity. No Brahmin could be more concerned for the preservation of insect life, and the only occasion on which he destroyed a venomous reptile was a source of long regret, to which he could never refer without manifesting sadness. He had selected a suitable place for planting apple seeds on a small prairie, and in order to prepare the ground he was mowing the long grass, when he was bitten by a rattlesnake. In describing the event he sighed heavily, and said, "Poor fellow, he only just touched me, when I, to the beat of my ungodly passion put the heel of my scythe in him, and went away. Some time afterward I went back, and there lay the poor fellow dead."

Numerous anecdotes bearing upon his respect for every form of life are preserved, and form the staple of pioneer recollections. On one occasion, a cool autumnal night, when Johnny, who always camped out in preference to sleeping in a house, had built a fire near which he intended to pass the night, he noticed that the blaze attracted large numbers of mosquitoes, many of whom flew too near to his fire and were burned. He immediately brought water and quenched the fire, accounting for his conduct afterward by saying "God forbid that I should build a fire for my comfort which should be the means of destroying any of His creatures!" At another time he removed the fire he had built near a hollow log, and slept on the snow, because he found that the log contained a bear and her cubs, whom, he said, he did not wish to disturb. And this unwillingness to inflict pain or death was equally strong when he was a sufferer by it, as the following will show. Johnny had been assisting some settlers to make a road through the woods, and in the course of their work they accidentally destroyed a hornets' nest. One of the angry insects soon found a lodgment under Johnny's coffee-sack cloak, but although it stung him repeatedly he removed it with the greatest gentleness. The men who were present laughingly asked him why he did not kill it. To which he gravely replied that "It would not be right to kill the poor thing, for it did not intend to hurt me."

Theoretically he was as methodical in matters of business as any merchant. In addition to their picturesqueness, the locations of his nurseries were all fixed with a view to a probable demand for the trees by the time they had attained sufficient growth for transplanting. He would give them away to those who could not pay for them. Generally, however, he sold them for old clothing or a supply of corn meal; but he preferred to receive a note payable at some indefinite period. When this was accomplished he seemed to think that the transaction was completed in a business-like way; but if the giver of the note did not attend to its payment, the holder of it never troubled himself about its collection. His expenses for food and clothing were so very limited that, notwithstanding his freedom from the *auri sacra fanes,* ["the cursed thirst for gold"] he was frequently in possession of more money than he cared to keep, and it was quickly disposed of for wintering infirm horses, or given to some poor family whom the ague had prostrated or the accidents of border life impoverished. In a single instance only he is known to have invested his surplus means in the purchase of land, having received a deed from Alexander Finley, of Mohican Township, Ashland County, Ohio, for a pat of the southwest quarter of section twenty-six; but with his customary indifference to matters of value, Johnny failed to record the deed, and lost it. Only a few years ago the property was in litigation.

* * *

In 1838—thirty-seven years after his appearance on Licking Creek—Johnny noticed that civilization, wealth, and population were pressing into the wilderness of Ohio. Hitherto he had easily kept just in advance of the wave of settlement; but now towns and churches were making their appearance, and even, at long intervals, the stage-driver's horn broke the silence of the grand old forests, and he felt that his work was done in the region in which he had labored so long. He visited every house, and took a solemn farewell of all the families. The little girls who had been delighted with his gifts of fragments of calico and ribbons had become sober matrons, and the boys who had wondered at his ability to bear the pain caused by running needles into his flesh were heads of families. With parting words of admonition he left them, and turned his steps steadily toward the setting sun.

During the succeeding nine years he pursued his eccentric avocation on the western border of Ohio and in Indiana. In the summer of 1847, when his labors had literally borne fruit over a hundred thousand square miles of territory, at the close of a warm day, after traveling twenty miles, he entered the house of a settler in Allen County, Indiana, and was, as usual, warmly welcomed. He declined to eat with the family, but accepted some bread and milk, which he partook of sitting on the door-step and gazing on the setting sun. Later in the evening he delivered his "news right fresh from heaven" by reading the Beatitudes. Declining other accommodation, he slept, as usual, on the floor, and in the early morning he was found with his features all aglow with a supernal light, and his body so near death that his tongue refused its office. The physician, who was hastily summoned, pronounced him dying, but added that he had never seen a man in so placid a state at the approach of death. At seventy-two years of age, forty-six of which had been devoted to his self-imposed mission, he ripened into death as naturally and beautifully as the seeds of his own planting had grown in to fiber and bud and blossom and the matured fruit.

Thus died one of the memorable men of pioneer times, who never inflicted pain or knew an enemy—a man of strange habits, in whom there dwelt a comprehensive love that reached with one hand downward to the lowest forms of life, and with the other upward to the very throne of God. A laboring, self-denying benefactor of his race, homeless, solitary, and ragged, he trod the thorny earth with bare and bleeding feet, intent only upon making the wilderness fruitful. Now "no man knoweth of his sepulcher;" but his deeds will live in the fragrance of the apple blossoms he loved so well, and the story of his life, however crudely narrated, will be a perpetual proof that true heroism, pure benevolence, noble virtues, and deeds that deserve immortality may be found under meanest apparel, and far from gilded halls and towering spires.

Harper's New Monthly Magazine, 43:258, November 1871.

On FATHER DAMIEN DE VEUSTER (1840–1889)

[Revered as the godly priest who went to live with the lepers of Hawaii in order to serve their material and spiritual needs, Damien de Veuster remains an exemplar in American history. In the twentieth century, Mother Theresa, whose work with the ill and dying in India combined practical care and a spiritual attitude, led a life similar to Father Damien's. Those who today work with AIDS patients are perhaps the closest we have to those who ministered to lepers in the times before effective treatments were developed for leprosy. The first piece below is a letter written by Father Damien listing the practical needs of his mission and assessing his own health. The second is a papal document describing his character, written on the occasion of Damien's beatification (a phase in the process toward sainthood). Damien's life is an exemplary illustration of the Catholic ideal of giving "time, talent, and treasure" for the welfare of others.]

A Hand Extended [Letter from Father Damien to Archbishop Gross 1/10/1888]

Your Excellency,

Your good letter of December 16 containing a check in the amount of $218.50 has been received. I thank your Excellency with all my heart, and each of the charitable donors. This sum gives witness to the generosity of your diocese and came just in time to pay a major portion of the supplies which I bought to distribute to the poor during the winter. I purchase only those things which are seldom provided, such as towels, calico, and quality shirts which the merchants give me at ten per cent discount. Our merchants in Honolulu save me many hundreds of dollars, and this helps me greatly in providing the necessities for those who are in need, having spent their six-dollar-a-year allowance for clothing.

We are well enough off with regard to good nourishment and lodging.

The number of lepers grows daily. They come to us from all points of our islands by order of the Board of Health, which does all in its power to make life comfortable for all the unfortunate lepers in our colony. [The leprosy] has now spread to my limbs and throughout my body. At present the sickness is only exterior, and I continue to be robust and attend to my duties.

Richard Stewart, *Leper Priest of Moloka'i: The Father Damien Story*. Honolulu: University of Hawai'i Press. 2000, 322.

Pope John Paul II : Beatification of Damien de Veuster (Given June 4, 1995 in Brussels, Belgium)

4. Down the centuries the Church has never ceased growing and bringing the Gospel to the ends of the earth, in response to Christ himself, who gave the Holy Spirit, the indispensable strength for men to carry out the task of evangelization. The Church gives thanks to the Holy Spirit for Fr. Damien, since it is the Spirit who inspired him with the desire to devote himself unreservedly to lepers on the islands of the Pacific, particularly on Molokai. Today, through me, the Church acknowledges and confirms the value of Fr. Damien's example along the path of holiness, praising God for having guided him to the end of his life on an often difficult journey. She joyfully contemplates what God can achieve through human weakness, for "it is he who gives us holiness and it is man who receives it" (Origen, *Homilies on Samuel*, I, 11, 11).

Fr. Damien displayed a particular form of holiness in his ministry; he was at once a priest, religious and missionary. With these three qualities, he revealed the face of Christ, showing the path of salvation, teaching the Gospel and working tirelessly for development. He organized religious, social and fraternal life on Molokai, at the time an island of banishment from society; with him everyone had a place, each one was recognized and loved by his brothers and sisters. . . .

5. Today's celebration is also a call to solidarity. While Damien was among the sick, he could say in his heart: "Our Lord will give me the graces I need to carry my cross and follow him, even to our special Calvary at Kalawao." The certainty that only things that count are love and the gift of self was his inspiration and the source of his happiness. The apostle of the lepers is a shining example of how the love of God does not take us away from the world. . . .

7. My heart turns to those who today are still suffering from leprosy. In Damien they now have an intercessor, because, before contracting the disease, he had already identified with them and often said: "We others, the lepers." In urging his cause for beatification with Paul VI, Raoul Follereau had a glimpse of the spiritual influence that Damien could have after his death. My prayer is for all those who are stricken by grave and incurable diseases, or are close to death. However, prayer also unites all who are afflicted with serious, incurable illnesses, or who are at the point of death. As the Bishops of your country have recalled, all men have the right to receive from their brothers and sisters a hand extended, a word, a glance, a patient and loving presence, even if they have no hope of being cured. Brothers and sisters who are ill, you are loved by God and the Church! For the human race, suffering is an inexplicable mystery; if it crushes the man left to his own forces, it finds meaning in the mystery of Christ who died and rose again, who remains close to every person and whispers to him: "Take courage! I have overcome the world" (John 16:33). I thank the Lord for those who accompany and assist the sick, the young, the weak and defenseless, the outcasts: I am thinking especially of health-care professionals, priests and lay people in pastoral care, hos-

Figure 3.14 Photo of Father Damien

pital visitors and those dedicated to the cause of life, to the protection of children and to providing each individual with shelter and a place in society. By their deeds, they call to mind the incomparable dignity of our brothers and sisters who suffer in mind or body; they show that every life, even the most frail and suffering, has importance and value in God's sight. With the eyes of faith, beyond appearances, we can see that every person bears the rich treasure of his humanity and the presence of God, who fashioned him from the beginning (cf. Psalm 139 [138]).

From *L'Osservatore Romano Weekly Edition* in English, Baltimore: The Cathedral Foundation, 7 June 1995. [*L'Osservatore Romano* is the newspaper of the Holy See.]

On MOTHER THEODORE GUERIN (1798–1856)

[Missionary generosity accounts for many charitable ventures in education and health care across America and abroad. Sacrifice and suffering, hard work and endurance—these are at the root of many of these ventures. Without the institutions that train and nurture, support and inspire, our world would lack some of its most influential leaders and humane workers for a better world. In 2006 Mother Theodore Guerin was canonized as a saint in the Roman Catholic Church. At that time a flurry of articles appeared about her life. The following is a distillation of biographical information from those pieces.]

An Indiana Educator
by William Jackson

In 1798 a baby girl was born to the Guerin family in Etables-sur-Mer, a village on the Brittany peninsula extending from France into the Atlantic Ocean. They named her Anne-Therese, and as she grew, her mother taught her at home. She had two brothers, but they both died in childhood in a fire. When she was fifteen bandits attacked her father, a lieutenant in Napoleon's navy returning home, and killed him. Anne-Therese's mother never recovered from that loss, becoming an invalid. It fell to Anne-Therese to be the caregiver for her mother and also to take care of her sister, Marie Jeanne.

When she was twenty, Anne-Therese wished to become a nun, but her mother would not hear of it. Four years later, after getting her mother's permission, she entered the order of the Sisters of Providence of Ruille-sur-Loir, taking the name Sister St. Theodore. She took first vows in 1825 and perpetual vows in 1831. For eight years, she ran a school in the industrial town of Rennes, in the west of France, before being transferred to Soulaines. There she ran a school and also studied medicine.

Meanwhile in America, Bishop Simon Brute de Remur (who also happened to be a Breton), as the first bishop of the Diocese of Vincennes, Indiana, saw a need for a convent to serve the Catholic settlers. (The area of this diocese today comprises the Archdiocese of Indianapolis but at that time comprised all of Indiana and eastern Illinois as well.) The bishop sent an emissary to France to find helpers to care for the sick in Indiana and to teach school there. Sister St. Theodore and a number of sisters of Providence seemed a likely choice. At first she was uncertain, because of her poor health. She had smallpox when she was a postulant (candidate seeking admission to an order), and the treatment she received caused lifelong problems in her digestive system. But after a time of prayer and reflection, she agreed. In 1840 she departed by ship from France along with five others—two sisters and three novices. The sisters landed in New York and several weeks later reached the forest clearing in Indiana named St. Mary-of-the-Woods. Overcoming difficulties and hardships, the sisters opened a girls' school, which later became St. Mary-of-the-Woods College. They also began a new religious congregation, modeling it after their convent in France.

Although Mother Theodore suffered from ill health, living on a diet of broth and soft foods, she and the other sisters in her order worked hard and established new schools in various Indiana towns and founded and ran two orphanages in Vincennes. They were also active in dispensing medicines to the settlers. The college they founded at St. Mary-of-the Woods was the first Catholic liberal arts college for women.

Mother Guerin's path was not always easy and her work was not always appreciated, but faith and devotion gave her the strength to undertake her mission and the stamina to persevere in the face of opposition. She died in 1856, and was buried near a small chapel.

In 1907 her body was exhumed and her brain was said to be intact. The proof of a saint's holiness is sometimes established by his or her body seeming to be impervious to decay, either in whole or in part. The case for her sainthood was put forward in 1909. Church authorities in America, France, and Rome examined her lifetime of good works and her writings. In 1992 Pope John Paul II declared her venerable and beatified her in1998. On October 15, 2006, she was canonized.

The American Sisters of Providence teaching ministry, which began in Indiana, multiplied across the state and expanded west into Illinois, and east to Massachusetts. They established schools in California, Florida, Texas, and Oklahoma. They sent missions to China, Taiwan, and the Philippines. A current member of the order, Sister Marie Kevin, summed up the Sisters' mission as one manifesting "God's providence by works of love, mercy and justice."

William J. Jackson, based on information found in Nancy Hartnagel, "Mother Theodore Guerin's Life: Sainthood Seen as Summons to Holiness," Catholic News Service, http://www.catholicnews.com/data/stories/cns/0605689.htm, and several news articles in the *Indianapolis Star* during October 2006.

EPILOGUE

EMILY DICKINSON (1830–1886)

[Emily Dickinson was raised as a New England Calvinist, but she rebelled against orthodox religion in her adult life after she failed to experience the requisite Calvinist conversion during her studies at Mount Holyoke College. A biographer noted that "she joined no church for doctrine and dogma could not convince the soul" (Emily Dickinson, Concise Dictionary of American Literary Biography: Realism, Naturalism, and Local Color, 1865–1917, Gale Research, 1988), but others point out that many of her poems are spiritual, with a hymnlike quality. Living a reclusive life in Amherst, Massachusetts, Dickinson published almost none of her poetry during her lifetime. She eventually was recognized as the greatest woman poet of her era. Simplicity and freshness of language are hallmarks of her verses. Small in size, concise in form, and artful in composition, her poems offer profound glimpses into enduring themes. Small acts of kindness not only make the world a better place, but they give meaning to life.]

If I Can Stop One Heart from Breaking

If I can stop one heart from breaking,

I shall not live in vain;

If I can ease one life the aching,

Or cool one pain,

Or help one fainting robin

Unto his nest again,

I shall not live in vain.

Poems of Emily Dickinson, eds. Martha Dickinson Bianchi and Alfred Leete Hampson. Boston: Little, Brown & Co., 1935, 5.

PART IV

GIVING IN "THE AMERICAN CENTURY" AND ITS SECULARIZATION

1900·2007

EPIGRAPH

BOB DYLAN (b. 1941)

[Darling of the sixties, voice of America's collective consciousness and zeitgeist, Dylan has been a tireless reinventor of himself. The spectrum found in Dylan's many songs includes hilarity, anger, blues, sorrow, indignation, love, and calls for sympathy for the downtrodden. Everyone can find himself or herself reflected in the depths of his songs, if only they listen past the nasal twang. Dylan grew up in the Iron Range region of Northern Minnesota in a Jewish family. He became a folksinger while quite young and was soon performing in Greenwich Village and on college campuses. He pioneered a folk-rock revolution and won an international following, writing brilliant and haunting songs decade after decade. Dylan's religious background is multilayered, with influences from African American Christianity, Kaballah study, and a personal spirituality like that of Whitman, Thoreau, and bluesman Robert Johnson. Here Dylan speaks for anyone who is confronted by someone in need: the song calls out to our own consciences; what do we do in response to seeing fellow humans in desperate circumstances? The song's simplicity gives it a heart-to-heart quality of emotional realism.]

What Good Am I?

What good am I if I'm like all the rest,
If I just turn away, when I see how you're dressed,
If I shut myself off so I can't hear you cry,
What good am I?

What good am I if I know and don't do,

If I see and don't say, if I look right through you,

If I turn a deaf ear to the thunderin' sky,

What good am I?

What good am I while you softly weep

And I hear in my head what you say in your sleep,

And I freeze in the moment like the rest who don't try,

What good am I?

What good am I then to others and me

If I've had every chance and yet still fail to see

If my hands tied must I not wonder within

Who tied them and why and where must I have been

What good am I if I say foolish things

And I laugh in the face of what sorrow brings

And I just turn my back while you silently die,

What good am I?

Bob Dylan, "What Good Am I?" *Oh Mercy*. Copyright ©1989 Special Rider Music.

FOLKTALES

TWO EAST TEXAS FOLK TALES

[Many selections in this anthology are about giving for the common good. The first story below is about what happens when people take too much from the common good. It is a story like the biblical losing of Eden, the destruction of Shel Silverstein's Giving Tree, or the killing of the golden goose. It is also like the Northwest Indian tale of the loss of a natural bridge related earlier in the book. Some read this as a cautionary tale about trust in others and community loyalty. It poignantly expresses "the tragedy of the commons," the decline of fellowship and common welfare. It expresses a basic motif of the Western psyche: a loss of better times due to temptation, vanity, greed. The second story is a Kafkaesque fantasy about gaining great wealth, about riches offered and withdrawn. Receiving the gift is contingent upon deciphering and remembering a warning; the odd clue is the key to accessing a fortune. The tale raises the question of whether giving with stipulations is a way to keep one's wealth. The game seems rigged, fixed to ensure that the giver will retain what is his. Or perhaps the story is about the elusiveness of dreamed-of riches; to "remember the best" may mean to hold fast, not be distracted, and not forsake one's priority.]

The Golden Log

There used to be a place where the sawmill and the commissary were on one side of a big deep creek and the settlement on the other. But the people never had any trouble getting across because there was a big golden log spanning the creek and it was easy to walk across.

Since this was the only crossing for many miles either way, the mill boss and everybody really kept an eye on this golden log to keep anything from happening to it, and there was a general understanding that the log was to walk on and nothing else. But the women got to chipping off a little every once in a while and trading it in to the commissary agent for new clothes and bedspreads and things like that. Everybody in the settlement was doing real well and they didn't need the money, but that's the way they were.

Well, they chipped and whittled on the sly and the log got smaller and smaller, but they cut it down so slowly that nobody ever noticed it. There were a few more people than usual falling in the creek, but still nobody thought much about it—except the women, of course; they knew.

Finally one day a new bride came across, going over to get some flour and a new enamel water dipper. She got to the middle of the log, looked all around, but didn't see anybody, so she bent over and chinked herself out a piece of gold and said to herself, "I believe I'll get me a new dress to look pretty in for the dance next Saturday night." She walked a little farther and said to herself, "It won't hurt to have some new shoes to go with it"; and she looked all around and then cut another little chunk out. She got across the log, stopped, and thought, "Takes a new hat to really get started in." One more look and she stepped back to the log, leaned out a little, and sliced a long sliver right off the top.

That last sliver was all it took. The log cracked and popped real loud and sank right to the bottom of the deepest hole in the creek. The mill boss heard the noise and came running down from the office. He caught her standing there and she had to tell what she had done, so he told her and her husband to pack up and leave the settlement. He took the commissary agent to the county seat and had him thrown in jail.

After that nothing seemed to go right at the mill. Every time the creek rose nobody came to work. They tried to build a bridge but it washed out every time there was a heavy dew. Finally it got so bad that the mill had to shut down and everybody left.

Nobody can tell you where that place is now. Some say it's in the Thicket; others say it's in Louisiana. But they all agree that a man could sit in a rocking chair on his front porch and shoot a deer any afternoon and that they baited their trotlines with five-pound bass. It must have been some place!

Francis E. Abernethy, "The Golden Log," in *The Golden Log*, ed. Mody C. Boatright, Wilson M. Hudson, and Allen Maxwell. Dallas: Southern Methodist University Press, 1962, 3–4.

Don't Forget the Best

Well, once upon a time they was a young friend of a very rich man visited him, and he had a beautiful cave of everything imaginable on earth in his cave. And the young man was so thrilled with the thoughts of just being in there with his rich friend, that he was thrilled to death. And the rich friend told him, now says, "if you don't forget the best," says, "you can have everything in this cave. Everything is yours."

So they went through and he admired everything so much. He was thrilled to death. And the rich man said to him, again now says, "Everything in here will be yours if you don't forget the best."

And they still went on in throughout the place, and the young man was thrilled to death. And they finally come on out towards the front and everything, and this rich man say now, "This is everything is yours, if you don't forget the best."

Finally they went to the door and walked on out on the outside, and rich man says, "Now," he says, "you forgot the best." And the door locked to, and he says, "That was the key."

Church Thomas, "Don't Forget the Best," in *The Golden Log*, ed. Mody C. Boatright, Wilson M. Hudson, and Allen Maxwell. Dallas: Southern Methodist University Press, 1962, 25–26.

FRAN STRIKER (1903–1962)

[Born in Buffalo, New York, Francis Hamilton Striker worked in amateur theater in New York City, and in radio stations in Buffalo, Cleveland, and Detroit. He produced early radio series and in 1932 worked on an idea about a Texas Ranger, which became the Lone Ranger story. It was first a very popular radio series and became the subject of novels, comic strips, and a TV program. The Lone Ranger is an archetypal cowboy hero of the American imagination circa mid-twentieth century. This hero is a helper of the unprotected, a lawman who had a near-death experience and came back to life. He lives outside the law, in service of a higher law. Not a killer, he brings the stray lambs back to the fold— or at least to jail. "Hi-ho Silver!" he cried before anyone could thank him. Lenny Bruce parodied this figure, implying suspicious motives behind the masks of do-gooders. Aren't there always some who impute ulterior motives to altruistic acts? For those who grew up

in the fifties, the Lone Ranger was an American hero like Superman, showing children an example of a charismatic figure helping ordinary folks in need.]

The Lone Ranger (Legend of the West)

They rode slowly, saving their strength and the strength of the two big stallions, the snow-white one called Silver and the slightly smaller paint horse that Tonto had named Scout. Yet, despite the easy manner of both the Lone Ranger and his faithful Indian companion, Tonto, they were alert and watchful. They had to be. There were many people who would have liked nothing more than to put bullets through the hearts of these two men. People who had sworn to kill the Lone Ranger because he had served justice by sending their friends to jail or to the hangman's noose.

He was an astonishing man, this Lone Ranger. He had become an almost legendary character throughout the length and breadth of seven states in the early West. Some folks regarded him as a myth, but countless others who had seen him in thrilling action told astounding stories of his skill with rope or gun, his hard riding, and uncanny judgment.

"Look ahead," the Lone Ranger told Tonto, speaking from behind a mask. "The moon is rising and we can see the top of the hill now."

"That's right," agreed the Indian. "There plenty cottonwood on top of hill. Maybe we hide horse there. Go to Snake River on foot."

"We'll see," promised the Lone Ranger. He had not yet told Tonto his purpose in heading toward the town of Snake River which bordered on the stream of water for which it was named. He had not told Tonto that he intended to leave him behind when he made his entry into the town itself. There was time enough for that later.

The Lone Ranger had his own peculiar way of serving justice. There were frequent times when sheriffs and other officers of the law disagreed with his methods, but the results of those methods generally found the lawless in jail and the people they oppressed happier for the Lone Ranger's appearance. For several minutes, the two rode toward the distant cottonwoods in silence.

Tonto glanced across the small space that separated the two horsemen, and pride showed in his dark eyes as he studied the fine profile of the masked man. Tonto felt that he had done much to bring this heroic figure to the West. And it was true. It was Tonto who had rescued the one remaining member of the small band of Texas Rangers who had engaged in a fierce battle with an outlaw army. Of the entire band, only one lived, and even this man was more nearly dead than alive.

Tonto remembered vividly how he had carried the still form to his cave, and there applied all the instinctive knowledge of his people in a tireless fight to fan the feeble spark of life to a new flame. For days the Texas Ranger tossed in fever on a crude pallet of straw in the cave. Then, slowly, he regained his health, to learn from Tonto the fate of his friends. He swore then that he would not rest until the last of that marauding band had been made to pay for the massacre. Tonto remembered the steely expression of grim determination that had shown in the Texas Ranger's face when he said, "The last one living—the *Lone Ranger.*" He remembered how the white man had unpinned his Texas Ranger's badge, and put it into his pocket; and how he had masked himself, so that none of the outlaws would know that he still lived. Then he had ridden out, masked, sometimes looked upon as an outlaw, while he brought one after another of the killers into the hands of the law.

"We can't stop now," the Lone Ranger had told Tonto when the last of the murderers was finally jailed. "There is too great a need for someone who can at times take the law into his own hands. The people of the West need help, and we're going to try to give it to them."

And that was just the beginning. The Lone Ranger and Tonto became inseparable. Each was the counterpart of the other. Where the Lone Ranger excelled in shooting and roping, Tonto was the superior in following a trail, in healing the sick, and in treating the wounded. When decisive action was required to secure information upon which to plan their actions, the Lone Ranger acted; when quiet stolid waiting in the hope of overhearing certain facts would accomplish the best results, then Tonto took charge.

✻   ✻   ✻

He made certain his two holsters were well tied to his thighs, and that his brace of heavy six-guns was fully loaded, and in smooth working order. Those guns held bullets that had become a symbol of the Lone Ranger—bullets of solid silver! The gleaming weapons had barked many times in self-defense and in the defense of others, but they had yet to take a life. When the Lone Ranger shot, he shot to disarm or to wound, but he never shot to kill.

Fran Striker, *The Lone Ranger and Tonto* (based on the original Lone Ranger adventures by George W. Trendle); New York: Grosset & Dunlap, 1940, 1–4, 6.

AFRICAN AMERICAN FOLKLORE

ZORA NEAL HURSTON (1891–1960)

[The daughter of a Baptist preacher, Zora Neal Hurston was three when she moved with her family to the first incorporated black community in the United States, Eatonville, Florida, where her father was later elected mayor. Hurston attended Howard University and Barnard College at Columbia University. She studied anthropology and became a respected folklorist and novelist. Her classic novel Their Eyes Were Watching God earned an honored place in the canon of American literature. Hurston also gained renown as an authority on African American culture and the Harlem Renaissance. The following fanciful folktale sermon collected by Hurston is about how the church was built and split into denominations and sects, and how Peter determined the way it would all turn out. This imaginative story displays humor with a twist of wry truth. Our greed may determine more than we realize; so might our generosity. Too, the story tells us something about factionalism, that it is inevitable because of human nature. The way we give our contributions matters, although, like Peter in this story, we may not fully realize it at the time.]

Folk-Sermon: Built on a Pieced-Up Rock

Christ was walkin' long one day wid all his disciples and he said, "We're goin' for a walk today. Everybody pick up a rock and come along." So everybody got their selves a nice big rock 'ceptin' Peter. He was lazy so he picked up a li'l bit of a pebble and dropped it in his side pocket and come along.

Well, they walked all day long and de other 'leven disciples changed them rocks from one arm to de other but they kept on totin' 'em. Long towards sundown they come 'long by de Sea of Galilee and Jesus tole 'em, "Well, le's fish awhile. Cast in yo' nets right here." They done like he tole 'em and caught a great big mess of fish. Then they cooked 'em and Christ said, "Now, all y'all bring up yo' rocks." So they all brought they rocks and Christ turned 'em into bread and they all had a plenty to eat wid they fish exceptin' Peter. He couldn't hardly make a moufful offa de li'l bread he had and he didn't like dat a bit.

Two or three days after dat Christ went out doors and looked up at de sky and says, "Well, we're goin' for another walk today. Everybody git yo'self a rock and come along."

They all picked up a rock apiece and as ready to go. All but Peter. He went and tore down half a mountain. It was so big he couldn't move it wid his hands. He had to take a pinch-bar to move it. All day long Christ walked and talked to his disciples and Peter sweated and strained wid dat rock of his'n.

Way long in de evenin' Christ went up under a great big ole tree and set down and called all of his disciples around 'im and said, "Now everybody bring up yo' rocks."

So everybody brought theirs but Peter. Peter was about a mile down de road punchin' dat half a mountain he was bringin'. So Christ waited till he got dere. He looked at de rocks dat de other 'leven disciples had, den he seen dis great big mountain dat Peter had and so he got up and walked over to it and put one foot up on it and said, "Why Peter, dis is a fine rock you got here! It's a noble rock! And Peter, on dis rock Ah'm gointer build my church."

Peter says, "Naw you ain't either. You won't build no church house on *dis* rock. You gointer turn dis rock into bread."

Christ knowed dat Peter meant dat thing so he turnt de hillside into bread and dat mountain is de bread he fed de 5,000 wid. Den he took dem 'leven other rocks and glued 'em together and built his church on it

And that's how come de Christian churches is split up into so many different kinds—cause it's built on pieced-up rock.

Zora Neale Hurston, *Mules and Men*. Bloomington: Indiana University Press, 1978, 29–30.

LANGSTON HUGHES (1902–1967) AND ARNA BONTEMPTS (1902-1973), EDITORS

[Slaves who were brought to America carried with them West African traditions of stories and styles, but slaveowners forbid them to use African languages. Some old African patterns turn up in stories told in English by slaves and their descendents, and new expressions of the African American community obliquely bespeak its views of the world based on experiences of the people. Typically, myths use symbolic, poetic, and sometimes humorous ways to tell us how things got to be the way they are; parables teach life lessons with simple anecdotes. The first of these stories, from an anthology of African American folklore edited by Hughes and Bontempts, two great writers of the Harlem Renaissance, is an extravagantly imaginative myth about a gift. The second is more like a parable, teaching that we should appreciate blessings in disguise and realize that silver linings are often the saving grace in life.]

Two African-American Folktales

God's Christmas Gift to the Devil

Well, one Christmas time, God was goin' to Palatka. De Devil was in de neighborhood too and seen God goin' long de big road, so he jumped behind a stump and hid. Not dat he was skeered uh God, but he wanted to git a Christmas present outa God but he didn't wants give God nothin'.

So he squatted down behind dis stump till God come along and then he jumped up and said, "Christmas gift!"

God just looked back over his shoulder and said, "Take de East Coast," and kept on walkin'. And dat's why we got storms and skeeters—it's de Devil's property.

Thanksgiving that Things Aren't Worse

A man named Simon Suggs was sitting in church listening to the Thanksgiving sermon and hearing the minister tell about all the things there were to be thankful for—even though Simon Suggs and all the folks sitting around him did not have much, since luck that year had been unlucky, crops had been bad and weather awful.

When the minister got through preaching and asked for testimonials, this is what Simon Suggs got up and said: "Give thanks for what? Me! The branch has flooded and washed away my barn. My hound dog died, my mule broke his leg and boll weevils et up my crops."

"Yes, brother," replied the minister, "I is heard—
And neither me nor God could doubt your word—
So let's bow down anyhow in all dis muss
And thank the Lord it ain't no wuss."

Langston Hughes and Arna Bontemps, ed., *The Book of Negro Folklore*. New York: Dodd, Mead, 1958, 125, 159–60.

DARYL CUMBER DANCE

[Dance, a prominent folklorist of African American traditions, grew up in the age of segregation, hearing legends and proverbs all around her in rural Virginia. She collected the pieces below in the second half of the twentieth century. The first brief folk story shows what a privileged person's situation looks like from another point of view. People are often oblivious to their unearned advantages, taking their status and inherited comforts in life for granted. The second piece, a humorous comparison, suggests that in the end, differences between wealthy and poor may not be so great after all.]

Why Whites Have Everything

God was making the worl' and He called de people, you know, de white people to get a bag and de colored people to get a bag. De colored people went to get the little light bag and the white people get the big, heavy bag; and the heavy bag [there] was money in it, and the light bag ain't have nothin' in it. And they say dat's why us ain't got nothin' today; white people got it all.

All a Matter of Money

They say, when you got money, you have a nervous breakdown and they put you in a mental institution; but when you ain't got no money, they say you crazy, and they put you in a 'sylum.

Daryl Cumber Dance, *Shuckin' and Jivin': Folklore from Contemporary Black Americans*. Bloomington: Indiana University Press, 1978, 312–13.

J. MASON BREWER (1896–1975)

[John Mason Brewer, after a stint in the army, taught in colleges in and around Austin, Texas. His grandparents had been slaves, and Brewer became a dedicated collector of slaves' tales; when he published them with the Texas Folklore Society, they were acclaimed as "the best collection of Negro folklore since Uncle Remus." For decades, Brewer traveled the Southern states and Texas, recording black folk traditions, and is known as one of the greatest folklorists of the twentieth century. The following ghost story collected by Brewer from an African American community in Texas presents a comforting image: when the collection plate is passed, scary ghosts hurry away. The invitation to give may make some scurry off, but it is a source of well-being for others. Why do they scurry off? Is this a dig at skinflints, symbolic of the ungenerous side of human nature? Few of us would care to identify with the inauspicious fleeing ghosts; we want to be solid contributors to the well-being of worthy ventures. The short pieces that follow the sermon are examples of imaginative hyperbole in folklore. In a few words, these jokes paint a picture of extreme stinginess, combining truth and humor. These visions of selfishness and cosmic-sized greed are tragicomic, making fun of cheapness the way the blues laugh about bothersome things—in order to keep it at bay.]

The Haunted Church and the Sermon on Tithing

Oncet down on de ole Washin'ton fawm dere was a Mefdis' preachuh by de name of Revun Logan what stay at de same charge for thirty yeah or mo'. He hol' de membuhship togedduh an' bul' de fuss chu'ch house in Eloise. Evuhbody in de Bottoms hab a good feelin' for Revun Logan, so when de new bishop dey 'lected hol' de annul conference down to Chilton one yeah, he change Revun Logan from de Wes' Texas Conference an' move 'im to de Texas Conference. Dis heah hurt Revun Logan's feelin's pow'ful bad, 'caze he bred an' bawn in de Bottoms, an' he ain't wanna trace his steps outen de Bottoms way dis late in life. He wropped up in de membuhship an' de settlement, but de new bishop lack de 'pos'l' Paul dat de Word tell 'bout. He say don' none of dese things move 'im an' keep 'im from 'bidin' by de law what done been writ in de displin'.

Revun Logan all bowed down in sorrow an' his haa't moughty heaby wid de partin' from his chu'ch starin' 'im in de face; so de nex' mawnin' atthuh he comed back from de conference de ole man what sweep up de chu'ch go by de li'l' pawsonage to pass de time of day wid 'im an' fin' 'im dead on the kitchen flo'. So dey buries 'im in de graveyard on de chu'ch groun's what he done hab de membuhship buy.

De nex' Sunday de preachuh what de bishop done sen't to teck Revun Logan's place come to preach his fuss sermon. De new preachuhs in dem days comin' up allus preach dey fuss sermon in de night time, so dis new preachuh gits up in de pulpit dat fuss night an' pray; den he raise his voice to lead a song; nex' he light out to preachin', but no sooner'n he staa't, de oil lamps all goes out an' ghostes staa'ts to comin' into de chu'ch house thoo de windows and de doors. Sump'n lack a gust of win' come thoo de whole chu'ch house. De pastuh, de membuhship, an' de chilluns all lights out from dere for de dirt road. De new preachuh saddle his hoss rail quick an' rides clear on outen de Bottoms, an' dey ain't pleased wid de fashion de bishop done treat Revun Logan.

Fin'ly, de bishop sen's a rail young preachuh what done finish up in a Mefdis' Preachuh school way somewhar. Dis his fuss charge an' he brung his wife wid 'im. De membuhship jes' know dis heah young preachuh gonna be scairt to deaf Sunday night when he staa't to preachin' an' de ghostes staa't to comin' in de windows, so dey meck hit uop dat dey ain't narry one of 'em goin' in de chu'ch dat night; 'stid, dey gonna all conjugate on t'ohuh side de dirt road 'cross from de chu'ch house an' crack dey sides laffin' when de young preachuh an' his wife come runnin' outen de chu'ch house when de lamps goes uot an' de ghostes staa'ts to comin' in.

Dey lines up cross de road from de chu'ch house long 'fo' de young preachuh an' his wife goes into de chu'ch house dat night an' lights all de lamps in de pulpit an' 'roun' de walls. Den de preachuh tuch his Bible an' his hymn book out, turnt to a pate in de hymn book an' raised a hymn. Den he put de hymn book down, open up his Bible, an' read a passage of scripture. When he done did dis, he offuh up a short prayer, den 'nounce his tex'. But de minnit he 'nounce his texs' de lamps goes out an' de ghostes staa'ts comin' in thoo de windows lack ez befo'. But de preachuh an' his wife don' budge. He keep rat on wid his sermon lack nothin' ain't done happen an' de sperrits an' ghostes all teck seats in de pews till he finish his sermon. He preach a sermon 'bout tithin'—you gib one tent' of you' wages to de chu'ch, he say. So when he git thoo wid de sermon, he say to his wife, "Sistuh White, git de collection plate an' pass hit 'roun' do's do Brothuhs an' Sistuhs kin th'ow in de collection." An' when he say dis, de ghostes staa'ts flyin' outen de windows faster'n dey comed in, an' de lamps come to be lighted again.

When de membuhship see dis dey all staa't runnin' cross de road to de chu'ch house whar de young preachuh an' his wife was gittin' dey things togethuh to leave de chu'ch house. Dey rushes up to de new preachuh, shakes his han' an tells 'im de bishop sho' done sen' de rat preachuh to dis charge. Dey tells 'im he done broke de spell of de ghostes, an' dis must have been de truf, 'caze de ghostes ain't nevuh showed up no mo', form dat day to dis one.

J. Mason Brewer, collector, "The Haunted Church and the Sermon on Tithing," in *The Word on the Brazos: Negro Preacher Tales from the Brazos Bottoms of Texas*. Austin: University of Texas Press, 1953, 64–66.

Tall Tales

The Stingiest Man

Question: What de stingiest man you done ever saw?
Answer: De stingiest man Ah ever done see go in de darkest room to chew his tobacco, so his shadow won't beg him fer none.

The Greediest Man

Question: What de greediest man you ever see?
Answer: De greediest man Ah ever saw—he ate up evuhthing on earth, ate all de angels out o' heaven, and snapped at God.

J. Mason Brewer, *American Negro Folklore.* Chicago: Quadrangle Books, 1968, 375, 377.

TALES OF GIVING AND CHEAPNESS

OKLAHOMA OIL JOKES AND A GENEROUS OIL MAN

[There's some truth in any joke; humor can harbor serious points of criticism. Woody Guthrie was a legendary folksinger and prolific songwriter of post-Depression America. He traveled the country, working odd jobs and singing about the experiences of the ordinary man. He gave the following imaginative spiel about the get-rich-quick ethos of a booming sector of exploitation: the American oil field. The final "can" in his piece means "jail." Following Guthrie's piece is a sermon based on folk material from Arkansas, collected by the WPA. In it, there are jokes, but also premonitions and a warning. The riches of the earth are a gift, hence the teaching that people should be good stewards.]

Oil and Hell (A Sermon)

"Brethren," he said, "The Lord made the world round like a ball."

"Amen!" agreed the congregation.

"And the Lord made two axles for the world to go round on, and He put one axle at the North Pole and one axle at the South Pole."

"Amen!" agreed the congregation.

"And the Lord put a lot of oil and grease in the center of the world so as to keep the axles well greased and oiled."

"Amen!" cried the congregation.

"And then a lot of sinners dig wells in Pennsylvania and steal the Lord's oil and grease. And they dig wells in Kentucky, Louisiana, Oklahoma, and Texas, and in Mexico and Russia, and steal the Lord's oil and grease. And some day they will have all the Lord's oil and grease, and them axles is gonna git hot. And then that will be hell, brethren, that will be hell!"

Velma Sample, Little Rock, Arkansas, January, 1937. Manuscripts of the Federal Writers' Project of the Works Progress Administration for the State of Arkansas. Also in *A Treasury of Southern Folklore*, ed. B. A. Botkin. New York: Crown, 1966, 112.

Religion of the Oil Field

Oil was more than gold ever was or ever will be, because you can't make any hair salve or perfume, TNT, or roofing material or drive a car with just gold. You can't pipe that gold back East and run them big factories, either.

The religion of the oil field, guys said, was to get all you can, and spend all you can as quick as you can, and then end up in the can.

Woody Guthrie, *Bound for Glory.* New York: Dutton, 1943, 115. Also in *A Treasury of Southern Folklore*, ed. B. A. Botkin. New York: Crown, 1966, 52.

The Petroleum Geologist: A Folk Image [Oil Man Edgar Davis]

[Hard work and fortune making are part of the American dream. President Calvin Coolidge, who served 1923-1929, is often quoted as saying "the business of America is business," but this leaves out the rest of his sentence: "but the ideal of the American people is idealism." Not every businessman who becomes wealthy becomes a folk hero—far from it—but sometimes the ones who have humanitarian ideals do. In memory of his generosity, Edgar Davis' name appears on a variety of public facilities in Texas—educational, medical, and cultural. The largesse of this controversial oil man was integral to his belief in divine guidance. Davis' generosity led his supporters to stand up for him. Faith and giving go together, as do magnanimous caring and fond remembrance. But faith and giving are not inextricably linked; some givers are not members of religions. Some are dedicated to social justice for complex reasons not easily categorized by denomination.]

The Commonwealth of Massachusetts had filed a suit against Edgar B. Davis of Luling, Texas. Davis had lived in Luling since 1922, but the commonwealth maintained that he had been a citizen of Massachusetts until 1926 and that he owed the state income taxes on a sum estimated as high as twelve million dollars. When a lawyer called on one citizen of Luling in search of evidence that Davis was not a legal resident of Texas, he was promptly informed that any man who said Davis was not a bona fide citizen of Luling, Texas, was a lying son of a bitch.

This was hardly legal evidence, and Massachusetts eventually obtained a judgement; but it is indicative of what the people of Luling and the surrounding country thought of Davis. He was emphatically a hero. Not only had he brought wealth to the community by discovering oil, but he had distributed his personal fortune in giving generous bonuses to his employees, in sponsoring art, in building community clubhouses, and in chartering and endowing the Luling foundation for the betterment of agriculture. And in the search for oil he had personally spent considerably more than a million dollars.

The people of Luling, in recounting his exploits to Stanley Walker, repeated the legend of his singlehanded struggle to find oil. They reported that "most geologists and most of the oil companies were convinced that there was no oil in Caldwell County." Of the same import had been an article in the historical edition of the Lockhart *Post-Register* for August 3, 1936, in which the only reference to geology was the statement that Davis had begun his seventh, and first successful, well against the advice of his geologist. There was no reference to the origin of the search for oil.

This search was quite typical of the times in that it was initiated by local men motivated at least in part by the desire to add a new resource to the not overly prosperous agricultural economy. Two lawyers, Norman Dodge and Carl C. Wade, asked a geologist, Verne Woolsey, to look for a place to drill. Woolsey remarked that they were sitting on a fault at the moment. He located the fault plane, and Dodge and Wade took leases. Wade then went East seeking capital to drill. He succeeded in interesting Oscar Davis, who took stock amounting to $75,000 in the newly organized Texas Southern Oil and Lease Syndicate, and asked his brother Edgar to manage his interests for a third of the profits. When the capital of the syndicate was exhausted, Edgar Davis paid off the stockholders, including his brother, and organized the North and South Oil Company to continue exploration.

He had been so confident of success that he had begun three wells. After a total of six dry holes which used up the fortune of a million and a half dollars he had made in rubber plantations, he made, against the advice of his geologist, a location on the Raphael Rios property. The well came in August 8, 1922, and led to further development in Caldwell and Hays counties.

In making this location Davis said he was guided by a deep faith in divine providence, and it was to divine guidance and not to geology that he ever afterward attributed his success. The preamble to the charter of the Luling Foundation (it is significant that it was not called the Edgar B. Davis Foundation) begins:

> Believing that a kind and gracious Providence, who guides the Destinies of all humanity, directed me in the search for and the discovery of oil, and in our successful management and favorable outcome of the business, and believing that the wealth which has resulted has not come through any virtue or ability of mine, and desiring to discharge in some measure the trust which has been reposed in me; and in a spirit of gratitude to the Giver of all good for his beneficence . . .

So successful was he in giving his money away that, although the state of Massachusetts secured a judgment, its representatives could find no assets to attach. The people of Caldwell and Hays counties resented the attempted raid by a Yankee state. Not all of them shared Davis' piety, but whatever their views on divine providence, Davis was their hero.

Mody Boatright, "The Petroleum Geologist: A Folk Image," in *The Golden Log*, ed. Mody C. Boatright, Wilson M. Hudson, and Allen Maxwell. Dallas: Southern Methodist University Press, 1962, 66–68.

DONALD M. HINES (b. 1931)

[Hines closely studied American folklore of the Pacific Northwest. His Ph.D. thesis, never published, contains wonderful nuggets in American vernacular. A man who would skimp even when he could not profit by it, unwilling to give what was needed for his own care— now that's cheap! It's the sign of a deep habit, so incorrigible it's funny. This kind of humor has many examples. For instance, an Arkansas editor once said that the stingiest man in his town talked through his nose to save the wear and tear on his false teeth. Such stories are funny but also serve to caution us against becoming caricatures ourselves.]

A Dreadful Mean Man [Cheap Even to Himself]

Old Ira Thornton was a dreadful mean man, and had difficulty, sometimes, in drawing his breath, because he begrudged the air necessary for that operation. One day the old fellow was at work upon the high beams of his barn, when he lost his balance and fell heavily upon the floor, twenty feet below. He was taken up for dead, with a fractured skull, and carried into the house. All efforts to bring him to consciousness were unavailing, and the doctor was called. Finally, the doctor having trepanned [performed surgery on] him, turned and asked Mrs. Thornton for a silver dollar to put where the piece of skull was wanting. At this remark, Ira, who had been breathing heavily, turned in bed and groaned out, "Wouldn't a cent do as well?"

Donald M. Hines, "Dust devils in the great desert: a study of the impress of the frontier in traditional anecdotes of humor and exaggeration, in fold beliefs, and in traditional speech gleaned from some of the old-time weekly newspapers from the inland empire of the Pacific Northwest," vol. 4, #00446. PhD diss., Indiana University, 1969, 1502. [Arkansas editor comment: Hines, "Dust devils," vol. 4, #00437, p. 1497.]

PAULETTE ATENCIO (b. 1937)

[Atencio grew up in Northern New Mexico. She describes herself as a traditional Hispanic storyteller who developed her repertoire of stories by listening closely to grandmothers, aunts, mother, father, and other elders as they told tales. She has published her stories and also performed them in public, using costumes, sound effects, and music to bring them alive. The plight of a poor man trying to improve his life makes for a story of struggle and hope. Faith brings a turning point. Doing good to others, the "poor" man is blessed with good fortune. His good deeds are validated and rewarded. In the second story, we see how cruel deeds bring misery, while good deeds ultimately protect and bring rewards. These are reassuring and life-affirming stories from the Southwest with morals that encourage helpfulness.]

Two Folktales from Northern New Mexico

The Poor Rich Man

Once there was a family that was very poor. The wife and husband had such a hard life that both appeared much older than they really were. The children looked undernourished. The husband would leave each morning in hopes of finding a job. Every night, he returned the same as he had left in the morning—without a job. One night, the wife overheard the husband saying, "Oh, my great father of heaven! What are we going to do? We have to eat." "*Viejo* (old man)," interrupted the wife. "Why don't you plead with Mr. Pacheco? Maybe he'll hire you to work at the store." The next morning, all the remaining tortillas were eaten. The poor man prayed and asked for help. With that, he left. When he got to town, he went to Mr. Pacheco's store and begged like never before. It was useless. Mr. Pacheco was not hiring.

Again, the poor man searched everywhere for a job but found none. The husband came home feeling discouraged and told his wife one more time, "I don't know what we're going to do. I have done everything possible but it seems God is either too far away to hear me or He is just tired and doesn't want to help. Tomorrow I'm going to look for God and ask Him point blank why we are so poor." "Don't go," the wife said. "You know that God is everywhere. Talk to Him here." Without paying attention to her words, the husband left.

He walked for miles until he arrived at the foothills of the Santa Clara Valley. The sun was shining brightly and, for a few seconds, it blinded him. He then saw what appeared to be a person. He moved closer to the man, who was sitting on a rock tending to his sheep. The mysterious man asked, "What are you looking for?" The poor man answered, "I'm looking for God. I have to talk to him. All I want to know is why we are so poor. I have faith that when I find him, he will help me and my family." The mysterious man looked deeply into the poor man's eyes and in a loving voice assured the poor man that things would change. "Your prayers have been answered. Go and enjoy your good fortune for seven years."

The poor man was very confused. Feeling ashamed, he thanked the mysterious man and walked slowly home. He couldn't believe his childish behavior. But, upon arriving home, he found his family in a happy state. One of his children had discovered bags of gold and jewelry. With this newfound fortune, their lives began to change for the better. During the next seven years, they became a wealthy family and were well known throughout the land. The poor man was very generous and shared their good fortune. He was given the nickname "the poor rich man."

After seven years passed, the poor man journeyed again to the Santa Clara Valley in search of the mysterious man. He thanked him for his kind generosity. He exclaimed that he and his family would gladly return to the way they used to be. The mysterious man replied, "You are indeed a good and just man. You have never stopped helping the poor. I will continue to bless you." The poor rich man returned home. Everyday he was grateful and lived to repay the mysterious man by providing services to the less fortunate, as we all should do!

The Beggar

Many years ago, there was a poor man and his wife who lived far away from town. Their only neighbor was a mean, selfish, and grouchy man. One evening, a beggar walking down the road stopped at the mean and selfish man's house. The beggar knocked and asked for a drink of water and something to eat. The horrid man swore at the beggar and chased him away. The beggar immediately took off and continued walking. Shortly, he arrived at the house where the poor but kind man lived with his wife. They were known by the name of Lopez. The beggar knocked. When the kind old man opened the door, he did not hesitate to invite the beggar in, they were so happy to have a visitor. The beggar informed them that he was very hungry. The old lady hurried to set the table. All they had to offer were three small pieces of hard tortilla and some water. The beggar ate the first piece of tortilla in one bite, so the old man gave him his share, and so did the kind lady. The beggar had now eaten enough. They asked the beggar to stay for the night but he felt it was best to be on his way.

Before the beggar left, he advised the couple to walk toward a small cave located in the area. "Inside," he told them, "you will find a round, flat rock. Move the rock and dig underneath. Because you have been so kind to me, you will find a reward." The beggar left. The kind man and his wife decided it was late and they would go to the cave in the morning. They did not know that the mean and selfish man had been listening to everything that was said. He took off running and didn't stop until he reached the cave. He began to dig and dig. Finally, he discovered a large glass jar. He took off the lid and thrust his hand inside. All of a sudden, hundreds of horrible insects crawled out and stung him. The jar was full of bees, tarantulas, and scorpions. Soon his body was covered with hives. The mean and selfish man was yelling, crying, and jumping up and down. He hurried to place the lid back on the jar. He was so angry that all he could do was swear. He ran back to the house where the kind old man and his wife lived. He climbed on top of the roof and yelled down the chimney at the top of his voice, "I dug out the gift that was left for you! Here it is! You stupid old fools! Here is your treasure! This is what you get for feeding a beggar!" He took off the lid, turned the jar upside down, and began to shake it. Down the chimney went all the horrible insects, creating a big pile at the bottom of the fireplace. Suddenly, they stopped moving and began to sparkle. The insects had turned to diamonds, rubies, sapphires, and other precious gems! The mean and selfish man ran off laughing to himself. Little did he know that the joke was on him. As for the old man and his wife, they just looked at each other and smiled. They would never be poor again!

Paulette Atencio, *Cuentos from My Childhood: Legends and Folktales of Northern New Mexico*. Santa Fe: Museum of New Mexico Press, 1991, 29–31, 60–61.

TENNESSEE STORY

[This Southern folk tale evokes the widespread idea, explored earlier in this anthology, that generosity brings good luck. The good news is that this idea encourages giving; the bad news is that someone who takes the idea too literally and gives to others expecting immediate returns might be disappointed. If his luck is not good, he may feel cheated and condemn the belief as a scam. The story implies that there are no guarantees in charity and philanthropy, except that these activities are learning experiences, potentially expansive and fulfilling endeavors.]

A Paying Business

At the close of a great meeting a Presbyterian minister gave notice that a collection would be taken up for Gospel purposes in the neighborhood. A Methodist preacher, also present, and who had just preached the sermon, it being his regular Sabbath at the place, then rose, and remarked that very little had been done toward the proper support of the Gospel or himself; that he had begun his circuit with two horses—one was used; he expected the other would soon go, and he would have to go afoot; Charity began at home; and "Besides, brethren, Christianity is a paying business—it pays a profit even in this world. Did you ever hear the story of the infidel in the Tennessee camp-meeting? Well, I'll tell you: Up in Tennessee once there was a camp-meeting held in a notorious bad neighborhood; and when, at the close of the exercises, the hat was sent round, a roll of notes, about fifty dollars, was found. The brethren in those parts, in those days being rather poor, considerable speculation was had as to whar that fifty dollars come from; and next year it was decided to keep an eye on that hat, and see if it was done over agin. Sure enough, next year's meeting there was another fifty just as before, and it was traced to an infidel reviling country store-keeper near the camp, and who was never known to say or do a good thing for God's people. So the elders called the man aside, and says, 'Did you put that 'ere fifty in that hat?' 'Well, I did.' 'Mistake, ain't it?' 'No, Sirs; I never makes mistakes. It's all right. Afore you chaps cum around these diggings preaching I couldn't keep ne'er a

261

shoat, ne'er a yearling no whar, and I lost a powerful sight of truck; and now, gentle-men, I keeps the most of 'em! It's a paying business to keep you here, and I goes in for it!'"

<hr>

A Treasury of Southern Folklore, ed. B. A. Botkin. New York: Crown, 1966, 97. (From "Editor's Drawer," *Harper's New Monthly Magazine* 18, no. 108 [April 1859]: 709–10.)

ANONYMOUS

[This Creole folktale from Louisiana tells how a bequest to ghosts benefited the poor. Members of various cultures perform rituals in which food offerings to ancestors are eaten by invited guests or nonhuman species, such as crows or fish; the desire to stay in touch with those who have died thus benefits others. Or sometimes the offerings are simply gifts for the spirits of the dead.]

The Bridal Ghost Dinner in New Orleans

I went to New Orleans and there a lawyer friend told me the ghost tale of the Mardi Gras dinner that has been told for many years.

New Orleans is the gayest city in Louisiana, and it is famous for its ghosts, its conjuring, and its Mardi Gras (which is Shrove Tuesday). People come to the Mardi Gras from every part of the country, and there is always a great ball at the French Opera House. On the stage, actors show beautiful living scenes of history and Greek tales, and the great crowd, dressed in silks and satins, watch and talk and make merry.

Many years ago, there sat in that gay Mardi Gras crowd at the Opera House a young gentleman who had come from up East. He didn't know anyone, so he sat alone and just looked at the gay goings on. Accidentally, his eyes wandered up to the boxes of the theater, and he saw in one of them the most beautiful girl he had ever seen in his life. She was a Creole, with eyes like black stars. He could not take his gaze off her. Soon she looked at him, and the moment their eyes met they fell in love with each other.

He left his seat and went into the lobby where the chandeliers sparkled and gleamed. Soon the girl entered, blushing like a rose in the morning.

"I should not have come," she whispered. "I left my parents and a young gentleman who was with us. He is courting me."

"I love you," he said, "and that excuses everything."

"My parents will be angry and worried."

"I will marry you, and I know they will forgive you." He took her arm. "Come, let us go, I am hungry," he said. "We will eat and then we will go to the church and be married."

She went with him without saying a word. They walked from the Opera House to Royal Street and went into a brilliantly lit restaurant and sat down at a table.

"Waiter," the young man said, "this is our bridal dinner. Put flowers on the table and bring us the finest meal you have."

The flowers were set on the table, and the waiter brought food fit for such a celebration.

They ate and they drank and talked of how much they loved each other. The hours passed quickly as they sat happily at that dinner and, before they realized it, there was a rosy dawn in the sky; it was Ash Wednesday.

The two went to the beautiful St. Louis Cathedral for early Mass, and then they went to the priest and were married.

Hand in hand, both came back to the girl's parents and they were forgiven.

Soon after, the newlyweds said goodbye to all and went up North where the groom had his home.

It was cold up in the North and the lovely Creole bride began ailing. Before long the girl wilted away like a delicate flower taken from its warmth and sunshine. She died and the young husband's heart was broken. Nothing could console him.

Shrove Tuesday, the day when he first set eyes on his beautiful bride who was no more and the time of the Mardi Gras in New Orleans, was nearing.

"I will have dinner with her at my side, like the first night I met her . . . in my imagination . . . in my memory," he said to himself.

He wrote a letter to the restaurant man on Royal Street and sent him the exact amount of money the dinner had cost that night. In the letter, he said:

"Set the table for the same dinner I had with my bride at your restaurant last Mardi Gras. Set it with flowers and the same food we ate that night. The finest food you have. My bride and I will be there, though you won't see us. Whatever is left, give to a young couple who have no money for a dinner that night."

The restaurant man did as he was told. He set flowers on the table and the finest food in the house. The waiter stood behind the chairs with a napkin on his arm. He stood there a long time, as had been ordered, but no one came. He felt cold and eerie standing there, with no one in the seats. It seemed like a death-dinner.

The restaurant man found a poor couple and gave them the food that had not been touched by human hands.

The next year, the restaurant man again received a letter and money ordering him to serve the meal, just as he had done the year before. There were to be flowers on the table and fine food and wine and a waiter in attendance. Then the food was to be given to a poor couple.

The restaurant man did as he was ordered, but this time the waiter thought there were two ghosts sitting at that table. He felt the air moving over the food and all around him. . . .

Every year thereafter a letter came to that restaurant with money for the same order, and the table was set accordingly. Folks in all New Orleans knew of that ghostly dinner for the beautiful dead Creole girl and her lover. And everyone believed her ghost and her husband's ghost came to that dinner.

One Mardi Gras the restaurant man received a letter from a lawyer up North telling him the man had died and had left an order, and money, for the dinners to be continued every Mardi Gras, just the same.

And so it was done for many, many years. Folks spoke about this strange bridal ghost dinner and came to see it set with the waiter standing behind the empty chairs. Many said they saw the flitting ghosts of the lovely Creole and the handsome young man at that table. Whether they saw the ghosts or not, the dinner was served on Mardi Gras night and people still tell of it in New Orleans.

M. A. Jagendorf, *Folk Stories of the South*. New York: Vanguard, 1972, 135–37.

WILLIAM J. LEDERER (b. 1912)
AND EUGENE BURDICK (1918–1965)

[Lederer was a career naval officer who served in World War II before becoming a novelist. Burdick wrote a novel titled Fail-Safe about a nuclear war started in error. Together they wrote The Ugly American, first published in 1958 during the Cold War. The novel shows how good intentions are not enough in a complex and conflicted world. Its publication caused President Eisenhower to appoint a committee to study foreign-aid policy in South-east Asia. The novel implies that without intelligence and knowledge, even well-meaning gifts can go astray, and that to be truly effective the philanthropist must be worldly wise, not naive. The episode related below, based on a true story according to the authors, shows how a lack of knowledge of another culture's language can be a serious drawback in gift giving. The term "Ugly American" is still used today.]

The Ugly American

There was some bad fortune that year in Sarkhan. Several typhoons blustered over the land just before the harvesting period, and destroyed most of the crops. Several months later, there was famine in the southern areas. The mobs already had ransacked the granaries of the rich.

At the Russian Embassy they learned from one of their informers who was employed as translator at the American Embassy that the United States was shipping 14,000 tons of rice to the stricken area. Soon after, the Russians learned from another informer—the American Ambassador's chauffeur—that the first of the American grain ships would be arriving in two days.

Krupitzyn acted with initiative and boldness. He bought up several tons of rice at black market prices in the capital, loaded the rice into a truck, and drove 300 miles south to the area where the famine was most intense.

When he arrived at Plutal, the main city of the south, a large crowd was gathered. The Communist newspaper there had come out with a special edition whose headlines announced that Russia, the friend of Sarkhan, would relieve the famine; and that the Russian Ambassador would personally arrive that day with the first token contribution of rice.

And then Krupitzyn himself came.

Speaking over a loudspeaker system and over all available radio stations in the area, Krupitzyn said that Russia was bending every effort to help her friends. The five tons of rice which he had brought along with him were all they could find locally. But be patient, he told them, in excellent Sarkhanese; several Russian grain ships would be arriving in a few days with thousands and thousands of tons of rice which would be distributed free. He then went on to say that Sarkhan and Russia were friends and allies and had to stand by each other because it was obvious that the colonial and capitalistic countries would not assist another nation unless they could profit from it.

The first American grain ship arrived two days later in the harbor of Haidho, the capital of Sarkhan. The USIS was there with cameramen and tape recorders. The Prime Minister was present to accept the relief grain from His Excellency Louis Sears, the American Ambassabor to Sarkhan. The sirens blew and there were a few fine speeches. When the speeches were over, the stevedores began unloading the bags of rice, carrying them down the dock, and placing them into the American trucks which were waiting to take the rice to the stricken area.

Half-way down the dock, each stevedore stopped at a weighing station so that his bag of rice could be weighed. It is customary in Sarkhan for stevedores to be paid by how much they carry, not by the hour. As each bag was removed from the scale, the checker came up to it and stencilled a few words in Sarkhanese on each of the white bags.

When the trucks arrived in Plutal, they were met by a crowd of perhaps 10,000 people. A loudspeaker announced that here was the rice which had been promised them a short time ago by the Russian Ambassador; and here was proof that Russia keeps her word.

There were objections from the crowd. "But these are American trucks and they are driven by American drivers."

"We have hired them all from the Americans," answered the Sarkhanese Communists. "Didn't the Russian Ambassador warn you that the capitalists would do anything for profit?"

The crowd was still doubtful. They had heard that the ships which brought the rice were flying the American flag; and the rice had been delivered by American trucks. But when the trucks were unloaded and the rice was handed out, then the populace knew that what the Communist propagandists were announcing over the loudspeakers was true. The Russian Ambassador had carried out his promise.

On each bag of rice there was stencilled in Sarkhanese for every citizen to see and read for himself: "This rice is a gift from Russia."

The Americans took pictures of the distribution of the rice and the smiling faces of the now happy people. There were no comments from any of the Americans present. None of them could read or understand Sarkhanese and they did not know what was happening.

About a week later, the American Embassy found out what had happened. Ambassador Louis Sears made a fiery speech; and from Washington came angry rumblings about instant retaliation. Subsequent American grain ships were properly safeguarded, but the people of Sarkhan continued to believe Russia was their friend and protector.

William J. Lederer and Eugene Burdick, *The Ugly American.* New York: W.W. Norton, 1965, 37–40.

O. HENRY (1862–1910)

[Born in Greensboro, North Carolina, William Sydney Porter was three years old when his mother died. He quit school at fifteen and eventually moved to Texas, where he worked at a variety of jobs. In 1894 he tried publishing a weekly humor journal called "The Rolling Stone," which failed in 1895, after which he worked as a reporter for the Houston Post. He began writing short stories, using the pen name O. Henry and moved to New York City in 1902, where he published a steady stream of these stories. The self-sacrifice in his following story makes the janitor a kind of disguised Christ image, selflessly giving his life in an act of gratuitous generosity so that another may live more fully. Heroes give of themselves to various degrees. Someone who saves your life is greatly appreciated. Someone who dies so that you may live has done more; he has given his very being. No greater love or larger gift can the imagination picture, and we keep the memory of the sacrifice alive as a reminder of the heights of generosity that are possible.]

The Last Leaf

In a little district west of Washington Square the streets have run crazy and broken themselves into small strips called "places." These "places" make strange angles and curves. One street crosses itself a time or two. An artist once discovered a valuable possibility in this street. Suppose a collector with a bill for paints, paper and canvas should, in traversing this route, suddenly meet himself coming back, without a cent having been paid on account!

So, to quaint old Greenwich Village the art people soon came prowling, hunting for north windows and eighteenth-century gables and Dutch attics and low rents. Then they imported some pewter mugs and a chafing dish or two from Sixth Avenue, and became a "colony."

At the top of a squatty, three-story brick Sue and Johnsy had their studio. "Johnsy" was familiar for Joanna. One was from Maine; the other from California. They had met at the table d'hôte of an Eighth Street "Delmonico's," and found their tastes in art, chicory salad and bishop sleeves so congenial that the joint studio resulted.

That was in May. In November a cold, unseen stranger, whom the doctors called Pneumonia, stalked about the colony, touching one here and there with his icy fingers. Over on the east side this ravager strode boldly, smiting his victims by scores, but his feet trod slowly through the maze of the narrow and moss-grown "places."

Mr. Pneumonia was not what you would call a chivalric old gentleman. A mite of a little woman with blood thinned by California zephyrs was hardly fair game for the red-fisted, short-breathed old duffer. But Johnsy he smote; and she lay, scarcely moving, on her painted iron bedstead, looking through the small Dutch window-panes at the blank side of the next brick house.

One morning the busy doctor invited Sue into the hallway with a shaggy, gray eyebrow.

"She has one chance in—let us say, ten," he said, as he shook down the mercury in his clinical thermometer. "And that chance is for her to want to live. This way people have of lining-up on the side of the undertaker makes the entire pharmacopoeia look silly. Your little lady has made up her mind that she's not going to get well. Has she anything on her mind?"

"She—she wanted to paint the Bay of Naples some day," said Sue.

"Paint?—bosh! Has she anything on her mind worth thinking twice—a man for instance?"

"A man?" said Sue, with a jew's-harp twang in her voice. "Is a man worth—but, no, doctor; there is nothing of the kind."

"Well, it is the weakness, then," said the doctor. "I will do all that science, so far as it may filter through my efforts, can accomplish. But whenever my patient begins to count the carriages in her funeral procession I subtract 50 per cent from the curative power of medicines. If you will get her to ask one question about the new winter styles in cloak sleeves I will promise you a one-in-five chance for her, instead of one in ten."

After the doctor had gone Sue went into the workroom and cried a Japanese napkin to a pulp. Then she swaggered into Johnsy's room with her drawing board, whistling ragtime.

Johnsy lay, scarcely making a ripple under the bedclothes, with her face toward the window. Sue stopped whistling, thinking she was asleep.

She arranged her board and began a pen-and-ink drawing to illustrate a magazine story. Young artists must pave their way to Art by drawing pictures for magazine stories that young authors write to pave their way to Literature.

As Sue was sketching a pair of elegant horseshow riding trousers and a monocle of the figure of the hero, an Idaho cowboy, she heard a low sound, several times repeated. She went quickly to the bedside.

Johnsy's eyes were open wide. She was looking out the window and counting—counting backward.

"Twelve," she said, and little later "eleven"; and then "ten," and "nine"; and then "eight" and "seven," almost together.

Sue look solicitously out of the window. What was there to count? There was only a bare, dreary yard to be seen, and the blank side of the brick house twenty feet away. An old, old ivy vine, gnarled and decayed at the roots, climbed half way up the brick wall. The cold breath of autumn had stricken its leaves from the vine until its skeleton branches clung, almost bare, to the crumbling bricks.

"What is it, dear?" asked Sue.

"Six," said Johnsy, in almost a whisper. "They're falling faster now. Three days ago there were almost a hundred. It made my head ache to count them. But now it's easy. There goes another one. There are only five left now."

"Five what, dear? Tell your Sudie."

"Leaves. On the ivy vine. When the last one falls I must go, too. I've known that for three days. Didn't the doctor tell you?"

"Oh, I never heard of such nonsense," complained Sue, with magnificent scorn. "What have old ivy leaves to do with your getting well? And you used to love that vine so, you naughty girl. Don't be a goosey. Why, the doctor told me this morning that your chances for getting well real soon were—let's see exactly what he said—he said the chances were ten to one! Why, that's almost as good a chance as we have in New York when we ride on the street cars or walk past a new building. Try to take some broth now, and let Sudie go back to her drawing, so she can sell the editor man with it, and buy port wine for her sick child, and pork chops for her greedy self."

"You needn't get any more wine," said Johnsy, keeping her eyes fixed out the window. "There goes another. No, I don't want any broth. That leaves just four. I want to see the last one fall before it gets dark. Then I'll go, too."

"Johnsy, dear," said Sue, bending over her, "will you promise me to keep your eyes closed, and not look out the window until I am done working? I must hand those drawings in by to-morrow. I need the light, or I would draw the shade down."

"Couldn't you draw in the other room?" asked Johnsy, coldly.

"I'd rather be here by you," said Sue. "Beside, I don't want you to keep looking at those silly ivy leaves."

"Tell me as soon as you have finished," said Johnsy, closing her eyes, and lying white and still as fallen statue, "because I want to see the last one fall. I'm tired of waiting. I'm tired of thinking. I want to turn loose my hold on everything, and go sailing down, down, just like one of those poor, tired leaves."

"Try to sleep," said Sue. "I must call Behrman up to be my model for the old hermit miner. I'll not be gone a minute. Don't try to move 'till I come back."

Old Behrman was a painter who lived on the ground floor beneath them. He was past sixty and had a Michelangelo's Moses beard curling down from the head of a satyr along with the body of an imp. Behrman was a failure in art. Forty years he had wielded the brush without getting near enough to touch the hem of his Mistress's robe. He had been always about to paint a masterpiece, but had never yet begun it. For several years he had painted nothing except now and then a daub in the line of commerce or advertising. He earned a little by serving as a model to those young artists in the colony who could not pay the price of a professional. He drank gin to excess, and still talked of his coming masterpiece. For the rest he was a fierce little old man, who scoffed terribly at softness in any one, and who regarded himself as especial mastiff-in-waiting to protect the two young artists in the studio above.

Sue found Behrman smelling strongly of juniper berries in his dimly lighted den below. In one corner was a blank canvas on an easel that had been waiting there for twenty-five years to receive the first line of the masterpiece. She told him of Johnsy's fancy, and how she feared she would, indeed, light and fragile as a leaf herself, float away, when her slight hold upon the world grew weaker.

Old Behrman, with his red eyes plainly streaming, shouted his contempt and derision for such idiotic imaginings.

"Vass!" he cried. "Is dere people in de world mit der foolishness to die because leafs dey drop off from a confounded vine? I haf not heard of such a thing. No, I will not bose as a model for your fool hermit-dunderhead. Vy do you allow dot silly pusiness to come in der prain of her? Ach, dot poor little Miss Johnsy."

"She is very ill and weak," said Sue, "and the fever has left her mind morbid and full of strange fancies. Very well, Mr. Behrman, if you do not care to pose for me, you needn't. But I think you are a horrid old—old flibbertigibbet."

"You are just like a woman!" yelled Behrman. "Who said I will not bose? Go on. I come mit you. For half an hour I haf peen trying to say dot I am ready to bose. Gott! dis is not any blace in which one so goot as Miss Yohnsy shall lie sick. Some day I vill baint a masterpiece, and ve shall all go away. Gott! yes."

Johnsy was sleeping when they went upstairs. Sue pulled the shade down to the window-sill, and motioned Behrman into the other room. In there they peered out the window fearfully at the ivy vine. Then they looked at each other for a moment without speaking. A persistent, cold rain was falling, mingled with snow. Behrman, in his old blue shirt, took his seat as the hermit miner on an upturned kettle for a rock.

When Sue awoke from an hour's sleep the next morning she found Johnsy with dull, wide-open eyes staring at the drawn green shade.

"Pull it up; I want to see," she ordered, in a whisper.

Wearily Sue obeyed.

But, lo! after the beating rain and fierce gusts of wind that had endured through the livelong night, there yet stood out against the brick wall one ivy leaf. It was the last one on the vine. Still dark green near its stem, with its serrated edges tinted with the yellow of dissolution and decay, it hung bravely from the branch some twenty feet above the ground.

"It is the last one," said Johnsy. "I thought it would surely fall during the night. I heard the wind. It will fall today, and I shall die at the same time."

"Dear, dear!" said Sue, leaning her worn face down to the pillow, "think of me, if you won't think of yourself. What would I do?"

But Johnsy did not answer. The lonesomest thing in all the world is a soul when it is making ready to go on its mysterious, far journey. The fancy seemed to possess her more strongly as one by one the ties that bound her to friendship and to earth were loosed.

The day wore away, and even through the twilight they could see the lone ivy leaf clinging to its stem against the wall. And then, with the coming of the night the north wind was again loosed, while the rain still beat against the windows and pattered down from the low Dutch eaves.

When it was light enough Johnsy, the merciless, commanded that the shade be raised.

The ivy leaf was still there.

Johnsy lay for a long time looking at it. And then she called to Sue, who was stirring her chicken broth over the gas stove.

"I've been a bad girl, Sudie," said Johnsy. "Something has made that last leaf stay there to show me how wicked I was. It is a sin to want to die. You may bring me a little broth now, and some milk with a little port in it, and—no; bring me a hand-mirror first, and then pack some pillows about me, and I will sit up and watch you cook."

An hour later she said. [*sic*]

"Sudie, some day I hope to paint the Bay of Naples."

The doctor came in the afternoon, and Sue had an excuse to go into the hallway as he left.

"Even chances," said the doctor, taking Sue's thin, shaking hand in his. "With good nursing you'll win. And now I must see another case I have downstairs. Behrman, his name is—some kind of an artist, I believe. Pneumonia, too. He is an old, weak man, and the attack is acute. There is no hope for him; but he goes to the hospital to-day to be made more comfortable."

The next day the doctor said to Sue: "She's out of danger. You've won. Nutrition and care now—that's all."

And that afternoon Sue came to the bed where Johnsy lay, contentedly knitting a very blue and very useless woolen shoulder scarf, and put one arm around her, pillows and all.

"I have something to tell you, white mouse," she said. "Mr. Behrman died of pneumonia to-day in the hospital. He was ill only two days. The janitor found him the morning of the first day in his room downstairs helpless with pain. His shoes and clothing were wet through and icy cold. They couldn't imagine where he had been on such a dreadful night. And then they found a lantern, still lighted, and a ladder that had been dragged from its place, and some scattered brushes, and a palette with green and yellow colors mixed on it, and—look out the window, dear, at the last ivy leaf on the wall. Didn't you wonder why it never fluttered or moved when the wind blew? Ah, darling, it's Behrman's masterpiece—he painted it there the night that the last leaf fell."

O. Henry (William Sidney Porter), *The Trimmed Lamp and Other Stories of the Four Million*. Garden City, N.Y.: Doubleday, Page, 1919, http://www.gutenberg.org/etext/3707.

LANGSTON HUGHES (1902–1967)

[Langston Hughes was a leader of the Harlem Renaissance in the 1920s, a great poet, playwright, and storyteller. He was a master of African American vernacular language used in eloquent literary expression. Hughes wrote, "I am the darker brother. They send me to eat in the kitchen when company comes." He prayed hopefully for the well-being of his country: "Let America be the dream the dreamers dreamed. Let it be that great strong

land of love where never kings connive nor tyrants scheme that any man be crushed by one above." Hughes knew the street life of the ghetto, its sorrows and its songs, and the world of the white establishment as well. In this story, a black professor is an intermediary between the wealthy and the poor and sees both sides of the story. He bridges their different views of themselves and of America. The story's dynamics portraying an educated representative of disadvantaged people in the home of powerful philanthropists form a microcosm of some of the race relations of our country. The story dramatizes the complexities of philanthropy and social uplift, the attitudes and unconscious prejudices of the civic minded, and the frustrations of the token minority.]

Professor

Promptly at seven a big car drew up in front of the Booker T. Washington Hotel, and a white chauffeur in uniform got out and went toward the door, intending to ask at the desk for a colored professor named T. Walton Brown. But the professor was already sitting in the lobby, a white scarf around his neck and his black overcoat ready to button over his dinner clothes.

As soon as the chauffeur entered, the professor approached. "Mr. Chandler's car?" he asked hesitantly.

"Yes, sir," said the white chauffeur to the neat little Negro. "Are you Dr. Walton Brown?"

"I am," said the professor, smiling and bowing a little.

The chauffeur opened the street door for Mr. Brown, then ran to the car and held the door open there, too. Inside the big car and on the long black running board as well, the lights came on. The professor stepped in among the soft cushions, the deep rug, and the cut glass vases holding flowers. With the greatest of deference the chauffeur quickly tucked a covering of fur about the professor's knees, closed the door, entered his own seat in front beyond the glass partition, and the big car purred away. Within the lobby of the cheap hotel a few ill-clad Negroes watched the whole procedure in amazement.

"A big shot!" somebody said.

At the corner as the car passed, two or three ash-colored children ran across the street in front of the wheel, their skinny legs and poor clothes plain in the glare of the headlights as the chauffeur slowed down to let them pass. Then the car turned and ran the whole length of a Negro street that was lined with pawn shops, beer joints, pig's knuckle stands, cheap movies, hairdressing parlors, and other ramshackle places of business patronized by the poor blacks of the district. Inside the big car the professor, Dr. Walton Brown, regretted that in all the large Midwestern cities where he had lectured on his present tour in behalf of his college, the main Negro streets presented the same sleazy and disagreeable appearance: pig's knuckle joints, pawn shops, beer parlors and houses of vice, no doubt—save that these latter, at least, did not hang out their signs.

The professor looked away from the unpleasant sight of this typical Negro street, poor and unkempt. He looked ahead through the glass at the dignified white neck of the uniformed chauffeur in front of him. The professor in his dinner clothes, his brown face even browner above the white silk scarf at his neck, felt warm and comfortable under the fur rug. But he felt, too, a little unsafe at being driven through the streets of this city on the edge of the South in an expensive car, by a white chauffeur.

"But, then," he thought, "this is the wealthy Mr. Ralph P. Chandler's car, and surely no harm can come to me here. The Chandlers are a power in the Middle West, and in the South as well. Theirs is one of the great fortunes of America. In philanthropy, nobody exceeds them in well-planned generosity on a large and highly publicized scale. They are a power in Negro education, too. That is why I am visiting them tonight at their invitation."

Just now the Chandlers were interested in the little Negro college at which the professor taught. They wanted to make it one of the major Negro colleges of America. And in particular the Chandlers were interested in his Department of Sociology. They were thinking of endowing a chair of research there and employing a man of ability for it. A Ph.D. and a scholar. A man of some prestige, like the professor. For his *The Sociology of Prejudice* (that restrained and conservative study of Dr. T. Walton Brown's) had recently come to the attention of the Chandler Committee. And a representative of their philanthropies, visiting the campus, had conversed with the professor at some length about his book and his views. This representative of the Committee found Dr. Brown highly gratifying, because in almost every case the professor's views agreed with the white man's own.

"A fine, sane, dependable young Negro," was the description that came to the Chandler Committee from their traveling representative.

So now the power himself, Mr. Ralph P. Chandler, and Mrs. Chandler, learning that he was lecturing at one of the colored churches of the town, had invited him to dinner at their mansion in this city on the edge of the South. Their car had come to call for him at the colored Booker T. Washington Hotel, where the hot water was always cold, the dresser drawers stuck, and the professor shivered as he got into his dinner clothes; and the bellboys, anxious for a tip, had asked him twice that evening if he needed a half pint or a woman.

But now he was in this big warm car and they were moving swiftly down a fine boulevard, the black slums far behind them. The professor was glad. He had been very much distressed at having the white chauffeur call for him at this cheap hotel in what really amounted to the red light district of the town. But, then, none of the white hotels in this American city would house Negroes, no matter how cultured they might be. Marian Anderson herself had been unable to find decent accommodations there, so the colored papers said, on the day of her concert.

Sighing, the professor looked out of the car at the wide lawns and fine homes that lined the beautiful well-lighted boulevard where white people lived. After a time the car turned into a fashionable suburban road and he saw no more houses, but only ivy-hung walls, neat shrubs, and boxwoods that indicated not merely homes beyond but vast estates. Shortly the car whirled into a paved driveway, past a small lodge, through a park full of fountains and trees, and up to a private house as large as a hotel. From a tall portico a great hanging lantern cast a soft glow on the black and chrome body of the big car. The white chauffeur jumped out and deferentially opened the door for the colored professor. An English butler welcomed him at the entrance and took his coat, hat, and scarf. Then he led the professor into a large drawing room where two men and a woman were standing chatting near the fireplace.

The professor hesitated, not knowing who was who; but Mr. and Mrs. Chandler came forward, introduced themselves, shook hands, and in turn presented their other guest of the evening, Dr. Bulwick of the local Municipal College—a college that Dr.

Brown recalled did *not* admit Negroes.

"I am happy to know you," said Dr. Bulwick. "I am also a sociologist."

"I have heard of you," said Dr. Brown graciously.

The butler came with sherry in a silver pitcher. They sat down, and the whites began to talk politely, to ask Dr. Brown about his lecture tour, if his audiences were good, if they were mostly Negro or mixed, and if there was much interest in his college, much money being given.

Then Dr. Bulwick began to ask about his book, *The Sociology of Prejudice*, where he got his material, under whom he had studied, and if he thought the Negro Problem would ever be solved.

Dr. Brown said genially, "We are making progress," which was what he always said, though he often felt he was lying.

"Yes," said Dr. Bulwick, "that is very true. Why, at our city college here we've been conducting some fine interracial experiments. I have had several colored ministers and high-school teachers visit my classes. We found them most intelligent people."

In spite of himself Dr. Brown had to say, "But you have no colored students at your college, have you?"

"No," said Dr. Bulwick, "and that is too bad! But that is one of our difficulties here. There is no Municipal College for Negroes—although nearly forty per cent of our population is colored. Some of us have thought it might be wise to establish a separate junior college for our Negroes, but the politicians opposed it on the score of no funds. And we cannot take them as students on our campus. That, at present, is impossible. It's too bad."

"But do you not think, Dr. Brown," interposed Mrs. Chandler, who wore diamonds on her wrists and smiled every time she spoke, "do you not think *Your people* are happier in schools of their own—that it is really better for both groups not to mix them?"

In spite of himself, Dr. Brown replied, "That depends, Mrs. Chandler. I could not have gotten my degree in any schools of our own."

"True, true," said Mr. Chandler. "Advanced studies, of course, cannot be gotten. But when your colleges are developed—as we hope they will be, and our Committee plans to aid in their development—when their departments are headed by men like yourself, for instance, then you can no longer say, 'That depends.'"

"You are right," Dr. Brown agreed diplomatically, coming to himself and thinking of his mission in that house. "You are right," Dr. Brown said, thinking too of that endowed chair of sociology and himself in the chair, the six thousand dollars a year that he would probably be paid, the survey he might make and the books he could publish. "You are right," said Dr. Brown diplomatically to Ralph P. Chandler. But in the back of his head was that ghetto street full of sleazy misery he had just driven through, and the segregated hotel where the hot water was always cold, and the colored churches where he lectured, and the Jim Crow schools where Negroes always had less equipment and far less money than white institutions; and that separate justice of the South where his people sat on trial but the whites were judge and jury forever; and all the segregated Jim Crow things that America gave Negroes and that were never equal to the things she gave the whites. But Dr. Brown said, "You are right, Mr. Chandler," for, after all, Mr. Chandler had the money!

So he began to talk earnestly to the Chandlers there in the warm drawing room about the need for bigger and better black colleges, for more and more surveys of *Negro* life, and a well-developed department of sociology at *his* own little institution.

"Dinner is served," said the butler.

They rose and went into a dining room where there were flowers on the table and candles, white linen and silver, and where Dr. Brown was seated at the right of the hostess and the talk was light over the soup, but serious and sociological again by the time the meat was served.

"The American Negro must not be taken in by communism," Dr. Bulwick was saying with great positiveness as the butler passed the peas.

"He won't," agreed Dr. Brown. "I assure you, our leadership stands squarely against it." He looked at the Chandlers and bowed. "All the best people stand against it."

"America has done too much for the Negro," said Mr. Chandler, "for him to seek to destroy it."

Dr. Brown bobbed and bowed.

"In your *Sociology of Prejudice*," said Dr. Bulwick, "I highly approve of the closing note, your magnificent appeal to the old standards of Christian morality and the simple concepts of justice by which America functions."

"Yes," said Dr. Brown, nodding his dark head and thinking suddenly how on six thousand dollars a year he might take his family to South America in the summer where for three months they wouldn't feel like Negroes. "Yes, Dr. Bulwick," he nodded, "I firmly believe as you do that if the best elements of both races came together in Christian fellowship, we would solve this problem of ours."

"How beautiful," said Mrs. Chandler.

"And practical, too," said her husband. "But now to come back to your college—university, I believe you call it—to bring that institution up to really first-class standards you would need . . . ?"

"We would need . . ." said Dr. Brown, speaking as a mouthpiece of the administration, and speaking, too, as mouthpiece for the Negro students of his section of the South, and speaking for himself as a once ragged youth who had attended the college when its rating was lower than that of a Northern high school so that he had to study two years in Boston before he could enter a white college, when he had worked nights as redcap in the station and then as a waiter for seven years until he got his Ph.D., and then couldn't get a job in the North but had to go back down South to the work where he was now—but which might develop into a glorious opportunity at six thousand dollars a year to make surveys and put down figures that other scholars might study to get their Ph.D.s, and that would bring him in enough to just once take his family on a vacation to South America where they wouldn't feel that they were Negroes. "We would need, Mr. Chandler . . ."

And the things Dr. Brown's little college needed were small enough in the eyes of the Chandlers. The sane and conservative way in which Dr. Brown presented his case delighted the philanthropic heart of the Chandlers. And Mr. Chandler and Dr. Bulwick both felt that instead of building a junior college for Negroes in their own town they could rightfully advise local colored students to go down South to that fine little campus where they had a professor of their own race like Dr. Brown.

Over the coffee, in the drawing room, they talked about the coming theatrical season. And Mrs. Chandler spoke of how she loved Negro singers, and smiled and smiled.

In due time the professor rose to go. The car was called and he shook hands with Dr. Bulwick and the Chandlers. The white people were delighted with Dr. Brown. He could see it in their faces, just as in the past he could always tell as a waiter when he had pleased a table full of whites by tender steaks and good service.

"Tell the president of your college he shall hear from us shortly," said the Chandlers. "We'll probably send a man down again soon to talk to him about his expansion program." And they bowed farewell.

As the car sped him back toward town, Dr. Brown sat under its soft fur rug among the deep cushions and thought how with six thousand dollars a year earned by dancing properly to the tune of Jim Crow education, he could carry his whole family to South America for a summer where they wouldn't need to feel like Negroes.

Langston Hughes, "Professor," in *Laughing to Keep from Crying*. New York: Holt, 1952.

VERSES AND SONGS

ANONYMOUS

[One of the morals of this poem published in a newspaper in the small Texas town of Grapevine is that charity begins at home, but that also, ideally, charity should be active throughout the week—not just on Sunday. This poem humorously imagines and lampoons the fate of an industrious man heedless of that ideal—he gets his just deserts in a surprising way.]

Ebenezer Gray's Religion

He thought he was a Christian—
Did Ebenezer Gray,
He never missed church meetings
And was always glad to pray.
He did not let religion
Hurt his business through the week,
But on Sunday morning
He was righteous like a meek.

He used to have a manner
That would make a clown feel blue
He used to chill his neighbors,
And his home was chilly, too,
But in the church on Sunday
You could never find him late,
And when it came to rooting
In religion, he was great.

He used to skin all comers
Through the week and like the game,
Yet claimed to run his business
In the Master's holy name.
He never let the doctrine
Used on Sunday, understand,

Affect upon a week day,
Any deal he had on hand.

Some people called him "brother,"
And great numbers called him names
The latter people being
Those who fathomed all his aims.
He died in proper season—
Crossed unto another shore—
And this is what St. Peter
Told the fellow at the door:

While you were good on Sundays,
Through the week, Eb, you were tough;
Hence, when I speak your sentence,
Do not think that I am rough;
Now you can spend your Sundays
Up here where the angels dwell,
but during all the week days
We're going to give you hell!

Grapevine Sun, Grapevine Texas, February 14, 1903.

WILLIAM M. GOLDEN (1878–1934)

[William Matthew Golden's biography is known only sketchily. He wrote several gospel hymns around the turn of the century, composing the tunes as well as the words. His best-known song is "Where the Soul of Man Never Dies," beginning "To Canaan's land I'm on my way," which was recorded by the Carter Family and Hank Williams. "A Beautiful Life" has been recorded by a number of artists, including the Statler Brothers and Bill Monroe. Golden wrote most of his songs while serving an eight-year sentence in the Mississippi state penitentiary. His lyrics are remembered and still sung today. This is a simple song appreciating daily life as the constant chance to be of help in small ways and to be worthy of one's blessings. It is a kind and gentle song, meditating on the happiness found in lending a hand to serve those in need.]

A Beautiful Life

Each day I'll do a golden deed,
By helping those who are in need;
My life on earth is but a span,
And so I'll do the best I can.

Refrain:
Life's evening sun is sinking low,
A few more days, and I must go
To meet the deeds that I have done,

Where there will be no setting sun.

To be a child of God each day,
My light must shine along the way;
I'll sing His praise while ages roll,
And strive to help some troubled soul.

The only life that will endure,
Is one that's kind and good and pure;
And so for God I'll take my stand,
Each day I'll lend a helping hand.

I'll help someone in time of need,
And journey on with rapid speed;
I'll help the sick and poor and weak,
And words of kindness to them speak.

While going down life's weary road,
I'll try to lift some trav'ler's load;
I'll try to turn the night to day,
Make flowers bloom along the way.

http://library.timelesstruths.org/music/A_Beautiful_Life/.

MAMIE DESDUME (1879–1911)

[Mamie Desdume (or Desdunes) mentored the great jazz pianist Ferdinand "Jelly Roll" Morton. She had only eight fingers but could play with greater facility than most ten-fingered piano players. Mamie was said to have been "good-natured, a fine dresser, and extremely popular with the sporting crowd." She played the blues with soul, and Jelly Roll heard her and was inspired. In memory of her, he gratefully named a piece that featured her lyrics "Mamie's Blues." The song dramatizes a poignant situation, and the plea speaks for itself. In such a situation you want to help. But will a donation make a difference? If you don't help, will the woman die of pneumonia?]

Mamie Desdume's Blues

I stood on the corner, my feet was dripping wet
I asked every man I met . . .

If you can't give me a dollar, give me a lousy dime.
Can't give a dollar, give me a lousy dime,
I wanna feed that hungry man of mine.

Langston Hughes and Arna Bontemps, eds., *The Book of Negro Folklore.* New York: Dodd, Mead: 1958, 349, 444.

EDWIN MARKHAM (1852–1940)

[Born in Oregon, Markham has been called "a poet of conscience and cause." He left behind a number of sayings about lending a helping hand: "A good action is never lost; it is a treasure laid up and guarded for the doer's need." "We have committed the Golden Rule to memory; let us now commit it to life." "There is a destiny that makes us brothers; None goes his way alone; All that we send into the lives of others comes back into our own." His following verse suggests that the power of love is a mystery not to be underestimated. Where there is a will and a wisdom to embrace others, a way may appear and prevail.]

Outwitted

He drew a circle that shut me out—
Heretic, rebel, a thing to flout.
But love and I had the wit to win;
We drew a circle that took him in.

---

http://www.theotherpages.org/poems/mark01.html (accessed February 26, 2008).

FOLK RHYMES

[These lines are said to be from "an endless song to which verses are made up on the spur of the moment and immediately forgotten." It jokingly speaks of the onus of "being on the dole."]

On Relief

I kin tell by the shape of your head
That you been eatin' charity bread.

Response:
And I kin tell by the bend in your knees
That you been eatin' charity cheese, etc.

American Life Histories: Manuscripts from the Federal Writers' Project, 1936–1940, http://lcweb2.loc.gov/cgi-bin/query/D?wpa:1:./temp/~ammem_jT1D.

GEORGIA DOUGLAS JOHNSON (1880–1966)

[Johnson was a poet of the Harlem Renaissance. This poem tells a truth in rhyme about begging: people often don't respect a beggar. Obviously the attitude of pleading is not a winning one in a culture of individualism—it bespeaks a lack of self-sufficiency. The beggar is usually not highly esteemed by others because he lacks clout and independence. Charity may be necessary in emergencies, but it does not engender a sense of self-respect in the recipients. Knowing this, the giver learns to be careful not to damage self-esteem further and sometimes finds ways to help people pull themselves up by their own efforts.

Observations in the following verses suggest that pleading and praying and pounding on doors are weak and desperate approaches; the punchline presents a bolder way. Unfortunately, the weak often do not feel able to "demand" and "contend." They have suffered loss and been weakened, and they feel at the mercy of those from whom they seek aid.]

The Suppliant

Long have I beat with timid hands upon life's leaden door,
Praying the patient, futile prayer my fathers prayed before,
Yet I remain without the close, unheeded and unheard,
And never to my listening ear is borne the waited word.

Soft o'er the threshold of the years there comes this counsel cool:
The strong demand, contend, prevail; the beggar is a fool!

Georgia Douglas Johnson, Poets' Corner, http://www.theotherpages.org/poems/2001/johnson0101.html.

PAUL LAURENCE DUNBAR (1872–1906)

[Dunbar was a renowned African American poet who often wrote in Southern dialect. This poem is in a more classical style than many of his others. It is a fable about a Queen (Nature) and an elf (Art). When offered a gift, few would think to ask instead for the giver. In this story, Nature, the giver, is much greater than any of the gifts she offers. Indeed, the giving of oneself is the most meaningful kind of giving. In this story, as in many fairy tales, there are boons offered. The hero shows his worthiness in his response to gifts from among which he may choose. Magnanimity of the recipient evokes magnanimity in the giver. Nature in this poem wishes for self-awareness; only Art can bring the gift of reflecting her beauty, making it known and shown to others. Art, in giving this gift which is enriching to the world at large, wins the love and self-giving of Nature.]

Nature and Art

TO MY FRIEND CHARLES BOOTH NETTLETON

I. The young queen Nature, ever sweet and fair,
  Once on a time fell upon evil days.
  From hearing oft herself discussed with praise,
  There grew within her heart the longing rare
  To see herself; and every passing air
  The warm desire fanned into lusty blaze.
  Full oft she sought this end by devious ways,
  But sought in vain, so fell she in despair.

  For none within her train nor by her side
  Could solve the task or give the envied boon.

So day and night, beneath the sun and moon,
She wandered to and fro unsatisfied,
Till Art came by, a blithe inventive elf,
And made a glass wherein she saw herself.

II. Enrapt, the queen gazed on her glorious self,
Then trembling with the thrill of sudden thought,
Commanded that the skilful wight be brought
That she might dower him with lands and pelf.
Then out upon the silent sea-lapt shelf
And up the hills and on the downs they sought
Him who so well and wondrously had wrought;
And with much search found and brought home the elf.
But he put by all gifts with sad replies,

And from his lips these words flowed forth like wine:
"O queen, I want no gift but thee," he said.
She heard and looked on him with love-lit eyes,
Gave him her hand, low murmuring, "I am thine,"
And at the morrow's dawning they were wed.

Paul Laurence Dunbar Digital Collection, http://www.libraries.wright.edu/special/dunbar/poetryindex
/nature_and_art.html.

VACHEL LINDSAY (1879–1931)

[Born in Springfield, Illinois, Lindsay rejected a medical career for writing and in 1905 sold the following poem as a pamphlet on the streets of New York. Self-printing his poems and reciting them as he traveled, he was a modern-day troubadour. For years he walked across regions of America selling his poetry and living hand to mouth. This poem, harkening back to the romantic wandering-minstrel image, dramatizes the poet as a beggar. The listener who supports him also hungers for something. Each offers gifts to the other.]

Rhymes to Be Traded for Bread [Prologue]

Even the shrewd and bitter,
Gnarled by the old world's greed,
Cherished the stranger softly
Seeing his utter need.
Shelter and patient hearing,
These were their gifts to him,
To the minstrel chanting, begging,
As the sunset-fire grew dim.
The rich said "you are welcome."
Yea, even the rich were good.
How strange that in their feasting

His songs were understood!
The doors of the poor were open,
The poor who had wandered too,
Who slept with never a roof-tree
Under the wind and dew.
The minds of the poor were open,
There dark mistrust was dead:
They loved his wizard stories,
They bought his rhymes with bread.

Those were his days of glory,
Of faith in his fellow-men.
Therefore to-day the singer
Turns beggar once again.

Vachel Lindsay, *Collected Poems*. New York: Mamillan, 1925.

ANONYMOUS

[This charming song, with a melody by Albert E. Brumley, is still sung in the south and is regularly played on Christian and country-music radio stations. Brumley was born into a poor tenant-farming family in Oklahoma. Following his musical inspiration, he became a preeminent southern gospel songwriter, widely known for his song "I'll Fly Away" and many others. The lyrics describe the joys of a contented life in a roadside cabin where one is in a position to be neighborly and to assist travelers on their journeys. The pastimes of scattering flowers and light, and easing others' loads, are sweeter and more satisfying than being the most powerful king, according to this spiritual lyric.]

I'd Rather Live by the Side of the Road

There are people who would rather live in splendor
Brag about their silver and their gold
People who would trade God's promise
For its glory to hold
There are people who would rather live in mansions
People who would rather live abroad
But I'd rather have a little log cabin
By the side of the road

Chorus:
I'd rather live by the side of the road
And try to point souls to the blest abode
Than to be a king or a millionaire
And live in mansions in bright array
I'd rather do a neighborly deed
For some traveler or a friend in need

I'd rather live by the side of the road
And help some pilgrim along life's way

I'd rather have a cabin by the roadside
Where the pilgrimage of man is passing by
Help to point souls to Jesus
And that city on high
Everyday I want to help to scatter roses
Every night I want my lamp to shine abroad
With a welcome from my little bay window
By the side of the road

http://jason.hannan.net/b_tab.html.

SARAH NORCLIFFE CLEGHORN (1876–1959)

[American socialist, pacifist Quaker, reformer, and poet, Cleghorn was a passionate advocate for social-justice causes such as women's suffrage, antilynching, prison reform, and opposition to child labor. This brief poem is a powerful plea for greater charitableness from industrial tycoons. It subtly presents the reverse of our expectations, to show us something is wrong. It heightens our sympathy for the children, making us want to reverse the equation. The shadow of the wisdom of generosity is the shortsightedness of greed, the ignorance of miserliness. Sometimes pointing out the shadow is a way of shedding light and encouraging reform.]

The Golf Links

The golf links lie so near the mill
That almost every day
The laboring children can look out
And see the men at play.

Sarah Norcliffe Cleghorn, Poets' Corner, http://www.theotherpages.org/poems/cleghorn.html.

PETER MAURIN (1877–1949)

[Maurin was a wanderer—a monkish Woody Guthrie—inspired by Catholic faith. He mentored Dorothy Day, the social activist, and together they founded the Catholic Worker Movement in 1933. Both were dedicated to nonviolence and lives of service to the poor. Dorothy Day wrote, "I felt that the Church was the Church of the poor, that St. Patrick's had been built from the pennies of servant girls, that it cared for the emigrant, it established hospitals, orphanages, day nurseries, houses of the Good Shepherd, homes for the aged, but at the same time, I felt that it did not set its face against a social order which made so much charity in the present sense of the word necessary. I felt that charity was a word to choke over. Who wanted charity? And it was not just human pride but a strong sense of man's dignity and worth, and what was due to him

in justice . . ." (Cited in Dorothy Day: A Radical Devotion, by Robert Coles, Reading, Mass.: Addison Wesley Publishing, 1987, p. 58.) Maurin heartily agreed. In the following verses Maurin skillfully uses symmetries and echoes of images and sounds to make his points. He wrote of the fulfillment found in a life lived for others, avoiding excesses and embracing simplicity.]

EASY ESSAYS

Go-getters vs. Go-givers

A personalist
    is a go-giver
    not a go-getter.
He tries to give
    what he has,
    and does not
    try to get
    what the other fellow has.
He tries to be good
    by doing good
    to the other fellow.
He is altro-centered,
    not self-centered.
He has a social doctrine
    of the common good
    through words and deeds.
He speaks through deeds
    as well as words,
    for he knows that deeds
    speak louder than words.
Through words and deeds
    he brings into existence
    a common unity,
    the common unity
    of a community.

Ambassadors of God

What we give to the poor
    for Christ's sake
    is what we carry with us
    when we die.
We are afraid
    to pauperize the poor
    because we are afraid
    to be poor.
Pagan Greeks used to say

that the poor
"are the ambassadors
of the gods."
To become poor
is to become
an ambassador of God.

St. Francis thought
that to choose to be poor
is just as good
as if one should marry
the most beautiful girl in the world
We seem to think
that poor people
are social nuisances
and not ambassadors of God.
We seem to think
that Lady Poverty
is an ugly girl
and not the beautiful girl
that St. Francis of Assisi
says she is.
And because we think so,
we refuse to feed the poor
with our superfluous goods
and let the politicians
feed the poor
by going around
like pickpockets,
robbing Peter
to pay Paul,
and feeding the poor
by soaking the rich.

Theory of Revolution

I want a change,
and a radical change.
I want a change
from an acquisitive society
to a functional society,
from a society of go-getters
to a society of go-givers.

Peter Maurin, "Go-getters vs. Go-givers" (excerpt); "Theory of Revolution" (excerpt); "Ambassadors of God" (entire), in *Easy Essays,* ed. Chuck Smith. West Hamlin, W.Va.: Green Revolution Catholic Worker Farm, 1973, 12, 17, 35.

JOHN TREVILLE LATOUCHE (1914–1956)

[John Treville Latouche wrote this cantata's lyrics, and Earl Robinson composed the music. Originally titled "The Ballad for Uncle Sam," this enthusiastic piece found fame when Paul Robeson sang it on the CBS radio network, accompanied by chorus and orchestra; it remained popular throughout World War II. Because of Robeson's left-wing politics, the song faded from the American popular music scene during the Red Scare of the late forties and early fifties, but it was performed again during the U.S. Bicentennial in 1976. The piece refers to many historical events in America's story and celebrates the diversity that is America's strength. The New York City Labor Chorus updated it; the added lyrics are indicated by parentheses. The song presents America as the composite figure Uncle Sam, whose identity is made up of many cultural backgrounds—as the nations motto expresses it: "e pluribus unum." Also, the song expresses the spirit of generosity—magnanimous and inclusive, optimistic and appreciative of all who make the great social quilt of America possible. Future generations of Americans can add to it their own experiences, including examples of Americans' expansive spirit of generosity in times of great need.]

The Ballad for Uncle Sam, or, Ballad for Americans

In seventy-six the sky was red
thunder rumbling overhead
Bad King George couldn't sleep in his bed
And on that stormy morn, Ol' Uncle Sam was born.
Some birthday!

Ol' Sam put on a three cornered hat
And in a Richmond church he sat
And Patrick Henry told him that while America drew breath
It was "Liberty or death."

What kind of hat is a three-cornered hat?
Did they all believe in liberty in those days?

Nobody who was anybody believed it.
Ev'rybody who was anybody they doubted it.
Nobody had faith.
Nobody but Washington, Tom Paine, Benjamin Franklin,
Chaim Solomon, Crispus Attucks, Lafayette. Nobodies.
The nobodies ran a tea party at Boston. Betsy Ross
organized a sewing circle. Paul Revere had a horse race.

And a little ragged group believed it.
And some gentlemen and ladies believed it.
And some wise men and some fools, and I believed it too.
And you know who I am.
No. Who are you mister? Yeah, how come all this?
Well, I'll tell you. It's like this . . . No let us tell you.

Figure 4.1 Cartoon images of Uncle Sam from Alton Ketchum. In the national imagination, figures such as Yankee Doodle and Uncle Sam are well known, and so are often used to graphically express ideas and current events in broad strokes. While the "Yankee Doodle" figure always has a rather whimsically youthful and foolish trickster quality, the Uncle Sam figure is more responsible, avuncular, and elderly like the nation's conscience. Uncle Sam as seen in cartoons is a convenient personification for the authority of America. He is often troubled, harassed, with his deep pockets stocked to dispense needed goods. As Santa Claus personifies the gift-giving spirit of Christmas, and the Statue of Liberty personifies America welcoming those seeking freedom, Uncle Sam personifies the fatherly power of America to pitch in and dutifully provide what is needed.

Mister Tom Jefferson, a mighty fine man.
He wrote it down in a mighty fine plan.
And the rest all signed it with a mighty fine hand
As they crossed their T's and dotted their I's
A bran' new country did arise.

And a mighty fine idea. "Adopted unanimously in
　　　Congress July 4, 1776,
We hold these truths to be self-evident, that all men
　　　are created equal.
That they are endowed by their creator with certain
　　　inalienable rights.
That among these rights are Life, Yes sir! Liberty, That's right!
And the pursuit of happiness."
Is that what they said? The very words.
That does sound mighty fine.

Building a nation is awful tough.
The people found the going rough.
(Some lived in cities, some worked the land,
And united they did stand, to make our country grand.)

Still nobody who was anybody believed it.
Everybody who anybody they stayed at home.
But Lewis and Clarke and the pioneers,
Driven by hunger, haunted by fears,
The Klondike miners and the forty niners,
Some wanted freedom and some wanted riches,
Some liked to loaf while others dug ditches.
But they believed it. And I believed it too,
And you know who I am.
No, who are you anyway, Mister?

Well, you see it's like this. I started to tell you.
I represent the whole . . . Why that's it!
Let my people go. That's the idea!
Old Abe Lincoln was thin and long,
His heart was high and his faith was strong.
But he hated oppression, he hated wrong,
And he went down to his grave to free the slave.

A man in white skin can never be free while his black
　　　brother is in slavery,
"And we here highly resolve that these dead shall not
　　　have died in vain.
And this government of the people, by the people and for the people
Shall not perish from the Earth."

Abraham Lincoln said that on November 19, 1863 at
    Gettysburg, Pennsylvania.
And he was right. I believe that too.

Say, we still don't know who you are, mister.
Well, I started to tell you . . .
The machine age came with a great big roar,
As America grew in peace and war.
And a million wheels went around and 'round.

Figure 4.2 Thomas Nast, engraving of "Uncle Sam's Thanksgiving."

The cities reached into the sky,
And dug down deep into the ground.
And some got rich and some got poor.
But the people carried through,
So our country grew.
(With Susan B. Anthony and the Suffragettes,
We women fought with all our might
And we made voting our right.
Our struggle continues to this day.
And the people carried through,
So our country grew.)

Still nobody who was anybody believed it.
Everybody who was anybody they doubted it.
And they are doubting still,
And I guess they always will,
But who cares what they say when I am on my way

Say, will you please tell us who you are?
What's your name, Buddy? Where you goin'? Who are you?
Well, I'm the everybody who's nobody,
I'm the nobody who's everybody.
What's your racket? What do you do for a living?

Well, I'm an
Engineer, musician, street cleaner, carpenter, teacher,
How about a farmer? Also. Office clerk? Yes sir!
That's right. (Homemaker?) Certainly!
Factory worker? You said it. (Mail carrier?) Yes ma'am.
(Hospital worker?) Absotively! (Social worker?) Posolutely!
Truck driver? Definitely!
Miner, seamstress, ditchdigger, all of them.
I am the "etceteras" and the "and so forths" that do the work.
Now hold on here, what are you trying to give us?
Are you an American?

Am I an American?
I'm just an Irish, (African), Jewish, Italian,
French and English, Spanish, Russian, Chinese, Polish,
Scotch, Hungarian, (Jamaican), Swedish, Finnish, (Dominican), Greek
and Turk and Czech
and (Native American).

And that ain't all.
I was baptized Baptist, Methodist, Congregationalist, Lutheran,
Atheist, Roman Catholic, (Moslem) Jewish, Presbyterian,
        Seventh Day Adventist,
Mormon, Quaker, Christian Scientist and lots more.
You sure are something.

Our country's strong, our country's young,
And her greatest songs are still unsung.
From her plains and mountains we have sprung,
To keep the faith with those who went before.

We nobodies who are anybody believe it.
We anybodies who are everybody have no doubts.
Out of the cheating, out of the shouting,
(Out of the greed and polluting,
Out of the massacre at Wounded Knee,
Out of the lies of McCarthy,
Out of the murders of Martin and John,
It will come again,
Our song of hope is here again.)

(Precious as our planet),
Deep as our valleys,
High as our mountains,
Strong as the people who made it.
For I have always believed it, and I believe it now,
And now you know who I am.
Who are you?
America! America!

John LaTouche (revised by NYC Labor Chorus). Available at http://www.cpsr.cs.uchicago.edu/robeson/links/NYlabor.ballad.lyrics.html.

ROBERT FROST (1874–1963)

[Frost said he was brought up on Universalist Unitarian, Presbyterian, and Swedenborgian religious traditions. As with a number of other American thinkers, he was not much of a churchgoer; his religious sensibility was an inward affair. Frost recited the following poem, written in 1942, at the inauguration of John F. Kennedy in 1961. It tells America's story as a series of paradoxes and causes us to ponder our past, present, and future. We might assume that withholding would make us stronger and giving of ourselves would lessen us, but Frost reverses that common sense, asserting that withholding weakens. The poem suggests that giving back deepens Americans' relationship to their homeland, that in giving ourselves for our country, we more genuinely become hers.]

The Gift Outright

The land was ours before we were the land's.
She was our land more than a hundred years
Before we were her people. She was ours
In Massachusetts, in Virginia,
But we were England's, still colonials,
Possessing what we still were unpossessed by,
Possessed by what we now no more possessed.
Something we were withholding made us weak
Until we found out that it was ourselves
We were withholding from our land of living,
And forthwith found salvation in surrender.
Such as we were we gave ourselves outright
(The deed of gift was many deeds of war)
To the land vaguely realizing westward,
But still unstoried, artless, unenhanced,
Such as she was, such as she would become.

Robert Frost, *Complete Poems [by] Robert Frost*. London: Cape, 1967, 467.

HANK WILLIAMS (1923–1953)

["Men with Broken Hearts" is a recitation piece written by Hank Williams, Sr., under the pen name Luke the Drifter. Those who knew him said this was his favorite of all the lyrical pieces he wrote. It was later used as an introduction to "Walk a Mile in My Shoes" sung by Elvis Presley. Both Williams and Presley were Southerners who came from backgrounds of poverty. As George Eliot wrote, "One must be poor to know the luxury of giving." Similarly, someone who has known brokenness can best appreciate the healing hand of kindness. Simple rhymes seem to speak Williams' heartfelt convictions in this passionate call for compassion and respect for broken people in their time of need.]

Men with Broken Hearts

You'll meet many just like me upon life's busy streets
With shoulders stooped and heads bowed low and eyes that stare in defeat
Or souls that live within the past where sorrow plays all parts
Where a living death is all that's left for men with broken hearts

Now you have no right to be the judge to criticize and condemn
Just think but for the grace of God it'd be you instead of him
One careless step a thoughtless deed and then the misery starts
And to those who weep death comes cheap these men with broken hearts

Oh so humble you should be when they come passin' by
For it's written that the greatest men they never get too big to cry
Some lose faith in love and life when sorrow shoots her darts
And with hope all gone they walk alone these men with broken hearts

Now you've never walked in that man's shoes or saw things through his eyes
Or stood and watched with helpless hands while the heart inside you dies
Some were paupers and some were kings and some were masters of the arts
But in their shame they're all the same these men with broken hearts

You know life sometimes can be so cruel that a heart will pray for death
God why must these living dead know pain with every breath
So help your neighbor along the road no matter where you start
For the God that made you made them too these men with broken hearts

Hank Williams, Acuff-Rose Music, 1951.

EDGAR GUEST (1881–1959)

[Edgar Guest was born in England; his family moved to America when he was ten years old. A poet of the common man, Guest wrote memorable jingling rhymes and was honored as Michigan's poet laureate. This poem, a friendly argument about friendship, is an advertisement for good will and companionable affection. There was a time when encour-

aging sociable graces was a motive force behind traditional poetry around the world. Take, for example, the following, attributed to Henry Burton: "Have you had a kindness shown? Pass it on. 'Twas not given for thee alone, Pass it on; Let it travel down the years, Let it wipe another's tears, 'Til in Heaven the deed appears—Pass it on." And this verse by Henry VanDyke: "Say not, 'Too poor,' but freely give; Sigh not, 'Too weak,' but boldly try, You never can begin to live—Until you dare to die." In the following poem Guest plays the role of intimate guide advising the reader about how and why to be a good friend.]

Be a Friend

Be a friend. You don't need money;
Just a disposition sunny;
Just the wish to help another
Get along some way or other;
Just a kindly hand extended
Out to one who's unbefriended;
Just the will to give or lend,
This will make you someone's friend.

Be a friend. You don't need glory.
Friendship is a simple story.
Pass by trifling errors blindly,
Gaze on honest effort kindly,
Cheer the youth who's bravely trying,
Pity him who's sadly sighing;
Just a little labor spend
On the duties of a friend.

Be a friend. The pay is bigger
(Though not written by a figure)
Than is earned by people clever
In what's merely self-endeavor.
You'll have friends instead of neighbors
For the profits of your labors;
You'll be richer in the end
Than a prince, if you're a friend.

Edgar A. Guest, *A Heap o' Livin'*. Chicago: Reilly & Lee, 1916, 97.

BOB DYLAN (b. 1941)

[Written in Bob Dylan's early phase of folk and protest songs accompanied by acoustic guitar, before his style morphed into a more freewheeling artistic and electric folk rock, this song powerfully voices a soulful vision of freedom's promise. It is filled with images of the troubled. The neediest and most forgotten feel the greatest hope for freedom. Dramatizing the bells' call, with their cosmic ringing in the skies, the lyrics reach out to the unprivi-

leged, those bereft of even the bare necessities, the endangered desperate seeking a way out of misfortune, which only freedom could provide. Dylan, the American bard singing to Americans, was also heard by people all around the world responding to oppression.]

Chimes of Freedom

Far between sundown's finish an' midnight's broken toll
We ducked inside the doorway, thunder crashing
As majestic bells of bolts struck shadows in the sounds
Seeming to be the chimes of freedom flashing

Flashing for the warriors whose strength is not to fight
Flashing for the refugees on the unarmed road of flight
An' for each an' ev'ry underdog soldier in the night
An' we gazed upon the chimes of freedom flashing.

In the city's melted furnace, unexpectedly we watched
With faces hidden while the walls were tightening
As the echo of the wedding bells before the blowin' rain
Dissolved into the bells of the lightning
Tolling for the rebel, tolling for the rake
Tolling for the luckless, the abandoned an' forsaked
Tolling for the outcast, burnin' constantly at stake
An' we gazed upon the chimes of freedom flashing.

Figure 4.3 Bob Dylan

Through the mad mystic hammering of the wild ripping hail
The sky cracked its poems in naked wonder
That the clinging of the church bells blew far into the breeze
Leaving only bells of lightning and its thunder
Striking for the gentle, striking for the kind
Striking for the guardians and protectors of the mind
An' the unpawned painter behind beyond his rightful time
An' we gazed upon the chimes of freedom flashing.

Through the wild cathedral evening the rain unraveled tales
For the disrobed faceless forms of no position
Tolling for the tongues with no place to bring their thoughts
All down in taken-for-granted situations
Tolling for the deaf an' blind, tolling for the mute
Tolling for the mistreated, mateless mother, the mistitled prostitute
For the misdemeanor outlaw, chased an' cheated by pursuit
An' we gazed upon the chimes of freedom flashing.

Even though a cloud's white curtain in a far-off corner flashed
An' the hypnotic splattered mist was slowly lifting
Electric light still struck like arrows, fired but for the ones
Condemned to drift or else be kept from drifting
Tolling for the searching ones, on their speechless, seeking trail

For the lonesome-hearted lovers with too personal a tale
An' for each unharmful, gentle soul misplaced inside a jail
An' we gazed upon the chimes of freedom flashing.

Starry-eyed an' laughing as I recall when we were caught
Trapped by no track of hours for they hanged suspended
As we listened one last time an' we watched with one last look
Spellbound an' swallowed 'til the tolling ended
Tolling for the aching ones whose wounds cannot be nursed
For the countless confused, accused, misused, strung-out ones an' worse
An' for every hung-up person in the whole wide universe
An' we gazed upon the chimes of freedom flashing.

Bob Dylan, *Lyrics 1962–2001*. New York: Simon & Schuster, 2004, 116–17.

REED WHITTEMORE (b. 1919)

[Whittemore was born in New Haven, Connecticut, and graduated from Yale University in 1941. He began publishing collections of his own poetry in books in 1946, after serving in the Army Air Corps during World War II, and taught at Carleton College and at the University of Maryland in College Park. He served as Consultant in Poetry (now Poet Laureate Consultant in Poetry) to the Library of Congress for two terms (1964–1965 and 1984–1985). His poetry seems to laugh at pretense and delight in asserting realistic appraisals of human behavior where flattery is often found instead, thanks to politicians' rhetoric, marketplace hype, and conventions of pious politeness. Whittemore found both humor and sadness in everyday life, writing about them with a deft touch. The poem below offers a humane and soulful take on giving, capturing the drama of the issues at stake, as well as the feelings of the man appealed to by noble causes. The man knows his help is needed, but he doesn't know what to do or quite where to start. He seems to shrug and do what he can.]

Philanthropist

The ads keep asking his help for the poor,
    the distressed,
The aged, the orphaned, the whatnot.
Now here is one asking him cleverly
    what he can do
For the earth's three hundred million
Illiterate.

He can burn books.

He is overextended.
He is bringing the peace already, and
    saving the ghetto

293

He feels helpless.
He would ask them to help him, if they
  could read him.
He feels death far off and high, in
  open places.
Help! he is lying in orchards on
  steep slopes.
Help! he is bones, he is wind flesh.
  Send money,
Hope.

But the plight of the Indian.

And the whooping crane.

What avails?
He draws two gravely wounded bucks from
  his sad wallet
For Christmas Seals.

Reed Whittemore, "Philanthropist," in *The Past, the Future, the Present: Poems Selected and New.* Fayetteville: University of Arkansas Press, 1990.

GWENDOLYN BROOKS (1917–2000)

[Those who would do good may have good intentions, but in reaching out to those in need, they may feel out of their element, fearful of all they don't know, worried that the needy might endanger them. In the following poem, when middle-class suburban women enter an unfamiliar environment to engage in social uplift, their identities seem questioned by the textures of the slums. That is, the extreme poverty seems to expose their own superficialities, self-doubts, and vulnerabilities. So far from home, they feel a strange glare and are embarrassed by a self-consciousness that their work is but a drop in the bucket. This is itself an education, if they can accept it. Gwendolyn Brooks was born in Topeka, Kansas, and grew up in Chicago. She explored ways of voicing African American experiences in poetry, and her work has won the respect of the literary world and many honors as well.]

The Lovers of the Poor

arrive. The Ladies from the Ladies' Betterment League
Arrive in the afternoon, the late light slanting
In diluted gold bars across the boulevard brag
Of proud, seamed faces with mercy and murder hinting
Here, there, interrupting, all deep and debonair,
The pink paint on the innocence of fear;
Walk in a gingerly manner up the hall.
Cutting with knives served by their softest care,

Served by their love, so barbarously fair.
Whose mothers taught: You'd better not be cruel!
You had better not throw stones upon the wrens!
Herein they kiss and coddle and assault
Anew and dearly in the innocence
With which they baffle nature. Who are full,
Sleek, tender-clad, fit, fiftyish, a-glow, all
Sweetly abortive, hinting at fat fruit,
Judge it high time that fiftyish fingers felt
Beneath the lovelier planes of enterprise.
To resurrect. To moisten with milky chill.
To be a random hitching post or plush.
To be, for wet eyes, random and handy hem.
Their guild is giving money to the poor.
The worthy poor. The very very worthy
And beautiful poor. Perhaps just not too swarthy?
Perhaps just not too dirty nor too dim
Nor—passionate. In truth, what they could wish
Is—something less than derelict or dull.
Not staunch enough to stab, though, gaze for gaze!
God shield them sharply from the beggar-bold!
The noxious needy ones whose battle's bald
Nonetheless for being voiceless, hits one down.
But it's all so bad! and entirely too much for them.
The stench; the urine, cabbage, and dead beans,
Dead porridges of assorted dusty grains,
The old smoke, heavy diapers, and, they're told,
Something called chitterlings. The darkness. Drawn
Darkness, or dirty light. The soil that stirs.
The soil that looks the soil of centuries.
And for that matter the general oldness. Old
Wood. Old marble. Old tile. Old old old.
Note homekind Oldness! Not Lake Forest, Glencoe.
Nothing is sturdy, nothing is majestic,
There is no quiet drama, no rubbed glaze, no
Unkillable infirmity of such
A tasteful turn as lately they have left,
Glencoe, Lake Forest, and to which their cars
Must presently restore them. When they're done
With dullards and distortions of this fistic
Patience of the poor and put-upon.
They've never seen such a make-do-ness as
Newspaper rugs before! In this, this "flat,"
Their hostess is gathering up the oozed, the rich
Rugs of the morning (tattered! the bespattered . . .),
Readies to spread clean rugs for afternoon.
Here is a scene for you. The Ladies look,

In horror, behind a substantial citizeness
Whose trains clank out across her swollen heart.
Who, arms akimbo, almost fills a door.
All tumbling children, quilts dragged to the floor
And tortured thereover, potato peelings, soft-
Eyed kitten, hunched-up, haggard, to-be-hurt.
Their League is allotting largesse to the Lost.
But to put their clean, their pretty money, to put
Their money collected from delicate rose-fingers
Tipped with their hundred flawless rose-nails seems . . .
They own Spode, Lowestoft, candelabra,
Mantels, and hostess gowns, and sunburst clocks,
Turtle soup, Chippendale, red satin "hangings,"
Aubussons and Hattie Carnegie. They Winter
In Palm Beach; cross the Water in June; attend,
When suitable, the nice Art Institute;
Buy the right books in the best bindings; saunter
On Michigan, Easter mornings, in sun or wind.
Oh Squalor! This sick four-story hulk, this fibre
With fissures everywhere! Why, what are bringings
Of loathe-love largesse? What shall peril hungers
So old old, what shall flatter the desolate?
Tin can, blocked fire escape and chitterling
And swaggering seeking youth and the puzzled wreckage
Of the middle passage, and urine and stale shames
And, again, the porridges of the underslung
And children children children. Heavens! That
Was a rat, surely, off there, in the shadows? Long
And long-tailed? Gray? The Ladies from the Ladies'
Betterment League agree it will be better
To achieve the outer air that rights and steadies,
To hie to a house that does not holler, to ring
Bells elsetime, better presently to cater
To no more Possibilities, to get
Away. Perhaps the money can be posted.
Perhaps they two may choose another Slum!
Some serious sooty half-unhappy home!—
Where loathe-lover likelier may be invested.
Keeping their scented bodies in the center
Of the hall as they walk down the hysterical hall,
They allow their lovely skirts to graze no wall,
Are off at what they manage of a canter,
And, resuming all the clues of what they were,
Try to avoid inhaling the laden air.

Gwendolyn Brooks, *Selected Poems*. New York: Harper & Row, 1963), 90–93. Also in *The Bean Eaters* (New York: Harper & Row, 1960, 35–38.

STUART SCHARF (b. 1941)

[This pop song from the late sixties demands concern for the welfare of our fellow human beings, the poor and disadvantaged. The rats and hunger and fires it describes are realistic features in a genre that had often been escapist and formulaic until Bob Dylan and others expanded the American songwriting palette. This song, sung by Spanky & Our Gang became a hit in 1968, four years after President Lyndon Johnson introduced legislation for a "War on Poverty." Scharf was born to a Jewish family in Brooklyn and was active in the Civil Rights movement of the sixties. Despite a lack of formal training, he became a successful songwriter and guitarist, working in recording studios in New York City. Today he runs his own record label (Takya Music) and says he tries to work in a "Zen compatible" manner.]

Give a Damn

If you'd take the train with me
Uptown, thru the misery
Of ghetto streets in morning light,
It's always night.
Take a window seat, put down your Times,
You can read between the lines,
Just meet the faces that you meet
Beyond the window's pane.

And it might begin to teach you
How to give a damn about your fellow man.
And it might begin to teach you
How to give a damn about your fellow man.

Or put your girl to sleep sometime
With rats instead of nursery rhymes,
With hunger and your other children
By her side,
And wonder if you'll share your bed
With something else which must be fed,
For fear may lie beside you
Or it may sleep down the hall.

[chorus]

Come and see how well despair
Is seasoned by the stif'ling air,

See your ghetto in the good old
Sizzling summertime.
Suppose the streets were all on fire
The flames like tempers leaping higher

297

Suppose you'd lived there all your life,

D'you think that you would mind?
And it might begin to reach you
Why I give a damn about my fellow man;
And it might begin to teach you
How to give a damn about your fellow man.

Stuart Scharf, "Give a Damn." Available at http://www.top40db.net/Lyrics/?SongID=68514&By=Artist &Match=Spanky+%26+Our+Gang (accessed February 26, 2008).

WENDELL BERRY (b. 1934)

[A lifelong Baptist, Berry continues to farm the Kentucky land his family has farmed for two hundred years. Highly regarded as a great spokesman for the family farm and as a poet and social critic, Berry has contributed a lively and substantial literature to modern America. His many books have found a sizable readership, and his rural-wise take on America merits attention. This poem shows a contrarian spirit, an urge to seek beyond clichés to find the expansive spirit of America.]

Manifesto: The Mad Farmer Liberation Front

So, friends, every day do something
that won't compute. Love the Lord.
Love the world. Work for nothing.
Take all that you have and be poor.
Love someone who does not deserve it.
Denounce the government and embrace
the flag. Hope to live in that free
republic for which it stands.

Wendell Berry, "Manifesto: The Mad Farmer Liberation Front," in *The Country of Marriage*. New York: Harcourt, Brace, Jovanovich, 1973.

ROBERT LOPEZ (b. 1975) AND JEFF MARX (b. 1970)

[This song passage from a popular Broadway musical offers a tuneful revelation of our inter-connectedness. The song is new, but the idea in the song is not. In 1901 Arthur T. Hadley, then president of Yale, wrote: "Humanity is made up of two classes. Individuals of the one participate in the business of life for what they can get out of it, of the other for what they can put into it. It is not, however, a paradox that those who put most into life are also, in the largest and best sense, those who get most out of it." This observation has been voiced in many ways in a variety of cultures and wisdom traditions. Consider, for example, this teaching of the Dalai Lama, speaking from the Buddhist perspective: "If you want others to be happy, practice compassion. If you want to be happy, practice compassion."]

The Money Song

....When you help others,
You can't help helping yourself!
When you help others,
You can't help helping yourself!
Every time you
Do good deeds
You're also serving
Your own needs.
When you help others,
You can't
Help
Helping yourself!....

Robert Lopez and Jeff Marx, "The Money Song," *Avenue Q—The Musical* (RCA, 2000), publisher: Hal Leonard Corporation, 2004.

THANKS, GOOD WILL, AND A GENEROUS HEART

WILLIAM JAMES (1842–1910)

[William James was the psychologist-philosopher brother of novelist Henry James. William James' classic, The Varieties of Religious Experience, from which this excerpt is taken, presents a variety of personality types based on the predominance of certain qualities. The saintly type has an excess of tenderhearted idealism and naiveté, trusting that others are good. But generous souls often spark others' spiritual sense of possibilities. This passage includes talk about "nonresistance" such as Gandhi practiced in South Africa and Martin Luther King, Jr., would later use in the American civil rights struggle. Discussing the saintly person's gift to society, James explores a radical rethinking of our unacknowledged assumptions about service. It is an example of spiritual values and pragmatic actions mutually joined in dynamic union—a situation often seen in history when progress is being made.]

The Value of Saintliness

Proceeding onwards in our search of religious extravagance, we next come upon excesses of Tenderness and Charity. Here saintliness has to face the charge of preserving the unfit, and breeding parasites and beggars. "Resist not evil," "Love your enemies," these are saintly maxims of which men of this world find it hard to speak without impatience. Are the men of this world right, or are the saints in possession of the deeper range of truth?

No simple answer is possible. Here, if anywhere, one feels the complexity of the moral life, and the mysteriousness of the way in which facts and ideals are interwoven.

Perfect conduct is a relation between three terms: the actor, the objects for which he acts, and the recipients of the action. In order that conduct should be abstractly perfect, all three terms, intention, execution, and reception, should be suited to one another. The best intention will fail if it either work by false means or address itself to the wrong recipient. Thus no critic or estimator of the value of conduct can confine himself to the actor's animus alone, apart from the other elements of the performance. As there is no worse lie than a truth misunderstood by those who hear it, so reasonable arguments, challenges to magnanimity, and appeals to sympathy or justice, are folly when we are dealing with human crocodiles and boa-constrictors; the saint may simply give the universe into the hands of the enemy by his trustfulness. He may by non-resistance cut off his own survival.

Herbert Spencer tells us that the perfect man's conduct will appear perfect only when the environment is perfect: to no inferior environment is it suitably adapted. We may paraphrase this by cordially admitting that saintly conduct would be the most perfect conduct conceivable in an environment where all were saints already; but by adding that in an environment where few are saints, and many the exact reverse of saints, it must be ill adapted. We must frankly confess, then, using our empirical common sense and ordinary practical prejudices, that in the world that actually is, the virtues of sympathy, charity, and non-resistance may be, and often have been, manifested in excess. The powers of darkness have systematically taken advantage of them. The whole modern scientific organization of charity is a consequence of the failure of simply giving alms. The whole history of constitutional government is a commentary on the excellence of resisting evil, and, when one cheek is smitten, of smiting back and not turning the other cheek also.

You will agree to this in general, for in spite of the Gospel, in spite of Quakerism, in spite of Tolstoi, you believe in fighting fire with fire, in shooting down usurpers, locking up thieves, and freezing out vagabonds and swindlers.

And yet you are sure, as I am sure, that were the world confined to these hard-headed, hard-hearted, and hard-fisted methods exclusively, were there no one prompt to help a brother first, and find out afterwards whether he were worthy; no one willing to drown his private wrongs in pity for the wronger's person; no one ready to be duped many a time rather than live always on suspicion; no one glad to treat individuals passionately and impulsively rather than by general rules of prudence; the world would be an infinitely worse place than it is now to live in. The tender grace, not of a day that is dead, but of a day yet to be born somehow, with the golden rule grown natural, would be cut out from the perspective of our imaginations.

The saints, existing in this way, may, with their extravagances of human tenderness, be prophetic. Nay, innumerable times they have proved themselves prophetic. Treating those whom they met, in spite of the past, in spite of all appearances, as worthy, they have stimulated them to be worthy, miraculously transformed them by their radiant example and by the challenge of their expectation.

From this point of view we may admit the human charity which we find in all saints, and the great excess of it which we find in some saints, to be a genuinely creative social force, tending to make real a degree of virtue which it alone is ready to assume as possible. The saints are authors, auctores, increasers, of goodness. The potentialities of development in human souls are unfathomable. So many who seemed irretrievably hardened have in point of fact been softened, converted, regenerated, in ways that amazed the subjects even more than they surprised the spectators, that we never can be sure in advance of any man that his salvation by the way of love is hopeless. We have no right to speak of human crocodiles and boa-constrictors as of fixedly incurable beings. We know not the complexities of personality, the smouldering emotional fires, the other facets of the character-polyhedron, the resources of the subliminal region. St. Paul long ago made our ancestors familiar with the idea that every soul is virtually sacred. Since Christ died for us all without exception, St. Paul said, we must despair of no one. This belief in the essential sacredness of every one expresses itself to-day in all sorts of humane customs and reformatory institutions, and in a growing aversion to the death penalty and to brutality in punishment. The saints, with their extravagance of human tenderness, are the great torch-bearers of this belief, the tip of the wedge, the clearers of the darkness. Like the single drops which sparkle in the sun as they are flung far ahead of the advancing edge of a wave-crest or of a flood, they show the way and are forerunners. The world is not yet with them, so they often seem in the midst of the world's affairs to be preposterous. Yet they are impregnators of the world, vivifiers and animaters of potentialities of goodness which but for them would lie forever dormant. It is not possible to be quite as mean as we naturally are, when they have passed before us. One fire kindles another; and without that over-trust in human worth which they show, the rest of us would lie in spiritual stagnancy.

Momentarily considered, then, the saint may waste his tenderness and be the dupe and victim of his charitable fever, but the general function of his charity in social evolution is vital and essential. If things are ever to move upward, some one must be ready to take the first step, and assume the risk of it. No one who is not willing to try charity, to try non-resistance as the saint is always willing, can tell whether these methods will or will not succeed. When they do succeed, they are far more powerfully successful than force or worldly prudence. Force destroys enemies; and the best that can be said of prudence is that it keeps what we already have in safety. But non-resistance, when successful, turns enemies into friends; and charity regenerates its objects. These saintly methods are, as I said, creative energies; and genuine saints find in the elevated excitement with which their faith endows them an authority and impressiveness which makes them irresistible in situations where men of shallower nature cannot get on at all without the use of worldly prudence. This practical proof that worldly wisdom may be safely transcended is the saint's magic gift to mankind. Not only does his vision of a better world console us for the generally prevailing prose and barrenness; but even when on the whole we have to confess him ill adapted, he makes some converts, and the environment gets better for his ministry. He is an effective ferment of goodness, a slow transmuter of the earthly into a more heavenly order.

In this respect the Utopian dreams of social justice in which many contemporary socialists and anarchists indulge are, in spite of their impracticability and non-adaptation to present environmental conditions, analogous to the saint's belief in an existent kingdom of heaven. They help to break the edge of the general reign of hardness and are slow leavens of a better order.

William James, *Varieties of Religious Experience*. New York: Modern Library, 1902, 347–52.

FULTON J. SHEEN (1895–1979)

[Fulton J. Sheen was born to a farm family in El Paso, Illinois. He received a master's degree from St. Viator College in Illinois and went on to study for the priesthood at St. Paul Seminary in Minnesota, receiving ordination in 1919. Sheen preached sermons on WLWL radio in New York, and for several years had an NBC radio program called The Catholic Hour. Known for his eloquent and dramatic presentation of religious ideas, he gave half-hour talks on his long-running nationally broadcast television program Life is Worth Living beginning in 1952. Sheen had a gift for putting classical Catholic theology into modern American vernacular with humor and warmth. He deftly summed up deep ideas in lines such as, "There are 200 million poor in the world who would gladly take the vow of poverty if they could eat, dress and have a home like I do!" and, "Love is a mutual self-giving that ends in self-recovery." He asked, "Show me your hands. Do they have scars from giving? Show me your feet. Are they wounded in service? Show me your heart. Have you left a place for divine love?" And he taught that "Our highest happiness consists in the feeling that another's good is purchased by our sacrifice." The following are excerpts from two of his books, Three to Get Married and Guide to Contentment.]

Qualities of Love[†]

The saint, like Vincent de Paul, has such a love of God's poor that he forgets to feed himself . . . Love does not thrive on moderation. Zeal is generosity. The love that measures the sacrifices it will make for others takes the edge off aspirations. Our Lord said that zealous love had two characteristics: first, it is forgiving, and second, it recognizes no limits. It is forgiving, because it knows that God's forgiveness of me is conditioned upon my forgiveness of others. Love never wears magnifying glasses in looking on the faults of others. Married life requires this zeal in the shape of forbearance, which is not a gritting of teeth in the face of annoyance, nor the cultivation of indifference; it is, rather, a positive and constructive action putting love where it is not found. One feels under an obligation more exquisite and divine than a marriage contract.

Zeal knows no limits. It never pronounces the word "enough." Our Lord said that after His followers had done all they were supposed to do, they were to consider themselves as "unprofitable servants." Knocking the boundaries out of love, He said: "But I tell you that you should not offer resistance of injury; if a man strikes thee on the right cheek, turn the other cheek also towards him; if he is ready to go to law with thee over thy coat, let him have it and thy cloak with it; if he compels thee to attend him on a mile's journey, go two miles with him of thy own accord." (Matt 5:39, 41)

In Divine service and in marriage, therefore, there should be a generosity which goes quite beyond the limits of justice. The neighbor who offers to come in for an hour to help and stays two; the doctor who in addition to a professional call "drops in just to see how you are"; the husband and wife who vie with one another in love; all have understood one of the most beautiful effects of love: its zeal, which makes them fools for one another. "We are fools for Christ's sake" (1 Cor 4:10).

Fulton J. Sheen, *Three to Get Married*. New York: Appleton-Century-Crofts, 1951, chap. 3. http://www.ewtn.com/library/MARRIAGE/3GETMARR.TXT.

[†] Title is the author's own.

Distinguishing Joy from Pleasure

Joy is not the same as pleasure or happiness. A wicked and evil man may have pleasure, while any ordinary mortal is capable of being happy. Pleasure generally comes from things, and always through the senses; happiness comes from humans through fellowship. Joy comes from loving God and neighbor. Pleasure is quick and violent, like a flash of lightning. Joy is steady and abiding, like a fixed star. Pleasure depends on external circumstances, such as money, food, travel, etc. Joy is independent of them, for it comes from a good conscience and love of God.

Fulton J. Sheen, *Guide to Contentment*. New York: Maco, 1967, 120.

KURT VONNEGUT (1922–2007)

[Vonnegut was a novelist of great imagination, painting life's sometimes grotesque absurdities and often adding fresh twists to our understanding of things. Of his friend Joseph Heller, he wrote that they were at a billionaire's party and someone asked Heller how he felt in comparing his book's profits with the amount the billionaire made in one day. Heller said he had something the billionaire could never have: "The knowledge that I've got enough." Vonnegut in the piece below points to a hopeful fact that brightens a sometimes-bleak landscape: often it's the widow's mite that cheers us. As Mother Teresa said, "We cannot do great things, we can only do small things with great love." Inspired, ordinary people are inspiring. Seeing their graceful acts makes us grateful, and we seek to realize a state of grace ourselves. Acts of kindness give joy and bring satisfaction.]

Ordinary Day Saints

About five years ago I got a letter from a woman who said she was about to have a baby and did I think it was a terrible thing to bring such a sweet, innocent animal into a world this terrible. So I replied that what made being alive almost worthwhile for me was saints I met—people who behave decently in an indecent society. They're all over the place. I ran into them in the army, and I ran into one just today. Think about the saints you meet in the course of an ordinary day. And then I tell people, "Perhaps some of you will be saints for this woman's child to meet."

Quoted by Studs Terkel in *Will the Circle Be Unbroken?* New York: New Press, 2001, 224.

MARGARET DAVIS (1951)

[Margaret Davis, of South Bend, Indiana, reflected on community spirit in a 1995 piece for Notre Dame Magazine. Her following notes on experiences in South Bend evoke the spirit of neighborliness that people in many communities share. As an African American preacher during a civil rights protest in the sixties once said, "Everything shines by perishing. The sun uses up its energy at a fantastic rate of speed and so does a candle perish as it shines. And so do you and me. We all shine by perishing." All things live by giving and sacrifice.]

Gestures of Grace

This spring, one of the neighborhood guardians was telling me her plans to restore the area. The idea amused me. This is hardly a historic neighborhood in the sense of stately old homes fallen into disrepair, then gentrified back to their former glory. This part of South Bend, Indiana, has always been a working class neighborhood, built up around Muessel Brewery. My house stands across from a school, the one where the man beat his companion into the gutter. Many of the people who first lived here were Germans who came to work in the brewery. In 1930, one of the owners was murdered during a robbery at his brewery, a few blocks away.

* * *

Once, when a man stole my wallet, I was so incoherent with rage that the police dispatcher had to ask me several times to calm down. But now, calling 911, my voice is steady. I describe the man, what he's done, where he is, where the victim is. Very calm, very controlled. I urge the police to hurry before he gets away. When I hang up, my hands are shaking so hard the headpiece clatters back into its holder. I doubt they're going to hurry.

* * *

My housemate worries that the young woman is dead or, if she isn't, that she may be hit by a car; while I am still on the phone, she is heading for the door with a blanket in one hand and a hammer in the other, in case the man, who has begun to move down the street, should return. Her courage and compassion, her willingness to act, strike me as one of those gestures of grace which soften the brutality of life.

* * *

Apparently this is the only part of town where crimes occur. Some time back a woman stood up in church to ask for our prayers because her car had been vandalized. She was outraged that such a thing should happen to her in her neighborhood. Later she remarked to me, "It's not like I live down the street from you, for heaven's sake."

After this latest incident, several people asked me if now I will finally move.

* * *

"I expect to pass through life but once . . . ," wrote Quaker William Penn. "If therefore there be any kindness I can show, or any good that I can do to my fellow beings, let me do it now and not defer or neglect it, as I shall not pass this way again."

* * *

I do not choose to live in my neighborhood in order to make any statements, or with the idea that I will make any profound difference. This is my home, that's all. Circumstances chose it and circumstances keep me here. Until circumstances change, it is my home.

* * *

Here is what I do know about these things: You cannot act with the expectation of performing miracles, but only with the hope of somehow coming close to doing that which needs to be done. The bumper stickers that urge us to perform random acts of kindness—what other kind are there? Our intrusions into another's life may prove to be the snowflake finally triggering the avalanche. Or, if we are lucky, a gesture of grace for the benefit of those who will not pass this way again, and a benediction upon ourselves for the circumstances that placed us in their path in the first place.

Margaret Davis, *Notre Dame Magazine* 24, no. 3 (Autumn 1995), http://www.nd.edu/~ndmag/daviau95.html.

LEWIS THOMAS (1913–1993)

[Thomas held leadership positions in medical schools, served as president and chancellor of Sloan-Kettering Cancer Center, and wrote provocative exploratory essays. He wrote about the natural basis for cooperation and helping others, and was concerned with eco-logical requirements for our survival in an environment of which we are a part. Here he presents a scientific and humanistic view on cooperation and helping others based on modern research findings. Such knowledge should inform our view of how the web of life works; otherwise, ours is a worldview derived from a previous era.]

Altruism: Self-Sacrifice for Others

Altruism has always been one of biology's deep mysteries. Why should any animal, off on its own, specified and labeled by all sorts of signals as its individual self, choose to give up its life in aid of another being? Nature, long viewed as a wild, chaotic battlefield swarming with more than 10 million different species, comprising unnumbered billions of competing selves locked in endless combat, offers only one sure measure of success: survival. Survival, in the cool economics of biology, means simply the persistence of one's own genes in the generations to follow.

At first glance, it seems an unnatural act, a violation of nature, to give away one's life, or even one's possessions, to another. And yet, in the face of improbability, examples of altruism abound. When a worker bee, patrolling the frontiers of the hive, senses the nearness of an intruder, its attack is pure, unqualified suicide; the bee's sting is barbed, and in the act of pulling away, the insect is fatally injured. Among other varieties of social insects, such as ants and higher termites, there are castes of soldiers for whom self-sacrifice is an everyday chore.

It is easy to dismiss the problem by saying that altruism is the wrong technical term for behavior of this kind. The word is a human word, strung together to describe an unusual aspect of human behavior, and we should not be using it for scientific, reductionist, genetic grounds. For we have cousins more than we can count, and they are all over the place, run by genes so similar to ours that the differences are minor technicalities. All of us—men, women, children, fish, sea grass, sandworms, dolphins, hamsters and soil bacteria, everything alive on the planet roll ourselves along through all our generations by replicating DNA and RNA, and although the alignments of nucleotides within these molecules are different in different species, the molecules themselves are fundamentally the same substance.

This is, in fact, the way it should be. If cousins are defined by common descent, the human family is only one small and very recent addition to a much larger family in a tree extending back at least 3.5 billion years. Our common ancestor was a single cell from which all subsequent cells derived, most likely a cell resembling one of today's bacteria in today's soil. For almost three-fourths of the earth's existence, cells of that first kind were the only life there was. It was less than a billion years ago that cells like ours appeared in the first marine invertebrates, and these were somehow pieced together by the joining up and fusion of the earlier primitive cells, retaining the same bloodlines. Some of the joiners, bacteria that had learned how to use oxygen, are with us still, part of our flesh, lodged inside the cells of all animals, all plants, moving us from place to place and doing our breathing for us. Now there's a set of cousins!

Even if I try to discount the other genetic similarities linking human beings to all other creatures by common descent, the existence of these beings in my cells is enough, in itself, to relate me to the chestnut tree in my backyard and to the squirrel in that tree.

There ought to be a mathematics for connections like this before anyone claims any kinship function, but the numbers are too big. At the same time, even if we wanted to, we cannot think the sense of obligation away. It is there, maybe in our genes for the recognition of cousins or, if not, because we have learned about the matter. Altruism, in its biological sense, is required of us. We have an enormous family to look after, or perhaps that assumes too much, making us sound like official gardeners and zoo keepers for the planet, responsibilities for which we are probably not yet grown-up enough. We need new technical terms for concern, respect, affection, substitutes of altruism. But at least we can acknowledge the family ties and, with them, obligations. If we do it wrong, scattering pollutants, clouding the atmosphere with too much carbon dioxide, extinguishing the thin carapace of ozone, burning up the forests, dropping the bombs, rampaging at large through nature as though we owned the place, there will be a lot of paying back to do and, at the end, nothing to pay back with.

Lewis Thomas, *Late Night Thoughts on Listening to Mahler's Ninth Symphony*. Boston: G. K. Hall, 1984.

BRIAN SWIMME (b. 1950)

[Philosophical cosmologist Brian Swimme names our mysterious source—the source of the universe and the source of life—"Ultimate Generosity," and he reminds us that all creation actively shares the energy and creative nature of the origin. This is a scientific fact, as well as a theme for philosophical thought. One implication is that generosity should come naturally to us as creatures of the energy-abundant cosmos. This philosophical interpretation of science is something Native Americans knew in their own way: we are not outside and above the natural world; we are within it, and as mutual participants, it is within us. The following is from Swimme's book, written as a dialogue between a youth and an elder, on the implications of cosmological research.]

The Universe Is a Green Dragon

We can use another word: the ground of being is *generosity*. The ultimate source of all that is, the support and well of being, is Ultimate Generosity. All being comes forth and shines, glimmers and glistens, because the root reality of the universe is generosity of being. That's *why* the ground is empty—every thing has been given over to the universe; all existence has been poured forth; all being has gushed forth because Ultimate Generosity retains no thing . . .

Take supernovas as your models. When they had filled themselves with riches, they exploded in a vast cosmic celebration of their work. What would you have done? Would you have had the courage to flood the universe with your riches? Or would you have talked yourself out of it by pleading that you were too shy? Or hoarded your riches by insisting that they were yours and that others did not deserve them because they did not work for them? Remember the supernova's extravagant generosity and celebration of being. It reminds us of our destiny as celebration become self-aware. We are Generosity-of-Being evolved into human form.

You are the elementary particles of the fireball, elements of the supernovas, and the generosity of the ground of all being. That is your fundamental nature. Our deepest desire is to share our riches, and this desire is rooted in the dynamics of the cosmos. What began as the outward expansion of the universe in the fireball ripens into your desire to flood all things with goodness. Whenever you are filled with a desire to fling your gifts into the world, you have become this cosmic dynamic of celebration, feeling its urgency to pour forth just as the stars felt the same urgency to pour themselves out. We know we feel this, whereas the star simply feels it and responds . . . Dance! See your most ordinary activities as the dance of the galaxies and all living beings. If we attempt to constrain the self-emergent expressions of joy, we bottle up the exuberance of the universe. Imagine trying to hold back a supernova! It's the same with human celebration, generosity and creativity; try to bottle them up and you only get neurosis and destruction. . . .

Brian Swimme, *The Universe Is a Green Dragon: A Cosmic Creation Story*. Santa Fe, N.Mex.: Bear, 1984, 146–48.

GARY SNYDER (b. 1930)

[Gary Snyder is a West Coast poet and essayist who first gained fame as a member of the beat generation in the 1950s. He has been a Buddhist for more than half a century, studying Japanese and Chinese culture as well as Native American traditions and ecology. His writing encourages us to relate fully to the world around us, wherever we may be. In the first piece, we are reminded that we often find paradoxes in the dynamics of giving when we reflect on our experiences. Being reduced to nothing, or experiencing loss of all, we are made aware of what we have in our depths to give back to the world we live in. As Ijugarjuk the Eskimo said, "All true wisdom is only to be learned far from the dwellings of men, out in the great solitudes, and is only to be attained through suffering. Privation and suffering are the only things that can open the minds of men to those things which are hidden from others," including our deepest inner resources. In the second piece, Snyder suggests reasons for being thankful in our participation in the earth's life. Buddhists are often thought of as world renouncers, but Snyder reminds us that there is far more to the tradition than that. Gratitude and work to promote the well-being of all are important Buddhist ideals.]

Back Home

The etiquette of the wild world requires not only generosity but a good-humored toughness that cheerfully tolerates discomfort, an appreciation of everyone's fragility, and a certain modesty. Good quick blueberry picking, the knack of tracking, getting to where the fishing's good ("an angry man cannot catch a fish"), reading the surface of the sea or sky—these are achievements not to be gained by mere effort. Mountaineering has the same quality. These moves take practice, which calls for a certain amount of self-abnegation, and intuition, which takes emptying of yourself. Great insights have come to some people only after they reached the point where they had nothing left. Álvar Núñez Cabeza de Vaca became unaccountably deepened after losing his way and spending several winter nights sleeping naked in a pit in the Texas desert under a north wind. He truly had reached the point where he had nothing. ("To have nothing, you must *have nothing!*" Lord Buckley says of this moment.) After that he found himself able to heal sick native people he met on his way westward. His fame spread ahead of him. Once he had made his way back to Mexico and was again a civilized Spaniard he found he had lost his power of healing—not just the ability to heal, but the *will* to heal, which is the will to be whole: for as he said, there were "real doctors" in the city, and he began to doubt his powers. To resolve the dichotomy of the civilized and the wild, we must first resolve to be whole.

One may reach such a place as Álvar Núñez by literally losing everything. Painful and dangerous experiences often transform the people who survive them. Human beings are audacious. They set out to have adventures and try to do more than perhaps they should. So by practicing yogic austerities or monastic disciplines, some people make a structured attempt at having nothing. Some of us have learned much from traveling day after day on foot over snowfields, rockslides, passes, torrents, and valley floor forests, by "putting ourselves out there." Another—and most sophisticated—way is that of Vimalakirti, the legendary Buddhist layman, who taught that by directly intuiting our condition in the actually existing world we realize that we have had nothing from the beginning. A Tibetan saying has it: "The experience of emptiness engenders compassion."

For those who would seek directly, by entering the primary temple, the wilderness can be a ferocious teacher, rapidly stripping down the inexperienced or the careless. It is easy to make the mistakes that will bring one to an extremity. Practically speaking, a life that is vowed to simplicity, appropriate boldness, good humor, gratitude, unstinting work and play, and lots of walking brings us close to the actually existing world and its wholeness.

People of wilderness cultures rarely seek out adventures. If they deliberately risk themselves, it is for spiritual rather than economic reasons. Ultimately all such journeys are done for the sake of the whole, not as some private quest. The quiet dignity that characterizes so many so-called primitives is a reflection of that. Florence Edenshaw, a contemporary Haida elder who has lived a long life of work and family, was asked by the young woman anthropologist who interviewed her and was impressed by her coherence, presence, and dignity, "What can I do for self-respect?" Mrs. Edenshaw said, "Dress up and stay home." The "home," of course, is as large as you make it.

The lessons we learn from the wild become the etiquette of freedom. We can enjoy our humanity with its flashy brains and sexual buzz, its social cravings and stubborn tantrums, and take ourselves as no more and no less than another being in the Big Watershed. We can accept each other all as barefoot equals sleeping on the same ground. We can give up hoping to be eternal and quit fighting dirt. We can chase off mosquitoes and fence out varmints without hating them. No expectations, alert and sufficient, grateful and careful, generous and direct. A calm and clarity attend us in the moment we are wiping the grease off our hands between tasks and glancing up at the passing clouds. Another joy is finally sitting down to have coffee with a friend. The wild requires that we learn the terrain, nod to all the plants and animals and birds, ford the streams and cross the ridges, and tell a good story when we get back home.

And when the children are safe in bed, at one of the great holidays like the Fourth of July, New Year's, or Halloween, we can bring out some spirits and turn on the music, and the men and the women who are still among the living can get loose and really wild. So that's the final meaning of "wild"—the esoteric meaning, the deepest and most scary. Those who are ready for it will come to it. Please do not repeat this to the uninitiated.

Gary Snyder, "The Etiquette of Freedom," in *The Practice of the Wild*. San Francisco: North Point, 1990, 22–24.

Grace and Gratitude [A Buddhist View]

Eating is a sacrament. The grace we say clears our hearts and guides the children and welcomes the guest, all at the same time. We look at eggs, apples, and stew. They are evidence of plenitude, excess, a great reproductive exuberance. Millions of grains of grass-seed that will become rice or flour, millions of codfish fry that will never, and must never, grow to maturity. Innumerable little seeds are sacrifices to the food-chain. A parsnip in the ground is a marvel of living chemistry, making sugars and flavors from earth, air, water. And if we do eat meat it is the life, the bounce, the swish, of a great alert being with keen ears and lovely eyes, with foursquare feet and a huge beating heart that we eat, let us not deceive ourselves.

We too will be offerings—we are all edible. And if we are not devoured quickly, we are big enough (like the old down trees) to provide a long slow meal to the smaller critters. Whale carcasses that sink several miles deep in the ocean feed organisms in the dark for fifteen years. (It seems to take about two thousand to exhaust the nutrients in a high civilization.)

At our house we say a Buddhist grace—

We venerate the Three Treasures {teachers, the wild, and friends}
And are thankful for this meal
The work of many people
And the sharing of other forms of life.

Anyone can use a grace from their own tradition (and really give it meaning)—or make up their own. Saying some sort of grace is never inappropriate, and speeches and announcements can be tacked onto it. It is a plain, ordinary, old-fashioned little thing to do that connects us with all our ancestors.

A monk asked Dong-shan: "Is there a practice for people to follow?"

Doug-shan answered: "When you become a real person, there is such a practice."

Sarvamangalam, Good luck to All.

Gary Snyder, *The Practice of the Wild*. San Francisco: North Point, 1994, 184–85.

OSEOLA MCCARTY (1908–1999)

[Oseola McCarty became a symbol of how an ordinary person can, through faith, thrift, and high ideals, contribute significantly to worthy causes. She saved her wages as a wash-erwoman for years to be able to contribute $150,000 to the University of Southern Mississippi in 1995 to establish a scholarship for deserving African American students. Her thoughts on saving money, building communities, and going home after being away, are simple and clear, with broad application. As English essayist Arthur Warwick wrote, "He gives not best who gives most; but he gives most who gives best." Below are some of Oseola McCarty's reflections.]

Simple Wisdom for Rich Living

We are responsible for the way we use our time on this earth, so I try to be a good steward. I start each day on my knees, saying the Lord's Prayer. Then I get busy about my work. I get to cleaning or washing. I find that my life and my work are increasing all the time. I am blessed beyond what I hoped.

The secret to building a fortune is compounding interest. It's not the ones that make the big money, but the ones who know how to save who get ahead.

You've got to leave your investment alone long enough for it to increase. I don't like to waste. I keep everything—clothes, furniture, housewares—until it wears out. Usefulness often outlasts style.

Building community is not that hard. It just takes ordinary friendliness. The woman who took me to the doctor when my arthritis got bad is a checkout person at my grocery store.

When she helped me with my groceries all those years, we spoke. I didn't stand there looking at the floor or the ceiling. We became acquainted.

I once took a trip to Niagra Falls. Law, the sound of the water was like the sound of the world coming to an end.

In the evenings we spread blankets on the ground and ate picnic dinners outdoors. I met people from all over the world.

On the return trip, we stopped in Chicago. I liked the city, but was ready to get back home. I missed the place where I belonged—where I was needed and making a contribution. No place, no matter how majestic, compares to the piece of earth where you have put down your roots.

I am not afraid of dying. I am ready to go anytime God calls me home. I am at peace with my life and my work. I don't think I have any enemies.

When I leave this world, I can't take nothing away from here. I'm old and I won't live always—that's why I gave the money to the school and put my affairs in order. I planned it and I am proud of it. I am proud that I worked hard and that my money will help young people who have worked hard to deserve it. I'm proud that I am leaving something positive in this world. My only regret is that I didn't have more to give.

Some people make a lot of noise about what's wrong with the world, and they are usually blaming somebody else. I think people who don't like the way things are need to look at themselves first. They need to get right with God and change their own ways. That way, they will know that they are making a difference in at least one life. If everybody did that, we'd be all right.

Oseola McCarty, *Simple Wisdom for Rich Living*. Atlanta: Longstreet, 1996, 10, 18, 22, 57, 64, 75, 79.

DWIGHT DAVID EISENHOWER (1890–1969)

[Eisenhower's family originally belonged to a sect of the Mennonites. When he was five years old, his parents joined the Watch Tower Society, later known as the Jehovah's Witnesses. In later years, Eisenhower became a member of the Presbyterian Church. Eisenhower served as the Supreme Allied Commander in Europe during World War II and was elected thirty-fourth president of the United States. The "Chance for Peace" or "Iron Cross Speech" was delivered at the American Society of Newspaper Editors on April 16, 1953. He

showed his humanitarian spirit and wisdom in noting costs of weaponry in comparison with costs of peaceful constructive acts. In 1896 William Jennings Bryan gave the greatest speech of his lifetime, about the gold standard, ending with the point: "you shall not press down upon the brow of labor this crown of thorns. You shall not crucify mankind upon a cross of gold." Eisenhower, speaking against the Cold War and the Iron Curtain, used the powerful image of humanity hanging from a cross of iron thanks to leaders' decisions to fund militarism. The practical dire needs of humanity and the highest American ideals of improving human life have not changed since this speech was given, except that the needs he described have grown greater.]

Chance for Peace (Iron Cross Speech)

The way chosen by the United States was plainly marked by a few clear precepts, which govern its conduct in world affairs.

First: No people on earth can be held, as a people, to be enemy, for all humanity shares the common hunger for peace and fellowship and justice.

Second: No nation's security and well-being can be lastingly achieved in isolation but only ineffective cooperation with fellow-nations.

Third: Any nation's right to form of government and an economic system of its own choosing is inalienable.

Fourth: Any nation's attempt to dictate to other nations their form of government is indefensible.

And fifth: A nation's hope of lasting peace cannot be firmly based upon any race in armaments but rather upon just relations and honest understanding with all other nations.

In the light of these principles the citizens of the United States defined the way they proposed to follow, through the aftermath of war, toward true peace.

This way was faithful to the spirit that inspired the United Nations: to prohibit strife, to relieve tensions, to banish fears. This way was to control and to reduce armaments. This way was to allow all nations to devote their energies and resources to the great and good tasks of healing the war's wounds, of clothing and feeding and housing the needy, of perfecting a just political life, of enjoying the fruits of their own free toil. . . .

. . . Every gun that is made, every warship launched, every rocket fired signifies, in the final sense, a theft from those who hunger and are not fed, those who are cold and are not clothed.

This world in arms in not spending money alone.

It is spending the sweat of its laborers, the genius of its scientists, the hopes of its children.

The cost of one modern heavy bomber is this: a modern brick school in more than 30 cities.

It is two electric power plants, each serving a town of 60,000 population. It is two fine, fully equipped hospitals.

It is some fifty miles of concrete highway.

We pay for a single fighter with a half million bushels of wheat.

We pay for a single destroyer with new homes that could have housed more than 8,000 people.

This, I repeat, is the best way of life to be found on the road the world has been taking.

This is not a way of life at all, in any true sense. Under the cloud of threatening war, it is humanity hanging from a cross of iron. . . .

The details of . . . disarmament programs are manifestly critical and complex.

Neither the United States nor any other nation can properly claim to possess a perfect, immutable formula. But the formula matters less than the faith—the good faith without which no formula can work justly and effectively.

The fruit of success in all these tasks would present the world with the greatest task, and the greatest opportunity, of all. It is this: the dedication of the energies, the resources, and the imaginations of all peaceful nations to a new kind of war. This would be a declared total war, not upon any human enemy but upon the brute forces of poverty and need.

The peace we seek, founded upon decent trust and cooperative effort among nations, can be fortified, not by weapons of war but by wheat and by cotton, by milk and by wool, by meat and by timber and by rice. These are words that translate into every language on earth. These are needs that challenge this world in arms.

This idea of a just and peaceful world is not new or strange to us. It inspired the people of the United States to initiate the European Recovery Program in 1947. That program was prepared to treat, with like and equal concern, the needs of Eastern and Western Europe.

We are prepared to reaffirm, with the most concrete evidence, our readiness to help build a world in which all peoples can be productive and prosperous.

This Government is ready to ask its people to join with all nations in devoting a substantial percentage of the savings achieved by disarmament to a fund for world aid and reconstruction. The purposes of this great work would be to help other peoples to develop the underdeveloped areas of the world, to stimulate profitability and fair world trade, to assist all peoples to know the blessings of productive freedom.

The monuments to this new kind of war would be roads and schools, hospitals and homes, food and health.

We are ready, in short, to dedicate our strength to serving the needs, rather than the fears, of the world.

We are ready, by these and all such actions, to make of the United Nations an institution that can effectively guard the peace and security of all peoples.

I know of nothing I can add to make plainer the sincere purpose of the United States.

I know of no course, other than that marked by these and similar actions, that can be called the highway of peace.

http://www.eisenhower.archives.gov/speeches/Chance_For_Peace.html (accessed February 26, 2008).

BARRY GOLDWATER (1909–1998)

[A conservative Republican leader of the 1960s, Goldwater spoke for some of America's core values—freedom, peace, and extending a helping hand. As a presidential candidate, he was demonized by the left; today, his ideas are better appreciated by both left and right. His ideal expressed below, of "never abandoning the needy or forsaking the helpless" is a

tall order. It is debatable how well wealthy nations have lived up to this ideal. Goldwater voiced his warnings and encouragements, and Americans are still impressed by his good sense and durable values.]

Acceptance Speech

... .I seek an America proud of its past, proud of its ways, proud of its dreams, and determined actively to proclaim them. But our example to the world must, like charity, begin at home.

In our vision of a good and decent future, free and peaceful, there must be room for deliberation of the energy and talent of the individual, otherwise our vision is blind at the outset.

We must assure a society here which while never abandoning the needy, or forsaking the helpless, nurtures incentives and opportunity for the creative and the productive.

We must know the whole good is the product of many single contributions....

Barry Goldwater, acceptance speech—1964 Republican presidential nomination (Republican National Convention, Cow Palace, San Francisco, July 16, 1964), http://www.nationalcenter.org/Goldwater.html.

RONALD REAGAN (1911–2004)

[The fortieth U.S. president, Reagan took office after the Vietnam War and Watergate, when many Americans felt disillusioned about politics and patriotic fervor. He led a conservative movement aimed at reinvigorating the American people with purpose and pride and reducing their reliance on government. He pledged in 1980 that if elected he would strive to restore "the great, confident roar of American progress and growth and optimism." His presidency strove to rekindle the ideal of serving America and good causes. In this speech he asks listeners to never take for granted the way of life Americans enjoy, and to imagine the price paid for it. Acts of giving and sacrifice large and small gave birth to America, and each generation is called upon to keep the enterprise going, to remember that it takes continual efforts of self-offering.]

First Inaugural Address

... Those who say that we are in a time when there are no heroes just don't know where to look. You can see heroes every day going in and out of factory gates. Others, a handful in number, produce enough food to feed all of us and then the world beyond. You meet heroes across a counter, and they are on both sides of that counter. There are entrepreneurs with faith in themselves and faith in an idea who create new jobs, new wealth and opportunity. They are individuals and families whose taxes support the Government [*sic*] and whose voluntary gifts support church, charity, culture, art, and education. Their patriotism is quiet but deep. Their values sustain our national life.

I have used the words "they" and "their" in speaking of these heroes. I could say "you" and "your" because I am addressing the heroes of whom I speak—you, the citizens of this blessed land ...

This is the first time in our history that this ceremony has been held, as you have been told, on the West Front of the Capitol. Standing here, one faces a magnificent vista, opening up on the city's special beauty and history. At the end of this open mall are those shrines to the giants on whose shoulders we stand.

Directly in front of me, the monument to a monumental man: George Washington, Father of our country. A man of humility who came to greatness reluctantly. He led America out of revolutionary victory into infant nationhood. Off to one side, the stately memorial to Thomas Jefferson. The Declaration of Independence flames with his eloquence.

And then, beyond the Reflecting Pool the dignified columns of the Lincoln Memorial. Whoever would understand in his heart the meaning of America will find it in the life of Abraham Lincoln.

Figure 4.4 Photo of President Ronald Reagan

Beyond those monuments to heroism is the Potomac River, and on the far shore the sloping hills of Arlington National Cemetery with its row upon row of simple white markers bearing crosses or Stars of David. They add up to only a tiny fraction of the price that has been paid for our freedom.

Each one of those markers is a monument to the kind of hero I spoke of earlier. Their lives ended in places called Belleau Wood, The Argonne, Omaha Beach, Salerno and halfway around the world on Guadalcanal, Tarawa, Pork Chop Hill, the Chosin Reservoir, and in a hundred rice paddies and jungles of a place called Vietnam.

Under one such marker lies a young man—Martin Treptow—who left his job in a small town barber shop in 1917 to go to France with the famed Rainbow Division. There, on the western front, he was killed trying to carry a message between battalions under heavy artillery fire.

We are told that on his body was found a diary. On the flyleaf under the heading "My Pledge," he had written these words: "America must win this war. Therefore I will work, I will save, I will sacrifice, I will endure, I will fight cheerfully and do my utmost, as if the issue of the whole struggle depended on me alone."

The crisis we are facing today does not require of us the kind of sacrifice that Martin Treptow and so many thousands of others were called upon to make. It does require, however, our best effort, and our willingness to believe in ourselves and to believe in our capacity to perform great deeds; to believe that together, with God's help, we can and will resolve the problems which now confront us.

And, after all, why shouldn't we believe that? We are Americans....

Ronald Reagan, first inaugural address (Washington, DC, January 20, 1981), http://www.bartleby.com/124/pres61.html.

GEORGE HERBERT WALKER BUSH (b. 1924)

["A Thousand Points of Light" was a philanthropic catch phrase and a government program associated with the Bush presidency (1989–1993). It referred to the many American people and agencies working to make the world a better place, kinder and gentler. The idea resonated with many Americans, though to some it seemed a glittering generality needing

more goal-oriented specifics and systematic encouragement. Each administration empha-
sizes an approach, developing programs and distinctive rhetorical devices in addressing
social needs, to call Americans to engage in the challenges at hand.]

Inaugural Address

... America is never wholly herself unless she is engaged in high moral principle. We
as a people have such a purpose today. It is to make kinder the face of the Nation and
gentler the face of the world. My friends, we have work to do. There are the homeless, lost and roaming. There are the children who have nothing, no love, no normalcy.
There are those who cannot free themselves of enslavement to whatever addiction—
drugs, welfare, the demoralization that rules the slums. There is crime to be conquered,
the rough crime of the streets. There are young women to be helped who are about to
become mothers of children they can't care for and might not love. They need our care,
our guidance, and our education, though we bless them for choosing life.

The old solution, the old way, was to think that public money alone could end these
problems. But we have learned that is not so. And in any case, our funds are low. We
have a deficit to bring down. We have more will than wallet; but will is what we need.
We will make the hard choices, looking at what we have and perhaps allocating it differently, making our decisions based on honest need and prudent safety. And then we
will do the wisest thing of all: We will turn to the only resource we have that in times of
need always grows—the goodness and the courage of the American people.

I am speaking of a new engagement in the lives of others, a new activism, hands-
on and involved, that gets the job done. We must bring in the generations, harnessing
the unused talent of the elderly and the unfocused energy of the young. For not only
leadership is passed from generation to generation, but so is stewardship. And the generation born after the second World War has come of age.

I have spoken of a thousand points of light, of all the community organizations that
are spread like stars throughout the Nation, doing good. We will work hand in hand,
encouraging, sometimes leading, sometimes being led, rewarding. We will work on this
in the White House, in the Cabinet agencies. I will go to the people and the programs
that are the brighter points of light, and I will ask every member of my government to
become involved. The old ideas are new again because they are not old, they are time-
less: duty, sacrifice, commitment, and a patriotism that finds its expression in taking
part and pitching in. ...

George Herbert Walker Bush, inaugural address (Washington, DC, January 20, 1989), http://www.
nationalcenter.org/BushInaugural.html.

TROUBLES, NEEDS AND HOPEFUL REMEDIES

W. E. B. DUBOIS (1868–1915)

[DuBois was a thinker and activist who recognized the potential of African Americans
and suggested ways to realize that potential in his insightful analyses laced with soul-
ful eloquence. His Harvard doctoral thesis, The Suppression of the African Slave Trade

in America, made a lasting contribution to the study of slavery; he later accepted a fellowship at the University of Pennsylvania to research Philadelphia's slums, studying the black community as a social system. DuBois was editor in chief of The Crisis, the NAACP publication, for twenty-five years. A trip to Russia in 1927 inspired him with a new sense of possibilities. DuBois stirred the ire of the American government with his sharp arguments against racism, and his communist sympathies caused dismay. In the following pieces from The Souls of Black Folk, he explains the necessity of educational opportunities for blacks and the power of African American churches to sustain both individuals and the community. The final piece is an obituary he wrote when the first self-made African American woman millionaire died.]

Functions of African American Colleges and Churches

The function of the Negro college, then, is clear: it must maintain the standards of popular education, it must seek the social regeneration of the Negro, and it must help in the solution of problems of race contact and co-operation. And finally, beyond all this, it must develop men. Above our modern socialism, and out of the worship of the mass, must persist and evolve that higher individualism which the centers of culture protect; there must come a loftier respect for the sovereign human soul that seeks to know itself and the world about it; that seeks a freedom for expansion and self-development; that will love and hate and labor in its own way, untrammeled alike by old and new. Such souls aforetime have inspired and guided worlds, and if we be not wholly bewitched by our Rhine-gold, they shall again. Herein the longing of black men must have respect: the rich and bitter depth of their experience, the unknown treasures of their inner life, the strange rendings of nature they have seen, may give the world new points of view and make their loving, living, and doing precious to all human hearts. And to themselves in these days that try their souls, the chance to soar in the dim blue air above the smoke is to their finer spirits boon and guerdon for what they lose on earth by being black.

* * *

The Negro church of today is the social center of Negro life in the United States, and the most characteristic expression of African character. Take a typical church in a small Virginia town: it is the "First Baptist"—a roomy brick edifice seating five hundred or more persons, tastefully finished in Georgia pine, with a carpet, a small organ, and stained-glass windows. Underneath is a large assembly room with benches. This building is the central club-house of a community of a thousand or more Negroes. Various organizations meet here,—the church, the Sunday-school, two or three insurance societies, women's societies, secret societies, and mass meetings of various kinds. Entertainments, suppers, and lectures are held beside the five or six regular weekly religious services. Considerable sums of money are collected and expended here, employment is found for the idle, strangers are introduced, news is disseminated and charity distributed. At the same time this social, intellectual, and economic center is a religious center of great power. Depravity, Sin, Redemption, Heaven, Hell, and Damnation are preached twice a Sunday after the crops are laid by; and few indeed of the community have the hardihood to withstand conversion. Back of this more formal religion, the Church often stands as a real conserver of morals, a strengthener of family life, and the final authority on what is Good and Right. . . . A great church like the Bethel of

Philadelphia has over eleven hundred members, an edifice seating fifteen hundred persons and valued at one hundred thousand dollars, an annual budget of five thousand dollars, and a government consisting of a pastor with several assisting local preachers, an executive and legislative board, financial boards and tax collectors; general church meetings for making laws; sub-divided groups led by class leaders, a company of militia, and twenty-four auxiliary societies. The activity of a church like this is immense and far-reaching, and the bishops who preside over these organizations throughout the land are among the most powerful Negro rulers in the World.

Such churches are really governments of men, and consequently a little investigation reveals the curious fact that, in the South, at least, practically every American Negro is a church member. Some, to be sure, are not regularly enrolled, and a few do not habitually attend services; but practically, a proscribed people must have a social center, and that center for this people is the Negro church. . . .

. . . We the darker ones come even now not altogether empty-handed: there are today no truer exponents of the pure human spirit of the Declaration of Independence than the American Negroes; there is no true American music but the wild sweet melodies of the Negro slave; the American fairy tales and folklore are Indian and African; and all in all, we black men seem the sole oasis of simple faith and reverence in a dusty desert of dollars and smartness. . . .

*   *   *

DuBois' Obituary for Madame C. J. Walker (1919)

One-tenth of the million dollar estate of the late Madame C. J. Walker, the Negro hair culturist, is bequeathed to charity. Among institutional bequests are Tuskegee Institute, $2,000; Daytona Normal and Industrial Institute, Manassas Industrial School, Old Folks' Home at Indianapolis, Old Folks' Home at St. Louis, and Haynes Institute, $5,000 each; Charlotte Hawkins-Brown Institute, $1,000; Sojourner Truth House, New York City, $500; Wilberforce University, $500; Music School Settlement, New York City, $600; Y.W.C.A., Louisville, Ky., $500; and the Old Folks' Home at Pittsburgh, $500. The bulk of the estate is bequeathed to her daughter, Lelia Walker Robinson, who succeeds the late Madame Walker as president of the firm. Since the death of her mother, Mrs. Robinson has been married to Dr. Wiley M. Wilson, a graduate of Howard University Medical School.

W. E. B. Dubois, *The Souls of Black Folk*. Chicago: A. C. McClurg, 1903; also New York: Signet, 1995, 138–39, 213–14, 52. *The Crisis* 18, no. 4 (August 1919): 20.

BOOKER T. WASHINGTON (1856–1915)

[Born into slavery in Virginia, Washington became a prominent educator, known for his eloquence as a public speaker. He became a spokesman for African Americans during the post-slavery transition era and helped build Tuskegee Institute. He appealed to philanthropists and raised funds to set up small community schools to advance educational opportunities for blacks living in southern states. He helped smooth relations between blacks and whites. In this passage, we see his practical insights and his appreciation for the many small contributions of the poor. W. E. B. Dubois criticized Booker T. Washington's acceptance of gradual progress for blacks, calling for more immediate civil rights, more

substantial political power, and more higher education for black youths. Two approaches, two personalities; both made important contributions to American society.]

On Getting Donations: The Science of Begging and Joys of Self-Forgetting[†]

Time and time again I have been asked, by people who are trying to secure money for philanthropic purposes, what rule or rules I followed to secure the interest and help of people who were able to contribute money to worthy objects. As far as the science of what is called begging can be reduced to rules, I would say that I have had but two rules. First, always to do my whole duty regarding making our work known to individuals and organizations; and, second, not to worry about the results. This second rule has been the hardest for me to live up to. When bills are on the eve of falling due, with not a dollar in hand with which to meet them, it is pretty difficult to learn not to worry, although I think I am learning more and more each year that all worry simply consumes, and to no purpose, just so much physical and mental strength that might otherwise be given to effective work. After considerable experience in coming into contact with wealthy and noted men, I have observed that those who have accomplished the greatest results are those who "keep under the body"; are those who never grow excited or lose self-control, but are always calm, self-possessed, patient, and polite. I think that President William McKinley is the best example of a man of this class that I have ever seen.

In order to be successful in any kind of undertaking, I think the main thing is for one to grow to the point where he completely forgets himself; that is, to lose himself in a great cause. In proportion as one loses himself in this way, in the same degree does he get the highest happiness out of his work.

Figure 4.5 Photo of Booker T. Washington

My experience in getting money for Tuskegee has taught me to have no patience with those people who are always condemning the rich because they are rich, and because they do not give more to objects of charity. In the first place, those who are guilty of such sweeping criticisms do not know how many people would be made poor, and how much suffering would result, if wealthy people were to part all at once with any large proportion of their wealth in a way to disorganize and cripple great business enterprises. Then very few persons have any idea of the large number of applications for help that rich people are constantly being flooded with. I know wealthy people who receive as many as twenty calls a day for help. More than once, when I have gone into the offices of rich men, I have found half a dozen persons waiting to see them, and all come for the same purpose, that of securing money. And all these calls in person, to say nothing of the applications received through the mails. Very few people have any idea of the amount of money given away by persons who never permit their names to be known. I have often heard persons condemned for not giving away money, who, to

[†] Title is the author's own.

my own knowledge, were giving away thousands of dollars every year so quietly that the world knew nothing about it.

* * *

Although it has been my privilege to be the medium through which a good many hundred thousand dollars have been received for the work at Tuskegee, I have always avoided what the world calls "begging." I often tell people that I have never "begged" any money, and that I am not a "beggar." My experience and observation have convinced me that persistent asking outright for money from the rich does not, as a rule, secure help. I have usually proceeded on the principle that persons who possess sense enough to earn money have sense enough to know how to give it away, and that the mere making known of the facts regarding Tuskegee, and especially the facts regarding the work of the graduates, has been more effective than outright begging. I think that the presentation of facts, on a high, dignified plane, is all the begging that most rich people care for.

While the work of going from door to door and from office to office is hard, disagreeable, and costly in bodily strength, yet it has some compensations. Such work gives one a rare opportunity to study human nature. It also has its compensations in giving one an opportunity to meet some of the best people in the world—to be more correct, I think I should say *the best* people in the world. When one takes a broad survey of the country, he will find that the most useful and influential people in it are those who take the deepest interest in institutions that exist for the purpose of making the world better.

* * *

Some people may say that it was Tuskegee's good luck that brought to us this gift of fifty thousand dollars. No, it was not luck. It was hard work. Nothing ever comes to one, that is worth having, except as a result of hard work. When Mr. Huntington gave me the first two dollars, I did not blame him for not giving me more, but made up my mind that I was going to convince him by tangible results that we were worthy of larger gifts.

* * *

I have found that strict business methods go a long way in securing the interest of rich people. It has been my constant aim at Tuskegee to carry out, in our financial and other operations, such business methods as would be approved of by any New York banking house.

I have spoken of several large gifts to the school; but by far the greater proportion of the money that has built up the institution has come in the form of small donations from persons of moderate means. It is upon these small gifts, which carry with them the interest of hundreds of donors, that any philanthropic work must depend largely for its support.

In my efforts to get money I have often been surprised at the patience and deep interest of the ministers, who are besieged on every hand and at all hours of the day for help. If no other consideration had convinced me of the value of the Christian life, the Christlike work which the Church of all denominations in America has done during the last thirty-five years for the elevation of the black man would have made me a Christian. In a large degree it has been the pennies, the nickels, and the dimes which have come from the Sunday-schools, the Christian Endeavour societies, and the missionary societies, as well as from the church proper, that have helped to elevate the Negro at so rapid a rate.

Booker T. Washington, *Up from Slavery: An Autobiography*. Garden City, N.Y.: Doubleday, 1901), 180–82, 183–84, 188, 192–93. Available at http://docsouth.unc.edu/fpn/washington/washing.html.

ST. CLAIR DRAKE (1911–1990)
AND HORACE R. CAYTON (1903–1970)

[The decades between 1880 and 1920 mark deep changes in America—a turn away from agrarian and small-town community patterns toward a more industry-centered and bureaucratically organized society. The formation of mutual-benefit societies among ethnic immigrants shows the sorts of needs new citizens experienced and their relationship to America. French Americans built orphanages, schools, and hospitals to preserve their identity. Jews used social-welfare agencies in their quest for assimilation. African Americans established mutual-aid societies when they experienced being left out of the larger society, according to Daniel Levine's study Immigrant/Ethnic Mutual Aid Societies, ca. 1880–1920. The following piece describes some of the details of membership in an African American burial association.]

Urban Burying Leagues

The burial association represents the impact of a southern culture pattern upon the northern community. The church "burying leagues" and lodges had, by 1920, been replaced in many sections of the South with associations organized by the undertaker. Each member paid weekly or monthly dues and the undertaker guaranteed an impressive burial. When a person had a policy with an insurance company and could not keep up the payments, the burial association would take over the policy in the role of beneficiary and continue to pay the premiums. The founder of the first burial association in Chicago defended the innovation thus:

> There was a need for one here in Chicago—you know they are a common thing in the South. Since the Depression, you will find more people in funeral systems than previously carried life insurance. I suppose it's because they had to cash in the policies for what they could and didn't have any protection left.

The largest burial association in Chicago was founded in 1922 by an undertaker with an eye for increased business. At this time, the masses of the migrants were unprotected except for lodge benefits. Many who had insurance policies had let them lapse or had cashed them in. White companies were charging exorbitant premiums. Northern Negro companies had not yet attained prestige. Into the breach stepped the burial association, offering a policy which, while it had no "turn-in" or borrowing value, assured the holder of a funeral, required no medical examination, and imposed no age limit. The association buried its policy-holders from its own funeral parlors, thus seriously threatening the ordinary undertaker. The Depression made burial societies even more popular, since when a policy was turned over to the association it did not need to be listed as an asset when applying for relief. A white doctor with a large Negro clientele commented somewhat patronizingly on the funeral system as follows:

> Doug and his brother had a funeral parlor. I think he is now the owner of the Eureka Funeral Association. You pay him so much a year to get a high-class funeral—something like ten cents a week. These Negroes will do a lot to be sure of a classy funeral. You see, Doug is in the insurance end of this just as much as the funeral business. He has a $15,000 Lincoln hearse and a whole string of Lincoln limousines. He

offers an "All-Lincoln" funeral. He tells them they are getting a thousand-dollar funeral; what he really does costs him probably a hundred dollars. He uses cheap coffins with a lot of paint. The way the thing is worked, they sign over their insurance policy for maybe a thousand dollars and are promised a big funeral. So Doug gets a cut two ways because he is in the insurance company, too. You should see his funeral parlors; they are elegant.

St. Clair Drake and Horace R. Cayton, "Urban Burying Leagues," in *The Book of Negro Folklore*, ed. Langton Hughes and Arna Bontemps. New York: Dodd, Mead, 1958, 589–90. (Originally published in *Black Metropolis*, 1945.)

HUEY P. LONG (1893–1935)

[Long, a Depression-era politician from Louisiana, has been portrayed in a novel and two movies titled All the King's Men. *His speeches were famous for their appeal to the sentiments and imagination of the ordinary person. Promising to dry the tears of the disappointed sounds noble, but raising false hopes can lead to further disappointment. Evangeline's story, extracted from one of Long's speeches, is a tragedy told in Cajun Louisiana, so the appeal of this imagery would be especially strong there. The populist appeal draws on known archetypal figures of the past and promises a more glorious future, persuading by skillfully playing on listeners' heartstrings.]*

The Tears of Evangeline [A Politician's Promise]

And it is here under this oak where Evangeline waited for her lover, Gabriel, who never came. This oak is an immortal spot, made so by Longfellow's poem, but Evangeline is not the only one who has waited here in disappointment.

Where are the schools that you have waited for your children to have, that have never come? Where are the roads and the highways that you send your money to build, that are no nearer now than ever before? Where are the institutions to care for the sick and disabled? Evangeline wept bitter tears in disappointment, but it lasted through only one lifetime. Your tears in this country, around this oak, have lasted for generations. Give me the chance to dry the eyes of those who still weep here.

Speech "delivered under the historic oak where Evangeline waited for her lover Gabriel, as described by Longfellow," in *Every Man a King, The Autobiography of Huey P. Long*. New Orleans: National Book, 1933, 99.

ISAAC ERWIN AVERY (1871–1904)

[This passage, taken from a book of writings by North Carolina journalist Isaac Erwin Avery, raises questions about helping the vulnerable. A white dress is easily dirtied; unfortunate missteps can cause lifetimes of suffering. To help the underprivileged regain their balance or to help them keep from falling requires resources, knowledge, and a dedication of energies. The piece asks, if the will to help is lacking among those who have the means, what hope do the vulnerable have?]

The Rescue Home [For Girls in Trouble]

The rescue home has assumed a task that will require all fortitude and delicacy, and it deserves the large encouragement that should support a heroic cause. Among the unfortunates that the mission will endeavor to reform there are those who will die with the paint on their faces, and alone, as dogs die. But there are others who have not lost good or womanliness, and they are sick at heart with an existence that now offers no release from bondage. They have found that in the long run their way is a disordered way that will permit naught of pleasure, naught of consolation, naught of heart's ease; and they would be clean because the wish for cleanness dies hard in a woman. But they are suspicious by training and sensitive beyond their rights, and they must be dealt with carefully. If you would reform a man you pat him on the back and make him sit at your table; but you would visit a fallen woman secretly, and you would consider yourself good if you kept reproach and lashing pity from showing in your eyes. Adopt a new plan here if you wish to do the right, and give to the unfortunates a kindness that does not patronize and a sympathy that is not feigned. They will need, not tracts, but gentleness, and not the preached painting of their scarlet sins, but a tender, insistent holding by the hand and a soft word of understanding. If you are going to do this hazardous thing, then, in God's name, go the limit in love.

How would it do to make the proposed rescue home a place for the prevention, rather than a cure, for the saddest evil in the world? The home proposes to pluck girls from an abyss. Why not make it lift a hand to keep them out of it? That little girl who came here from Reidsville last week, and went hellward in Springs' Alley, was hungry. She hadn't a cent of money. She was in a strange place; she was young, healthy, lonely and—hungry. She is now in Springs' Alley, but suppose she had known that there was some place she could go to and be cared for till she got work to do? Last year a "blue-eyed girl, wearing a clean, white dress," left her home in Cleveland County and came here—alone. She knew not sin. But she was penniless, and in the darkened city there was welcome to her only from foulmouthed hags who trade in human souls. And so the child stumbled on into the night, and her blue eyes became dulled and her white dress was besmirched. Suppose—but why suppose? You know the condition that exists. Continually there come to this town young girls who seek work. They are helpless, ignorant, unprotected. What salvation might come if they knew that when temptation is hardest they can flee to a house of refuge that is gentle and shames not? It is all right to drag the unfortunates from their painted misery, but is it not better to fight for the clear-eyed children who do not want to fall, yet must fall?

Isaac Erwin Avery, *Idle Comments*. Charlotte, N.C.: Avery, 1905, 108–09.

TWO PIECES FROM GRAPEVINE (TEXAS)

[Civil society takes constant renewal and encouragement of the philanthropic spirit. This piece from a small-town newspaper shows local community spirit. Note the use of a simple image—cultivating a garden—to urge townspeople to give of themselves to the community, so that they might see life blossom rather than wither in the Texas sun. The second piece, a historical note from the Grapevine Historical Museum, shows how the impulse of generosity generated a friendship that girdled the earth, bonding two distant communities.]

Cultivate Your Community as You Would Cultivate Your Garden

Gardens are cultivated for the pleasures they give us, in color, beauty and fragrance, pleasures which satisfy the sensual part of our natures. Gardeners and those who own them realize that they must be carefully cultivated to yield this loveliness, for without cultivation the most beautiful flower will die.

The same is true of one's community; unless you cultivate it there will be no well-regulated, happy place in which you can live. A community is cultivated with as much care as a garden—the money spent now in the stores at home is the seed planted toward a blooming of prosperity later on; the interest shown in community legislation is the pruning that shapes its future and the consideration and kindness shown one's town-folks and neighbors results in blossoming friendships and good fellowship. Spring is here and with it are new economic standards to meet, new acceleration to be applied to buying, building, industry, and financial strengthening. Exercise your power in these things that mean a return to normalcy for all of us, but exercise them in your own community, which will mean not only better living for you, but for those who live with you and around you.

The result will be a renewal of faith, of hope and of strength—flowers that bloom in the garden of human endeavor.

W. E. Keeling, editor and publisher, *The Grapevine Sun*, March 8, 1934.

Docents Notebook, Grapevine Historical Museum: How Grapevine Helped Pitcairn Islanders

In 1912 Grapevine mayor Benjamin R. Wall learned that the inhabitants of Pitcairn Island in the Pacific, many of whom were the descendents of Fletcher Christian and the other mutineers of the H. M. S. *Bounty*, were in need of clothing and other items. Thus began a long-term relationship in which Grapevine residents sent monthly parcels to Pitcairn Island, including dry goods, seeds, the first sewing machine and typewriter. In return, the islanders sent homemade presents, such as wood carvings, strings of beads, mats, candleholders, and flying fish carved from rare miro wood. Later Robert Stark, a Grapevine resident and ham radio operator, had almost weekly contacts with ham operator Tom Christian, conducting all types of business for the Pitcairn residents.

History from Docents Notebook:

In 1912, B. R. Wall, the benevolent mayor of Grapevine was attending a Redman Lodge meeting in Charleston, South Carolina where he met an old sea captain who had placed an ad in a paper asking if anyone was interested in doing a good deed, to please send magazines or newspapers to Lincoln Clark at Pitcairn Island.

After returning to Grapevine, Mayor Wall sent a parcel of magazines and papers to Lincoln Clark. After an extended period of time, Mayor Wall received a thank you letter from Mr. Clark. Correspondence was exchanged, and the mayor asked if there were other items they needed other than reading material. Mr. Clark wrote back that since they had no money, only souvenirs they made were used to barter with passing ships. He also added that there was a particular shortage of bloomers which the modest Pitcairn girls wore when climbing coconut trees, with only three pairs left on the entire island. (Does anyone know if Mayor Wall sent bloomers?)

So in 1912 a warm friendship began which continued over 50 years between the citizens of Grapevine and the descendants of the H. M. S. *Bounty* mutineers on Pitcairn Island.

Grapevine Area History. Grapevine, Tex.: Grapevine Historical Society, 1979, 99–100.

HERBERT HOOVER (1874–1964)

[The thirty-first president, Herbert Hoover served in office from 1929–1933. Hoover believed in the Efficiency Movement, which claimed that all problems have technical solutions. He took office the same year that the Great Depression began; although his new programs did some good, they were not enough, and his missteps and seeming callousness led to his defeat in 1932. From a Quaker background, Hoover worked for humanitarian causes before becoming president, helping thousands of Americans stranded in Europe at the outset of World War I, and aiding people in Belgium, Germany, and Russia during severe food crises.]

Never Before

Our national resources are not only material supplies and material wealth but a spiritual and moral wealth in kindliness, in compassion, in a sense of obligation of neighbor to neighbor and a realization of responsibility by industry, by business, and the community for its social security and its social welfare. . . . We can take courage and pride in the effective work of thousands of voluntary organizations for the provision of employment, for the relief of distress, that have sprung up over the entire nation. Industry and business have recognized a social obligation to their employees as never before. . . . Never before in a great depression has there been so systematic a protection against distress. . . . Never before has there been such an outpouring of the spirit of self-sacrifice and service. . . . The ultimate goal of the American social ideal is equality of opportunity and individual initiative. These are not born of bureaucracy. This ideal is the expression of the spirit of our people. This ideal obtained at the birth of the Republic. It was the ideal of Lincoln. [I]t is the ideal upon which the Nation has risen to unparalleled greatness.

Herbert Hoover, radio address on Lincoln's Birthday, February 12, 1931. The whole text may be accessed at John Woolley and Gerhard Peters, The American Presidency Project. Santa Barbara: University of California (hosted), Gerhard Peters (database), http://www.presidency.ucsb.edu/ws/?pid=22975.

FERDINAND LUNDBERG (1905–1995)

[Abraham Epstein, known as "the father of the Social Security Act," in 1933 declared that there was a false belief that private philanthropy had done a good job of relieving distress during the early years of the Great Depression. He said that in reality private charity never addressed more than a third of the nation's struggles and that the Depression's ongoing problems eventually brought attention to philanthropy's shortfall. Ferdinand Lundberg, an economist and journalist, agreed with Epstein's assessment and went even further. Lun-

dberg wrote an acerbic book about America's sixty wealthiest "dynastic" families of power. Buttressed by ninety less-wealthy families, this powerful group, according to Lundberg, was the hidden industrial oligarchy that dominated America's decision-making processes and determined her fate.]

Mirrors . . . and Pervasive Ballyhoo

The field of contemporary philanthropy, or noncommercial investment, is a labyrinth of mirrors, flashing lights, fitful shadows and pervasive ballyhoo . . . very little money—a trivial amount, in fact—has been given away by the wealthy of fabulously rich America, and most of that has been given since the income tax took effect in 1913. . . . The word "gift" might properly be discarded in this connection in favor of more precise words like "allocation" and "transfer."

Ferdinand Lundberg, *America's 60 Families*. New York: Vanguard, 1937, 320–21.

JANE ADDAMS (1860–1935)

[Born in Cedarville, Illinois, and raised a Quaker, Addams studied at what is now Rockford College. The death of her father launched a decade of soul-searching. While traveling in England, she encountered workers trying to help the poor. Returning home, she and friends founded Hull House in Chicago, dedicated to uplifting the disadvantaged, where she worked for many years. In Chicago she joined a Presbyterian church and remained a lifetime member, but it is said that on most Sundays she would attend Unitarian church services or take part in activities at the Ethical Culture Society. She was awarded the Nobel Peace Prize in 1931. In her writing we see the modern soul dealing with problems of the poor. Her honesty, clarity, uncertainty, shrewdness, and kindness shine through. She is aware of the theory of evolution and the idea of survival of the fittest but did not accept "social Darwinism" as an excuse to let the unfortunate suffer. Her life's work and thought earned her a high place in the history of American philanthropy.]

Charitable Effort

A very little familiarity with the poor districts of any city is sufficient to show how primitive and genuine are the neighborly relations. There is the greatest willingness to lend or borrow anything, and all the residents of the given tenement know the most intimate family affairs of all the others. The fact that the economic condition of all alike is on a most precarious level makes the ready outflow of sympathy and material assistance the most natural thing in the world. There are numberless instances of self-sacrifice quite unknown in the circles where greater economic advantages make that kind of intimate knowledge of one's neighbors impossible. An Irish family in which the man has lost his place, and the woman is struggling to eke out the scanty savings by day's work, will take in the widow and her five children who have been turned into the street, without a moment's reflection upon the physical discomforts involved. The most maligned landlady who lives in the house with her tenants is usually ready to lend a scuttle full of coal to one of them who may be out of work, or to share her supper. A woman for whom the writer had long tried in vain to find work failed to appear at the appointed time when employment was secured at last. Upon investigation it transpired that a neighbor further down the street was taken ill, that the children ran for the family friend, who went of course, saying simply when reasons for her non-appearance were demanded, "It broke my heart to leave the place, but what could I do?" A woman whose husband was sent up to the city prison for the maximum term, just three months, before the birth of her child found herself penniless at the end of that time, having gradually sold her supply of household furniture. She took refuge with a friend whom she supposed to be living in three rooms in another part of town. When she arrived, however, she discovered that her friend's husband had been out of work so long that they had been reduced to living in one room. The friend, however, took her in, and the friend's husband was obliged to sleep upon a bench in the park every night for a week, which he did uncomplainingly if not cheerfully. Fortunately it was summer, "and it only rained one night." The writer could not discover from the young mother that she had any special claim upon the "friend" beyond the fact that they had formerly worked together in the same factory. The husband she had never seen until the night of her arrival, when he at once went forth in search of a midwife who would consent to come upon his promise of future payment.

The evolutionists tell us that the instinct to pity, the impulse to aid his fellows, served man at a very early period, as a rude rule of right and wrong. There is no doubt that this rude rule still holds among many people with whom charitable agencies are brought into contact, and that their ideas of right and wrong are quite honestly outraged by the methods of these agencies. When they see the delay and caution with which relief is given, it does not appear to them a conscientious scruple, but as the cold and calculating action of a selfish man. It is not the aid that they are accustomed to receive from their neighbors, and they do not understand why the impulse which drives people to "be good to the poor" should be so severely supervised. They feel, remotely, that the charity visitor is moved by motives that are alien and unreal. They may be superior motives, but they are different, and they are "agin nature." They cannot comprehend why a person whose intellectual perceptions are stronger than his natural impulses, should go into charity work at all. The only man they are accustomed to see whose intellectual perceptions are stronger than his tenderness of heart, is the selfish and avaricious man who is frankly "on the make." If the charity visitor is such a person, why does she pretend to like the poor? Why does she not go into business at once?

We may say, of course, that it is a primitive view of life, which thus confuses intellectuality and business ability; but it is a view quite honestly held by many poor people who are obliged to receive charity from time to time. In moments of indignation the poor have been known to say: "What do you want, anyway? If you have nothing to give us, why not let us alone and stop your questionings and investigations?" "They investigated me for three weeks, and in the end gave me nothing but a black character," a little woman has been heard to assert. This indignation, which is for the most part taciturn, and a certain kindly contempt for her abilities, often puzzles the charity visitor. The latter may be explained by the standard of worldly success which the visited families hold. Success does not ordinarily go, in the minds of the poor, with charity and kind-heartedness, but rather with the opposite qualities. The rich landlord is he who collects with sternness, who accepts no excuse, and will have his own. There are moments of irritation and of real bitterness against him, but there is still admiration, because he is rich and successful. The good-natured landlord, he who pities and spares his poverty-pressed tenants, is seldom rich. He often lives in the back of his house, which he has owned for a long time, perhaps has inherited; but he has been able to accumulate little. He commands the genuine love and devotion of many a poor soul, but he is treated with a certain lack of respect. In one sense he is a failure. The charity visitor, just because she is a person who concerns herself with the poor, receives a certain amount of this good-natured and kindly contempt, sometimes real affection, but little genuine respect. The poor are accustomed to help each other and to respond according to their kindliness; but when it comes to worldly judgment, they use industrial success as the sole standard. In the case of the charity visitor who has neither natural kindness nor dazzling riches, they are deprived of both standards, and they find it of course utterly impossible to judge of the motive of organized charity. . . .

The neighborhood understands the selfish rich people who stay in their own part of town, where all their associates have shoes and other things. Such people don't bother themselves about the poor; they are like the rich landlords of the neighborhood experience. But this lady visitor, who pretends to be good to the poor, and certainly does talk as though she were kind-hearted, what does she come for, if she does not intend to give them things which are so plainly needed?

The visitor says, sometimes, that in holding her poor family so hard to a standard of thrift she is really breaking down a rule of higher living which they formerly possessed; that saving, which seems quite commendable in a comfortable part of town, appears almost criminal in a poorer quarter where the next-door neighbor needs food, even if the children of the family do not.

✳   ✳   ✳

Just when our affection becomes large enough to care for the unworthy among the poor as we would care for the unworthy among our own kin, is certainly a perplexing question. To say that it should never be so, is a comment upon our democratic relations to them which few of us would be willing to make.

Of what use is all this striving and perplexity? Has the experience any value? It is certainly genuine, for it induces an occasional charity visitor to live in a tenement house as simply as the other tenants do. It drives others to give up visiting the poor altogether, because, they claim, it is quite impossible unless the individual becomes a member of a sisterhood, which requires, as some of the Roman Catholic sisterhoods do, that the member first take the vows of obedience and poverty, so that she can have nothing to give save as it is first given to her, and thus she is not harassed by a constant attempt at adjustment.

Both the tenement-house resident and the sister assume to have put themselves upon the industrial level of their neighbors, although they have left out the most awful element of poverty, that of imminent fear of starvation and a neglected old age.

The young charity visitor who goes from a family living upon the most precarious industrial level to her own home in a prosperous part of the city, if she is sensitive at all, is never free from perplexities which our growing democracy forces upon her.

Jane Addams, *Democracy and Social Ethics*. New York: Macmillan, 1902, http://www.gutenberg.org/files/15487/15487-h/15487-h.htm.

HOWARD HUSOCK (n.d.)

[Husock's historical research into his family's experiences uncovers detailed information about life in Philadelphia in the 1930s and work of the "Agency"—the Juvenile Aid Society. The charitable women ("Jewish Victorians," as Husock calls them) were following scriptural teachings as well as social-conscience imperatives of the time in helping parentless children. The plight of orphans is an ongoing situation that every society must continue to help resolve; the challenges do not diminish. Attempts to address these problems may change, but it's not certain that the new ways are always going to be better. Husock concludes with a statement of values expressed in the Agency's literature.]

How the Agency Saved My Father

(Summary: His mother was dead; his ne'er-do-well father couldn't support him; an Agency put him into foster care at age nine. My quest to find out why and how yielded surprises—and public policy questions for today.)

The biggest mystery of my childhood was the question of how my father had survived his. Though the details were fuzzy, the facts seemed clear: an auto accident outside Trenton, in which his parents were seriously injured; orphaned, not long after, in South Philadelphia in the depth of the Depression, ultimately raised in foster homes . . . and yet, by 18, off by streetcar to engineering school and, after the war, to life in the middle class.

What had made it possible? The most intriguing explanation involved something he called the Agency. "Once a year," he would say, "the Agency took us to get a suit—one pair of long pants, one pair of knickers." Or: "The Agency even paid to get my teeth fixed—before antibiotics, so you had to go once a week to get the root canal drained so it wouldn't get infected." Or: "Even though it was the Depression and everyone was poor, my sister would insist on getting off the streetcar a block away from the Agency, so when we went to see the doctor no one would know we were getting charity."

In a thousand ways, the world of my father's childhood amid the row houses of South Philly—a world where fish were kept alive in the bathtub so they'd stay fresh, where teenagers enjoyed classical music, where sunflower seeds were the junk food of choice—is as gone as any European *shtetl* [emphasis added; pre-WWII Eastern European ghettos where Jews were supposed to live in semi-autonomous communities headed by a rabbi]. But to me, the Agency was the most distant part of it: my own father, it appeared, had been raised without parents and without the support of public funds, under the auspices of a charitable organization. Though recent talk about how "faith-based charity" should have a role in "social-service delivery" has made my father's experience seem a little less outlandish, the mystery haunted me. I wanted to solve it, both as a personal matter and a policy one. What exactly was the Agency? How did it compare with its successors? And—here's the personal part of the query—what effects of its work have I, unknowingly, lived with myself?

My father provided the crucial clue. Once a month, he recalled, an older woman, connected with the Agency, would arrive in a chauffeur-driven black Cadillac to check on him. Her name: Mrs. Sternberger.

I found her traces a few blocks from Independence Hall, at the Balch Institute for

Ethnic Studies, which houses the records of Philadelphia's myriad Jewish charities. On the founding board of directors of the Juvenile Aid Society, I discovered, was a woman named Matilda K. Sternberger. And looking through the Juvenile Aid Society's pile of typed case records, I turned up the March 2, 1934, proceedings of its Placement Committee's monthly meeting—which took up the case of Bernard Husock and his elder sister Sylvia.

It is a powerful thing to come across such a record only minutes before library closing time. It is sobering to read about one's own family as the object of intervention and help—especially when you're used to identifying with those providing the help, and even more especially when such records contain powerful revelations, as these did. I learned that my father's parents had not died at the same time; his father had outlived his mother and become a single father, responsible for two young children, aged five and ten, in the early years of the Depression. I learned that in June 1932, three years before the Social Security Act became law, at a time when state and local governments provided only short-term emergency relief, my grandfather had first turned to private charity for support. So my father and his sister were not, as I had believed, simple examples of orphans cared for by charity. Their situation was more like that so common today: a single-parent family in search of help, a family for which outsiders were deciding whether help was deserved and, if so, what form that help should take.

By the time it considered the case of my father, the Juvenile Aid Society had been making such decisions for more than 20 years. It grew out of the Young Women's Union, which was part of a movement, beginning in the 1880s, in which (as Philadelphia's *Jewish Exponent* later wrote) "the noxious tenements of South Philadelphia were invaded by an unlikely little army of well-bred, carefully nurtured Jewish young ladies from the safely upper-middle-class environs of Spring Garden Street." Led by banking heiress Bella Loeb Selig, the union began to move from children's recreation and nursery programs to an effort its members called "baby snatching"—by which they meant persuading the Juvenile Court (founded in 1901) to release children in trouble into their custody. To handle these kids, the union gave birth to the Juvenile Aid Society in 1911.

By 1932, it was a big organization, paying for the care of 350 children in any given week (rising to 450 in the high-immigration early 1920s) with an annual budget of $100,000, almost all raised from private donations. It was part of a larger system of some 80 private nonprofit and religious organizations, which cared for the vast majority of abused, abandoned, or orphaned children in Pennsylvania—many more than the 600 or so children housed in five state institutions at a cost of around $150,000 a year.

Through the Juvenile Aid Society, the wealthy German-Jewish women on its board expressed their sense of responsibility for the children of poor "Russian" immigrants, their generic term for eastern European Jews. So it was that women named Deutsch and Guckenheimer—members, many of them, of the city's grand Moroccan-style Reform temple, Congregation Rodeph Shalom—came to take some responsibility for children named Lazarowitz and Katz, then piling into South Philadelphia and crowding it with what ultimately would be more than 200 small, dark synagogues, squeezed in among the row houses.

These charitable women can be thought of as Jewish Victorians, combining a religious impulse with the Victorian commitment to "child saving." They were moved by the Talmudic injunction that "the blessed man is the man that brings up an orphan boy or girl until marriage has given him another home," and—fearing that the Russians would abandon Judaism as they acculturated to America—they required all children they assisted to attend religious schools, known formally as Jewish Education Centers. For them, religion was the guarantor of the bourgeois values and the self-discipline they cherished. "Moral behavior," the Agency's literature observes, "is the result of right habit and daily practice. . . . Cultivate the child's natural desires for leadership, for justice, for independence, for self-respect, for hero-worship. Morality is an inner driving force. Religion is an inner light and revelation. These cannot be forced from without. Open the windows of the soul through which the inner splendor may shine."

City Journal, Spring 1999, http://www.city-journal.org/html/9_2_how_the_agency.html.

DANIEL J. BOORSTIN (1914–2004)

[Boorstin was a renowned historian and scholar of American politics, who wrote insightfully about democracy and great Americans such as Thomas Jefferson. The following passage by Boorstin is useful in helping us think about what is distinctive in American nonprofit public institutions. Often we understand things better by making comparisons; considering the institutions in Europe helps us see how America is unique. Americans have vastly more private "voluntary" hospitals, universities, and social-service agencies— but this is a difference of degree rather than kind. The extent to which we have institutionalized our belief in the values of philanthropy into our lives—and distanced many of these values from government—and the pride we have in our philanthropic identity are also key differences. We often hear, "Americans are the most generous people on earth." Whether that is true or not, it's important for us to believe it, and for our leaders to repeat it, as part of our American identity. Like noble knights in the old legend, awaking from the cave, we feel it is our duty to be on the noble quest.]

From Charity to Philanthropy

If you are an American interested in education and public institutions and you travel about France today, you find something strangely missing from the landscape. . . . You are apt to feel puzzled, a bit lost and disoriented, simply because what you see there, like much else in Europe, is classifiable with an unfamiliar neatness. The sites and buildings are, with few exceptions, either public or private. They are monuments of the wealth and power, *either* of individuals *or* of the state. . . . If you are not in a private building, you are in an institution created and supported and controlled by the government.

In a great American city, by contrast, many—even most—of the prominent public buildings and institutions are of a quite different character. They do not fall into either of these sharply separated classes. Strictly speaking, they are not private, nor are they run by the government. They are a third species, which in many important respects is peculiarly American. They have many unique characteristics and a spirit all their own. They are monuments to what in the Old World was familiar neither as private charity nor as government munificence. They are monuments to community. They originate in the community, depend on the community, are developed by the community, serve the community, and rise or fall with the community.

They are such familiar features of our American landscape that we can easily forget, if we have ever noticed, that they are in many ways a peculiar American growth—peculiar both in their character and in their luxuriance, in what has made them grow and in what keeps them alive and flourishing. I need hardly remind you of such prominent features of Chicago life as the Art Institute, the Chicago Museum of Natural History (sometimes called the Field Museum), the Shedd Aquarium, the Adler Planetarium, the Museum of Science and Industry (commonly called the Rosenwald Museum), and The University of Chicago (founded by John D. Rockefeller). Each of these—in fact, nearly all the major philanthropic, educational, and public-serving institutions of the city (with some conspicuous exceptions)—was founded and is sustained voluntarily by members of the community. One finds comparable institutions in every other American city. Of course, there are numerous hospitals, universities, and other enterprises supported by our government; but these are far more often the creatures of local or state than of the national government. Scattered examples of community institutions of this type are not unique to the United States. Something like them—some of the Oxford and Cambridge colleges, for example—existed even before the New World was settled by Europeans. In one form or another a few such institutions are found today probably in every country in the world, except in Communist countries, where the autonomous public spirit is prohibited. But in extent, power, influence, and vitality our community institutions are a peculiarly American phenomenon.

Here in the United States, even some of our institutions ostensibly run by one or another of our governments are in fact community institutions in a sense in which they are not elsewhere in the world. Take, for example, our "public" schools. In the great nations of western Europe, the schools which are supported by the general citizenry and which anyone can attend free of charge are run not by separate communities through school boards but from the center by the national government headquartered, say, in Paris or in Rome. It was once a familiar boast of the French minister of education that he could look at his watch at any moment during the day and tell you exactly what was being taught in every classroom in the country. Nothing is more astonishing to a European than to be told that in the United States we have no corresponding official and that, except for a few constitutional safeguards (for example, of freedom of religion, or of free entry to public facilities, regardless of race), the conduct of our public instruction is decentralized. It is in local community hands.

Daniel J. Boorstin, *The Decline of Radicalism.* New York: Random House, 1963, 40–43.

NELSON ALGREN (1909–1981)

[Nelson Algren, a writer from Chicago, felt that monumental philanthropy let the wealthy off the hook too easily. He noted that the skeptical poor sometimes take a jaundiced view of public gifts like monuments and museums intended for their edification. Washington Gladden, a Congregationalist leader, criticized John D. Rockefeller's philanthropy: "His fortune is laid in the most relentless rapacity known in modern commercial history . . .[It is a] system of plunder . . . of brigandage." When Chicago Theological Seminary took a $100,000 gift, Gladden said it made the seminary a participant in Rockefeller's "iniquity." Fellow Congregationalist leader Graham Taylor disagreed, saying what matters in a penny is "not its pedigree but its destiny." This is a perennial issue debated in philanthropic circles.]

Something Fishy

"The slums take their revenge," the white-haired poet warned us thirty-two American League seasons and Lord-Knows-How-Many-Swindles-Ago. "Always somehow or other their retribution can be figured in any community."

The slums take their revenge. And you can take your pick of the avengers among the fast international set at any district-station lockup on any Saturday night. The lockups are always open and there are always new faces. Always someone you never met before, and where they all come from nobody knows and where they'll go from here nobody cares.

The giants cannot come again; all the bright faces of tomorrow are careworn hustlers' faces.

And the place always gets this look of some careworn hustler's tomorrow by night, as the arch of spring is mounted and May turns into June. It is then that the women come out of the summer hotels to sit one stone step above the pavement, surveying the men curb-sitting one step below it. Between them pass the nobodies from nowhere, the nobodies nobody knows, with faces cut from the same cloth as their caps, and the women whose eyes reflect nothing but the pavement.

The nameless, useless nobodies who sleep behind the taverns, who sleep beneath the El. Who sleep in burnt-out busses with the windows freshly curtained; in winterized chicken coops or patched-up truck bodies. The useless, helpless nobodies nobody knows: that go as the snow goes, where the wind blows, there and there and there, down any old cat-and-ashcan alley at all. There, unloved and lost forever, lost and unloved for keeps and a day, there far below the ceaseless flow of TV waves and FM waves, way way down there where no one has yet heard of phonevision nor considered the wonders of

"My wish is simple—to give something back to the community."

Figure 4.6 Eldon Dedini cartoon

technicolor video—there, there below the miles and miles of high-tension wires servicing the miles and miles of low-pressure cookers, there where they sleep on someone else's pool table, in someone else's hall or someone else's jail, there where they chop kindling for heat, cook over coal stoves, still burn kerosene for light, there where they sleep the all-night movies through and wait for rain or peace or snow: there, there beats Chicago's heart.

There, unheard by the millions who ride the waves above and sleep, and sleep and dream, night after night after night, loving and well beloved, guarding and well guarded, beats the great city's troubled heart.

And all the stately halls of science, the newest Broadway hit, the endowed museums, the endowed opera, the endowed art galleries, are not for their cold pavement-colored eyes. For the masses who do the city's labor also they keep the city's heart. And they think there's something fishy about someone giving them a museum for nothing and free admission on Saturday afternoons.

They sense somebody got a bargain, and they are so right. The city's arts are built upon the uneasy consciences that milked the city of millions on the grain exchange, in traction and utilities and sausage-stuffing and then bought conscience-ease with a minute fraction of the profits. A museum for a traction system, an opera building for a utilities empire. Therefore the arts themselves here, like the acres of Loredo Taft's deadly handiwork, are largely statuary. Mere monuments to the luckier brokers of the past. So the people shy away from their gifts, they're never sure quite why . . .

Nelson Algren, *Chicago: City on the Make*. Chicago: University of Chicago Press, 1987, 67–69.

KENNETH W. MORGAN (b. 1908)

[Harvard University, one of the oldest philanthropic institutions in America, was founded in 1638 when Rev. John Harvard died of consumption. "When his will was opened, it was found that he had left his whole library of two hundred and sixty volumes and one half of his estate to the proposed college—his estate being worth nearly 1600 pounds sterling. Provided thus with a fund of nearly 1200 pounds, the trustees went forward, erected a building, established the college and conferred upon it the name of its first benefactor. The example of John Harvard was more beneficial even than the money which he bequeathed, for it inspired a large number of other persons with generous feelings toward the infant institution" (Cyclopedia of Biography, cited in Historical Lights, Six Thousand Quotations from Standard Histories and Biographies, complied by Charles E. Little [New York: Funk & Wagnalls, n.d.], no. 2288, p. 270). After World War II, Americans realized they needed to learn more about other cultures and began to found institutions for that purpose. This narrative describes the founding of a center at Harvard to study the religions of the world, fulfilling this newly felt desire to learn about the languages and faiths of others. The center thrives today as a multidisciplinary forum for scholars of religion from around the world.]

Establishment of the Center for the Study of World Religions, Harvard University

The whole thing goes back to a little lady—we always called her the Little Lady because she never wanted her name to be used—the reason was, she said, "I'm almost 90, and soon I'll go to the other side and see all my friends there and if I did something for the Lord, and added my name on it, I'd be ashamed to see them." It is possible to find out her name here because there has been some carelessness, but if you do know her name, please forget it for her sake. I think her friends must be satisfied by now, since she's been dead for quite a few years . . . she died in 1958—almost 90.

Around the end of the 19th century there was a group of young people, mostly Protestant, well to do, rather self-consciously from "old" New York families, who decided that they wanted to live their Christian faith in a way that would make a difference in the community. So they decided to find some of the most deplorable blocks in the city of New

York and to bring Christ to the block. They went to the Village, but very soon ran out of steam. They were worried because they were convinced that their ideas were right—they decided that they were not worshiping enough to maintain the fervor of their religious faith. So they made a little chapel as part of their building and spent a great deal of time there in prayer, so much so that it became for them a very sacred place. Then, because they saw that they were not wise enough to answer all the questions that they needed to answer, they began to study, first in the Bible and then in devotional writings. They made the discovery—remember they were Protestant, mostly Episcopalian—that the Catholics had more devotional writings that were worth studying than the Protestants, and so they turned to Catholic materials, and through chance they began to study Asian sacred writings, and became quite excited about the *Bhagavad Gita* and some of the Buddhist writings. They developed a library and their work in the Village went on—until about 1950, when the chapel was finally closed. Some of the people remained there right through—one of them was Annette Lewis. Others, as they got married and had children, moved out of the building or would come back to the building occasionally to work.

The Little Lady had become clearly the head of the group—a remarkable woman, very sure of herself, regarded almost with awe by the members. In addition to the project in the Village they developed a place they called Chapel Farm on a rocky hill on the outskirts of New York City, with a high fence around it; there the Little Lady built a big house and others built little cottages nearby. At first it was a place they used in the summer, and later they lived there all year. At the end of her life, the Little Lady lived in a cottage and only went to the big house when she was going to meet someone. I had seen her quite a few times before I was allowed to go to the little cottage where she lived. To get to the big house she would call Charles the chauffeur and if it was someone really important she would go down in the Rolls Royce, but she much preferred her other car. She had a gorgeous Hispaño-Suiza in the First World War which she gave to the French army. After the War she bought another Hispaño-Suiza. Now the nice thing about her Hispaño-Suiza was that since she was a little lady she could walk into the car with dignity. The Rolls Royce wasn't so convenient. When the Hispaño-Suiza wore out she bought a Cadillac chassis and had them put the Hispaño-Suiza body on it and that was the car she preferred to come to the house in. I felt accepted when she quit coming down in her Rolls Royce and started coming down in the Hispaño-Suiza. It was fun to talk with her about cars, and places she had seen, and old New York—at 89 she was knowledgeable, keenly observant, and an interesting conversationalist. As members of the group grew older they didn't recruit the younger people and finally they closed down the chapel. One of the last people to leave the chapel was Miss Lewis, who came up to live at Chapel Farm in a house just a little way from the Little Lady's cottage—I didn't ever meet Annette there. Now the problem was: as the people who had been part of the group died they had such confidence in the Little Lady that they would leave their estates to her—they didn't know what she would do with their money but they knew that whatever she did would be agreeable to them. When she was a little girl she had met J. P. Morgan, and thought he was a very able person, and she put the money in a fund in J. P. Morgan's bank. A brother of one of the most faithful followers was a broker on Wall Street who helped her invest wisely; working with the Morgan Bank they did rather well. You may wonder about the money that Annette Lewis had—at first, she didn't have a great deal, but if you had a modest fund in 1910 and you had a good broker and Morgan's bank to take care of it for you, and you didn't spend much of the money on yourself, it would grow. I think it likely that Miss Lewis expected to die before the Little Lady and to leave her estate to the Little Lady too, so she wouldn't have to decide what to do with it.

Well, coming up to 1950, the lawyer for the Little Lady was nervous because she didn't have a proper will, and the bank, which is conscientious about its trust accounts, was increasingly concerned, so they sent handsome young men to explain to her that she should make clear how she wanted them to encourage the study of the great religions of the world because, as she said to me later, "When we were starting the chapel in the Village and were discouraged, and seemed to be losing our way, we found that by prayer and studying the devotional writings from all different parts of the world we gained a new insight and power that we hadn't had before and we feel that people ought to be encouraged to study the great religions of the world." That was her dream, but she had not decided how to carry it out.

About the time that the bank and her lawyer were pressing her to decide how the funds at her disposal should be used, the Little Lady heard of a new organization in England, the Union for the Study of the Great Religions of the World, created by H. N. Spalding of Oxford, and she decided that she would like to do something like that. Spalding had endowed the World Religions chair at Oxford occupied by Radhakrishnan at that time, and his organization was making small grants for research and publication in religion, particularly the religions of Asia. Since the Little Lady, in 1954, was about 85 years old and not able to travel about, she asked a good friend, Dr. Godfrey Dewey of Lake Placid, New York, to help her explore the possibilities for encouraging the study of the great religions of the world. He visited England that year for talks with Spalding, with Professor Thacker at Durham and with D. D. D. Henderson who was executive secretary for the Spalding Trust; later, Thacker and Henderson were in this country for further consultations and recommended that whatever funds might be available should be used in this country. Godfrey Dewey was then asked to explore the various academic centers to see if one would be the best place. (Some of his friends have suggested that he was biased because he is a Harvard man, but he insists that his judgment concerning Harvard has always been affectionately objective.)

I came into the picture by chance. Someone, I can't remember who, had suggested that when I was in England on my way to India I should visit Dr. Spalding at Oxford since we shared an interest in the study of Asian religions. We had an interesting conversation and I remember his saying that he had some friends in the States who shared our interests and that he would write to them. In 1954, when I was back at Colgate University, I received a letter inviting me to come to the University Club, in New York, to talk with a Wall Street broker concerning Asian religions. He did not mention any names, but told me that he had friends who had been studying Asian religions and had some funds they would like to use to encourage a better understanding of the great religions of the world. He said they were thinking of starting a library of Asian religious books, perhaps starting with their own collections, and maybe with a place where people could come together to discuss religious ideas. I suggested that such a plan would be futile, that if they wanted to encourage the study of the religions of the world they should be connected with an educational institution so the work would go on even when the people involved were changed, and all the resources of the university, the books, the scholars in related fields, the museums and galleries, would support the program without the expense of duplicating them. I suggested that the serious study of the religions of the world is just beginning, that we need a graduate center to train teachers and encourage research, one that would bring people from different parts of the world to work and study together; and related with that we should be encouraging the study of Asian religions in undergraduate programs so we would have more students coming up for graduate study in the field and would introduce the Asian perspective more effectively into the educational experience of college students. . . . She was persuaded that Harvard would be the best place for the graduate program, even though she was suspicious that Harvard was not sufficiently interested in the study of religion and would almost certainly attempt to divert to other uses the funds she might contribute. . . . She was sure that universities tend to accept endowment happily and then spend it according to the whims of the trustees and faculty without remembering the purposes for which the money was given, so she had me write out the terms of the gift explicitly to make as sure as possible that the funds would be used in ways that would encourage undergraduate understanding of the religions of the world.

*   *   *

So much for the past. Just a word about the future.

Many years ago I had an instructive conversation with Arthur Dunham, former head of the Business School at Harvard and a skillful fund raiser. He told me how he helped develop the China program at Harvard from a small initial gift to a substantial endowment. He said, "Remember this, young man: if a person has money to invest he can either seek a large return on his funds in stocks or bonds or real estate, or look for his returns in accomplishing things he thinks should be done. Either way, you must be sure that he is told what the income is: it is disgraceful to accept someone's money and then never report to them what has been accomplished." We don't have many people to report to now, for most of the people who knew the Little Lady and her friends are dead. Of course, if the Little Lady's theories about heaven are correct, she undoubtedly knows all about what is going on here; I'm not sure that is how things work, but I wouldn't want to quibble about it. Either way, we have invested over $3,000,000 in the Center and now we are getting the income. The dividends are in a doctor's thesis, in the classroom, in counseling, in articles written, books read, new ideas shared as you live together here, and in the teaching and research going on in many parts of the world by people who have lived here for awhile. The income on this investment is compounded in the lives of many people whose religious insight has been sharpened, broadened, and deepened because they have had opportunities to study religious ways other than their own here at the Center. The Little Lady, and her crusty old lawyer, and the trustees at the Morgan bank and Marjorie Kilpatrick, and Annette Lewis would be happy that they had invested so wisely here, and that their investments have been so ably nurtured at the Center.

Kenneth W. Morgan, "The Establishment of the CSWR, Harvard," *Bulletin*. Cambridge: Center for the Study of World Religions, Harvard University, Summer, 1977.

MARTIN LUTHER KING, JR. (1929–1968)

[Born at the onset of the Great Depression, King was an exceptional learner, entering Morehouse University at the age of fifteen. After graduation he studied at Crozer Theological Seminary, earning his degree with high honors. He then studied for his doctorate in Systematic Theology at Boston University. King was an eloquent Baptist minister. His

powerful voice, rooted in his Christian conscience, addressed the complexities and social problems of America in the middle of the twentieth century. He became a prophetic figure in the sixties, seeking justice and equality for African Americans and other minorities. Inspired by Gandhi, he called upon Americans to live up to their ideals, their Constitution, and their highest vision. He challenged America to practice what she preached and learn to love and give liberty and justice to all. His was an unforgettable voice of the twentieth century, bringing alive the ancient teachings of "love thy neighbor" and making relevant other Christian wisdom teachings by applying them to issues of the day. He won the Nobel Peace Prize at age thirty-five—the youngest recipient ever given the award. He worked tirelessly for justice through non-violent resistance, even when he knew his own life was in danger and, like Gandhi, died from an assassin's bullet. In a sermon in 1956, King said, "You may give great gifts to charity. You may tower high in philanthropy. But if you have not love it means nothing. You may even give your body to be burned, and die the death of a martyr. Your spilt blood may be a symbol of honor for generations yet unborn, and thousands may praise you as history's supreme hero. But even so, if you have not love your blood was spilt in vain. Without love benevolence becomes egotism, and martyrdom becomes spiritual pride."]

Remaining Awake Through a Great Revolution

It is always a rich and rewarding experience to take a brief break from our day-to-day demands and the struggle for freedom and human dignity and discuss the issues involved in that struggle with concerned friends of goodwill all over our nation. And certainly it is always a deep and meaningful experience to be in a worship service. And so for many reasons, I'm happy to be here today.

I would like to use as a subject from which to preach this morning: "Remaining Awake Through a Great Revolution." The text for the morning is found in the book of Revelation. There are two passages there that I would like to quote, in the sixteenth chapter of that book: "Behold I make all things new; former things are passed away."

I am sure that most of you have read that arresting little story from the pen of Washington Irving entitled "Rip Van Winkle." The one thing that we usually remember about the story is that Rip Van Winkle slept twenty years. But there is another point in that little story that is almost completely overlooked. It was the sign in the end, from which Rip went up in the mountain for his long sleep.

When Rip Van Winkle went up into the mountain, the sign had a picture of King George the Third of England. When he came down twenty years later the sign had a picture of George Washington, the first president of the United States. When Rip Van Winkle looked up at the picture of George Washington—and looking at the picture he was amazed—he was completely lost. He knew not who he was.

And this reveals to us that the most striking thing about the story of Rip Van Winkle is not merely that Rip slept twenty years, but that he slept through a revolution. While he was peacefully snoring up in the mountain a revolution was taking place that at points would change the course of history—and Rip knew nothing about it. He was asleep. Yes, he slept through a revolution. And one of the great liabilities of life is that all too many people find themselves living amid a great period of social change, and yet they fail to develop the new attitudes, the new mental responses, that the new situation demands. They end up sleeping through a revolution.

There can be no gainsaying of the fact that a great revolution is taking place in the world today. In a sense it is a triple revolution: that is, a technological revolution, with the impact of automation and cybernation; then there is a revolution in weaponry, with the emergence of atomic and nuclear weapons of warfare; then there is a human rights revolution, with the freedom explosion that is taking place all over the world. Yes, we do live in a period where changes are taking place. And there is still the voice crying through the vista of time saying, "Behold, I make all things new; former things are passed away."

Now whenever anything new comes into history it brings with it new challenges and new opportunities. And I would like to deal with the challenges that we face today as a result of this triple revolution that is taking place in the world today.

First, we are challenged to develop a world perspective. No individual can live alone, no nation can live alone, and anyone who feels that he can live alone is sleeping through a revolution. The world in which we live is geographically one. The challenge that we face today is to make it one in terms of brotherhood.

Now it is true that the geographical oneness of this age has come into being to a large extent through modern man's scientific ingenuity. Modern man through his scientific genius has been able to dwarf distance and place time in chains. And our jet planes have compressed into minutes distances that once took weeks and even months. All of this tells us that our world is a neighborhood.

Through our scientific and technological genius, we have made of this world a neighborhood and yet we have not had the ethical commitment to make of it a brotherhood. But somehow, and in some way, we have got to do this. We must all learn to live together as brothers or we will all perish together as fools. We are tied together in the single garment of destiny, caught in an inescapable network of mutuality. And whatever affects one directly affects all indirectly. For some strange reason I can never be what I ought to be until you are what you ought to be. And you can never be what you ought to be until I am what I ought to be. This is the way God's universe is made; this is the way it is structured.

John Donne caught it years ago and placed it in graphic terms: "No man is an island entire of itself. Every man is a piece of the continent, a part of the main." And he goes on toward the end to say, "Any man's death diminishes me because I am involved in mankind; therefore never send to know for whom the bell tolls; it tolls for thee." We must see this, believe this, and live by it if we are to remain awake through a great revolution.

Secondly, we are challenged to eradicate the last vestiges of racial injustice from our nation. I must say this morning that racial injustice is still the black man's burden and the white man's shame.

It is an unhappy truth that racism is a way of life for the vast majority of white Americans, spoken and unspoken, acknowledged and denied, subtle and sometimes not so subtle—the disease of racism permeates and poisons a whole body politic. And I can see nothing more urgent than for America to work passionately and unrelentingly—to get rid of the disease of racism.

Something positive must be done. Everyone must share in the guilt as individuals and as institutions. The government must certainly share the guilt; individuals must share the guilt; even the church must share the guilt.

We must face the sad fact that at eleven o'clock on Sunday morning when we stand to sing "In Christ there is no East or West," we stand in the most segregated hour of America.

The hour has come for everybody, for all institutions of the public sector and the private sector to work to get rid of racism. And now if we are to do it we must honestly admit certain things and get rid of certain myths that have constantly been disseminated all over our nation.

One is the myth of time. It is the notion that only time can solve the problem of racial injustice. And there are those who often sincerely say to the Negro and his allies in the white community, "Why don't you slow up? Stop pushing things so fast. Only time can solve the problem. And if you will just be nice and patient and continue to pray, in a hundred or two hundred years the problem will work itself out."

There is an answer to that myth. It is that time is neutral. It can be used either constructively or destructively. And I am sorry to say this morning that I am absolutely convinced that the forces of ill will in our nation, the extreme rightists of our nation—the people on the wrong side—have used time much more effectively than the forces of goodwill. And it may well be that we will have to repent in this generation. Not merely for the vitriolic words and the violent actions of the bad people, but for the appalling silence and indifference of the good people who sit around and say, "Wait on time."

Somewhere we must come to see that human progress never rolls in on the wheels of inevitability. It comes through the tireless efforts and the persistent work of dedicated individuals who are willing to be co-workers with God. And without this hard work, time

Figure 4.7 Photo of Dr. Martin Luther King, Jr.

itself becomes an ally of the primitive forces of social stagnation. So we must help time and realize that the time is always ripe to do right.

Now there is another myth that still gets around: it is a kind of over reliance on the bootstrap philosophy. There are those who still feel that if the Negro is to rise out of poverty, if the Negro is to rise out of the slum conditions, if he is to rise out of discrimination and segregation, he must do it all by himself. And so they say the Negro must lift himself by his own bootstraps.

They never stop to realize that no other ethnic group has been a slave on American soil. The people who say this never stop to realize that the nation made the black man's color a stigma. But beyond this they never stop to realize the debt that they owe a people who were kept in slavery two hundred and forty-four years.

In 1863 the Negro was told that he was free as a result of the Emancipation Proclamation being signed by Abraham Lincoln. But he was not given any land to make that freedom meaningful. It was something like keeping a person in prison for a number of years and suddenly discovering that that person is not guilty of the crime for which he was convicted. And you just go up to him and say, "Now you are free," but you don't give him any bus fare to get to town. You don't give him any money to get some clothes to put on his back or to get on his feet again in life.

Every court of jurisprudence would rise up against this, and yet this is the very thing that our nation did to the black man. It simply said, "You're free," and it left him there penniless, illiterate, not knowing what to do. And the irony of it all is that at the same time the nation failed to do anything for the black man, though an act of Congress was giving away millions of acres of land in the West and the Midwest. Which meant that it was willing to undergird its white peasants from Europe with an economic floor.

But not only did it give the land, it built land-grant colleges to teach them how to farm. Not only that, it provided county agents to further their expertise in farming; not only that, as the years unfolded it provided low interest rates so that they could mechanize their farms. And to this day thousands of these very persons are receiving millions of dollars in federal subsidies every year not to farm. And these are so often the very people who tell Negroes that they must lift themselves by their own bootstraps. It's all right to tell a man to lift himself by his own bootstraps, but it is a cruel jest to say to a bootless man that he ought to lift himself by his own bootstraps.

We must come to see that the roots of racism are very deep in our country, and there must be something positive and massive in order to get rid of all the effects of racism and the tragedies of racial injustice.

There is another thing closely related to racism that I would like to mention as another challenge. We are challenged to rid our nation and the world of poverty. Like a monstrous octopus, poverty spreads its nagging, prehensile tentacles into hamlets and villages all over our world. Two-thirds of the people of the world go to bed hungry tonight. They are ill-housed; they are ill-nourished; they are shabbily clad. I've seen it in Latin America; I've seen it in Africa; I've seen this poverty in Asia.

I remember some years ago Mrs. King and I journeyed to that great country known as India. And I never will forget the experience. It was a marvelous experience to meet and talk with the great leaders of India, to meet and talk with and to speak to thousands and thousands of people all over that vast country. These experiences will remain dear to me as long as the cords of memory shall lengthen.

But I say to you this morning, my friends, there were those depressing moments. How can one avoid being depressed when he sees with his own eyes evidences of millions of people going to bed hungry at night? How can one avoid being depressed when he sees with his own eyes God's children sleeping on the sidewalks at night? In Bombay more than a million people sleep on the sidewalks every night. In Calcutta more than six hundred thousand sleep on the sidewalks every night. They have no beds to sleep in; they have no houses to go in. How can one avoid being depressed when he discovers that out of India's population of more than five hundred million people, some four hundred and eighty million make an annual income of less than ninety dollars a year. And most of them have never seen a doctor or a dentist.

As I noticed these things, something within me cried out, "Can we in America stand idly by and not be concerned?" And an answer came: "Oh no!" Because the destiny of the United States is tied up with the destiny of India and every other nation. And I started thinking of the fact that we spend in America millions of dollars a day to store surplus food, and I said to myself, "I know where we can store that food free of charge—in the wrinkled stomachs of millions of God's children all over the world who go to bed hungry at night." And maybe we spend far too much of our national budget establishing military bases around the world rather than bases of genuine concern and understanding.

Not only do we see poverty abroad, I would remind you that in our own nation there are about forty million people who are poverty-stricken. I have seen them here and there. I have seen them in the ghettos of the North; I have seen them in the rural areas of the South; I have seen them in Appalachia. I have just been in the process of touring many areas of our country and I must confess that in some situations I have literally found myself crying.

I was in Marks, Mississippi, the other day, which is in Whitman County, the poorest county in the United States. I tell you, I saw hundreds of little black boys and black girls walking the streets with no shoes to wear. I saw their mothers and fathers trying to carry on a little Head Start program, but they had no money. The federal government hadn't funded them, but they were trying to carry on. They raised a little money here and there; trying to get a little food to feed the children; trying to teach them a little something.

And I saw mothers and fathers who said to me not only were they unemployed, they didn't get any kind of income—no old-age pension, no welfare check, no anything. I said, "How do you live?" And they say, "Well, we go around, go around to the neighbors and ask them for a little something. When the berry season comes, we pick berries. When the rabbit season comes, we hunt and catch a few rabbits. And that's about it."

And I was in Newark and Harlem just this week. And I walked into the homes of welfare mothers. I saw them in conditions—no, not with wall-to-wall carpet, but wall-to-wall rats and roaches. I stood in an apartment and this welfare mother said to me, "The landlord will not repair this place. I've been here two years and he hasn't made a single repair." She pointed out the walls with all the ceiling falling through. She showed me the holes where the rats came in. She said night after night we have to stay awake to keep the rats and roaches from getting to the children. I said, "How much do you pay for this apartment?" She said, "A hundred and twenty-five dollars." I looked, and I thought, and said to myself, "It isn't worth sixty dollars." Poor people are forced to pay more for less. Living in conditions day in and day out where the whole area is constantly drained without being replenished. It becomes a kind of domestic colony. And the tragedy is, so often these forty million people are invisible because America is so affluent, so rich. Because our expressways carry us from the ghetto, we don't see the poor.

Jesus told a parable one day, and he reminded us that a man went to hell because he didn't see the poor. His name was Dives. He was a rich man. And there was a man by the name of Lazarus who was a poor man, but not only was he poor, he was sick. Sores were all over his body, and he was so weak that he could hardly move. But he managed to get to the gate of Dives every day, wanting just to have the crumbs that would fall from his table. And Dives did nothing about it. And the parable ends saying, "Dives went to hell, and there were a fixed gulf now between Lazarus and Dives."

There is nothing in that parable that said Dives went to hell because he was rich. Jesus never made a universal indictment against all wealth. It is true that one day a rich young ruler came to him, and he advised him to sell all, but in that instance Jesus was prescribing individual surgery and not setting forth a universal diagnosis. And if you will look at that parable with all of its symbolism, you will remember that a conversation took place between heaven and hell, and on the other end of that long-distance call between heaven and hell was Abraham in heaven talking to Dives in hell.

Now Abraham was a very rich man. If you go back to the Old Testament, you see that he was the richest man of his day, so it was not a rich man in hell talking with a poor man in heaven; it was a little millionaire in hell talking with a multimillionaire in heaven. Dives didn't go to hell because he was rich; Dives didn't realize that his wealth was his opportunity. It was his opportunity to bridge the gulf that separated him from his brother Lazarus. Dives went to hell because he was passed by Lazarus every day and he never really saw him. He went to hell because he allowed his brother to become invisible. Dives went to hell because he maximized the minimum and minimized the maximum. Indeed, Dives went to hell because he sought to be a conscientious objector in the war against poverty.

And this can happen to America, the richest nation in the world—and nothing's wrong with that—this is America's opportunity to help bridge the gulf between the haves and the have-nots. The question is whether America will do it. There is nothing new about poverty. What is new is that we now have the techniques and the resources to get rid of poverty. The real question is whether we have the will.

In a few weeks some of us are coming to Washington to see if the will is still alive or if it is alive in this nation. We are coming to Washington in a Poor People's Campaign. Yes, we are going to bring the tired, the poor, the huddled masses. We are going to bring those who have known long years of hurt and neglect. We are going to bring those who have come to feel that life is a long and desolate corridor with no exit signs. We are going to bring children and adults and old people, people who have never seen a doctor or a dentist in their lives.

We are not coming to engage in any histrionic gesture. We are not coming to tear up Washington. We are coming to demand that the government address itself to the problem of poverty. We read one day, "We hold these truths to be self-evident, that all men are created equal, that they are endowed by their Creator with certain inalienable Rights, that among these are Life, Liberty, and the pursuit of Happiness." But if a man doesn't have a job or an income, he has neither life nor liberty nor the possibility for the pursuit of happiness. He merely exists.

We are coming to ask America to be true to the huge promissory note that it signed years ago. And we are coming to engage in dramatic nonviolent action, to call attention to the gulf between promise and fulfillment; to make the invisible visible.

Why do we do it this way? We do it this way because it is our experience that the nation doesn't move around questions of genuine equality for the poor and for black people until it is confronted massively, dramatically in terms of direct action.

Great documents are here to tell us something should be done. We met here some years ago in the White House conference on civil rights. And we came out with the same recommendations that we will be demanding in our campaign here, but nothing has been done. The President's commission on technology, automation and economic progress recommended these things some time ago. Nothing has been done. Even the urban coalition of mayors of most of the cities of our country and the leading businessmen have said these things should be done. Nothing has been done. The Kerner Commission came out with its report just a few days ago and then made specific recommendations. Nothing has been done.

And I submit that nothing will be done until people of goodwill put their bodies and their souls in motion. And it will be the kind of soul force brought into being as a result of this confrontation that I believe will make the difference.

Yes, it will be a Poor People's Campaign. This is the question facing America. Ultimately a great nation is a compassionate nation. America has not met its obligations and its responsibilities to the poor.

One day we will have to stand before the God of history and we will talk in terms of things we've done. Yes, we will be able to say we built gargantuan bridges to span the seas, we built gigantic buildings to kiss the skies. Yes, we made our submarines to penetrate oceanic depths. We brought into being many other things with our scientific and technological power.

It seems that I can hear the God of history saying, "That was not enough! But I was hungry, and ye fed me not. I was naked, and ye clothed me not. I was devoid of a decent sanitary house to live in, and ye provided no shelter for me. And consequently, you cannot enter the kingdom of greatness. If ye do it unto the least of these, my brethren, ye do it unto me." That's the question facing America today.

I want to say one other challenge that we face is simply that we must find an alternative to war and bloodshed. Anyone who feels, and there are still a lot of people who feel that way, that war can solve the social problems facing mankind is sleeping through a great revolution. President Kennedy said on one occasion, "Mankind must put an end to war or war will put an end to mankind." The world must hear this. I pray God that America will hear this before it is too late, because today we're fighting a war.

I am convinced that it is one of the most unjust wars that has ever been fought in the history of the world. Our involvement in the war in Vietnam has torn up the Geneva Accord. It has strengthened the military-industrial complex; it has strengthened the forces of reaction in our nation. It has put us against the self-determination of a vast majority of the Vietnamese people, and put us in the position of protecting a corrupt regime that is stacked against the poor.

It has played havoc with our domestic destinies. This day we are spending five hundred thousand dollars to kill every Vietcong soldier. Every time we kill one we spend about five hundred thousand dollars while we spend only fifty-three dollars a year for every person characterized as poverty-stricken in the so-called poverty program, which is not even a good skirmish against poverty.

Not only that, it has put us in a position of appearing to the world as an arrogant nation. And here we are ten thousand miles away from home fighting for the so-called freedom of the Vietnamese people when we have not even put our own house in order. And we force young black men and young white men to fight and kill in brutal solidarity. Yet when they come back home they can't hardly live on the same block together.

The judgment of God is upon us today. And we could go right down the line and see that something must be done—and something must be done quickly. We have alienated ourselves from other nations so we end up morally and politically isolated in the world. There is not a single major ally of the United States of America that would dare send a troop to Vietnam, and so the only friends that we have now are a few client-nations like Taiwan, Thailand, South Korea, and a few others.

This is where we are. "Mankind must put an end to war or war will put an end to mankind," and the best way to start is to put an end to war in Vietnam, because if it continues, we will inevitably come to the point of confronting China which could lead the whole world to nuclear annihilation.

It is no longer a choice, my friends, between violence and nonviolence. It is either nonviolence or nonexistence. And the alternative to disarmament, the alternative to a greater suspension of nuclear tests, the alternative to strengthening the United Nations and thereby disarming the whole world, may well be a civilization plunged into the abyss of annihilation, and our earthly habitat would be transformed into an inferno that even the mind of Dante could not imagine.

This is why I felt the need of raising my voice against that war and working wherever I can to arouse the conscience of our nation on it. I remember so well when I first took a stand against the war in Vietnam. The critics took me on and they had their say in the most negative and sometimes most vicious way.

One day a newsman came to me and said, "Dr. King, don't you think you're going to have to stop, now, opposing the war and move more in line with the administration's policy? As I understand it, it has hurt the budget of your organization, and people who once respected you have lost respect for you. Don't you feel that you've really got to change your position?" I looked at him and I had to say, "Sir, I'm sorry you don't know me. I'm not a consensus leader. I do not determine what is right and wrong by looking at the budget of the Southern Christian Leadership Conference. I've not taken a sort of Gallup Poll of the majority opinion." Ultimately a genuine leader is not a searcher for consensus, but a molder of consensus.

On some positions, cowardice asks the question, is it expedient? And then expedience comes along and asks the question, is it politic? Vanity asks the question, is it popular? Conscience asks the question, is it right?

There comes a time when one must take the position that is neither safe nor politic nor popular, but he must do it because conscience tells him it is right. I believe today that there is a need for all people of goodwill to come with a massive act of conscience and say in the words of the old Negro spiritual, "We ain't goin' study war no more." This is the challenge facing modern man.

Let me close by saying that we have difficult days ahead in the struggle for justice and peace, but I will not yield to a politic of despair. I'm going to maintain hope as we come to Washington in this campaign. The cards are stacked against us. This time we will really confront a Goliath. God grant that we will be that David of truth set out against the Goliath of injustice, the Goliath of neglect, the Goliath of refusing to deal with the problems, and go on with the determination to make America the truly great America that it is called to be.

I say to you that our goal is freedom, and I believe we are going to get there because however much she strays away from it, the goal of America is freedom. Abused and scorned though we may be as a people, our destiny is tied up in the destiny of America.

Before the Pilgrim fathers landed at Plymouth, we were here. Before Jefferson etched across the pages of history the majestic words of the Declaration of Independence, we were here. Before the beautiful words of the "Star Spangled Banner" were written, we were here.

For more than two centuries our forebearers labored here without wages. They made cotton king, and they built the homes of their masters in the midst of the most humiliating and oppressive conditions. And yet out of a bottomless vitality they continued to grow and develop. If the inexpressible cruelties of slavery couldn't stop us, the opposition that we now face will surely fail.

We're going to win our freedom because both the sacred heritage of our nation and the eternal will of the almighty God are embodied in our echoing demands. And so, however dark it is, however deep the angry feelings are, and however violent explosions are, I can still sing "We Shall Overcome."

We shall overcome because the arc of the moral universe is long, but it bends toward justice.

We shall overcome because Carlyle is right—"No lie can live forever."

We shall overcome because William Cullen Bryant is right—"Truth, crushed to earth, will rise again."

We shall overcome because James Russell Lowell is right—as we were singing earlier today, "Truth forever on the scaffold,/Wrong forever on the throne./Yet that scaffold sways the future./And behind the dim unknown stands God,/Within the shadow keeping watch above his own."

With this faith we will be able to hew out of the mountain of despair the stone of hope. With this faith we will be able to transform the jangling discords of our nation into a beautiful symphony of brotherhood.

Thank God for John, who centuries ago out on a lonely, obscure island called Patmos caught vision of a new Jerusalem descending out of heaven from God, who heard a voice saying, "Behold, I make all things new; former things are passed away."

God grant that we will be participants in this newness and this magnificent development. If we will but do it, we will bring about a new day of justice and brotherhood and peace. And that day the morning stars will sing together and the sons of God will shout for joy. God bless you.

Martin Luther King, Jr., "Remaining Awake Through a Great Revolution," sermon (National Cathedral, Washington, D.C., March 31, 1968), *Congressional Record*, 9 April 1968.

ALLEN GINSBERG (1926–1997)

[When Beat poet and controversial modern-day prophet-iconoclast Allen Ginsberg was in Indianapolis in 1991, he spoke of "sleepwalkers," saying that before he died he wanted to write an epic poem to break through America's "sleepwalking consciousness." He said a taxi driver had recently used the phrase "cultural fascism" in asking him what difficulty "sleepwalking" Americans are trying to avoid. The following was Ginsberg's answer, a sense that America has an intermittent amnesia, forgetting who we are and what needs to be done. It will take great philanthropic fervor and resources to make progress in addressing the needs of our age. Republican president Dwight Eisenhower said, "Every gun that is made, every warship launched, every rocket fired, represents, in the final analysis, a theft from those who hunger and are not fed, who are cold and are not clothed." That statement from a great American president is not too distant from Ginsberg's view.]

Why Americans Are Sleepwalkers

My view there was the fact that with a small portion of the world's population, 7 or 8 %, we're consuming almost half the world's raw materials, living, as I said earlier, high on the hog, and that to confront this understanding and lower our standard of living and begin to spread the wealth is just the opposite of what's happening in America now, so people are "sleepwalking" in the sense that they don't know what's gonna come. And then you get premonitions of it among fundamentalists talking about the "rapture," "Armageddon," the "apocalypse," . . . and you get premonitions among the old ladies and grandmas who say, "I never saw the world like this, things are really outta hand!" And you get premonitions among young punks who have a sense of despair about the future, you get premonitions from the mayors who say "these cities are never going to be repaired," but nobody wants actually to acknowledge that progress is over and it's time to figure out where we are, so it's like alcoholics in a state of denial—you know Alcoholics Anonymous terminology—that's what I mean by "sleepwalking." As the lone superpower of the world America is anxious, paranoid, fearful of losing what it has. Going along pretending nothing needs special attention, because it's all so frighteningly massive. . . . How do kids wake up to social rebellion, when you doubt that your voice will carry any weight against [corporations and government agencies]. . . . Poetry is about candor, information, "news that stays news," emotional news, because "only emotion objectified endures" rather than covering over, dulling.

Allen Ginsberg, TV interview, Indianapolis, October 1991. The text I include above is a transcription made from a tape of the Butler University TV show.

REPRESENTATIVE SERVICE AND CHARITABLE ORGANIZATIONS

JANET LUNDQUIST

[The origin stories of service groups are useful—understanding a group's roots is helpful in grasping the group's aims and trajectory. Regaining small-town friendliness and giving back to the world are valuable philanthropic goals. Probably each of us could name American organizations dedicated to the values we would like to see thrive, and each organization shows how, under the right conditions, people together can accomplish far more than one person alone.]

Origins and Aims of the Rotary Club[†]

History. Rotary was not always this large of an organization.

According to the Rotary International Web site, Paul P. Harris founded Rotary on Feb. 23, 1905. The attorney, who wished to recapture in a professional club the same friendly spirit he had felt in the small towns of his youth, decided to gather his business acquaintances together.

In those early years, Rotary members simply met to enjoy camaraderie and enlarge their circle of business and professional acquaintants.

The first four members—Harris; Silvester Schiele, a coal dealer; Hiram Shorey, a merchant tailor; and Gustavus Loehr, a mining engineer—gathered in Loehr's business office in Room 711 of the Unity Building in downtown Chicago. After enlisting a fifth member, printer Harry Ruggles, the group was formally organized as the Rotary Club of Chicago.

[†] Title is the author's own.

The original club emblem, a wagon wheel design, was the precursor of the familiar cogwheel emblem now used by Rotarians worldwide. The name "Rotary" derived from the early practice of rotating meetings among members' offices . . .

Rotary International has grown to a group of about 1.2 million members who belong to more than 31,000 Rotary clubs.

Ask Rotary members why they joined the club, and often they will first say they wanted the opportunity to help other people. Many of the Rotarians in town Saturday said they were drawn to the generosity of the group as well as the camaraderie.

In addition to enlarging the members' circles of business contacts and professional acquaintants, Rotary International has come to be a service club with lofty goals, such as the complete eradication of polio as part of its PolioPlus program.

"They like to give, and I like that philosophy," Morimoto said. "Whenever I meet Rotarians from other areas, they're all cut from the same cloth. There's no selfishness.

"It's not just a social club. Their real intent is to serve the community," he said.

Janet Lundquist, "Rotarians Welcome the World," *Herald News,* http://www.jolietrotary.com/rotarians_welcome_world.htm.

ALPHA PHI ALPHA FRATERNITY

[This distinguished fraternal organization—the first intercollegiate fraternity founded by African Americans—has a reputation for service and excellence. Thurgood Marshall and Martin Luther King, Jr., were members; philosopher Cornell West is a member. He and others speak highly of the fraternity's dedication to acts of service, including volunteering for voter education and voter registration drives, working with Habitat for Humanity, raising money for the March of Dimes, and building a $100 million memorial to Martin Luther King, Jr., in Washington.]

Servants of All

Motto: "First of All, Servants of All, We Shall Transcend All." Chapters: 700+. Cardinal Principles: Manly Deeds, Scholarship, and Love For All Mankind.

Alpha Phi Alpha is an intercollegiate service fraternity generally recognized as the first established by African Americans. Founded on December 4, 1906, on the campus of Cornell University in Ithaca, New York, the fraternity has initiated over 175,000 men into the organization and has been open to men of all races since 1945. The fraternity utilizes motifs and artifacts from Ancient Egypt to represent the organization and preserves its archives at the Moorland-Spingarn Research Center.

Founders Henry A. Callis, Charles H. Chapman, Eugene K. Jones, George B. Kelley, Nathaniel A. Murray, Robert H. Ogle and Vertner W. Tandy are collectively known as the "Seven Jewels" and they swiftly expanded the fraternity when a second chapter was chartered at Howard University in 1907. Beginning in 1908, the Howard chapter became the prototype for six of the remaining eight National Pan-Hellenic Council members, a predominantly African American fraternal council. Today, there are over 700 Alpha chapters in the Americas, Africa, Europe, Asia, and the West Indies. The Alphas have encountered problems similar to other fraternities, including a two-year suspension for a 2001 hazing episode at Ohio State University.

The fraternity has provided leadership and service during the Great Depression, World War II, Civil Rights Movements, and addressed social issues such as apartheid and urban housing, and other economic, cultural, and political issues affecting people of color. The Martin Luther King Jr. National Memorial is a project of Alpha Phi Alpha and the fraternity jointly leads philanthropic programming initiatives with March of Dimes, Head Start, Boy Scouts of America and Big Brothers Big Sisters of America.

Members of Alpha Phi Alpha include former Jamaican Prime Minister and Rhodes Scholar Norman Manley; Nobel Peace Prize winner Martin Luther King Jr.; former U.S. Vice President Hubert Humphrey; Olympian Jesse Owens; Justice Thurgood Marshall; and former Atlanta Mayors Maynard Jackson and Andrew Young. Numerous other American leaders are among the men who have adopted the fraternity's principles—manly deeds, scholarship, and love for all mankind.

National Programs

National programs are projects adopted by the General Convention and the national office is tasked with overall fraternity supervision and program management.

The fraternity combines its efforts in conjunction with other philanthropic organizations such as Head Start, Boy Scouts of America, Big Brothers Big Sisters of America, Project Alpha with the March of Dimes, NAACP, Habitat for Humanity, and Fortune 500 companies. The Washington, D.C. Martin Luther King Jr. National Memorial Project Foundation is a project of Alpha Phi Alpha to construct the Martin Luther King Jr. National Memorial. Alpha Phi Alpha provides for charitable endeavors through the Fraternity's Education and Building Foundations, providing academic scholarships and shelter to underprivileged families. Alpha's "Designated Charity" benefits from the approximately $10,000, one-time contribution fund-raising efforts at the fraternity's annual general convention. The Fraternity also has made commitments to train leaders with national mentoring programs.

Alpha Phi Alpha, http://www.alphaphialpha.net/. Also, Wikipedia, http://en.wikipedia.org/wiki/Alpha_Phi_Alpha.

CHINESE CONSOLIDATED BENEVOLENT ASSOCIATION

[Active in thirty-five American cities, CCBA has served Chinese immigrants during the last century and is in some ways a model for other groups that form to help people arriving on America's shores. Classical Chinese thought includes strong philanthropic ideas rooted in Confucian philosophy. Jen is the Chinese word for the inborn capacity to feel compassion and benevolence toward others. Confucius saw it as the foundational virtue, necessary for all other virtues to develop. Confucians teach that the humane feeling of sympathy and the ability to commiserate and help others are signs of one's humanity. Through neglect and abuse, people can lose their inborn humanity; through practice, they can develop this natural sense of goodwill toward others.]

Eight Questions Answered

1. What is the Chinese Consolidated Benevolent Association, New York? The Chinese Consolidated Benevolent Association (CCBA) was founded in 1883 to serve and pro-

tect the interests of the Chinese people in New York City. Historically it has performed a quasi-government role in the Chinese community, so that the President of the CCBA is sometimes referred to as the "Mayor of Chinatown."

2. What are the functions of the CCBA? Externally, we represent the Chinese-Americans living in the Greater New York area. Internally, we are the hinges that keep the Chinese-American community intact and vigorous. More specifically, we

- Provide social services
- Mediate personal and commercial disputes
- Preserve Chinese traditions and cultural heritage
- Serve as a bridge between Chinese and American groups
- Promote Chinese-American interests
- Engage in charitable activities
- Sponsor educational and recreational activities.

3. Who are the members of your Association? The Association is made up of 60 member organizations. They represent a cross-section of the Chinese community in New York: fellow-provincial organizations such as the Hoy Sun Ning Yeung Association and the Lin Sing Association; clansmen organizations such as the Lee, Eng, or Chan Family Association; political organizations such as the Kuo Min Tang (Nationalist Party) Eastern Region Office; professional and trade organizations such as the Chinese Chamber of Commerce and the Chinese American Restaurant Association; as well as religious, cultural and women's organizations. In other words, the CCBA is an umbrella organization.

4. How is your Association President chosen or elected? The Association President is elected by the CCBA General Assembly from among the two candidates nominated by the Hoy Sun Ning Yeung Association and the Lin Sing Association. The term is for two years and the President's position alternates between someone from the Hoy Sun Ning Yeung Association and the Lin Sing Association. The President takes office on March 1st of even years.

This form of election has been practiced since 1922, because early Chinese immigrants came predominantly from the county of Hoy Sun in Kwangtung Province, while those from all other counties outside of Hoy Sun formed the Lin Sing Association. In Chinese, Lin Sing denotes "united formation."

5. How did your Association come into being? Chinese presence in New York was noted since the clipper ship days. Some were merchants and sailors. Others were transmigrants from Cuba, Peru, and the Caribbean. The larger numbers did not come until after the Gold Rush of 1849 and the completion of the transcontinental railroad. When the tracks of the Union Pacific and the Central Pacific were joined at Promontory Point, Utah, in 1869, about 30,000 Chinese railroad workers lost their jobs. Some chose to come to New York because of the virulent anti-Chinese climate in the West.

An 1870 census shows there were only 23 Chinese living in New York City. But the number increased to 120 in 1872, 853 in 1880, 2,559 in 1890, and 6,321 in 1900. They were mostly in such lines of business as laundry, cigar and tobacco, groceries and restaurants.

However, anti-Chinese feelings ran high. The Chinese were persecuted and attacked. Discriminatory laws were passed against them, forbidding them to become citizens. In 1882, Congress passed the Chinese Exclusion Act, which prohibited Chinese persons from entering the country except for a few exempt classes. The hostility created a lot of problems for the Chinese already in this country.

To deal with these problems, community leaders proposed the formation of an organization representing all the Chinese groups in the New York area.

But the proposition did not materialize until 1883, when the Imperial Manchu Court established a Consulate in New York. The organization was then known as the Chinese Charitable and Benevolent Association of the City of New York. It was incorporated in New York State in 1890.

In the beginning, there were seven member organizations: the Hoy Sun Ning Yeung Association, Lin Sing Association, Chinese Merchants Association, Hip Sing Association, Chinese Chamber of Commerce, Chinese Masonic Association, and Kuo Min Tang Eastern Region Office. By 1948, organization membership had increased to 60 and remains the same today. That same year, the Association was renamed the Chinese Consolidated Benevolent Association. New York.

6. How does your Association fulfill its functions? By working like a skillful Chinese artist who uses two brushes to paint a picture at the same time. On the one hand, we maintain close contact with all Chinese-American organizations in the nation; on the other, we try hard to get integrated into the mainstream of American society.

Our efforts were reciprocated in 1954 with an epochmaking event. Robert Wagner, who had been Manhattan Borough President, visited Chinatown after taking office as Mayor of New York City. Mr. Wagner was the first incumbent NYC Mayor to have set foot in the CCBA.

In May of the following year, a Congressional group arrived in Chinatown. This was the first fact-finding mission from Capitol Hill. Five months later, on October 10th, a number of U.S. political and business leaders attended a gala party hosted by the CCBA at the Waldorf-Astoria in Midtown Manhattan, in celebration of the "Double 10th" National Day of the Republic of China. Also present were Governor K. C. Wu of Taiwan and Paul Cardinal Yupin of Taipei.

7. Is the CCBA linked to other organizations like yours in other cities? Yes. There are sister CCBA organizations in many of the major cities of the United States with large Chinese populations. In early 1957, we initiated the convocation of the first National Convention of Chinese in America. It was held in Washington, D.C., with 124 delegates attending from 35 cities.

The Convention called on all Chinese-Americans to strengthen solidarity, abide by the U.S. Constitution, and seek equality with other ethnic groups. It also called upon the U.S. Government to increase the immigration quota for China and for immigration officials to refrain from harassing Chinese immigrants without a warrant.

This Convention has since met every other year.

8. What educational facilities do you maintain? We have three levels of schools—for the young, the very young, and adults in Chinese and English.

- The New York Chinese School was founded in 1910, with the purpose of providing young Chinese in the United States with an opportunity to learn the language and culture of their ancestral land. Enrollment has multiplied from the initial two dozen to the present 3,000, ranging in levels from kindergarten to 12th grade. The school is open seven days a week. It also conducts classes in such specialized subjects as piano, Chinese music, painting, dance, handicrafts, and martial arts. The school's 70-member drum-and-fife corps is a Chinatown institution. It has been invited to perform at innumerable occasions inside and outside the community.

- The Chinatown Day Care Center was established in 1976 by the Chinese Service Center. When the Center ran into financial problem in 1987, the CCBA took over. The Day Care Center now has an enrollment of 200 toddlers each month.
- The CCBA English School for Adults opened in the fall of 1970 to meet the needs of an increasing number of newly arrived immigrants to learn English. In the beginning, 400 students were enrolled in 21 evening classes. Day classes were added during the 1980s. At present, the average monthly enrollment is between 400 and 500.
- The Cascades Center for Teaching & Learning is a special high school for new immigrants, who have been out of school owing to family or financial reasons. The first class opened in February 1998 with 100 students, ranging in ages from 17 to 20.

Chinese Consolidated Benevolent Association, http://ccbanyc.org/eaboutus.html#01.

S. S. RAMA RAO PAPPU AND J. K. BHATTACHARJEE

[Hindu traditions include the teaching of karma yoga—working for the welfare of the world without regard for personal reward, dedicating one's service as a form of worship. The Sanskrit word "dana" comes from the same root as the English "donate." The following appeal (to raise the awareness of fellow Bengalis in America regarding Hindu traditions of giving, encouraging them to be generous to worthy causes) to an immigrant Asian community hearkens to old cultural roots while seeking to explain current needs, urging community members to "give until it hurts." The first Asian to win the Nobel Prize for literature, Bengali poet Rabindranath Tagore of India, wrote: "Our society exists to remind us, through its various voices, that the ultimate truth in man is not in his intellect or his possessions; it is in his illumination of mind, in his extension of sympathy across all barriers of caste or color; in his recognition of the world, not merely as a storehouse of power, but as a habitation of man's spirit, with its eternal music of beauty and its inner light of the divine presence." Pappu and Bhattacharjee are professors at Miami University, Oxford, Ohio. They are members of the Indian immigrant community in America.]

Leadership in Giving: An Appeal for Philanthropy and Service by the Indian/Bengali Community [in America]

Recent studies of the Indian community show that, as an ethnic minority, the Indians in North America are excelling in the arts and sciences, medicine, education and business. The Indian community is also said to be one of the more prosperous and flourishing communities in America. As the first generation of Indians is graying, and the second generation is coming on its own, we must reflect on taking a leadership role in philanthropy, community service and volunteerism, fields largely neglected, if not ignored by us as a community.

The Importance of DANA in Indian Tradition: Dana (Sanskrit for "charity, sharing"), *asteya* ("non-possession"), *tyaga* ("sacrifice") and *samnyasa* ("life-renunciation") play an important role in the Indian life-world. *Tyaga, asteya* and *samnyasa* are considered *ideals,* and are therefore morally optional, whereas *dana* is morally *obligatory,* which everyone must engage in. It is said in the *Rig Veda* that "riches come now to one, now to another, and like the wheels of cars, are ever rolling" and "all guilt is he who eats with no partaker" (X. 117). According to *Mahabharata (Anusasanaparva),* one should spend one-third of one's possession for dharmic duties which include philanthropic acts like planting trees, digging wells, construction of poor homes, etc. There are many examples in the Hindu Scriptures such as Isa Upanishad, Bhagavad Gita, and Manusmriti which encourage philanthropy and volunteerism. In our own times, Mahatma Gandhi had adopted the lifestyle of *daridranarayana* (the poorest and lowliest) to emphasize the importance of *dana* in modern India. Other Indian leaders, like Sri Ramakrishna, Vivekananda and Vinoba Bhave advocated that in addition to service to humanity, a part of our wealth should be committed for the service of God, community and the preservation of our cultural and religious heritage

Philanthropy as an Obligation: From Ashoka to Gandhi, charity is considered a strict obligation. Dana or gifting is the method which the Indians have adopted from times immemorial to promote art, architecture, music, literature, philosophy, temple building, construction of dharmasalas (rest houses), hospitals for humans, birds and beasts. Imagine how poor Indian culture and civilization would have been, if there was no large-scale gifting activities by the kings and emperors, the rich and the business community. By their giving activities, Indians have also maintained a stable economic and social order. For gifting is the method of transfer of private ownership to communal ownership, from those who have to those who need. In return, gifting is also the means of attaining social reputation and honor. According to the Isa Upanishad everything that exists belongs to the Lord, and therefore one should enjoy by renunciation. While singing our aarati, we say *"tana mana dhana jo kuch hai sab hii hai teraa* etc. i.e. "O Lord, whatever I have—body, mind and wealth—belong to You, what do I lose by giving up everything which you have given to me and which does not belong to me."

The Need for Gifting by the Indian Americans: The duty of gifting by the Indian American community needs no emphasis because (i) we are all cultural ambassadors to the best Indian traditions and dana as an obligation does not cease when we leave the shores of India; (ii) as citizens of America, we are receivers from and beneficiaries of the American (economic) dream, but not "givers" in any adequate way; (iii) that by giving, we will be creating a stable multi-dimensional relationship with other ethnic groups and the community at large (imagine whether the "dot buster" movement would have arisen in New Jersey a few years ago if we had been engaged in social welfare programs also along with our business activities there); (iv) that we shall build our reputations in the Indian and American communities (like the Watumull family in Hawaii whose name is a household word there, or the Hinduja family which is well-known all over the world); (v) and finally by giving we will set a good example for our children to follow.

What is our fair share in gifting? "Give till it hurts" is the principle of dana. Dana unlike tyaga, aims at the minimum, not at the maximum. The concept of "hurting" may be interpreted as "the principle of least inconvenience." Thus, when our giving up anything does not involve something of great significance, but involves only minimal inconvenience, then we have an obligation to give that up for charitable purposes. For example, if giving up a beer, or eating out or buying an extra new dress, causes us only a minimal inconvenience, but will bring about a much larger good for someone, like feeding a hungry child from starvation, we have an obligation to donate the money so saved for dana. Dana, however, is more than gifting material goods *(dhana)*. It also includes offering physical and mental *(tana, mana)* support—physically helping and showing sympathy to those who are suffering and engaging in acts of compassion *(karuna)* to care for them. The beneficiaries of gifting our material possessions (dhana) are the poor, the "have nots," but everyone, poor and rich, can be the recipient of karuna. In the modern context, this includes volunteerism, community service, good samaritanship etc. Thus, following volunteerism and service, we have an obligation to utilize our time in alleviating suffering wherever it exists, in rich homes and poor homes alike.

How much and to whom shall we give? We should make a resolution, in the beginning of every year, as to how much we can give monetarily and in service activities. We should set our priorities between local (e.g. building a temple, a community hall) and global projects (e.g. building a school or hospital in India); projects which are of an emergency nature (famine relief in Sudan and hurricane relief in Florida, flood or earthquake relief in India) and those which benefit and enrich the culture of the community in the long run (construction of an Arts Center). We should find the right cause or project and ask if not us who, and if not now, when, we will support the project. Most people set up a part of their estate for charity, but by giving while living, one can see for oneself the results that make the difference.

(a) *Local Projects:* What project to select and how? Experts recommend that we support local credible projects and to be cautious of "mail order projects" (projects of unknown credibility), no matter how noble they may appear. Suggested local projects to volunteer our time and provide support for are: schools, Little League and colleges as booster, scholarships, mentoring disadvantaged students, special projects (civil and political) of the community; local hospitals, retirement homes, soup kitchens in downtowns (Cincinnati, Dayton), the United Way, Red Cross, Salvation Army, weekend free clinics by physicians, Indian community blood drive, etc. In our own backyard, the ongoing local projects of the Indian (Bengali) community include the Gandhi Jayanthi canned food drive for the Cincinnati Freestore Food Bank, temple projects, cultural and educational activities for our children; community Gandhi House in Dayton for homeless single mothers; Rabrindranath Tagore Chair and India Studies Center at Indiana University in Bloomington, Emergency Disaster relief, etc.

(b) *Global Projects:* Our global commitments should, to a large extent, include India but should not be limited to India, like helping in projects to alleviate the current famine situation in Sudan. Suggested projects for India, but not limited to are: the village literacy projects being pursued in Andhra Pradesh, share and care projects in Gujarat and elsewhere, the medical clinics of Dr. Vijayanagar, the Calcutta slum development project of Ramakrishna Mission, AIDS projects, free clinics by visiting physicians, free exchange of information and technical know-how by visiting researchers and entrepreneurs.

(c) *Examples for Children:* Such giving and services not only give us personal satisfaction and visibility/recognition in the local community, but will also provide our children with excellent examples for them to emulate and the donors act as role-models when they grow up.

(d) *Partnership with Community Groups:* Last, but not least, members of the Indian community should join appropriate local civic and service organizations such as the Lions Club, Kiwanis Club, Rotary Club and Jaycees to provide service, leadership, recognition, visibility and support to the local, national and international projects and needs.

Text by courtesy of Rama Rao Pappu and J. K. Bhattacharjee, 2006. Samanway, Bangamela (Bengali cultural/musical festival) brochure, Chicago: 2006.

SHARIQ SIDDIQUI

[Shariq Siddiqui is an Indianapolis lawyer and Ph.D. candidate in Philanthropic Studies at Indiana University-Purdue University in Indianapolis. When asked to compile a description of some of the active philanthropic and service organizations for Muslims in America, he gathered the following. The organizations named here, and many more besides, remind us that besides zakah, the tradition of giving to the poor, widows, and orphans, Muslims have a variety of ways of giving generously, cooperating, and coordinating resources to help others.]

Muslim Charitable Organizations

Islam suggests that the best form of giving would be the kind that is given at the right time for the right reason for the right cause. The Prophet echoes this when he states, "There is no envy except in two things: a person whom Allah has given wealth and he spends it, all, in the proper way, and a person whom Allah has given wisdom and he uses it in judgment and teaches it." Sunnah Islam has specific guidelines on how one can give charity to obtain approval from God. "If ye disclose acts of charity it is well but if ye hide them and give them to the poor that is best for you, and will remove from you some of your stains of evil. And Allah is well acquainted with what ye do" (Quran II.271). God knows our intent and gives us credit for good intent. If the motivation behind giving is glory or material gain, it defeats the spiritual purpose of the gift. Rather than helping the giver, it hurts in spiritual terms. Furthermore, while it is permissible to give publicly, it is preferable to give anonymously.

Connecting Muslims with others relies on the power of association. Muslims have established numerous organizations in the United States for the support of those who practice the Islam faith as well as to educate Muslims and non-Muslims alike in the tenets and values of Islam. The Islamic Society of North America is considered to be the largest Muslim organization in North America. Its annual convention brings together over thirty-five thousand American Muslims. The Islamic Assembly of North America also promotes the understanding of Muslim teachings in America and serves English-speaking Muslims. Many associations support Muslims from specific heritages. The Islamic Circle of North America is an organization of Indian and Pakistani families in America; Muslim American Society members are primarily Arab American. The membership of Mosque Cares is primarily African American as is the Nation of Islam's, composed of followers of Minister Farakhan and followers of Elijah Muhammad.

Advocacy to advance the understanding of Islam and the rights of Muslims is also an important effort. The Council of American Islamic Relations is the largest civil-rights advocacy organization in America, and the MAS Freedom Foundation is the civil-rights and media wing of the Muslim American Society. The Muslim Public Affairs Council focuses on engaging the American government and media to bring forth the American Muslim perspective, while the American Muslim Alliance is committed to establishing grass-roots organizations to increase American Muslims involvement in politics.

Hundreds of other organizations promote the educational objectives of Muslims in this country as well as bring relief to Muslims in need both here and around the world. Other associations serve youth, support professionals, and connect Muslims in various ways with others in their community.

Shariq Siddiqui is a lawyer and Ph.D. student in philanthropic studies at IUPUI.

MORMON SERVICE PROJECT (2005)

[Clean-up and recovery work after a catastrophe is a challenging kind of service. One leaves behind the orderly routines of one's own world and enters a transitional world of loss and trauma. The following describes the experience of a Mormon group working to help victims of Hurricane Katrina, which slammed Louisiana and Mississippi in 2005. Mormon charities are extensive—this is just one example. Other groups also gave their time and energy to this crisis. Chainsaws and brooms, pickup trucks and shovels, ladders and backhoes—many tools were used and herculean tasks performed. We seldom hear about these work crews, but what it means to one person or one family to be rescued and helped in a traumatic time is something very great and often cannot be put into words.]

Hurricane Katrina Chainsaw Brigade[†]

Latter-day Saints to Mobilize Another 4,000 Volunteers in Chainsaw Brigade's Second Wave

SALT LAKE CITY, Sept. 16 [2005] The buzz of chainsaws will again fill the air this weekend as thousands of volunteers from The Church of Jesus Christ of Latter-day Saints descend on the Gulf Coast to help victims of Hurricane Katrina.

Setting aside their weekday routines as bankers, accountants, contractors, attorneys, managers, dentists, retirees, students and salesmen, volunteers are on their way to Louisiana and Mississippi in carpools and buses, bringing with them tents, sleeping bags, food, water, clothing, chainsaws, ladders and even backhoes.

These volunteers, dubbed the "chainsaw warriors," are expected to drive late into the night from their homes in Alabama, Florida, Georgia, Louisiana, South Carolina and Texas.

By Saturday morning tent cities will again surround Latter-day Saint chapels in Collins, Columbia, Covington, Gulfport, Hattiesburg, LaPlace, Laurel, Meridian, Pascagoula, Picayune, Slidell and Waveland.

In the days immediately preceding the mobilization, Church leaders from the volunteers' home congregations divided them into crews and gave them instruction, while

† Title is the author's own.

those at the points of destination identified community residents in greatest need and drafted work orders in preparation for an early start the next day.

The volunteers will work through the daylight hours on Saturday and to midday on Sunday, cutting and clearing debris from fallen trees and covering damaged roofs with tarps to prevent water damage as residents await insurance settlements and repairs.

Last weekend volunteers cleared literally thousands of yards in a mission of mercy. As of Monday evening, a tally of the Church's combined volunteer efforts in hurricane-stricken areas included 9,204 man-days and 4,832 work orders, providing assistance to over 4,800 people.

"I don't think that we've ever had that kind of effort in a sustained way," said Elder D. Todd Christofferson (a member of the Presidency of the Seventy, one of the bodies that provide leadership to the worldwide Church from its headquarters in Salt Lake City, Utah). The ongoing relief effort to which he referred began as soon as the receding storm allowed trucks loaded with relief supplies to enter the stricken areas. "And it's not the end," he promised.

Over the next two weekends, Latter-day Saint congregations in Alabama, Arkansas, Florida, Georgia, Louisiana, North Carolina and Texas have committed an additional 4,000 weekend workers to the ongoing cleanup and relief effort, which will extend to some areas hardest hit by Katrina that are only gradually becoming accessible to volunteer work crews. Another 1,800 will follow over three weekends in October.

Behind the numbers lie the individuals. Tales of struggle and survival emerged as the visitors and local residents worked side by side in the cleanup effort:

- Chelsey (age 7 and an energetic helper with the debris removal) and James Barron (10) of Hattiesburg, Mississippi, spoke animatedly of their experience in the hurricane, with its loud wind, "limbs flying around," the crash of the wall that surrounded their property that "sounded like dynamite," and the "scary" time when a tree—one of several that was to litter their property—fell onto their home.

- A Hattiesburg mother, whose battle with multiple sclerosis makes her particularly susceptible to the loss of power in the oppressive late-summer heat, has chosen to stay with her family and help with the cleanup, which seemed an insurmountable task after the magnitude of the work led to the demise of both of the family's chainsaws.

- An observer of a crew's labors in Petal, Mississippi, asked if they would be able to clear the debris from the yard of that town's police chief, who had been too busy helping others in the storm's aftermath to clean up his own property; that became their next stop.

- A grandmother raising her three grandchildren in a beautifully kept mobile home outside of Toomsuba, Mississippi, found her life disrupted when a falling tree tore a floor-to-roof gash in its back wall, rendering it uninhabitable for the children—until the "Mormon Helping Hands" crew, working well past sunset, provided the necessary stopgap repair that allowed the children to return.

At the same time that their chainsaws were taking apart fallen trees, the Latter-day Saint volunteers forged bonds with people of other faiths.

- A Baptist family in Mississippi, surprised at the offer of help from a Latter-day Saint work crew, named the mountain of debris that they and their newfound friends from Georgia jointly hauled to their curbside their "Mormon pile."

• In Louisiana, after losing two trucks, a fully stocked freezer and more in the flooding that accompanied the hurricane and forced her family's evacuation, Slidell Harts United Methodist Church member Mildred Eden found her attempt to return to her home thwarted by a jumble of fallen trees and wires spread across her yard and driveway. "You are the best thing that has happened to me since the hurricane," she said. "I'm a volunteer, so when we get back in our home and you need help, I'll help you."

That spirit of reciprocity played out repeatedly, with people of other denominations contributing spontaneously to the effort.

• As one crew was cutting and clearing debris from a home in Picayune, Mississippi, a neighbor pulled up with his four-wheel drive and front-end loader. After moving the accumulating debris to the curbside with his loader, he exclaimed, "You go back and tell your group that Mr. Seal from the Pine Grove Baptist Church helped you."

• A United Methodist congregation in Slidell, Louisiana, allowed volunteers descending on that community from Houston, Texas, to sleep in their church. When the local congregants arrived at their church on Sunday, they found the debris cleared from their churchyard and their hurricane-damaged flag mounted as a keepsake while a bright new banner flew from the flagpole. In a shared worship service, the pastor voiced a feeling of unity shared by those of both denominations: "The Mormons are now our friends."

"When I hear these stories, I am humbled by the tremendous service that is being rendered between people of all faiths," said Elder John S. Anderson, director of the Church's Emergency Operations Center in Slidell, which coordinates the relief effort throughout the Southeast. "We are all children of God, and that's what matters."

As volunteer workers and those they were assisting bade farewell, a common realization emerged that all parties involved were beneficiaries. A crew leaving the home of an elderly couple in Meridian, Mississippi, after removing the debris from several large trees that had fallen in their yard, reported hearing their last tearful "thank-yous" as they pulled away.

"Before last weekend, most of us had experienced the satisfaction of contributing money to relief agencies," said B. Jeffrey Strebar, bishop of the Whitewater congregation near Atlanta, Georgia. "But the pure joy of looking into the tear-filled eyes of those whose lives have been so overwhelmingly altered was an experience that will never be forgotten."

Church of Jesus Christ of Latter-day Saints, http://www.prnewswire.com/cgi-bin/stories. pl?ACCT=104&STORY=/www/story/09-16-2005/0004109396&EDATE= (September 17, 2005, PR Newswire Association LLC).

CHARMAYNE "CHARLI" SHAW AND JOHNNY FLYNN

[*Native American leaders have been active in ecological and community-oriented philanthropic activities for generations. Rebecca Adamson, a Cherokee social entrepreneur, for example, is the founder of First Nations Development Institute and president of First Peoples Worldwide. There are national Indian organizations such as Native Americans in Philanthropy, which operates The Native Philanthropy Institute. There are also a large number of local Native American organizations helping solve problems and serving peoples' needs at the grass-roots level; the following group is but one example. Charli Shaw is president of the Native American Student Alliance, and Johnny Flynn, a Potawatami Indian, is a professor of Religious Studies at IUPUI. The organization described below, I-NASHEN, is a nonprofit group of students, faculty, staff, and interested parties formed to advocate on behalf of Native American educational issues in Indiana. Teaching about Native American traditional values to current and future generations involves the marshalling of resources for education so that children grow up knowing their people's history and identity. Without teachers' dedicated service to the community, key treasures of heritage are in danger of being lost.]*

I-NASHEN (Indiana-Native American Scholars in Higher Education Network)

I-NASHEN is a not-for-profit organization set up in Indiana after the first Native American Education conference was held at Indiana University Purdue University Indianapolis (IUPUI) in late September 2006. The principal purpose of I-NASHEN is to advocate for the development of programs and services for and about Native Americans in the educational system K–12 and in Higher Education in the state of Indiana. However, since its original formation in a series of meetings in the Fall of 2006, the organization has the potential to expand its commitment throughout the United States.

There are more treaties with the Indian tribes native to Indiana than in any other state, more than thirty with the Miami, Potawatomi, Shawnee, Delaware, Wea, Chippewa, Ottawa, Mahican, Seneca, and other bands. With the exception of some of the treaties that drove most of the tribes out of the state, Indian leaders in those days consistently identified the development of educational facilities for Indians as one of their primary goals. Now, nearly two hundred years after the last series of treaties, the state of Indiana and the Federal government still have not fulfilled those promises.

Members of I-NASHEN have identified three goals which address the issues of Indian education in Indiana.

1. The development of programs of instruction, tutoring, and other vital services for the Indian students of Indiana in grades K–12. Along with those programs for Indians, public schools in Indiana need to address the lack of curriculum regarding the long history of Indian nations in the state. More than fifteen thousand years of Indian history and culture receives little or no notice in the K–12 curriculum and I-NASHEN intends to address that glaring discrepancy in the education of Indian and non-Indian students.

2. The development of outreach to all tribes to recruit Native American students and faculty into the Indiana system of Higher Education. Recruiting students and faculty into Higher Education is directed principally, but not limited to, state sponsored schools in the Indiana University system.

3. The development of courses, programs, and departments of Native American studies in the Indiana system of Higher Education. In order to address the need for curriculum at the K–12 level of Indiana's educational system, we need the resources to inform teachers and leaders of the future regarding Native American contributions to American history and culture.

Currently, I-NASHEN is seeking 501(c)(3) status as a non-profit organization with the ability to raise and administer funds devoted to the development of a network of students, faculty, and staff of like minds regarding American Indian education here in the state of Indiana. Membership or affiliation with I-NASHEN is not limited to Native American ancestry but is open to all people, regardless of ethnicity or educational backgrounds.

Courtesy of Johnny Flynn and Charmayne Shaw, IUPUI, May 2007. Used with permission.

THE LIFE AND WORKS OF PHILANTHROPISTS

On JULIUS ROSENWALD (1862–1932)

[Julius Rosenwald, the son of Jewish immigrants, is best known as a business executive, part-owner and leader of Sears, Roebuck and Company, and for his philanthropic activities. The Rosenwald Fund gave millions to support the education of African Americans. The idea that doing good and helping others helps oneself is found in various American philanthropic ventures. As seen below in Daniel Boorstin's reflections on philanthropy in the life of Rosenwald, the works of a generous person offer lessons in themselves. More recent major Jewish philanthropists in America include Eli and Edythe Broad, Dora Donner Ide, Edmond Safra, Laurence Tisch, Judah Touro, and Gene and Marilyn Glick. The Talmudic injunction "Justice, justice you shall seek" is interpreted to mean one should seek justice and well-being for oneself, and justice and well-being for others as well.]

From Conscience to Community by Daniel J. Boorstin

There are few better illustrations of this central concept—perhaps it might better be called a sentiment—in American life than the history of American philanthropy. And there has been no more effective exponent of the community spirit in philanthropy than Julius Rosenwald, the centennial of whose birth was celebrated on October 15, 1962. I will not try to tell the story of Rosenwald's philanthropies. I will, rather, describe some of the distinctiveness of certain American developments and show how Julius Rosenwald participated in them.

Philanthropy or charity throughout much of European history has been a predominantly private virtue. In most of Western Europe the national states and their organs were elaborated before the needs of modern industrial society came into being. The state and its organs had therefore preempted most of the areas of public benevolence, improvement, education, and progress even before the appearance of the great fortunes which modern industry made possible. The creators of the modern state—for example, Queen Elizabeth I in England, Napoleon in France, and Bismarck in Germany—developed arms of the state to do more and more jobs of public service, public enrichment, public enlightenment, and cultural and scientific progress. The charitable spirit was a kind of residuum; it inevitably tended to become the spirit of almsgiving. Of course, everybody was required to contribute by taxes or gifts to state or church institutions. But because the state—and its ancient partner, the church—had taken over the business of wholesale philanthropy, the independent charities of wealthy men were generally left to alleviating the distress of the particular individuals whom they noticed.

By the nineteenth century in France *or* Italy—even in England—it was by no means easy, though one had the means and the desire, to found a new university (the legislature might not charter it; it might confuse or compete against the state-organized system; it might become a center of "revolutionary" or of "reactionary" ideology; etc.), a new museum, or a new research institute. The right to establish new institutions, like the right to bear arms, was jealously guarded by the sovereign, which, of course, usually meant the single national government at the center.

Meanwhile Christian teachings had long exalted the spirit of charity and the practice of almsgiving. "If thou wilt be perfect, go and sell that thou hast, and give to the poor, and thou shalt have treasure in heaven: and come and follow me . . . Verily I say unto you, that a rich man shall hardly enter into the kingdom of heaven" (Matt 19:21-23); "Knowledge puffeth up, but charity edifieth" (1 Cor 8:1); "And now abideth faith, hope, charity, these three; but the greatest of these is charity" (1 Cor 13:13). Charity ennobled the giver; it was more blessed to give than to receive.

The first characteristic of the traditional charitable spirit, then, was that it was private and personal. This fact has made difficulties for scholars trying to chronicle philanthropy, especially outside the United States. Donors have often been reluctant to make known the size (whether because of the smallness or the largeness) of their donations. They have sometimes feared that signs of their wealth might bring down on them a host of the poor, confiscatory demands from the tax farmer, or jealousy from the sovereign. For more reasons than one, therefore, charity, which was a salve for the conscience, became an innermost corner of consciousness, a sanctum of privacy. A man's charities were a matter between him and his God. Church and conscience might be intermediaries, but the community did not belong in the picture.

Second, the traditional charitable spirit was perpetual, unchanging, and even in a certain sense, rigid. "The poor," said Jesus, "ye always have with you" (John 12:8). The almsgiver was less likely to be trying to solve a problem of this world than to be earning his right to enter into the next. There hardly seemed to be any problem of means or of purpose. Since it was always a greater virtue to give than to receive, the goodness of charity came more from the motive of the giver than from the effect of the gift. Only a hypocrite, a proud man, or one impure of heart would hesitate while he chose among the objects of the gift.

The philanthropic spirit as it has developed, changed, flourished, and become peculiarly institutionalized in America, has been very different. In some respects it has even been opposed to these two characteristics of the time-honored virtue. Here, again, the dominant note, the pervading spirit, the peculiar characteristic, has been a preoccupation with community. This transformation of the charitable spirit has been expressed in at least three peculiarly American emphases.

1. Community Enrichment: The Purposes of Philanthropy

The focus of American philanthropy has shifted from the giver to the receiver, from the salving of souls to the solving of problems, from conscience to community. No one better expressed this spirit than Julius Rosenwald, when he said: "In the first place 'philanthropy' is a sickening word. It is generally looked upon as helping a man who hasn't a cent in the world. That sort of thing hardly interests me. I do not like the 'sob stuff' philanthropy. What I want to do is to try to cure the things that seem to be wrong. I do not underestimate the value of helping the underdog. That, however, is not my chief concern but rather the operation of cause and effect. I try to do the thing that will aid groups and masses rather than individuals."

This view, which we should probably call (in William James's phrase) "tough minded" rather than hardhearted, has long dominated what has been the peculiarly American charitable spirit.

The patron saint of American philanthropy is not Dorothea Dix or any other saintly person but rather Benjamin Franklin, the man with a business sense and an eye on his community. For Franklin, doing good was not a private act between bountiful giver and grateful receiver; it was a prudent social act. A wise act of philanthropy would sooner or later benefit the giver along with all other members of the community. While living in Philadelphia, Franklin developed philanthropic enterprises which included projects for establishing a city police, for the paving and the better cleaning and lighting of city streets, for a circulating library, for the American Philosophical Society for Useful Knowledge, for an Academy for the Education of Youth (origin of the University of Pennsylvania), for a debating society, and for a volunteer fire department.

Like Julius Rosenwald, Franklin did not go in for "sob-stuff philanthropy." Few, if any, of his enterprises were primarily for the immediate relief of distress or misfortune. Notice, also, that in Franklin's mind and in his activities the line between public and private hardly existed. If an activity was required and was not yet performed by a government—by city, state, or nation—he thought it perfectly reasonable that individuals club together to do the job, not only to fill the gap, but also to prod or shame governments into doing their part. A large number, but by no means all, of his activities have been taken over by the municipality of Philadelphia, the state of Pennsylvania, or the federal government. From this point of view the important thing was not whether the job was done by government or by individuals: both governments and individuals were agencies of community. The community was the thing. Notice also that Franklin's opportunity to step into the breach with community enterprises arose in large part because the community was relatively new, because state activities were still sparse—in a word, because the community existed before the government. . . .

2. Community Participation: The Means of Philanthropy

While, as we have just observed, the focus of American philanthropy has shifted from giver to receiver, there has occurred another equally important shift in point of view. The clear lines between the roles of the giver and the receiver, which in the traditional European situation were so distinct, in America became blurred. In an American equalitarian, enterprising, fluid society the ancient contrasts between the bountiful rich and the grateful poor, the benefactor and the beneficiary, on which the almsgiving situation had depended, became obsolete. In America a community—the ultimate beneficiary—was increasingly expected to be its own benefactor. The recipient here (who became more difficult to identify as a member of a fixed social class) was now viewed less as a target of individual generosity than as an integral part of the social capital, an item of community investment.

It is not surprising, then, that the time-honored notion that it is more blessed to give than to receive, like some other ancient fixed axioms of charity, began to be dissolved. When you no longer believe the ancient axiom that the "poor are always with you," a recipient is no longer a member of a permanent social class. So far did we move from the old notion; now the ideal recipient of philanthropy was himself viewed as a potential donor. Just as the value of a charitable gift tended to be judged less by the motive of the giver than by the social effect of the gift, so the suitability of a recipient was judged less by his emotional response, his gratitude or his personal loyalty to a benefactor than by his own potential contribution to the community. A free citizen who receives assistance is no mere receptacle of benevolence; he prepares himself to become a fountain of benevolence.

By a twist of New World circumstances, by the transformation of the charitable spirit, in the United States it often happened that those who received most from an act of philanthropy were also those who gave most. Julius Rosenwald, and some other characteristically American philanthropists, have viewed this as the ideal philanthropic situation. Take, for example, a scene in Boligee, Alabama, in the winter of 1916–17. This was one of the so-called arousement meetings to raise money from the local Negro community to meet Julius Rosenwald's offer of a matching sum to build a simple schoolhouse. We are fortunate to have an eyewitness account:

> We gathered together in a little old rickety building, without any heat, only from an old rusty stove with the stove pipe protruding out of the window where a pane had been removed for the flue . . . The Farmers had been hard hit that year as the boll weevil had figured very con-spicuously in that community, and most of the people were tenants on large plantations. When we reached the scene where the rally was to be staged, the teacher with thirty-five or forty little children had prepared a program which consisted of plantation melodies . . . They sang with such fervor and devotion, until one could hardly restrain from crying . . . The patrons and friends were all rural people, and crudely dressed. The women had on home spun dresses and aprons, while the men in the main were dressed in blue overalls. Their boots and shoes were very muddy, as they had to trudge through the mud from three to four miles . . . When the speaking was over we arranged for the silver offering, and to tell the truth I thought we would do well to collect ten dollars from the audience; but when the Master of Cer-emonies, Rev. M. D. Wallace, who had ridden a small mule over the county through the cold and through the rain, organizing the people, began to call the collection the people began to respond. You would have been over-awed with emotion if you could have seen those poor people walking up to the table, emptying their pockets for a school . . . One old man, who had seen slavery days, with all of his life's earnings in an old greasy sack, slowly drew it from his pocket, and emptied it on the table. I have never seen such a pile of nickels, pennies, dimes, and dollars, etc., in my life. He put thirty-eight dollars on the table, which was his entire savings.

These were the people who would benefit most from the Rosenwald gift, yet they were the people who in proportion to their means were giving most.

Someone with less faith in his fellow men might simply have given the sums out-right without asking any matching funds, for the Negroes of Alabama were surely depressed and underprivileged. In a recent previous year, when the state of Alabama had appropriated $2,865,254 for public education, only $357,585, or less than 15 percent, went to Negro schools—this despite the fact that Negroes made up about half the population of the state. Rosenwald had faith in the Negroes of Alabama—not only in their potentiality but, still more important, in their present determination and their ability to help themselves.

By the time of his death, Rosenwald had contributed to the construction of 5,357 public schools, shops, and teachers' homes in 883 counties of fifteen southern states at a total cost of $28,408,520. Julius Rosenwald's personal contribution was monumental: $4,366,519. But a fact of which he would have been still prouder was that his contribution had induced others to contribute still more. . . .

3. Adaptation to Community: The Flexibility of Philanthropy

Faith, hope, and charity were as changeless as God or human nature, but philanthropy must change with its community. American philanthropists were citizens of fast-growing cities with shifting populations, novel enterprises, and as speedy an obsolescence of social problems as of everything else. To do their job, they had to keep their eyes open and their feet on the ground. They had to be alert to new needs which required new investments by everybody in a progressive community.

Julius Rosenwald, who had grown up with the West and with Chicago, was well aware of all this. He warned vain men against seeking immortality by attaching their names to institutions; he reminded them of Nesselrode, "who lived a diplomat, but is immortal as a pudding."

Rosenwald never tired of pointing to the dangers of rigid philanthropy, of gifts in perpetuity for unchanging purposes, which might become a burden rather than a blessing. Since Julius Rosenwald's day, two new kinds of problems in the application of the American community ideal to philanthropic institutions have become acute. The first has arisen from the vast foundations which appeared in the first decades of our century. While in many respects these foundations were squarely in the American tradition which I have described, they faced new problems and themselves created some. Many of these are not unrelated to the dangers against which Julius Rosenwald warned, although they arise from some opposite causes. The perpetuities, the rigidities, and the bureaucracies against which Rosenwald inveighed were in charities whose purposes were too specific and hence likely are extremely general in their purpose. The public dangers which arise from them come precisely from the fact that there is no prospect that they will ever become obsolete. The Ford Foundation's purpose is to serve the public welfare.

Spontaneity, drift, fluidity, and competition among American institutions have given our future much of its vitality. Some of the dangers which come from the new large foundations spring from the very vagueness and generality of their purposes as well as from their sheer size. They have already become powerful, independent, self-perpetuating institutions. They are in the wholesale (some might say the "mail-order") philanthropy business. Instead of encouraging latent energies in the community, they are naturally tempted to initiate projects; and the more spectacular and more novel are often most attractive from a public relations point of view. They show few signs of that self-liquidating tendency that Rosenwald rightly insisted to be a feature of a healthy foundation. The entry into our language of certain phrases is a clue to the changing spirit of our large-scale philanthropy and to the new dangers. We all have heard of the "foundation executive"—a person who makes his living from administering philanthropy, from inventing, developing, and publicizing worthy projects. He is often a refugee from academic life; he is seldom underpaid (at least by academic standards); ideally, he is a person of driving energy, of aggressive organizing power, and of all the affable virtues. He is a new breed of the American college president, another expert on things in general, who has the new advantage of being able to exert his affability on the disbursement rather than on the collection of funds. But some might ask whether one such breed is not enough and perhaps all that our culture can stand. Amusement is sometimes expressed by professors when they find themselves solemnly presenting their appeals for support of their research to foundation officials who left university life precisely because they were unable to produce research which satisfied these very same professors.

Another telltale phrase which has entered our vocabulary is the so-called "foundation project." Generally speaking, a foundation project must be collaborative; it must have defined and predictable results; it must be noncontroversial; and yet it must have some popular interest. The fact that we in academic life know what kind of project will appeal or will not appeal to the foundations is one of the worst things that can be said about them. Generally speaking, instead of being an incentive to the initiative of individuals or communities, our largest foundations have tended to foster (as, indeed, they created) the vogue for concocted projects cast in the foundation mold. Thus foundations become freezing agents in the world of scholarship and of community projects. Their proper role is as catalyst.

Daniel J. Boorstin, *The Decline of Radicalism*. New York: Random House, 1963, 52–67.

On HELEN KELLER (1880–1968)

[Helen Keller became ill at nineteen months and lost her sight and hearing. Her mother pursued authorities in the field (including Alexander Graham Bell) and found the best help to educate her. Helen overcame great obstacles in her struggle to learn and is a symbol of hope and realization of human potential. She earned a B.A. degree from Radcliffe College in 1904. She wrote reflections such as: "I long to accomplish a great and noble task, but it is my chief duty to accomplish small tasks as if they were great and noble. . . . Although the world is full of suffering, it is also full of the overcoming of it. . . . Optimism is the faith that leads to achievement. Nothing can be done without hope or confidence. . . . It is hard to interest those who have everything in those who have nothing. . . . Until the great mass of the people shall be filled with the sense of responsibility for each other's welfare, social justice can never be attained." For inspiration and understanding, Helen Keller studied the world's philosophers and religious thinkers, including the spiritual teachings of Immanuel Swedenborg, whose work also influenced John Chapman, William Blake, Coleridge and Emerson, Charles Sanders Peirce and William James. The following account evokes some of the generous and courageous spirit of this celebrated American.]

Helen Keller [An Example of Courageous Human Spirit]
by C. W. B.

One of Helen Keller's most touching observations was that, due to her double handicap, conversations with God were quite often easier than discourse with man, and this might be why she availed herself of the opportunity to participate in them. That the participation had been elevating no one could doubt who ever entered her consciousness for conversation—even fleetingly.

Helen Keller directed the attention of her friends on the right to action for social justice; the attention of her friends on the left to the idea of God and the soul. Each had a tendency to prefer and covet the sacrament she offered the other. As the world descended more deeply year by year into doubt and cynicism, it was little short of irksome to her liberal friends that Helen Keller never doubted that her Maker would ultimately take her unto Himself in a new dimension of life. Yet it was quite plain to them also she was already much larger than life as we know it. . . .

. . . Early in the century Helen Keller's espousal of social justice caused her to dream dreams and think thoughts which few Americans dared to dream or think at the time. A good few people, who were drifting into the illusion that they were Helen Keller's brains, hastened to prove they were not when she advanced into areas of conflict for which they had no taste and which they could not believe a woman who was "both deaf and blind" could comprehend. It was quite amusing how preoccupied with her "deafness" and "blindness" people became when she disagreed with them. . . .

Toward the end of her book *Midstream*, written in 1929, there is a chapter entitled, "Thoughts That Will Not Let Me Sleep," among the most important and discerning chapters in American literature. She says, "I know it would be an advantage to express my disapproval with captivating grace. If I could deliver my indictments with an urbanity so exquisite that every reader would feel implicitly exempted from the charge, and feel free to relish the strokes administered to the rest, this chapter would be more enjoyed."

Figure 4.8 Photo of Helen Keller

She then goes on to write a bill of particulars with respect to poverty and social justice in 1929, which only the most forward-looking American newspapers have managed to get onto their editorial pages in the 60s.

In the midst of this comes a paragraph: "I love my country. To say that is like saying I love my family. I did not choose my country any more than I chose my parents, but I am her daughter just as I am truly the child of my Southern mother and father. What I am my country has made me. She has fostered the Spirit which made my education possible. Neither Greece nor Rome, nor all China, nor Germany, nor Great Britain has surrounded a deaf-blind child with the devotion and skill and resources which have been mine in America.

"But my love of America is not blind. Perhaps I am more conscious of her faults because I love her so deeply. Nor am I blind to my own faults. It is easy to see there is little virtue in the old formulas, and that new ones must be found. . . ."

This, so long as she was physically able to maintain direct communication with the world, was the essence of Helen Keller. It is not fair to her memory to recall only her "captivating grace," so spontaneous and puzzling to her self, which she feared would mask her profound ethical, moral and mystical observations.

"C.W.B." wrote this obituary in 1968. Printed copy found among the Clara Barton papers at the National Archives, College Park, Maryland, Box 1, folder 004.

On JULIAN PRICE (1941–2001)

[Asheville, North Carolina, entered a phase of revitalization in the 1990s, a process that transformed it into a cultural oasis and a favorite tourist destination. Those formative years brought new investors in Asheville's business future. Artists and craftspeople were drawn there, and the picturesque town developed as a retirement haven. The city's cultural life was renewed and intensified, its reputation greatly enhanced. Businessman and visionary Julian Price was at the forefront of Asheville's transformation and development. Other towns across the nation might look to Price's work as an object lesson in how revitalization happens.]

Julian Price, Visionary Business and Civic Investor

A native of Greensboro, North Carolina, Julian Price grew up in the Irving Park neighborhood, attended public schools, and then went to Woodbury Forest, Virginia, private high school and Guilford College. Julian spent the next twenty years in Oregon and California. While there, he generously gave seed money for environmental causes too risky for most, while he worked for $3.50 an hour at a photo lab. He built two houses, the first one with the help of his then-wife Barbara Stanley and their neighbor. He grew and sold organic vegetables and marketed English seaweed fertilizer. He produced and distributed cutting-edge public-radio interviews, with people such as a former Grand Dragon of the KKK who helped integrate Durham, North Carolina, schools and a man who helped "unskilled" people in an economically depressed part of North Carolina to begin and run a successful shitake mushroom business.

When Julian decided to return to North Carolina, he thought he was going to move to New Bern and had put down a deposit on a house there. But when in Asheville, as he walked down Walnut Street between two big empty buildings, he was overcome with emotion and knew that Asheville would be his new home. Those two buildings would later become crown jewels of his firm, Public Interest Projects: the Malaprops Bookstore with apartments above it and the Smith-Carrier Condominiums. Two months after moving to town, Julian went to the French Broad Food Coop's Open House and there met his soon-to-be-sweetheart and wife Meg MacLeod.

From his apartment home in the heart of downtown Asheville, Julian used his experience and distinct perspective to invest time and resources in local businesses and nonprofit organizations and the people who run them. [He made] countless contributions between 1990 and 2001.

* * *

Change is always accompanied by controversy and by energy that some read as tumult and others read as positive energy. The period of the 1990s in Asheville has been a model of how energetic individuals can shape community and can turn the lethargy of tradition into a vibrant and thriving cultural milieu. Julian Price was a central figure in reshaping Asheville. His numerous initiatives stand at the center of many of the significant cultural shifts the city has seen in the last two decades.

Change can not be effected without capital. The 1990s was a period when considerable capital flowed into Asheville's cultural rebirth. The generous philanthropic and civic contributions of individuals like Julian Price and others came at a time in our nation's history that allowed for great freedom of creative expression and development. Asheville's reputation as a counterculture stimulated individual creativity, and many of the cities finest galleries, art museums, theaters, music, and civic projects grew out of this youthful creative wellspring and the growing and generous retirement community. This diverse influx of people contributed money and civic involvement to shape "their" community. Julian Price is among those vibrant and visionary individuals whose contributions have left a lasting legacy. Julian's legacy is Asheville's reconstruction in the 1990s and continuing today. His gentle vision and kind generosity helped to give Asheville an aura that is unique and comfortable. Julian Price wanted to "come home again," and he helped to make Asheville the kind of place that many would want to call home.

The Julian Price papers [at the University of North Carolina] are a record of Asheville's evolution during the 1990s and Julian's contributions to that evolution. Collectively, the papers are a comprehensive record for anyone wishing to document and study the rebirth and revitalization of a small city in the American southeast and the role of individual advocacy and philanthropy. It is a record for the public who may be interested in specific civic projects in Asheville, in Julian Price, and in the process of community advocacy, creativity, and community building.

University of North Carolina at Asheville, D. H. Ramsey Library, Special Collections/University Archives—Julian Price Papers (1941–2001). Partially transcribed from the Memorial Service for Julian Price, December 9, 2001.

On THOMAS G. COUSINS

[A housing project that moves from illness to health plays a key role in helping others make a better life and a better America. East Lake Meadows in Atlanta, Georgia, was in material disrepair and social dysfunction, in dire need of remedies. Thomas G. Cousins, with faith and vision, started the transformation. The real-estate businessman initiated the effort through his family foundation and showed that there are viable solutions for solving the problems of public housing and demoralizing inner-city conditions. Through Cousins' efforts, the health of the total community was vastly improved—with decent housing, full employment, strong after-school programs, as well as facilities for recreation and other necessities of life. This success story is an example of what is possible. Cousins shows how wise investments in the future of our nation's communities can make all the difference in the world.]

The Transformation of East Lake Meadows
by Philippa Strum

In 1995, the East Lake Meadows housing project was among the worst places in the United States to live. Its crime rate was 3.3 times higher than the rest of Atlanta and 18 times higher than the national average. The neighborhood experienced an average of one murder a week. As Mayor Shirley Franklin commented, in a program organized by the Division of U.S. Studies and cosponsored by the Comparative Urban Studies

Project, it was the only neighborhood in Atlanta she would not drive through alone. Its median household income was $4,536. Fifty-nine percent of the adults living in East Lake Meadows were on welfare. Its employment rate was 13.5 percent, and only five percent of the fifth graders at its elementary school met state mathematics standards. Sixty percent of its housing units did not meet safety and sanity standards; 30 percent were uninhabitable. City officials referred to the neighborhood as "Little Viet Nam."

Today, violent crime in East Lake is down by 95 percent. Only five percent of its adults rely on welfare. While 69 percent of all Atlanta public school system students meet or exceed state math standards, the figure for East Lake's Charles R. Drew Charter School is 78 percent, and 80 percent of its eighth graders meet or exceed state reading standards. Not a single recent graduate of the Drew school has dropped out of high school. As an East Lake resident and activist in its neighborhood association has commented, "We tore down hell and built heaven."

The change was made possible by the East Lake Foundation, an entity organized to transform and revitalize East Lake. The endeavor was the idea of Thomas G. Cousins, an Atlanta businessman who realized that successful urban renewal depended upon a holistic approach. Working with members of the East Lake community, the Foundation tore down the substandard public housing and replaced it with small mixed-income rental apartment buildings organized around crescent-shaped streets. It turned Drew Elementary School into a charter school and housed it in a bright, light-filled building connected to a YMCA that is used by the community for both recreation and meetings. The community has an early childhood learning center, playgrounds, senior citizen programs, and job skills programs. Its renewal has also transformed the surrounding neighborhood, as the median home value has jumped from $47,000 to $153,000.

The project's success, the panelists agreed, stems in large part from its holistic approach, combining attractive and well-maintained housing, education, and family services. Former Mayor William Hudnut of Indianapolis, Indiana, and Chevy Chase, Maryland, spoke about the need for mixed-income housing as a major element in urban renewal, emphasizing that it can be both profitable for investors and the creator of enormous social capital. Fifty percent of East Lake's housing is market rate. Apartments are organized, Cousins said, so that the few families on welfare live in-between two working families and are literally surrounded by examples of what they can accomplish. That, along with job training and education, helps move additional members of the community into the paid workforce.

Charles Knapp, the Foundation's president, described East Lake as an ongoing process. The Foundation has now bought nearby land and plans to put working class housing on it, both so that low-income homeowners can build up equity and so that the neighborhood does not become gentrified rather than mixed-income. An urban renewal project such as East Lake requires a long-term commitment, Knapp said. The panelists commented that it also requires the ability to be flexible, a strong funding plan, an equally strong board of directors, and extensive neighborhood involvement. The lessons of East Lake have now been utilized by a number of other communities, and the premise behind the day's program is that other urban areas may well find it a useful example of best practices.

Philippa Strum, "Creating Communities of Hope and Opportunity: The Revitalization of East Lake," Woodrow Wilson International Center for Scholars, United States Studies, http://www.wilsoncenter. org/index.cfm?topic_id=1427&fuseaction=topics.event_summary&event_id=230460.

BOB AND SHERRY WECHSLER

[Contributing money and donating time and energy in service are not the only ways to participate in philanthropic activities. Statistics in a recent study titled Health Related Philanthropy show that sixty-two percent of American adults have donated blood at least once. Advances in medical science have made organ donation and donations of tissue and DNA a modern form of giving. Fifty-two percent of Americans have formally expressed, by signing organ-donor cards or indicating on driver's licenses, a wish to be an organ donor. Seven percent have arranged to donate their physical remains to science. With more than ninety-two thousand Americans currently on a waiting list to receive an organ transplant, the need exceeds the supply. The gift of one's organs is a deeply unique offering to help improve and extend the quality of life of those in need. "Every gift of noble origin is breathed upon by Hope's perpetual breath," wrote William Wordsworth. The following personal account of organ and tissue donation is from a newspaper in Rock Island, Illinois.]

Giving Gift of Many Lives

It was Saturday morning when we received the call. Crist, our 28-year-old son, had fallen down his basement steps and sustained severe head injuries. He was undergoing his second brain surgery to remove blood clots which meant part of the frontal brain lobe had to be removed.

When we arrived at Hennepin County doctors gave us the worst possible news a parent could ever receive. Crist's injuries were so severe there was very little hope of his surviving. There were two more procedures they would try in an effort to reduce his inter-cranial pressure. However, prayer was the order of the day. The rest of the evening and early morning hours we spent performing the procedures to no avail. After a CT scan, the doctors showed us where he was beginning to undergo brain death, meaning he would not be able to breathe on his own.

At this point we knew our priority was to honor Crist's wish to be an organ donor. The doctors and staff were pleased to help us carry out his wish. "Life Source," the organ procurement organization that serves Minnesota, North Dakota and South Dakota was called in and the donation process began.

This is how it works. The next of kin, in our case Crist's wife, his mother and his father spent time with the coordinator filling out the consent forms. Meanwhile, an assessment of Crist was going on which included his condition, medical history, etc.

A search then went on for recipients. The organs included his heart, lungs, kidneys, liver, pancreas and intestine. These are the most critical organs and must be transplanted within a very short time—so time and distance are critical factors. These organs are harvested by the surgical team that actually does the transplants. An amazing amount of coordination is necessary for this to be successful. Tissue to recover includes the eyes, bones, ligaments, skin, every other disc and every other rib. These tissues are used for reconstructive surgeries, cancer treatment, sports injuries, burn patients, and so on. Many of the tissues are processed and then used as need arises. Some are also used for medical research. These tissues could help 40 to 50 people.

Everything that is removed from the donor is replaced with a prosthesis so an open casket funeral is possible.

We asked about the age of donors since we have stated on our driver's licenses that we are donors. There really aren't any age restrictions. In fact recently they received the liver from an 80-year-old woman and the transplant went well because the veins in the liver were harder and they didn't have concern about them collapsing.

We have received the following information about Crist's recipients:

His heart was given to a 47-year-old man from Minnesota, who had heart disease. He is feeling well and we've received two cards from him.

A 39-year-old man from Minnesota, who was in liver failure, received Crist's healthy liver. He is married with four children. He is feeling well and has been discharged from the hospital.

A 40-year-old woman from Minnesota received one of Crist's kidneys. She suffered from kidney disease and had been waiting for a kidney since February 2000.

Crist's other kidney and pancreas went to a 39-year-old South Dakota man who has diabetes. He is a single parent with two sons and has been waiting for a transplant since May 1999.

Crist's lung and intestine were sent to research organizations to help scientists find cures for such diseases as Cystic Fibrosis and Crohn's.

The Minnesota Lions Eye Bank informed us that two people received cornea implants from Crist's eyes.

We would be remiss if we didn't mention the fact that this entire process was handled in the most compassionate, caring manner possible; from the doctors, nurses and staff at Hennepin County Memorial Hospital to the people with Life Source to the surgical team and the recipients themselves.

Knowing that all these people are being helped comforts us as we grieve the loss of our wonderful son. He is truly a hero. Our wish is for continued prayers for the recipients of Crist's organs and tissues that they will regain their health and they will know Jesus as their Savior. To register as an organ donor in Illinois, simply sign the back of your driver's license or state ID card and have two people witness your signature. And most important, let your family know of your wish to be a donor. If you would like more information regarding organ donation, contact the Gift of Hope Organ & Tissue Donor Network at 1-888-307-3668. In loving memory of Crist Wechsler; Feb. 28, 1976–June 15, 2004.

Bob and Sherry Wechsler, *Rock Island Argus* (October 9, 2004).

CRITICAL THINKING ON HELPING AND GIVING

C. WEST CHURCHMAN (1913–2004)

[Churchman was a leading philosopher in systems theory and management science, presenting systems theory without jargon. How we conceive of the world and our stance in it often determines our approach to solving problems and accomplishing goals. Churchman's Systems Theory analysis helps us think about the complexities of realist and idealist presuppositions, providing a useful corrective to one-sidedness; ultimately, both sides are entangled in the overall dynamics, and balance is needed for the system's optimal functioning. This thinking is an antidote to ideologues confusing themselves for realogues, and realogues confusing themselves for ideologues. Example from history: "For more than half

a century, over-enthusiastic idealists of one variety or another have gotten themselves and the country into trouble abroad and had to be bailed out by prudent successors brought in to clean up the mess. When the crisis passes, however, the realists' message about the need to act carefully in a fallen world ends up clashing with the American loftier impulses. The result is a tedious cycle that plays itself out again and again." (Gideon Rose, "Get Real," New York Times, August 18, 2005.) In thinking about ameliorating complex social problems through philanthropy, we need to consider a number of complicating factors. Naive oversimplifying may make matters worse, while cynicism may dismiss possibilities out of hand. We disregard whole-systems thinking at our own peril.]

Idealism and Realism [Systems Theory and Philanthropic Decision-making]

Not only do we assume that one system can be meaningfully regarded as better than another system, but in our praising and complaining we also assume that we can actually do something to improve the systems we inhabit. . . . Today we are capable in some countries of nourishing those who for various physical and economic reasons are not able to find resources for the sustenance of their life. Our abundance of food is like a huge cornucopia compared to the supply of food in generations past. The next generation will adequately feed the world. The ideal is a perfect meal, whenever required, tailored to the specific tastes of each person on earth. . . . The utopians of the nineteenth century actually hoped to find a society that would supply to every man what he really required for his life. What they often failed to realize was that once man is supplied in such a manner, he may well find that life is no longer worth living, or at least has become far from "satisfactory" for him. . . . Brilliance of mind [in scientific specialists] is not a quality that necessarily leads to the best type of judgment concerning the ethics of whole systems. Indeed, there is often an inclination of the brilliant mind to select one aspect of the total situation that can be most precisely formulated and to give this aspect far greater weight than it deserves, simply because it can be so formulated in comparison with other, far more important aspects. . . .

. . . There seems to be no successful way in which the expert of large-scale systems can become a "generalist." There is no such thing as the "universal" man in the area of the ethics of large-scale systems.

Therefore, the need for a well-informed public is a true need. The underlying ethical principle here is that every man ought to feel that by his nature he can acquire knowledge about how society should be designed. . . .

The founders of our nation were geniuses of organization. They saw that the only adequate answer to the problem of a free society was a system of "checks and balances": The people elect the law makers and executives, who freely appoint the courts, who control the people, the law makers, and the executives.

But how reflective is the U.S.A. today? Who tells the people that the national goals are satisfactory? Who tells the people that they no longer truly elect their representatives? Or that the courts are honest? Or that the executive has failed to be merely an executive.

How can man ever come to be self-reflective about his own goals? . . .

*　　*　　*

The cast of characters . . . is made up of two extremists. The first is called a *realist*, and believes that reality is what exists in the world of the senses, the hard-fact world.

371

He also believes that reality does not exist in "wholes." He is fond of saying that "there is no such thing as a group mind, or an organization, and certainly no such thing as a 'whole system.'" . . . The second character is an *idealist*. . . . For him the question "What is real?" means what is realizable? Since the realizable is an idea, he believes that ideas are primary; what we observe is the result of what we think about. Hence he interprets the first challenge to be a challenge to thought: How can we be sure that we have thought about everything that is relevant? . . .

Managers, the people who make decisions, also recognize a distinction between the "practical" decision maker and the "visionary" decision maker. . . .

The practical short-range planner believes that the only objectives that are realistic are those that we can see out to the "horizon." The visionary long-range planner believes that the only objectives that mean anything to us are those that determine our whole lives, that is, the objectives that lie beyond every horizon of human aspiration. . . .

The characters in the story become blurred and indistinguishable, because the realist . . . must consider that nebulous, abstract idea called whole system: he must do this if he is to be realistic about his plans . . . it seems as though we can't keep the two characters of our story apart: The realist and idealist merge. . . .

It is easy to recognize the "hard-headed" politician or businessman who shies away from the abstract, nebulous ideas, who deals in tangibles, who wants the facts and not the theories, who above all exists in the world of the feasible. Whenever ideas drive him to consider superworlds and vague consequences, he abandons the idea for the world he can deal with. He is not a great, over all planner, but a man who charges in where real opportunity exists and deals with the factors that really matter. . . .

As I have said, in a system the parts have reality only by virtue of their relationship to other parts. The wheel of a car is really a wheel only because there is an axle and the axle is real only because there is a frame. . . .

Perhaps we can say that a realist is one who believes in concentrating his attention on the parts, all other things being equal; he believes it is realistic for us simply to consider the part and not bother our heads about the obscure whole. . . .

The Governor of the State of California once issued a mandate that all parts of the [state] system reduce expenditures by 10 percent. This is an application of the realist philosophy because it is based on the notion that if one looks into each part, it will be possible to remove sufficient waste of time and money to make the required reduction in expenditure. One can do this part by part, says the realist, without having to concern oneself about the effect on the whole system. . . . In other words, to the realist a part can be realistically considered because the parts can be made separable. . . .

[The idealist says one cannot perfect the operations of one component of the system without looking at the way it reacts with other parts of the system.]

. . . Many realists become very puzzled and annoyed by what they consider the irrationalities of the social world, crime, slums, discrimination, cheating in social welfare; they wish to clear up the mess wherever they find it. But in their attempts to "improve things" they create disturbances in other parts of the system, disturbances that come back on them and forestall their improvements. We are all aware of the instances where, under the claim of instituting new freedoms, government agencies indulge in spying, wire tapping, suppressing freedom of speech and political action. Slums become cleared away only to be replaced by ugly parking lots, and the slum dwellers reappear in some other ghetto of the city. The idealist and long-range planner argue that the whole system has to be understood as a complex of competing parts, each wanting something that constrains the others. Consequently the parts of the system cannot be looked at as separable from one another. . . .

The paradox of the idealist is that he himself believes in a vicious separability of thinking and action. . . .

The practical decision maker knows that he must act. The idealist and long-range planner ramble on endlessly about all kinds of ramifications and postpone the moment of action . . . The practical aspect of the realist lies in his belief in action even when action entails risks. The realist in other words is sensitive to the problems of timing. The idealist on the other hand believes in the reality of the plan; the action is secondary.

In this distinction it's the realist who seems to come out on top, because he believes, along with common sense, in the reality of the act and the actor, the decision and the decision maker. Wonderful! The idealist of course, believing instead in the reality of the plan and especially the ideal plan, looks impractical and absurd. But who is this actor, this hero of the realist philosophy? For example, in the model of the producer's world it was assumed that the producer [of goods] was the actor who acted as a unit with a well-defined preference and with well-defined alternative choices. From the realist's point of view the actor and the action were embedded in this concept of the completely responsible and authoritative decision maker. This picture is sheer nonsense. The producer is not a unit, no matter how forceful a personality he may be. He is at least a coalition of many people—stockholders, government, consumers, labor, public. He is also a self, that is a very complicated system of conflicting psychological beings, or ego and id, or persona and archetype. . . .

The paradox of the realist continues. He thinks that the actor and action are the basis of reality, but the actor and his action turn out to be two ideas in the head of the realist—and not very good ideas at that. . . .

Try as I will, I can't keep realism from looking absurd. The realist wants to thump hard, look hard, and "what happens" to him is supposed to be reality! He's not even childish, because even a child knows better than to trust his senses alone; the imaginary also complements the sensory in his reality.

Idealism is an absurdly easy philosophy because its opponent is so ridiculous.

Yet the strange situation still continues. Realism in our culture is the more popular philosophy. People admire the straightforward man of action, just as in science they admire the individual who does not drift off too vaguely into ill-defended theories. . . .

According to the realist all science needs of him is his ability to observe and reason dispassionately. The pictures he draws of reality thereby are supposed to become accurate, whatever may be his emotional life, . . . or . . . the . . . politics of his age.

But the idealist has no difficulty whatsoever in systematically destroying this realist hero, who thrives on the concept of this separable and disinterested observation. . . .

Though realism from the idealist's point of view is easy to attack, and its hero is easy to make ridiculous, very much the same is the fate of the idealist in the hands of an astute realist. How can one possibly maintain the doctrine that no man is realistic unless he represents in his specific acts all the relevant world of his life, conscious and unconscious, political and apolitical, future and past? The gods could not demand more of themselves. Men have always known how unrealistic it is to aspire to be like gods. To the realist, the idealist's doctrine amounts to saying that to be realistic one must be utterly unrealistic. . . .

To the realist, constraints on system design are like doors to the outside world; if the designer opens the doors, he allows to enter the evil spirits of other designs, frighteningly obscure, deeply complex. . . . The hero of the idealist is the system guarantor. The idealist concocts such a hero, the guarantor, to take care of all the unknowns and evils that he so threateningly permits to come into the conscious mind. The monism of the old-fashioned idealist implied that the guarantor is the ideal, or the God, or the Good. . . .

To the realist it seems that idealism only makes sense in terms of its basic evidence. Where it jumps to after it's stated its evidence is something else again, an unreality that has no philosophical significance. In other words, says the realist, the only meaning that lies in idealism is its adherence to hard, unalterable fact.

Thus our argument seems always to take us back to the same point. Try as hard as we can to develop a distinction between realism and idealism based on historical thought, the two seem to merge as thought presses on. The realist turns into idealist, and the idealist into realist every time we press him to make his arguments clear about his general notion of systems . . . one cannot tackle the problem of what is real in a system without going through on one's own thinking process the opposition between the real and the ideal. . . .

Social science has been dominated by a realist philosophy, an uncritical belief in the disinterested observer. But the idealist's counterthought is that most of social science does not produce information, and that social scientists' claim for objectivity is unwarranted. . . .

Finally, we also recognize that the realist has the best technology even if he has the weakest philosophy, and the idealist has the soundest philosophy with the weakest technology. This position characterizes our culture.

C. West Churchman, *Challenge to Reason*. New York: McGraw Hill, 1968, 1, 49, 61, 65, 84, 112, 171–72, 180–87, 191, 193, 197.

JOHN D. ROCKEFELLER (1839–1937)

[Rockefeller helped establish the oil industry in America and was influential in the development of modern philanthropy. He helped found Standard Oil and during his lifetime built it into the largest and most profitable company in the world, becoming the world's wealthiest man. A religious man, Rockefeller nurtured a lifelong interest in the Protestant church and an involvement in the interfaith movement; he wished that the sects of Christianity could become more united. For years he taught a Young Men's Bible Class at the Fifth Avenue Baptist Church in New York. He donated millions to building Riverside Church and to the Interchurch Center, which is headquarters of a variety of church groups. He was not bound by sectarianism in making his contributions, giving to Jewish and Roman Catholic groups as well as Protestant ones. Part of his credo was, "I believe that the rendering of useful service is the common duty of mankind and that only in the purifying fire of sacrifice is the dross of selfishness consumed and the greatness of the human soul set free." He spent his last four decades deeply involved in philanthropic activities in education and public health. Foundations run by experts distributed his donations of hundreds of millions of dollars, and this became a model for many others. He recognized giving as an art, and seeing the pitfalls philanthropists often stumble into, he developed useful ideas about how to give with expertise, making a great impact on the blossoming forms of philanthropic activities in his time.]

The Difficult Art of Giving

It is, no doubt, easy to write platitudes and generalities about the joys of giving, and the duty that one owes to one's fellow men, and to put together again all the familiar phrases that have served for generations whenever the subject has been taken up. . . . It is most difficult, however, to dwell upon a very practical and businesslike side of benefactions generally, without seeming to ignore, or at least to fail to appreciate fully, the spirit of giving which has its source in the heart, and which, of course, makes it all worth-while.

In this country we have come to the period when we can well afford to ask the ablest men to devote more of their time, thought, and money to the public well-being. I am not so presumptuous as to attempt to define exactly what this betterment work should consist of. Every man will do that for himself, and his own conclusion will be final for himself. It is well, I think, that no narrow or preconceived plan should be set down as the best.

I am sure it is a mistake to assume that the possession of money in great abundance necessarily brings happiness. The very rich are just like all the rest of us; and if they get pleasure from the possession of money, it comes from their ability to do things which give satisfaction to someone besides themselves.

Limitations of the Rich

The mere expenditure of money for things, so I am told by those who profess to know, soon palls upon one. The novelty of being able to purchase anything one wants soon passes, because what people most seek cannot be bought with money. These rich men we read about in the newspapers cannot get personal returns beyond a well-defined limit for their expenditure. They cannot gratify the pleasures of the palate beyond very moderate bounds, since they cannot purchase a good digestion; they cannot lavish very much money on fine raiment for themselves or their families without suffering from public ridicule; and in their homes they cannot go much beyond the comforts of the less wealthy without involving them in more pain than pleasure. As I study wealthy men, I can see but one way in which they can secure a real equivalent for money spent, and that is to cultivate a taste for giving where the money may produce an effect which will be a lasting gratification; and I would respectfully present this as a Christmas thought, even though crudely expressed, to the so-called "money kings," great and small.

A man of business may often most properly consider that he does his share in building up a property which gives steady work for few or many people; and his contribution consists in giving to his employees good working conditions, new opportunities, and a strong stimulus to good work. Just so long as he has the welfare of his employees in his mind and follows his convictions, no one can help honoring such a man. It would be the narrowest sort of view to take, and I think the meanest, to consider that good works consist chiefly in the outright giving of money.

The Best Philanthropy

The best philanthropy, the help that does the most good and the least harm, the help that nourishes civilization at its very root, that most widely disseminates health, righteousness, and happiness, is not what is usually called charity. It is, in my judgment, the investment of effort or time or money, carefully considered with relation to the power of employing people at a remunerative wage, to expand and develop the resources at hand,

and to give opportunity for progress and healthful labor where it did not exist before. No mere money-giving is comparable to this in its lasting and beneficial results.

If, as I am accustomed to think, this statement is a correct one, how vast indeed is the philanthropic field! It may be urged that the daily vocation of life is one thing, and the work of philanthropy quite another. I have no sympathy with this notion. The man who plans to do all his giving on Sunday is a poor prop for the institutions of the country.

The excuse for referring so often to the busy man of affairs is that his help is most needed. I know of men who have followed out this large plan of developing work, not as a temporary matter, but as a permanent principle. These men have taken up doubtful enterprises and carried them through to success often at great risk, and in the face of great skepticism, not as a matter only of personal profit, but in the larger spirit of general uplift.

Disinterested Service: The Road to Success

If I were to give advice to a young man starting out in life, I should say to him: If you aim for a large, broad-gauged success, do not begin your business career, whether you sell your labor or are an independent producer, with the idea of getting from the world by hook or crook all you can. In the choice of your profession or your business employment, let your first thought be: Where can I fit in so that I may be most effective in the work of the world? Where can I lend a hand in a way most effectively to advance the general interests? Enter life in such a spirit, choose your vocation in that way, and you have taken the first step on the highest road to a large success. Investigation will show that the great fortunes which have been made in this country, and the same is probably true of other lands, have come to men who have performed great and far-reaching economic services—men who, with great faith in the future of their country, have done most for the development of its resources. The man will be most successful who confers the greatest service on the world. Commercial enterprises that are needed by the public will pay. Commercial enterprises that are not needed fail, and ought to fail.

The Generosity of Service

Probably the most generous people in the world are the very poor, who assume each other's burdens in the crises which come so often to the hard pressed. The mother in the tenement falls ill and the neighbor in the next room assumes her burdens. The father loses his work, and neighbors supply food to his children from their own scanty store. How often one hears of cases where the orphans are taken over and brought up by the poor friend whose benefaction means great additional hardship! This sort of genuine service makes the most princely gift from superabundance look insignificant indeed. The Jews have had for centuries a precept that one-tenth of a man's possessions must be devoted to good works, but even this measure of giving is but a rough yardstick to go by. To give a tenth of one's income is well nigh an impossibility to some, while to others it means a miserable pittance. If the spirit is there, the matter of proportion is soon lost sight of. It is only the spirit of giving that counts, and the very poor give without any self-consciousness. But I fear that I am dealing with generalities again.

The education of children in my early days may have been straightlaced, yet I have always been thankful that the custom was quite general to teach young people to give systematically of money that they themselves had earned. It is a good thing to lead children to realize early the importance of their obligations to others but, I confess, it is increasingly difficult; for what were luxuries then have become commonplaces now. It should be a greater pleasure and satisfaction to give money for a good cause than to earn it, and I have always indulged the hope that during my life I should be able to help establish efficiency in giving so that wealth may be of greater use to the present and future generations.

Perhaps just here lies the difference between the gifts of money and service. The poor meet promptly the misfortunes which confront the home circle and household of the neighbor. The giver of money, if his contribution is to be valuable, must add service in the way of study, and he must help to attack and improve underlying conditions. Not being so pressed by the racking necessities, it is he that should be better able to attack the subject from a more scientific standpoint; but the final analysis is the same: his money is a feeble offering without the study behind it which will make its expenditure effective.

Great hospitals conducted by noble and unselfish men and women are doing wonderful work; but no less important are the achievements in research that reveal hitherto unknown facts about diseases and provide the remedies by which many of them can be relieved or even stamped out.

To help the sick and distressed appeals to the kindhearted always, but to help the investigator who is striving successfully to attack the causes which bring about sickness and distress does not so strongly attract the giver of money. The first appeals to the sentiments overpoweringly, but the second has the head to deal with. Yet I am sure we are making wonderful advances in this field of scientific giving. All over the world the need of dealing with the questions of philanthropy with something beyond the impulses of emotion is evident, and everywhere help is being given to those heroic men and women who are devoting themselves to the practical and essentially scientific tasks. It is a good and inspiring thing to recall occasionally the heroism, for example, of the men who risked and sacrificed their lives to discover the facts about yellow fever, a sacrifice for which untold generations will bless them; and this same spirit has animated the professions of medicine and surgery.

The Fundamental Thing in All Help

If the people can be educated to help themselves, we strike at the root of many of the evils of the world. This is the fundamental thing and it is worth saying even if it has been said so often that its truth is lost sight of in its constant repetition.

The only thing which is of lasting benefit to a man is that which he does for himself. Money which comes to him without effort on his part is so seldom a benefit and often a curse. That is the principal objection to speculation—it is not because more lose than gain, though that is true—but it is because those who gain are apt to receive more injury from their success than they would have received from failure. And so with regard to money or other things which are given by one person to another. It is only in the exceptional case that the receiver is really benefited. But, if we can help people to help themselves, then there is a permanent blessing conferred.

Some Underlying Principles

My own conversion to the feeling that an organized plan was an absolute necessity came about in this way.

About the year 1890, I was still following the haphazard fashion of giving here and there as appeals presented themselves. I investigated as I could, and worked myself almost to a nervous break-down in groping my way, without sufficient guide or chart, through this ever-widening field of philanthropic endeavor. There was then forced upon me the necessity to organize and plan this department of our daily tasks on as distinct lines of progress as we did our business affairs; and I will try to describe the underlying principles we arrived at, and have since followed out, and hope still greatly to extend.

It may be beyond the pale of good taste to speak at all of such a personal subject—I am not unmindful of this—but I can make these observations with at least a little better grace because so much of the hard work and hard thinking are done by my family and associates, who devote their lives to it.

Every right-minded man has a philosophy of life, whether he knows it or not. Hidden away in his mind are certain governing principles, whether he formulates them in words or not, which govern his life. Surely his ideal ought to be to contribute all that he can, however little it may be, whether of money or service, to human progress.

Certainly one's ideal should be to use one's means, both in one's investments and in benefactions, for the advancement of civilization. But the question as to what civilization is and what are the great laws which govern its advance have been seriously studied. Our investments not less than gifts have been directed to such ends as we have thought would tend to produce these results. If you were to go into our office, and ask our committee on benevolence or our committee on investment in what they consider civilization to consist, they would say that they have found in their study that the most convenient analysis of the elements which go to make up civilization runs about as follows:

1st. Progress in the means of subsistence, that is to say, progress in abundance and variety of food-supply, clothing, shelter, sanitation, public health, commerce, manufacture, the growth of the public wealth, etc.

2nd. Progress in government and law, that is to say, in the enactment of laws securing justice and equity to every man, consistent with the largest individual liberty, and the due and orderly enforcement of the same upon all.

3rd. Progress in literature and language.

4th. Progress in science and philosophy.

5th. Progress in art and refinement.

6th. Progress in morality and religion.

If you were to ask them, as indeed they are very often asked, which of these they regard as fundamental, they would reply that they would not attempt to answer, that the question is purely an academic one, that all these go hand in hand, but that historically the first of them—namely, progress in means of subsistence—had generally preceded progress in government, in literature, in knowledge, in refinement, and in religion. Though not itself of the highest importance, it is the foundation upon which the whole superstructure of civilization is built, and without which it could not exist.

John D. Rockefeller, "Some Random Reminiscences of Men and Events," article 3 in Rockefeller's series, in *The World's Work* (1907 and 1908), later retitled "The Difficult Art of Giving."

BILL MOYERS (b. 1934)

[Bill Moyers has interviewed more thinkers, creative people, and social activists seeking to improve their communities and America than has any other interviewer. Videotapes of these interviews constitute an archive of the voices of our greatest writers, artists, and leaders. Moyers grew up in a family that attended a Baptist church, which was a formative

influence in his spiritual life. He is best known as a broadcast journalist and former host of the PBS program NOW with Bill Moyers. Moyers is president of the Schumann Center for Media and Democracy. Below he discusses serious issues of philanthropy and presents hopeful examples of the ablest givers. His work is an invitation to join together to realize what democracy means. Some of Moyers' insightful ideas on philanthropy and successful societies reflect new situations and understandings that have emerged since Carnegie and Rockefeller wrote their philanthropic prescriptions.]

Finding Justice in Charity [On Getting Philanthropy Right]

Some people I know love money for its own sake. Some I know love power for its own sake. Sometimes they are the same people.

But over the years, I have found that the people of means who are the happiest and most deeply satisfied are those who use their money to empower others. They feel more than lucky; they feel blessed.

It's not easy giving money away. I found that out during my 13 years on the board of the Rockefeller Foundation and over the past 14 years as president of the Florence and John Schumann Foundation (now the Schumann Center for Media and Democracy) where I have been working with a family who decided to spend down their assets in their lifetime and asked my help in doing so. In that role, I've wound up working with and advising a score of other foundations. But I've also been on the other side of philanthropy. As a public broadcaster, I've had to raise every penny for every production I mount on PBS—millions of dollars over the past 30 years, much of it from foundations. I have had a window on the world of philanthropy that enables me to see both sides—supply and demand. I know first-hand the hazards, limitations and frustrations of the field.

For one thing, when you make a mistake, people are loath to tell you. Unlike investing, where the market delivers quick verdicts on mistakes, or business, where bad decisions cannot go long undetected, the feedback loop in philanthropy rarely turns up irrefutable evidence that you blew one. I have long wished to talk to the great British economist Walter Bagehot, who once wrote that "the most melancholy of human reflection, perhaps, is that on the whole, it is a question whether the benevolence of mankind does more harm than good." I'd like to know where he came down on the matter.

. . . I am not at all surprised that John D. Rockefeller thought it was harder to give money away than to earn it.

But when you get it right—when you have squared your expectations and your reach and know as only you can know that what you have done matters—it can be sweet.

John Wesley got it right. If you have made a passage of faith similar to mine, you will recognize the name. In the 18th century, in Britain, with his brother Charles, John Wesley founded the Methodist movement that gave rise to benevolent impulses and institutions that survive to this day. In my seminary days, one of the wisest of my own mentors, a professor of social ethics named T. B. Maston, believed that we Baptists had a lot to learn from our Methodist kin. So he suggested that I read John Wesley's *Journal*. It's a remarkable account of a discerning man who lived almost the whole of that tumultuous and transformative century. People were flocking from the rural areas to the cities as agriculture gave way to industrialization. The cities choked on crime, disease and pollution. The poor were crushed under debt and often found their only escape in alcohol and drugs. The five percent of the population at the top controlled nearly one third of the national income and did what elites often do—they spent their money walling themselves off from the lived experience of ordinary people.

Not John Wesley. The best-known evangelist of his time—the Billy Graham of his day—was so popular the offerings poured in, making him a well-to-do man. But Wesley put himself on a budget of 30 pounds a year and gave the rest of it away—over the course of his lifetime, he gave away nearly all of what he earned. "If I leave behind me ten pounds," he wrote, "you and all mankind [can] bear witness against me, that I have lived and died a thief and a robber." In one of his most famous sermons, he spoke on the Biblical passage that says "the love of money is the root of all evil"—but he had in mind "not the thing itself":

"The fault does not lie in the money, but in them that use it. . . . In the hands of [God's] children, it is food for the hungry, drink for the thirsty, raiment for the naked. It gives to the traveler and the stranger where to lay his head. By it we may supply the place of a husband to the widow, and of a father to the fatherless. It may be a defense for the oppressed, a means of health to the sick, of ease to them that are in pain; it may be as eyes to the blind, as feet to the lame; yea, a lifter up from the gates of death."

I don't think philanthropy has had a more compelling mandate than John Wesley's. It was his inspiration to see that while charity may be good for the soul, justice is the salvation of society. Social justice became his great passion, the moral purpose of his calling.

Eliot Rosewater got it right. He's the multimillionaire protagonist in Kurt Vonnegut's satiric novel, *God Bless You, Mr. Rosewater, or Pearls Before Swine*. As Vonnegut put it, "A sum of money is a leading character in this tale about people, just as a sum of honey might properly be a leading character in a tale about bees." Read the book if you haven't, but be sure to wrap it in plain brown paper, because it can be quite subversive, as I discovered when I gave copies to some fellow trustees of the Rockefeller Foundation back in the late '60s.

Eliot Rosewater is not your typical buttoned-down philanthropoid. He is the heir to the fabulous Rosewater fortune—the 14th largest in the nation, created, Vonnegut tells us, during the Civil War "through cowardice and knavery." He decides to leave the life of an international playboy to go home to his native Indiana—to the town of Rosewater, no less—to take over the family foundation. There he undergoes a transformation, becomes a volunteer fireman, throws open the office to all comers and simply asks those who show up, "How can we help you?" He even runs ads in the local paper that say "Don't kill yourself, call the Rosewater Foundation." When they do call, he answers the phone himself. The town fathers are alarmed, to put it mildly, when they realize Eliot Rosewater intends to give all the money away to poor people—many of them poor dirty people. They decide they must stop him, and the only way they can do so is to prove him insane, which they set out to do. I won't spoil the story for you, but I will say it's a witty and wise book. One reviewer said that "Kurt Vonnegut managed to write a book about money and love without the ugly word versus between them" (and in doing so) shows that "money and love can exist together." Although the story does not end with the promise of a perfect world, its message—as other readers will tell you on Marek Vit's Kurt Vonnegut Corner—is worth hearing today: That if we can't change the world, we can at least help it, and that while "we may not be able to undo the harm that has been done, we can certainly love, simply because they are people, those who have been made useless by our past stupidity and greed, our previous crimes against our brothers. And if that seems insane, then the better the world for such folly."

Rachel Naomi Remen got it right. You may have heard of Rachel. She's a physician, teaches community medicine at the University of California in San Francisco, and co-founded (with Michael Lerner) Commonweal, the center for cancer patients in northern California. Several years ago, I featured her work in a series for PBS called "Healing and the Mind"—about the impact of emotions on our health. In her recent book, *My Grandfather's Blessings*, Rachel writes about how one day she came into an unexpected legacy of $20,000 on the condition that she give it away in any way she saw best. Even for so modest an amount of money, she found herself on a steep learning curve, learning that "giving away money can be demanding and even lonely." She had developed a therapist's eye for growth in people, but "had never before noticed the places where things were trying to move forward in the culture, groups of people or individuals whose vision, if nurtured, could lead to a better world." She writes:

> I suppose that I never saw them because I did not think I personally had the means to be of help to them and so they had nothing to do with me. You might never notice plants struggling to grow around you, either, until someone hands you a full watering can. But I could see them now. They were everywhere.

She was still trying to figure out what to do with the money when one evening she and a friend went out to eat at a local restaurant. At the very next table two men were dining so close she couldn't help overhearing them. One was telling the other about a program he and some of his Spanish-speaking colleagues had been running as volunteers, providing support groups for poor families who had lost children to illness, accident or violence. More than a hundred couples had been helped to preserve marriages torn open by grief and blame and to parent their remaining children. But now many of the city's hospitals had merged or gone out of business or been taken over by organizations that had no interest in supporting such a program. For lack of money, it was about to close.

Rachel says that by now she was eavesdropping shamelessly. She heard the second fellow ask the first one—whose name was Steve—"How much do you need to keep things going?" Steve answered sadly, "A great deal of money. More than we could ever raise." "How much is it?" his friend asked again. "Four thousand dollars," Steve replied. At this, Rachel Remen reached across the few feet separating the tables, touched the man lightly on the arm, and said: "You got it, Steve." And reaching into her purse for her checkbook, she filled it out on the spot.

Without this admittedly modest opportunity, Rachel says, "I doubt that I would have responded to the conversation at the next table or even heard it. I knew [now] that I had something of value to give [and once I gave it away] an odd thing has happened. . . . I still notice the growing edge of things and I still respond to it. I give away my time, my skills, my network of friends, my life experience. You do not need money to be a philanthropist. We all have assets. You can befriend life with your bare hands."

This seems to me philanthropy at its most basic—to spot people at the "growing edge of things"—people whose vision, if nurtured, could lead to a better world—and give them the means to do more than they could do with just their bare hands.

It's what the Schumann brothers—Robert and Ford—were doing when they asked me to join them in 1991. We had become acquainted when their foundation underwrote some of my work on PBS. We discovered a mutual obsession about the state of democracy, including a belief that the fate of our country is bound up in the quality and integrity of news and information. Over the years, many of our grants have gone to alternative media—to independent journalism and non-commercial public radio and television. Commercial media had made its peace with the little lies and fantasies that are the byproducts of the merchandising process. From that Faustian bargain has come a steady gusher of the nonsense, violence and trivia that today are the opiate of democracy. As the late scholar Cleanth Brooks wrote, on every front we are being assaulted by "the bastard muses:"

- Propaganda, which pleads, sometimes unscrupulously, for a special cause at the expense of the total truth;
- Sentimentality, which works up emotional responses unwarranted by and in excess of the occasion;
- Pornography, which focuses on one powerful drive at the expense of the total human personality.

Day and night, the media pipe these images into our culture and consciousness, bombarding us with mass-produced and mass-consumed carnage masquerading as amusement. We can no more escape their effects by turning off our own television or radio than we can escape the effect of automobile emissions in the neighborhood by leaving our own car in the garage. This coarsening of popular culture and public discourse has created a society where vulgarity, banality and brutality are profitable commodities for corporations but at a great cost to democracy. The philosopher Leo Strauss once told his students that the Greek word for vulgarity—*apeirokalia*—means "the lack of experience in things beautiful." It would perhaps have come as no surprise to Strauss, as it came as no surprise to me, to read a few years ago that 50 million children in America are afflicted with a sickness for which our society has no name—the writer simply called it "intellectual poverty." Another version of "the lack of experience in things beautiful." The educator Herbert Kohl warned us: "If television does not provide time for the consideration of people and events in depth, we may end up training another generation of TV adults who know what kind of toilet paper to buy, who know how to argue and humiliate others, but who are thoroughly incapable of the social and political literacy necessary to preserve and extend democracy." His plea fell on the deaf ears of the media tycoons who decide so much of what we see, read and hear. But you and I can do something about that by putting money in the hands of creative spirits—producers, writers, journalists and filmmakers and editors who share Henry David Thoreau's conviction that "to affect the quality of the day is the highest of the arts."

*   *   *

A profound transformation is occurring in America. Inequality is greater than it's been since 1929. Forty years ago, the gap in terms of wealth between the top 20 percent and the bottom 20 percent was 30-fold. Now it's more than 75-fold. Such concentrations of wealth would be far less of an issue if the rest of society were benefiting proportionately. But that's not the case. Middle-class and working people have to run harder and harder just to stay even, and our social stratification has become alarming. Just this week, the conservative journalist David Brooks, quoted in *Time*, points out that if you come from a family earning over $96,000 a year, your odds of getting a bachelor's degree by age 24 are one in three. If you come from a family earning under $36,000, it's one in 17.

Time is no Marxist rag. Neither is *The Economist*, which is considered by many to be the most principled and ablest defender of capitalism in the world. Earlier this year, *The Economist* produced a sobering analysis of what is happening to the old notion that any American can get to the top. A growing body of evidence led the editors to conclude that with income inequality reaching levels not seen since the Gilded Age and social mobility not increasing at anything like the same pace as inequality, "The United States risks calcifying into a European-style class-based society." Let me repeat that: "The United States risks calcifying into a European-style class-based society." That alarm echoed a report last year by the American Political Science Association, which found that "increasing inequalities threaten the American ideal of equal citizenship and that progress toward real democracy may have stalled in this country and even reversed."

Our political class seems indifferent to these warnings. Indifferent to the fact that more children are growing up in poverty in America than in any other industrial nation. Indifferent to the fact that millions of workers are actually making less money today in real dollars than they did 20 years ago. Indifferent to the fact that while we have the most advanced medical care in the world, nearly 44 million Americans—eight out of 10 of them in working families—are uninsured and cannot get the basic care they need.

There's a book I wish we could make required reading for every member of Congress: Jared Diamond's new book, *Collapse: How Societies Choose to Fail or Succeed.* The Pulitzer Prize winner tells us that one of the main factors in the decline of earlier societies was the insulation of elites. Mayans on the Yucatan Peninsula, for example, suffered as environmental degradation—deforestation, soil erosion and poor water management—diminished food supplies. Chronic warfare made matters worse as more and more people fought over less and less land and resources. Although Mayan kings could see their forests vanishing and their hills eroding, "They were able to insulate themselves from problems afflicting the rest of society. By extracting wealth from commoners, they could remain well fed while everyone else was slowly starving." Too late, the elites realized they could not reverse the deteriorating environment, and they became casualties of their own privilege.

Any society, Diamond warns, contains a built-in blueprint for failure if people at the top insulate themselves from the consequences of their actions and from an awareness of the commonplace experiences of life. He goes on to describe an America where elites cocoon themselves "in gated communities, guarded by private security patrols, and filled with people who drink bottled water, depend on private pensions, and send their children to private schools." Gradually, they lose the motivation "to support the police force, the municipal water supply, Society Security, and public schools." At the end of this road is a state of nature—a war of all against all—"where the strong take what they can, and the weak suffer what they must."

Here is one of the great moral issues of democracy—and it's one you have the means to address. I applaud you for wrestling with the challenge of wealth, for coming together to explore how people of means can engage life's realities and the perils to democracy instead of denying or running from them. And I am honored that you asked me to join you. As I thought about this occasion, I remembered my introductory course in anthropology taught by Gilbert McAllister at the University of Texas half a century ago. I can see "Dr. Mac" right now, in my mind's eye, recounting the years he had spent among the Apaches as a young graduate student. They had taught him the meaning of reciprocity. In the Apache tongue, he said, the word for grandfather and the word for grandson are one and the same, indicating the bond between the generations, linked to one another in an embrace of mutual obligation. With that he was off, expounding on the conviction that through the ages human beings have advanced more through collaboration than competition. For all the chest-thumping about rugged individuals and self-made men, he said, an ethic of cooperation inspired the social compromise that is the basis of civilization. Civilization, after all, is but a thin layer of civility stretched across the passions of the human heart. "Live and let live" is not enough to sustain a civilization; we have to move toward an active commitment of "live and help live."

My own father used to reminisce about growing up on the Red River, between Oklahoma and Texas. He was 14 when his own father died during the flu epidemic in 1918. Neighbors washed my grandfather's body, neighbors dug his grave and neighbors laid him in the earth. Through the years, my father was one of several men in our church who took turns sitting beside the corpse of a departed friend or fellow congregant. He often drew the midnight shift and would go directly from his vigil to his job. Shortly before his own death, as we sat talking on the front porch, I asked him: "Why did you sit up all night when you had to drive your truck all the next day?" He seemed surprised by the question, as if it had never occurred to him, and then, without hesitation, he answered: "Because it was the thing we did."

The thing *we* did!

There, I suggest, in the commonplace philosophy of an ordinary man, is the antidote to the cynicism that grips our embattled and endangered democracy.

There is "the growing edge of things" that awaits your resources, and mine; your bare hands, and mine.

Democracy is the thing we do *together*, if it is to be done at all.

Bill Moyers, "Finding Justice in Charity," adapted from his speech presented to a wealth and giving forum on October 22, 2005. http://www.tompaine.com/print/finding_justice_in_charity.php.

WENDELL BERRY (b. 1934)

[In this essay Berry speaks for the land—the soil of our planet—and brings us back to basics. He explores the Judeo-Christian understanding of believers' obligations to the earth. Having been given the land, he asks, what is required of human beings? This question involves a deep paradigm, the gift of the Promised Land, which has implications for our relationship to the health of the soil and with others who inhabit America and the world at large. Once again, we see how charity begins at home—with responsible care, not profligate rapacity. This is an old theme in American writing. Captain John Smith in the early 1600s tried to convince his contemporaries that the true value of America was not in her precious metals, but in the produce of her waters and soils. Each generation needs to realize and reaffirm the gifts of our land, upon which we all depend. Berry points out that science and academia are often not concerned about humanity's welfare, but rather with their own goals and institutions, and he inquires into the Christian commitment to good stewardship.]

The Gift of Good Land

"Dream not of other Worlds . . ." —PARADISE LOST 8:175

The story of the giving of the Promised Land to the Israelites is more serviceable than the story of the giving of the Garden of Eden, because the Promised Land is a divine gift to a *fallen* people. For that reason the giving is more problematical, and the receiving is more conditional and more difficult. In the Bible's long working out of the understanding of this gift, we may find the beginning—and, by implication, the end—of the definition of an ecological discipline.

The effort to make sense of this story involves considerable difficulty because the tribes of Israel, though they see the Promised Land as a gift to them from God, are also obliged to take it by force from its established inhabitants. And so a lot of the "divine sanction" by which they act sounds like the sort of rationalization that invariably accompanies nationalistic aggression and theft. It is impossible to ignore the similarities to the westward movement of the American frontier. The Israelites were following their own doctrine of "manifest destiny," which for them, as for us, disallowed any human standing to their opponents. In Canaan, as in America, the conquerors acted upon the broadest possible definition of idolatry and the narrowest possible definition of justice. They conquered with the same ferocity and with the same genocidal intent.

But for all these similarities, there is a significant difference. Whereas the greed and violence of the American frontier produced an ethic of greed and violence that justified American industrialization, the ferocity of the conquest of Canaan was accompanied from the beginning by the working out of an ethical system antithetical to it—and antithetical, for that matter, to the American conquest with which I have compared it. The difficulty but also the wonder of the story of the Promised Land is that, there, the primordial and still continuing dark story of human rapaciousness begins to be accompanied by a vein of light which, however improbably and uncertainly, still accompanies us. This light originates in the idea of the land as a gift—not a free or a deserved gift, but a gift given upon certain rigorous conditions.

It is a gift because the people who are to possess it did not create it. It is accompanied by careful warnings and demonstrations of the folly of saying that "My power and the might of mine hand hath gotten me this wealth" (Deut 8:17). Thus, deeply implicated in the very definition of this gift is a specific warning against *hubris* which is the great ecological sin, just as it is the great sin of politics. People are not gods. They must not act like gods or assume godly authority. If they do, terrible retributions are in store. In this warning we have the root of the idea of propriety, of *proper* human purposes and ends. We must not use the world as though we created it ourselves.

*　*　*

The ability to be good is not the ability to do nothing. It is not negative or passive. It is the ability to do something well—to do good work for good reasons. In order to be good you have to know how—and this knowing is vast, complex, humble and humbling; it is of the mind and of the hands, of neither alone.

The divine mandate to use the world justly and charitably, then, defines every person's moral predicament as that of a steward. But this predicament is hopeless and meaningless unless it produces an appropriate discipline: stewardship. And stewardship is hopeless and meaningless unless it involves long-term courage, perseverance, devotion, and skill. This skill is not to be confused with any accomplishment or grace of spirit or of intellect. It has to do with everyday proprieties in the practical use and care of created things—with "right livelihood."

If "the earth is the Lord's" and we are His stewards, then obviously some livelihoods are "right" and some are not. Is there, for instance, any such thing as a Christian strip mine? A Christian atomic bomb? A Christian nuclear power plant or radioactive waste dump? What might be the design of a Christian transportation or sewer system? Does not Christianity imply limitations on the scale of technology, architecture, and land holding? Is it Christian to profit or otherwise benefit from violence? Is there not, in Christian ethics, an implied requirement of practical separation from a destructive or wasteful economy? Do not Christian values require the enactment of a distinction between an organization and a community?

Wendell Berry, *The Gift of Good Land: Further Essays Cultural & Agricultural*. San Francisco: North Point, 1981, 269–70, 275–76.

THOMAS MOORE (b. 1940)

[Moore, a Catholic, entered a religious community of monks embracing voluntary poverty but ultimately decided not to take vows. Moore's first passage is about begging; he reflects that asking for donations in our time takes many forms. His reflections prompt us to examine what we are asking for in our own lives. This theme of mortals as beggars is an old one—Thomas Hooker, the legendary American preacher of the seventeenth century, wrote a sermon on the topic, saying we are all beggars at the gate of mercy. The Book of Mormon asks: "For behold, are we not all beggars?" And Bob Dylan sings: "Name me someone that's not a parasite and I'll go out and say a prayer for him." We all depend, but we do not all acknowledge our dependence; we all have reason to feel humble, but not all are humble. Humility can make us more generous; who but one who realizes his debts feels a deep urge to pay back? Moore's second piece is about the experiential richness of acts of service, bringing out hidden truths about the relationships of those who would play a positive part in others' lives, deepening our understanding of the subtle dynamics involved in our interactions.]

Meditations

My community was called a mendicant order—begging, living off alms. Today begging is shameful to the middle class, a scandal to those who think everyone can and should work for a living. The homeless person on the street is surrounded by the emotional shadows of reprobation.

Yet, the most spiritual activities are funded by begging: public radio and television, charities, programs for the disadvantaged, medicine, education. Even today many who enter the most meaningful professions become mendicants.

If we are not beggars, we might ask ourselves if we have any spirituality in our lives.

Thomas Moore, *Meditations: On the Monk Who Dwells in Daily Life*. New York: HarperCollins, 1994, 79.

Voices from the Heart: In Celebration of America's Volunteers

People say they are looking for happiness, but happiness is usually a passing sensation. As a way of life, it always seems out of reach. What we may be looking for is something deeper, some fulfillment of our potential, experiences, perhaps, that we can look back on and say to ourselves, "Life has been worth living."

In the temper of the times we turn inward when we look for this kind of meaning. We develop skills and talents, try yoga and meditation, and buy any new gadget that promises deliverance from the ennui of modern living. With many exceptions to the rule, we have forgotten that turning outward and making a positive contribution to our family, our community, and the world at large may provide that meaning and purpose without which we feel aimless and empty.

Over the years I have sat in therapy with many men and women whose chief complaint was loneliness. They felt it bitterly and did crazy things to chase it away or fill the emptiness. In those painful moments of dialogue, I would avoid psychological analysis and instead ask if there were someone, a child or a sick person in the family or neighborhood perhaps, who needed attention. Loneliness is not always resolved by finding a partner or a group of friends—you can be very lonely in a crowd of people—but by becoming absorbed in service to nature and community.

We are a profoundly egocentric culture. Popular psychology recommends a strong sense of self, well-maintained ego boundaries, and wholesome self-esteem—all ego concerns that turn our attention inward and increase anxiety. The religious and spiritual traditions offer a completely different point of view. They say that we find our soul only when we lose our highly prized sense of self. As Jesus said, "Finding his soul he loses it; losing it because of me he finds it."

The pleasure we are looking for that makes sense of life and provides the feeling of being grounded comes from a deep place—not from the surface ego but from the deep soul. We could spend our lives at the complicated project of making a healthy ego, but real satisfaction comes as a grace from the depths. And often it comes in paradoxical ways. The *Tao Te Ching* says: "The sage never tries to store things up. The more he does for others, the more he has. The more he gives to others, the greater his abundance."

Spiritual sayings like these could be taken sentimentally and not mean much for practical living. On the other hand, they could offer a radically different philosophy of life, wherein we give up the entire effort of modern psychology to manufacture a conflict-free existence and instead discover an intense and deep sense of identity and purpose in service to others. Service is not just something we do out of the goodness of our hearts or from principle; it is a deep, archetypal experience of the soul, for which we have both a need and an instinct. Satisfying this need fulfills us at the very same time that it contributes to the world.

There is another paradox to be found in service, one that volunteers discover quickly. The real beauty of nature and of persons is often revealed within the ugliness of pain and suffering. One motivating reward for the volunteer is to discover the beauty and grace hiding beneath the veneer of suffering and deprivation.

✻   ✻   ✻

With courage and heart the volunteer may surrender free time, personal security, and attention to self in service that often appears unremarkable. But the reward is immeasurable because it fills the heart and soul rather than the wallet or the ego. The volunteer is granted a vision of deep human beauty and grace that is covered over to the person unwilling to get that close to life without a personal agenda. And this vision is transforming. It offers the elusive joy and happiness that others often expect to find in inadequate, less humble substitutes.

It's interesting to notice how the many attractions and preoccupations in modern life contrast precisely with the concerns of the volunteer. Many people look for pleasure in the endless supply of technological gadgetry that industry continues to provide. While the volunteer is on the streets or in the woods, the rest of us sit in front of televisions and computer screens. "Tele-vision" means "seeing at a distance." The volunteer is in the midst of life and therefore finds personal vitality in service. The television addict looks at life through a glass partition, at a safe distance, and develops a strange numbed interpretation of life. . . . I am led to think that volunteering is one of the best therapies in our society. Through active and giving involvement in our own communities and around the world we break through the dominant neurosis of our age—the emptiness we feel from the protective distance with which we view life today.

Everyone could and should be a volunteer. To be paid for service is certainly legitimate, but it doesn't have the personal effect that the volunteer enjoys. Volunteering is a stepping out of the supposed prudent ways of smart society and entering life through another door.

It isn't a way of helping as much as it is a way of being.

In stores I often find my books in a section labeled self-help. I have serious problems with both words. "Self," no matter how carefully defined, is inseparably linked to ego. I prefer the ancient word "soul" because it addresses both the important sense of "I," identity, and other. I also have trouble with the idea of helping. I don't see how to remove from that word a feeling of superiority. Sometimes people offer to help me in various ways, and if I haven't asked for help, I usually get a sinking feeling. I feel nudged deeper into my inferiority. So as a therapist and a writer, I try to keep my intentions clean. I don't start out with the idea of helping. If help happens, I guess that is all right.

I see a volunteer more as an adventurer than as someone pursuing a helping avocation. The volunteer has a good balance between service and self-realization. He or she enters more fully into life, and I assume that the desire for vitality inspires the volunteer. If all we do is do our paid work and see the side of experience limited by our social class and ethnic background, we only half live. The volunteer sees the promise for a fuller life in deeper engagement. The people he "helps," as any volunteer might confess, are usually his teachers.

The volunteer takes seriously and puts into simple, concrete practice the wisdom of the ages. The Self is neither within nor without, say the Upanishads. Just as salt dissolved in water spreads its taste everywhere, so the soul permeates everything. Accordingly, the volunteer finds her soul in the little world she pours herself into. The volunteer also disregards the modern idea that we are all independent atoms living in our isolated neighborhoods and homes. The volunteer doesn't argue the point, but lives out the philosophy that sees us all profoundly connected and mutually dependent. "Every atom belonging to me as good belongs to you," says Walt Whitman. Or, in the unsurpassed words of John Donne, who gradually found his way from a life of abandon to one of service as a father of seven and a pastor of countless souls:

> Every man is a piece of the continent.
> A part of the main.
> Any man's death diminishes me,
> Because I am involved in mankind.

Thomas Moore, in Brian O'Connell, *Voices from the Heart: In Celebration of America's Volunteers*. San Francisco: Jossey-Bass, 1999, 8–11.

JAMES HILLMAN (b.1926)

[Hillman, an insightful and influential thinker on matters of psychological understanding, is known as the originator of post-Jungian archetypal psychology. Just as Rockefeller saw giving as an art, Hillman sees service as an art. He explores the question, what is really involved in the kind of service people care about? And, how can we best serve? Hillman suggests that the ideal servant has a certain "precision consciousness" that falls within the tradition of aesthetic practice, and he helps us think about service as an activity so characterized. In this piece from his book Kinds of Power, he reminds us that service is a species of power. Other voices speak of giving with persuasive feeling and calculative logic; Hillman analyzes the gift of service with unique psychological insights. Like other Jewish thinkers of the modern era—Freud, Marx, and Einstein to name three—Hillman is original and iconoclastic.]

On Service and Philanthropy

Good service as measured by the standards of the well-heeled elite moves away from impersonal delivery toward a more personal and individualized touch. A concierge on each hotel floor, private hospital room with private nurse, more attendants per passenger in first-class air travel, chauffeured car or valet parking, a flow of personal hands-on attention: decorators, hairstylists, tailors, masseurs, financial planners. Good service by this standard simply wants "someone to talk with who can do well, and respectfully, what I ask for." Notice the five components in this definition: a human person, with language skills and sensitivity, adequate to the task, as judged by the recipient or customer. This is a far cry from automatic electronic devices. So which way do we go in thinking about service: more systematized or more personalized?

✳ ✳ ✳

Because we have had more than a hundred and fifty years of rapid, innovative, technological solutions that improve service delivery, we continue to imagine along the same paths, sometimes deaf to suggestions that service can improve by *non*-technological means. The old cliche holds: new wars are fought with the last war's weapons and by the last war's generals. Past ideas that once worked determine approaches to new problems.

As service machines replace physical labor—washing clothes, washing cars, washing floors—and as computer chips and software replace mental labor, our ideas of service remain tied to labor-saving devices. At the same time, surplus and inadequately paid labor have become the major concerns of futurists as well as the major parasite sucking the vitality of Western capitalism.

In the 1950s the Western idea of an efficient steel mill employed the fewest people per ton of product: in China the most efficient steel plant gave the most employment and had the highest ratio of persons per ton. Today we may be tilting toward that Chinese thinking as employment becomes as important as productivity for the well being of the nation. And it is in the service sector where the new jobs are found even as the imagination of that sector remains fastened to the old paradigms of productivity.

Because the imagination of business and industry remains under the spell of the productivity paradigm, a paradigm that favors high tech/low touch employment, we continue to devalue the obverse side of the coin so necessary for service: high touch/ low tech. And so our society continues to foment an under-rewarded, disrespected, resentful and recalcitrant work force, waiting for the lottery to lift them from the degra-dation inherent in the very idea of their jobs. So long as good service means "eliminat-ing what does not need to be done" (the "form follows function" theory of modernist architecture applied to human services), we will have barren no-frills service stripped of fantasy, restricting the imaginative power in those who serve. Good service takes the extra step, "goes out of its way," shows imaginative variations, finds precise ways of pleasing. It calls on imagination and delights the imagination as well as the senses. It is more Baroque than Bauhaus.

To move our ideas of service, we will have to clear away the usual discourse obses-sively focused on delivery, implementation, rationalization and performance, with mod-els drawn from McDonald's quick-serve systems and Federal Express's quick telephone response rule. The reduction to simplistics of the human delight in serving—caring, mending, nursing, teaching, cleaning, answering, helping, fixing, greeting, conserving, easing, feeding, leading—can only vitiate all our attempts at quality improvement on which the economy depends.

What after all is "quality" but the approximation to an ideal—that is, the idea of quality closes the gap between an actual material event and an idealized perfect form. By aiming at perfection, quality reminds the soul of ideal beauty. "Perfect service," we say. A quality chemical has not been degraded by substitutes, attempting to be 100 percent pure. A quality machine tool tolerates only micro dimensional imperfections. A quality service brings otherworldly expressions of praise: superb, graceful, beautiful, divine, marvelous, wonderful. As an *aesthetic* gesture, good service pleases both giver and recipient by the beauty of the performance, thereby enhancing life and adding value to an event that would otherwise be only a transaction.

This aesthetic idea of quality offers a different base for the acknowledged superiority of Japanese quality. I believe we have wrongly attributed that superiority to a set of eco-nomic and psychological factors only: the conformity of their work force and the homo-geneity of their population; their intense school pressure assuring habits of concentration and long attention span; their management-labor teamwork; their disciplined competi-tiveness from top to bottom; their traditions of obedience to rules (specifications), even to their "shame culture," in which errors become psychologically intolerable.

To these factors supposedly accounting for Japanese quality, I would add their aes-thetic sensibility that is essential both to the decorum of Japanese daily life and to the complexities of their imagistic language. From the beginning, the Japanese mind is set in a culture that pays devout attention to sensate details. Their hobbies in the refined arts—flower arrangement, tea ceremony, calligraphy, martial arts and weapons, min-iaturization, painstaking handcrafts, garden appreciation, food preparation, traditional dance—as well as the subtle infinitesimal variety of gestures in the Noh performances bespeak a "precision consciousness" of sensate aesthetic qualities in an attempt at the ideal. Precision consciousness is what we call "quality control."

Of course, this objective, aesthetic—impersonality can lead to empty formalism and the stultifying stiff mannerism that Americans see all too often in Japanese procedures. Any mode casts its shadow. I am not suggesting that we imitate the Japanese mode of service because it is better. I am rather suggesting that we notice that Japanese delivery of quality results from a precision consciousness based in an aesthetic tradition.

Quality service, then, enhances life by keeping one eye always on the ideal, striv-ing for the purity of perfection. Of course, the ideal cannot be achieved, for that is the nature of "ideal," which explains why an ideal is not simply a benchmark standard. "Ideal" implies qualities that are beyond any preset description. They are only pointers to how things should be and, perhaps, how they desire to be, as if something in each moment of life wants to transcend itself. Perhaps improvement is not only a human desire. Perhaps progress toward perfection, toward the realization of the ideal, is inherent in the very nature of things, which service recognizes by doing what it can to support this desire for enhancement, bringing out of each thing its best possible performance. This is the spiritual impulse that is the true root of service. Our service in life and our service to life attempt to return whatever we do to a utopic vision, the ideal of heaven, which each of us feels in the heart as an aesthetic joy whenever something is done really right.

In recent years service has been imagined more in human than in heavenly terms. Quality service has more and more come to be defined as "personalized service." This is due to the influence of therapeutic psychology with its needling insistence on personal feelings and personal relationships, a focus that disturbs the formal "codes" of conduct in business affairs. For business observes rituals that serve the task and the organization impersonally—cold, uncaring and patriarchal as that may seem.

When personalized service becomes the criterion of quality service, then more attention is paid to the relationship between receiver and provider than to the objective nature of the task. "Would you do this for me?" says the cabin attendant, asking me to pull my seat to an upright position for landing. Why do it for her? As a favor? As a personal kindness? Instead, we are performing the impersonal rituals of landing, the correct procedures that approximate an ideal form and have little to do with the human relations between her and me. The waiter's name does not bear upon the dinner for which I came to the restaurant—I'm not there to make his acquaintance. His concern for my dining will be shown neither by his imperative, "enjoy," as I begin, nor by his interrogation about the dishes afterward, but by his precision consciousness regarding each and every act, the rituals that he is there to perform, thereby doing his job beautifully.

Personalized service puts the person before the service. One person serves the other; I am in service to you, or you to me, so that the master/slave situation of servile servitude immediately lurks in the shadow, splitting surface sweetness on the one hand and aggressive resentment on the other. Only a saintly Sister of Charity can perform personalized service without being caught by the suppressed hostility emanating from this shadow.

It is the job that demands service; the objectivity of the job turns service into a ritual activity. Then we might regard service as less for the sake of a person than for a thing, an event or situation, less a disempowering servitude than an enhancement, less a subjective kindness than an objective ritual. Like waxing the floor to enhance its luster, like airing a room after everyone else has gone to bed.

By objective ritual, I mean the way a nurse bathes an immobile patient, a priest says Mass, an interpreter translates the text, an actor plays the part. In each of these cases the personal may interfere with the objective performance of the service and the specifications of the job. Not only persons call for service; their things do, too—the oil changed, the VCR cleaned, the dryer repaired, the message transmitted. Ceremonies of the repairman. Objects have their own personalities that ask for attention, just as the ads show the smiling bathtub that enjoys the new cleanser or the wood siding that likes the fresh stain which protects it from decay. Treating things as if they had souls, carefully, with good manners—that's quality service.

We have now sailed by, rather scornfully, the two main lines of discourse regarding service; the first, with reference to the deliverer's performance (the high-tech production model), and the second, with reference to the recipient's satisfaction (the model of personalized needs). We have left the arguments and measurements of delivery, satisfaction, performance, personal and impersonal altogether in order to return to where this chapter began. Let's look again into the old idea of service that is so abhorrent: service as servitude, inescapable bondage unto death. Not to a technical system of productive efficiency (Stangl [Commandant of a Nazi concentration camp; he claimed that the work he did there was service, and he had done nothing wrong]; and also what Japanese youth are beginning to rebel against), and not to a personal customer who is always right (Hegel's "master" become the consumer whose every wish one must obey). Rather, an idea of servitude to the Other, the Other as the planet as a whole and in each of its smallest components.

The idea of service that I am imagining would derive from deep ecology. The Gaia hypothesis holds that our world, this planet, is a breathing organism. It is all and everywhere alive and enjoys degrees of consciousness, where consciousness is no longer defined as an exclusive property of human beings and so no longer restricted to location only inside human skins and skulls. Although the Gaia hypothesis is recent and uses biological, physical and chemical evidence, the idea is as old as the pre-Socratic philosophers, Stoic cosmology, the Neoplatonic world soul (*anima mundi*), the universal dreaming Soul of Leibniz, and is founded in strata of myths of the earth which the name Gaia, Greek earth Goddess, deliberately indicates.

The careful reader will already have noticed, and perhaps been disturbed by, a characteristic of this book's style which reflects the Gaia hypothesis. The aberration endows all sorts of nouns with subjectivity. You have been reading sentences that attribute consciousness and intention, power even, to ideas, to things and especially to words. Words are given biographies, the book is said to have a task, and phenomena are described as displaying themselves without me or anyone else doing it for them. The book shares the power of agency between the human as subject of the sentences and other kinds of subjects that in most prose, other than children's books and science-fiction fantasy, are not entitled to the right to life. The very way the sentences are composed attempts to liberate the idea of soul from confinement in the human person, especially the first person singular, "I."

Service to a world ensouled implies that human life serves inescapably this large organic system. Our exhalations, our excreta, our emotions—whatever we humans generate—serve in one way or another this interdependent complexity we call the biosphere, and which other cultures describe with the names of powers, gods and goddesses. As servers in this organism we are inevitably both providers and recipients. Good service would be defined by estimations of what's good for the world's soul and bad service by what is neglectful and diffident.

*   *   *

This idea of service demands surrender, a continuous attention to the Other. It feels like humiliation and servitude only when we identify with a ruling willful ego as mirror of a single dominating god. But what if a God is in each thing, the other world distributed within this world?

Theology calls this distribution of the divine within all things the theory of immanence, and, sometimes, pantheism. Whether God is right here in things, whether each thing has its own God, whether there is one God or many Gods, or *any* Gods—these theological questions may fascinate but they are not immediately relevant to the practical point: service treats each particular thing as carrying its own specific value—including that airplane seat which I am asked to place in an upright position. By treating that seat as if it were animated with its own spirit I will be less likely to rough it up and more likely to show care. A cared-for seat will also perform better and provide longer-lasting service.

A theology of immanence means treating each thing, animate and inanimate (perhaps the distinction no longer clearly obtains), natural and man-made, as if it were alive, requiring what each living thing requires above all else: careful attention to its properties, their specific qualities. This plant needs little water; this wood won't bear great weight and burns with a smoky fire. Look at me carefully: I am an aspen, not an oak. Notice differences, pay attention, give respect (re-spect = look again). Notice what is right under your nose, at your fingertips, and attend to it as it asks, according to its needs. Aesthetic sensitivity. Precision consciousness.

These notions of attending and serving are the meanings of the Greek word *therapeia*, from which our word "therapy" comes. The Greek idea of a *therapeutes* was one who attended, was a servant of, and thereby could heal. A service relation to the planet could bring about its healing or at least maintain its health.

An aesthetic idea of service fits with what newer theory calls "high-touch" (rather than high-tech) service. This idea is aesthetic because it requires a sensitivity to the nature of that which is, calling for careful perception and sensitive reactions. These words, "sensation" and "perception," are the English translation of *aisthesis*, which referred in Greek not to some abstract theory of beauty, but to the perception of the sensate world as it appears. I am proposing the idea that service can be relocated *from* a purely functional concept allied with mechanical efficiency to a qualitative participation of the senses in systemic relations. Service then becomes *fitting ecological response*. Tasks now imagined mainly as duties, or penalties—cleaning up, detoxification, repair, scrubbing, recycling—become models for a therapeutic and aesthetic idea of service.

Suzi Gablik's book on the role of art in an ecologically conscious society describes compassionate action toward things as a new mode for Western art—art in service to the world [Suzi Gablik, *The Reenchantment of Art* (New York: Thames & Hudson, 1991)]. One chapter, describing an artist's devotion to the regular cleaning of the banks of the upper Rio Grande, portrays a ritual of service that is in keeping with a definition of art in its most extreme old-fashioned sense, "art for art's sake," but here no longer a private "creation" by a socially detached elite, separate from life and the surroundings, but in dedication to life and the surroundings. It is pure art, without compensation. It has no motive beyond the act, no program, no tendentious message—for the river cannot be cleaned by one person, if ever cleaned at all. It is ritual gesture, meditative devotion and service for its own sake, unprofitable and pleasing no customer.

We are now past conflicting definitions of our topic: one measured by corporate profitability, the other by consumer satisfaction, and have landed on a wider shore. Here I would risk defining service with two fundamentals: first, as *harmlessness*; second, as *enhancement*. The best service does the least harm and enhances as value or beauty. It offers the least possible offense to the gods in its performance, its materials and its purpose. Such service follows the ancient medical caution *primum nihil nocere* (first, to do no harm), allowing us to imagine service as a way of healing the world's ills, which it does by raising the quality of whatever it touches. Such service also fulfills the oldest idea of the

Hero who once was imagined to be a person who sought the ideal and whose courage and extraordinary gifts were in service to the Gods for the welfare of the community.

*   *   *

Subtle Power

Think of the harvest Goddess Demeter/Ceres with her cornucopia stuffed with edible pleasures. Think of the power of feasting in many non-Western societies, where the mark of prestige, authority and leadership, as well as the aim of ambition, is to give away to everyone all they can ever possibly eat [Lewis Hyde, *The Gift: Imagination and the Erotic Life of Property* (New York: Random House/Vintage, 1979)]. "Lean and mean" as the main means of productive power neglects the ultimate aim of the accumulation of profit in the history of American capitalism. The notable names give it all back: altruism, charity, endowment, magnanimity. The foundation fathers have become as important in American history as the Founding Fathers. Must generosity be put off until the end as part of the last will rather than incorporated into the good will of daily living?

Philanthropy, which means love of mankind, goes beyond the gifts of money and is not the privilege of only eminent persons of admirable character. Even the mean and the miscreant can be philanthropists, exercising power in daily life by pouring out their vitality in service to their work or their friends, like Picasso and Ezra Pound. The power of generosity has little to do with the personal intention of the giver and much to do with the impersonal effect of the gift. Philanthropy is also a propitiatory rite, an attempt to give back some of the power that was given to you lest you become a victim of your own gifts. King Midas in the old Greek story received the marvelous boon from Dionysos that whatever Midas touched would become gold. But as even his food and drink turned to gold, he had to pray again to Dionysos to take away the very gift that had made him so rich.

James Hillman, *Kinds of Power: A Guide to Its Intelligent Uses.* New York: Currency, 1997, 68–82, 205–6.

WILLIAM A. SCHAMBRA (b. 1933)

[Constitutional scholar William A. Schambra is director of the Hudson Institute's Bradley Center for Philanthropy and Civic Renewal in Washington and was appointed to the board of directors of the Corporation for National and Community Service in 2002. Neoconservative thinking on philanthropy offers perspectives that need to be seriously considered, whether one agrees with them or not. Politicians sometimes claim that the values of family, faith, and neighborhood are associated with a political affiliation, but like the differences between idealist and realist views, the deeper we look, the more we see good qualities as complexly distributed. This biographical memorial looks at one life in terms of effective leadership in conservative philanthropy.]

Michael Joyce's Mission: Using Philanthropy to Wage a War of Ideas

It was typical of Michael S. Joyce, who died last month at age 63, to focus one of his last major speeches about conservative philanthropy not on abstract ideologies or arcane public-policy concepts, but rather on his memories of a sultry evening in the late summer of 1995, when he appeared in the pulpit of Holy Redeemer Institutional

Church of God in Christ, Milwaukee's largest African-American congregation.

He was there as the chief executive of the Lynde and Harry Bradley Foundation, one of the nation's foremost conservative backers of "school choice," an effort to provide low-income parents with government-subsidized vouchers they could use to send their children to private schools.

The Wisconsin Supreme Court had just issued an injunction against Milwaukee's groundbreaking school-choice program, and several thousand parents who had been counting on it to escape what they considered failing public schools suddenly faced an uncertain and foreboding future.

That setback "was but one of many on the road to parental school choice—there will no doubt be more," Mr. Joyce noted in a lecture at Georgetown University. But that moment "demonstrates the patience of the approach we took and the abiding faith in the possibilities of active citizenship, even in the poorest communities, that undergirded our giving philosophy."

Mr. Joyce's rousing speech was capped by the announcement of $1-million [*sic*] in Bradley Foundation grants to tide the voucher families over until the program was reaffirmed. As he often noted afterward, this was the moment when school choice stopped being a dry-as-dust policy idea, and assumed a human face—the face of the desperate mother quoted in *The New York Times* who "would rather go to jail" than send her children back to the public schools.

Most of the accounts of Mr. Joyce's career will no doubt focus on the central role he played in training, supplying, and deploying conservatism's intellectual troops in modern America's war of ideas. Indeed, as fellow conservative foundation leader James Piereson has already noted, "he basically invented the field of modern conservative philanthropy."

Born into one of Cleveland's proudly blue-collar, Democratic, Irish Catholic neighborhoods in 1942, Mr. Joyce soon joined the ranks of the neoconservatives, who found that the liberalism of their fathers had turned against the sturdy, working-class values of family, church, and neighborhood that had boosted generations of Americans out of poverty.

Under the patronage of "godfather of neoconservatism" Irving Kristol, Mr. Joyce became executive director of the John M. Olin Foundation from 1979 to 1985, and then president and CEO of the Lynde and Harry Bradley Foundation from 1985 to 2001.

In those posts, backed by boards of directors scrupulously devoted to carrying out the original intentions of Mr. Olin and the Bradley brothers, Mr. Joyce helped direct millions of grant dollars to the scholars, writers, nonprofit organizations, and think tanks that today represent the intellectual infrastructure of the conservative movement.

It was necessary, in his view, to construct a set of parallel intellectual institutions, because the virulent radical doctrines of the 1960s counterculture had ruthlessly and systematically expelled conservative views from the primary cultural and intellectual organs of American life—the universities, the news media, Hollywood, and the professions of law, education, and theology.

Against liberalism's belief in compulsory governmental redistribution of wealth, Mr. Joyce's grantees helped revive the defense of a vigorous, free marketplace that had generated and generously dispersed historically unparalleled amounts of wealth.

Against liberalism's apparent abandonment of the defense of the West under the influence of morale-sapping, relativist doctrines of multiculturalism, Mr. Joyce's grantees argued for a vigorous, unabashedly patriotic defense of our nation's freedoms.

395

Against liberalism's moral doctrine of "if it feels good, do it," Mr. Joyce sought to shore up traditional commitments to family, faith, neighborhood, and voluntary associations—the local, value-generating institutions that he had known in Cleveland, and that taught personal and political self-governance, reflecting the dignity of the individual's divinely endowed, immortal soul.

Mr. Joyce summed up his work as "using philanthropy to support a war of ideas to defend and help recover the political imagination of the founders."

*　　*　　*

. . . Mr. Joyce came to understand the centrality of small, grass-roots, faith-based institutions as the means by which low-income people could, as the founders intended, solve their own problems in ways that social-service professionals often overlooked or ridiculed.

In pursuit of the faith-based notion, Mr. Joyce directed funds not only to the analysts in Washington and New York who argued for it.

He also supported the smallest, scrappiest community groups a few blocks from Bradley headquarters in Milwaukee's inner city, who were, as he often pointed out, creating jobs, tackling crime, tutoring young people, and conquering drug addiction without a single condescending social-service professional or overbearing government-contract officer in sight.

When George W. Bush began to formulate his own "compassionate conservative" proposals for advancing faith-based solutions to social problems as a part of his campaign for President, he called on Bradley-supported activists and scholars like Robert Woodson, Marvin Olasky, Myron Magnet, and James Q. Wilson. But he also consulted Milwaukee neighborhood leaders like Cordelia Taylor of Family House, a local community-based center that provides care to poor elderly people, and Holy Redeemer's Bishop Sedgwick Daniels. It was hardly coincidence that President Bush should have included in his first inaugural address a call to Americans to be "citizens, not spectators."

Inasmuch as one element in conservatism's recent success has been its ability to overcome a deep-seated, historic image of indifference to the poor, it was possible precisely through the development of serious conservative programs for reform in the way low-income Americans gain access to education and social services.

Mr. Joyce was at the very heart of such efforts. He fought to the end of his life to ensure that conservatism would never forget the faces of those parents at Holy Redeemer, and would continue to craft social policies that reflected the founders' commitments to individual spiritual dignity and citizen engagement through voluntary, civic associations.

William A. Schambra, The Chronicle of Philanthropy, March 2, 2006, http://www.philanthropy.com/free/update/2006/03/2006030201.htm.

MARVIN OLASKY (b. 1950)

[Olasky is a professor of journalism at the University of Texas, a conservative columnist and editor-in-chief of World magazine. Born into a Russian Jewish family, Olasky became an atheist, then a Communist, before finding Christianity and neoconservative thought. His ideas about compassion have influenced such national political leaders as Newt Gin-

grich, William Bennett, and George W. Bush. The principles Olasky discusses below are a checklist of good qualities he believes characterize compassionate conservatism.]

Seven Principles of Compassionate Conservatism

Assertive

The preamble to the Constitution speaks of government promoting the general welfare but not providing it. Alexis de Tocqueville was astounded to see Americans forming associations to fight poverty and other social ills rather than waiting for government to act. Such assertiveness surprised Europeans well into the twentieth century. This quality is depicted well in one of my family's favorite movies, *The Great Escape.* In it, captured pilot Steve McQueen refuses to kiss up to the prison camp commandant, who asks, "Are all American officers as ill-mannered as you are?" McQueen breezily responds, "About 99 percent, yeh." Recently, however, many Americans have become better mannered, meekly paying taxes and expecting a paternalistic government to fight poverty. Compassionate conservatism is the opposite of a wimpy doctrine; it emphasizes a renewal of the citizen assertiveness that so impressed the first great foreign journalist to come here, de Tocqueville.

Basic

Compassionate conservatives choose the most basic means of bringing help to those who need it. The goal is to look within the family first; if the family cannot help, maybe an individual or group within the neighborhood can; if not, then organizations outside the neighborhood but within the community should be called on. If it is necessary to turn to government, compassionate conservatives typically look first to municipal, then to county, then to state, and only then to federal offices. At each governmental level, the basics should be in order before proceeding to the more complicated stages. For example, a group that protects teenage ex-hookers from pimps should have adequate police protection. Good Samaritan laws should be enacted so that a person who helps a mugging victim does not have to fear a lawsuit. When such basic protection is in place and counterproductive regulations have been replaced, the next goal is improve information flow concerning an organization and to facilitate contributions. Then it is time to bring in questions of direct grants, tax credits, and so forth, always looking to the most basic level of government that can act efficiently on a particular problem.

Challenging

The tendency of affluent Americans has been to turn poor people into pets, giving them food and an occasional pat on the head but not pushing them to be all they can be. Over time, bad charity has tended to drive out good, because people given a choice of pampering or needed pressure generally take the easy route. But those who consider the good of others as more important than their own satisfaction challenge clients (and themselves) to stretch self-perceived limits. Hard, character-building work is often particularly important in this process. Compassionate conservatives do not merely give the poor a safety net that may turn into a hammock; they provide a trampoline. The goal is to have the affluent stretch their limits also. It's easy to write a check but hard to check pride and arrogance at the door when dealing with those who don't get much respect, or to travel to a part of town that is outside the middle-class comfort zone.

Diverse

Since the 1960s, the vast majority of agencies to which those in trouble are supposed to turn have all had similar three-step approaches. First, *take a number.* The egalitarian goal is to ensure that everyone is treated exactly alike so that no one has any legal standing to complain. Second, *take your money.* Make sure that everyone entitled to benefits receives those benefits, even if the process enables people to stay in misery, instead of pushing them to become financially independent. Third, *take your religious beliefs outside.* God is supposedly banished from the premises. The compassionate conservative goal is to offer a choice of programs: Protestant, Catholic, Jewish, Islamic, Buddhist, atheist. Some programs may emphasize education, some family, some work. Compassionate conservatives make sure that no one is placed in a particular type of program against his will, but they also try to make sure that religious people are free to communicate their values.

Effective

While understanding the severe limitations of government poverty fighting, compassionate conservatives do not assume that all private philanthropy is good and all government programs are automatically bad. Some private charities can be as bureaucratic, unchallenging, and downright foolish as their governmental counterparts, so the goal is to ask tough questions. Does a program have a success rate that can be quantified? Is the amount a group spends per person sensible in relation to services offered and their outcome? Does a group mobilize community strengths by efficiently using volunteers? Does a program use the professional capabilities of those who volunteer? The two bottom lines of helping organizations—lives changed, funds used efficiently—need assessment. The quantity of people fed or bedded down is not as significant as the quality question: What happens to those human beings?

Faith Based

Judging by the historical record and contemporary testimony, well-managed, faith-based programs are more effective in fighting poverty, on the average, than their nonreligious counterparts. Research studies show that church attendance tracks closely with lower dropout rates, less drug use, and fewer crimes committed. Faith-based organizations have shown that the best way to teach self-esteem and respect for law is to teach that we are esteemed by a wonderful God who set out for us rules of conduct that benefit society and ourselves. For civil rights reasons also, the First Amendment's guarantee of freedom *for* religion should not be taken to mean freedom *from* religion. Therefore, for both pragmatic and philosophical reasons, compassionate conservatives insist that the Bible (or the Koran) should not be excluded by judicial fiat from any antipoverty work, including that financed by government, as long as individuals have a choice of programs.

Gradual

The pragmatism of compassionate conservatives suggests careful checking on what works and what does not, each step of the way. A typical process (to use a Texas example) would be to start with one faith-based prison program, check results, and then expand it if graduates of that program have a reduced rate of recidivism. Similarly, to see if tax credits will increase the resources of nongovernmental antipoverty groups in a way that benefits society, the plan is to start with a limited program and then expand it if the pluses outweigh the minuses. The goal throughout is gradual, sustainable change, tested at each step of the way, rather than a revolution that could be quickly followed by counterrevolution.

Marvin Olasky, *Compassionate Conservatism: What It Is, What It Does, and How It Can Transform America*. New York: Simon and Schuster, 2001, 16–20.

JEFFREY SACHS (b. 1954)

[Sachs, director of the Earth Institute at Columbia University, Quetelet Professor of Sustainable Development, professor of health policy and management, and special advisor to the UN on the Millennium Development Goals, has proposed a plan to end world poverty. To some, this sounds audacious; to others, like common sense. If not us, who? If not now, when? The interview below is from Mother Jones, an alternative nonprofit magazine known for investigative reporting, the most read progressive periodical in the United States. In it, Sachs answers questions about his plan. Sachs is an economist, and his approach to helping the poor is neither religious nor philosophical but pragmatic and statistical, based in social sciences. The self-interest motive is often neglected when considering world poverty, but the well-being of others can be an important component in attaining our own well-being.]

The End of Poverty: An Interview with Jeffrey Sachs

Mother Jones: What makes your plan to end poverty so different from the development efforts that were tried in the 1950s and 60s? Why hasn't five decades worth of development work been very successful thus far?

JEFFREY SACHS: I think so far there's been a lack of appropriate effort, which includes many things. For development to work, rich countries need to help poor countries make certain practical investments that are often really very basic. Once you get your head around development issues and realize how solvable many of them are, there are tremendous things that can be done. But for decades we just haven't tried to do many of these basic things. For instance, one issue that has been tragically neglected for decades now is malaria. That's a disease that kills up to 3 million people every year. It's a disease that could be controlled quite dramatically and easily if we just put in the effort. It's truly hard for me to understand why we aren't.

MJ: What do you say to critics who argue that it's a waste to put more money into a development system that hasn't used that money very effectively thus far?

JS: Well, we have to be smart about whatever we're doing. But I'm quite convinced that, broadly speaking, economic development works. The main arguments of the Millennium Project Report, and the main argument of my book is that there are certain places on the planet that, because of various circumstances—geographical isolation, burden of disease, climate, or soil—these countries just can't quite get started. So it's a matter of helping them get started, whether to grow more food or to fight malaria or to handle recurring droughts. Then, once they're on the first rung of the ladder of development, they'll start climbing just like the rest of the world.

MJ: So do you believe that past efforts, to get these less-developed countries on the "first rung," haven't been pragmatic enough?

JS: Part of it is that many of these countries are invisible places, neglected by us politically, neglected by our business firms, by international markets, and by trade. We tend to focus on these countries only when they're in such extraordinary crises that they get shown on CNN because they're in a deep drought or a massive war, which is something that impoverished countries are much more prone to falling to. There haven't been too many stories in our press about Senegal, Ghana, Tanzania, Malawi, or Ethiopia, other than when the disasters hit. And yet these are places that are in very deep trouble all of the time, but with largely solvable problems. And those are the kinds of the places that I'm talking about as being stuck in extreme poverty.

MJ: If there's been no real effort to draw the world's attention to those places, is there any hope that funding will go there?

JS: The world got side-tracked from development issues during the post-9/11 crisis period. During the war in Iraq there were bitter divisions in the world community, and the idea of being able to focus on the problems of extreme poverty or malaria or drought and chronic hunger in Africa were just not at the top of the world's debate.

But I think the tsunami in the Indian Ocean last December, in which we could all see the scope of the devastation on our television screens, shifted discussion towards the plight of the world's poor. So now there are some positive signs. Tony Blair has pushed for an Africa Commission which just produced a report in March that focuses on poorest of the poor in Africa. There will be a UN poverty summit this September which is predicted to be the largest gathering of world leaders in history. And I'm traveling extensively around the world talking about these issues. So I think that even in our country, there is a growing discussion.

*　　*　　*

MJ: Some critics have expressed concern that the Millennium Goals may set unrealistic targets for certain countries. What if those countries fail to meet the specified level of development and then disillusioned donors decide to lower their funding?

JS: First, it should be understood that the goals in most cases are set proportionate to a given country's situation. So we'll reduce by 2/3 the child mortality rate, or by 3/4 the maternal mortality rate. We're not aiming at the same absolute standard in every country. I think that the other thing that is really important to understand is that I have been working with the UN on this for the last 3 years and meeting leaders all over the world. What I've found is that their concern isn't that the goals are too high. Exactly the opposite: They actually *want* these UN goals, they want them to be ambitious, and they want to be held to account. And they want their development partners, the developed world, to be held to account on following through on commitments. Again, this all goes towards pressuring rich nations to set aside 0.7 percent of GNP for development aid. That is not a goal that I set, or that the UN set, this is a goal that was adopted 35 years ago by the world community and the goal that was set again in the Monterrey consensus signed by the U.S. in 2002.

MJ: What about aid being sent to countries that have a serious problem with corruption? Some have argued that large amounts of aid will merely prop up those regimes. Can poverty be eradicated while corrupt politicians are in office?

JS: My experience is that there's corruption everywhere: in the U.S., in Europe, in Asia, and in Africa. It's a bit like infectious disease—you can control it, but it's very hard to eradicate it. And yes, there are some cases where the corruption is so massive that unless you are really, really clever and come up with some radically new approach to the issue, you're going to have a hard time accomplishing many development goals. It's quite hard in a place like Zimbabwe, now, where the current government, in a quite despicable way, clings to power. Or, in a country where there is absolutely no transparency or where you have a family ruling violently to stay in power. It's very hard to do a lot of the things that really need to be done to build an effective school system, a health system, and so on. I don't have any magic solution for those situations.

But, let me note that the world successfully eradicated small pox, and not just in countries that scored high on a governance index but in all parts of the world. This was an international effort which targeted a specific outcome undertaken by professionals using a proven technology and a very extensive monitoring system. And that's the general model for our aid proposals. Nothing is done on trust. Everything should be done on a basis of measurement and monitoring. When you really focus, there are so many ways to be clever about how to do this to make it work better. Don't just send money; send bed nets, send in auditors, make targets quantitative. There are a lot of tricks, a lot of ways, that if one is practical about this, one can get results.

But what happens is that everyone's wringing their hands about corruption without trying to solve practical problems. And right now, we're not even helping the *well-governed* places, the places where we are capable of finding absolutely practical and effective approaches to turning help into real success on the ground. The basic issue is not to lecture about morality and governance. The basic issue is, is there a way for us to help to fight AIDS, TB, malaria, and other killers which are taking an incredible number of lives? I've seen these children dying, each time I visit these clinics. And these are absolutely preventable deaths.

*   *   *

MJ: In your book, you recount some of your experiences in developing countries. In one passage you note, "One day in Goni's office we were brainstorming and hit on the idea of establishing an emergency social fund that would direct money to the poorest communities to help finance local infrastructure like water harvesting, or irrigation, or road improvements. I picked up the phone and called the World Bank. Katherine Marshall, the head of the Bolivia team at the Bank immediately responded, "You're right, let's do this." [sic] Why is it that a whole World Bank team specializing in Bolivia hadn't come up with the idea that you had?

JS: Well, sometimes they have ideas, sometimes I have ideas. It just so happened in this case that the idea came from me. But I do feel that in Washington over the last 25 years, especially during this era called "the structural adjustment era," there hasn't been a lot of actual problem-solving. There has been a lot of concern about budget-saving on the part of the rich countries. A lot of what was really happening in Washington had a subtext: "Keep poor people away from our taxpayers, tell them to tighten their belts, tell them to solve their own problems, tell them to keep sending their debt payments to us."

It was, in my view, a very unhappy and unsatisfactory period and there were, no doubt, a lot of creative people that were prepared to do a lot of things but they weren't given assignments to do that. I was absolutely shocked and aghast when I learned that in the late 1990s the World Bank and other donors weren't paying a penny to help treat people dying of AIDS.

Rarely do rich countries say, "Look, we're just not prepared to spend money to save poor people's lives." Instead, you get a lot of skepticism. "You can't do this, this is impossible. We're doing everything we can after all. We've tried everything. Let's go slowly.

401

Let's do one thing at a time." I don't buy those arguments. I think that they all essentially stem from a vision that has been forced on the professional staff of these agencies because they have no money to spend. And they have no money to spend because in the end, the United States and other rich countries aren't giving them the resources to enable them to think ambitiously enough. One of the reasons why that is, is because the American people think we're doing everything we can be doing and frankly because they're told that there's nothing more we can do.

MJ: Do you think the U.S. will ever agree to dedicate 0.7 percent of its GNP to development aid?

JS: I don't think that any leading politician believes we're going to do that right now. It's not the conventional wisdom. The way it's going to happen is if the public tells the politicians, "Yes, we want to do this, we want to follow through on our word, it's good for us, and it's good for the world."

I've found in talks and discussion about the Millennium Project that people are very surprised to find out what the U.S. is and is not doing vis-à-vis the world's poor. Opinion surveys show, and I find this verified in audiences, e-mails, and discussion groups, that people tend to overestimate U.S. assistance efforts, usually by a factor of about 25 or 30. People think that we give several percent of our annual income and several percent, maybe even a quarter of our budget to foreign aid and they're shocked to find out that it's actually much less than 1 percent of our budget. They're shocked to find that throughout Africa, the kind of practical investments that I'm talking about run to about 1 penny out of every $100 of our GNP. They can't believe it, but that's the unfortunate situation. When they find that out, and they see that we're spending $500 billion on the military and only about $1 to $2 billion on investments in Africa, they're concerned because I think that they feel this is probably not the best choice for America . . .

What the Africa Commission, the Millennium Development Report, the World Bank and IMF have all found is that right now poor countries could usefully absorb a tremendous increase of money and use it properly. The IMF and World Bank recently released a report called the Global Monitoring Report which said that aid should be doubled. There is a professional understanding that the money is needed to break the poverty trap and save lives and that the money can be effectively used.

Jeff Sachs interview with Onnesha Roychoudhuri in *Mother Jones,* May 6, 2005, http://www. motherjones.com/news/qa/2005/05/jeffrey_sachs.html.

CELEBRITY PHILANTHROPY

[In contemporary society, the story of America expands to include celebrities who are known around the globe. Prominent media figures bring attention to causes and make notable contributions to charities and nonprofit organizations. Fame brings responsibilities today, more so than in decades past— much is expected from Americans who have been given much. Who does not know something about Oprah and her charitable works? Who has never heard of Angelina Jolie and Brad Pitt's work, or Madonna's health-care center in Malawi? Willy Nelson and Farm Aid? Many celebrities have found that giving back is a soulful way to stay grounded. Helping others keeps one joined to basic human life; by forgetting oneself in addressing others' problems, one can find satisfaction and escape the infamous disasters of excessive egoism.]

The Public Face of Generosity

Who is generous? If we look at stories in the media, we might answer: certain celebrities and prominent people are striving to be generous.

Entertainers—high profile celebrities—can give something back by bringing attention to charities. In the various religions and wisdom systems of the world, we are not supposed to treat another person as an "it," an object to exploit, but as a "thou," revered and loved with a sense of mutual relationship. But some celebrities seem to say that perhaps there are times when it is good to treat our own egos as "its"—to selflessly treat one's fame as an object useful for generating support for a worthy cause. When they find a mission, some stars go all out for it, traveling the world, giving their time and resources, lending their support in various ways. Celebrities can attract fans to a cause and make it hip to be involved in solving problems that otherwise might languish in neglect.

For example, consider longtime Hollywood stars known for their benefit events. Bob Hope and Bing Crosby had their charity golf tournaments, and Jerry Lewis devoted his time to annual telethons for muscular distrophy and the March of Dimes. (Bob Hope quipped "If you haven't any charity in your heart, you have the worst kind of heart trouble.") Johnny Cash did prison outreach, charity concerts, and raised money for SOS Children and other good works. Danny Thomas and his daughter Marlo are known for their work for St. Jude Children's Research Hospital. (The hospital was built in Memphis because Thomas heard of an African American child being refused treatment in a segregated southern hospital. Today it is the fourth largest charitable health-care institution in America.) Paul Simon founded, and Marc Anthony and Jennifer Lopez are active in supporting, the Children's Health Fund. Matt Damon founded OneXOne to help the poverty stricken in Africa.

George Burns raised funds for Ben Gurion Hospital in Israel. Marlon Brando made efforts for Native American causes, sometimes stirring up controversy in the process. Sally Struthers raised awareness of hungry children around the world by making appeals on TV and in magazine ads. Actor Paul Newman founded "Newman's Own" food products company and has given all profits (totalling over $200 million) from it to thousands of charities. He and his wife, Joanne Woodward, are known for Hole in the Wall Gang camps for children with cancer and other life-threatening illnesses. Kirk Douglas and his wife are known for their funding of Harry's Haven, a facility for people suffering from Alzheimer's. Singer Lou Rawls raised funds for a quarter of a century for the United Negro College Fund. Bill Cosby has contributed millions to support African American educational institutions, including Spelman College and Fisk University.

Elizabeth Taylor raises awareness and funds for AIDS research, and a galaxy of other stars join her. Comics Billy Crystal, Whoopi Goldberg, and Robin Williams raise money by hosting a fundraiser named Comic Relief. Established in 1986 by Bob Zmuda and held from time to time, Comic Relief is televised on HBO and has raised and paid out $50 million for health-care services to homeless people in America. In 2006 Comic Relief raised money for victims of Hurricane Katrina. Don Cheadle and Mia Farrow have been hard-working activists trying to call attention to the plight of the victims of the Janjaweed militia in Darfur. Garth Brooks speaks for many around the country when he sings "The Change," a song explaining that he's reaching out not to change the world, but so that the world won't change him.

Bette Midler buys vacant lots in New York City, helping residents turn them into gardens for neighborhood people to enjoy. Edward Norton works with the BP Solar Neighbors program connected with the Enterprise Foundation, which helps low-income homeowners cut down on energy bills by means of solar power. Richard Gere (and Sharon Stone and Steven Segal and Adam Yauch) benefit Dalai Lama and Tibetan Buddhist causes. Doris Day worked for animal protection. Texas singer Kinky Friedman has a kennel to care for stray dogs. Ed Asner, Alec Baldwin, Ed Begley Jr., Berk Breathed, Dixie Carter, Mary Chapin Carpenter, Whoopi Goldberg, Steve Guttenberg, Anne Heche, Tippi Hedren, Anjelica Huston, Diane Keaton, Ali MacGraw, Bill Maher, Mary Tyler Moore, Frankie Muniz, Kevin Nealon, Victoria Principal, Christina Ricci, Britney Spears, Jerry Stiller, Betty White, Montel Williams, and Robin Williams are all active in causes protecting animals from cruelty.

In recent years Oprah has been named the most generous show-biz celebrity. She is said to have given $300 million of her own money to charity. She is highly respected in South Africa for her support of schools there. In 2006 she established a school for bright South African girls showing the promise of leadership. Her Angel Network, which benefits people in need, draws support from other stars—such as Jon Bon Jovi who gave her a million dollar check. (His cause is to help remedy urban blight.) Rosie O'Donnell has organized "Rosie's Broadway Kids" to give theater-arts opportunities to children in New York's public schools. A galaxy of stars including Quincy Jones, Michael Jackson, and Lionel Richie joined forces to make the song "We Are the World," which benefited those who were suffering in an African famine in 1985. Although Bono of U2 is not an American, he is a celebrity who has had an impact on American foreign policy regarding AIDS and the forgiving of Third World debt. Don Imus' offering the facilities of a Texas ranch to be used by kids with cancer and autism is another example of a celebrity giving back to society.

Leonardo DiCaprio is associated with support for TreePeople, which works to encourage Los Angeles citizens to care for urban trees. Angelina Jolie serves as ambassador for the United Nations High Commissioner for Refugees, an agency that helps 20 million displaced people with humanitarian aid in over 120 countries. She also gives one third of her income to the causes she believes in. Brad Pitt has donated money and garnered support for African and other Third World charities. Jon Seda works for patients suffering with reflex sympathetic dystrophy syndrome. Bob Sagit works for Jewish charitable causes.

Russell Simmons contributes generously to Rush Philanthropic Arts, which gives city kids more access to arts and opportunities to minority artists. Playwright Wendy Wasserstein created a mentoring program that served to open New York theaters to public-high-school students. As a memorial to Tupac, his mother founded Tupac Amaru Shakur Foundation for the Arts to offer art programs to youths. "What we do now matters forever," is a motto at the foundation website. The Tavis Smiley Foundation also encourages and empowers youth with a variety of programs. As Jesse Jackson said, "Never look down on anybody unless you're helping him up."

"Success for Good," an Arizona-based national nonprofit organization dedicated to supporting and raising awareness for the nonprofit sector, honored in 2006 four high-profile recipients of the annual "Golden Karma Awards": (1) actress Jane Seymour for her work with the American Red Cross. (Her work with the Red Cross in Kenya was the subject of a documentary by her husband, James Keach, and led her to form the

J & J Foundation to benefit children in need.); (2) actress Jessica Biel for charitable works supporting Best Friends Animal Sanctuary and Serving Those Who Serve and PETA. (Her own charitable organization, the Make the Difference Network, provides a national "wish list" where those in need can find funding from nonprofit organizations.); (3) actress Marlee Matlin works for The Children Affected by AIDS Foundation; (4) Hollywood Mayor Johnny Grant for his years of service to the USO. (For more information see http://www.goldenkarmaawards.org/news.html.) In 2007 American Idol Gives Back raised $70 million in two nights to change the lives of children and young people trapped in extreme poverty. Such generosity is a hopeful sign.

Who's generous? Sports heroes are often seen as role models in America today. Muhammad Ali has championed numerous causes, including forgiveness of Third World debt. Tiger Woods Charities Foundation is devoted to the benefit of youths and promotion of excellence in their endeavors. Andre Agassi has a charitable trust that founded a college-prep school in Las Vegas to encourage underserved kids. He has spent over $14 million on children's charities. The Lance Armstrong Foundation was formed to inspire and empower cancer patients through various education, advocacy, public health, and research programs. Doug Flutie is a strong supporter of autism research. New York Yankee catcher Jorge Posada is a spokesman for craniosynostosis. Distinguished sports writer Frank Deford presently serves as chairman emeritus for the Cystic Fibrosis Foundation, an organization he has worked with for years.

We could go on and on, but this indicates something of celebrity philanthropy. Each person has his or her own reasons for helping others. Often some personal experience has opened their hearts. Perhaps the well rewarded feel the need to give back and benefit the less rewarded. As the saying derived from the New Testament (Luke 12:48) goes, "From those to whom much has been given, much will be expected."

William J. Jackson, compiled from a variety of news stories, press releases, and articles in magazines and on the Internet.

BILL CLINTON (b. 1946)

[The responses of individuals and groups to tragedies like the 2004 tsunami, Hurricane Katrina, and Darfur and to problems like the AIDS epidemic are often as important as the response of government agencies. Bill Clinton, since serving as president, has worked energetically on international crises of great magnitude. His philanthropic work, like Jimmy Carter's, is influential. Both former presidents come from Baptist backgrounds, and the ethos of Christian compassion is shown in the causes they support and in the efforts they make. In this piece, Clinton discusses emerging patterns in philanthropy.]

On Philanthropy

It's important to point out that not only the ways of giving are changing but the people—when I saw that film I was so proud that there was a federal employee that had given every single month for 25 years. [The film was a videotape titled "Philanthropic Heroes," the federal employee was a woman named Mary Grayson.] Someone obviously of modest means, doubtless a lot of other claims on her income. So I want to thank people like Mary Grayson and others who are giving. And I think we ought to think about new opportunities, or I think the buzz word is "portals," that are opening in the world of on-line philanthropy and how we can make sure that we can continue not only to increase the volume of money but to broaden the base of giving. We'll hear today about venture philanthropists and start-up charities and other ways in which the entrepreneurial spirit is invading and energizing this field.

I would like to also point out that volunteering is another important way of giving. This week, Hillary and I celebrated the fifth anniversary of AmeriCorps. And we've already had 150,000 young people serve. And I'm very, very proud of that. (Applause.) I think that is an important thing to say. In a lot of ways, the measure of our life and our happiness is—to paraphrase one of the many wonderful things Martin Luther King said, can be answered by the question: what are you doing for others?

So I'm encouraged by this conference, by the energy here. Some of my favorite people in all our country are out here in this audience today, people I have admired, some of you for 20 or 30 years, for all the things that I have watched you do for others. And I thank you for coming.

I am glad that the sheer volume of charitable giving is going off the charts. But I think, as we've had this phenomenal increase in wealth in our country, I would feel even better if the percentage of our national income devoted to charitable giving had gone up just a little bit. You heard Hillary say what we could do if we could just increase it by 1 percent. But going from 2 to 3 percent is a huge increase. We've been sort of stuck at 2 percent. Now, when the stock market triples, 2 percent is a lot more than it used to be. That's not real pocket change; it's real money.

But if you think about what we could do with just a little more, I think it is really worth pondering. We're having the same debate in Congress now, and I don't want to get into any kind of political dispute about that, but just let me give you an example. I very much want the United States to take the lead with the rest of the wealthy countries in alleviating the debt of the poorest countries in the world. And the Pope has asked us to do it for the millennium—(applause.) Now, this is a campaign with a broad base: it's being spearheaded by the Pope and Bono, the lead singer for U2. (Laughter.) And even though I am not a candidate for anything anymore, I can spot a big tent when I see it. (Laughter.)

So, you know, we ought to do this. And this is just a little bit of all the money we've got. And it's just like de Tocqueville said a long time ago, this is not just charity; this is good citizenship. We take this burden off these people. If they are well governed and they are working hard, we give them a chance to be our partners and friends in a more equal and balanced way for the future.

So there are things for all of us to do. I would like to—I would hope today that I will learn something and that we will learn something about how we can at least incrementally increase the percentage of our income we are devoting to philanthropy. I hope we will learn something, as I already said, about the ways we can do it. And I hope we will learn a little bit about whether we can all give smarter and whether we can make sure that the money we are giving is spent in the most effective possible way.

I take it we all begin by accepting that we no longer believe that there is a choice out there—which was never a real choice—between government meeting all of our society's needs, and government walking away from them all and letting philanthropy do it. We have to have a better partnership, and it will work better if we do.

We need to think about, in government, whether we can do more things to generate more constructive philanthropy. The Treasury Department will meet with representatives of the nonprofit sector next month to discuss this. And I, in the meanwhile, am going to establish an inter-agency task force to strengthen our philanthropic partnership between government, nonprofit groups, and citizens; and to ask the Council of Economic Advisors to do me a study on the role of philanthropy in the American economy, and how they believe I can increase it.

By analyzing trends in charitable giving, by assessing the impact of the baby boomers' retirement, which—it's going to be interesting to see whether it makes us more or less generous when we retire, this largest of all generations of Americans. It should make us more generous, because the kids in school are finally the first generation bigger than the baby boomers, and they need our help.

But we need to think about that. What's our message going to be to the baby boomers as they move toward retirement? What's our message going to be to people thinking about the shape of our social tensions as we double the number of people over 65 in the next 30 years? What's our message going to be to ourselves, those of us in the baby boom generation, about how our citizenship responsibilities should grow when we lay down the burdens of retirement, particularly if we've been lucky enough to have a secure way to maintain our standard of living.

This is deserving of an awful lot of thought because there is a whole bunch of us. And on the whole, those who manage to escape a career in politics are going to be better off than any generation in American history. (Laughter.) So some serious thought needs to be given to this.

Well, I've had a little fun with this today. (Laughter.) But I am really grateful to you all for being here. This is a big deal. We all know—the truth is we're all fairly pleased with ourselves for being here because you feel better about your life when you've spent a portion of it doing something for somebody else. And you feel better about the good fortune you have financially if you spend at least a little of it giving something to someone else.

So what we want to do is to start the new millennium poised to do more and to do it better. And to give more chances to more people to participate.

Remarks by President William Jefferson Clinton (White House Conference on Philanthropy, "Gifts to the Future," October 22, 1999).

EPILOGUE

WENDELL BERRY (b. 1934)

[This poem envisions the gifts of existence in a God-given world and speaks of the dependence and responsibilities of humans. Berry's words urge us to go beyond our habits and limits to experience deeper relations to earth and fellow humans. His poetry is informed by experiences of the natural world, such as the ways of a river. He speaks suggestively of the gifts we receive, how they shape who we are, and how our use of them, as well as their abuse and loss, form our story and our legacy.]

The Gift of Gravity

All that passes descends,
and ascends again unseen
into the light: the river
coming down from sky
to hills, from hills to sea,
and carving as it moves,
to rise invisible,
gathered to light, to return
again. "The river's injury
is its shape." I've learned no more.
We are what we are given
and what is taken away;
blessed be the name
of the giver and taker.
For everything that comes

is a gift, the meaning always
carried out of sight
to renew our whereabouts,
always a starting place.
And every gift is perfect
in its beginning, for it
is "from above, and cometh down
from the Father of lights."
Gravity is grace.
All that has come to us
has come as the river comes,
given in passing away. And if our wickedness
destroys the watershed,
dissolves the beautiful field,
then I must grieve and learn
that I possess by loss
the earth I live upon
and stand in and am.

Wendell Berry, *The Gift of Gravity*. New York: Workman, 1979, 1–2.

✦ CONCLUSION ✦

Who Is Generous?

With the interconnectedness that we share as one
Every action that we take affects everyone
—FROM "BODHISATTVA VOW" BY THE BEASTIE BOYS

Born with "mirror neurons,"[1] humans soon develop sympathy for others; an extension of sympathy is generosity. Trained by parents at home, by parables in religious teachings, and by heroic acts in stories we hear, we are confirmed in our caring for others. We are called by voices without and within. Unless we mourn with humanity in humanity's mourning, our "griefs grieve on no universal bones"[2] but only on small potatoes. With larger hearts, we can help make lives better.

The creative work of philanthropy is a kind of expansive performance art producing a drama of transformation, helping humanity realize potentials. Just as we have invented the fractal-like cluster bomb that multiplies the scale of explosive power, so, too, we can innovate fractal-like forces for good, generating life-supportive effects, multiplying them.

The first generations of Europeans in America had to help each other, both to survive and to make life humane and worth surviving.

The Puritans sailed forth to found a new Promised Land, feeling they were God's elect. Their ideals included charity to improve the lives of Native Americans they encountered here. Although fully developed voluntary associations were not a significant aspect of colonial society, the Puritans carried some of the necessary values found in voluntary associations.

English philosopher John Locke, born of Puritan parents, developed the concept of Civil Society, which influenced the Scottish Enlightenment, which in turn influenced the American expression of philanthropy. The Enlightenment, with thinkers like Franklin and Jefferson, endeavored to return to a more ideal state of nature, discerning the way with reason and liberty. Philanthropy meant founding educational and social-uplift institutions. After the Revolution, new voluntary associations came into existence at the town and state levels to face emerging social challenges. In 1790, America's population was 3.9 million. The era from 1790 to 1840 has been called a burgeoning Age of Benevolence. Where in earlier times charitable actions were undertaken by individuals, the scale and organization of actions to benefit others now grew and became more systematic and institutionalized.

The Jacksonian era (1829–1837) had its tragedies, including the banishment of Indian tribes to western regions, but it brought also a time of imagination. The visions of Whitman, Emerson, Thoreau, Hawthorne, and Melville, infused with spiritual philosophies and intuitions, sought the soul of America to understand America's unique destiny. By 1880, America's population had grown to 50 million. Immigrant aid societies grew, helping newcomers get a start and assimilate into American culture. By 1915, 100 million people were living in America.

The generations who built up America's industries and wealth and attained greatness through innovations and creativity found that by becoming philanthropists, they could make their material success a fulfillment of human meaning. By 1950, America was home to 5 percent of the world's population, had more wealth than the rest of the world, and produced the majority of what it consumed. By 1967 we were 200 million; by 2006, 300 million. The ever-growing scale comes with new needs to be addressed.

Who is generous? Society pages of newspapers run headlines and photos of "celebutantes" at charity balls and fund-raising dinners. It seems the socially conscious wealthy are generous. But are our casually gathered impressions accurate? What do statistics tell us?

Recent research (Arthur C. Brooks' book *Who Really Cares* [New York: Basic Books, 2006]) indicates that those who go to church or another place of worship as children are more giving as adults. It suggests that we learn charity as children from our families, ministers, Sunday-school teachers, synagogue and mosque leaders, and other communicators of community values.[3] Secular liberals and secular conservatives give less to religious organizations, often donating more to secular ones.

Conservative Americans, according to this research, give significantly more (30 percent more per head of a family) than those who believe their tax dollars should be used by the government to help the poor and other charitable causes. Another recent research project[4] suggests, "Baby Boom religious giving is much less than that of their parents' generation (at similar points in the life-course); the transmission of religious giving from parents to children is much stronger than the transmission of secular giving; poverty and family disruption during adolescence affects later giving and volunteering; and a moral principle of care has a stronger direct relationship with pro-social behavior than does empathy."[5] So the religiously raised tend to be generous. And the spirit of giving is expressed and enabled in ever-new ways; some megachurches are installing ATMs to make giving easier for congregants. But statistics also indicate that smaller churches often have higher levels of individual-member giving, so congregation size is not an absolute factor.

Who is generous? The working poor are generous—more so than average middle-class Americans. The working poor who attend religious services regularly are especially generous and may sport license plates that say BN BLST (Been blessed), and feeling gratitude, give to others. "There are a million ways to give to charity. Toy drives, food drives, school-supply drives…telethons, walkathons, and danceathons. But just who is giving? Three quarters of American families donate to charity, giving $1,800 each, on average. Of course, if three quarters give, that means that one quarter don't give at all."[6] The wealthy give more in total dollars donated,[7] but those with less income give away almost 30 percent more of their income. Why? Perhaps because they know what it's like to be in need, and so they commiserate and do something about it.

In our postmodern age, simple old formulas and categories have grown in complexity. For many Americans in their thirties, religiosity and church membership do not constitute the mainspring of motivation or primary channel of giving. Instead, an individual sense of spirituality is at play. Many report tithing to social concerns; conscience and personal ethics, rather than religious organizations per se, are important to them. Online philanthropy is a new avenue used increasingly by contributors. Bloggers seeking donations for worthy charities, and MySpace and Facebook personal profiles making appeals for support of important humanitarian causes are multiplying. In the twenty-first century, cyberspace giving is growing far beyond what it was in the previous century.

Who is generous? Ethnic and religious groups and nonprofits helping the vulnerable—African American philanthropy, Hispanic philanthropy, the Korea Society, Muslim charities, Catholic Charities USA, American Friends Service Committee, Universalist Unitarians Service Committee, Latter-day Saints Charities, Lutheran World Relief, The Association of Evangelical Relief and Development Organizations, Native American philanthropy such as the work of United National Indian Tribal Youth (UNITY). The Combined Jewish Philanthropies (CJP) was founded in 1895 with the aims of promoting communal responsibility, generous giving, compassion, and justice and has worked for over a century "to care for people in need, to preserve Jewish learning, and to enrich Jewish culture worldwide." The Native American Seventh Generation Fund helps many individuals and tribes, improving reservation life and urban Indian lives. United Way, American Red Cross, American Refugee Committee, Presbyterian Disaster Assistance, Save the Children USA, Stop Hunger Now, National Immigration Forum, AmeriCares, World Vision (a Christian humanitarian organization "working for the well being of all people, especially children," including child soldiers), Baptist World Aid, Habitat for Humanity, Oxfam America, Sathya Sai Baba Service organizations, Covenant House, and other generous problem-solving groups engaged in charitable activities, including the Vincent de Paul Society. "It is only because of your love that the poor will forgive you the bread you give them," as Saint Vincent de Paul said.

Women In Need (WIN) is an organization formed to serve homeless and disadvantaged women in Manhattan, Brooklyn, and the Bronx with shelter, child care, job training, and AIDS education, as well as alcohol and substance-abuse treatment. The Global Fund for Women (GFW) was founded in Palo Alto, California, in 1987 by three women who saw that the lack of substantial resources for women's human-rights causes constituted a serious obstacle to the improvement of women's status. GFW raises funds for the support of women's human-rights organizations. It is the largest organization of its kind, funding grants to women's groups active in overcoming poverty, violence, and discrimination.

The Case Foundation, actively involved since 1997 in solving social problems, invests in grants to fund such endeavors as improving the water supply to African villages, projects benefiting children and young adults, and work encouraging collaboration, entrepreneurship and leadership development, such as Accelerate Brain Cancer Cure (ABC2).

The John Weidner Foundation for Altruism is a growing organization founded by the widow of a Dutch Seventh-day Adventist who during World War II saved many lives; she wanted to recognize the spirit of generosity and service in people's lives today. "The John Henry Weidner Foundation seeks to identify, support and emulate the behavior of these quiet altruists who brighten the darkest periods of history and darkest corners of the planet to speak for the voiceless, even at the risk of losing their lives." Bard College is an example of outreach to men serving time, offering an excellent prisoner education program. Dan Duncan, of Houston, Texas, who earned his fortune in the oil and gas industries, and his wife donated $100 million to the Cancer Center at Baylor College of Medicine.

Who is generous? Well-known business and political leaders are prominent givers. Ted Turner, who says he was inspired to be more giving by Dickens' *Christmas Carol* (and by worries about an apocalypse) in 1997 gave a billion dollar gift to the UN. This exemplary act has sparked other philanthropy.[8] *Forbes* annually lists the four hundred richest people in America. While this list is a status symbol for some, it now has competition; the online magazine *Slate* now annually lists the "60 largest American personal charitable givers," and *Business Week* offers an annual list of "Most Generous Philanthropists."

In an earlier age, Americans like Andrew Carnegie and John D. Rockefeller found that the satisfaction of amassing a fortune could be matched or surpassed by using their wealth to help those in need. Today a new generation is at work using their fortunes in ways that are useful and satisfying. For example, Charles F. Finney, a New Jersey businessman and strong believer of "giving while living," quietly gave over $2.6 billion to worthy causes. The Bill and Melinda Gates Foundation, saving lives in Africa from AIDS and malaria, is building a living cathedral of life-saving healthcare for many in need today. Warren Buffet has augmented the amount the foundation has to work with by putting his own great philanthropic resources under Gates' management. In 1998 Pierre Omidyar, billionaire founder of eBay, began a charity supporting nonprofit foundations. In 2004 he changed his philanthropy to invest in for-profit businesses that make a positive contribution to social change. Texas oilman Sid Richardson gave a gift of $25 million to the Metropolitan Opera of New York. Veronica Atkins' contributions to research on obesity and diabetes are also considerable.

Former president Jimmy Carter helps Habitat for Humanity and other organizations. Bill Clinton has focused on AIDS and raising money for the 2004 tsunami relief work and other causes. (Indeed, individuals in America gave over $2 billion in food, clothing, and cash to tsunami victims, far more than the U.S. government gave.) Al Gore has performed significant work for environmental awareness. Teresa Heinz Kerry runs a large philanthropic operation—Heinz endowment foundations, including those devoted to environmental concerns, are worth $1.3 billion. Betty Ford raised awareness of breast cancer, and alcohol and drug addiction, founding Betty Ford Center in 1982.[9]

If men like Rockefeller and Carnegie and Mellon (founding donor of the National Gallery in Washington) were "second founders" of our nation, then Turner and Gates and other generous givers are "third founders," joining a continuous stream of able people refounding democracy and furthering its philanthropic ideals. Civilization is not a *fait accompli* but a process continually being renewed. The Russell Sage Foundation was established with $10 million by Margaret O. Sage as a memorial to her financier husband, Russell, in 1907. It supports research in the social sciences, funding scholarship that develops social-policy ideas in such areas as health care, labor law, and city planning. "Impact 100" is the name of a growing network of philanthropic activities; in it, groups of women in various American cities pool contributions of $1,000 each, to constitute grants of $100,000 to deserving organizations in their areas. MIT professor Nicholas Negroponte initiated the "One Laptop per Child" project, a nonprofit organization to put personal computers within reach of poor children. This educational project will help level the learning field for the world's children, providing five to ten million laptops to kids in Nigeria, Brazil, India, China, and Argentina.

Former Microsoft executive John Wood founded "Room to Read," which has established 2,500 libraries and 210 schools in Nepal, Cambodia, Sri Lanka, and elsewhere. William Norris, a pioneer in computers who founded Control Data Corporation, has used business resources not just to increase profits, but for the common good, undertaking actions with unknown social dividends in people's lives, such as bringing jobs and training opportunities to inner cities. Since then, Starbucks and other companies have caught the idea and continue to develop it. Whether you call it corporate philanthropy or good citizenship, it has that pragmatic sign of American character—it works! The builder Eli Broad, founder of the Broad Foundation, works to create new opportunities for Americans, funding projects in education and the arts.

American businesses are increasingly recognizing that entrepreneurial philanthropy has a strong appeal to young Americans who like the idea that they can buy products they want and simultaneously express their good-heartedness, with a percentage of their spending going toward worthy causes. The Hilton Family of Hotels sponsors behospitable.com, a website that tracks acts of kindness helping strangers. Conrad Hilton's original philosophy was "to fill the earth with the light and warmth of hospitality." The Random Acts of Kindness Foundation offers resources, ideas, and inspiration to those seeking to practice kindness and "pass it on" to others (http://www.actsofkindness.org/about/).

Social entrepreneur Jeff Skoll founded the Skoll Foundation in 1999 "to pursue his vision of a world where all people, regardless of geography, background or economic status, enjoy and employ the full range of their talents and abilities." Skoll, the first employee as well as the first president of eBay, describes his plan as "strategic investments in the right people," leading to enduring social change—"uncommon heroes dedicated to the common good," as the Skoll Foundation puts it. Socially concerned businesses are in the news more and more these days;[10] *Giving* magazine, *Good* magazine, and other publications tell us about them. Ben Goldhirsh, founder of *Good* (the subscription fees for which are donated to charity), was inspired by his father's generosity to his employees. Like his father, he believes that engaging in work, charity, and creativity leads people to happiness.

Who is generous? American foundations,[11] which today are more diversified and ever more concerned with funding high-impact concerns. The Robert Wood Johnson Foundation, William and Flora Hewlitt Foundation, the Lilly Endowment, and the W. K. Kellogg Foundation are substantial givers. Ronald McDonald House, for children with serious illnesses, has awarded over $400 million in grants to children's programs since 1974. Fisher House helps veterans and their families. The largest corporate cash givers are: Wal-Mart, Altria Group, Ford Motor, Exxon Mobil, Target, J. P. Morgan Chase, Johnson & Johnson, Wells Fargo, and Bank of America. ("Cash giving" here includes grants made by a company foundation, contributions made by the company to the foundation, as well as employee gifts matched by corporation donations.) Target has been giving 5 percent of its income before taxes to community causes and organizations since 1946. Avon Breast Cancer Crusade has given more than $300 million since 1992. Dawn Saves Wildlife is another example of brand-name products involved in funding charitable causes and nonprofit concerns. The Apple/Motorola/Sprint/Gap (and others) Red Campaign donates some profits from certain designated products to the fight against AIDS in Africa. The list goes on and on.

The social entrepreneurs are diversified. Filmmaker and attorney Gillian Caldwell founded a company named Witness. (Motto: "See it. Film it. Change it.") It trains people in various nations to take video footage that can be used as evidence of human-rights crimes, such as taking children and turning them into child soldiers. Bill Drayton founded Ashoka, an association of social entrepreneurs offering innovative solutions to pressing problems around the world. Like Muhammad Yunus, who pioneered micro-financing, which invests in individuals needing only small funding to start businesses, these businessmen and women are working out practical answers to problems large and small, not just theorizing or protesting. Too, there is Kiva.org, a microcredit web-site where small-scale start-up businesses can profile their plans and where individual lenders can make small loans, often of a few hundred dollars, to help the individual entrepreneurs in their potential endeavors.

Ordinary people can be amazingly generous. Mary Clarke was a middle-aged Cali-fornia mother who, after raising her family, decided to become a nun. For the next twenty-five years she ministered to prisoners inside La Mesa State Penitentiary Tijuana, Mexico. As Sister Antonia, she has devoted her life to serving the needs of prisoners, earning the nickname "Prison Angel." Also generous are small local organizations, like the Optimist Club. This group has been busy "Bringing out the Best in Kids" since 1919. Optimist Clubs are known for conducting positive service projects that provide a help-ing hand to young people. Club members are known in their communities for their contagious upbeat attitudes. Optomist volunteers have faith in young people and help them to be the best they can be, making a difference in the world. At present, 105,000 members belong to over 3,200 local branches of the Optimist Club. They engage in 65,000 service projects annually, being of service to over six million young people. Optimist Clubs spend about $78 million on activities in their communities every year. The Optimist's motto is "Friend of Youth." Big Brothers Big Sisters programs are also time-proven ways volunteers can be friends with children and widen their horizons— "Little moments. Big magic."

Compassionate end-of-life care for individuals and their families is made possi-ble in many communities across America. The Community Hospice Foundation is an organization that raises funds and manages charitable contributions to help support hospice care. Hospice Patients Alliance is a nonprofit charitable organization dedicated to promoting quality hospice services. A service organization, The Living/Dying Proj-ect, grew out of the Hanuman Foundation Dying Center, and it offers spiritual support for persons of all spiritual paths facing life-threatening illnesses.

Who is generous? Anonymous givers. "Guerilla philanthropy" is a growing kind of giving practiced by those disenchanted with organizations. Tired of institutionalized giv-ing and seeking to avoid the limelight, they rediscover the fresh vitality at the heart of giving. Mystery donors hear a story of need and make personal gifts. They say that money changes relationships and so prefer anonymity, like crouching tigers and hidden drag-ons—unseen forces for good—with no public or private thanks necessary. "Secret Santas" give without fanfare, and time will tell how contagious this kind of generosity may be. There are websites—such as justgiving.org and networkforgood.org—that allow donors to select from a variety of causes and enable givers to preserve their anonymity.

Who is generous? The wounded seeking healing. Family members sometimes wish to memorialize loved ones who have passed away. Thus out of loss comes gain—out of heartache, happiness and well-being for others. It is therapeutic, the psyche's way to cope and heal, thriving and growing with life rather than giving in to death. Paul

Newman and Joanne Woodward founded Hole in the Wall Gang Camp and the Scott Newman Foundation to treat drug addiction in memory of Newman's son who died of an overdose in 1978.

William Payton's son Joseph died in Kigali, Rwanda, in 1982; his son Matthew died at eighteen from lymphoma in 1973. In their memory, Payton built and donated a library for philanthropic studies at Indiana University-Purdue University at Indianapolis, the first library dedicated solely to philanthropy.

Taylor's Closet was founded by the sixteen-year-old twin sister of a girl who died at birth. Lindsay Giambattista wrote to relations, friends, and businesses asking them to donate clothes and has created a place where foster children can receive clothing. Information about the organization (taylorscloset.com) quotes Matthew 25:36: "I was naked and you clothed me, I was sick and you visited me, I was in prison and you came to me" (RSV). Giambattista began her project on a small scale, appealing to friends and family and then with the Web site. Contribution raising has never been more democratic—the Internet has leveled the field.[12]

The large-heartedness involved in turning one's own disappointments into expansive joy for others comes in many forms. Jilted six weeks before her wedding, Kyle Paxman changed her plans, inviting 125 women to a party, the proceeds of which went to Vermont Children's Aid Society and CARE USA. As Kyle planned this charity event, she said, "It's going to be hard, of course. But the end of my story now isn't so awful."[13]

There is wisdom in generosity. Wisdom is an understanding that takes the long view, encouraging patience and sharing and promoting an expanded sense of identity and participation in the lives around us. Helping others takes one out of oneself; contributing to the world's well-being, we share in the common good. Self-centeredness has its limits, while caring for others brings a sense of indefinite expansion. Giving allows the light of love to scatter the shadows and bring thaw, as part of the soul's learning process.[14] Knowing you've done what you could changes your own self-consciousness. A subtle music lifts your spirit, and "you are like a rich man entering heaven through the ear of a raindrop,"[15] knowing you and your camel never could get through the eye of a needle. Those who give and volunteer regularly often are happier, healthier, and live longer than those who do not. The "helper's high" is an inner smile that comes from seeing the smiles of those we help.

Through generosity we may make great saves; what was tragic loss, a ruinous mistake, can be transformed into new life, new hope. The great thing about human beings is that they are able to forget themselves, offer themselves. The human impulse to give comes in many forms and springs from many reasons. We don't know when we follow a generous impulse how our work will turn out. We take a leap of faith that "he who began a good work in you will complete it." And that, too, shows our interconnectedness with a larger reality than our small selves.

Young and old can find satisfaction in giving of themselves. Take the example of Lucious Newsome, an African American man now in his nineties. He is a Catholic who was once a Baptist minister. He runs The Lord's Pantry and is known as "the Lord's beggar for the poor." For two decades he has worked to feed the poor in Indianapolis. He and others founded "Anna's House," a clinic and learning center, food pantry and tutoring center. It is named for Anna Molloy, a child in Lucious' parish (Nativity of Our Lord Jesus Christ). Anna helps feed the poor from her wheelchair, wearing an oxygen respirator. They distribute vegetables and other donated food to Hispanic immigrants, homeless people, and others in need and serve meals, including a large Thanksgiving dinner to hundreds each year. Such tireless dedication is an inspiration to all who see it.

To discuss giving realistically, we cannot limit ourselves to positive examples, painting an overly rosy picture. Sometimes philanthropy is used negatively, as seen in a number of selections in this anthology. Giving can be used for self-aggrandizement or to gain power. It can be employed to advance a particular social agenda. Paternalism, amateurism, and fiscal limitations may come into play. Particularism—the fact that inclusion in some associations implies exclusion of those who are not like-minded—can also mar generosity. Such examples illustrate how generosity, without the broad, deep vision wisdom brings, can be misguided, useless, even harmful. *Good Intentions: Moral Obstacles and Opportunities*, edited by David H. Smith, usefully delves into such issues. Wisdom is what allows generosity to expand beyond mere personal self-gratification, avoid pitfalls, and become a creative force in the larger social context. Wisdom sidesteps egotism and delusions of grandeur, bringing humility and clarity.

Thomas Merton's poem "A Letter to America" evokes America's promise. "America, when you were born and when the plains/Spelled out their miles of praises in the sun/ What glory and what history/The rivers seemed to prepare."[16] Thankfully, new generations of Americans, interacting at Liberty's crossroads of generosity, still strive to fulfill that promise, and their self-giving does not happen by chance; it flows from wisdom and lives up to the land's long preparation. In times of crisis, America's generous spirit soars. Famous Americans have given donations to help New Orleans recover, but over one million ordinary Americans have volunteered to help in the post-Katrina clean-up and reconstruction effort along the Gulf Coast.

Who is generous? We are generous. The stories of others' creativity are stories of our creativity; the stories of others' generosity are stories of our generosity. We count our blessings and give of our gifts, rediscovering the magic of sharing and the satisfaction of helping repair what's been broken, laboring to give birth in the ever-hopeful new world we help bring into existence.

ENDNOTES

PREFACE

*Thomas Jefferson, letter to Robert Skipwith, 1771. This sentence shows a strong influence from Francis Hutcheson. *The Cambridge Companion to the Scottish Enlightenment*, ed., Alexander Broadie, Cambridge: Cambridge University, 2003, p. 335.

[1]For example, the *Tao Te Ching*, the *I Ching*, the *Dhammapada*.

[2]My sense of fractals (geometric patterns that depict the parts of a whole as self-similar to the whole) gives me a confidence that I can make valid representations of complex topics on a variety of scales. One can collect a library of hundreds of books on a single topic; one can select a variety of culled books and make one shelf of representative books; one could collect texts and make a 2500 page anthology, one could make a 1000 page anthology, a 500 page anthology, a 250 page anthology—each work could present the same topic and have its uses. In fact, this compendium of passages from four centuries represents the distillation of a library.

[3]Merle Miller, *Plain Speaking; an oral biography of Harry S Truman*, New York: 1974, p. 69.

[4]Walt Whitman's poem "I hear America singing," in his book *Leaves of Grass*, colorfully lists the everyday voices Whitman heard in his day. For the text of the poem see http://lcweb2.loc.gov/cocoon/ihas/html/whitman/whitman-home.html.

[5]This is the title of Robert D. Putnam's book on Americans becoming disconnected from a sense of community. *Bowling Alone: The Collapse and Revival of American Community*, New York: Simon & Schuster, 2000.

[6]Shakespeare used this phrase in his play *The Tempest* (II.1.253), to suggest that what happened yesterday leads up to what is happening today.

[7]See Wilfred Cantwell Smith, *Faith and Belief: The Difference Between Them*, Oxford: Oneworld Publications, 1998.

[8]David Hackett Fischer's book, *Albion's Seed*, on regions in colonial America, explores their varied backgrounds. The formative early era of British culture left legacies. After a couple of generations three distinct cultures emerged: planter society of the South, with aristocratic customs; New England ethos, egalitarian but controlled by Puritan power structure; and Middle colonies like Pennsylvania, varied, agrarian, mercantile. Even today America reflects remnant aspects of regional, religious, and class divisions of 17th and 18th century regions of England that were transplanted here by the first settlers.

[9]I like the idea represented by the term "immediatist" which David Hackett Fischer uses to characterize thinking about relations of past to present; in his view every period of the past, understood in its own terms, is immediate to the present because the past is not past but lives on in trends and potentials. In this view empirical knowledge of the past is necessary to understand moral decisions and make choices in the present. Considering the contributions of the old style of history (telling a story) and the new history (which asks specialized questions and answers them with statistics and other specialized techniques of analysis), I agree that knowledge will be best served by creatively integrating when possible the good qualities of both approaches.

[10]Such as Alpha Phi Alpha; Optimist Club, Knights of Columbus; Kiwanis; Rotary Club.

[11]A recent study shows this. Rene Bekkers and Mark O. Wilhelm, "Helping Behavior, Dispositional Empathic Concern, and the Principle of Care," Mimeo, IUPUI, September 8, 2006.

[12]Among the surprises: I found that Andrew Carnegie wanted to take Helen Keller over his knees and spank her because she said she was a socialist. I found that a famous philanthropic family in Texas, the Hoggs, named their daughter Ima—how could one not become a philanthropist if one was named "Ima Hogg"? I found that the Mayor of Grapevine, Texas, asked his

townspeople to send care packages to Pitcairn Island, where the illegitimate children of Christian Fletcher (of "Mutiny on the Bounty" fame) needed bloomers.

[13]Bob Dylan, "Wedding Song," Planet Waves album, 1974.

CONCLUSION

[1]Research on "mirror neurons" opens new understanding of the processes of empathy. See for example, "Grasping the Intentions of Others with One's Own Mirror Neuron System," by Marco Iacoboni, Istvan Molnar-Szakacs, Vittorio Gallese, Giovanni Buccino, John C. Mazziotta, Giacomo Rizzolatti. *PLoS Biol.* 2005 March; 3(3): e79. Published online 2005 February 22 at http://biology.plosjournals.org/perlserv/ ?request=get-document&doi=10.1371/ journal. pbio.0030079. Researchers are beginning to understand empathy better at the neuron level in the brain. Empathy involves interiorizing and truly reflecting on others' plights.

[2]William Faulkner, Nobel Prize speech, 1950.

[3]"Syracuse University professor Arthur C. Brooks argues in *Who Really Cares,* New York: Basic Books, 2006, that there are many misconceptions regarding charitable giving and volunteering. He finds that statistical studies prove our ideas about "bleeding heart liberals" and uncaring conservatives are empty cliches. If conservatives give 30 percent more money than liberals, and donate more blood and engage in service for more hours, our stereotypes are skewed. He finds that religious people are three times more generous than secularists in giving to all charities, and 14 percent more generous in donations to nonreligious charities. In his findings those in a religious tradition are 57 percent more likely than secularists to offer help to homeless people.

[4]"An Interdisciplinary Approach to Charitable Giving and Prosocial Behavior," Mark Wilhelm. Sabbatical Speakers Series, Indiana University-Purdue University at Indianapolis School of Liberal Arts, January 12, 2007. This study was multidisciplinary, making use of approaches from sociology, economics, demography, and psychology.

[5]Ibid.

[6]John Stossel and Kristina Kendall, "Who Gives and Who Doesn't?" ABC News 20/20, http://abcnews.go.com/2020/story?id=2682730&page=1.

[7]See "The Social Capital Community Benchmark Survey." http://www.cfsv.org/community survey/.

[8]Turner was one of the recipients of the Carnegie Medal award for new approaches to philanthropy and desire to make an immediate impact on society. The other honorees were Leonore Annenberg, Brooke Astor, Irene Diamond, William H. Gates Sr., David Rockefeller, and George Soros.

[9]A list of celebrities and links to information about their causes is at http://www.fundraisers.com/giving/causeceleb93.html.

[10]Muhammad Yunus, Nobel prize winning economist, suggests that socially concerned businesses can help unleash creative entrepreneurship in the lives of the disadvantaged—his example is a non-profit bank that is meant to help poor women start small businesses.

[11]See Joel L. Fleishman, *The Foundation: A Great American Secret; How Private Wealth is Changing the World,* New York: Public Affairs, 2007.

[12]For example, Stephen Posts' "Works of Love Newsletter."

[13]Stephanie Strom, "Wedding Off, Jilted Bride Turns party Into a Benefit," *The New York Times,* September 8, 2006, p. A17.

[14]Psychologist James Hillman observed: "Love is painful, it breaks the heart; the broken heart is no longer the innocent heart—it has experiential knowledge, so love is the learning of the soul." The loving ones who lose someone learn a lesson and do something loving in the memory of the loved one. Love means a change of self—expanded identity, experience of 'we.' So we grow in soul.

"At first, loss can render us into withdrawn, immobile shells. Frozen in grief, unfocussed, we feel so much has been taken from us we can't go on. But then we realize that giving can render us flowing with the stream of life again."

[15]Seamus Heaney, "The Rain-Stick." This is the first poem in Heaney's *The Spirit Level,* London: Faber and Faber, 1996.

[16]Thomas Merton, *The Collected Poems,* New York: New Directions, 1977, p. 153.

INDEX

Figure 4.10 "Blessed Art Thou," painting by Kate Kretz